Mastering French Vocabulary

A THEMATIC APPROACH

SECOND EDITION

WOLFGANG FISCHER AND
ANNE-MARIE LE PLOUHINEC

BARRON'S

Mastering French Vocabulary
A Thematic Approach

Second Edition

by
Professor Wolfgang Fischer
and
Anne-Marie Le Plouhinec

All inquiries should be addressed to:
Barron's Educational Series, Inc.
250 Wireless Boulevard
Hauppauge, NY 11788
http://www.barronseduc.com

ISBN-13: 978-0-7641-2394-8
ISBN-10: 0-7641-2394-7

Library of Congress Catalog Card Number: 2002106702

Printed in China
19 18 17 16 15 14 13 12 11

Contents

Foreword   5

List of Abbreviations   8

1 Personal Information   9
1.1   Personal Data 10
1.2   Nationality, Language,
      Country 13

2 The Human Body   17
2.1   Body Parts, Organs 18
2.2   Sexuality and Reproduction . . 20
2.3   Birth, Stages of Development,
      Death 23
2.4   Senses and Physical
      Reactions 26
2.5   Movements and Activities . . 30
2.6   Appearance 34
2.7   Cosmetics and Personal
      Grooming 36

3 Health and Medicine   41
3.1   General Condition, Health,
      and Disease 42
3.2   Medical Care 49
3.3   Drugs, Tobacco, Alcohol . . . 53

**4 Mental Processes and States,
    Behavior   57**
4.1   Feelings 58
4.2   Thinking, Imagining,
      Wanting 63
4.3   Character, Behavior 68
4.4   Activities and Abilities 76

5 Food and Drink, Clothing, Shopping 84
5.1   Eating and Drinking 85
5.2   Cooking, Baking, and
      Utensils 93
5.3   Articles of Clothing 97
5.4   Jewelry and Accessories 104
5.5   Shopping 106

6 Living Arrangements   111
6.1   Construction, Houses,
      Buildings, and Inhabitants . . 112
6.2   Accommodations and
      Furnishings 116
6.3   Housekeeping and
      Household Chores 119

7 Private Life, Social Relations   123
7.1   Individuals, Families 124
7.2   Greetings and Farewells 128

7.3   Young People 129
7.4   Social Groups, Living
      Conditions, and Ways of
      Behavior 132
7.5   Relationships and Ties 137
7.6   Possession and Ownership . . 145

8 Education, Learning   147
8.1   Education 148
8.2   School, Classroom
      Instruction 150
8.3   University Study, Science,
      and Research 160

9 Occupations and the Job World 165
9.1   Tools and Skilled Trades 166
9.2   Office, Office Items 167
9.3   Vocational and Professional
      Training, Occupations 170
9.4   Work and Working
      Conditions 178

**10 Leisure Time, Recreation, Sports,
     and Games   184**
10.1 Leisure Time, Hobbies,
      and Games 185
10.2 Sports 188
10.3 Theater, Film, and
      Television 195
10.4 Celebrations 201

11 Travel and Tourism   204
11.1 Trips and Travel
      Preparations 205
11.2 Accommodations 212
11.3 Dining Out 214
11.4 Sights of Interest 217

12 Visual Arts, Music, Literature 220
12.1 Visual Arts 221
12.2 Music and Musical Events . . 224
12.3 Literature 229
12.4 Prose, Nonfiction 231
12.5 Poetry 235
12.6 Drama 237
12.7 Working with Texts 239

13 History, Religion, Philosophy   245
13.1 History 246
13.2 Religion 251
13.3 Philosophy 254

Contents

14 The State, Society, Politics   259
14.1 Constitution, State Institutions 260
14.2 Public Administration 265
14.3 Parties, Political Systems . . . 268
14.4 Laws, Justice System, Crime . . 271
14.5 Associations, Unions 278
14.6 Domestic Politics 280
14.7 International Relations 285
14.8 Peace, War, Military 289

15 The Economy and Business   294
15.1 Agriculture, Fishing, and Mining 295
15.2 Industry and Handicrafts . . . 298
15.3 Company Operations 300
15.4 Technology 302
15.5 Trade and Services 304
15.6 Money, Banking 306
15.7 Insurance 311

16 Communications and Mass Media   314
16.1 Telecommunications 315
16.2 Postal Service 317
16.3 Television, Radio 319
16.4 Video and Sound Carriers . . 322
16.5 Newspapers, Magazines, and Books 323
16.6 Multimedia, Computers 328

17 Traffic, Means of Transportation   332
17.1 Individual Transportation . . . 333
17.2 Public Transportation System 342

18 Nature, the Environment, Ecology   348
18.1 Universe, Earth 349
18.2 Geography 351
18.3 Climate, Weather 356
18.4 Substances, Materials 360
18.5 Plants, Gardens, Agriculture . . 363
18.6 Animals, Keeping an Animal . . 367
18.7 Ecology, Environmental Protection, and Catastrophes 372
18.8 Town, Country, Buildings, and Infrastructure 378

19 Time and Space   384
19.1 Days of the Week and Dates 385
19.2 Time and Time of Day 387
19.3 Months and Seasons 389
19.4 Other Time Concepts 391
19.5 Spatial Relationships 396
19.6 Length, Circumference, Distance 399
19.7 Place and Direction 401

20 Colors and Shapes   404
20.1 Colors 405
20.2 Shapes 407

21 Quantities, Measures, Numbers   409
21.1 Designations of Quantity . . . 410
21.2 Numbers and Counting Words 414
21.3 Measures and Weights 417

22 General Concepts   420
22.1 Classification 421
22.2 Degree, Comparison, Contexts 422
22.3 Properties 426
22.4 Way and Manner 429
22.5 Cause, Effect, Goal, Purpose . . 431
22.6 State, Motion, and Change . . 433

23 Linguistic Communication   439
23.1 Speaking, Informing, Asking, Answering 440
23.2 Excusing, Regretting, Consoling 444
23.3 Allowing, Forbidding, Suggesting, Advising 446
23.4 Pain, Anger, Aggression 447
23.5 Agreeing, Confirming, Qualifying, Refusing 451
23.6 Praising and Thanking, Criticizing 456
23.7 Taking a Position and Evaluating 458
23.8 Exhorting and Wishing 465
23.9 Phrases Used in Letters 467

24 Structural Words   469
24.1 Adjuncts and Pronouns 470
24.2 Interrogatives 474
24.3 Conjunctions 476
24.4 Auxiliary Verbs 479
24.5 Negations 480
24.6 Adverbs and Adverbial Expressions 481
24.7 Prepositions 483
24.8 Linguistic Terminology 487

Index of All French Entries   491

List of Phonetic Symbols Used in This Book   545

Foreword

Target Groups and Purpose of This Thematic Vocabulary

Mastering French Vocabulary: A Thematic Approach is intended for use by several groups, including **middle school and high school students** who want to practice the basic vocabulary they have learned and to add to it in an organized way. More advanced students may feel overwhelmed at times by the sheer volume of new words they encounter in assigned or independent work: reading French books and magazines, watching films, and listening to music. The division of this book into basic and advanced sections will help them reinforce or expand what they already know, add new words and phrases in a systematic way, and separate essential vocabulary items from those of secondary importance. Moreover, it will help them produce written and spoken French as they analyze texts, write commentaries and papers, work on projects, and prepare for quizzes and exams, including competitive exams at the national level.

College students of French also will find this volume useful in their work with more challenging materials, as they translate, read, learn about French culture, analyze and interpret demanding historical or literary texts, and communicate with increasing sophistication in a foreign language.

Adults who are learning French independently also will benefit from *Mastering French Vocabulary*, whether they are acquiring the language for professional use, preparing for a stay in France, or simply wish to increase their enjoyment by reading French literature and seeing French television programs and films in the original versions.

What Does This Book Contain?

In putting together this comprehensive volume of **basic** and **advanced vocabulary items** based on current usage, the authors examined and evaluated the following sources, among others:
  ▷ vocabulary lists of textbooks currently used in schools and universities;
  ▷ vocabulary and frequency lists used in adult evening courses;
  ▷ portions of the electronic EU dictionary (available on the internet; use the search term EURODICAUTOM);
  ▷ articles and other relevant materials from the field of French area studies;
  ▷ lists of neologisms drawn from the latest dictionaries.

The basis for the book was **modern standard French**, the so-called *langue courante*. Where appropriate, terms from more **colloquial speech** and from current slang – *français familier* or *populaire* – were included as well.

Structure and Presentation of the Vocabulary

There are numerous ways to structure a theme-based vocabulary learning aid, of course. The present book focuses on human beings and the areas of their experience. The resulting 24 **major subject areas** were broken down into 122 detailed **subsections**. Within these subsections, the vocabulary items are **clustered according to content**; thus they are easy to grasp and can be learned in small, comfortably managed units.

The user-friendly **layout** reflects principles of **educational psychology**. It is easy to find one's way around in the book, and the material is readily retained.

▷ The use of **color-shaded areas** makes it simple to distinguish the basic vocabulary from the advanced vocabulary.

▷ The 9,305 **main entries** (basic vocabulary, 5,632; advanced vocabulary, 3,673) are printed in blue; the 4,741 **subentries** (basic vocabulary, 3,168; advanced vocabulary, 1,573) appear in black type. Important or typical expressions, as well as significant differences between English and the target language, are set off by the use of boldface.

▷ **Triangular symbols** as well as **dotted lines** separate the **word clusters**.

▷ A **phonetic transcription** is provided for each entry. (See the List of Phonetic Symbols Used in This Book on the inside of the back cover.)

▷ Verbs that form the *passé composé* with *être* are marked with an asterisk (*) (with the exception of the reflexive verbs).

▷ Deviations from *français courant* are indicated by the addition of *fam (familier)* or *pop (populaire)*.

▷ If the entry can be classified in **several categories**, as in the case of *(un,e) célibataire*, that fact is indicated (*n* = noun, *adj* = adjective).

▷ There are 133 "i-boxes," which provide information about certain hard-to-learn features of the language.

▷ At the end of almost every chapter, there is a list of possible **"false friends"** to help users avoid annoying pitfalls.

The Main Thrust

The primary goal of this book is to help the user **learn words efficiently**. Therefore, a purely alphabetical arrangement of the material in each chapter would not have served our purpose.

Our memory stores words and their meanings in "networks." Thus, everything that can create a connection between the foreign word and its equivalent will promote understanding and strengthen retention. That principle of educational psychology is reflected in the way the material in this book is organized: the words were divided into **easy-to-grasp semantic units**, so-called **word clusters**, dealing with a certain subject matter. Within these semantic building blocks, **synonyms** *(terrible, horrible)* and **antonyms** *(chaud — froid)*, as well as **subordination** *(meuble — siege — chaise)*, **semantic fields** *(une rue; une route; une chausée; une avenue)*, and **families of words** *(dessiner; un dessin; un,e dessinateur, -trice)* create contexts that provide lasting impressions and promote memorization.

This kind of organization, which reflects an effort to achieve coherency of content and language, means that words are no longer assigned to the basic or advanced vocabulary exclusively on the basis of their statistical frequency. Moreover, words with several meanings may appear in the basic vocabulary in their primary meaning, and in the advanced vocabulary in their secondary meaning (*une action,* for example, appears as "action" in the basic vocabulary and as "stock" in the advanced vocabulary).

How Do We Deal With the Dangers of Equating Isolated Words from the Two Languages?

Word equations are definitely significant in the language reception process, but in the area of language production they entail certain risks. Because they lead the learner to engage in constant translation and analysis, they quite frequently result in transfer of speech habits from the mother tongue to the target language.

To avoid such risks, this book places special emphasis on **syntactic embedding** of most words:

▷ Relevant words or phrases (adjuncts) used with **verbs** (for example, *demander qc à qn*) make the syntactic connection easier.

▷ **Sample sentences** provide situational contexts that make understanding and retention easier. They show how the target word is connected with other parts of the sentence and illustrate possible differences between the French and English systems.

▷ In language production, words cannot always be joined with other words indiscriminately. Often they are part of fixed combinations involving nouns, adverbs, or verbs; these are known as **collocations** (for example: *prendre du poids – gain weight; faire attention à – watch out for, mind*). It is these set phrases that differentiate languages most clearly; they give learners the greatest difficulty and require clearly focused practice. The authors of this book felt a special obligation to take that fact into account.

▷ **Idiomatic expressions** (*locutions*) and **proverbs** (*proverbes*) illustrate the extent to which imagination and a playful mind can shape a language. In many cases, they range quite far from the basic meanings of the target word, but mastering them is part and parcel of achieving competence in using another language and understanding another culture.

List of Abbreviations

adj	adjectif	adjective
adv	adverb	adverb
f	féminin	feminine
fam	familier	colloquial
loc	locution	phrase, form of speech
m	masculin	masculine
n	nom	noun
péj	péjoratif	pejorative
pop	populaire	highly colloquial, slang
prov	proverbe	proverb
qc	quelque chose	something
qn	quelqu'un	someone
s.o.	someone	
s.th.	something	
subj	subjonctif	subjunctive
v	verbe	verb

Nom

Lebrun

Prénom

Dominique

Né(e) le <u>12/7/1982</u>

à <u>Colmar</u>

Nationalité <u>française</u>

Adresse <u>38, avenue des Vosges</u>

<u>67 000 Strasbourg</u>

FRANCE РОССИЯ

USA DEUTSCHLAND

ESPAÑA ITALIA

GREAT BRITAIN

1.1 Personal Data

le **nom** [nɔ̃]	name
le **nom de famille**	surname, family name
le **prénom** [pʀenɔ̃]	first name
s'appeler [saple]	be called, be named
Comment t'appelles-tu ?/Tu t'appelles comment ?/Comment tu t'appelles ?	What's your name?

monsieur, messieurs [məsjø, mesjø]	Mr.
madame, mesdames [madam, medam]	Mrs.
Madame Martin, née Dupont	Mrs. Martin, née Dupont
mademoiselle, mesdemoiselles [madmwazɛl, medmwazɛl]	Miss

---

i

Monsieur ...

The following *abbreviations* are in common use:
M. (Monsieur), **Mme** (Madame), **Mlle** (Mademoiselle),
MM. (Messieurs), **Mmes** (Mesdames), **Mlles** (Mesdemoiselles).

These are used as *forms of address:*
Monsieur/Messieurs, Madame/Mesdames, Mademoiselle/Mesdemoiselles.

In *polite social address,* the name is not mentioned:
Bonjour monsieur/madame/   *Good morning.*
mademoiselle.
Oui/Non/Merci messieurs/mesdames/   *Yes./No./Thank you.*
mesdemoiselles.

When *greeting acquaintances,* the name is often added:
Bonjour Monsieur/Madame/   *Good morning, Mr./Mrs./Miss Rigot.*
Mademoiselle Rigot.

---

habiter qc/à [abite]	live in
J'habite une maison neuve.	I live in a new house.
J'habite à Paris.	I live in Paris.
l'**adresse** f [adʀɛs]	address
un **domicile** [dɔmisil]	(place of) residence
les **coordonnées** f; fam [kɔɔʀdɔne]	address and telephone number
Donne-moi les coordonnées de Paul.	Give me Paul's address and phone number.
une **rue** [ʀy]	street
26, rue du Labrador	26, rue du Labrador
une **route** [ʀut]	road, way; route

une rue – une route

Note the difference between:
J'ai rencontré Martine <u>dans la rue</u>.   *I met Martine on the street (in town).*
Attention, il y a du verglas <u>sur la route</u>.   *Watch out, there's ice on the (country) road.*

une **avenue** [avny]	avenue
un **boulevard** [bulvaʀ]	boulevard
une **place** [plas]	plaza, square

le **numéro** [nymeʀo]	number
C'est **au numéro** 6 de la rue Rambuteau.	It's on rue Rambuteau, number 6.
le **numéro de téléphone** [nymeʀod(ə)telefɔn]	telephone number
le **code postal** [kɔdpɔstal]	postal code, zip code number

la **situation de famille** [sitɥasjɔ̃d(ə)famij]	marital status
le **mari** [maʀi]	husband
la **femme** [fam]	wife
Julie est la deuxième femme de Pierre.	Julie is Pierre's second wife.
marié,e [maʀje]	married

le **sexe** [sɛks]	sex
masculin,e [maskylɛ̃, in]	male
féminin,e [feminɛ̃, in]	female

l'**âge** *m* [aʒ]	age
J'ai dix-huit ans. Et toi, **quel âge as-tu ?**	I'm 18. And how old are you?
âgé,e de [aʒe]	old
Elle est âgée de 24 ans.	She is 24 years old.
un **an** [ã]	year
(un,e) **adulte** *n; adj* [adylt]	adult
un,e **enfant** [ãfã]	child
C'est un film **pour enfants.**	This is a children's film.
un,e **adolescent,e**; un,e **ado** *fam* [adɔlesã, ãt]	adolescent, youth
(un,e) **jeune** *n; adj* [ʒœn]	young person; young
Il ne comprend pas les jeunes d'aujourd'hui.	He doesn't understand the youth of today.

une **religion** [ʀ(ə)liʒjɔ̃]	religion

(un,e) **chrétien,ne** n; adj [kʀetjɛ̃, jɛn]	Christian
(un,e) **catholique** n; adj [katɔlik]	Catholic
Il ne m'a pas l'air très catholique. fam	He seems rather mysterious to me.
(un,e) **protestant,e** n; adj [pʀɔtɛstã, ãt]	Protestant

un **métier** [metje]	business, calling, trade, profession
C'est un métier d'avenir.	That's a profession for the future.
une **profession** [pʀɔfesjɔ̃]	profession
un **boulot** fam [bulo]	job
Elle cherche un boulot pour les vacances.	She's looking for a vacation job.

l'**état civil** m [etasivil]	civil status; civil registrar's office
Il faut aller faire signer ce formulaire à l'état civil.	This form has to be signed at the civil registrar's office.
(un,e) **célibataire** n; adj [selibatɛʀ]	bachelor, spinster; single
une mère célibataire	a single mother
(un,e) **fiancé,e** n; adj [fjãse]	fiancé, fiancée; engaged
séparé,e [sepaʀe]	separated
Michel et Alice se sont séparés.	Michel and Alice have separated.
la **séparation** [sepaʀasjɔ̃]	separation
(un,e) **divorcé,e** n; adj [divɔʀse]	divorced person; divorced
Ils ont divorcé l'année dernière.	They got a divorce last year.
le **divorce** [divɔʀs]	divorce
(un,e) **veuf, veuve** n; adj [vœf, vœv]	widower, widow; widowed
(un,e) **orphelin,e** n; adj [ɔʀfəlɛ̃, in]	orphan; orphaned
l'**époux**, l'**épouse** m; f [epu, uz]	husband, wife
Dites bien le bonjour de notre part à Madame votre épouse.	Please give your wife our regards.
un **père de famille** [pɛʀdəfamij]	family man
une **mère de famille** [mɛʀdəfamij]	married woman with children

la **date de naissance** [datdənɛsãs]	date of birth
le **lieu de naissance** [ljød(ə)nɛsãs]	place of birth
(**être**) **d'origine** ... [dɔʀiʒin]	(be) of . . . origin
C'est un Français d'origine italienne.	He is a Frenchman of Italian origin.

majeur,e [maʒœʀ]	of (full legal) age

la **majorité** [maʒɔʀite]	majority (full legal age)
mineur,e [minœʀ]	minor
un film **interdit aux mineurs**	a film not approved for viewing by minors
(l')**aîné,e** n; adj [ene]	firstborn; older, oldest
C'est notre fils aîné.	That's our eldest son.
(le/la) **cadet,te** n; adj [kadɛ, ɛt]	junior; younger, youngest
Il a une sœur cadette.	He has a younger sister.

l'**appartenance à une religion** f [apaʀtənãsaynʀəliʒjõ]	religious affiliation
(un,e) **musulman,e** n; adj [myzylmã, an]	Muslim
(un,e) **juif/juive** n; adj [ʒɥif, ʒɥiv]	Jew/Jewess; Jewish
(un,e) **athée** n; adj [ate]	atheist

1.2 Nationality, Language, Country

un **passeport** [paspɔʀ]	passport
les **papiers d'identité** m [papjedidãtite]	identification documents
une **carte d'identité** [kaʀtdidãtite]	identification card
valable [valabl]	valid
périmé,e [peʀime]	expired
Ma carte d'identité est périmée depuis trois mois.	My ID card expired three months ago.
un **signe particulier** [siɲpaʀtikylje]	distinguishing characteristic

un **continent** [kõtinã]	continent
un **pays** [pei]	country
une **nation** [nasjõ]	nation
la **nationalité** [nasjɔnalite]	nationality, citizenship
Fatima va demander la nationalité française.	Fatima is going to apply for French citizenship.

une **frontière** [fʀõtjɛʀ]	border
(un,e) **étranger, -ère** n; adj [etʀãʒe, ɛʀ]	foreigner; foreign
immigrer [imigʀe]	immigrate
un,e **immigré,e** [imigʀe]	immigrant
Les immigrés ont parfois du mal à s'intégrer.	Integration is sometimes difficult for immigrants.
l'**immigration** f [imigʀasjõ]	immigration
émigrer [emigʀe]	emigrate

une **langue** [lãg]	language
la **langue maternelle**	mother tongue, native language
une **langue étrangère**	foreign language
bilingue [bilɛ̃g]	bilingual

l'**Europe** f [øʀɔp]	Europe
l'**Afrique** f [afʀik]	Africa
l'**Amérique** f [ameʀik]	America
l'**Asie** f [azi]	Asia
l'**Australie** f [ɔstʀali]	Australia

ℹ **Inhabitant – Language**

To designate *members of a people* or of an *ethnic group*, use the capitalized form of the adjective:

un,e Espagnol,e; un,e Allemand,e	*a Spaniard; a German*
un,e Breton,ne	*a Breton*

Languages, on the other hand, are not capitalized in French:

l'espagnol; l'allemand; le français; le breton	*Spanish; German; French; Breton*

---

la **France** [fʀãs]	France
français,e [fʀãnsɛ, ɛz]	French
l'**Allemagne** f [almaɲ]	Germany
allemand,e [almã, ãd]	German
la **Grande-Bretagne** [gʀãdbʀətaɲ]	Great Britain
britannique [bʀitanik]	British
l'**Angleterre** f [ãglətɛʀ]	England
anglais,e [ãglɛ, ɛz]	English

ℹ **être – aller – venir + country name**

être/aller	**en** France (**la** France)	*be in France/go to France*
to be, to go	**en** Italie (**l'**Italie f)	*be in Italy/go to Italy*
	en Iran (**l'**Iran m)	*be in Iran/go to Iran*
	au Portugal (**le** Portugal)	*be in Portugal/go to Portugal*
	aux Etats-Unis (**les** Etats-Unis)	*be in the United States/go to the United States*
venir	**de** Belgique (**la** Belgique)	*come from Belgium*
to come	**d'**Allemagne (**l'**Allemagne f)	*come from Germany*
	d'Irak (**l'**Irak m)	*come from Iraq*
	du Mexique (**le** Mexique)	*come from Mexico*
	des Etats-Unis (**les** Etats-Unis)	*come from the United States*

l'**Italie** f [itali]   Italy
italien,ne [italjɛ̃, jɛn]   Italian
l'**Espagne** f [ɛspaɲ]   Spain
espagnol,e [ɛspaɲɔl]   Spanish
le **Portugal** [pɔʀtygal]   Portugal
portugais,e [pɔʀtygɛ, ɛz]   Portuguese
la **Belgique** [bɛlʒik]   Belgium
belge [bɛlʒ]   Belgian
les **Pays-Bas** m [peiba]   the Netherlands
néerlandais,e [neɛʀlɑ̃dɛ, ɛz]   Dutch
la **Hollande** ['ɔlɑ̃d]   Holland
hollandais,e ['ɔlɑ̃dɛ, ɛz]   Dutch
le **Luxembourg** [lyksɑ̃buʀ]   Luxembourg
luxembourgeois,e   Luxembourger, Luxembourg
[lyksɑ̃buʀʒwa, waz]
l'**Autriche** f [otʀiʃ]   Austria
autrichien,ne [otʀiʃjɛ̃, jɛn]   Austrian
la **Grèce** [gʀɛs]   Greece
grec, grecque [gʀɛk]   Greek
l'**Irlande** f [iʀlɑ̃d]   Ireland
irlandais,e [iʀlɑ̃dɛ, ɛz]   Irish
la **Finlande** [fɛ̃lɑ̃d]   Finland
finlandais,e [fɛ̃lɑ̃dɛ, ɛz]   Finnish
la **Suède** [sɥɛd]   Sweden
suédois,e [sɥɛdwa, waz]   Swedish
la **Norvège** [nɔʀvɛʒ]   Norway
norvégien,ne [nɔʀveʒjɛ̃, jɛn]   Norwegian
le **Danemark** [danmaʀk]   Denmark
danois,e [danwa, waz]   Danish
scandinave [skɑ̃dinav]   Scandinavian
la **Suisse** [sɥis]   Switzerland
suisse; un,e **Suisse**, une **Suissesse** Swiss
adj; n [sɥis, ɛs]

les **Etats-Unis** m [etazyni]   the United States
les **USA** m [yɛsa]   the USA
américain,e [ameʀikɛ̃, ɛn]   American
le **Canada** [kanada]   Canada
canadien,ne [kanadjɛ̃, jɛn]   Canadian
le **Mexique** [mɛksik]   Mexico
mexicain,e [mɛksikɛ̃, ɛn]   Mexican
le **Brésil** [bʀezil]   Brazil
brésilien,ne [bʀeziljɛ̃, jɛn]   Brazilian

la **Russie** [ʀysi]   Russia
russe [ʀys]   Russian

la **Pologne** [pɔlɔɲ]	Poland
polonais,e [pɔlɔnɛ, ɛz]	Polish
la **République tchèque**	Czech Republic
[ʀepybliktʃɛk]	
tchèque [tʃɛk]	Czech
la **Slovaquie** [slɔvaki]	Slovakia
slovaque [slɔvak]	Slovak
la **Turquie** [tyʀki]	Turkey
turc, turque [tyʀk]	Turkish

l'**Albanie** f [albani]	Albania
la **Bulgarie** [bylgaʀi]	Bulgaria
la **Roumanie** [ʀumani]	Romania
la **Hongrie** ['ɔgʀi]	Hungary
l'**Estonie** f [ɛstɔni]	Estonia
la **Lettonie** [lɛtɔni]	Latvia
la **Lituanie** [lityani]	Lithuania
la **Biélorussie** [bjelɔʀysi]	Belarus
l'**Ukraine** f [ykʀɛn]	Ukraine
la **Yougoslavie** [jugɔslavi]	Yugoslavia
la **Croatie** [kʀoasi]	Croatia
la **Serbie** [sɛʀbi]	Serbia
la **Slovénie** [slɔveni]	Slovenia
la **Bosnie-Herzégovine**	Bosnia-Herzegovina
[bɔsniɛʀzegɔvin]	

la **Chine** [ʃin]	China
chinois,e [ʃinwa, waz]	Chinese
le **Japon** [ʒapɔ̃]	Japan
japonais,e [ʒapɔnɛ, ɛz]	Japanese
l'**Inde** f [ɛ̃d]	India
indien,ne [ɛ̃djɛ̃, jɛn]	Indian

l'**Algérie** f [alʒeʀi]	Algeria
algérien,ne [alʒeʀjɛ̃, jɛn]	Algerian
le **Maroc** [maʀɔk]	Morocco
marocain,e [maʀɔkɛ̃, ɛn]	Moroccan
la **Tunisie** [tynizi]	Tunisia
tunisien,ne [tynizjɛ̃, jɛn]	Tunisian
le **Maghreb** [magʀɛb]	the Maghreb (Morocco, Algeria, Tunisia)
maghrébin,e [magʀebɛ̃, in]	Maghreb
l'**Egypte** f [eʒipt]	Egypt

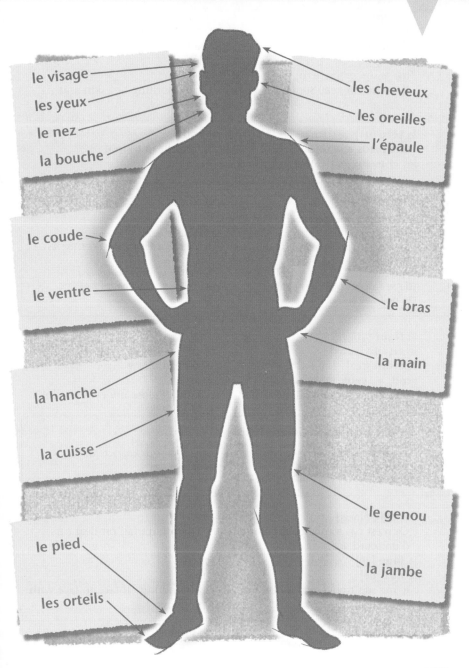

le visage

les yeux

le nez

la bouche

les cheveux

les oreilles

l'épaule

le coude

le ventre

le bras

la main

la hanche

la cuisse

le genou

le pied

la jambe

les orteils

2.1 Body Parts, Organs

le **corps** [kɔʀ]	body
le corps humain	the human body
la **peau** [po]	skin
le **sang** [sɑ̃]	blood
l'**os**, les **os** m [lɔs, lezo]	bone
Il n'a que la peau sur les os. loc	He's nothing but skin and bones.

la **tête** [tɛt]	head
des pieds à la tête	from head to foot
les **cheveux** m [ʃ(ə)vø]	hair

---

cheveux – poil

Note the difference between:
le(s) **cheveu(x)**	*hair (of the head)*
Mon père n'a presque plus de <u>cheveux</u>.	*My father has almost no hair left (on his head).*
le **poil**	*(human) body hair; animal hair*
Elle se rase les <u>poils</u> des jambes.	*She shaves the hair on her legs.*
On **poil**, see also p. 20.	

---

la **figure** [figyʀ]	face
le **visage** [vizaʒ]	face
le **front** [fʀɔ̃]	forehead, brow
l'**œil**, les **yeux** m [lœj, lezjø]	eye
Je n'ai pas **fermé l'œil de la nuit**.	I didn't close my eyes all night.

---

avoir + physical characteristics

The *definite* or the *indefinite article* can be used for physical characteristics:
Il a <u>les/des</u> cheveux roux.	*He has red hair*
Elles ont <u>les/des</u> yeux noirs/clairs.	*They have black/light eyes.*

---

l'**oreille** f [ɔʀɛj]	ear
Ce n'est pas tombé dans l'oreille d'un sourd. loc	That didn't fall on deaf ears.
la **joue** [ʒu]	cheek
le **nez** [ne]	nose
Je me suis trouvé **nez à nez** avec mon chef.	I found myself face to face with my boss.

la **bouche** [buʃ]	mouth
la **lèvre** [lɛvʀ]	lip

la **langue** [lãg]	tongue
tirer la langue à qn	stick one's tongue out at s.o.
la **dent** [dã]	tooth
le **menton** [mãtɔ̃]	chin

le **cou** [ku]	neck
sauter au cou de qn	fall on s.o.'s neck
la **gorge** [gɔRʒ]	throat
avoir un chat dans la gorge *loc*	have a frog in one's throat

l'**épaule** *f* [epol]	shoulder
le **dos** [do]	back
la **taille** [taj]	waist; size

un **organe** [ɔRgan]	organ
la **poitrine** [pwatRin]	chest, breast, bosom
le **cœur** [kœR]	heart
Son cœur bat trop vite.	Her heart beats too fast.
le **ventre** [vãtR]	belly, abdomen
l'**estomac** *m* [ɛstɔma]	stomach

le **bras** [bRa]	arm
le **coude** [kud]	elbow
la **main** [mɛ̃]	hand
le **doigt** [dwa]	finger
montrer qn/qc du doigt	point one's finger at s.o./s.th.

la **jambe** [ʒãb]	leg
Elle s'est cassé la jambe.	She broke her leg.
le **genou,** les **genoux** [ʒ(ə)nu]	knee
le **pied** [pje]	foot
casser les pieds à qn *fam*	get on s.o.'s nerves

le **crâne** [kRan]	skull
avoir mal au crâne	have a headache
le **cerveau** [sɛRvo]	brain
C'est le **cerveau** de la bande.	He's the brains of the outfit.
le **nerf** [nɛR]	nerve
le **système nerveux** [sistɛmnɛRvø]	nervous system
l'**artère** *f* [aRtɛR]	artery
la **veine** [vɛn]	vein
le **muscle** [myskl]	muscle
le **tendon** [tãdɔ̃]	tendon
Il souffre d'une déchirure du tendon d'Achille.	He tore his Achilles tendon.

la **paupière** [popjɛR]	eyelid
le **cil** [sil]	eyelash
le **sourcil** [suRsil]	eyebrow
froncer les sourcils	knit one's brows
le **poil** [pwal]	(human) body hair; animal hair
être à poil	be naked
Il a un poil dans la main. *loc*	He is work-shy.

le **poignet** [pwaɲɛ]	wrist
le **poing** [pwɛ̃]	fist
serrer les poings	ball one's fists
le **pouce** [pus]	thumb
A six ans, il suce toujours son pouce.	At the age of six, he still sucks his thumb.

la **nuque** [nyk]	nape (of the neck)
la **colonne vertébrale** [kɔlɔnvɛRtebRal]	spine, vertebral column
le **sein** [sɛ̃]	breast
les seins	bosom
la **hanche** ['ɑ̃ʃ]	hip
les **fesses** *f* [fɛs]	buttocks, bottom
donner une claque sur les fesses	give a slap on the bottom
le **derrière** [dɛRjɛR]	bottom, behind

le **poumon** [pumɔ̃]	lung
le **foie** [fwa]	liver
le **rein** [Rɛ̃]	kidney
l'**intestin** *m* [ɛ̃tɛstɛ̃]	intestine

la **cuisse** [kɥis]	thigh
la **cheville** [ʃ(ə)vij]	ankle
Il s'est foulé la cheville.	He sprained his ankle.
le **talon** [talɔ̃]	heel
l'**orteil** *m* [ɔRtɛj]	toe
le **doigt de pied** [dwad(ə)pie]	toe

2.2 Sexuality and Reproduction

un **sentiment** [sɑ̃timɑ̃]	feeling
l'**amour** *m* [amuR]	love
aimer [ɛme]	love, be fond of; like

Je ne l'aime pas d'amour, mais je l'aime bien	I don't love him/her, but I like him/her.
(être) amoureux, -euse (de qn) [amuʀø, øz]	be in love (with s.o.)
tomber* amoureux, -euse de qn	fall in love with s.o.
Ils sont tombés amoureux l'un de l'autre.	They fell in love with each other.
l'**affection** f [afɛksjɔ̃]	affection

faire la cour à qn [fɛʀlakuʀ]	court s.o., woo s.o.
Il lui fait la cour depuis des mois.	He's been courting her for months.
flirter avec [flœʀte]	flirt with
draguer qn fam [dʀage]	hit on s.o.
Il l'a draguée toute la soirée.	He was hitting on her all evening.

un,e **ami,e** [ami]	friend
C'est son **petit ami**.	That's her boyfriend.
un **copain**, une **copine** fam [kɔpɛ̃, in]	pal, chum
un **compagnon**, une **compagne** [kɔ̃paɲɔ̃, kɔ̃paɲ]	life partner
un **amant** [amɑ̃]	lover
une **maîtresse** [mɛtʀɛs]	lover, mistress

embrasser [ɑ̃bʀase]	kiss
un **baiser** [beze]	kiss
caresser [kaʀɛse]	caress
la **tendresse** [tɑ̃dʀɛs]	tenderness
tendre [tɑ̃dʀ]	tender
faire l'amour avec qn [fɛʀlamuʀ]	make love with s.o.
coucher avec qn fam [kuʃe]	sleep with s.o., go to bed with s.o.
Tout ce qu'il veut, c'est coucher avec elle.	All he wants is to sleep with her.

le **sexe** [sɛks]	sex
sexuel, le [sɛksɥel]	sexual
sexy fam [sɛksi]	sexy
désirer [deziʀe]	desire, want

(être) enceinte [ɑ̃sɛ̃t]	(be) pregnant
attendre un enfant [atɑ̃dʀɛ̃nɑ̃fɑ̃]	expect a baby
accourcher de [akuʃe]	give birth to, deliver
Elle a accouché d'un beau garçon.	She gave birth to a handsome boy.
l'**accouchement** m [akuʃmɑ̃]	birth, delivery

mettre au monde [mɛtʀomɔ̃d] Elle veut mettre son bébé au monde chez elle.	bring into the world She would like to bring her baby into the world at home.

une **liaison** [ljɛzɔ̃]
avoir une liaison orageuse avec qn

(être) fidèle (à qn) [fidɛl]
(être) infidèle (à qn) [ɛ̃fidɛl]
tromper qn [tʀɔ̃pe]

liaison, relationship
have a stormy (love) affair with s.o.

(be) faithful (to s.o.)
(be) unfaithful (to s.o.)
deceive s.o.

vierge [vjɛʀʒ]
la **virginité** [viʀʒinite]
les **rapports sexuels** m [ʀapɔʀsɛksɥɛl]
le **comportement sexuel** [kɔ̃pɔʀt(ə)mɑ̃sɛksɥɛl]
la **puberté** [pybɛʀte]
Mon fils est **en pleine puberté**.
les **règles** f [ʀɛgl]

virginal
virginity
sexual relations
sexual conduct
puberty
My son is in the midst of puberty.
(menstrual) period

le **plaisir** [plɛziʀ]
exciter [ɛksite]
érotique [eʀɔtik]
l'**érotisme** m [eʀɔtism]

pleasure
excite
erotic
eroticism

le **sperme** [spɛʀm]
Le virus du sida **se transmet par** le sperme.
impuissant,e [ɛ̃pɥisɑ̃, ɑ̃t]
l'**impuissance** f [ɛ̃pɥisɑ̃s]
jouir [ʒwiʀ]
frigide [fʀiʒid]

sperm
The AIDS virus is transmitted through sperm.
impotent
impotence
have an orgasm
frigid

hétéro(sexuel, le) [eteʀo(sɛksɥɛl)]
homo(sexuel, le) [ɔmɔ(sɛksɥɛl)]
(un) **pédé** n; adj; fam [pede]
(une) **lesbienne** n; adj [lɛsbjɛn]

heterosexual
homosexual
gay man; gay
lesbian

la **reproduction** [ʀ(ə)pʀɔdyksjɔ̃]
la **conception** [kɔ̃sɛpsjɔ̃]
la **grossesse** [gʀosɛs]
une **fausse-couche** [foskuʃ]
Elle a peur de **faire une fausse-couche**.

reproduction
conception
pregnancy
miscarriage
She is afraid of having a miscarriage.

stérile [steʀil]	sterile
la stérilité [steʀilite]	sterility
fécond,e [fekɔ̃, ɔ̃d]	fertile
la fécondité [fekɔ̃dite]	fertility
féconder [fekɔ̃de]	fertilize
la fécondation [fekɔ̃dasjɔ̃]	fertilization
la fécondation artificielle/in vitro	artificial insemination
un moyen de contraception [mwajɛ̃d(ə)kɔ̃tʀasɛpsjɔ̃]	contraceptive
la pilule [pilyl]	pill (oral contraceptive)
Elle a arrêté de prendre la pilule.	
un préservatif [pʀezɛʀvatif]	condom
un distributeur de préservatifs	condom-vending machine
avorter [avɔʀte]	abort
se faire avorter	have an abortion
un avortement [avɔʀtəment]	abortion
une I.V.G. (une interruption volontaire de grossesse) [iveʒe]	voluntary interruption of pregnancy
le contrôle des naissances [kɔ̃tʀoldenɛsɑ̃s]	birth control

2.3 Birth, Stages of Development, Death

la vie [vi]	life
risquer sa vie	risk one's life
Que la vie est belle !	How beautiful life is!
vivre [vivʀ]	live
vivant,e [vivɑ̃, ɑ̃t]	living, alive
survivre à qn/qc [syʀvivʀ]	survive s.o./s.th.
Le blessé n'a pas survécu long-temps à l'accident.	The injured man did not survive the accident for long.
la survie [syʀvi]	survival
la naissance [nɛsɑ̃s]	birth
naître* [nɛtʀ]	be born
être né,e	be born
De Gaulle est né à Lille.	De Gaulle was born in Lille.
un anniversaire [anivɛʀsɛʀ]	birthday
Bon anniversaire !	Happy birthday!
exister [ɛgziste]	exist, live
l'existence f [ɛgzistɑ̃s]	existence

les **parents** m [paʀɑ̃]	parents; relatives
le **père** [pɛʀ]	father
la **mère** [mɛʀ]	mother
le **bébé** [bebe]	baby
Ma sœur **attend un bébé** pour le mois d'avril.	My sister is expecting a baby in April.
le **fils** [fis]	son
la **fille** [fij]	daughter, girl

grandir [gʀɑ̃diʀ]	grow
Il a grandi dans une famille pauvre.	He grew up in a poor family.
un,e **enfant** [ɑ̃fɑ̃]	child
l'**enfance** f [ɑ̃fɑ̃s]	childhood
(un,e) **jeune** n; adj [ʒœn]	young person; young
les jeunes d'aujourd'hui	the youth of today
la **jeunesse** [ʒœnɛs]	youth
l'**éducation** f [edykasjɔ̃]	education
éduquer [edyke]	educate
élever [el(ə)ve]	rear, bring up
un enfant mal élevé	an ill-bred child
un,e **adolescent,e**; un,e **ado** fam [adɔlɛsɑ̃, ɑ̃t]	adolescent, youth
l'**adolescence** f [adɔlɛsɑ̃s]	adolescence, youth
(un,e) **adulte** n; adj [adylt]	adult, grown-up

le **mariage** [maʀjaʒ]	marriage
un **mariage civil/religieux**	a civil/religious wedding
se marier avec qn [s(ə)maʀje]	marry s.o.
un **couple** [kupl]	(married) couple
Ils forment un beau couple, tous les deux.	The two of them make an attractive couple.

---

i

se marier (avec qn), marier qn à/avec qn, épouser qn

Note the difference between:

se marier (avec qn)	*marry (s.o.)*
Elle s'est mariée à l'église.	*She got married in church.*
Elle s'est mariée avec mon frère.	*She married my brother.*
marier qn avec/à qn	*marry s.o. to s.o.*
Ils ont marié leur fille au fils/avec le fils d'un gros industriel.	*They married their daughter to the son of a big industrialist.*
épouser qn	*marry s.o.*
Céline a épousé son chef.	*Céline married her boss.*

l'**âge** m [aʒ]	age
être d'un certain âge	be not so young anymore
le **3ᵉ âge** [tʀwazjema]	retirement age
Il vit dans une **résidence pour le 3ᵉ âge.**	He lives in a home for senior citizens.
âgé,e de [aʒe]	old; of age
Je suis âgé de 30 ans.	I'm 30 years old.
vieux, vieil, vieille [vjø, vjɛj]	old, aged
Il est très vieux. Un vieil homme. Une vieille dame.	He is very old. An old man. An old lady.
mourir* [muʀiʀ]	die
mourir d'un cancer du poumon	die of lung cancer
(le, la) **mort,e** n; adj [mɔʀ, mɔʀt]	dead person; dead
Elle est morte d'un infarctus.	She died of a heart attack.
L'accident a fait deux morts.	The accident claimed two lives.
mortel,le [mɔʀtɛl]	fatal
une maladie mortelle	a fatal illness
la **mort** [mɔʀ]	death
Attention, danger de mort !	Caution, danger!
se suicider [səsɥiside]	commit suicide
le **suicide** [sɥisid]	suicide

ℹ️ la mort, etc.

Pay attention to the *article* and the *pronunciation:*

la mort [mɔʀ]	*the death*
le mort [mɔʀ], la morte [mɔʀt]	*the dead man, the dead woman*

---

un **nourrisson** [nuʀisɔ̃]	infant
un,e **gamin,e** fam [gamɛ̃, in]	little boy, little girl
un,e **gosse** fam	brat, urchin, kid
Quel sale gosse !	What a little brat!

---

vieillir [vjejiʀ]	grow old, age
la **vieillesse** [vjɛjɛs]	(old) age
un **vieillard** [vjɛjaʀ]	old man
sénile [senil]	senile
la **retraite** [ʀ(ə)tʀɛt]	retirement
une **maison de retraite (médicalisée)**	retirement home (nursing home)
partir/être à la retraite	retire/be retired
un,e **retraité,e** [ʀətʀete]	pensioner, retired person
(un,e) **centenaire** n; adj [sɑ̃t(ə)nɛʀ]	centenarian; one hundred years old
l'**espérance de vie** f [ɛspeʀɑ̃sdəvi]	life expectancy

L'espérance de vie des femmes est plus élevée que celle des hommes.	The life expectancy of women is greater than that of men.

se fiancer avec [s(ə)fjɑ̃se]	become engaged to
épouser [epuze]	marry
uni,e [yni]	united
un **couple très uni**	a very close couple
conjugal,e [kɔ̃ʒygal]	conjugal, marital, matrimonial
le **lit conjugal**	marriage bed
un **ménage** [menaʒ]	household, married couple
faire une **scène de ménage à qn**	make a scene with s.o.

se séparer de qn [səsepaʀe]	separate from s.o.
la **séparation** [sepaʀasjɔ̃]	separation
divorcer de qn/(d')avec qn [divɔʀse]	divorce s.o., get a divorce from s.o.
Cet acteur a divorcé de sa quatrième femme.	This actor has divorced his fourth wife.
le **divorce** [divɔʀs]	divorce

décéder* [desede]	die, pass away
Il est décédé lundi dernier.	He died last Monday.
le **décès** [dese]	demise, death
défunt,e [defɛ̃, ɛ̃t]	deceased
son défunt mari	her deceased husband
le **deuil** [dœj]	mourning
être en deuil	be in mourning
porter le deuil de qn	wear mourning for s.o.
un **cimetière** [simtjɛʀ]	cemetery
la **tombe** [tɔ̃b]	tomb, grave
le **cercueil** [sɛʀkœj]	coffin
enterrer [ɑ̃teʀe]	bury, inter
Elle a été enterrée près de ses parents.	She was buried next to her parents.
l'**enterrement** m [ɑ̃tɛʀmɑ̃]	burial, interment
les **obsèques** f [ɔbsɛk]	funeral
les **condoléances** f [kɔ̃dɔleɑ̃s]	condolences, sympathy
présenter ses condoléances	express one's condolences

2.4 Senses and Physical Reactions

voir [vwaʀ]	see, perceive
Je n'ai rien vu; le brouillard était trop épais.	I didn't see anything; the fog was too heavy.

la **vue** [vy]	vision, sight
avoir la vue basse	be nearsighted; have poor vision
visuel,le [vizɥɛl]	visual
visible [vizibl]	visible
C'est **visible à l'œil nu.**	It is visible to the naked eye.
regarder [ʀ(ə)gaʀde]	look at
un **regard** [ʀ(ə)gaʀ]	look, glance
remarquer [ʀ(ə)maʀke]	notice
observer [ɔpsɛʀve]	observe
une **observation** [ɔpsɛʀvasjɔ̃]	observation
avoir le **sens de l'observation**	have a good sense of observation
aveugle [avœgl]	blind

| **entendre** [ãtãdʀ] | hear |
| **écouter** [ekute] | listen (to) |

---

entendre – écouter

Note the difference between:

entendre	*hear (perceive)*
Qu'est-ce que c'est ? J'entends des bruits.	*What's that? I hear noises.*
écouter	*hear (pay attention to); listen to*
Tais-toi, s'il te plaît. J'écoute les infos.	*Please be quiet. I'm listening to the news.*

---

le **son** [sɔ̃]	sound
le son du piano	the sound of the piano
le **bruit** [bʀɥi]	noise
le **silence** [silɑ̃s]	silence
La parole est d'argent et le silence est d'or. *prov*	Talk is silver, and silence is golden.
silencieux, -euse [silɑ̃sjø, jøz]	silent

| **sentir** [sãtiʀ] | smell |
| **Ça sent bon/mauvais.** | It/That smells good/bad. |

---

sentir

Note the *shades of meaning* conveyed by **sentir**:

Je ne sens rien, j'ai un rhume.	*I can't smell anything, I have a cold.*
Beurk! Ce poisson sent.	*Ugh, this fish smells (bad).*
Tu sens le tabac.	*You smell of tobacco.*
Viens sentir ces fleurs, elles sentent très bon/mauvais.	*Smell these flowers; they smell very good/bad.*

When used adverbially, the adjective **bon/mauvais** remains unchanged.

| une **odeur** [ɔdœʀ] | odor, smell |
| L'argent n'a pas d'odeur. *loc* | Money has no odor. |

goûter [gute] — taste, try
le **goût** [gu] — (sense of) taste
Ça a un goût de pomme. — That tastes like apple.

toucher [tuʃe] — touch
N'y touche pas! — Don't touch it!
froid,e [fʀwa, fʀwad] — cold
chaud,e [ʃo, ʃod] — warm, hot
tiède [tjɛd] — lukewarm, tepid
Elle n'a pas inventé l'eau tiède. *loc* — She's not the brightest.
dur,e [dyʀ] — hard
un **œuf dur** — a hard-boiled egg
mou, molle [mu, mɔl] — soft
doux, douce [du, dus] — soft, smooth
un tissu **doux au toucher** — a fabric that is soft to the touch

la **fatigue** [fatig] — fatigue, tiredness
Je suis morte de fatigue. — I'm dead tired.
fatigué,e [fatige] — tired, fatigued
dormir [dɔʀmiʀ] — sleep
s'endormir [sɑ̃dɔʀmiʀ] — fall asleep
le **sommeil** [sɔmɛj] — sleep
Je n'ai pas sommeil. — I'm not sleepy.
se réveiller [s(ə)ʀevɛje] — awake, wake, wake up
le **réveil** [ʀevɛj] — waking, awakening; alarm clock
avoir le réveil difficile — have a hard time waking up

réagir [ʀeaʒiʀ] — react
une **réaction** [ʀeaksjɔ̃] — reaction
un **réflexe** [ʀeflɛks] — reflex
un **geste** [ʒɛst] — gesture, movement (of the hands)
Il n'a pas fait un geste pour m'aider. — He didn't lift a finger to help me.

grandir [gʀɑ̃diʀ] — grow
Ma fille a beaucoup grandi depuis Noël. — My daughter has grown a lot since Christmas.

---

i **Verbs ending in -ir**

Some *verbs ending in* -ir whose stem is derived from an adjective express a *development*, a process of *becoming*:
rougir *blush;* **pâlir, blêmir** *become pale;* **grandir** *grow;* **grosser** *become fatter, gain weight;* **maigrir** *lose weight.*

---

grossir [grosir]
Il a **grossi** de cinq kilos.
maigrir [megrir]

gain weight, get fat
He has gained five kilos.
lose weight

reconnaître [r(ə)konɛtr]
apercevoir [apɛrsəvwar]
Je l'ai aperçu de loin.

recognize
catch sight of, perceive
I caught sight of him from a
distance.

s'apercevoir de qc [sapɛrsəvwar]
Je ne me suis pas aperçu de son
absence.
perceptible [pɛrsɛptibl]

notice s.th.
I haven't noticed his absence.

perceptible

baisser les yeux [beselezjø]
détourner le regard
[deturnel(ə)r(ə)gar]
un **coup d'œil** [kudœj]
  jeter un coup d'œil sur qn/qc
cligner (des yeux) [kliɲe]
loucher [luʃe]
(être) myope [mjɔp]
(être) presbyte [prɛsbit]
la **cécité** [sesite]

lower one's eyes; look down
look away

glance, look
  glance at s.o./s.th.
blink
squint
be nearsighted/myopic
be farsighted/presbyopic
blindness

l'**ouïe** f [wi]
  avoir l'ouïe très fine
auditif, -ive [oditif, iv]
(un,e) **malentendant,e** n; adj
[malɑ̃tɑ̃dɑ̃, ɑ̃t]
(un,e) **sourd,e** n; adj [sur, surd]
Il est sourd comme un pot. loc
(un,e) **sourd-muet,te**
la **surdité** [syrdite]

(sense of) hearing
  have excellent hearing
auditory
person who is hard of hearing;
hard of hearing
deaf person; deaf
He's as deaf as a doorpost.
deaf-mute
deafness

rougir [ruʒir]
Elle est timide, elle rougit dès
qu'on la regarde.
pâlir [palir]
Il a pâli quand il a entendu cette
nouvelle.

blush
She is shy; she blushes when
you look at her.
become pale
He turned pale when he heard
that news.

2.5 Movements and Activities

agir [aʒiʀ]	act, do
une **action** [aksjɔ̃]	action, deed
une **femme d'action**	a woman of action
actif, -ive [aktif, iv]	active
une **activité** f [aktivite]	activity
un **mouvement** [muvmã]	movement
bouger [buʒe]	move, budge
Hier je n'ai pas **bougé de chez moi.**	Yesterday I didn't budge from home.
s'arrêter [saʀɛte]	stop, pause
se trouver [tʀuve]	be; find oneself
Où te trouves-tu en ce moment?	Where are you at the moment?
rester* [ʀɛste]	stay, remain

marcher [maʀʃe]	go on foot, walk; march
la **marche**	walk, walking; march
La **marche à pied** est excellente pour la santé.	Walking is excellent for one's health.
le **pas** [pa]	step
Les soldats **marchent au pas.**	The soldiers march in step.
fair qc **pas à pas**	do s.th. step by step

> **go**
>
> To express *go* as a **form of movement,** use either **marcher** or **aller** (+ **à pied,** for example):
>
> | | |
> |---|---|
> | **Pas si vite. Marche plus lentement.** | *Not so fast. Go slower.* |
> | **On y va à pied ou en voiture?** | *Are we going on foot or by car?* |
>
> **Aller** expresses pure *(forward) movement,* locomotion.
>
> | | |
> |---|---|
> | **Je vais à Nantes.** | *I'm going (driving, flying, traveling) to Nantes.* |

---

aller* [ale]	go
Va dans la cuisine!	Go in the kitchen!
venir* [v(ə)niʀ]	come
Tu viens avec moi?	Are you coming with me?
revenir* [ʀəv(ə)niʀ, ʀ(ə)vəniʀ]	return
revenir sur ses pas	retrace one's steps
suivre qn/qc [sɥivʀ]	follow s.o./s.th.
se diriger vers [s(ə)diʀiʒe]	go toward, make for

---

avancer [avãse]	move forward, advance

reculer [ʀ(ə)kyle]	draw back, move back
reculer de trois pas	go three steps back
retourner* [ʀ(ə)tuʀne]	return, go back
On continue ou on retourne à la maison ?	Are we going on or going back home?
se retourner [səʀ(ə)tuʀne]	turn around
Tout le monde se retourne **sur son passage.**	Everyone turns around when he/she goes past.
le **retour** [ʀ(ə)tuʀ]	return

partir* [paʀtiʀ]	depart, leave, go; set out
Il veut **partir pour** l'Afrique.	He wants to go to Africa.
repartir* [ʀ(ə)paʀtiʀ]	go away again
le **départ** [depaʀ]	departure
sortir* [sɔʀtiʀ]	go out; leave, depart
une **sortie** [sɔʀti]	exit
Sortie de secours	emergency exit
entrer* [ãtʀe]	enter, come in
une **entrée** [ãtʀe]	entrance, entry
rentrer* [ʀãtʀe]	enter again; return
Ils sont rentrés de vacances.	They have returned from vacation.
arriver* [aʀive]	arrive
l'**arrivée** f [aʀive]	arrival

courir [kuʀiʀ]	run, race
parcourir [paʀkuʀiʀ]	travel through; go through
Il a parcouru toute la ville.	He went all over town.
une **course** [kuʀs]	run; course; race
se dépêcher de faire qc [s(ə)depɛʃe]	hurry to do s.th.
rapide [ʀapid]	fast
Il est plus rapide que toi.	He is faster than you.
vite adv [vit]	fast, quickly
Il court plus vite que toi.	He runs faster than you.
lent,e [lã, lãt]	slow

sauter [sote]	jump, leap
un **saut** [so]	jump
un **saut périlleux**	somersault
tomber* [tɔbe]	fall, drop
une **chute** [ʃyt]	fall, drop

monter* [mɔ̃te]	climb; go up, ascend
une **montée** [mɔ̃te]	slope, ascent
descendre* [desɑ̃dʀ]	descend; go down; get out
descendre de voiture	get out of the car
une **descente** [desɑ̃t]	descent; disembarkment

---

monter, descendre, sortir, rentrer, retourner

The verbs **monter, descendre, sortir, rentrer,** and **retourner** change their meaning, depending on whether they are followed by a *direct object* (transitive use) or not (intransitive use). When used *intransitively,* they form the compound tenses with **être,** and when used *transitively,* the auxiliary verb is **avoir.**

Elle <u>est</u> montée/descendue.	*She went up/down.*
Elle <u>a</u> monté/descendu la valise.	*She carried the suitcase up/down.*
Ils <u>sont</u> sortis/rentrés.	*They went out/came back.*
Il <u>a</u> sorti/rentré la poubelle.	*He took out/brought in the garbage can.*
Elle <u>est</u> retournée à Paris.	*She has returned to Paris.*
Il <u>a</u> retourné les cartes.	*He turned over the cards.*

---

voler [vɔle]	fly
le **vol** [vɔl]	flight

---

voler, le vol

Voler and le vol are *homonyms:* depending on the context, **voler** means either *fly* or *steal,* and **le vol** is either *flight* or *theft.*

Les hirondelles volent bas aujourd'hui.	*The swallows are flying low today.*
On m'a volé le porte-monnaie dans le métro.	*My wallet was stolen in the subway.*
un vol régulier/charter	*a regularly scheduled/charter flight*
un vol à l'étalage	*shoplifting*

---

nager [naʒe]	swim
nager le crawl	do the crawl (stroke)
la **natation** [natasjɔ̃]	swimming
danser [dɑ̃se]	dance
danser le rock	dance to rock music
la **danse** [dɑ̃s]	dance
s'exercer [sɛgzɛʀse]	(do) exercise
un **exercice** [ɛgzɛʀsis]	exercise

---

debout adj; adv [d(ə)bu]	upright, standing up
se mettre debout	get up
être debout	be up
se **lever** [s(ə)lɔve]	get up, rise

se baisser [s(ə)bɛse]	bend over
assis,e [asi, iz]	seated, sitting down
être/rester assis,e	sit/remain seated
une **place assise/debout**	seat/standing room
s'asseoir [saswaʀ]	sit down
Asseyez-vous.	Have a seat.
couché,e [kuʃe]	lying down
se coucher [kuʃe]	lie down
se reposer [s(ə)ʀ(ə)poze]	rest

montrer [mõtʀe]	show
présenter [pʀezãte]	present, offer
présenter ses vœux	offer one's congratulations
donner [dɔne]	give
distribuer [distʀibɥe]	distribute, deal out
Le facteur distribue le courrier.	The postman delivers the mail.
rendre [ʀãdʀ]	return, give back
tendre [tãdʀ]	hold out
tendre la main à qn	hold out one's hand to s.o.
tenir [t(ə)niʀ]	hold
attraper [atʀape]	catch
Je cours pour **attraper le bus.**	I'm running to catch the bus.
prendre [pʀãdʀ]	take
voler [vɔle]	steal
Qui vole un œuf vole un bœuf.	It starts with small things and
prov	ends with big ones.

un **acte** [akt]	deed, action, act
Il faut le **juger sur ses actes.**	He has to be judged by his deeds.
un **acte de bonté**	an act of kindness
remuer [ʀəmye]	move
se rendre à [s(ə)ʀãdʀ]	betake oneself, go
Il s'est rendu à Brest.	He has gone to Brest.
s'approcher de qn/qc [sapʀɔʃe]	approach s.o./s.th
se rapprocher de qn/qc [s(ə)ʀapʀɔʃe]	approach s.o./s.th. again
accourir* [akuʀiʀ]	hasten, rush up to
Je suis accouru dès que tu m'as appelé.	I rushed over as soon as you called me.
s'éloigner de [selwaɲe]	go away, absent oneself
se déplacer [s(ə)deplase]	travel; change one's place
se précipiter [s(ə)pʀesipite]	hurl oneself
s'élancer [selãse]	rush; bound forth
s'élancer au secours de qn	rush to s.o.'s aid

la **fuite** [fɥit]	flight
s'**enfuir** [sɑ̃fɥiʀ]	flee
s'**échapper** [seʃape]	escape
se **sauver** *fam* [səsove]	save oneself
Sauvez-vous avant qu'il soit trop tard.	Clear out before it's too late.
glisser [glise]	slip, slide
J'ai glissé sur une peau de banane.	I slipped on a banana peel.
traîner [tʀɛne]	drag along; loiter, linger

à **genoux** [aʒ(ə)nu]	kneeling, on one's knees
être/se mettre à genoux	be on one's knees/kneel down
s'**appuyer (sur)** [sapɥje]	lean (on), rest (on)
s'**allonger (sur)** [salɔ̃ʒe]	lie down (on)
Allonge-toi sur le canapé.	Lie down on the sofa.
se **redresser** [s(ə)ʀ(ə)dʀɛse]	straighten up again; right oneself

se **détendre** [s(ə)detɑ̃dʀ]	relax
Nous jouons du piano pour nous détendre.	We play the piano to relax.
la **détente** [detɑ̃t]	relaxation

2.6 Appearance

beau, bel, belle [bo, bɛl]	beautiful, fine, nice
un beau bébé; un bel enfant; une belle jeune fille	a beautiful baby; a beautiful child; a beautiful little girl
la **beauté** [bote]	beauty
joli,e [ʒɔli]	pretty
laid,e [lɛ, lɛd]	ugly
Il est laid à faire peur. *loc*	He is as ugly as sin.
la **laideur** [lɛdœʀ]	ugliness

la **taille** [taj]	size
un homme de petite taille	a man of small stature
grand,e [gʀɑ̃, gʀɑ̃d]	large, big
petit,e [p(ə)ti, it]	small, little
Elle est toute petite.	She is quite tiny.

le **poids** [pwa]	weight
prendre/perdre du poids	gain/lose weight
gros,se [gʀo, gʀos]	fat

gras,se [gra, gras]	corpulent, obese
mince [mɛ̃s]	slender
maigre [mɛgr]	thin, lean
fort,e [fɔr, fɔrt]	stout, sturdy, robust

les **cheveux** m [ʃ(ə)vø]	hair
long,ue [lɔ̃, lɔ̃g]	long
avoir les cheveux longs	have long hair
court,e [kur, kurt]	short
(un,e) **blond,e** n; adj [blɔ̃, blɔ̃d]	blond
C'est une fausse blonde.	She's not a true blonde.
roux, rousse [ru, rus]	red-haired
brun,e [brɛ̃, bryn]	dark-haired

l'**aspect physique** [aspɛfizik]	(physical) appearance
le **physique** [fizik]	outward appearance; physique
avoir un physique avantageux	have a becoming appearance, be good-looking
l'**apparence** f [aparɑ̃s]	appearance
avoir l'air (de) m [avwarlɛr]	look (like)
Il a l'air d'un clochard.	He looks like a vagrant.

---

i **avoir l'air + adjective**

After **avoir l'air**, the adjective ending generally is determined by the *subject*, but with *female persons* the masculine form may be used as well. In that case, **air** m is considered to be the antecedent.

Elle a l'air heureuse/heureux.	*She looks happy.*
Ces devoirs ont l'air difficiles.	*These tasks look difficult.*

---

la **constitution** [kɔ̃stitysjɔ̃]	constitution
avoir une robuste constitution	have a robust constitution
fragile [fraʒil]	fragile
musclé,e [myskle]	muscular
baraqué,e fam [barake]	large and sturdy
souple [supl]	supple, flexible; lithe
la **souplesse** [suplɛs]	suppleness, flexibility
élancé,e [elɑ̃se]	slender, slim; lanky
une silhouette élancée	a slender silhouette
svelte [svɛlt]	slender, svelte
corpulent,e [kɔrpylɑ̃, ɑ̃t]	corpulent, stout
la **corpulence** [kɔrpylɑ̃s]	corpulence
une dame **de forte corpulence**	an extremely corpulent lady
trapu,e [trapy]	squat, dumpy, stocky

mignon,ne [miɲɔ̃, ɔn]	dainty, pretty; sweet; cute
affreux, -euse [afʁø, øz]	frightful, hideous, repulsive
moche *fam* [mɔʃ]	ugly; dowdy
ridé,e [ʁide]	wrinkled
ridé comme une vieille pomme	as wrinkled as an old apple
voûté,e [vute]	stooped, bent
Il marche voûté comme un vieillard.	He walks stooped over like an old man.

le **teint** [tɛ̃]	complexion
avoir le teint frais	have a fresh complexion
bronzé,e [bʁɔ̃ze]	tanned
pâle [pal]	pale
Tu es pâle comme un linge. *loc*	You're as pale as a corpse.
avoir des boutons *m* [avwaʁdebutɔ̃]	have pimples

chauve [ʃov]	bald
châtain [ʃatɛ̃]	chestnut, nut-brown, auburn
Elle a les cheveux châtains.	She has auburn hair.
Elle est châtain.	She is chestnut-haired.
foncé,e [fɔ̃se]	light, bright
clair,e [klɛʁ]	light
avoir les yeux clairs	have light eyes

2.7 Cosmetics and Personal Grooming

la **toilette** [twalɛt]	dress, attire; personal grooming
faire sa toilette	dress; wash up
un gant de toilette	washcloth
se laver [s(ə)lave]	wash (oneself)
un **bain** [bɛ̃]	bath
se faire couler un bain	run a bath for oneself
une **douche** [duʃ]	shower
prendre une douche	take a shower
le **savon** [savɔ̃]	soap

chaud,e [ʃo, ʃod]	hot, warm
tiède [tjɛd]	lukewarm
froid,e [fʁwa, fʁwad]	cold
propre [pʁɔpʁ]	clean
la **propreté** [pʁɔpʁəte]	cleanliness

propre ...

Some adjectives change their *meaning*, depending on whether they *precede* or *follow* the noun modified:

un hôtel propre	*a clean hotel*
Il l'a écrit de sa propre main.	*He wrote it in his own hand.*
C'est une histoire vraie.	*It's a true story.*
C'est un vrai problème.	*It's a real problem.*
une histoire drôle	*a funny story*
une drôle d'histoire	*a strange story*
un homme brave	*a good man*
un brave type	*a decent/good guy*
un ancien ministre	*a former minister*
un monument ancien	*an ancient building*

sale [sal]　　　　　　　　　　　dirty, filthy
　être sale comme un peigne *loc*　be very dirty
la **saleté** [salte]　　　　　　　dirt, filth

sécher [seʃe]　　　　　　　　　dry
　Mes cheveux sèchent vite.　　　My hair dries quickly.
sec, sèche [sɛk, sɛʃ]　　　　　dry
une **serviette (de toilette/de bain)** [sɛRvjɛt]　hand towel/bath towel
s'essuyer [sesɥije]　　　　　　dry (oneself)
　Essuie-toi les mains avec cette serviette de toilette.　Dry your hands with this hand towel.
se nettoyer [s(ə)netwaje]　　clean (oneself)

le **dentifrice** [dãtifRis]　　　　toothpaste
　un **tube de dentifrice**　　　　tube of toothpaste
une **brosse (à dents)** [bRɔs(adã)]　toothbrush
se brosser les dents [s(ə)bRɔseledã]　brush one's teeth

une **brosse (à cheveux)** [bRɔs(aʃ(ə)vø)]　(hair)brush
un **peigne** [pɛɲ]　　　　　　　comb
se peigner [s(ə)pɛɲe]　　　　comb one's hair
se coiffer [s(ə)kwafe]　　　　dress one's hair
une **coiffure** [kwafyR]　　　　hairdo
　Tu as changé de coiffure?　　　Do you have a new hairdo?
un,e **coiffeur, -euse** [kwafœR, øz]　hairdresser
　aller chez le coiffeur　　　　　go to the hairdresser
une **coupe de cheveux** [kupdəʃ(ə)vø]　haircut

Hairdresser

Note:

un coiffeur, une coiffeuse	*hairdresser*
(se) coiffer	*dress (one's) hair*

Though English has the nouns *coiffure* and *coif* and the verb *coiffure*, all borrowed from French, they are not common in modern usage.

les **ciseaux** *m* [sizo]	scissors

ciseaux ...

Note:

des ciseaux *m*, une paire de ciseaux	*(a pair of) scissors*
deux paires de ciseaux	*two pairs of scissors*

Similarly:

des lunettes *f*, une paire de lunettes	*(a pair of) eyeglasses*
trois paires de lunettes	*three pairs of eyeglasses*
des tenailles *f*, une paire de tenailles	*(a pair of) pliers*
deux paires de tenailles	*two pairs of pliers*

Along with **des tenailles, une tenaille** is now in common use in French.

un **shamp(o)oing** [ʃɑ̃pwɛ̃]	shampoo
fair son shamp(o)oing	shampoo one's hair
une **crème** [kʀɛm]	face cream
une crème de jour/de nuit	a day/night cream
un tube de crème solaire	a tube of sunscreen

l'**hygiène** [iʒjɛn]	hygiene
rincer [ʀɛ̃se]	rinse (out)
se rincer les cheveux	rinse one's hair
une **éponge** [epɔ̃ʒ]	sponge
frotter [fʀɔte]	scrub
Frotte-moi le dos, s'il te plaît.	Scrub my back, please.

un **brushing** [bʀœʃiŋ]	blow-dry
un **sèche-cheveu(x)** [sɛʃʃəvø]	hairdryer

For information on the plural of compound nouns of the **verb + noun** type, see p. 94.

la **laque** [lak]	hair spray

la **barbe** [baʀb]	beard
porter la barbe	wear a beard

la **moustache** [mustaʃ]	mustache
se **raser** [s(ə)ʀaze]	shave (oneself)
la **crème à raser**	shaving cream
un **après-rasage** [apʀɛʀazaʒ]	aftershave
un **rasoir** [ʀazwaʀ]	razor
un **rasoir électrique**	electric razor
un **ongle** [ɔ̃gl]	nail
une **lime à ongles**	nail file
un **vernis à ongles**	nail polish
se **couper les ongles**	cut one's nails
le **dissolvant** [disɔlvɑ̃]	nail polish remover
un **coton** [kɔtɔ̃]	cotton pad/swab
le **maquillage** [makijaʒ]	makeup
se **démaquiller** [s(ə)demakije]	remove one's makeup
s'**épiler** [sepile]	pluck out one's hairs
une **pince à épiler**	tweezers
se **parfumer** [s(ə)paʀfyme]	use perfume, put on perfume
le **parfum** [paʀfɛ̃]	perfume
une **eau de toilette** [odtwalɛt]	eau de toilette, toilet water
un **flacon d'eau de toilette**	a bottle of eau de toilette
une **trousse de toilette** [tʀusdətwalɛt]	cosmetics bag
un **produit de beauté** [pʀɔdɥidbote]	cosmetic item, beauty product
une **lotion** [lɔsjɔ̃]	lotion
un **pot de crème (hydratante)** [podkʀɛm(idʀatɑ̃t)]	jar of (moisturizing) cream
un **déodorant** [deɔdɔʀɑ̃]	deodorant
la **poudre** [pudʀ]	powder
la **mascara** [maskaʀa]	mascara
le **rouge à lèvres** [ʀuʒalɛvʀ]	lipstick
la **ligne** [liɲ]	figure
surveiller sa ligne	watch one's figure
se **peser** [s(ə)pəze]	weigh oneself
Je me pèse tous les matins.	I weigh myself every morning.
(**être) soigné,e** [swaɲe]	(be) well groomed
un **institut de beauté** [ɛ̃stitydbote]	beauty salon
la **manucure** [manykyʀ]	manicure
la **pédicure** [pedikyʀ]	pedicure

French Word	English Equivalent	False Friend	French Equivalent
la figure	face	figure *(body shape)* figure *(person)*	la taille, la ligne, la silhouette; le personnage
impotent,e	infirm, crippled	impotent	impuissant,e
la toilette	personal grooming; dressing	toilet	les toilettes *f;* les WC *m*

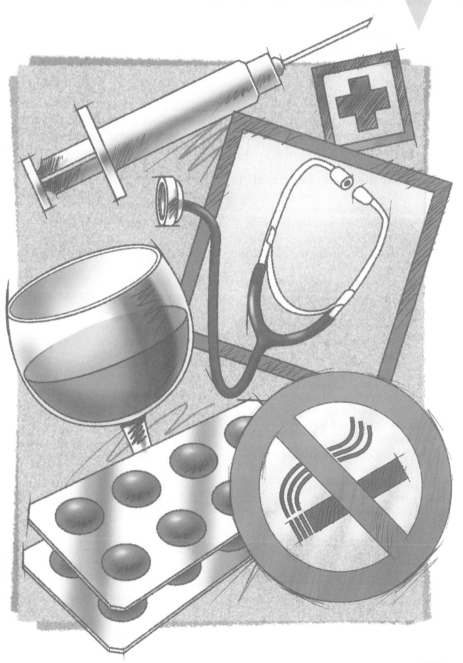

3.1 General Condition, Health, and Disease

vivre [vivʀ]	live
la **vie** [vi]	life
vivant,e [vivã, ãt]	alive
Il est **sorti vivant** de cette catastrophe.	He survived that catastrophe.

la **santé** [sãte]	health
être en **bonne santé**	be healthy, be in good health
sain,e [sɛ̃, sɛn]	healthy
sain et sauf	safe and sound
l'**état (de santé)** [eta(d(ə)sãte)]	state, condition (of health)
Elle est dans un **état grave.**	She is in serious condition.
être en forme [ɛtʀãfɔʀm]	be fit and well
avoir bonne/mauvaise mine [avwaʀbɔn/movɛzmin]	look good/bad
Tu n'es pas en forme? Tu as mauvaise mine.	Aren't you well? You look bad.
se sentir bien/mal [səsãtiʀbjɛ̃/mal]	feel good/ill
Je ne me sens pas très bien aujourd'hui.	I don't feel very good today.
aller bien/mal [allebjɛ̃/mal]	be well/unwell
Comment allez-vous? Bien, j'espère.	How are you? Fine, I hope.

la **fatigue** [fatig]	fatigue, tiredness
être mort,e de fatigue	be dead tired
(être) fatigué,e [fatige]	(be) tired, fatigued
fatiguer [fatige]	tire; get on s.o.'s nerves
Cette longue promenade m'a fatigué.	That long walk tired me out.
avoir sommeil [avwaʀsɔmɛj]	be sleepy
Je vais me coucher, j'ai sommeil.	I'm going to bed, I'm sleepy.
tomber de sommeil	be overcome with sleep
le **repos** [ʀ(ə)po]	rest
se reposer [səʀ(ə)poze]	(take a) rest

faible [fɛbl]	weak
Depuis sa maladie, il se sent faible.	Since his illness he has felt weak.
la **faiblesse** [fɛblɛs]	weakness
fragile [fʀaʒil]	fragile, weak

Elle a une **santé fragile**.	Her state of health is fragile.

une **maladie** [maladi]
  attraper une maladie
  C'est une **maladie grave**, mais elle n'est pas mortelle.
(un,e) **malade** n; adj [malad]

  tomber* gravement malade

disease, illness
  catch a disease, become ill
  It's a serious illness, but it's not fatal.
sick person, invalid, patient; sick, ill
  fall seriously ill

le **mal**, les **maux** [mal, mo]
  Ses maux de tête sont terribles.
(se) faire mal [(s(ə))fɛʀmal]
  Ça me fait mal quand je bouge la jambe.
  Elle s'est fait mal en tombant.
avoir mal (à) [avwaʀmal]
  J'ai mal aux dents.
la **douleur** [dulœʀ]

pain
  Her headaches are terrible.
hurt (oneself)
  It hurts when I move my leg.

  She hurt herself when she fell.
have pain
  I have a toothache
pain

prendre froid [pʀɑ̃dʀ(ə)fʀwa]
  Ne reste pas sous la pluie, tu vas prendre froid.
le **rhume** [ʀym]
  avoir/attraper un rhume
  le **rhume des foins**
éternuer [etɛʀnɥe]
  A tes souhaits! Ça fait trois fois que tu éternues.
le **mal de gorge** [maldəgɔʀʒ]
avoir mal à la gorge [avwaʀmalalagɔʀʒ]
la **toux** [tu]
tousser [tuse]

catch cold
  Don't stay out in the rain; you're going to catch cold.
cold
  have/catch a cold
  hay fever
sneeze
  God bless you! That's the third time you've sneezed.
sore throat
have a sore throat

cough
cough

la **fièvre** [fjɛvʀ]
  un **accès de fièvre**
la **grippe** [gʀip]
qn a chaud/froid [ʃo/fʀwa]
(être) brûlant,e [bʀylɑ̃, ɑ̃t]
transpirer [tʀɑ̃spiʀe]
trembler [tʀɑ̃ble]
garder le lit [gaʀdel(ə)li]
un **thermomètre** [tɛʀmɔmɛtʀ]

fever
  attack of fever
flu
s.o. is hot/cold
(be) burning (with fever)
sweat, perspire
tremble
stay in bed
thermometer

prendre sa température [pʀɑ̃dʀsatɑ̃peʀatyʀ]	take one's temperature

---

une **attaque** [atak] — attack, fit
Il a eu une **attaque** (d'apoplexie). — He has had a(n) (apoplectic) fit/a stroke.
une **crise** [kʀiz] — crisis, attack
une crise cardiaque — heart attack
une crise de foie — liver attack
un **infarctus** [ɛ̃faʀktys] — heart attack

---

un **choc** [ʃok] — shock
être en état de choc — be in a state of shock
un **allergie** [alɛʀʒi] — allergy
(être) allergique à [alɛʀʒik] — (be) allergic to
Je suis allergique aux fraises. — I'm allergic to strawberries.
urgent,e [yʀʒɑ̃, ɑ̃t] — urgent

---

un **accident** [aksidɑ̃] — accident
une **chute** [ʃyt] — fall
Il a fait une **chute** mortelle. — He fell to his death.
(se) blesser [s(ə)blɛse] — injure (oneself)
(un,e) blessé,e n; adj [blɛse] — injured person; injured
Les victimes de l'accident sont grièvement blessées. — The accident victims are seriously injured.
Cette collision a fait **trois blessés graves**. — That collision resulted in three seriously injured persons.
une **blessure** [blɛsyʀ] — wound, injury

---

gravement/grièvement

grièvement (*grievously, gravely, seriously*) is used in connection with injuries (**blessé** *injured, wounded*; **brûlé** *burned*).
Ils se sont grièvement brûlés. — *They were seriously burned.*

Otherwise, **gravement** is used as the *adverbial* form of **grave**.
Il est gravement malade. — *He is gravely ill.*

(se) couper [s(ə)kupe] — cut (oneself)
la **coupure** [kupyʀ] — cut
saigner [seɲe] — bleed
le **sang** [sɑ̃] — blood
Il a perdu beaucoup de sang. — He has lost a lot of blood.
se brûler [s(ə)bʀyle] — burn oneself, get burned
une **brûlure** [bʀylyʀ] — burn

---

le **régime** [ʀeʒim] — diet

Nous sommes **au régime** sans sel.	We're on a salt-free diet.
suivre un régime	be on a diet
l'**exercice** m [ɛgzɛʀsis]	exercise
Tu devrais **faire un peu d'exercice.**	You ought to get a little exercise.
maigre [mɛgʀ]	thin, lean
maigrir [mɛgʀiʀ]	lose weight
gros,se [gʀo, gʀos]	fat
grossir [gʀosiʀ]	gain weight

se porter bien/mal [s(ə)pɔʀtebjɛ̃/mal]	be well/unwell
être bien/mal portant,e [ɛt(ʀə)bjɛ̃/malpɔʀtɑ̃, ɑ̃t]	be in good/ill health
être bien/mal en point [ɛt(ʀə)bjɛ̃/malɑ̃pwɛ̃]	be in good health/be in a bad way
(être) épuisé,e [epɥize]	(be) exhausted

les **symptômes** m [sɛ̃ptom]	symptoms
Il **présente tous les symptômes** de la grippe.	He shows all the symptoms of the flu.
les **troubles** m [tʀubl]	troubles
souffrir de qc [sufʀiʀ]	suffer from s.th.
Il **souffre d'** une bronchite aiguë.	He suffers from acute bronchitis.
se déclarer [s(ə)deklaʀe]	show itself, break out
La maladie **s'est déclarée** au bout de deux jours.	The disease broke out two days later.
la **tension** [tɑ̃sjɔ̃]	blood pressure
L'infirmière **a pris ma tension.**	The nurse took my blood pressure.

malin, maligne [malɛ̃, maliɲ]	malignant
bénin, bénigne [benɛ̃, beniɲ]	benign
une **tumeur bénigne**	a benign tumor
héréditaire [eʀeditɛʀ]	hereditary
une **maladie héréditaire**	hereditary illness
génétique [ʒenetik]	genetic
la **manipulation génétique**	genetic manipulation
contagieux, -euse [kɔ̃taʒjø, jøz]	contagious
contaminer [kɔ̃tamine]	contaminate
s'aggraver [sagʀave]	deteriorate, worsen
Son état **s'est aggravé** rapidement.	His condition has deteriorated rapidly.
une **aggravation** [agʀavasjɔ̃]	deterioration, worsening
une **rechute** [ʀəʃyt]	relapse
Elle a fait une rechute.	She has had a relapse.

les **courbatures** f [kuʀbatyʀ]	stiffness in the back and limbs
avoir les jambes molles	have wobbly legs
[avwaʀleʒɑ̃bmɔl]	
trempé,e [tʀɑ̃pe]	soaked, drenched
être trempé,e de sueur	be drenched in sweat
avoir des vertiges f	have vertigo
[avwaʀdevɛʀtiʒ]	
pâle [pal]	pale
Tu devrais aller te coucher, tu es	You ought to go lie down; you're
tout pâle.	quite pale.

un **refroidissement**	cold
[ʀ(ə)fʀwadismɑ̃]	
une **infection** [ɛ̃fɛksjɔ̃]	infection
un **microbe** [mikʀɔb]	germ, microbe
un **virus** [viʀys]	virus

une **angine** [ɑ̃ʒin]	tonsillitis; sore throat
Il a chopé une angine. fam	He's picked up developed tonsillitis.
une **inflammation** [ɛ̃flamasjɔ̃]	inflammation
une **bronchite** [bʀɔ̃ʃit]	bronchitis
une **pneumonie** [pnømɔni]	pneumonia
une **otite** [ɔtit]	middle-ear infection
uen **appendicite** [apɛ̃disit]	appendicitis
se faire opérer de l'appendicite	have an appendectomy

la **rougeole** [ʀuʒɔl]	measles
la **rubéole** [ʀybeɔl]	German measles, rubeola
la **varicelle** [vaʀisɛl]	chicken pox
les **oreillons** m [ɔʀɛjɔ̃]	mumps
la **démangeaison** [demɑ̃ʒɛzɔ̃]	itching
un **abcès** [absɛ]	abscess

une **indigestion** [ɛ̃diʒɛsjɔ̃]	indigestion
la **diarrhée** [djaʀe]	diarrhea
le **poison** [pwazɔ̃]	poison
un **poison violent**	fast-acting poison
s'**empoisonner** [sɑ̃pwazɔ̃ne]	poison oneself
une **intoxication** [ɛ̃tɔksikasjɔ̃]	poisoning
une **intoxication alimentaire**	food poisoning
vomir [vɔmiʀ]	vomit

le **cholestérol** [kɔlɛsteʀɔl]	cholesterol
le **diabète** [djabɛt]	diabetes

les **rhumatismes** m [Rymatism]	rheumatism
le **cancer** [kɑ̃seR]	cancer
le **SIDA** [sida]	AIDS
(être) séropositif, -ive [seRopozitif, iv]	(be) HIV positive
(faire) une dépression nerveuse [depResjɔ̃nɛRvøz]	(have) a nervous breakdown
dépressif, -ive [depREsif, iv]	depressive, depressed
névrosé,e [nevRoze]	neurotic
une **maladie mentale** [maladimɑ̃tal]	mental illness
étouffer [etufe]	suffocate, choke
s'asphyxier [sasfiksje]	asphyxiate, suffocate
s'évanouir [sevanwiR]	faint
perdre connaissance [pɛRdR(ə)kɔnɛsɑ̃s]	lose consciousness
tomber* dans les pommes fam [tɔ̃bedɑ̃lepom]	pass out, faint
Dès qu'il voit du sang, il tombe dans les pommes.	As soon as he sees blood, he faints.
une **ampoule** [ɑ̃pul]	blister

---

i **Inflatables**

The notion of a receptacle that swells, such as a blister, bladder, bubble, vesicle, or balloon, is expressed in various ways in French:

une ampoule	*(water, burn) blister*
Je me suis fait des ampoules aux pieds.	*I walked until my feet were blistered.*
une bulle	*balloon (in comic strips)*
Dans les bandes dessinées, les personnages s'expriment par bulles.	*In the comics, the people express themselves in balloons.*
une bulle de savon	*soap bubble*
la vessie	*urinary bladder*
la vésicule biliaire	*gallbladder*

---

une **plaie** [plɛ]	wound
une **plaie ouverte**	open wound
un **bleu** [blø]	bruise
un **hématome** [ematom]	hematoma, effusion of blood
une **bosse** [bɔs]	boil
enflé,e [ɑ̃fle]	swollen
Après sa chute, il avait le genou enflé.	After his fall, his knee was swollen.
une **commotion cérébrale** [komosjɔ̃seRebRal]	concussion

se **démettre qc** [s(ə)demɛtʀ] — dislocate s.th.
  Elle s'est démis l'epaule. — She has dislocated her shoulder.
une **déchirure** [deʃiʀyʀ] — tear
  Je souffre d'une déchirure musculaire. — I'm suffering from a torn muscle.
un **claquage** [klakaʒ] — strain, pull
se **tordre qc** [s(ə)tɔʀdʀ] — twist
  Je me suis tordu la cheville. — I've twisted my ankle.
une **entorse** [ɑ̃tɔʀs] — sprain
se **fouler qc** [s(ə)fule] — slightly sprain s.th.
une **foulure** [fulyʀ] — slight sprain

---

une **fracture** [fʀaktyʀ] — fracture, break
se **fracturer qc** [s(ə)fʀaktyʀe] — break s.th.
se **casser le bras** [s(ə)kasel(ə)bʀa] — break one's arm
  Mon fils s'est cassé le bras. — My son has broken his arm.
un **plâtre** [platʀ] — (plaster) cast
un **lumbago** [lɛ̃bago] — low back pain
un **handicap** [ɑ̃dikap] — handicap
(un,e) **handicapé,e** [ɑ̃dikape] — handicapped (person)
  un **handicapé physique/mental** — a physically/mentally handicapped person

infirme [ɛ̃fiʀm] — crippled; invalid; disabled
un,e **invalide** [ɛ̃valid] — invalid
  un **invalide de guerre** — war invalid

---

s'améliorer [sameljɔʀe] — improve
  Son état s'améliore peu à peu. — His condition is improving bit by bit.
une **amélioration** [ameljɔʀasjɔ̃] — improvement
la **convalescence** [kɔ̃valɛsɑ̃s] — convalescence
guérir de [geʀiʀ] — recover from
  On ne guérit pas du sida. — AIDS is incurable.
guérir qn de qc [geʀiʀ] — cure s.o. of s.th.
  L'homéopathe m'a guéri de mon allergie. — The homeopathic physician cured me of my allergy.
la **guérison** [geʀizɔ̃] — healing
guéri,e [geʀi] — healed, cured

---

une **précaution** [pʀekosjɔ̃] — precaution(ary measure)
  Depuis son infarctus, il **prend beaucoup de précautions**. — Since his heart attack, he takes a lot of precautions.
récupérer [ʀekypeʀe] — recuperate

Je trouve qu'il met du temps à récupérer.	I think he's taking a lot of time to recuperate.
se remettre qc [sǝʀ(ǝ)mɛtʀ]	recover from s.th.
reprendre des forces [ʀ(ǝ)pʀɑ̃dʀdefɔʀs]	regain one's strength

3.2 Medical Care

la **médecine** [med(ǝ)sin]	medicine
médical,e [medikal]	medical
une **visite médicale**	medical examination
un **médecin** [medsɛ̃]	doctor, physician
le **médecin de famille**	family doctor
un **docteur** [dɔktœʀ]	doctor
un,e **généraliste** [ʒeneʀalist]	general practitioner
un,e **spécialiste** [spesjalist]	specialist
C'est un **spécialiste en pédiatrie**.	He's a specialist in pediatrics.
un,e **chirurgien,ne** [ʃiʀyʀ ʒjɛ̃, jɛn]	surgeon
un,e **infirmier, -ière** [ɛ̃fiʀmje, jɛʀ]	nurse

un,e **patient,e** [pasjɑ̃, ɑ̃t]	patient
un,e **malade** [malad]	patient, invalid
un **hôpital** [ɔpital]	hospital
hospitalier, -ière [ɔspitalje, jɛʀ]	hospital attendant
le **personnel hospitalier**	hospital staff
une **clinique** [klinik]	clinic
une **pharmacie** [faʀmasi]	pharmacy
un,e **pharmacien,ne** [faʀmasjɛ̃, jɛn]	pharmacist

un **rendez-vous** [ʀɑ̃devu]	appointment
Le docteur **reçoit sur rendez-vous**.	The doctor sees people by appointment.
la **consultation** [kɔ̃syltasjɔ̃]	consultation
les **heures de consultation**	office hours
consulter [kɔ̃sylte]	consult
Tu devrais consulter un spécialiste.	You ought to consult a specialist.
un **cabinet médical** [kabinɛmedikal]	practice, office (of a doctor)
une **salle d'attente** [saldatɑ̃t]	waiting room
une **visite à domicile** [visitadɔmisil]	house call
un **examen** [ɛgzamɛ̃]	examination
examiner [ɛgzamine]	examine

se faire examiner par qn	have oneself examined by s.o.

soigner [swaɲe]	treat
Son docteur le soigne très bien.	His doctor treats him very well.
Il soigne sa grippe en restant au chaud.	He's treating his flu by staying indoors where it's warm.
le **soin** [swɛ̃]	treatment, care
les **premiers soins**	first aid
le **traitement** [tʀɛtmã]	treatment
traiter [tʀɛte]	treat
traiter une maladie	treat a disease
une **piqûre** [pikyʀ]	hypodermic injection
faire une piqûre à qn	give s.o. an injection

---

i **Injection**

Note the difference:

une piqûre	*a shot, a hypodermic injection*
une seringue	*a syringe, a hypodermic needle*

---

un **médicament** [medikamã]	medication, medicament
prendre un médicament	take a medication
un **comprimé** [kɔ̃pʀime]	tablet
prescrire qc à qn [pʀɛskʀiʀ]	prescribe s.th. for s.o.

une **aide** [ɛd]	aid
opérer [ɔpeʀe]	operate
une **opération** [ɔpeʀasjɔ̃]	operation
subir une opération	have an operation, undergo surgery, be operated on
sauver qn [sove]	save s.o.

un,e **dentiste** [dãtist]	dentist
la **dent** [dã]	tooth
avoir mal aux dents	have a toothache
les **soins dentaires** *m* [swɛ̃dãtɛʀ]	dental care, dental treatment
un **cabinet dentaire** [kabinɛdãtɛʀ]	dentist's office

un,e **toubib** *fam* [tubib]	doctor, physician
un,e **ophtalmologue**; un,e **oph-talmo** *fam* [ɔftalmɔlɔg, ɔftalmo]	ophthalmologist, eye doctor
un,e **oto-rhino (-laryngologiste)**; un,e **ORL** [ɔtɔʀino/laʀɛ̃gɔlɔʒist; ɔɛʀɛl]	ear, nose, and throat doctor, otorhinolaryngologist
un,e **gynécologue**; un,e **gynéco** *fam* [ʒinekɔlɔg, ʒineko]	gynecologist

un,e **orthopédiste** [ɔʀtopedist]	orthopedist
un,e **pédiatre** [pedjatʀ]	pediatrician
un,e **dermatologue**; un,e **dermato** fam [dɜʀmatɔlɔg, dɜʀmato]	dermatologist
un,e **psychiatre**; un,e **psy** fam [psikjatʀ, psi]	psychiatrist
la **Sécurité sociale**; la **Sécu** fam [sekyʀitesɔsjal]	social and health insurance plan
une **feuille de maladie/de soins** [fœjdəmaladi/dəswɛ̃]	illness/treatment form (presented by patient to health-insurance carrier for reimbursement of expenses)
remplir sa feuille de maladie	fill out one's treatment form
les **honoraires** m [ɔnɔʀɛʀ]	doctor's fee, honorarium
rembourser [ʀɑ̃buʀse]	reimburse
Ce médicament n'est pas remboursé par la Sécu.	This medication is not paid for by health insurance.
un **certificat (médical)** [sɛʀtifika(medikal)]	medical certificate
ausculter qn [ɔskylte]	listen to s.o.'s chest with a stethoscope
un **diagnostic** [djagnɔstik]	diagnosis
faire un diagnostic	make a diagnosis
prendre le pouls [pʀɑ̃dʀ(ə)ləpu]	take the pulse
une **ordonnance** [ɔʀdɔnɑ̃s]	prescription
Le medecin a rédigé/délivré une ordonnance.	The doctor wrote out/issued a prescription.
une **ambulance** [ɑ̃bylɑ̃s]	ambulance
le **SAMU (Service d'aide médicale d'urgence)** [samy]	emergency medical service
Il faut appeler le SAMU.	You have to call the emergency medical service.
un **C.H.U. (Centre hospitalier universitaire)** [seaʃy]	university hospital center
la **Croix-Rouge** [kʀwaʀuʒ]	Red Cross
le **mercurochrome** [mɛʀkyʀokʀom]	mercurochrome
le **coton** [kɔtɔ̃]	cotton pad/swab
le **sparadrap** [spaʀadʀa]	Band-Aid
un **pansement** [pɑ̃smɑ̃]	dressing
un **pansement adhésif**	adhesive tape
une **pommade** [pɔmad]	salve, ointment

un **remède** [ʀ(ə)mɛd]	remedy, cure
C'est un **remède miracle** contre la toux.	It's a miracle remedy for coughs.

un **cachet** [kaʃɛ]	tablet
une **pilule** [pilyl]	pill
la **pilule**	birth control pill
des **gouttes** f [gut]	drops
des **gouttes pour le nez**	nose drops
un **antibiotique** [ãtibjɔtik]	antibiotic
un **calmant** [kalmã]	sedative

l'**homéopathie** f [ɔmeɔpati]	homeopathy
les **médecines douces** f [med(ə)sindus]	alternative medicine
l'**acupuncture** f [akypɔ̃ktyʀ]	acupuncture

une **radio(graphie)** [ʀadjo(gʀafi)]	X ray (image)
Il vaudrait mieux faire une radio de votre jambe.	It would be better to x-ray your leg.
radiographier [ʀadjogʀafje]	(take an) X ray
les **rayons** m	rays
les rayons X ont été découverts par Röntgen.	X rays were discovered by Röntgen.
une **anesthésie** [anɛstesi]	anesthesia
une anesthésie locale/générale	local/general anesthesia
une **échographie** [ekogʀafi]	sonogram, ultrasound exam
A l'**échographie**, on a bien vu le bébé.	In the sonogram the baby was clearly visible.
un **électrocardiogramme (ECG)** [elɛktʀokaʀdjɔgʀam]	electrocardiogram (ECG, EKG)
(passer) un scanneur/scanner [(pase)ɛ̃skanœʀ/ɛʀ]	(have a) CT scan
un **stimulateur cardiaque**; un **pacemaker** [stimylatœʀkaʀdjak/pɛsmɛkœʀ]	pacemaker

une **prise de sang** [pʀizdəsã]	blood sample
vacciner qn contre qc [vaksine]	vaccinate s.o. against s.th.
J'ai été vacciné contre le tétanos.	I've been vaccinated against tetanus.
un **vaccin** [vaksɛ̃]	vaccine
une **transfusion sanguine** [tʀãsfyzjɔ̃sãgin]	blood transfusion
une **perfusion** [pɛʀfyzjɔ̃]	infusion

Il doit **rester sous perfusion** jusqu'à demain.	He has to stay on the intravenous drip until tomorrow.
une **greffe** [gʀɛf]	transplant
une **greffe d'organe**	organ transplant

une **carie** [kaʀi]	decay
un **plombage** [plɔbaʒ]	filling
plomber une dent [plɔbeyndã]	fill a tooth
une **couronne** [kuʀɔn]	(dental) crown
un **dentier** [dãtje]	set of teeth, dentures
un **appareil dentaire** [apaʀɛjdãtɛʀ]	brace
arracher [aʀaʃe]	pull
On lui a arraché une dent de sagesse.	She had a wisdom tooth pulled.

3.3 Drugs, Tobacco, Alcohol

se droguer [s(ə)dʀɔge]	use/take drugs
une **drogue** [dʀɔg]	drug
une **drogue douce/dure**	soft/hard drug
consommer de la drogue	use drugs
procurer de la drogue	obtain drugs
fournir de la drogue	deal, supply drugs
écouler de la drogue	deal drugs
(un,e) **drogué,e** n; adj [dʀɔge]	drug addict; drug-addicted
(être) dépendant,e [depãdã, ãt]	(be) addicted, dependent
(être) accro fam [akʀo]	(be) hooked

le **haschisch**; le **hasch** fam [aʃiʃ, aʃ]	hash(ish)
la **marijuana** [maʀiʀwana/maʀiʒɥana]	marijuana
un **joint**; un **pétard** fam [ʒwɛ̃, petaʀ]	joint
l'**ecstasy** f [ɛkstazi]	ecstasy

une **thérapie** [teʀapi]	therapy
se soumettre à une thérapie	undergo therapy
se désintoxiquer [dezɛ̃tɔksike]	go into detox
la **désintoxication** [dezɛ̃tɔksikasjɔ̃]	detox
suivre une cure de désintoxication	go into detox
(être) clean fam [klin]	(be) clean

fumer [fyme]	smoke
Défense de fumer.	No smoking.

la **fumée** [fume]	smoke
un,e **fumeur, -euse** [fymœr, øz]	smoker
C'est un **gros fumeur.**	He's a heavy smoker.
une **zone non-fumeurs**	no-smoking area

le **tabac** [taba]	tobacco
un **bureau de tabac**	tobacco shop
une **cigarette** [sigarɛt]	cigarette
une **cigarette bout filtre/avec filtre; sans filtre**	filter cigarette; unfiltered cigarette
un **paquet de cigarettes**	a pack of cigarettes
rouler une cigarette	roll a cigarette
Veuillez éteindre vos cigarettes.	Please extinguish your cigarettes.
un **cigare** [sigar]	cigar
une **pipe** [pip]	pipe
un **briquet** [brikɛ]	cigarette lighter
Auriez-vous du feu ? – Oui, voilà mon briquet.	Do you have a light? Yes, here's my lighter.
une **allumette** [alymɛt]	match

boire [bwar]	drink
boire un coup (de trop)	have a glass (too many)
boire dans un verre	drink from a glass
boire à la bouteille	drink from the bottle
un,e **buveur, -euse** [byvœr, øz]	drinker
prendre un verre [prɑ̃drɛ̃ver]	have a drink
Viens prendre un verre à la maison.	Come on, let's have a drink at home.

l'**alcool** m [alkɔl]	alcohol
l'**alcoolisme** m [alkɔlism]	alcoholism
(un,e) **alcoolique** n; adj [alkɔlik]	alcoholic
l'**abus** m [aby]	abuse
L'abus d'alcool est dangereux pour la santé.	The abuse of alcohol is dangerous to one's health.

un **stupéfiant** [stypefjɑ̃]	narcotic
absorber des stupéfiants	use narcotics
la **came** fam [kam]	stuff
se camer fam [s(ə)kame]	take drugs, use
la **cocaïne**; la **coke** fam, la **neige** fam [kɔkain, kɔk, nɛʒ]	cocaine (coke, snow)
l'**héroïne** f [erɔin]	heroin
se piquer/se shooter fam [s(ə)pike/səʃute]	shoot up

le **crack** [kRak]	crack
la **méthadone** [metadɔn]	methadone
La méthadone est un produit de substitution.	Methadone is a substitute drug.
le **LSD** [ɛlɛsde]	LSD

une **dose** [doz]	dose
s'**injecter** une dose d'**héroïne**	inject a dose of heroin
une **overdose**/une **surdose**	overdose
le **manque** [mãk]	withdrawal (symptoms)
être en **manque** (de)	have withdrawal symptoms, be in withdrawal
flipper fam [flipe]	be on a bad trip, freak out, flip out

la **toxicomanie** [tɔksikɔmani]	drug addiction
un,e **toxicomane**; un,e **toxico** fam [tɔksikɔman, tɔksiko]	drug addict, junkie
un,e **trafiquant,e** [tRafikã, ãt]	dealer, drug trafficker
un **dealer/dealeur** [dilœR]	dealer
le **trafic de drogue** [tRafikdədRɔg]	drug traffic

le **tabagisme** [tabaʒism]	nicotine addiction
une campagne de lutte contre le tabagisme	antismoking campaign
la **nicotine** [nikɔtin]	nicotine
le **goudron** [gudRã]	tar

un,e **clope** fam [klɔp]	smoke; drag; butt
Tu peux me **passer** une clope ?	Can you give me a drag?
une **cartouche de cigarettes** [kaRtuʃdəsigaRɛt]	carton of cigarettes
une **boîte d'allumettes** [bwatdalymɛt]	box of matches, matchbox

un **mégot** [mego]	butt
la **cendre** [sãdR]	ash
un **cendrier** [sãdRije]	ashtray

ivre [ivR]	drunk, intoxicated
l'**ivresse** f [ivRɛs]	drunkenness, intoxication
un,e **ivrogne** [ivRɔɲ]	drunk (person)
soûl,e [su, sul]	drunk
noir,e fam [nwaR]	drunk, inebriated
beurré,e fam [bœRe]	drunk, inebriated
prendre une cuite fam [pRãdRynkɥit]	get drunk

avoir la gueule de bois [avwaʀlagœldəbwa]	have a hangover, be hung over
un **alcootest** [alkɔtɛst]	alcohol test
le **taux d'alcoolémie** [todalkɔlemi]	blood alcohol content

French Word	English Equivalent	False Friend	French Equivalent
une infusion	herbal tea	infusion	une perfusion
un rendez-vous	appointment	(lovers') rendez-vous	un rendez-vous amoureux
blesser	injure, wound	bless	bénir
une blessure	injury, wound	blessing	une bénédiction

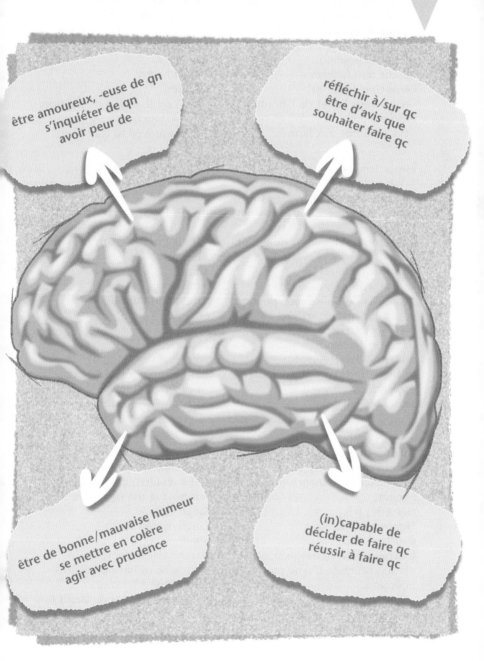

4.1 Feelings

le **sentiment** [sãtimã]	feeling, sentiment
éprouver un sentiment de joie	experience a feeling of joy
cacher ses sentiments	hide one's feelings
se sentir [səsãtiʀ]	feel
Je me sens heureux.	I feel happy.
l'**émotion** f [emosjɔ̃]	emotion
réagir **sous l'effet de l'émotion**	react on the basis of emotion
ému,e [emy]	moved, touched
Elle est **émue aux larmes.**	She is moved to tears.

aimer [ɛme]	love; like
J'aime bien Paul, mais j'aime encore mieux Jean.	I like Paul, but I like Jean even more.
(être) amoureux, -euse (de qn) [amuʀø, øz]	(be) in love (with s.o.)
Il est **tombé amoureux de** sa prof d'anglais.	He fell in love with his English teacher.
admirer [admiʀe]	admire
l'**admiration** f [admiʀasjɔ̃]	admiration
éprouver de l'admiration pour qn	feel admiration for s.o.
un,e **admirateur, -trice** [admiʀatœʀ, tʀis]	admirer
détester [detɛste]	hate, detest
adorer [adɔʀe]	adore; be very fond of
J'adore Nadine, mais je déteste son mari.	I'm terribly fond of Nadine, but I can't stand her husband.
adorable [adɔʀabl]	adorable, sweet, nice

la **joie** [ʒwa]	joy
sauter de joie	jump for joy
s'amuser (à) [samyze]	have fun, enjoy oneself
Les enfants s'amusent à embêter le voisin.	The children are having fun annoying the neighbor.
rire (de) [ʀiʀ]	laugh (at)
rigoler fam [ʀigɔle]	laugh, have fun
sourire [suʀiʀ]	smile
heureux, -euse (de) [øʀø, øz]	happy, glad (about)
Je suis heureuse d'avoir pris cette décision.	I'm glad to have made this decision.
Elle a été très heureuse de la naissance de ses jumeaux.	She was very happy about the birth of her twins.
le **bonheur** [bɔnœʀ]	happiness; good luck, good fortune

For more on the rendering of *(good) luck* in French, see p. 133.

Le malheur des uns fait le bonheur des autres. *prov*	One person's joy is another's sorrow.
content,e (de) [kɔ̃tɑ̃, ɑ̃t]	content, satisfied; pleased, glad
Je suis content de te voir en bonne santé.	I'm glad to see you in good health.

malheureux, -euse (de) [malørø, øz] — unhappy (about)

Il est malheureux de ne pas pouvoir partir en vacances. — He's unhappy about being unable to go on vacation.

le **malheur** [malœʀ] — unhappiness, misfortune, bad luck
pleurer [plœʀe] — cry, weep
pleurer de joie — weep tears of joy

espérer (faire) qc [ɛspeʀe] — hope (to do) s.th., hope for s.th.
J'espère te revoir bientôt. — I hope to see you again soon.
Elle est déçue parce qu'elle espérait une augmentation. — She's disappointed because she was hoping for a pay raise.
l'**espoir** *m* [ɛspwaʀ] — hope
perdre l'espoir — lose hope
l'**espérance** *f* [ɛspeʀɑ̃s] — hope
Sa réponse négative a brisé toutes mes espérances. — Her negative reply dashed all my hopes.
désespérer de qn/qc [dezɛspeʀe] — despair of s.th./s.o.
Je désespère de lui faire comprendre ça. — I despair of making him understand this.
(être) désespéré,e [dezɛspeʀe] — (be) desperate, disheartened
le **désespoir** [desɛspwaʀ] — despair
être au désespoir — be in despair

la **peur** [pœʀ] — fear

 Fear

The notion of *fear* is expressed in various ways in French, depending on context:
la peur — *fear (in general), dread*
une peur bleue — *a blue funk*
N'ayez pas peur! — *Don't be afraid!*
la crainte — *fear, apprehension*
Soyez sans crainte! — *Have no fear!*
l'angoisse *f* — *anguish, great distress*
un cri d'angoisse — *a cry of anguish*
l'anxiété *f* — *anxiety, inner uneasiness*
envisager l'avenir avec anxiété — *approach the future with great anxiety*

avoir peur (de)
J'ai peur des chiens.
J'ai peur que Martin soit malade.
la **crainte** [kʀɛ̃t]
craindre [kʀɛ̃dʀ]
Les marins craignent la tempête.
craindre que + *subj*
Je crains que nous ayons des
ennuis.

be afraid
I'm afraid of dogs.
I'm afraid that Martin is ill.
fear
fear, be afraid of
The sailors fear the storm.
fear that
I fear that we may have some
worries.

plaire [plɛʀ]
Carine plaît beaucoup à Pierre.
le **plaisir** [pleziʀ]
prendre plaisir à qc

please; be pleasing
Pierre likes Carine a lot.
pleasure
take pleasure in s.th.

la **honte** ['ɔ̃t]
Tu me **fais honte.**
avoir honte de qn/qc
se moquer de qn/qc [s(ə)mɔke]
Tou le monde se moque de son nez.
la **pitié** [pitje]
avoir pitié de qn

shame; disgrace
I am ashamed of you.
be ashamed of s.o./s.th.
make fun of s.o./s.th.
Everyone makes fun of his nose.
pity
have pity on s.o.

ressentir qc [ʀ(ə)sɑ̃tiʀ]
ressentir de la pitié pour qn
manifester [manifɛste]
manifester sa joie
refouler [ʀ(ə)fule]
refouler un sentiment de haine
surmonter [syʀmɔ̃te]
surmonter son chagrin
la **passion** [pasjɔ̃]
toucher [tuʃe]
Sa gentillesse me touche
beaucoup.

feel s.th.
feel sympathy for s.o.
show, make known
show one's delight
suppress, repress
suppress a feeling of hatred
overcome, subdue
overcome one's grief
passion
touch, move
His/Her kindness touches me
greatly.

haïr ['aiʀ]
Je le hais profondément.
la **haine** ['ɛn]
éprouver de la haine pour
qn/qc
le **dégoût** [degu]
Son égoïsme **m'inspire du**
dégoût.
(être) dégoûté,e [degute]

hate
I hate him profoundly.
hatred
feel hatred for s.o./s.th.

disgust
His egotism fills me with disgust.

(be) disgusted

joyeux, -euse [ʒwajø, øz]   glad; cheerful
être d'humeur joyeuse   be in a cheerful mood
l'**enthousiasme** *m* [ãtuzjasm]   enthusiasm
se réjouir de qc [s(ə)ʀeʒwiʀ]   be delighted about/at s.th.
Je me réjouis de la savoir   I'm delighted to know that she's
heureuse.   happy.
l'**excitation** *f* [ɛksitasjõ]   excitement
Il y a une lueur d'excitation dans   His eyes shone with excitement.
ses yeux.

la **mélancolie** [melãkɔli]   melancholy
mélancolique [melãkɔlik]   melancholic
la **nostalgie** [nɔstalʒi]   nostalgia, longing
avoir la nostalgie du temps passé   be nostalgic for the past
nostalgique [nɔstalʒik]   nostalgic; sad
pleurnicher [plœʀniʃe]   whimper, whine, snivel
Cet enfant pleurniche sans arrêt.   That child whines nonstop.
sangloter [sãglɔte]   sob
le **chagrin** [ʃagʀɛ̃]   grief; regret, sorrow
le **chagrin d'amour**   lover's grief
souffrir de qc [sufʀiʀ]   suffer from s.th.
Elle souffre de l'absence de son ami.   She suffers from the absence of
    her friend.
la **souffrance** [sufʀãs]   suffering, pain
la **dépression** [depʀesjõ]   depression
(être) déprimé,e [depʀime]   (be) depressed
le **deuil** [dœj]   mourning; grief, sorrow
être en deuil de qn   be in mourning for s.o.

la **confiance** [kõfjãs]   confidence, trust
Je lui **accorde toute ma confiance.**   I have complete confidence in him.
faire confiance à qn   trust s.o.
avoir confiance en qn   have confidence in s.o.
se méfier de qn/qc [s(ə)mefje]   mistrust, distrust s.o./s.th.
Je me méfie de ses sourires   I distrust his hypocritical smiles.
hypocrites.
la **méfiance** [mefjãs]   mistrust, distrust
considérer qc avec méfiance   view s.th. with mistrust

s'inquiéter de qc [sɛ̃kjete]   be anxious, be uneasy about s.th.
Je m'inquiète du retard de mon   I'm worried because my son is
fils.   late.
l'**inquiétude** *f* [ɛ̃kjetyd]   uneasiness, anxiety, concern

inquiet, -ète [ɛ̃kjɛ, ɛt]
concerned, uneasy, worried
Nous sommes inquiets de ne pas
avoir de ses nouvelles.
We're uneasy because we have
no news of him/her.

se faire du souci [s(ə)fɛʀdysusi]
worry
Pourquoi est-ce que tu n'as pas
appelé? On s'est fait du **souci pour**
toi.
Why didn't you phone? We were
worried about you.

l'**angoisse** f [ɑ̃gwas]
anguish, agony
horrible [ɔʀibl]
horrible
la **terreur** [teʀœʀ]
terror
terrifier qn [teʀifje]
terrify s.o.
L'explosion nous a terrifiés.
The explosion terrified us.

anxieux, -euse [ɑ̃ksjø, jøz]
anxious

mépriser qn [mepʀize]
despise, scorn
Après ce qui'il m'a fait, je ne peux
que le mépriser.
After what he has done to me,
I can only despise him.

le **mépris** [mepʀi]
contempt, scorn
la **jalousie** [ʒaluzi]
jealousy, envy
(être) jaloux, -ouse (de qn)
[ʒalu, uz]
(be) jealous/envious (of s.o.)
Il est jaloux de tous ses amis.
He is jealous of all his/her
friends.

la **déception** [desɛpsjɔ̃]
disappointment
(être) déçu,e [desy]
(be) disappointed
Sa réaction m'a beaucoup déçu.
His reaction disappointed me
greatly.

envieux, -euse [ɑ̃vjø, jøz]
envious, jealous
l'**envie** f [ɑ̃vi]
envy
s'en prendre à qn [sɑ̃pʀɑ̃dʀ]
lay the blame on s.o.
Pas la peine de t'en prendre à lui,
ce n'est pas sa faute.
It's not worthwhile to lay the
blame on him; it's not his fault.

en vouloir à qn [ɑ̃vulwaʀ]
bear s.o. a grudge; be angry with s.o.
Je lui en veux de m'avoir trompé.
I'm angry with him/her because
he/she deceived me.

l'**embarras** m [ɑ̃baʀa]
embarrassment; difficulty
Ces circonstances l'ont mise dans
l'embarras.
These circumstances caused
them a lot of trouble.

(être) embarrassé,e [ɑ̃baʀase]
(be) embarrassed.
Je ne sais pas quoi faire, je suis
très embarrassé.
I don't know what to do; I'm
really embarrassed.

la **résignation** [ʀeziɲasjɔ̃]
resignation
se résigner à [s(ə)ʀeziɲe]
resign oneself to, be resigned to

Il s'est résigné à ne plus la voir.	He has resigned himself to not seeing her again.
(être) vexé,e [vɛkse]	(be) annoyed
J'ai été vexé par sa remarque.	I was annoyed by his remark.
ne pas s'en faire [nəpasãfɛʀ]	not mind (it)
Ne t'en fais pas, demain ça ira mieux.	Never mind; it'll be better tomorrow.
l'**ennui** *m* [ãnɥi]	boredom
s'ennuyer de qn [sãnɥije]	miss s.o.
Elle s'ennuie de ses parents.	She misses her parents.
subir qc [sybiʀ]	undergo, suffer; sustain
Il a subi une lourde perte.	He has suffered a heavy loss.
supporter [sypɔʀte]	endure; tolerate, bear
Elle ne peut plus supporter ses avances.	She can't bear his advances any longer.
troubler [tʀuble]	disturb; trouble
s'effondrer [sefɔ̃dʀe]	collapse
Quand elle a appris la nouvelle, elle s'est effondrée.	When she heard the news, she collapsed.

4.2 Thinking, Imagining, Wanting

penser à [pãse]	think of
Elle pense souvent à Marc.	She often thinks of Marc.
la **pensée** [pãse]	thought, thinking
une **idée** [ide]	idea, thought
Il a eu l'idée de passer par Nîmes.	It occurred to him that he could drive by way of Nîmes.
changer d'idée	change one's opinion
réfléchir à/sur qc [ʀefleʃiʀ]	reflect upon s.th., consider s.th.
J'ai réfléchi à/sur votre argument.	I have considered your argument.
une **réflexion** [ʀeflɛksjɔ̃]	reflection, consideration
la **raison** [ʀɛzɔ̃]	reason
perdre la raison	lose one's sanity
l'**intelligence** *f* [ɛ̃teliʒãs]	intelligence
intelligent,e [ɛ̃teliʒã, ãt]	intelligent
intellectuel,le [ɛ̃telɛktɥɛl]	intellectual
un travail intellectuel	an intellectual task
comprendre [kɔ̃pʀãdʀ]	understand
Je n'y comprends rien.	I understand nothing (about it).

la **compréhension** [kɔ̃pReãsjɔ̃]	comprehension, understanding

le **sens** [sãs]	sense; senses; intelligence
le **bon sens**	good sense
le **non-sens**	nonsense
(la) **logique** *n; adj* [lɔʒik]	logic; logical
C'est la seule explication logique.	It's the only logical explanation.

une **opinion** [ɔpiɲɔ̃]	opinion, view
se faire une opinion sur qc	form an opinion about s.th.
la **vérité** [veRite]	truth
vrai,e [vRɛ]	true, correct

> **i** For information on *adjectives* that *change their meaning* depending on whether they *precede* or *follow* the noun modified, see p. 37.

une **erreur** [eRœR]	error
Vous avez commis une erreur.	You've made an error.
L'erreur est humaine. *prov*	To err is human.
se tromper [s(ə)tRɔ̃pe]	be mistaken

savoir [savwaR]	know; know how, be able
Je sais qu'il a raison.	I know that he's right.
le **savoir** [savwaR]	knowledge, learning
connaître [kɔnɛtR]	know; be acquainted with
connaître un poème **par cœur**	know a poem by heart
la **connaissance** [kɔnɛsãs]	knowledge; acquaintance
les **connaisances en francais**	knowledge of French
une **théorie** [teɔRi]	theory
théorique [teɔRik]	theoretical

retenir qc [R(ə)təniR]	retain s.th.; remember s.th.
Je n'arrive jamais à retenir votre nom.	I never manage to remember your name.
se rappeler qn/qc [səRap(ə)le]	remember s.o./s.th.

> **i** **rappeler**
>
> *Note the difference:*
>
> | | |
> |---|---|
> | **se rappeler qn/qc** | *remember s.o./s.th* |
> | Tu te rappeles notre prof de maths ? | *Do you remember our math teacher?* |
> | **rappeler qc à qn** | *remind s.o. of s.th.* |
> | Cela me rappelle mon enfance. | *That reminds me of my childhood.* |
> | **rappeler à qn de faire qc** | *remind s.o. to do s.th.* |
> | Rappelle-moi de mettre le réveil. | *Remind me to set the alarm clock.* |

se souvenir de [səsuv(ə)niR]	remember

Je ne me souviens plus de la date de ton anniversaire.
oublier qc/de faire qc [ublije]

I don't remember the date of your birthday anymore.
forget s.th./to do s.th.

analyser [analize]
comparer qn/qc à qn/qc [kɔ̃paʀe]
Il ne faut pas toujours le comparer à son frère.
distinguer de [distɛ̃ge]
distinguer le bien du mal
reconnaître [ʀ(ə)kɔnɛtʀ]
se rendre compte de qc [s(ə)ʀɑ̃dʀ(ə)kɔ̃t]
Elle ne s'est pas rendu compte de son erreur.

analyze
compare s.o./s.th. with s.o./s.th.
You can't always compare him with his brother.
distinguish from
distinguish good from evil
recognize
realize, get a clear idea of s.th.

She has not realized her error.

croire qn/qc [kʀwaʀ]

believe s.o./s.th.

For information on **croire** and the words associated with it, see p. 251.

un **avis** [avi]
A mon avis, tu devrais t'excuser.

opinion
In my opinion, you ought to apologize.

être d'avis que
un **point de vue** [pwɛ̃dvy]
partager le point de vue de qn
une **impression** [ɛ̃ʀesjɔ̃]
J'ai l'impression que tu te moques de moi.
la **proposition** [pʀɔpozisjɔ̃]
Sa proposition me paraît intéressante.
proposer qc à qn/à qn de faire qc [pʀɔpoze]

be of the opinion that
point of view
share s.o.'s point of view
impression
I have the impression that you're making fun of me.
suggestion, proposal
Her/His proposal seems interesting to me.
propose s.th. to s.o.; suggest that s.o. do s.th.

s'imaginer (faire) qc [simaʒine]
Les jeunes s'imaginent avoir toujours raison.
l'**imagination** f [imaʒinasjɔ̃]
supposer [sypoze]
Je suppose que tu es en colère contre lui.
rêver (de) [ʀeve]
Je rêve d'un voyage à Tahiti.
un **rêve** [ʀɛv]

imagine (doing) s.th.
Young people imagine that they're always right.
imagination
suppose
I suppose you're furious with him.
dream (of)
I dream of a trip to Tahiti.
dream

un **plan** [plã] tirer des plans	plan draw up plans

la **volonté** [vɔlɔ̃te] — will
vouloir [vulwaʀ] — will; wish, want
Je voudrais que tu viennes cette après-midi. — I would like you to come this afternoon.
Tu veux bien qu'on aille au cinéma? — Do you want to go to the movies with me?
demander [d(ə)mãde] — ask; demand; desire; want

---

demander

Pay close attention to the associated words!

demander qc	*ask for s.th., demand s.th.*
Je demande une explication.	*I demand an explanation.*
demander qn	*ask for s.o.*
On demande Mme Caradec au téléphone.	*Mrs. Caradec is wanted on the phone.*
demander qc à qn	*ask s.o. for/about s.th*
Tu pourrais demander le chemin à cet agent.	*You could ask this policeman the way.*
demander à qn de faire qc	*ask s.o. to do s.th.*
Demandez-lui de nous attendre.	*Ask him to wait for us.*

---

souhaiter (de) faire qc [swete] — wish to do s.th.
Ils souhaitent acheter une grande maison. — They wish to buy a large house.
désirer faire qc [deziʀe] — desire to do s.th.
Je désire parler au directeur. — I would like to speak to the manager.

le **désir** [deziʀ] — desire, wish
préférer (faire) qc [pʀefeʀe] — prefer (to do) s.th.
Je préfère ne pas la rencontrer. — I prefer not to meet her.
avoir envie de qc [avwaʀãvi] — want s.th.
J'ai envie d'une glace. — I want some ice cream.
il vaut mieux [ilvomjø] — it's better
Il vaut mieux ne pas le déranger. — It's better not to disturb him.
Il vaut mieux qu'on s'en aille maintenant. — We'd better go now.

---

un **objectif** [ɔbʒɛktif] — goal, object(ive)
un **but** [byt] — object, end, aim, purpose
poursuivre un but/un objectif précis — pursue a precise/clear goal
un **projet** [pʀɔʒɛ] — project, plan
faire des projets pour les vacances — make vacation plans

accepter [aksɛpte]
refuser (de faire) qc [ʀ(ə)fyze]
Elle refuse de nous aider.
Elle refuse qu'on lui vienne en aide.
renoncer à (faire) qc [ʀ(ə)nɔ̃se]
Nous renonçons à lui faire comprendre notre point de vue.

accept
refuse (to do) s.th.
She refuses to help us.
She refuses help.
give up (doing) s.th.
We're giving up trying to make her understand our point of view.

s'opposer à [sɔpoze]
éviter de faire qc [evited(ə)fɛʀ]
empêcher qn de faire qc [ɑ̃pɛʃe]
Son père veut l'empêcher de se marier.

oppose
avoid doing s.th.
prevent s.o. from doing s.th.
His father wants to prevent him from getting married.

conclure [kɔ̃klyʀ]
tirer une conclusion [tiʀeynkɔ̃klyzjɔ̃]
J'en tire les conclusions qui s'imposent.
juger qn/qc [ʒyʒe]
juger qn **sur ses actes**
le **jugement** [ʒyʒmɑ̃]
un **préjugé** [pʀeʒyʒe]
Les préjugés ont la vie dure.

conclude
draw a conclusion
I draw indispensable conclusions from it.
judge s.o./s.th.
judge s.o. by his deeds
judgment
prejudice
Prejudices are long-lived.

la **mémoire** [memwaʀ]
avoir une mémoire d'éléphant
douter de qc/que + *subj* [dute]
Je doute de sa sincérité.
On doute qu'il dise la vérité.

memory
have the memory of an elephant
doubt s.th.; doubt that
I doubt his sincerity.
We doubt that he's telling the truth.

un **doute** [dut]
confondre avec [kɔ̃fɔ̃dʀ]
Je l'ai confondue avec sa sœur.
la **confusion** [kɔ̃fyzjɔ̃]
confus,e [kɔ̃fy, yz]

doubt
confuse with
I confused her with her sister.
confusion
confused

deviner [d(ə)vine]
Devine qui j'ai rencontré dans le métro.
une **devinette** [dəvinɛt]
poser une devinette à qn
prévoir [pʀevwaʀ]
C'était à prévoir qu'il aurait un accident.

guess
Guess who I ran into in the subway.
riddle
ask s.o. a riddle
predict, foresee
It was foreseeable that he would have an accident.

une **prévision** [pʀevizjɔ̃]	prediction, prognosis
les **prévisions** **météorologiques**	weather forecast
constater **qc** [kɔ̃state]	state s.th.
une **constatation** [kɔ̃statasjɔ̃]	statement

une **intention** [ɛ̃tɑ̃sjɔ̃]	intention
Ma mère est **pleine de bonnes** **intentions.**	My mother is full of good intentions.
avoir l'intention de faire qc	intend to do s.th.
envisager (de faire) qc [ɑ̃vizaʒe]	consider (doing) s.th.
Nous envisageons de nous installer en Provence.	We are considering settling in Provence.
songer à [sɔ̃ʒe]	think of; mean
Elle songe à émigrer.	She is thinking of emigrating.
tenir à ce que + subj [t(ə)niʀ]	insist on s.th.; place value on s.th.
Je tiens à ce que tu fasses tes devoirs.	I insist that you do your homework.

volontaire [vɔlɔ̃tɛʀ]	voluntary; intentional
involontaire [ɛ̃vɔlɔ̃tɛʀ]	involuntary; unintentional
un **homicide involontaire**	negligent homicide
à volonté [avɔlɔ̃te]	at pleasure, at will
Il y a du caviar à volonté.	There's as much caviar as you want.
imposer qc à qn [ɛ̃poze]	force s.th. on s.o.
une **exigence** [ɛgziʒɑ̃s]	(unreasonable) demand; exigency
exiger qc [ɛgziʒe]	exact, require, demand
J'exige tes excuses.	I demand an apology from you.
(être) exigeant,e [ɛgziʒɑ̃, ɑ̃t]	(be) demanding, exacting
Il est très exigeant envers lui-même.	He places high demands on himself.
arbitraire [aʀbitʀɛʀ]	arbitrary
une **décision arbitraire**	an arbitrary decision

la **résolution** [ʀezɔlysjɔ̃]	decision; resolution
résolu,e [ʀezɔly]	resolved, decided, determined
Je suis bien résolu à lui dire ses quatre vérités.	I'm firmly resolved to tell him/her a few home truths.

4.3 Character, Behavior

le **caractère** [kaʀaktɛʀ]	character; nature, disposition
un **bon/mauvais caractère**	a good/bad character

Elle n'est pas méchante, mais elle
a mauvais caractère.
le **trait de caractère**
caractériser [kaʀakteʀize]
caractéristique de [kaʀakteʀistik]
Cette affirmation est caractéristique de sa pensée.
une **qualité** [kalite]
un **défaut** [defo]
Sois sincère, dis-moi mes qualités
et mes défauts.

She's not malicious, but she is
bad-tempered.
character trait
characterize
characteristic of
This assertion is characteristic of
his thinking.
quality
defect, fault
Be honest; tell me my strengths
and my faults.

le **tempérament** [tɑ̃peʀamɑ̃]
l'**état d'esprit** m [etadɛspʀi]
la **façon de voir les choses**
[fasɔ̃d(ə)vwaʀleʃoz]
Je n'apprécie pas ta façon de voir
les choses.

temperament
state of mind
way of seeing things

I don't like your way of seeing
things.

l'**humeur** f [ymœʀ]

humor, mood

humeur – humour

French uses different words to render English *humor*, which means both *a comic
quality* and *a mental disposition*. **Note the difference:**
l'**humeur** f
être de bonne/mauvaise humeur
Elle est d'humeur changeante.
l'**humour** m
Il manque totalement d'humour.

humor, mood
be in a good/bad mood
She has a changeable disposition.
humor
He is totally humorless.

agréable [agʀeabl]
aimable [ɛmabl]
l'**amabilité** f [amabilite]
charmant,e [ʃaʀmɑ̃, ɑ̃t]
Il est d'une humeur charmante.
le **charme** [ʃaʀm]
gentil,le [ʒɑ̃ti, ij]
Sois gentil, apporte-moi mes
lunettes.
la **gentillesse** [ʒɑ̃tijɛs]
sympa(thique) [sɛ̃pa(tik)]
la **sympathie** [sɛ̃pati]

agreeable, pleasant
kind, amiable, obliging
kindness
charming, delightful
He is in a delightful mood.
charm
nice, kind, sweet
Be sweet and bring me my
glasses.
kindness, niceness, sweetness
likeable, congenial
fellow-feeling, sympathy

désagréable [dezagʀeabl]
Je ne l'aime pas, je le trouve
désagréable.

disagreeable, unpleasant
I don't like him; I find him
unpleasant.

méchant,e [meʃã, ãt]	wicked; naughty; mean
la **méchanceté** [meʃãste]	wickedness; naughtiness; meanness
sévère [sevɛʀ]	severe, stern
la **sévérité** [seveʀite]	severity, sternness
la **colère** [kɔlɛʀ]	anger, fury
se mettre en colère	fly into a fury
être en colère	be angry
la **rage** [ʀaʒ]	rage
Ça m'a mis dans une rage folle.	It sent me into a mad rage.

---

i

-age

Polysyllabic nouns ending in **-age** are generally *masculine:*

un garage	a garage
un étage	a story, a floor
un passage	a passage
le massage	massage
le dopage	the doping (of horses, athletes, etc.)

Monosyllabic nouns, however, are usually *feminine:*

une cage	a cage
la rage	the rage
une page	a page

---

bon,ne [bɔ̃, bɔn]	good
la **bonté** [bɔ̃te]	goodness
tendre [tãdʀ]	tender
adresser un regard tendre à qn	cast a tender glance at s.o.
la **tendresse** [tãdʀɛs]	tenderness
sensible [sãsibl]	sensitive
la **sensibilité** [sãsibilite]	sensitivity
une **sensibilité à fleur de peau**	hypersensitivity
généreux, -euse [ʒeneʀø, øz]	generous
la **générosité** [ʒeneʀozite]	generosity

---

inhumain,e [inymɛ̃, ɛn]	inhumane
Je trouve son attitude inhumaine.	I find his/her attitude inhumane.

insensible (à) [ɛ̃sãsibl]	insensitive (to)
(un,e) **égoïste** *n; adj* [egɔist]	egotist; egotistic, selfish
Les hommes sont tous des égoïstes.	All men are egotistic.
l'**égoïsme** *m* [egɔism]	egotism
avare [avaʀ]	greedy, avaricious

---

juste [ʒyst]	just, fair
Elle est sévère mais juste.	She is strict, but fair.

la **justice** [ʒystis]	justice
honnête [ɔnɛt]	honest
l'**honnêteté** f [ɔnɛtte]	honesty
Ayez l'honnêteté de reconnaître votre erreur.	Have the honesty to confess your error.

injuste [ɛ̃ʒyst]	unjust, unfair
l'**injustice** f [ɛ̃ʒystis]	injustice, wrong
malhonnête [malɔnɛt]	dishonest
la **malhonnêteté** [malɔnɛtte]	dishonesty

gai,e [ge/gɛ]	cheerful
Tu n'as pas l'air très gai aujourd'hui.	You don't look very cheerful today.
la **gaieté** (la gaîté) [gete]	cheerfulness, gaiety
drôle [dʀol]	funny
Arrête, tu n'es vraiment pas drôle.	Stop it; you're really not very funny.
amusant,e [amyzɑ̃, ɑ̃t]	amusing, funny
comique [kɔmik]	comic(al), funny
Il est comique, il nous fait toujours rire.	He's really comical; he always makes us laugh.
original,e [ɔʀiʒinal]	original; quaint, odd

triste [tʀist]	sad
la **tristesse** [tʀistɛs]	sadness
(**être**) **mécontent,e** [mekɔ̃tɑ̃, ɑ̃t]	(be) discontented, displeased
Elle est mécontente de son nouveau chef.	She is displeased with her new boss.

calme [kalm]	calm
Ne t'énerve pas, reste calme.	Don't get excited; stay calm.
tranquille [tʀɑ̃kil]	calm, tranquil
Laisse-moi tranquille.	Leave me alone.
naturel,le [natyʀɛl]	natural
décontracté,e [dekɔ̃tʀakte]	relaxed

nerveux, -euse [nɛʀvø, øz]	nervous; excitable
énervant,e [enɛʀvɑ̃, ɑ̃t]	enervating, annoying
fatigant,e [fatigɑ̃, ɑ̃t]	tiring, fatiguing
bizarre [bizaʀ]	bizarre, strange
compliqué,e [kɔ̃plike]	complicated
Avec lui, rien n'est simple, il est tellement compliqué.	Nothing's simple with him; he's terribly complicated.
difficile [difisil]	difficult

rapide [Rapid] — rapid, fast
dynamique [dinamik] — dynamic
un jeune cadre dynamique — a dynamic young manager
avoir de la volonté — have a strong will
[avvaRd(ə)lavolɔ̃te]
énergique [enɛRʒik] — energetic
l'**énergie** f [enɛRʒi] — energy
déborder d'énergie — overflow with energy
autoritaire [ɔtɔRitɛR] — authoritarian

lent,e [lɑ̃, lɑ̃t] — slow
Il a l'esprit plutôt lent. — He's more of a slow thinker.
mou, molle [mu, mɔl] — soft; feeble; indolent, sluggish
Jamais je ne pourrais vivre avec lui, il est trop mou. — I could never live with him; he's too indolent.
faible [fɛbl] — weak
Elle est trop faible avec ses enfants. — She is too lenient with her children.
(un,e) **paresseux, -euse** n; adj — lazy, slothful
[paRɛsø, øz]
Tu y arriverais, si tu n'étais pas si paresseux. — You'd get it done if you weren't so lazy.
la **paresse** [paRɛs] — laziness

bête [bɛt] — stupid, silly
Il est bête comme ses pieds. loc — He's a blockhead.
la **bêtise** [betiz] — stupidity, stupid thing
faire des bêtises — do stupid things
stupide [stypid] — stupid, dumb
la **stupidité** [stypidite] — stupidity
(un,e) **idiot,e** n; adj [idjo, idjɔt] — idiot; idiotic, dumb

courageux, -euse [kuRaʒø, øz] — courageous
le **courage** [kuRaʒ] — courage
fier, fière de [fjɛR] — proud of
Ils sont fiers de leurs enfants. — They're proud of their children.
la **fierté** [fjɛRte] — pride

sage [saʒ] — wise; prudent; well-behaved
être sage comme une image loc — be good as gold
prudent,e [pRydɑ̃, ɑ̃t] — prudent, cautious
la **prudence** [pRydɑ̃s] — prudence, caution
agir avec prudence — act prudently
diplomate [diplɔmat] — diplomatic

Elle n'est pas assez diplomate pour les réconcilier.	She is not diplomatic enough to reconcile them.
raisonnable [Rɛzɔnabl]	reasonable
poli,e [pɔli]	polite
la **politesse** [pɔlitɛs]	politeness
discret, -ète [diskRɛ, ɛt]	discreet
la **discrétion** [diskResjɔ̃]	discretion, tact
faire preuve de discrétion	give proof of one's discretion
sérieux, -euse [seRjø, jøz]	serious; responsible, sound
Cet homme est très **sérieux dans son travail.**	This man is very responsible in his work.
être sérieux comme un pape *loc*	be deadly serious

imprudent,e [ɛ̃pRydɑ̃, ɑ̃t]	imprudent, unwise
l'**imprudence** *f* [ɛ̃pRydɑ̃s]	imprudence
impoli,e [ɛ̃pɔli]	impolite
indiscret, -ète [ɛ̃diskRɛ, ɛt]	indiscreet, tactless
poser des questions indiscrètes	ask indiscreet questions
une **indiscrétion** [ɛ̃diskResjɔ̃]	indiscretion
commettre une indiscrétion	commit an indiscretion
curieux, -euse [kyRjø, jøz]	curious
Il est curieux comme un singe. *loc*	He is very, very curious.
la **curiosité** [kyRjozite]	curiosity
bavard,e [bavaR, aRd]	talkative, chatty

la **mentalité** [mɑ̃talite]	mentality
la **personnalité** [pɛRsɔnalite]	personality
le **comportement** [kɔ̃pɔRtəmɑ̃]	behavior, deportment
se **comporter** [s(ə)kɔ̃pɔRte]	behave, act
Il s'est mal comporté envers toi.	He behaved badly toward you.
la **vertu** [vɛRty]	virtue
le **vice** [vis]	vice
L'oisiveté est mère de tous les vices. *prov*	Idleness is the root of all evil.

avoir le cœur sur la main [avwaRləkœRsyRlamɛ̃]	be very generous
avoir un faible pour [avwaRɛ̃fɛbl]	have a weakness for
Luc a un faible pour les blondes.	Luc has a weakness for blondes.
(un,e) **idéaliste** *n; adj* [idealist]	idealist; idealistic
(un,e) **réaliste** *n; adj* [Realist]	realist; realistic

agité,e [aʒite]	agitated, upset
insolent,e [ɛ̃sɔlɑ̃, ɑ̃t]	insolent, rude

arrogant,e [aʀɔgã, ãt] | arrogant
Je n'aime pas **ses airs arrogants.** | I don't like his arrogant mannerisms.
râleur, -euse *fam* [ʀalœʀ, øz] | nagging, bad-tempered
grossier, -ière [gʀosje, jɛʀ] | boorish, rude, unmannerly
Quel grossier personnage ! | What a rude person!
brutal,e [bʀytal] | brutal, surly; unexpected
une réaction brutale | a brutal/an unexpected reaction
une **brute** [bʀyt] | brute; brutal person; boor
une **sale brute** | dirty brute, dirty beast
la **brutalité** [bʀytalite] | brutality

franc, franche [fʀã, fʀãʃ] | frank, open
digne de foi [diɲdəfwa] | believable, deserving of credit
Ne crois pas tout ce qu'il dit, il n'est pas digne de foi. | Don't believe everything he says; he's not believable.
sincère [sẽsɛʀ] | sincere, honest
mes vœux les plus sincères | my sincerest wishes
la **sincérité** [sẽseʀite] | sincerity
modeste [mɔdɛst] | modest
la **modestie** [mɔdɛsti] | modesty
serviable [sɛʀvjabl] | helpful

(un,e) **menteur, -euse** *n; adj* [mãtœʀ, øz] | liar; lying, deceitful
traiter qn de menteur | call someone a liar
(un,e) **hypocrite** *n; adj* [ipokʀit] | hypocrite; hypocritical
l'**hypocrisie** *f* [ipokʀizi] | hypocrisy
orgueilleux, -euse [ɔʀgøjø, jøz] | proud, haughty, arrogant
l'**orgueil** *m* [ɔʀgœj] | pride, arrogance
L'orgueil précède la chute. *loc* | Pride comes before a fall.
vaniteux, -euse [vanitø, øz] | vain
la **vanité** [vanite] | vanity
rancunier, -ière [ʀãkynje, jɛʀ] | rancorous, spiteful
se venger de [səvãʒe] | revenge oneself for
Je vais me venger de vos moqueries. | I'm going to revenge myself for your jeers.
faire du tort à qn [fɛʀdytɔʀ] | wrong s.o., harm s.o.
Cet article dans le journal lui a fait du tort. | This newspaper article harmed him/her.

ouvert,e [uvɛʀ, ɛʀt] | open
avoir l'esprit ouvert | be open-minded
équilibré,e [ekilibʀe] | balanced, poised
(avoir de) l'humour *m* [ymuʀ] | (have a sense of) humor

manquer d'humour	lack a sense of humor
déterminé,e [detɛʀmine]	determined
un risque-tout [ʀiskətu]	daredevil
(un,e) optimiste n; adj [ɔptimist]	optimist; optimistic
l'optimisme m [ɔptimism]	optimism
J'envisage l'avenir avec optimisme.	I view the future with optimism.
satisfait,e [satisfɛ, ɛt]	satisfied, pleased
la satisfaction [satisfaksjɔ̃]	satisfaction
afficher sa satisfaction	proclaim one's satisfaction
obtenir satisfaction	obtain satisfaction
tolérant,e [tɔleʀɑ̃, ɑ̃t]	tolerant

timide [timid]	timid
la timidité [timidite]	timidity
complexé,e [kɔ̃plɛkse]	inhibited
Il est complexé à cause de son poids.	He has a complex because of his weight.
peureux, -euse [pøʀø, øz]	fearful

renfermé,e [ʀɑ̃fɛʀme]	retiring
Elle est renfermée sur elle-même.	She has withdrawn into herself.
déséquilibré,e [dezekilibʀe]	unbalanced
borné,e [bɔʀne]	narrow-minded; limited
têtu,e [tety]	stubborn
Tu es têtu comme une mule. loc	You're as stubborn as a mule.
(un,e) pessimiste n; adj [pesimist]	pessimist; pessimistic
le pessimisme [pesimism]	pessimism
intolérant,e [ɛ̃tɔleʀɑ̃, ɑ̃t]	intolerant

efficace [efikas]	effective, efficient
Pour cet emploi il faut quelqu'un d'efficace.	For this job you need someone efficient.
ambitieux, -euse [ɑ̃bisjø, jøz]	ambitious
l'ambition f [ɑ̃bisjɔ̃]	ambition
consciencieux, -euse [kɔ̃sjɑ̃sjø, jøz]	conscientious

désordonné,e [dezɔʀdɔne]	messy, disorderly
flemmard,e fam [flɛmaʀ, aʀd]	lazy, slack
indifférent,e [ɛ̃difeʀɑ̃, ɑ̃t]	indifferent
Il est indifférent à ce qui se passe autour de lui.	He's indifferent to what goes on around him.
l'indifférence f [ɛ̃difeʀɑ̃s]	indifference

compréhensif, -ive [kɔ̃pʀeɑ̃sif, iv]	understanding, broad-minded

attentif, -ive [atɑ̃tif, iv]	attentive
prêter une oreille attentive à qn	listen to s.o. attentively
conciliant,e [kɔ̃siljɑ̃, ɑ̃t]	conciliatory, open-minded
réfléchi,e [ʀefleʃi]	deliberate; thoughtful
Il n'agit pas à la légère, il est réfléchi.	He doesn't act inconsiderately; he's very thoughtful.
brave [bʀav]	brave; worthy, honest
C'est un **brave type**. *fam*	He's an honest fellow.
faire le brave	play the bully

> **i** For information on *adjectives* that *change their meaning* depending on whether they *precede* or *follow* the word modified, see p. 37.

malin, maligne [malɛ̃, maliɲ]	malicious; cunning, clever
A malin, malin et demi. *loc*	Even a cunning person can be outfoxed.
une **joie maligne**	malignant delight, spiteful glee
rusé,e [ʀyze]	crafty, sly
rusé comme un renard *loc*	sly as a fox
la **ruse** [ʀyz]	ruse, trick
arriver* à qc par la ruse	achieve s.th. by deceit

hésitant,e [ezitɑ̃, ɑ̃t]	hesitant, undecided
(un,e) **lâche** *n; adj* [laʃ]	coward; cowardly
Il s'est comporté **en lâche**.	He behaved in a cowardly way.
gâté,e [gate]	spoiled
un **enfant gâté**	a spoiled child
craintif, -ive [kʀɛ̃tif, iv]	fearful, timid
trouillard,e *fam* [tʀujaʀ, jaʀd]	cowardly
avoir la trouille *fam* [avwaʀlatʀuj]	be scared
Vas-y toi; moi, j'ai la trouille.	You go there; I've got the jitters.

distingué,e [distɛ̃ge]	distinguished
avoir de la classe	have class
[avwaʀd(ə)laklas]	
Elle a une classe folle !	She has a lot of class!
(un,e) **snob** *n; adj* [snɔb]	snob; snobbish
vulgaire [vylgɛʀ]	vulgar, common

4.4 Activities and Abilities

l'**activité** *f* [aktivite]	activity
Il est **débordant d'activité**.	He's bursting with activity.
(in)actif, -ive [(in)aktif, iv]	active; inactive
une **action** [aksjɔ̃]	action, deed

passer à l'action
agir [aʒiʀ]
Il agit souvent sans réfléchir.
une **réaction** [ʀeaksjɔ̃]
déclencher une réaction
réagir [ʀeaʒiʀ]

go into action
act
He often acts without thinking.
reaction
set off a reaction
react

adroit,e [adʀwa, wat]
l'**adresse** f [adʀɛs]
Ce sport demande beaucoup
d'adresse.
maladroit,e [maladʀwa, wat]
la **maladresse** [maladʀɛs]
capable (de) [kapabl]
Ne me mets pas en colère, sinon
je suis capable de tout.
incapable (de) [ɛ̃kapabl]
Elle est incapable de voyager seule.

ingenious, clever, skillful
skill, dexterity, cleverness
This sport requires a lot of skill.

awkward, clumsy
awkwardness, clumsiness
capable (of)
Don't make me angry, or else
I'm capable of anything.
incapable (of)
She's incapable of traveling alone.

une **décision** [desizjɔ̃]
prendre une décision importante
décider (de faire) qc [deside]
La fermeture de l'usine a été
décidée hier.
J'ai décidé de faire du sport
régulièrement.
se décider à faire qc [s(ə)deside]
Je me suis enfin décidé à lui dire
la vérité.
être décidé,e à [deside]
Je suis bien décidé à arrêter de
fumer.
préparer qc [pʀepaʀe]
une **préparation** [pʀepaʀasjɔ̃]
l'**hésitation** f [ezitasjɔ̃]
hésiter à faire qc [ezite]
J'hésite à lui prêter ma voiture.

decision
make an important decision
decide (to do) s.th.
The closing of the firm was
decided yesterday.
I've decided to play sports
regularly.
decide to do s.th.
I finally decided to tell her/him
the truth.
be determined, be resolved
I'm quite determined to stop
smoking.
prepare s.th.
preparation
hesitation
hesitate to do s.th.
I hesitate to lend him/her my
car.

essayer de faire qc [eseje]
un **essai** [esɛ]
faire un essai
risquer de faire qc [ʀiske]
On risque de tout perdre à vouloir
trop gagner. prov

try to do s.th.
attempt, try
make an attempt
risk doing s.th.
You risk losing everything when
you try to win too big.

réussir à faire qc [ʀeysiʀ]
Le 25 juillet 1909, Blériot a réussi à traverser la Manche en avion.

succeed in doing s.th.
On July 25, 1909, Blériot succeeded in flying across the English Channel.

une **réussite** [ʀeysit]

success

arriver* à faire qc [aʀive]
Je ne suis pas arrivé à réparer la voiture.

succeed in doing s.th.
I didn't succeed in repairing the car.

oser faire qc [oze]
Il n'ose pas l'inviter à dîner.

dare to do s.th.
He doesn't dare ask her out to dinner.

résoudre [ʀezudʀ]
résoudre un problème

solve, resolve
solve a problem

échouer à/dans [eʃwe]
Elle a échoué dans ses projets.

fail in
She failed in her plans.

un **échec** [eʃɛk]
Il aura du mal à se remettre de cet échec.

failure, flop
He will have a hard time recovering from this failure.

---

un **effort** [efɔʀ]
faire des efforts
avoir du mal à faire qc [avwaʀdymal]
J'ai du mal à croire tes explications.

effort
make efforts
have difficulty (in) doing s.th.
I have a hard time believing your explanations.

avoir de la peine à faire qc [avwaʀd(ə)lapɛn]
J'ai eu de la peine à porter ma valise.

be scarcely able to do s.th.
I was scarcely able to carry my suitcase.

se débrouiller [s(ə)debʀuje]
Débrouille-toi tout seul.

manage
See if you can manage alone.

---

créer [kʀee]
un parfum créé par Chanel

create
a perfume created by Chanel

la **création** [kʀeasjɔ̃]

creation

inventer [ɛ̃vɑ̃te]
Si tu n'existais pas, il faudrait t'inventer.

invent
If you didn't exist, they'd have to invent you.

une **invention** [ɛ̃vɑ̃sjɔ̃]
faire breveter une invention

invention
have an invention patented

réaliser [ʀealize]
réaliser ses projets

realize; carry out
realize one's plans

la **réalisation** [ʀealizasjɔ̃]

realization

imiter [imite]

imitate

une **imitation** [imitasjɔ̃]	imitation

faire attention à [fɛRatɑ̃sjɔ̃]
Il raconte des bêtises, ne fais pas attention à lui.
Fais attention à la marche.
faire exprès de faire qc [fɛRɛkspRɛ]
Ils font exprès de faire du bruit pour nous déranger.
faire semblant (de faire qc) [fɛRsɑ̃blɑ̃]
Il fait semblant de dormir.

pay attention to; watch out for, mind
He's talking nonsense; don't pay any attention to him.
Mind the step.
do s.th. intentionally
They're intentionally making noise to disturb us.
pretend (to do s.th.)

He is pretending to be asleep.

perdre [pɛRdR]
la **perte** [pɛRt]
une **grosse perte**
chercher [ʃɛRʃe]
Qui cherche trouve. *prov*
trouver [tRuve]
retrouver [R(ə)tRuve]
partager [paRtaʒe]
Je partage tout avec toi, mon chéri.

lose
loss
a serious loss
search
Search, and you will find.
find
find again
share
I share everything with you, my darling.

diriger [diRiʒe]
Mon père dirige une entreprise importante.
organiser [ɔRganize]
l'**organisation** f [ɔRganizasjɔ̃]
avoir le sens de l'organisation
choisir [ʃwaziR]
le **choix** [ʃwa]
faire son choix
Je n'ai pas le choix.

lead, direct, head
My father runs an important company.
organize
organization
have a sense of organization
choose
choice
make one's choice
I have no choice.

parler [paRle]
chanter [ʃɑ̃te]
chanter juste/faux
écouter [ekute]
Je peux dire ce que je veux, ils ne m'écoutent jamais.
entendre [ɑ̃tɑ̃dR]
Tu as entendu ce bruit?

speak
sing
sing true/out of tune
hear; listen to
I can say what I like; they never listen to me.
hear
Did you hear that noise?

For information on the difference between **écouter** and **entendre**, see p. 27.

lire [liʀ]	read
la **lecture** [lɛktyʀ]	reading
être plongé dans la lecture d'un roman	be immersed in reading a novel
écrire [ekʀiʀ]	write

regarder [ʀ(ə)gaʀde]	look at, take a look at
un **regard** [ʀ(ə)gaʀ]	look
jeter un regard sur	cast a glance at
observer [ɔpsɛʀve]	observe
une **observation** [ɔpsɛʀvasjɔ̃]	observation
avoir le sens de l'observation	have good powers of observation
remarquer [ʀ(ə)maʀke]	notice, observe; remark upon
une **remarque** [ʀ(ə)maʀk]	remark
s'intéresser à [sɛ̃teʀese]	be interested in
Je m'intéresse beaucoup à la politique.	I'm very interested in politics.
un **intérêt** [ɛ̃teʀɛ]	interest
C'est sans intérêt.	That's not interesting.

la **capacité** [kapasite]	capacity
Ça n'entre pas dans ses capacités.	That exceeds his capacities.
l'**incapacité** f [ɛ̃kapasite]	incapacity
être dans l'incapacité de faire qc	be incapable of doing s.th.
la **faculté** [fakylte]	faculty, ability
Dans son domaine, il **fait preuve de** facultés étonnantes.	In his field, he has surprising abilities.
le **savoir-faire** [savwaʀfɛʀ]	know-how
manquer de savoir-faire	lack the know-how

habile [abil]	clever, skillful
Il est très **habile de** ses mains.	He's very clever with his hands.
malhabile [malabil]	clumsy
l'**habileté** f [abil(ə)te]	cleverness; skill
compétente,e [kɔ̃petã, ãt]	competent
la **compétence** [kɔ̃petãs]	competence; skill, proficiency
Il est connu pour **ses compétences en informatique**.	He's known for his proficiency in information technology.
incompétent,e [ɛ̃kɔ̃petã, ãt]	incompetent
l'**incompétence** f [ɛ̃kɔ̃petãs]	incompetence

une **tâche** [taʃ]	task
entreprendre une tâche	undertake a task

i

tache – tâche

In speech it doesn't matter, but in writing it's fatal. *Don't forget the circumflex accent!*

une tache	*spot*
Ton pantalon est plein de taches.	*Your pants are full of spots.*
une tâche	*task*
Tu n'auras pas la tâche facile.	*You will not have an easy task.*

élaborer qc [elabɔʀe]
work out s.th.

se charger de qc [səʃaʀʒe]
take care of s.th.
Tu apportes le vin, et je me charge du dessert.
You bring the wine, and I'll take care of the dessert.

accomplir qc [akɔ̃pliʀ]
accomplish s.th.

se donner la peine [s(ə)dɔnelapɛn]
take the trouble
Il ne s'est même pas donné la peine de me répondre.
He didn't even take the trouble to answer me.

faire de son mieux [fɛʀdəsɔ̃mjø]
do one's best
J'ai fait de mon mieux, mais ce n'est pas très réussi.
I did my best, but it wasn't very successful.

(se) perfectionner [(s(ə))pɛʀfɛksjɔne]
improve, perfect
Elle veut aller aux Etats-Unis pour perfectionner son anglais.
She wants to go to the United States to improve her English.

se tirer d'affaire [s(ə)tiʀedafɛʀ]
get out of a difficulty

---

projeter [pʀɔj(ə)te]
plan, intend
Nous projetons d'aller passer un mois au Canada.
We plan to spend a month in Canada.

s'engager dans qc/à faire qc [sɑ̃gaʒe]
undertake s.th.; get involved in s.th.
Elle s'est engagée dans une aventure dangereuse.
She became involved in a dangerous adventure.
Il s'est engagé à me rendre l'argent avant Noël.
He has promised to return the money to me before Christmas.

se forcer à faire qc [s(ə)fɔʀse]
force oneself to do s.th.
Je me suis forcé à manger les légumes.
I forced myself to eat the vegetables.

s'efforcer de faire qc [sefɔʀse]
endeavor to do s.th.
Il s'efforçait de rester calme.
He endeavored to stay calm.

se garder de faire qc [s(ə)gaʀde]
refrain from doing s.th.

céder [sede]
give in, succumb
céder à une envie
succumb to a desire

---

faire qc en vain [fɛʀɑ̃vɛ̃]
do s.th. in vain
J'ai cherché en vain, je n'ai rien trouvé.
I searched in vain; I found nothing.

faire qc en personne [fɛʀãpɛʀsɔn] — do s.th. in person
faire qc en cachette [fɛʀãkaʃɛt] — do s.th. secretly
Les enfants ont fumé en cachette. — The children smoked in secret.
faire qc avec/sans peine [fɛʀavɛk/sãpɛn] — do s.th. with/without difficulty
Est-ce qu'on peut apprendre le français sans peine? — Can French be learned without difficulty?
faire qc avec/sans succès [fɛʀavɛk/sãsyksɛ] — do s.th. successfully/unsuccessfully
faire qc volontiers [fɛʀvɔlõtje] — do s.th. gladly, be glad to do s.th.
Merci de votre invitation, nous viendrons volontiers. — Thank you for your invitation; we'll be glad to come.

apercevoir [apɛʀsəvwaʀ] — catch sight of, glimpse
J'ai aperçu Jacques dans le métro. — I caught sight of Jacques in the subway.

s'apercevoir de qc [sapɛʀsəvwaʀ] — notice s.th.
Je me suis aperçu qu'il me manquait 100 francs. — I noticed that I was missing 100 francs.
concevoir [kõs(ə)vwaʀ] — imagine; comprehend
Je **conçois mal** que tu aies fait ça. — I don't understand how you could do that.

se faire une idée de [s(ə)fɛʀynide] — have an idea of
Je vous dis ça pour que vous puissiez vous faire une idée de la gravité de la situation. — I'm telling you this so that you'll have an idea of the seriousness of the situation.
tenir compte de qc [t(ə)niʀkõt] — bear in mind; take into account
Tu ne tiens jamais compte de mon avis. — You never take my opinion into account.

réclamer [ʀeklame] — claim; demand back
réclamer des dommages-intérêts — sue for damages
acquérir qc [akeʀiʀ] — acquire s.th.
Bien mal acquis ne profite jamais. — Ill-gotten gains never prosper.
prov
une **acquisition** [akizisjõ] — acquisition

attribuer [atʀibye] — attribute; confer
On a attribué le prix Nobel de Littérature à Günter Grass en 1999. — The Nobel Prize for Literature was conferred on Günter Grass in 1999.

(se) répartir [(s(ə))ʀepaʀtiʀ] — divide; share
On se répartit les tâches domestiques. — We share the household chores.
la **répartition** [ʀepaʀtisjõ] — distribution, division
accorder qc à qn [akɔʀde] — grant s.th. to s.o.

Je lui ai accordé 8 jours de réflexion.	I've granted him a week to think it over.
destiner qc à qn [destine]	to destine s.th. for s.o.
Cette lettre lui est destinée.	This letter is intended for him.

oublier (de faire qc) [ublie]	forget (to do s.th.)
J'ai oublié de passer à l'épicerie.	I forgot to go by the grocery store.
l'**oubli** m [ubli]	forgetfulness; oversight
tomber* dans l'oubli	sink into oblivion
négliger [negliʒe]	neglect
négliger ses obligations	neglect one's obligations
la **négligence** [negliʒãs]	negligence
se désintéresser de	lose interest in
[s(ə)dezẽteʀese]	
Je me désintéresse complètement de ce sujet.	I have lost all interest in that subject.
le **désintérêt** [dezẽteʀɛ]	disinterest

French Word	English Equivalent	False Friend	French Equivalent
gentil,le	nice, kind, sweet	gentle	doux, aimable
borné,e	narrow-minded	born	né,e

5.1 Eating and Drinking

manger [mɑ̃ʒe]
Le soir, on mange souvent froid.

l'appétit m [apeti]
manger de bon appétit
"L'appétit vient en mangeant; la
soif s'en va en buvant." *(Rabelais)*
la **faim** [fɛ̃]
avoir faim
avoir une **faim de loup** *loc*
mourir* de faim
avoir envie de qc [avwaʀɑ̃vi]
J'ai bien envie d'un sandwich.

eat
In the evening we often eat a
cold supper.
appetite
eat with good appetite
"Appetite increases when you eat;
thirst decreases when you drink."
hunger
be hungry
be as hungry as a wolf
die of hunger
have a desire for s.th.
I really want a sandwich.

boire [bwaʀ]
boire à la bouteille
boire dans un verre
une **boisson** [bwasɔ̃]
la **soif** [swaf]
avoir soif

drink
drink from the bottle
drink from a glass
beverage, drink
thirst
be thirsty

un **aliment** [alimɑ̃]
l'**alimentation** f [alimɑ̃tasjɔ̃]
la **nourriture** [nuʀityʀ]
se nourrir (de) [s(ə)nuʀiʀ]
Ce garçon ne se nourrit que de
choclat.
avaler [avale]
avaler de travers

food, nourishment
feeding, nourishment
nourishment, sustenance
live on
That boy lives on nothing but
chocolate.
swallow
swallow the wrong way

un **repas** [ʀ(ə)pa]
se mettre à table [s(ə)mɛtʀatabl]
servir qc (à qn) [sɛʀviʀ]
Je vous sers encore un peu de
viande?
se servir [səsɛʀviʀ]
Sers-toi, je t'en prie.
le **petit déjeuner** [p(ə)tideʒœne]
prendre le petit déjeuner
(le) **déjeuner** n; v [deʒœne]
(le) **goûter** n; v [gute]
Il faut absolument **goûter à** ce
fromage. Il est délicieux.

meal, repast
sit down to the table
serve s.th. (to s.o.)
May I serve you a little more
meat?
serve oneself
Please help yourself.
breakfast
eat breakfast
lunch; eat lunch
snack; try, taste
You absolutely have to taste this
cheese. It's delicious.

(le) **dîner** n; v [dine]
dinner; dine, eat dinner
Le soir, ils vont souvent dîner au restaurant.
In the evening they often dine in a restaurant.

le **régime** [ʀeʒim]
diet
René est de mauvaise humeur. Il **est au régime** depuis lundi.
René is in a bad mood. He's been on a diet since Monday.
Moi aussi, je vais **me mettre au régime**.
I'm going to put myself on a diet too.

le **goût** [gu]
taste
avoir du goût
have a good taste
Bizarre, ce poulet **a un goût de poisson**.
Strange, the chicken tastes like fish.
bon,ne [bɔ̃, bɔn]
good
sucré,e [sykʀe]
sweet
salé,e [sale]
salty, salted
La soupe est trop salée.
The soup is too salty.
poivré,e [pwavʀe]
peppery, pungent; spicy
amer, -ère [amɛʀ]
bitter
acide [asid]
sour

brûlant,e [bʀylɑ̃, ɑ̃t]
burning hot
chaud,e [ʃo, ʃod]
hot, warm
Mange pendant que c'est chaud.
Eat while it's hot.
tiède [tjɛd]
lukewarm, tepid
froid,e [fʀwa, fʀwad]
cold

cru,e [kʀy]
raw, uncooked
un camembert **au lait cru**
raw-milk Camembert
cuit,e [kɥi, kɥit]
cooked, done
dur,e [dyʀ]
hard
mou, molle [mu, mɔl]
soft
tendre [tɑ̃dʀ]
tender
Ce bifteck est vraiment tendre.
This steak is really tender.

épais,se [epɛ, ɛs]
thick, dense
gras,se [gʀa, gʀas]
fat, fatty
maigre [mɛgʀ]
lean
Je voudrais trois tranches de jambon bien maigre.
I'd like three slices of really lean ham.
lourd,e [luʀ, luʀd]
heavy, hard to digest
On ne va plus dans ce restaurant, la cuisine y est trop lourde.
We don't go to that restaurant anymore; the cooking there is too hard to digest.

léger, -ère [leʒe, leʒɛʀ]	light
allégé,e [aleʒe]	low-fat
un fromage allégé	a low-fat cheese
sec, sèche [sɛk, sɛʃ]	dry
du saucisson sec	hard sausage
frais, fraîche [fʀɛ,fʀɛʃ]	fresh
pur,e [pyʀ]	pure
100% pur jus de fruits	100% pure fruit juice

un **café** [kafe]	coffee
un **thé** [te]	tea
boire un **thé** au citron	drink tea with lemon
le **lait** [lɛ]	milk
un **chocolat** [ʃɔkɔla]	chocolate, cocoa
le **sucre** [sykʀ]	sugar
le **sucre** en morceaux	lump sugar, cube sugar
une **sucrette** [sykʀɛt]	artificial sweetener

une **baguette** [bagɛt]	baguette (long roll of French bread)
une **tartine** [taʀtin]	slice of bread with butter and jam
un **croissant** [kʀwasɑ̃]	croissant, crescent roll
le **pain** [pɛ̃]	bread
une tranche de **pain**	a slice of bread
le **pain** complet	wholegrain bread
un petit **pain**	roll
le **pain** de mie	toast
du **pain** grillé	toasted bread
un **grille-pain**	toaster
une **brioche** [bʀiɔʃ]	brioche
une **biscotte** [biskɔt]	zwieback, cracker

le **beurre** [bœʀ]	butter
la **confiture** [kɔ̃fityʀ]	jam
le **miel** [mjɛl]	honey
un **œuf** [œf]	egg
un **œuf** à la coque	a soft-boiled egg
un **œuf** sur le plat	a fried egg

le **hors-d'œuvre** ['ɔʀdœvʀ]	appetizer, hors d'oeuvre
une **entrée** [ɑ̃tʀe]	first course, starter
une **soupe** [sup]	soup
un **pâté** [pate]	pâté
le **jambon** [ʒɑ̃bɔ̃]	ham
le **jambon** cru	uncooked ham
le **jambon** blanc	boiled ham
le **saucisson** [sosisɔ̃]	sausage

une **omelette** [ɔmlɛt]	omelet
les **crudités** f [kʀydite]	raw vegetables
au choix [oʃwa]	of your choice (all at one price)
Vous pouvez prendre des crudités ou du pâté, au choix.	You have a choice of the raw vegetables or the pâté.

le **poisson** [pwasɔ̃]	fish
la **truite** [tʀɥit]	trout
la **sole** [sɔl]	sole
le **saumon** [somɔ̃]	salmon
le **saumon fumé**	smoked salmon
le **thon** [tɔ̃]	tuna
le **thon à l'huile**	tuna in oil
le **hareng** ['aʀɑ̃]	herring
la **sardine** [saʀdin]	sardine
les **fruits de mer** m [fʀɥidmɛʀ]	seafood
les **moules** f [mul]	mussels

la **viande** [vjɑ̃d]	meat
le **bœuf** [bøf]	beef
le **veau** [vo]	veal
le **porc** [pɔʀ]	pork
le **mouton** [mutɔ̃]	mutton
l'**agneau** m [aɲo]	lamb
le **poulet** [pulɛ]	chicken
le **canard** [kanaʀ]	duck
la **dinde** [dɛ̃d]	turkey
le **lapin** [lapɛ̃]	rabbit
poser un lapin à qn fam; loc	stand someone up
le **gibier** [ʒibje]	game

le **bifteck** [biftɛk]	(beef)steak
le **steak** [stɛk]	steak
le **rôti** [ʀoti/ʀɔti]	roast
la **sauce** [sos]	sauce, gravy
le **foie** [fwa]	liver

---

i

le foie – la foi – la fois

Same sound, different spelling; *note these homophones:*

le foie [fwa]	*the liver*
du foie gras	*goose or duck liver (paté)*
la foi [fwa]	*faith, belief*
Il n'y a que la foi qui sauve. loc	*That's a likely story!*
la fois [fwa]	*the time*
Une fois n'est pas coutume. loc	*Once does not constitute a habit.*

une **côtelette** [kotlɛt/kɔtlɛt]	cutlet, chop
une **escalope** [ɛskalɔp]	scallop (of veal or pork)
un **filet** [filɛ]	filet
une **entrecôte** [ãtʀəkot]	steak cut from between the ribs

le **légume** [legym]	vegetable

les légumes

The plural, **les légumes**, means *vegetables*. **Légumes verts** are *greens*. **Les grosses légumes** is an idiom meaning *bigwigs*.

la **pomme de terre** [pɔmdətɛʀ]	potato
les **pommes de terre à l'eau**	boiled potatoes
les **pommes de terre sautées**	pan-fried potatoes
les **(pommes) frites** *f* [(pɔm)fʀit]	French fries
la **purée** [pyʀe]	mashed potatoes
la **carotte** [kaʀɔt]	carrot
Les carottes sont cuites. *fam*	We're done for.
une **tomate** [tɔmat]	tomato
les **haricots verts** *m* [ˈaʀikovɛʀ]	green beans
les **petits pois** *m* [p(ə)tipwa]	peas
les **asperges** *f* [aspɛʀʒ]	asparagus
le **champignon** [ʃãpiɲɔ̃]	mushroom
le **champignon (de Paris)**	button mushroom
l'**oignon** *m* [ɔɲɔ̃]	onion

le **riz** [ʀi]	rice
les **nouilles** *f* [nuj]	noodles
les **pâtes** *f* [pat]	pasta

la **salade** [salad]	salad
une **salade composée**	mixed salad
une **salade de fruits**	fruit salad
la **vinaigrette** [vinɛgʀɛt]	vinaigrette dressing
la **mayonnaise** [majɔnɛz]	mayonnaise

les **produits laitiers** *m* [pʀɔdɥilɛtje]	dairy products
le **fromage** [fʀɔmaʒ]	cheese
le **fromage blanc**	cream cheese, farmer cheese
le **camembert** [kamãbɛʀ]	Camembert
le **gruyère** [gʀɥjɛʀ]	Gruyère
le **yaourt**/le **yog(h)ourt** [jauʀt/jɔguʀt]	yogurt
la **crème fraîche** [kʀɛmfʀɛʃ]	crème fraîche

les **fruits** *m* [fʀɥi]	fruit
les **fruits secs**	dried fruit
une **pomme** [pɔm]	apple
une **poire** [pwaʀ]	pear
une **pêche** [pɛʃ]	peach
une **banane** [banan]	banana
une **orange** [ɔʀɑ̃ʒ]	orange
un **ananas** [anana(s)]	pineapple
un **melon** [m(ə)lɔ̃]	melon
du **raisin** [ʀɛzɛ̃]	grapes
un **grain de raisin**	grape
une **cerise** [s(ə)ʀiz]	cherry
une **prune** [pʀyn]	plum
travailler pour des prunes *loc*	work for nothing, work in vain
une **fraise** [fʀɛz]	strawberry
une **framboise** [fʀɑ̃bwaz]	raspberry
le **dessert** [desɛʀ]	dessert

---

i

dessert – désert

Note the difference between:

le dessert [desɛʀ]	*dessert*
le désert [dezɛʀ]	*desert*

---

un **gâteau** [gato]	cake
Pour le dessert, il y a un **gâteau à la crème**.	For dessert there's a cream cake.
une **tarte** [taʀt]	tart
des **pâtisseries** *f* [patisʀi]	pastry
une **glace** [glas]	ice cream
Je prendrais bien une **glace à la vanille**.	I'd like vanilla ice cream.
le **parfum** [paʀfɛ̃]	flavor
Quel parfum? Fraise ou chocolat?	What flavor? Strawberry or chocolate?
une **mousse au chocolat** [musoʃɔkɔla]	chocolate mousse
la **crème** [kʀɛm]	cream; custard
un **bonbon** [bɔ̃bɔ̃]	candy

---

l'**eau (minérale)** *f* [o (mineʀal)]	(mineral) water
l'**eau gazeuse**	carbonated water, effervescent water
un **jus (de fruits)** [ʒy(d(ə)fʀɥi]	(fruit) juice
verser [vɛʀse]	pour

Verse-moi un peu de jus d'orange, s'il te plaît.

Please pour me a little orange juice.

une **limonade** [limɔnad]

lemonade; soft drink

un **sirop** [siʀo]

syrup

vider (son verre) [vide]

empty (one's glass)

Il a vidé son verre **d'une traite.**

He emptied his glass in a single swallow.

l'**alcool** *m* [alkɔl]

alcohol

une **boisson sans alcool**

a nonalcoholic beverage

la **bière** [bjɛʀ]

beer

une **bière blonde**

a light beer

une **bière brune**

a dark beer

le **vin** [vɛ̃]

wine

un **vin de table**

table wine

le **(vin) blanc**

white wine

Vous prendrez bien un **petit blanc sec,** M. Martin ?

You'll have a little glass of dry white wine, won't you, Mr. Martin?

le **(vin) rouge**

red wine

le **(vin) rosé**

rosé (wine)

le **champagne** [ʃɑ̃paɲ]

champagne

le **(vin) mousseux** [(vɛ̃)musø]

sparkling wine

le **cidre** [sidʀ]

cider

un **tire-bouchon** [tiʀbuʃɔ̃]

corkscrew

un **ouvre-bouteille** [uvʀəbutɛj]

bottle opener

A votre santé ! [avɔtʀəsɑ̃te]

To your health!

A la vôtre ! *fam*

Here's to you!

affamé,e [afame]

hungry

à jeun [aʒɛ̃]

fasting

Il faut prendre ce médicament à jeun.

This medication has to be taken on an empty stomach.

dévorer [devɔʀe]

devour

digérer [diʒeʀe]

digest

(le) **souper** *n; v* [supe]

(late) supper; eat a late-evening meal

la **saveur** [savœʀ]

taste; flavor

(un,e) **gourmand,e** *n; adj* [guʀmɑ̃, ɑ̃d]

gourmand, glutton; greedy

la **gourmandise** [guʀmɑ̃diz]

gluttony, greediness

un **gourmet** [guʀmɛ]

gourmet

grignoter [gʀiɲɔte]

nibble

Elle n'a pas d'appétit. Elle a juste grignoté une biscotte.

She has no appetite. She nibbled only on a cracker.

mâcher [maʃe]

chew

5   Food and Drink, Clothing, Shopping

trinquer à [tʀɛ̃ke]	toast, drink to
Trinquons à la santé des jeunes mariés !	Let's drink to the health of the young couple!
ivre [ivʀ]	drunk
soûl,e *fam* [su, sul]	drunk
saignant,e [sɛɲɑ̃, ɑ̃t]	rare
à point [apwɛ̃]	medium
bien cuit,e [bjɛ̃kɥi, it]	well done
Deux steaks saignants, et un bien cuit, s'il vous plaît.	Two rare steaks and one well done, please.
un **casse-croûte** [kaskʀut]	snack
le **potage** [pɔtaʒ]	soup
la **soupe à l'oignon** [supalɔɲɔ̃]	onion soup
une **aubergine** [obɛʀʒin]	eggplant
un **chou-fleur** [ʃuflœʀ]	cauliflower
un **artichaut** [aʀtiʃo]	artichoke
un **concombre** [kɔ̃kɔ̃bʀ]	cucumber
un **cornichon** [kɔʀniʃɔ̃]	gherkin
un **poivron** [pwavʀɔ̃]	green pepper
l'**ail** *m* [aj]	garlic
une **endive** [ɑ̃div]	endive, (broad-leaved) chicory
une **(chicorée) frisée** [(ʃikɔʀe)fʀize]	escarole, (wild) chicory
une **laitue** [lɛty]	lettuce
assaisonner [asɛzɔne]	dress (salad)
les **épices** *f* [epis]	spices
épicer [epise]	spice
épicé,e [epise]	spiced
le **thym** [tɛ̃]	thyme
le **laurier** [lɔʀje]	bay
le **persil** [pɛʀsi]	parsley
la **ciboulette** [sibulɛt]	chive
les **fines herbes** *f* [finzɛʀb]	herbs for seasoning, fines herbes
les **herbes de Provence** *f* [ɛʀbdəpʀɔ̃s]	herbes de Provence
la **vanille** [vanij]	vanilla
la **cannelle** [kanɛl]	cinnamon
une **coupe** [kup]	cup, goblet
Comme dessert, je vous recommande une **coupe de glace**.	For dessert I recommend that you have an ice cream sundae.

un **flan** [flã]	flan, baked custard
la **crème Chantilly** [kʀɛm ʃɑ̃tiji]	whipped cream
une **crêpe** [kʀɛp]	crêpe
une **gaufre** [gofʀ]	Belgian waffle
un **gâteau sec** [gatosɛk]	cookie

varié,e [vaʀje]	various, assorted
Il y a des hors-d'œuvre variés au menu.	There are assorted appetizers on the menu.
appétissant,e [apetisɑ̃t ɑ̃t]	appetizing
rafraîchissant,e [ʀafʀeʃisɑ̃, ɑ̃t]	refreshing
Cette boisson est très rafraîchissante.	This drink is very refreshing.
indigeste [ɛ̃diʒɛst]	indigestible, hard to digest
Ma mére trouve la cuisine à l'huile indigeste.	My mother thinks food cooked with oil is hard to digest.

5.2 Cooking, Baking, and Utensils

la **cuisine** [kɥizin]	kitchen; cooking; cooked food
un **livre de cuisine**	cookbook
cuisiner [kɥizine]	cook
un,e **cuisinier, -ière** [kɥizinje, jɛʀ]	cook
un **plat** [pla]	dish (the vessel and the food)
un **plat cuisiné**	ready-cooked dish
C'est mon plat préféré.	That's my favorite dish.

---

i

Cooking

Depending on the context, French expresses *cook* in various ways:

cuisiner/faire la cuisine	*cook*
Mon frère cuisine très bien.	*My brother is a very good cook.*
Tu sais faire la cuisine ?	*Can you cook?*
cuire	*cook (until done)*
cuire au four	*bake*
Les lentilles doivent cuire 40 minutes.	*The lentils have to cook for 40 minutes.*
faire cuire	*cook (until done or firm)*
faire cuire un œuf	*hard-boil an egg*
Va te faire cuire un œuf. *fam*	*Go jump in the lake!*
faire	*cook, prepare, make*
faire du thé/du café	*make tea/coffee*
bouillir	*boil*
L'eau bout à 100 degrés.	*Water boils at 100°C.*
faire bouillir qc	*bring to a boil*
faire bouillir du lait	*bring milk to a boil*

un **four** [fuʀ]	oven
mettre au four	put in the oven
un **(four à) micro-ondes**	microwave (oven)
un **réfrigérateur** [ʀefʀiʒeʀatœʀ]	refrigerator
un **frigidaire**; un **frigo** *fam*	refrigerator, fridge
[fʀiʒidɛʀ, fʀigo]	
un **congélateur** [kɔ̃ʒelatœʀ]	freezer
congeler [kɔ̃ʒ(ə)le]	freeze

griller [gʀije]	grill
rôtir [ʀotiʀ/ʀɔtiʀ]	roast
faire chauffer [fɛʀʃofe]	warm, heat
réchauffer [ʀeʃofe]	reheat
refroidir [ʀəfʀwadiʀ]	cool, chill

une **recette** [ʀəsɛt]	recipe
préparer [pʀepaʀe]	prepare
éplucher [eplyʃe]	peel
couper [kupe]	cut
découper [dekupe]	cut up
mélanger [melɑ̃ʒe]	mix
ajouter qc (à qc) [aʒute]	add s.th. (to s.th.)
Il n'y a pas assez de sel, il faut que tu en ajoutes un peu.	There's not enough salt; you have to add a little more.

une **boîte** [bwat]	can
un **ouvre-boîte (s)**	can opener
serrés comme des sardines (en boîte) *loc*	squeezed in like sardines (in a can)
une **conserve** [kɔ̃sɛʀv]	canned food

---

i **Plural**

In accordance with the new spelling rules (1990), compound nouns of the **verb + noun** type are treated as **simple nouns**; that is, the noun portion takes an ending only in the plural:

un porte-monnaie	des porte-monnaie<u>s</u>	wallets, billfolds
un ouvre-boîte	des ouvre-boîte<u>s</u>	can openers
un sèche-cheveu	des sèche-cheveu<u>x</u>	hairdryers

This new spelling is allowed.

The traditional spelling currently is fluctuating:

un porte-monnaie	des porte-monnaie
un ouvre-boîte(s)	des ouvre-boîte(s)
un sèche-cheveux	des sèche-cheveux

l'**huile** f [ɥil]	oil
une **goutte d'huile**	a drop of oil
le **vinaigre** [vinɛgʀ]	vinegar
une **cuillerée (de)** [kɥij(e)ʀe]	a spoonful (of s.th.)

le **sel** [sɛl]	salt
Ajoutez **une pincée de sel.**	Add a pinch of salt.
saler [sale]	salt
le **poivre** [pwavʀ]	pepper
poivrer [pwavʀe]	pepper
la **moutarde** [mutaʀd]	mustard

la **farine** [faʀin]	flour
la **levure** [l(ə)vyʀ]	yeast, leavening
la **pâte** [pat]	dough

la **table** [tabl]	table
mettre la table	set the table
débarrasser la table	clear the table
le **couvert** [kuvɛʀ]	cover (plate, spoon, knife, fork)
mettre le couvert	set the table
la **vaisselle** [vɛsɛl]	plates and dishes
faire la vaisselle	do/wash the dishes

une **assiette** [asjɛt]	plate
une **assiette plate**	flat plate
une **assiette creuse**	soup plate
un **verre** [vɛʀ]	glass
une **tasse** [tas]	cup

> For information on the use of **un verre/une tasse de**, see p. 216.

une **soucoupe** [sukup]	saucer
un **bol** [bɔl]	bowl, basin

un **couteau** [kuto]	knife
une **cuillère** (une **cuiller**) [kɥijɛʀ]	spoon
une **cuillère à soupe**	soupspoon, tablespoon
une **petite cuillère** (une **cuillère à café**)	teaspoon (coffee spoon)
une **fourchette** [fuʀʃɛt]	fork

une **nappe** [nap]	tablecloth
une **serviette (de table)** [sɛʀvjɛt]	napkin
une **corbeille à pain** [kɔʀbɛjapɛ̃]	breadbasket

Cooking, Baking, and Utensils

> ## ℹ With and without a handle
>
> *Note the difference between:*
> | | |
> |---|---|
> | une **corbeille** | *basket (without a handle)* |
> | une **corbeille à papier** | *wastepaper basket* |
> | un **panier** | *basket (with a handle)* |
> | un **panier à provisions** | *shopping basket* |
> | un **panier à salade** *(fam)* | *salad basket (for drying salad greens after washing)* |

---

une **plaque de cuisson** [plakdəkɥisɔ̃]	burner, stove plate
à feu doux [afødu]	on low heat, over a low flame
faire cuire à feu doux	cook on low heat/over a low flame, simmer

remuer [ʀəmɥe]	stir
fouetter qc [fwɛte]	whip, beat, whisk
la **crème fouettée**	whipped cream
battre [batʀ]	beat
battre les œufs **en neige**	beat egg whites until stiff

la **pâte brisée** [patbʀize]	shortcrust pastry
la **pâte feuilletée** [patfœjte]	puff pastry, flaky pastry
la **pâte levée** [patləve]	yeast dough

une **casserole** [kasʀɔl]	saucepan, casserole
une **marmite** [maʀmit]	cooking pot
C'est dans les vieilles marmites qu'on fait la meilleure soupe. *prov*	The best soup is made in old pots.
une **cocotte-minute** [kɔkɔtminyt]	pressure cooker
une **poêle** [pwal]	pan

> ## ℹ Masculine/feminine
>
> **Note the different articles:**
> | | |
> |---|---|
> | <u>une</u> poêle (à frire) | *(frying) pan* |
> | <u>un</u> poêle | *stove (for heating a room)* |
> | un poêle à bois | *wood stove* |

---

une **friteuse** [fʀitøz]	deep-fat fryer
la **graisse** [gʀɛs]	fat, grease
un **moule** [mul]	baking pan

une **cafetière** [kaftjɛʀ]	coffeepot
une **théière** [tejɛʀ]	teapot
une **carafe** [kaʀaf]	carafe
un **plateau** [plato]	tray
un **plateau de fromages**	cheese tray
un **saladier** [saladje]	salad bowl
une **soupière** [supjɛʀ]	soup tureen

5.3 Articles of Clothing

un **vêtement** [vɛtmã]	garment
les **habits** m [abi]	clothes, apparel
s'habiller [sabije]	dress (oneself)
Il a sauté dans l'eau **tout habillé.**	He jumped into the water fully clothed.
se déshabiller [s(ə)dezabije]	undress (oneself)
les **fringues** f; fam [fʀɛ̃g]	togs, duds
mettre [mɛtʀ]	put on
Mets un manteau, il fait froid.	Put on a coat; it's cold.
enlever [ãl(ə)ve]	take off, remove
enlever son chapeau	remove one's hat
porter [pɔʀte]	wear
changer de qc [ʃãʒe]	change s.th.
changer de chaussettes	change socks
se changer [səʃãʒe]	change (one's) clothes
Avec cette pluie, je suis tout mouillé; je vais me changer.	With this rain, I'm totally soaked; I'm going to change clothes.
se couvrir [s(ə)kuvʀiʀ]	dress warmly
Couvre-tio, il fait froid.	Dress warmly; it's cold.

à l'endroit [alãdʀwa]	right side out
à l'envers [alãvɛʀ]	wrong side out
Il a mis son pull à l'envers.	He put on his sweater wrong side out.

un **pantalon** [pãtalɔ̃]	pants
un **short** [ʃɔʀt]	shorts
un **jean** [dʒin]	jeans
une **robe** [ʀɔb]	dress
une **robe du soir**	evening dress
une **jupe** [ʒyp]	skirt
une **mini (jupe)**	miniskirt

une **chemise** [ʃ(ə)miz]	shirt
Il change d'avis comme de chemise. *loc*	He changes his opinion like his shirt.
un **chemisier** [ʃ(ə)mizje]	blouse
un **tee-shirt**; un **T-shirt** [ti'ʃœʀt]	T-shirt
un **pull** [pyl]	pullover, sweater
un **sweat** [swɛt]	sweatshirt
un **manteau** [mɑ̃to]	coat
un **imperméable**; un **imper** *fam* [ɛ̃pɛʀ(meabl)]	raincoat
un **anorak** [anɔʀak]	parka
un **blouson** [bluzɔ̃]	jacket, windbreaker
un **costume** [kɔstym]	suit
aller au bureau en **costume trois pièces**	go to the office in a three-piece suit

---

What to wear

Note the difference between:

une **veste**	jacket, blazer
un **veston**	jacket, suit coat
Le veston de mon costume est trop large.	My suit jacket is too big.
un **gilet**	cardigan; waistcoat, vest
un **gilet de sauvetage**	life vest

---

un **chapeau** [ʃapo]	hat
une **casquette** [kaskɛt]	cap
une **casquette de base-ball**	baseball cap
un **bonnet** [bɔnɛ]	knit cap
un **béret (basque)** [beʀɛ(bask)]	(Basque) beret
des **sous-vêtements** *m* [suvɛtmɑ̃]	underwear
un **soutien-gorge** [sutjɛ̃gɔʀʒ]	bra
un **slip** [slip]	briefs; panties
un **collant** [kɔlɑ̃]	pantyhose
un **bas** [ba]	stocking
une paire de bas nylon	a pair of nylon stockings
des **chaussettes** *f* [ʃosɛt]	socks
un **maillot de bain** [majodbɛ̃]	bathing suit
un **(maillot) deux-pièces** [døpjɛs]	two-piece bathing suit
un **bikini** [bikini]	bikini
un **slip de bain** [slipdəbɛ̃]	bathing trunks

un **pyjama** [piʒama]	pajamas
une **chemise de nuit** [ʃ(ə)mizdənɥi]	nightgown
une **robe de chambre** [ʀɔbdəʃɑ̃bʀ]	dressing gown, bathrobe

des chaussures f [ʃosyʀ]	shoes
une **paire de chaussures**	a pair of shoes
des **bottes** f [bɔt]	boots
en avoir plein les bottes fam	be fed up
des **baskets** m [baskɛt]	sneakers
des **sandales** f [sɑ̃dal]	sandals
des **tennis** m [tenis]	tennis shoes

laver [lave]	wash
une **machine à laver**	washing machine
la **lessive** [lɛsiv]	wash(ing), laundry
faire la lessive	do the laundry
le **linge** [lɛ̃ʒ]	linen, laundry, wash
mouillé,e [muje]	wet
humide [ymid]	damp
Le linge est encore humide.	The laundry is still damp.
sec, sèche [sɛk, sɛʃ]	dry
sécher [seʃe]	dry
Au soleil, le linge **séchera** plus vite.	The laundry will dry faster in the sun.

nettoyer [nɛtwaje]	clean, dry-clean
faire nettoyer une veste	have a jacket cleaned
une **tache** [taʃ]	spot
enlever une tache	remove a spot

 For the difference between **tache** and **tâche**, see p. 81.

repasser [ʀ(ə)pase]	iron
le **fer à repasser**	iron
une **table/planche à repasser**	ironing board
le **repassage** [ʀ(ə)pasaʒ]	ironing
froissé,e [fʀwase]	wrinkled

chic [ʃik]	chic, stylish
élégant,e [elegɑ̃, ɑ̃t]	elegant
la **mode** [mɔd]	fashion
à la mode	fashionable, in fashion
Les jupes courtes sont à la mode, cette année.	This year short skirts are in fashion.

---

mode

Same spelling, same pronunciation; it's the article that makes the difference.

la mode	*fashion*
Elle est habillée à dernière mode.	*She's dressed in the latest fashion.*
un défilé de mode	*fashion show*
le mode	*mode; way; (gram.) mood*
le mode d'emploi	*directions for use*

---

moderne [mɔdɛʀn]	modern
la **qualité** [kalite]	quality
un tissu de bonne qualité	a fabric of good quality
nouveau, nouvel; nouvelle	new
[nuvo, nuvɛl]	
neuf, neuve [nœf, nœv]	new
J'ai mal aux pieds dans mes chaus-	My feet hurt in my new shoes.
sures neuves.	

New ≠ new

Note the difference:

neuf, neuve	une voiture neuve	*a (brand-)new car*
nouveau, nouvel,	une nouvelle voiture	*a new (different) car*
nouvelle	(= une autre voiture)	

---

usé,e [yze]	used; worn-out, threadbare
un vieux jean **usé aux genoux**	old jeans with worn-out knees
propre [pʀɔpʀ]	clean
sale [sal]	dirty

---

la **taille** [taj]	size
C'est **à ma taille.**	That's my size.
Comme taille, je fais du 38.	I wear size 38.
court,e [kuʀ, kuʀt]	short
long, longue [lɔ̃, lɔ̃g]	long
large [laʀʒ]	large, big
étroit,e [etʀwa, etʀwat]	narrow, tight; small
serré,e [seʀe]	tight; narrow
une veste **serrée à la taille**	a narrow-waisted jacket

---

chaud,e [ʃo, ʃod]	warm
un vêtement chaud pour l'hiver	warm winter clothing
confortable [kɔ̃fɔʀtabl]	comfortable
épais,se [epɛ, ɛs]	heavy
léger, -ère [leʒe, ʒɛʀ]	light
un tissu épais/léger	a heavy/light fabric
fin, fine [fɛ̃, fin]	thin

un **tailleur** [tajœR]
Elle porte le plus souvent des tail-
leurs très classiques.
un **ensemble** [ãsãbl]
On ne peut pas acheter la veste
sans la jupe, c'est un ensemble.

tailor; tailor-made suit
She usually wears very classic
tailor-made suits.
(two- or three-piece) set
You can't buy the jacket without
the skirt; it's a set.

un **peignoir** [pɛɲwaR]
un **survêtement** [syRvɛtmã]
un **jogging** [dʒɔgiŋ]
Il a mis son jogging pour aller courir
en forêt.

dressing gown, bathrobe
tracksuit
jogging suit
He put on his jogging suit to go
for a run in the woods.

un **tablier** [tablije]
un **tablier de cuisine**
Ça lui va comme un tablier à une
vache. *fam; loc*
une **blouse** [bluz]
La femme de ménage porte une
blouse pour protéger ses vêtements.
une **salopette** [salɔpɛt]

apron
kitchen apron
That clashes./That doesn't suit
him/her at all.
smock
The cleaning lady wears a smock
to protect her clothes.
overalls, dungarees

la **lingerie** [lɛ̃ʒRi]
une **culotte** [kylɔt]
Chez les Dupont, c'est la femme qui
porte la culotte.
une **petite culotte** (en dentelle)
un **caleçon** [kalsɔ̃]
un **tricot**/un **maillot de corps**
[tRiko, majod(ə)kɔR]
un **body** [bɔdi]

ladies' underwear, lingerie
briefs, underpants
In the Dupont family, it's the
wife who wears the pants.
(lace) panties
men's (long) drawers
undershirt

bodysuit, one-piece undergarment

la **layette** [lɛjɛt]
Il s'est acheté un pull **bleu-layette**.

des **chaussons** *m* [ʃosɔ̃]

baby garments
He bought himself a baby-blue
sweater.
slippers; bootees

des **escarpins** *m* [ɛskaRpɛ̃]
à **talons hauts/plats** [atalõ/pla]
Dans ses **chaussures à talons hauts**,
elle fait 5 centimètres de plus.
à **talons aiguilles** [atalõegɥij]
des **pantoufles** *f* [pãtufl]
la **pointure** [pwɛ̃tyR]
Quelle pointure fais-tu ?

pumps
high-heeled/flat-heeled
In her high-heeled shoes, she's
five centimeters taller.
with stiletto heels
slippers
shoe size
What is your shoe size?

chausser [ʃose]	put on shoes; wear a shoe size
Je chausse du 46.	I wear size 46 shoes.

un **col** [kɔl]	collar
un **col en V**	a V neck
un **col roulé**	a turtleneck
une **manche** [mɑ̃ʃ]	sleeve
une **chemise à manches courtes**	a short-sleeved shirt
faire la manche *fam*	beg
une **poche** [pɔʃ]	pocket
Il n'a pas la langue dans sa poche.	He has a glib tongue.
loc	

une **corde (à linge)** [kɔrd(alɛ̃ʒ)]	clothesline
une **pince (à linge)** [pɛ̃s(alɛ̃ʒ)]	clothespin
étendre le linge [etɑ̃drlǝlɛ̃ʒ]	hang out washing
essorer le linge [esɔrel(ǝ)lɛ̃ʒ]	wring out washing
un **sèche-linge** [sɛʃlɛ̃ʒ]	clothes dryer

une **teinturerie** [tɛ̃tyrri]	dry cleaner
un **pressing** [prɛsiŋ]	dry cleaner
une **laverie (automatique)**	laundromat
[lavri]	
rétrécir [retresir]	shrink
Ce pull a rétréci au lavage.	This sweater shrank when it was washed.

un **tissu** [tisy]	fabric
une **étoffe** [etɔf]	fabric
le **cuir** [kɥir]	leather
un blouson **en cuir véritable**	a jacket made of real leather
le **coton** [kɔtɔ̃]	cotton
une **chemise 100% coton**	a 100% cotton shirt
la **laine** [lɛn]	wool
un pull **en pure laine**	a sweater made of pure wool
les **fibres synthétiques** *f*	synthetic fibers
[fibr(ǝ)sɛ̃tetik]	
les **microfibres** *f* [mikrofibr]	microfibers
la **soie** [swa]	silk

retoucher [r(ǝ)tuʃe]	alter
une **retouche** [r(ǝ)tuʃ]	alteration
On fait les retouches gratuitement.	We do free alterations.
raccourcir [rakursir]	shorten
J'ai raccourci mon pantalon.	I had my pants shortened.
rallonger [ralɔ̃ʒe]	lengthen

coudre [kudʀ]	sew
une **machine à coudre**	sewing machine
recoudre [ʀ(ə)kudʀ]	sew on
recoudre un bouton	sew on a button
une **aiguille** [egɥij]	sewing needle
Autant chercher une aiguille dans une botte de foin. *loc*	It's like looking for a needle in a haystack.
une **épingle** [epɛ̃gl]	pin
des **ciseaux** *m* [sizo]	scissors

 For information on *forming the plural* of French nouns of the **ciseaux** type, see p. 38.

un **fil** [fil]	thread

déchirer [deʃiʀe]	tear
repriser [ʀ(ə)pʀize]	darn, mend
Tu as déchiré ton pantalon neuf. Et qui va le repriser?	You've torn your new trousers. And who's going to mend them?
un **trou** [tʀu]	hole

broder [bʀɔde]	embroider
la **broderie** [bʀɔdʀi]	embroidery
un **crochet** [kʀɔʃɛ]	crochet hook
faire du crochet	crochet
tricoter [tʀikɔte]	knit
les **aiguilles à tricoter**	knitting needle
le **tricot** [tʀiko]	knitwear

la **dentelle** [dɑ̃tɛl]	lace
le **velours** [v(ə)luʀ]	velvet
la **fourrure** [fuʀyʀ]	fur
un **manteau de fourrure**	fur coat

une **ceinture** [sɛ̃tyʀ]	belt
Il va falloir se serrer la ceinture. *loc*	It's time to tighten our belts.
un **bouton** [butɔ̃]	button
une **fermeture éclair** [fɛʀmətyʀeklɛʀ]	zipper
Remonte ta fermeture éclair.	Pull up your zipper.
une **fermeture velcro**, le **velcro** [(fɛʀmətyʀ)vɛlkʀo]	Velcro closing

démodé,e [demɔde]	old-fashioned, out of fashion

Démodée, cette robe ? Elle est indémodable.	That dress, old-fashioned? It's timeless.
avoir du goût [avwaʀdygu]	have good taste
s'habiller avec beaucoup de goût	dress tastefully
un **modèle** [mɔdɛl]	model
C'est le même modèle mais en bleu.	It's the same model, but in blue.

essayer [eseje]	try on
Je voudrais essayer la **taille audessus**.	I'd like to try on the next size.
aller à qn [alea]	suit s.o., look good on s.o.
Cet ensemble lui va **à ravir**.	This suit looks divine on her.
aller avec qc [aleavɛk]	go with s.th.
Cette cravate ne va pas avec ta chemise.	That tie doesn't go with your shirt.
assorti,e [asɔʀti]	matching, coordinated
une jupe et un chemisier assortis	a skirt and a matching blouse

uni,e [yni]	self-colored, without a pattern
imprimé,e [ɛ̃pʀime]	printed
un tissu imprimé à petites fleurs	a fabric printed with little flowers
rayé,e [ʀeje]	striped
à rayures [aʀejyʀ]	striped
à carreaux [akaʀo]	checked
une **veste à carreaux écossais**	a Scottish plaid jacket
à pois [apwa]	dotted

doublé,e [duble]	lined
Ce blouson est entièrement doublé.	This jacket is completely lined.
la **doublure** [dublyʀ]	(clothes) lining
souple [supl]	soft, supple

5.4 Jewelry and Accessories

un **bijou**, des **bijoux** [biʒu]	jewel, gem, piece of jewelry
une **chaîne** [ʃɛn]	chain
une **montre** [mɔ̃tʀ]	watch
regarder l'heure à sa montre	look at one's watch

précieux, -euse [pʀesjø, jøz]	valuable, precious
en or [ãnɔʀ]	(made of) gold
une **montre en or**	a gold watch
doré,e [dɔʀe]	gilded
en argent [ãnaʀʒã]	(made of) silver
argenté,e [aʀʒãte]	silver-plated

un **accessoire** [akseswaʀ]	accessory
un **foulard** [fulaʀ]	scarf
une **écharpe** [eʃaʀp]	scarf, sash
un **gant** [gã]	glove
une **paire de gants**	a pair of gloves
Cela lui va comme un gant. *loc*	That fits him like a glove.
une **cravate** [kʀavat]	(neck)tie
un **nœud** [nø]	knot
faire un nœud (de cravate)	tie a knot (in a tie)
un **nœud papillon**	bowtie
un **mouchoir** [muʃwaʀ]	pocket handkerchief

un **sac** [sak]	bag
un **sac à main**	handbag
un **parapluie** [paʀaplɥi]	umbrella

une **bague** [bag]	ring
Il lui a mis la bague au doigt.	He put the ring on her finger (he married her).
une **alliance** [aljãs]	wedding ring
un **bracelet** [bʀaslɛ]	bracelet
un **collier** [kɔlje]	necklace
une **boucle d'oreille** [bukl(ə)dɔʀɛj]	earring
une **broche** [bʀɔʃ]	brooch

un **joyau** [ʒwajo]	jewel
les **joyaux de la couronne**	crown jewels
un **diamant** [djamã]	diamond
une **perle** [pɛʀl]	pearl
Ma cuisinière est une vraie perle.	My cook is a real jewel.
une **pierre précieuse** [pjɛʀpʀesjøz]	precious stone
un **bijou-fantaisie** [biʒufãtezi]	costume jewelry
du toc [tɔk]	fake or imitation jewelry, paste
C'est du toc, ça se voit au premier coup d'œil.	It's fake; you can see that right away.

5.5 Shopping

un **magasin** [magazɛ̃]	store, shop
un **magasin de jouets**	toy store
un **grand magasin**	department store
un **marché** [maʀʃe]	market
faire son marché	do the marketing
un **supermarché** [sypɛʀmaʀʃe]	supermarket
un **hypermarché** [ipɛʀmaʀʃe]	large supermarket
une **grande surface** [gʀɑ̃dsyʀfas]	supermarket, consumer warehouse
un **centre commercial** [sɑ̃tʀəkɔmɛʀsjal]	shopping center
une **boutique** [butik]	boutique, small shop
le **petit commerce** [p(ə)tikɔmɛʀs]	small tradesmen
Les grandes surfaces, c'est la mort du petit commerce.	The supermarkets are putting all the small tradesmen out of business.

une **boucherie** [buʃʀi]	butcher shop
aller* à la boucherie	go to the butcher shop
un,e **boucher, -ère** [buʃe, ɛʀ]	butcher
aller* chez le boucher	go to the butcher
une **charcuterie** [ʃaʀkytʀi]	pork butcher shop, deli, cold cuts store
un,e **charcutier, -ière** [ʃaʀkytje, ɛʀ]	pork butcher

---

i **Where to buy meat and sausage**

Note the difference between:

une charcuterie	*pork butcher shop (with sausages and cold cuts)*
une boucherie	*butcher shop (where primarily meat is sold)*
une boucherie-charcuterie	*pork butcher shop selling meat and sausage*

---

une **boulangerie** [bulɑ̃ʒʀi]	bakery
un,e **boulanger, -ère** [bulɑ̃ʒe, ɛʀ]	baker
une **pâtisserie** [patisʀi]	pastry shop
un,e **pâtissier, -ière** [patisje, jɛʀ]	pastry cook
une **épicerie** [episʀi]	grocery store
On trouve tout, à l'**épicerie du coin**.	You find everything at the corner grocery store.
un,e **épicier, -ière** [episje, jɛʀ]	grocer

---

une **librairie** [libʀɛʀi]	bookstore
un,e **libraire** [libʀɛʀ]	book dealer
une **papeterie** [papɛtʀi/pap(ə)tʀi]	stationery store
un **bureau de tabac** [byʀodtaba]	tobacco shop

une **parfumerie** [paʀfymʀi]
une **vitrine** [vitʀin]
Je voudrais essayer les chaussures
rouges qui sont dans la vitrine.
faire du lèche-vitrine(s)

perfume shop
store window, display window
I'd like to try on the red shoes
that are in the store window.
go window-shopping

un **achat**[aʃa]
J'aime bien **faire mes achats** dans
ce quartier.
acheter [aʃte]
faire les courses f [feʀlekuʀs]
un,e **client,e** [klijã, ãt]
être bon client
la **clientèle** [klijãtɛl]
Les prix bas attirent une clientèle
nombreuse.

purchase
I like to do my shopping in this
part of town.
buy, purchase
shop, go shopping
customer
be a good customer
customers, clientele
The low prices attract many
customers.

vendre [vãdʀ]
un,e **vendeur, -euse** [vãdœʀ, øz]
la **marchandise** [maʀʃãdiz]
Leur marchandise n'est pas toujours
très fraîche.
un,e **marchand,e** [maʀʃã, ãd]
le **marchand de journaux**
marchander [maʀʃãde]
un **article** [aʀtikl]
Nous n'avons pas cet article **en**
magasin.

sell
salesman, saleswoman
merchandise
Your merchandise is not always
very fresh.
merchant, dealer
newsdealer
ask the price of; dicker, haggle
article, item
We don't carry that item.

une **tranche** [tʀãʃ]
trois tranches de jambon
un **morceau** [mɔʀso]
Un morceau de bœuf pour quatre
personnes, s'il vous plaît.
un **litre** [litʀ]
un litre **de lait entier**
un **kilo(gramme)** [kilo(gʀam)]
un sac de cinq kilos de pommes de
terre
une **livre** [livʀ]
une livre de beurre

slice
three slices of ham
piece
a piece of beef for four people,
please
liter
a liter of whole milk
kilo(gram)
a five-kilo sack of potatoes

pound (500 grams)
a pound of butter

désirer [deziʀe]
Et à part ça, vous désirez ?

wish
What else would you like?

avoir besoin de qc [avwaʀbəzwɛ̃]
J'ai besoin d'un nouveau jean.
avoir envie de qc [avwaʀɑ̃vi]
J'ai bien envie de cette petite robe.
choisir [ʃwaziʀ]
Il a choisi un livre de Simenon.

need s.th.
I need a new pair of jeans.
want s.th., have a longing for s.th.
That little dress really tempts me.
choose, select
He chose a book by Simenon.

faire la queue [fɛʀlakø]
Eh, vous! Faites la queue comme tout le monde !
un **chariot** [ʃaʀjo]
la **caisse** [kɛs]
un,e **caissier, -ière** [kɛsje, jɛʀ]
combien ? [kɔ̃bjɛ̃]
coûter [kute]
Ça fait/coûte combien ?
Ça coûte une fortune.
cher, chère [ʃɛʀ]
Ça coûte trop cher.

get in line
Hey, you! Get in line like everybody else!
shopping cart
cashier's desk
cashier
how much?
cost
How much does that come to/cost?
That costs a fortune.
expensive, dear
That's too expensive.

> **Les erreurs se paient cher**
>
> In certain *fixed expressions*, the *adverb* is replaced by an *adjective:*
> coûter/acheter/payer cher   *be expensive/buy at a high price/pay dearly*
> travailler dur   *work hard*
> peser lourd   *be heavy*
> sentir bon/mauvais   *smell good/bad*

---

augmenter [ɔgmɑ̃te]
Les prix augmentent sans arrêt.
baisser [bese]
bon marché [bɔ̃maʀʃe]
   meilleur marché
Dans les grandes surfaces, beaucoup d'articles sont meilleur marché que chez les petits commerçants.
gratuit,e [gʀatɥi, ɥit]
une **réduction** [ʀedyksjɔ̃]
les **soldes** *m* [sɔld]
acheter un vêtement **en solde**

increase; rise
Prices are constantly rising.
drop
cheap
   cheaper
In the supermarkets, many items are cheaper than in small shops.
gratis, free
discount; reduction
clearance sales; reductions
buy a garment on sale

l'**argent** *m* [aʀʒɑ̃]
dépenser [depɑ̃se]
Il dépense plus qu'il ne gagne.

money
spend
He spends more than he earns.

la **monnaie** [mɔnɛ] — coin, money; change
  redre la monnaie — make change
  une **pièce de monnaie** — coin
  le **porte-monnaie** — wallet, billfold
le **franc** [fʀɑ̃] — franc
l'**euro** *m* [øʀo] — euro
  18 euros, ça fait combien, en francs ? — 18 euros; how much is that in francs?
un **billet (de banque)** [bijɛ] — bill, banknote
un **portefeuille** [pɔʀtəføj]
  Je ne mets jamais ma carte de crédit dans mon portefeuille. — I never put my credit card in my wallet.

payer [peje] — pay
  payer cher — pay dearly
le **prix** [pʀi] — price
  C'est **hors de prix** ! — That's extravagantly expensive!

un **traiteur** [tʀɛtœʀ] — caterer
un **étalage** [etalaʒ] — display of goods
un **rayon** [ʀejɔ̃] — department
  Vous trouverez ça **au rayon parfumerie**. — You'll find that in the cosmetics department.
un **distributeur automatique** [distʀibytœʀɔtɔmatik] — automatic dispenser, vending machine

coûteux, -euse [kutø, øz] — costly, expensive
les **coûts** *m* [ku] — costs
faire un prix à qn [feʀɛ̃pʀi] — give a discount to s.o.
  Vous me faites un prix, si je prends 10 paires de chaussettes ? — Can you give me a discount if I buy 10 pairs of socks?
une **offre spéciale** [ɔfʀ(ə)spesjal] — special offer
en promotion [ɑ̃pʀɔmosjɔ̃] — in a promotion
  acheter un article/un produit en promotion — buy an item/a product as part of a sales promotion

payer comptant [pejekɔ̃tɑ̃] — pay cash
  C'est moins cher, si on paie comptant ? — Is it cheaper if you pay cash?
payer cash [pejekaʃ] — pay cash
la **vente par correspondance** [vɑ̃tpaʀkɔʀɛspɔ̃dɑ̃s] — mail-order sales
un **catalogue** [katalog] — catalog
commander [kɔmɑ̃de] — order
  commander qc **sur catalogue** — order s.th. from the catalog

un **emballage** [ɑ̃balaʒ]	packaging, packing
emballer [ɑ̃bale]	pack up, wrap up
Je vous l'emballe, ou c'est pour consommer tout de suite?	Should I wrap it up for you, or will you eat it right away?
déballer [debale]	unwrap
un **paquet-cadeau** [pakɛkado]	gift package

French Word	English Equivalent	False Friend	French Equivalent
une blouse	(work) smock	blouse	un chemisier
une veste	jacket, blazer	vest	un gilet
des raisins	grapes	raisins	des raisins secs
une nappe	tablecloth	nap	un somme, une sieste

Legrand

Cartier

Simon

6.1 Construction, Houses, Buildings, and Inhabitants

bâtir [batiʀ]	build
un **terrain à bâtir**	lot, building site
un **bâtiment** [batimã]	building
la **construction** [kõstʀyksjõ]	building, construction; structure
construire [kõstʀɥiʀ]	construct, build
faire construire une maison	have a house built
transformer [tʀãsfɔʀme]	remodel
On a transformé une ancienne ferme.	We remodeled an old farmhouse.
l'**architecture** *f* [aʀʃitɛktyʀ]	architecture
un,e **architecte** [aʀʃitɛkt]	architect
un **plan** [plã]	plan

un **matériau** *m* [mateʀjo]	material
des **matériaux de construction**	building materials
une **pierre** [pjɛʀ]	stone, rock
une **brique** [bʀik]	brick
une **tuile** [tɥil]	(roof) tile
un **toit de tuiles**	tiled roof
le **béton** [betõ]	concrete
une construction **en béton armé**	a reinforced concrete structure

un **immeuble** [imœbl]	real estate
une **tour** [tuʀ]	tower, tall building
les **tours de la Défense**	the multistory office buildings of la Défense (*office district on the edge of Paris*)

For information on the *gender* of **tour**, see p. 191.

un,e **HLM** (une **habitation à loyer modéré**) [aʃɛlɛm]	rent-controlled housing
un **appartement** [apaʀtəmã]	apartment
un **appartement de luxe**	luxury apartment
un appartement modeste	modest apartment
l'**espace** *m* [ɛspas]	space, room
Notre appartement est très petit, **on manque d'espace.**	Our apartment is quite small; we don't have enough room.

une **maison** [mɛzõ]	house
une **maison individuelle**	single-family house
une **maison préfabriquée**	prefabricated house
un **pavillon** [pavijõ]	single-family house
un **pavillon de banlieue**	single-family house in a suburb
une **villa** [vila]	villa, country house

la **résidence** [ʀezidɑ̃s]	residence
le **lieu de résidence**	place of residence
une **résidence secondaire**	second residence, vacation home

un **logement** [lɔʒmɑ̃]	housing, accommodation, lodging
loger [lɔʒe]	live
loger dans un appartement moderne	live in a modern apartment
habiter qc [abite]	live in s.th.
habiter un quartier résidentiel	live in a (nice) residential area

déménager [demenaʒe]	move
Nous avons déménagé de Reims à Lyon.	We've moved from Reims to Lyon.
le **déménagement** [demenaʒmɑ̃]	move
emménager (dans) [ɑ̃menaʒe]	move (into)
Elle a emménagé dans l'appartement du troisième.	She's moved into the apartment on the third floor.
s'installer [sɛ̃stale]	settle
Il s'est installé à Tours.	He has settled in Tours.

un,e **propriétaire** [pʀɔpʀijetɛʀ]	owner
une **propriété** [pʀɔpʀijete]	property
posséder [dɔsede]	own, possess

un,e **locataire** [lɔkatɛʀ]	tenant
un,e **sous-locataire**	subtenant
louer [lue]	rent
Chambre à louer.	Room for rent.
le **loyer** [lwaje]	rent
Le loyer a encore augmenté.	The rent has gone up again.
la **location** [lɔkasiɔ̃]	renting
mettre en location	(offer for) rent

un,e **habitant,e** [abitɑ̃, ɑ̃t]	inhabitant, resident
un,e **voisin,e** [vwazɛ̃, in]	neighbor
un,e **concierge** [kɔ̃sjɛʀʒ]	concierge, caretaker
un,e **gardien,ne** [gaʀdjɛ̃, jɛn]	guard; watchman

la **porte** [pɔʀt]	door
Qui a frappé à la porte?	Who knocked at the door?
sonner [sɔne]	ring
On a sonné.	Someone rang the doorbell.
une **sonnette** [sɔnɛt]	bell
donner un coup de sonnette	ring the bell

une **serrure** [seRyR]	lock
une **clé** (**clef**) [kle]	key
fermer à clé	lock (a door)

une **entrée** [ãtRe]	entrance, entry
la **porte d'entrée**	front door, street door
un **couloir** [kulwaR]	passage, corridor
le **rez-de-chaussée** [Redʃose]	street floor, ground floor
un **étage** [etaʒ]	floor, story
J'habite au 3ᵉ (étage).	I live on the third (floor)

For information on the **gender of nouns** ending in **-age**, see p. 70.

un **escalier** [eskalje]	staircase, stairs
monter/descendre l'escalier	go up/down the stairs
Il a monté péniblement l'escalier.	He climbed the stairs with great difficulty.
l'**ascenseur** m [asãsœR]	elevator
appeler l'ascenseur	call the elevator

une **pièce** [pjɛs]	room
Mes parents ont acheté un (**appartement de**) **trois pièces.**	My parents have bought a three-room apartment.
une **salle à manger** [salamãʒe]	dining room
une **salle de séjour** [saldəseʒuR]	living room
un **salon** [salɔ̃]	living room
une **chambre** [ʃãbR]	(bed)room
Il a loué une chambre près de la fac.	He's rented a room near the university.
la **chambre (à coucher)**	bedroom
la **chambre d'amis**	guest room
une **cuisine** [kɥizin]	kitchen
une **kitchenette** [kitʃənɛt]	kitchenette

une **salle de bains** [saldəbɛ̃]	bathroom
les **W.-C.** m [vese]	toilet, lavatory
Les W.-C. sont occupés.	The toilet is occupied.
les **toilettes** f [twalɛt]	toilet
le(s) **cabinet(s)** m [kabinɛ]	toilet

un **toit** [twa]	roof
une **cheminée** [ʃəmine]	chimney; fireplace
le **sol** [sɔl]	ground; earth
le **sous-sol**	basement
la **cave** [kav]	cellar
Descends chercher du vin à la cave.	Go down to the cellar to get some wine.

une **terrasse** [teʀas]	terrace
un **balcon** [balkɔ̃]	balcony
un **jardin** [ʒaʀdɛ̃]	garden
un **garage** [gaʀaʒ]	garage
Tu as sorti la voiture du garage?	Have you taken the car out of the garage?

> ℹ️ For information on the *gender of nouns* ending in -**age**, see p. 70.

---

un **édifice** [edifis]	building, edifice
un **building** [b(y)ildiŋ]	tall building
la **façade** [fasad]	façade
l'**extérieur** *m* [ɛksteʀjœʀ]	exterior
L'extérieur du château **ne paie pas de mine.** *loc*	The exterior of the castle does not look good.
l'**intérieur** *m* [ɛ̃teʀjœʀ]	interior
le **hall d'entrée** ['oldɑ̃tʀe]	entrance hall
un **digicode** [diʒikɔd]	electronic (digital) lock (with entry code)
La porte d'entrée est **équipée** d'un digicode.	The front door is equipped with an electronic lock.
un **interphone** [ɛ̃teʀfɔn]	intercom

le **palier** [palje]	landing (on a staircase)
un **voisin de palier**	hall neighbor
le **grenier** [gʀənje]	attic

un **appartement en copropriété** [apaʀtəmɑ̃ɑ̃kɔ̃pʀɔpʀijete]	co-op apartment
un **studio** [stydjo]	studio or one-room apartment
un **deux-pièces** [døpjɛs]	two-room apartment
un **duplex** [dyplɛks]	duplex
un **F3** [ɛftʀwa]	three-room apartment
meublé,e [mœble]	furnished
Il a trouvé un **studio meublé.**	He's found a furnished apartment.
luxueux, -euse [lyksɥø, øz]	luxurious
spacieux, -euse [spasjø, jøz]	spacious, roomy
un grand appartement aux pièces spacieuses	a large apartment with spacious rooms
à l'étroit [aletʀwa]	narrow (in terms of space)
Nous cherchons un F3, parce que nous nous sentons à l'étroit dans notre deux-pièces.	We're looking for a three-room apartment because we feel cramped in our two-room apartment.

de grand standing [dəgʀɑ̃stɑ̃diŋ]   luxury
  un **appartement de grand standing** luxury apartment
les **charges** f [ʃaʀʒ]   subsidiary costs, extras, expenses
  Le loyer s'élève à 500 euros **sans** The rent is 500 euros, not
  les charges.   counting the expenses.

6.2 Accommodations and Furnishings

un **mur** [myʀ]   wall
le **plafond** [plafɔ̃]   ceiling
le **plancher** [plɑ̃ʃe]   floor
  recouvrir le plancher de moquette cover the floor with wall-to-wall
    carpeting
un **coin** [kwɛ̃]   corner
une **marche** [maʀʃ]   step
  rater une marche   miss a step

une **porte** [pɔʀt]   door
une **fenêtre** [f(ə)nɛtʀ]   window
  regarder par la fenêtre   look out the window
une **vitre** [vitʀ]   pane of glass

une **baignoire** [bɛɲwaʀ]   bathtub
un **lavabo** [lavabo]   sink, washbasin
une **douche** [duʃ]   shower
installer [ɛ̃stale]   install
  Je voudrais installer une nouvelle I'd like to install a new shower
  cabine de douche.   stall.

équiper [ekipe]   equip, furnish
  une cuisine **équipée d'une hotte** a kitchen equipped with a venti-
  aspirante   lator hood
un **four** [fuʀ]   oven
un **réfrigérateur**; un **frigo** fam   refrigerator, fridge
[ʀefʀiʒeʀatœʀ, fʀigo]
  Mets le coca au frigo.   Put the Coke in the fridge.

le **chauffage** [ʃofaʒ]   heating
  faire installer le chauffage central have central heating installed
un **radiateur** [ʀadjatœʀ]   radiator
un **poêle** [pwal]   (heating) stove
  un **poêle à mazout**   oil stove

l'**électricité** f [elɛktʀisite]	electricity
le **gaz** [gaz]	gas
une **cuisinière à gaz**	gas stove
la **lumière** [lymjɛʀ]	light

le **confort** [kɔ̃fɔʀ]	comfort, convenience
un **appartement tout confort**	apartment with all modern conveniences
confortable [kɔ̃fɔʀtabl]	comfortable
inconfortable [ɛ̃kɔ̃ʀtabl]	uncomfortable

un **meuble** [mœbl]	piece of furniture
des **meubles Louis XV**	furniture in the style of Louis XV
une **table** [tabl]	table
un **bureau** [byʀo]	desk; office
une **chaise** [ʃɛz]	chair; seat
un **fauteuil** [fotœj]	armchair
un **coussin** [kusɛ̃]	pillow, cushion

---

i **Getting comfortable ...**

Note the difference between:

un coussin	*pillow, cushion*
Il me faut un coussin, mon siège est trop bas.	*I need a cushion; my seat is too low.*
un oreiller	*(bed)pillow*
Il dort avec deux oreillers.	*He sleeps with two pillows.*

---

un **lit** [li]	bed
un **grand lit**	double bed
une **table de nuit/de chevet** [tabldənɥi/dəʃ(ə)vɛ]	nightstand, bedside table

une **armoire** [aʀmwaʀ]	armoire, wardrobe, cupboard
une **armoire à glace**	mirror wardrobe
un **placard** [plakaʀ]	wall cupboard, built-in closet
un **tiroir** [tiʀwaʀ]	drawer
une **commode** [kɔmɔd]	chest of drawers
une **étagère** [etaʒɛʀ]	set of shelves
ranger des livres sur les étagères	arrange books on the shelves

un **cadre** [kadʀ]	frame
un **tableau** [tablo]	picture
accrocher un tableau	hang a picture

une **lampe** [lãp]	lamp
allumer/éteindre une lampe	turn on/off a lamp
un **vase** [vaz]	vase

---

vase

Note the difference between:

le vase	*the vase*
un vase en cristal	*a crystal vase*
la vase	*the mud*
Cette carpe a un goût de vase.	*This carp has a muddy taste.*

---

une **glace** [glas]	mirror
Elle aime se regarder dans la glace.	She likes to look at herself in the mirror.
un **miroir** [miʀwaʀ]	mirror

---

un **volet** [vɔlɛ]	(window) shutter
ouvrir les volets	open the shutters
un **store** [stɔʀ]	(spring-roller) blind, shade
descendre le store	pull down the shade
un **rideau** [ʀido]	curtain
un **rideau de douche**	shower curtain
le **papier peint** [papjepɛ̃]	wallpaper
Il serait temps de **changer les papiers peints.**	It's about time to change the wallpaper.

---

un **tapis** [tapi]	carpet, rug
un **tapis persan**	Persian rug
la **moquette** [mɔkɛt]	wall-to-wall carpet
le **parquet** [paʀkɛ]	parquet floor

---

un **robinet** [ʀɔbinɛ]	water faucet
ouvrir/fermer le robinet	turn on/off the water faucet
un **évier** [evje]	sink
le **carrelage** [kaʀlaʒ]	tile flooring

---

un **interrupteur** [ɛ̃teʀyptœʀ]	(light) switch
L'interrupteur est à gauche de la porte.	The switch is to the left of the door.
le **courant (électrique)** [kuʀã]	(electrical) current
Il y a une **coupure de courant.**	There's a current outage.
une **prise (de courant)**	wall plug
un **bouton** [butɔ̃]	button, switch
l'**éclairage** *m* [eklɛʀaʒ]	lighting
un éclairage indirect	indirect lighting
éclairer [ekleʀe]	light
Cette lampe **éclaire mal.**	This lamp doesn't give much light.
un **lampadaire** [lãpadɛʀ]	floor lamp

l'**ameublement** *m* [amœbləmã]	furniture
un **canapé** [kanape]	couch, sofa
un **canapé en cuir**	leather couch
un **sofa** [sɔfa]	sofa
une **couette** [kwɛt]	feather comforter, quilted comforter
se glisser sous la couette	slip under the comforter
un **édredon** [edrədõ]	eiderdown comforter
un **traversin** [travɛrsẽ]	bolster

6.3 Housekeeping and Household Chores

le **ménage** [menaʒ]	household; housekeeping
faire le ménage	do the housekeeping
une **femme de ménage**	housekeeper; cleaning woman
le **désordre** [dezɔrdr]	disorder
ranger [rãʒe]	put in order
Tu pourrais ranger ta chambre, elle est en désordre.	You could tidy up your room; it's a total mess.

sale [sal]	dirty, filthy
la **saleté** [salte]	dirt, filth
salir [salir]	make dirty, soil
propre [prɔpr]	clean

> **i** For information on *adjectives* that *change meaning* depending on whether they *follow* or *precede* the word modified, see p. 37.

la **propreté** [prɔprəte]	cleanliness
laver [lave]	wash
laver qc à la main	wash s.th. by hand
le **lavage** [lavaʒ]	washing; wash, laundry
nettoyer [netwaje]	clean
le **nettoyage** [netwajaʒ]	cleaning
essuyer [esɥije]	dry, wipe dry
essuyer la vaisselle	dry the dishes
frotter qc [frɔte]	scrub s.th.

une **brosse** [brɔs]	brush
un **chiffon** [ʃifõ]	rag, cloth
passer un chiffon humide sur un meuble	go over a piece of furniture with a damp cloth
un **balai** [balɛ]	broom
donner un coup de balai	sweep up

balayer [baleje]	sweep
la **poussière** [pusjɛʀ]	dust
un **chiffon à poussière**	dustcloth, duster

un **appareil** [apaʀɛj]	appliance
les **appareils électro-ménagers**	electrical household appliances
une **machine** [maʃin]	machine
Je ne suis pas content de ma nou- velle **machine à laver.**	I'm not happy with my new washing machine.
électrique [elɛktʀik]	electric(al)
une **pile** [pil]	battery
fonctionner [fɔ̃ksjɔne]	function
la **garantie** [gaʀɑ̃ti]	guarantee
être sous garantie	be under warranty

la **vaisselle** [vɛsɛl]	plates and dishes
faire la vaisselle	wash the dishes
faire la cuisine [fɛʀlakɥizin]	cook

la **lessive** [lɛsiv]	wash; washing
le **linge** [lɛ̃ʒ]	linen; laundry
mettre le linge sale à la machine	put the dirty laundry in the washing machine
repasser [ʀ(ə)pase]	iron
le **fer à repasser**	iron

allumer [alyme]	turn on
éteindre [etɛ̃dʀ]	turn off
Tu as encore oublié d'éteindre la lumière.	You forgot to turn the light off again.
faire du feu [fɛʀdyfø]	make a fire
chauffer [ʃofe]	warm, heat
Il fait chauffer le lait.	He's warming the milk.

faire le lit [fɛʀləli]	make the bed
un **drap** [dʀa]	(bed)sheet
un **oreiller** [ɔʀɛje]	bed pillow

mettre la table [mɛtʀ(ə)latabl]	set the table
débarrasser [debaʀase]	clear the table
enlever [ɑ̃l(ə)ve]	clear; remove
N'enlève pas mon verre, s'il te plaît, j'ai encore soif.	Please don't take away my glass; I'm still thirsty.
la **poubelle** [pubəl]	trashcan
mettre les ordures à la poubelle	throw the trash in the trashcan

les **travaux ménagers** *m* [tʀavomenaʒe]	housework, household chores
la **ménagère** [menaʒɛʀ]	housewife
le **maître**, la **maîtresse de maison** [mɛtʀə, mɛtʀɛsdəmɛzɔ̃]	man/lady of the house
donner un coup de main à qn [dɔneɛ̃kud(ə)mɛ̃]	help s.o., give s.o. a hand
un **aspirateur** [aspiʀatœʀ]	vacuum cleaner
passer l'**aspirateur**	run the vacuum
épousseter [epuste]	dust
aérer [aeʀe]	air; ventilate
Il faudrait aérer, ça **sent le renfermé** dans cette pièce.	You need to air this room; it smells stuffy.
un **produit d'entretien** [pʀɔdɥidãtʀətjɛ̃]	cleaning products
un **équipement** [ekipmã]	equipment
un **équipement ménager**	household equipment
un **batteur** [batœʀ]	hand-held mixer
une **cafetière** [kaftjɛʀ]	coffeepot
une **cafetière électrique**	electric coffeemaker
une **cuisinière** [kɥizinjɛʀ]	stove
une **plaque de cuisson** [plakdəkɥisɔ̃]	burner, (stove) plate
une **machine à laver** [maʃinalave]	washing machine
un **sèche-linge** [sɛʃlɛ̃ʒ]	clothes dryer
un **lave-vaisselle** [lavvɛsɛl]	dishwasher
un **chauffe-eau** [ʃofo]	water heater
un **court-circuit** [kuʀsiʀkɥi]	short circuit
les **plombs** [plɔ̃]	fuses
Les plombs ont sauté.	The fuses are burned out
un **vide-ordures** [vidɔʀdyʀ]	garbage disposal
un appartement équipé d'un vide-ordures	an apartment equipped with a garbage disposal
les **déchets** *m* [deʃɛ]	garbage, waste
les **épluchures** *f* [eplyʃyʀ]	peelings (of fruit)

French Word	English Equivalent	False Friend	French Equivalent
sonner	ring	sun	exposer au soleil
la cave	cellar	cave	la caverne
un coin	corner	coin	une pièce de monnaie
un coussin	pillow, cushion	cousin	un cousin

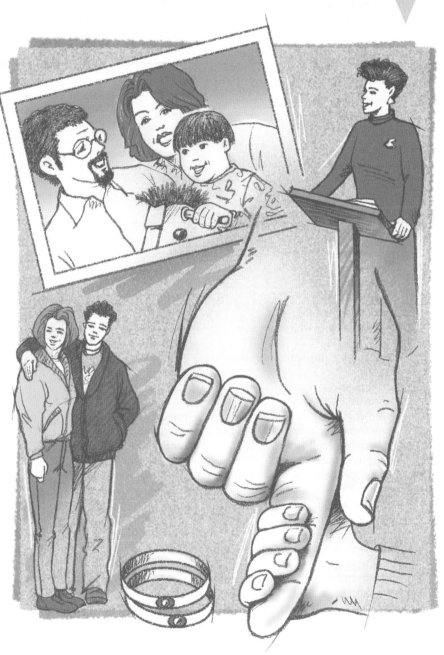

7.1 Individuals, Families

la **famille** [famij]	family
une **famille nombreuse**	family with many children
une **fête de famille**	family celebration
Elle fait partie de la famille.	She's part of the family.

ℹ️ **It's all in the family.**

Note the difference between:

familier, -ère	*familiar, well-known*	un **visage familier**	*a familiar face*
familier, -ère	*familiar, intimate*	un **comportement familier**	*overly familiar behavior*
familier, -ère	*unconstrained*	le **langage familier**	*colloquial speech*
familial, e	*familial, family*	une **entreprise familiale**	*a family business*
		Il a des ennuis **familiaux**.	*He has family troubles.*

---

les **parents** *m* [paʀɑ̃]	parents
le **père** [pɛʀ]	father
le **papa** [papa]	papa
la **mère** [mɛʀ]	mother
la **maman** [mamɑ̃]	mama

---

le **mari** [maʀi]	husband
Puis-je vous présenter mon mari ?	May I introduce my husband to you?
(un,e) **marié,e** *n; adj* [maʀje]	bridegroom/bride; married
l'**homme** *m* [ɔm]	man
la **femme** [fam]	woman; wife
une **femme enceinte**	pregnant woman
un **couple** [kupl]	couple
vivre en couple	live together (as a couple)
un **couple bien assorti**	a well-matched couple

---

l'**enfant** *m* [ɑ̃fɑ̃]	child
un **enfant unique**	only child
élever un enfant	raise a child
adopter un enfant	adopt a child
le **bébé** [bebe]	baby
Elle attend un bébé pour le mois de juin.	She's expecting a baby in June.
le **fils** [fis]	son
le **garçon** [gaʀsɔ̃]	boy
la **fille** [fij]	girl; daughter

le **frère** [fʀɛʀ]	brother
le **demi-frère**	half-brother
la **sœur** [sœʀ]	sister
la **demi-sœur**	half-sister

les **grands-parents** m [gʀɑ̃paʀɑ̃]	grandparents
la **grand-mère** [gʀɑ̃mɛʀ]	grandmother
la **mamie** fam [mami]	granny, grandma
la **mémé** fam [meme]	granny
le **grand-père** [gʀɑ̃pɛʀ]	grandfather
le **papy/papi** fam [papi]	grandpa
le **pépé** fam [pepe]	granddad

les **petits-enfants** m [p(ə)tizɑ̃fɑ̃]	grandchildren
la **petite-fille** [p(ə)titfij]	granddaughter
le **petit-fils** [p(ə)tifis]	grandson

l'**oncle** m [ɔ̃kl]	uncle
la **tante** [tɑ̃t]	aunt
le **neveu** [n(ə)vø]	nephew
la **nièce** [njɛs]	niece
le/la **cousin,e** [kuzɛ̃, in]	cousin
un **cousin germain**	first cousin
une **cousine au 2ᵉ degré**	second cousin

(un,e) **fiancé,e** n; adj [fjɑ̃se]	fiancé/fiancée; engaged
(un,e) **célibataire** n; adj [selibatɛʀ]	bachelor/spinster; single, unmarried
une **mère**/un **père célibataire**	single/unmarried mother/father
séparé,e [sepaʀe]	separated
la **séparation** [sepaʀasjɔ̃]	separation
divorcer de qn/(d)'avec qn [divɔʀse]	divorce/get a divorce from s.o.
M. Durand a **divorcé de/ (d')avec** sa troisième femme.	Mr. Durand has divorced his third wife.
(un,e) **divorcé,e** n; adj [divɔʀse]	divorced person, divorcée; divorced
le **divorce** [divɔʀs]	divorce
(un,e) **veuf, veuve** n; adj [vœf, vœv]	widower/widow; widowed

fonder une famille [fɔ̃deynfamij]	start a family
la **vie de famille** [vidfamij]	family life
avoir de la famille à … [avwaʀd(ə)lafamij]	have family in …
Nous avons de la famille à Quimper.	We have relatives in Quimper.
un **membre de la famille** [mɑ̃bʀ]	family member

le **planning familial** [planiŋfamiljal]	family planning
l'**époux** m [epu]	spouse, husband
l'**épouse** f [epuz]	spouse, wife
le **droit de garde** [dʀwad(ə)gaʀd]	custody
Lors du divorce, il a obtenu le droit de garde.	At the time of the divorce, he received custody.
la **pension alimentaire** [pɑ̃sjɔalimɑ̃tɛʀ]	alimony, maintenance payment
(un,e) **parent,e** n; adj [paʀɑ̃, ɑ̃t]	parent, relative; related
un,e parent, e proche/éloigné,e	close/distant relation
la **parenté** [paʀɑ̃te]	kinship, relationship
par alliance [paʀaljɑ̃s]	by marriage
C'est mon oncle par alliance.	He's my uncle by marriage.
le **lien** [ljɛ̃]	bond, tie, link
resserrer les **liens de parenté**	strengthen family ties
paternel,le [patɛʀnɛl]	paternal
maternel,le [matɛʀnɛl]	maternal
ma **grand-mère maternelle/ paternelle**	my grandmother on my mother's/father's side
fraternel,le [fʀatɛʀnɛl]	fraternal, brotherly
les **arrière-petits-enfants** m [aʀjɛʀp(ə)tizɑ̃fɑ̃]	great-grandchildren
un **arrière-petit-fils** [aʀjɛʀp(ə)tifis]	great-grandson
une **arrière-petite-fille** [aʀjɛʀp(ə)titfij]	great-granddaughter

Watch out for the plural!

As an element of *compound nouns,* **arrière** (adverb) is invariable.
ses arrière-petits-enfants *his great-grandchildren*
In compound nouns of the *adjective + noun* type, both elements add an -s in the plural.
mes grands-pères *my grandfathers*
des cartes postales *postcards*

un **jumeau**, une **jumelle** [ʒymo, ʒymɛl]	twin (brother/sister)
des **vrais jumeaux**	identical twins
des **sœurs jumelles**	twin sisters
(un,e) **majeur,e** n; adj [maʒœʀ]	adult; of full age

la **majorité** [maʒɔʀite]	majority
(un,e) **mineur,e** n; adj [minœʀ]	minor; under age
Ce film est **interdit aux mineurs.**	This film is not approved for viewing by minors.
(l')**aîné,e** n; adj [ene]	oldest, eldest *(of siblings)*
C'est l'aînée de trois filles.	She's the eldest of three girls.
(le/la) **cadet,te** n; adj [kadɛ, ɛt]	younger, junior
Elle a un frère cadet.	She has a younger brother

un,e **ancêtre** [ãsɛtʀ]	ancestor, forebear
nos ancêtres, les Gaulois	our ancestors, the Gauls
les **arrière-grands-parents** m [aʀjɛʀɡʀãpaʀã]	great-grandparents
un **arrière-grand-père** [aʀjɛʀɡʀãpɛʀ]	great-grandfather
une **arrière-grand-mère** [aʀjɛʀɡʀãmɛʀ]	great-grandmother
descendre de [desãdʀ]	be descended from
descendre d'une famille noble	be descended from an aristocratic family
les **descendants** m [desãdã]	descendants
la **descendance** [desãdãs]	descent, lineage
avoir une descendance nombreuse	have many descendants

le **parrain** [paʀɛ̃]	godfather
la **marraine** [maʀɛn]	godmother

les **beaux-parents** m [bopaʀã]	parents-in-law
le **beau-père** [bopɛʀ]	father-in-law
la **belle-mère** [bɛlmɛʀ]	mother-in-law
le **gendre** [ʒãdʀ]	son-in-law
la **belle-fille** [bɛlfij]	daughter-in-law

monoparental,e [mɔnopaʀãtal]	with only one parent
une **famille monoparentale**	one-parent family
adoptif, -ive [adɔptif, iv]	adoptive
le **fils adoptif** de mon ami	my friend's adopted son
l'**union libre** f [ynjɔlibʀ]	cohabitation without marriage
le **concubinage** [kɔ̃kybinaʒ]	cohabitation without marriage
vivre en concubinage/en union libre	live together without being married

7.2 Greetings and Farewells

arriver [aʀive]	arrive
On va arriver en retard.	We're going to get there late.
rencontrer qn [ʀɑ̃kɔ̃tʀe]	meet s.o.
saluer qn [salɥe]	greet
Saluez-le de ma part.	Remember me to him.
Bonjour ! [bɔ̃ʒuʀ]	Good morning/afternoon/day.
Bonjour M./Mme Pennec.	Good morning, Mr./Mrs. Pennec.
Salut ! [saly]	Hello. Hi.
Allô ! [alo]	Hello! *(on the telephone)*
Allô, qui est à l'appareil ?	Hello, who's calling?
Bonsoir ! [bɔ̃swaʀ]	Good evening.
partir* [paʀtiʀ]	leave, go away
Ils sont partis **chacun de son côté.**	They went off in different directions.
se séparer [səsepaʀe]	part
On s'est séparés au coin de la rue Daguerre.	We parted at the corner of rue Daguerre.
Bonne nuit ! [bɔnnɥi]	Good night.
Au revoir. [ɔʀvwaʀ]	Good-bye.

Madame/Mesdames [madam/medam]	Mrs., Ms.
une **dame**	a lady
Mademoiselle/Mesdemoiselles [madmwazɛl/medmwazɛl]	Miss
une **demoiselle**	a young lady
Monsieur/Messieurs [məsjø/mesjø]	Mr.
un **monsieur**	a gentleman
Dis bonjour au monsieur.	Say good morning to the gentleman.

A bientôt. [abjɛ̃to]	See you soon.
A plus tard. [aplytaʀ]	See you later.
A tout à l'heure. [atutalœʀ]	See you later.
A ce soir. [asəswaʀ]	See you this evening.
A demain. [ad(ə)mɛ̃]	See you tomorrow.

présenter qn à qn [pʀezɑ̃te]	introduce s.o. to s.o.
Permettez-moi de vous présenter M./Mme Moreau.	May I introduce Mr./Mrs. Moreau to you?
Je la leur présente.	I introduce her to them.
Je te présente à elle.	I introduce you to her.
se présenter	introduce oneself

Enchanté,e. [ɑ̃ʃɑ̃te] **Enchanté,e/Heureux, -euse de faire votre connaissance.**	Delighted. Delighted/Pleased to meet you/make your acquaintance.
chéri,e [ʃeʀi] **mon amour** [mɔ̃namuʀ] **mon/ma petit(e)** [mɔ̃p(ə)ti, map(ə)tit]	darling, dear my darling, my love my boy/girl, my little one
mon cher, ma chère [mɔ̃ʃɛʀ, maʃɛʀ] **mon vieux, ma vieille** *fam* [mɔ̃vjø, mavjɛj] **mon chou** *fam* [mɔ̃ʃu] **mon trésor** *fam* [mɔ̃tʀezɔʀ] **mon lapin** *fam* [mɔ̃lapɛ̃]	my dear old friend my dear, my darling my darling my pet

7.3 Young People

un,e **jeune** [ʒœn]
  Les jeunes de moins de 18 ans
  paient demi-tarif.
	young person, youth
	  Young people under 18 pay half-
	  price.

la **jeunesse** [ʒœnɛs]	youth
un **jeune homme** [ʒœnɔm]	young man
un **garçon** [gaʀsɔ̃]	young boy
une **(jeune) fille** [(ʒœn)fij]	(young) girl
les **jeunes gens** *m* [ʒœnʒɑ̃]	young people, youths
un,e **adolescent,e**; un,e **ado** *fam* [adɔlesɑ̃, ɑ̃t; ado]	adolescent, teen(ager)

un,e **ami,e** [ami]
  un,e **petit,e ami,e**
	friend
	  boyfriend, girlfriend

un **copain**, une **copine** [kɔpɛ̃, in]	friend, buddy, pal
se **rencontrer** [s(ə)ʀɑ̃kɔ̃tʀe]	meet

sortir* avec qn [sɔʀtiʀ]
  Il sort avec Sylvie depuis
  3 semaines.
  sortir* ensemble
	go out with s.o.
	  He's been going out with Sylvie
	  for three weeks.
	  go together; go out together

un **groupe** [gʀup]	group

une **bande** [bɑ̃d]
  faire partie d'une bande de jeunes
	group, gang, crowd
	  be part of a group/gang/crowd of
	  young people

une **association (sportive)** [asɔsjasjɔ̃(spɔʀtiv)]	(sports) association, club
devenir membre d'une association	join an association
faire du sport [fɛʀdyspɔʀ]	engage in/play a sport

> **i** **Let's play!**
>
> To express *engage in a sport,* French generally uses **faire de** + *definite article* + *type of sport.* Examples:
>
> | | |
> |---|---|
> | **Elle fait de la voile.** | *She sails.* |
> | **Nous faisons de la natation.** | *We swim.* |
> | **Il fait du tennis (= Il joue au tennis).** | *He plays tennis.* |
> | **Tu fais du ski ?** | *Do you ski?* |

une **MJC** (maison des jeunes et de la culture) [ɛmʒise]	youth center
une **discothèque** [diskɔtɛk]	disco(theque)
danser [dɑ̃se]	dance
Le samedi soir, on va danser.	On Saturday evening we go dancing.
aller*/sortir* en boîte *fam* [ale/sɔʀtiʀɑ̃bwat]	go to the disco/(night)club

un **concert** [kɔ̃sɛʀ]	concert
un **concert (de) rock**	rock concert
le **rap** [ʀap]	rap
un,e **rappeur, -euse** [ʀapœʀ, øz]	rapper
un **fan** [fan]	fan
C'est un fan de Tonton David.	He/She is a fan of Tonton David.
un **tube** *fam* [tyb]	hit
le **top 50** [tɔpsɛ̃kɑ̃t]	charts, hit parade
Ce tube est en tête du Top 50.	This hit is at the top of the charts.

un **conflit** [kɔ̃fli]	conflict
un **conflit de générations**	generational conflict
un **problème** [pʀɔblɛm]	problem
résoudre un problème	solve a problem
le **dialogue** [djalɔg]	dialogue
le dialogue entre jeunes et adultes	the dialogue between young people and adults

l'**autorité** *f* [ɔtɔʀite]	authority
Ce prof n'a aucune autorité.	This teacher lacks all authority.
la **révolte** [ʀevɔlt]	revolt, rebellion
(la) **critique** *n; adj* [kʀitik]	critique, criticism; critical

Elle trouve ses parents trop critiques à l'égard des ados.	She thinks her parents are too critical of teenagers.
contredire qn [kɔ̃tʀədiʀ]	contradict s.o.
Sa fille le contredit sans arrêt.	His daughter contradicts him constantly.
s'entendre bien/mal avec qn [sɑ̃tɑ̃dʀbjɛ̃/mal]	get along with s.o. well/poorly

l'agression f [agʀesjɔ̃]	aggression
être victime d'une agression	be the victim of aggression
une **bagarre** [bagaʀ]	scuffle; riot
la **violence** [vjɔlɑ̃s]	violence
violent,e [vjɔlɑ̃, ɑ̃t]	violent
détruire [detʀɥiʀ]	destroy
Ils ont détruit une cabine téléphonique.	They've destroyed a phone booth.

un,e **pote** *fam* [pɔt]	friend, chum, pal
une soirée sympa entre potes	a fun evening with friends
un **mec** *fam* [mɛk]	guy, fellow
une **nana** *fam* [nana]	babe, chick
le **look** *fam* [luk]	appearance, look
avoir un **look d'enfer**	look hot
l'âge ingrat m [aʒɛ̃gʀa]	awkward age
Mon fils est **en plein dans** l'âge ingrat.	My son is right at the awkward age.
la **puberté** [pybɛʀte]	puberty
pubertaire [pybɛʀtɛʀ]	pubescent, in puberty

la **confiance** [kɔ̃fjɑ̃s]	trust, confidence
avoir confiance en qn/faire confiance à qn	have confidence in s.o./trust s.o.
se confier à qn [s(ə)kɔ̃fje]	confide in s.o.
la **compréhension** [kɔ̃pʀeɑ̃sjɔ̃]	understanding, comprehension
Elle se plaint **du manque de compréhension** de ses parents.	She complains about her parents' lack of understanding.
compréhensif, -ive [kɔ̃pʀeɑ̃sif, iv]	understanding, broadminded
l'incompréhension f [ɛ̃kɔ̃pʀeɑ̃sjɔ̃]	lack of understanding, incomprehension
remettre qn/qc en question [ʀ(ə)mɛtʀɑ̃kɛstjɔ̃]	call s.o./s.th. into question
Est-ce que tu dois toujours tout remettre en question?	Do you always have to question everything?
se brouiller [s(ə)bʀuje]	quarrel with, fall out with
Elle s'est brouillée avec son copain.	She had a falling out with her friend.

en vouloir à qn (de qc/de faire qc) [ãvulwaʀ] J'en veux à mon frère de son égoïsme.	be angry with s.o. (because of s.th./for doing s.th.) I'm angry with my brother because of his egotism.
une **fugue** [fyg]	running away
fuguer [fyge]	run away

un,e **zonard,e** *fam* [zonaʀ, aʀd]	someone who lives in the poor part of town; asocial person
un,e **loubard,e** *fam* [lubaʀ, aʀd]	petty thief
mal tourner [maltuʀne] J'ai peur qu'il **finisse par mal tourner.**	go astray, go wrong I'm afraid he'll end up going astray.
s'en sortir [sãsɔʀtiʀ] Elle a des problèmes, mais je crois qu'elle va s'en sortir.	recover from; get out of She has problems, but I think she'll overcome them.
la **délinquance juvénile** [delɛkãsʒyvenil]	juvenile delinquency
un,e **casseur, -euse** *fam* [kasœʀ, øz]	demonstrator who uses violence

un **graffiti** [gʀafiti]	graffiti
un **tag** [tag] Les murs de la gare sont couverts de tags.	spray(ed) graffiti The walls of the station are covered with spray graffiti.
un,e **tagueur, -euse** [tagœʀ, øz]	sprayer
le **verlan** [vɛʀlã]	verlan *(form of language used by French youth)*

Verlan

Verlan is a language spoken primarily by young French people. It is based on the switching of syllables: **(à) l'envers** *with the syllables reversed* → **verlan**. Examples: metro → tromé, bizarre → zarbi, femme → meuf, blouson → zomblou.

7.4 Social Groups, Living Conditions, and Ways of Behavior

les **gens** *m* [ʒã]	people
la **population** [pɔpylasjɔ̃] faire partie de la **population active**	population be part of the working population
les **jeunes** *m* [ʒœn]	youth, young people
la **jeunesse** [ʒœnɛs]	youth

la **vieillesse** [vjɛjɛs]	old age
le **3ᵉ âge** [tʀwazjɛmaʒ]	senior years
Il y a des tarifs réduits **pour le 3ᵉ âge.**	There are discounts for senior citizens.

la **société** [sɔsjete]	society
social,e [sɔsjal]	social
une **couche sociale**	social stratum
le **milieu** [miljø]	milieu, social sphere
venir d'un **milieu social défavorisé**	come from an underprivileged sphere of society
une **communauté** [kɔmynote]	community
un **groupe** [gʀup]	group
appartenir à un **groupe ethnique minoritaire**	belong to an ethnic minority group
une **classe** [klas]	class, stratum
une **classe sociale**	social class

aisé,e [eze]	well-to-do
venir d'un **milieu aisé**	come from a well-to-do background
moyen,ne [mwajɛ̃, jɛn]	middle, average
les **classes moyennes**	the middle classes
la **bourgeoisie** [buʀʒwazi]	bourgeoisie, middle class
(un,e) **bourgeois,e** n; adj [buʀʒwa, waz]	(a) bourgeois person
populaire [pɔpylɛʀ]	popular; common
Il est **issu des couches populaires.**	He comes from a modest background.
(un,e) **ouvrier, -ière** n; adj [uvʀije, ijɛʀ]	worker; working
la **classe ouvrière**	the working class

riche [ʀiʃ]	rich
la **richesse** [ʀiʃɛs]	riches
la **fortune** [fɔʀtyn]	fortune

ⓘ Fortune – chance – bonheur

Note the difference between:

la fortune	*fortune; success; wealth*
faire fortune	*make a fortune*
la roue de la fortune	*wheel of fortune*
la chance	*chance; luck, good fortune*
avoir de la chance	*be lucky*
Bonne chance!	*Good luck!*
le bonheur	*happiness; good fortune, success*
un bonheur sans nuages	*unclouded happiness*

pauvre [povʀ]	poor
la **pauvreté** [povʀəte]	poverty
la **misère** [mizɛʀ]	misery, distress; want
tomber* dans la misère	fall on hard times
démuni,e [demyni]	destitute
un quartier pauvre où vivent les plus démunis	a slum where the most destitute live

un,e **propriétaire** [pʀɔpʀijetɛʀ]	owner
la **propriété** [pʀɔpʀijete]	property
Propriété privée.	Private property.

un,e **chômeur, -euse** [ʃomœʀ, øz]	unemployed person
le **chômage** [ʃomaʒ]	unemployment
Elle **est au chômage** depuis 6 mois.	She's been unemployed for six months.
un,e **RMIste** (RMI = revenu minimum d'insertion) [ɛʀɛmist]	social welfare recipient (RMI = minimum income paid by the state to persons over the age of 25 without means)
l'**aide sociale** f [ɛdsɔsjal]	welfare
un,e **SDF (sans domicile fixe)** [ɛsdeɛf]	person with no fixed place of residence
un,e **sans-abri** [sɑ̃zabʀi]	homeless person
un,e **clochard,e** [klɔʃaʀ, aʀd]	hobo
un,e **mendiant,e** [mɑ̃djɑ̃, ɑ̃t]	beggar
mendier [mɑ̃dje]	beg

un,e **immigré,e** [imigʀe]	immigrant
immigrer [imigʀe]	immigrate
Sa famille **a immigré** dans les années 60.	Her family immigrated in the sixties.
l'**immigration** f [imigʀasjɔ̃]	immigration
l'immigration clandestine	illegal immigration
s'intégrer [sɛ̃tegʀe]	become integrated
aider les immigrés à s'intégrer dans notre société	help immigrants become integrated into our society
l'**intégration** f [ɛ̃tegʀasjɔ̃]	integration

accepter [aksɛpte]	accept
rejeter [ʀ(ə)ʒəte/ʀəʒ(ə)te]	reject
Les étrangers se sentent souvent rejetés.	Foreigners often feel rejected.
s'adapter à [sadapte]	adapt to, adjust to
Il s'est bien adapté à sa nouvelle vie.	He's adapted well to his new life.
l'**adaptation** f [adaptasjɔ̃]	adaptation, adjustment

être en conflit avec qn [ɛtʀɑ̃kɔ̃fli] be in conflict with s.o.
respecter [ʀɛspɛkte] respect
tolérer [tɔleʀe] tolerate
la **tolérance** [tɔleʀɑ̃s] tolerance
l'**intolérance** f [ɛ̃tɔleʀɑ̃s] intolerance
avoir pitié de qn [avwaʀpitje] have pity on s.o.
  Ayez pitié de moi. Have pity on me.
faire pitié à qn [fɛʀpitje] move s.o. to pity
  Le voir dans un état pareil me fait Seeing him in such a state really
  vraiment pitié. moves me to pity.

aider qn (à faire qc) [ede] help s.o. (do s.th.)
  Je vous aide à pousser la voiture ? Shall I help you push the car?
encourager qn [ɑ̃kuʀaʒe] encourage s.o.
  Applaudissez pour les encourager. Applaud in order to encourage
  them.
décourager qn [dekuʀaʒe] discourage s.o.
  Ne te décourage pas si vite ! Don't be discouraged so quickly!
soutenir qn [sut(ə)niʀ] support s.o.
  Ils ont réussi parce que leurs amis They were successful because
  les ont beaucoup soutenus. their friends gave them lots of
  support.

avoir des problèmes m have problems
[avwaʀdepʀɔblɛm]
une **épreuve** [epʀœv] test; ordeal
  subir une dure épreuve undergo a difficult ordeal
le **souci** [susi] anxiety; care
  se faire du souci worry
la **difficulté** [difikylte] difficulty

dépendant,e (de) [depɑ̃dɑ̃, ɑ̃t] dependent (on)
dépendre de [depɑ̃dʀ] depend on
indépendant,e (de) [ɛ̃depɑ̃dɑ̃, ɑ̃t] independent (of)
libre [libʀ] free
se libérer de [s(ə)libeʀe] free oneself from/of
  Elle s'est libérée de l'influence de She has freed herself from her
  ses parents. parents' influence.
délivrer de [delivʀe] free from/of
  Nous voilà **délivrés de nos soucis**. Now we're free of our worries.

la **responsabilité** [ʀɛspɔ̃sabilite] responsibility
(être) responsable de [ʀɛspɔ̃sabl] (be) responsible for
  Je me sens responsable de ma I feel responsible for my sister.
  sœur.

protéger [pʀɔteʒe]	protect
la **protection** [pʀɔtɛksjɔ̃]	protection
sauver [sove]	save, rescue

les **vieux** *m* [vjø]	old people, the elderly
les **personnes âgées** *f* [pɛʀsɔn(z)aʒe]	seniors, elderly people
une **génération** [ʒeneʀasjɔ̃]	generation
la génération 68	the generation of 1968
Le fossé entre les générations s'agrandit.	The generation gap is increasing.

les **conditions de vie** *f* [kɔ̃disjɔ̃d(ə)vi]	living conditions
le **niveau de vie** [nivod(ə)vi]	standard of living
s'accroître [sakʀwatʀ]	grow; increase
Le taux de chômage **s'est encore accru**.	The number of unemployed has increased again.
une **augmentation** [ɔgmɑ̃tasjɔ̃]	increase; raise
J'ai demandé une **augmentation (de salaire)** à mon chef.	I've asked my boss for a raise (in salary).
une **réduction** [ʀedyksjɔ̃]	reduction
la **réduction du temps de travail**	reduction of working hours

privilégié,e [pʀivileʒje]	privileged
un **privilège** [pʀivilɛʒ]	privilege
fortuné,e [fɔʀtyne]	rich, well-to-do
Ils font partie d'une des familles les plus fortunées de France.	They belong to one of the richest families in France.
les **revenus** *m* [ʀəv(ə)ny/ʀ(ə)vəny]	income
l'**impôt sur le revenu**	income tax
la **prospérité** [pʀɔspeʀite]	prosperity
les **ressources** *f* [ʀəsuʀs]	resources, means
disposer de ressources illimitées	have unlimited resources

précaire [pʀekɛʀ]	precarious
se trouver dans une situation précaire	find oneself in a precarious situation
les **déshérités** *m* [dezeʀite]	the disadvantaged
un,e **sans-papiers** [sɑ̃papje]	illegal immigrant
Cette organisation lutte pour la légalisation des sans-papiers.	This organization fights for the legalization of illegal immigrants.
appauvri,e [apovʀi]	impoverished
(un,e) **économiquement faible** *n; adj* [ekɔnɔmikmɑ̃fɛbl]	economically disadvantaged (person)

une allocation réservée aux èconomiquement faibles	a benefit available to only the economically disadvantaged
le **prolétariat** [pʀɔletaʀja]	proletariat (lowest social or economic class)

(un,e) **marginal,e** n; adj [maʀʒinal]	marginalized (person), outsider
(un,e) **exclu,e** n; adj [ɛkskly]	excluded (person), outcast
aider les exclus à retrouver leur place dans la société	help outcasts find their place in society again
l'**exclusion** f [ɛksklyzjɔ̃]	exclusion; casting out
la **fracture sociale** [fʀaktyʀsɔsjal]	social gap
le **quart-monde** [kaʀmɔ̃d]	the poor, the Fourth World

inquiéter qn [ɛ̃kjete]	alarm s.o., disturb s.o.
L'augmentation de la criminalité inquiète les pouvoirs publics.	The increase in crime alarms the authorities.
l'**inquiétude** f [ɛ̃kjetyd]	uneasiness, concern
maltraiter qn [maltʀɛte]	mistreat s.o.
bousculer qn [buskyle]	jostle s.o.; bully s.o.

solidaire [sɔlidɛʀ]	bound up (with)
se sentir solidaire des marginaux	feel a sense of solidarity with marginalized groups
la **solidarité** [sɔlidaʀite]	solidarity
porter secours à qn [pɔʀtes(ə)kuʀ]	give aid to s.o., help s.o.

7.5 Relationships and Ties

un,e **ami,e** [ami]	friend
l'**amitié** f [amitje]	friendship
faire qc **par amitié pour qn**	do s.th. out of friendship for s.o.
amical,e [amikal]	friendly, amicable
aimable [ɛmabl]	kind, obliging
Merci beaucoup, vous êtes très aimable.	Thank you; you're very kind.
l'**amabilité** f [amabilite]	kindness
un **copain**, une **copine** [kɔpɛ̃, in]	friend, chum, buddy
un,e **camarade** [kamaʀad]	comrade; one's equal or peer
C'est un ancien **camarade de classe**.	He's a former classmate.
un,e **voisin,e** [vwazɛ̃, in]	neighbor
un,e **collègue** [kɔlɛg]	colleague

connaître [kɔnɛtʀ]	know, be acquainted with

faire la connaissance de qn
[fɛʀlakɔnɛsɑ̃s]
J'ai fait la connaissance d'une fille
très sympa.
être en contact avec [ɛtʀɑ̃kɔ̃takt]
Il est toujours en contact avec ses
anciens collègues.
une **relation** [ʀ(ə)lasjɔ̃]
**entretenir des relations amicales
avec qn**
des **rapports** m [ʀapɔʀ]
avoir des rapports tendus avec qn

make s.o.'s acquaintance
I've met a very nice girl.
be in contact with
He's still in contact with his
former colleagues.
relation
maintain friendly relations with
s.o.
relations
be on strained terms with s.o.

vouvoyer [vuvwaje]
tutoyer [tytwaje]
On se vouvoie ou on se tutoie?

faire la bise à qn [fɛʀlabiz]
serrer la main à qn [seʀelamɛ̃]
(être) poli,e [pɔli]
(être) gentil,le [ʒɑ̃ti, ij]
Tu pourrais être plus gentil avec ta
sœur.
l'**ambiance** f [ɑ̃bjɑ̃s]
froid,e [fʀwa, fʀwad]
Pendant toute la réunion,
l'ambiance a été froide.
agréable [agʀeabl]
détendu,e [detɑ̃dy]

address s.o. as *vous*
address s.o. as *tu*
Shall we say *vous* or *tu* to each
other?
give s.o. a kiss
shake s.o.'s hand
(be) polite
(be) nice
You could be nicer to your sister.

ambiance, mood
cold, chilly
During the entire meeting, the
mood was chilly.
agreeable, pleasant
relaxed

sympa(thique) [sɛ̃pa(tik)]
la **sympathie** [sɛ̃pati]
antipathique [ɑ̃tipatik]
Jean m'est très antipathique.
l'**antipathie** f [ɑ̃tipati]
Elle m'inspire une profonde
antipathie.

congenial, likable, nice
sympathy
not likable, uncongenial
I feel a great aversion to Jean.
antipathy, dislike
She provokes a profound dislike
in me.

embrasser [ɑ̃bʀase]
caresser [kaʀɛse]
Elle caresse tendrement les cheveux
de son copain.
courir après qn [kuʀiʀ]
Pourquoi est-ce que tu cours encore
après cette fille?
draguer qn *fam* [dʀage]

embrace; kiss
caress, stroke
She tenderly strokes her friend's
hair.
run after s.o.
Why are you still running after
that girl?
hit on s.o.

repousser [ʀ(ə)puse]   reject, spurn, rebuff

féliciter [felisite]   praise; congratulate
  féliciter qn pour/de son travail   praise s.o. for his work
un **compliment** [kɔ̃plimɑ̃]   compliment
imiter [imite]   imitate
  C'est son idole, elle l'imite en tout.   She's her role model; she imi-
                                              tates her in everything.
l'**imitation** f [imitasjɔ̃]   imitation
se moquer de [s(ə)mɔke]   make fun of, laugh at
  Ne mets pas cette chemise, tout   Don't wear that shirt; everybody
  le monde va se moquer de toi.   will laugh at you.
faire marcher qn fam [fɛʀmaʀʃe]   pull s.o.'s leg, put s.o. on
  Je ne te crois pas. Tu veux me   I don't believe you. Are you
  faire marcher, où quoi?   putting me on, or what?

attendre qn [atɑ̃dʀ]   wait for s.o.
aller* voir qn [alevwaʀ]   visit s.o., go see s.o.

---

i | **Visiting**

Note the difference:
aller/venir voir qn   *go see s.o, visit s.o.*
Cet(te) après-midi, on va voir notre tante. *This afternoon we're going to see our*
                                             aunt.
Venez me voir demain.   *Come see me tomorrow.*
rendre visite à qn   *pay a visit to s.o. (more formal)*
Si vous le permettez, nous vous rendrons   *With your permission, we will pay you a*
visite après-demain.   *visit the day after tomorrow.*
visiter qc   *visit s.th., view s.th.*
Tu as déjà visité le Louvre?   *Have you visited the Louvre yet?*

---

aller* chercher qn [aleʃɛʀʃe]   pick s.o. up
  Sois tranquille, on ira te chercher   Don't worry; we'll pick you up
  à la gare.   at the train station.
inviter à [ɛ̃vite]   invite to
  J'ai invité les Dupont à dîner.   I've invited the Duponts to
                                              dinner.
une **invitation** [ɛ̃vitasjɔ̃]   invitation
une **visite** [vizit]   visit
  rendre visite à qn   pay a visit to s.o.
recevoir [ʀ(ə)səvwaʀ/ʀəs(ə)vwaʀ]   receive
  Dans cette grande maison, on   In this big house we can receive
  peut recevoir beaucoup de   a great many people.
  monde.

s'intéresser à [sɛ̃teʁese]
be interested in

Il s'intéresse beaucoup trop à mon amie.
He's much too interested in my friend.

concerné,e [kɔ̃sɛʁne]
concerned

se sentir **concernè,e par** les problèmes d'un copain
feel concerned about a friend's problems

s'ennuyer [sɑ̃nɥije]
be bored

Qu'est-ce qu'on s'ennuie ici !
It's so boring here!

seul,e [sœl]
alone, lonely

Tu ne veux pas venir ce soir ? Je me sens si seul.
Don't you want to come over this evening? I feel so lonely.

la **solitude** [sɔlityd]
loneliness, solitude

---

retrouver qn [ʁ(ə)tʁuve]
meet s.o. (again)

revoir qn [ʁ(ə)vwaʁ]
see s.o. again; meet s.o. again

Ils se sont revus au bout de 20 ans.
They've met again after 20 years.

quitter qn [kite]
leave s.o.

Ne me quitte pas !
Don't leave me!

perdre de vue [pɛʁdʁ(ə)dəvy]
lose sight of

Après la fac, on s'est perdu de vue.
After college we lost sight of each other.

---

accompagner qn [akɔ̃paɲe]
accompany s.o.

Tu m'accompagnes au théâtre ce soir ?
Will you go to the theater with me this evening?

amener qn [am(ə)ne]
bring s.o. along

emmener qn [ɑ̃m(ə)ne]
take s.o. along

ramener qn [ʁam(ə)ne]
take/drive s.o. back

Je l'ai ramené en voiture.
I took him back (home) in the car.

Bringing/taking s.o./s.th. back

Mener (bring, take) and its compounds (**amener** = bring with, **ramener** = bring back, take home, **emmener** = take away) are used primarily with **persons**, while **porter** and its compounds (**apporter** = bring (with, here), **rapporter** = bring back, bring again, **emporter** = take away) are used with **things**, or when something is being **carried**.

Note the difference between:

Si tu veux, tu peux <u>amener</u> ton cousin.
If you like, you can bring your cousin along.

<u>Apporte-moi</u> mes lunettes, s'il te plaît.
Bring me my glasses, please.

Vous pourriez m'<u>emmener</u> à l'aéroport?
Could you take me to the airport?

une pizza à <u>emporter</u>
a take-out pizza

fort,e [fɔʀ, fɔʀt]	strong, powerful
la **force** [fɔʀs]	strength, force, power
faible [fɛbl]	weak
la **faiblesse** [fɛblɛs]	weakness
patient,e [pasjɑ̃, jɑ̃t]	patient
Elle ne s'énerve jamais, elle est très patiente.	She never gets upset; she's very patient.
la **patience** [pasjɑ̃s]	patience
impatient,e [ɛ̃pasjɑ̃, jɑ̃t]	impatient
l'**impatience** f [ɛ̃pasjɑ̃s]	impatience

regretter [ʀ(ə)gʀete]	regret
Nous regrettons de l'avoir laissé partir.	We regret having let him go.
le **regret** [ʀ(ə)gʀɛ]	regret

calmer qn [kalme]	calm s.o. (down)
J'ai eu du mal à la calmer.	I had trouble calming her down.
consoler qn [kɔ̃sɔle]	console s.o.
Elle était triste, mais son amie l'a consolée.	She was sad, but her friend consoled her.
la **consolation** [kɔ̃sɔlasjɔ̃]	consolation
s'énerver [senɛʀve]	get upset, become irritable
Ne t'énerve pas pour ça !	Don't get upset about it!
se fâcher [s(ə)faʃe]	get angry
Lorsqu'il a vu sa voiture abîmée, **il s'est fâché tout rouge.**	When he saw his damaged car, he got very angry.
furieux, -euse [fyʀjø, øz]	furious

reprocher qc à qn [ʀ(ə)pʀɔʃe]	reproach s.o. with/for s.th.
Je lui reproche beaucoup son attitude.	I greatly object to his attitude.
Je te reproche de ne penser qu'à toi.	I reproach you for thinking only of yourself.
un **reproche** [ʀ(ə)pʀɔʃ]	reproach
se disputer avec qn [s(ə)dispyte]	quarrel with s.o.
Ma fille se dispute sans arrêt avec son ami.	My daughter quarrels continually with her boyfriend.
une **dispute** [dispyt]	quarrel, dispute

la **chance** [ʃɑ̃s]	(good) luck; chance
Tu as de la chance d'avoir retrouvé ton porte-monnaie.	You were lucky to have found your billfold again.
avoir la chance de faire qc	have the good luck to do s.th.

J'ai eu la chance de travailler avec lui.	I've had the good luck to work with him.
Bonne chance !	Good luck!

For information on the use of *luck* in French, see also p. 133.

avoir du succès [avwaʀdysyksɛ]	be successful, have success
la **malchance** [malʃɑ̃s]	bad luck, misfortune
être poursuivi par la malchance	be pursued by misfortune

être bien/mal avec qn [ɛtʀbjɛ̃/mal]	be on good/bad terms with s.o.
Il vaut mieux être bien avec son chef.	It's better to get along well with your boss.
frapper [fʀape]	hit, strike
battre [batʀ]	hit, beat
Quand il a trop bu, il bat sa femme et ses enfants.	When he's had too much to drink, he beats his wife and his children.
un **coup** [ku]	blow, hit
un **coup de pied**	kick
un **coup de poing**	blow with the fist
tuer [tye]	kill

fréquenter qn [fʀekɑ̃te]	visit s.o. frequently, keep company with s.o.
une **liaison** [ljɛzɔ̃]	liaison; union; intimacy
être attiré,e par qn [atiʀe]	be attracted by/to s.o.
J'ai toujours été attiré par cette femme.	I was always attracted to that woman.
charmer qn [ʃaʀme]	charm s.o.
apprécier [apʀesje]	appreciate

l'**affection** f [afɛksjɔ̃]	affection
affectueux, -euse [afektyø, øz]	affectionate
chaleureux, -euse [ʃaløʀø, øz]	warm, animated, cordial
un accueil chaleureux	a warm reception
cordial,e [kɔʀdjal]	cordial, warm
une atmosphère cordiale	a cordial atmosphere

(être) fidèle (à qn) [fidɛl]	(be) faithful (to s.o.)
Elle a toujours été fidèle à ses amis.	She has always been faithful to her friends.
la **fidélité** [fidelite]	faithfulness, fidelity
l'**infidélité** f [ɛ̃fidelite]	infidelity, unfaithfulness
tromper qn [tʀɔ̃pe]	deceive s.o.
décevoir qn [des(ə)vwaʀ]	disappoint s.o.; deceive s.o.

Pierre m'a beaucoup déçu: je comptais pourtant sur lui.	Pierre has disappointed me greatly; still, I was counting on him.
la **déception** [desɛpsjɔ̃]	disappointment; deception, deceit
jaloux, -ouse (de) [ʒalu, uz]	jealous (of)
Elle ne peut jamais sortir seule, son mari est trop jaloux.	She can never go out alone; her husband is too jealous.
la **jalousie** [ʒaluzi]	jealousy

soupçonner qn [supsɔne]	suspect s.o.
Je le soupçonne de me tromper.	I suspect that he's deceiving me.
le **soupçon** [supsɔ̃]	suspicion
éveiller **les soupçons** de qn	arouse s.o.'s suspicions
le **mépris** [mepʀi]	contempt, scorn
s'attirer le mépris de qn	incur s.o.'s contempt
mépriser qn [mepʀize]	scorn s.o.
être hostile à qn [ɔstil]	be hostile to s.o.
Il a bien senti que tout le monde lui était hostile.	He certainly sensed that everyone was hostile to him.
l'**hostilité** f [ɔstilite]	hostility

faire une gaffe fam [fɛʀyngaf]	make a blunder, put one's foot in it, goof up
Il ne faisait que des gaffes, on l'a mis à la porte.	He did nothing but goof up, so they kicked him out.
gaffer fam [gafe]	put one's foot in it
faire de la peine à qn [fɛʀd(ə)lapɛn]	hurt s.o., pain s.o.; be sorry
Ça me fait de la peine de le voir si malheureux.	It pains me/I'm sorry to see him so unhappy.
humilier qn [ymilje]	humiliate s.o.
une **humiliation** [ymiljasjɔ̃]	humiliation
subir une humiliation	suffer a humiliation
gifler qn [ʒifle]	slap s.o.
une **gifle** [ʒifl]	slap
vexer qn [vɛkse]	annoy s.o.
Elle est vexée pour un oui ou pour un non.	She's annoyed over every little thing.
provoquer qn [pʀɔvɔke]	provoke s.o.
une **provocation** [pʀɔvɔkasjɔ̃]	provocation
Je n'ai pas réagi à ses provocations.	I didn't react to his provocations.
gêner qn [ʒene]	embarrass s.o.; annoy s.o.

récompenser [ʀekɔ̃pɑ̃se]	reward, recompense
une **récompense** [ʀekɔ̃pɑ̃s]	reward, recompense

punir [pyniʀ]
Quand son père va savoir ça, elle va **se faire punir**.
la **punition** [pynisjɔ̃]

punish
When her father learns about it, she will be punished.
punishment

---

contraindre qn à [kɔ̃tʀɛ̃dʀ]
Tu ne pourras pas le contraindre à partir.
la **contrainte** [kɔ̃tʀɛ̃t]
dominer qn [dɔmine]
la **domination** [dɔminasjɔ̃]
priver qn de qc [pʀive]
Si tu continues, **tu seras privé de dessert**.
poursuivre qn [puʀsɥivʀ]
poursuivre qn en justice

compel/force s.o. to
You can't force him to go.
constraint, coercion, compulsion
dominate s.o.
domination
deprive s.o. of s.th.
If you keep on, you won't get any dessert.
persecute s.o.
prosecute s.o. at law

---

la **compagnie** [kɔ̃paɲi]
Ils recherchent la compagnie des gens de leur âge.
accueillir qn [akœjiʀ]
un **accueil** [akœj]
adopter qn [adɔpte]
Ma famille a adopté mon nouveau copain tout de suite.

company
They seek the company of people their own age.
receive s.o., welcome s.o.
reception, welcome
adopt s.o.; embrace s.o.
My family immediately embraced my new friend.

---

traiter qn de qc/comme [tʀɛte]
Ils l'ont traité d'imbécile, et ça ne lui a pas plu du tout.
faire ses adieux m [fɛʀsezadjø]
une **rupture** [ʀyptyʀ]
rompre avec qn [ʀɔ̃pʀ]
Ella a rompu avec son fiancé.
faire une scène à qn [fɛʀynsɛn]
Chaque fois que je rentre tard, mes parents me font une scène.

call s.o. s.th.; treat s.o. like
They called him an imbecile, and he didn't like that at all.
say good-bye
break-up
break up with s.o.
She broke up with her fiancé.
have a fight with s.o.
Every time I come home late, my parents start a fight with me.

---

se réconcilier avec [s(ə)ʀekɔ̃silje]
la **réconciliation** [ʀekɔ̃siljasjɔ̃]
la **réconciliation franco-alle-mande**
s'arranger avec [saʀɑ̃ʒe]

reconcile with
reconciliation
the Franco-German reconciliation
come to an arrangement with

les **retrouvailles** *f* [ʀ(ə)tʀuvaj]	meeting again
On va fêter nos retrouvailles.	We'll celebrate our meeting again.

le **bien-être** [bjɛ̃nɛtʀ]	well-being
être à l'aise [ɛtʀalɛz]	feel well
s'épanouir [sepanwiʀ]	brighten up; bloom
Elle s'épanouit de jour en jour.	She blooms more each day.
le **prestige** [pʀɛstiʒ]	prestige
jouir d'un grand prestige auprès de qn	enjoy great prestige with s.o.

7.6 Possession and Ownership

avoir [avwaʀ]	have
Nous avons une maison en Bretagne.	We have a house in Brittany.
appartenir à qn [apaʀtəniʀ]	belong to s.o.
Ce sac ne m'appartient pas.	This bag doesn't belong to me.
A qui est ... ? [akiɛ]	Whose ... ?
A qui sont ces gants ?	Whose gloves are these?
être à qn [ɛtʀ]	belong to s.o.
Ce livre est à Nathalie.	This book belongs to Nathalie.
être à (moi; toi; lui, elle; nous; vous; eux, elles)	belong to (me; you; him, her, it; us, you; them)
N'y touche pas. **C'est à moi.**	Don't touch it. It belongs to me.
posséder [pɔsede]	possess, own
la **possession** [pɔsesjɔ̃]	possession
prendre possession de qc	take possession of s.th.
propre [pʀɔpʀ]	own
C'est son propre appartement.	It's his own apartment.

 For information on *adjectives* that *change their meaning* depending on whether they *follow* or *precede* the word modified, see p. 37.

un, e **propriétaire** [pʀɔpʀietɛʀ]	owner, proprietor
être le/la/les ... de qn [ɛtʀlə/la/le]	be the ... of s.o., be s.o.'s ...
C'est la voiture de Marcel.	That's Marcel's car.

le **capital** [kapital]	capital
amasser un **capital important**	amass considerable capital
la **richesse** [ʀiʃɛs]	riches
la **pauvreté** [povʀəte]	poverty
vivre dans la pauvreté	live in poverty

disposer de qn [dispɔze] — have s.th. at one's command
Il dispose d'une petite fortune. — He has a small fortune at his command.

détenir [det(ə)niʀ] — own
le(s) **bien(s)** m [bjɛ̃] — wealth, estate, property; goods
Elle a donné tous ses biens à l'Eglise. — She has given all her wealth to the Church.
la **prospérité** [pʀɔspeʀite] — prosperity
prospère [pʀɔspɛʀ] — prosperous, flourishing
une entreprise prospère — a prosperous undertaking

une **acquisition** [akizisjɔ̃] — acquisition
Ce Picasso, c'est sa **dernière acquisition**. — That Picasso is his latest acquisition.
acquérir qc [akeʀiʀ] — acquire s.th.
un **placement** [plasmɑ̃] — investment
faire un bon placement — make a good investment
une **action** [aksjɔ̃] — stock

le **testament** [tɛstamɑ̃] — will
coucher qn sur son testament — put s.o. in one's will
l'**héritage** m [eʀitaʒ] — inheritance
faire un bel héritage — inherit a fortune
hériter de qn; qc/de qc [eʀite] — inherit from s.o.; inherit s.th from s.o.
Elle a tout hérité de ses parents. — She's inherited everything from her parents.
Voilà la montre que/dont j'ai hérité(e) de ma tante. — That's the clock I inherited from my aunt.
un,e **héritier, -ière** [eʀitje, jɛʀ] — heir, heiress
le **patrimoine** [patʀimwan] — patrimony, inheritance
sauvegarder le patrimoine — safeguard the inheritance/legacy

$$233^2$$

$$8\left(512+324\right)^4 - \frac{3}{12}x$$

8.1 Education

élever [el(ə)ve]	educate; rear, bring up
éduquer [edyke]	educate
l'**éducation** f [edykasjɔ̃]	education
Elle a reçu une très bonne éducation.	She's received a very good education.
un,e **éducateur, -trice** [edykatœʀ, tʀis]	educator

la **culture** [kyltyʀ]	culture; education
la **culture générale**	general education
cultivé,e [kyltive]	cultivated; educated
la **formation** [fɔʀmasjɔ̃]	education; molding (of character)
Cette école assure une formation solide.	This school guarantees a solid education.
la **formation continue**	continuing education
la **formation permanente**	further education
former qn [fɔʀme]	educate, train, bring up s.o.

enseigner qc à qn [ɑ̃sɛɲe]	teach s.th. to s.o.
J'enseigne le japonais à des adultes.	I teach Japanese to adults.
l'**enseignement** m [ɑ̃sɛɲ(ə)mɑ̃]	instruction, teaching
entrer dans l'enseignement	become a teacher
l'**enseignement primaire**	primary education
l'**enseignement secondaire**	secondary education
l'**enseignement supérieur**	higher education
un,e **enseignant,e** [ɑ̃sɛɲɑ̃, ɑ̃t]	instructor, teacher

savoir [savwaʀ]	know
Cet enfant sait beaucoup de choses.	This child knows a lot.
le **savoir** [savwaʀ]	knowledge
connaître [kɔnɛtʀ]	know; understand, be versed in
Je n'y connais rien.	I don't understand any of it.
Il connaît bien sa **table de multiplication.**	He knows his multiplication table well.
les **connaissances** f [kɔnɛsɑ̃s]	knowledge
ignorer [iɲɔʀe]	not know; be ignorant of
J'ignore l'origine de cette expression.	I don't know the origin of this expression.

un **but** [byt]	end, goal
poursuivre un but	pursue a goal
la **motivation** [mɔtivasjɔ̃]	motivation

motiver [mɔtive] motivate
Il est parfois difficile de motiver Sometimes it is hard to motivate
les élèves. the students.
se concentrer [s(ə)kɔ̃sɑ̃tʀe] concentrate
la **concentration** [kɔ̃sɑ̃tʀasjɔ̃] concentration
faire attention à [fɛʀatɑ̃sjɔ̃] pay attention to
Il ne fait jamais attention à ce que He never pays attention to what
je dis. I say.
(être) attentif, -ive [atɑ̃tif, iv] (be) attentive
Elle n'est pas attentive en classe. She's never attentive in class.
faire des progrès [fɛʀdepʀɔgʀɛ] make progress
Ma fille a fait des progrès en My daughter has made progress
maths. in math.

présent,e [pʀezɑ̃, ɑ̃t] present
la **présence** [pʀezɑ̃s] presence
absent,e [absɑ̃, ɑ̃t] absent
l'**absence** f [absɑ̃s] absence
En cas d'absence, il faut apporter In case of absence, an excuse
un mot d'excuse. must be brought.

apprendre qc à qn [apʀɑ̃dʀ] teach s.th. to s.o.
Elle a appris le violon à tous ses She has taught all her children
enfants. to play the violin.
paresseux, -euse [paʀesø, øz] lazy
la **paresse** [paʀɛs] laziness
travailleur, -euse [tʀavajœʀ, jøz] hard-working, industrious
comprendre [kɔ̃pʀɑ̃dʀ] understand, comprehend
la **compréhension** [kɔ̃pʀeɑ̃sjɔ̃] understanding, comprehension

autoritaire [ɔtɔʀitɛʀ] authoritarian
l'**autorité** f [ɔtɔʀite] authority
exercer son autorité sur qn exercise one's authority over s.o.
sévère [sevɛʀ] severe, strict
la **discipline** [disiplin] discipline; (school) subject
refuser de **se plier à la discipline** refuse to accept discipline

servir de modèle à serve as a model for
[sɛʀviʀdəmɔdɛl]
Son grand frère lui a toujours His big brother always served as
servi de modèle. a model for him.
récompenser qn de qc reward s.o. for s.th.
[ʀekɔ̃pɑ̃se]
une **récompense** [ʀekɔ̃pɑ̃s] reward
indulgent,e [ɛ̃dylʒɑ̃, ɑ̃t] indulgent, lenient
l'**indulgence** f [ɛ̃dylʒɑ̃s] indulgence, leniency
faire preuve d'indulgence give proof of one's indulgence

exiger qc de qn [egziʒe]	demand s.th. of s.o.
J'exige de toi que tu fasses un effort.	I demand that you make an effort.
(être) exigeant,e v; adj [egziʒɑ̃, ɑ̃t]	(be) demanding
obéir à [ɔbeiʀ]	obey
obéir à un ordre	obey an order
punir [pyniʀ]	punish
une **punition** [pynisjɔ̃]	punishment
Il mérite une **bonne punition**.	He deserves a proper punishment.

le **talent** [talɑ̃]	talent
le **don** [dɔ̃]	gift
avoir un don pour les langues	have a gift for languages
(être) doué,e (pour) [due]	(be) gifted (in)
Elles sont douées pour le dessin.	They are gifted in drawing.
(être) fort,e/faible en [fɔʀ, fɔʀt/fɛbl]	(be) good/poor at/in
Il est vraiment fort en anglais.	He's really good at English.
la **mémoire** [memwaʀ]	memory

l'**instruction** f [ɛ̃stʀyksjɔ̃]	education, learning, instruction
Elle a de l'instruction.	She is well educated.
instruit,e [ɛ̃stʀɥi, it]	well educated
un,e **moniteur, trice** [mɔnitœʀ, tʀis]	instructor, coach
une **monitrice de ski**	ski instructor

8.2 School, Classroom Instruction

une **école** [ekɔl]	school
une **école publique**	public school
une **école privée**	private school
une **école primaire/élémentaire**	primary/elementary school
une **école mixte**	mixed school

le **jardin d'enfants** [ʒaʀdɛ̃dɑ̃fɑ̃]	kindergarten
l'**école maternelle**; la **maternelle** [(ekɔl)matɛʀnɛl]	kindergarten
le **cours préparatoire (CP)** [kuʀpʀepaʀatwaʀ (sepe)]	first grade
le **cours élémentaire (CE)** [kuʀelemɑ̃tɛʀ (see)]	second and third grades

le **cours moyen (CM)** [kuʀmwajɛ̃ (seɛm)]	fourth and fifth grades

....

le **collège** [kɔlɛʒ]	junior high school
Il entrera au collège en septembre.	He'll start junior high in September.
le **lycée** [lise]	high school
le **lycée d'enseignement professionnel (LEP)**	vocational high school
un,e **lycéen,ne** [liseɛ̃, ɛn]	high school student
un **échange (scolaire)** [eʃɑ̃ʒ(skɔlɛʀ)]	student exchange program
Les enfants sont partis à Nîmes **en échange scolaire.**	The children have gone to Nîmes on a student exchange program.
un,e **correspondant,e** [kɔʀɛspõdɑ̃, ɑ̃t]	pen pal

....

un **professeur** [pʀɔfesœʀ]	teacher; professor
un **professeur des écoles**	elementary school teacher
un,e **prof** fam [pʀɔf]	teacher; prof
un,e **instituteur, -trice**; un,e **instit** fam [ɛ̃stitytœʀ, tʀis; ɛ̃stit]	kindergarten/elementary school teacher

....

un,e **élève** [elɛv]	student, pupil
une **classe** [klas]	class; (school) grade
une salle (de classe)	classroom
Les Français **ont classe** l'après-midi aussi.	The French go to school in the afternoon too.
sauter une classe	skip a grade
passer dans la classe supérieure	be promoted to the next grade
redoubler (une classe)	repeat (a grade)

....

réussir qc/à faire qc [ʀeysiʀ]	succeed in s.th./in doing s.th.
réussir un contrôle	do well on a classroom quiz
Il réussit dans tout ce qu'il entreprend.	He succeeds in everything he undertakes.
Tu ne réussiras pas à me convaincre.	You won't succeed in convincing me.
la **réussite** [ʀeysit]	success
un **échec** [eʃɛk]	failure
échouer à qc [eʃue]	fail (in) s.th.
échouer à un examen	fail an exam

le **baccalauréat**; le **bac** *fam* [bakalɔʀea, bak]	high school diploma
passer le bac	pass the high school graduation exam
rater qc [ʀate]	fail a test, write a poor paper
rater le bac	flunk the high school graduation exam
les **devoirs** *m* [dəvwaʀ]	homework
Fais tes devoirs avant de sortir.	Do your homework before you go out.
un **exercice** [egzɛʀsis]	exercise
un exercice compliqué/simple	a complicated/simple exercise
une **difficulté** [difikylte]	difficulty
un texte **bourré de difficultés**	a passage filled with difficulties
une **question** [kɛstjɔ̃]	question
poser une question à qn	ask s.o. a question
répondre à une question	answer a question
interroger [inteʀɔʒe]	ask
une **interrogation (écrite)**; une **interro** *fam* [inteʀɔgasjɔ̃ekʀit, ɛ̃teʀo]	test
J'ai complètement raté l'interro d'anglais.	I really messed up on the English test.
une **composition** [kɔ̃pozisjɔ̃]	composition
un **contrôle** [kɔ̃tʀol]	classroom quiz
une **dictée** [dikte]	dictation
l'**orthographe** *f* [ɔʀtɔgʀaf]	spelling
une **faute** [fot]	mistake
Ta dictée est pleine de **fautes d'orthographe**.	Your dictation is full of mistakes.
correct,e [kɔʀɛkt]	correct, right
donner une réponse correcte	give a correct answer
le **corrigé** [kɔʀiʒe]	corrected exercise
la **grammaire** [gʀamɛʀ]	grammar
le **vocabulaire** [vɔkabylɛʀ]	vocabulary
avoir un vocabulaire riche/pauvre	have a rich/poor vocabulary
un **mot** [mo]	word
employer le mot juste	use the appropriate word
l'**usage** *m* [yzaʒ]	usage
parler [paʀle]	speak

une **expression** [ɛksprɛsjɔ̃]	expression
l'expression orale/écrite	oral/written expression
le **langage** [lɑ̃gaʒ]	language; speech
La grammaire définit les règles du langage.	Grammar defines the rules of a language.
la **langue** [lɑ̃g]	language; speech
s'exprimer dans la langue des jeunes	speak the language of the young people
le **niveau de langue**	speech level
familier, -ière [familje, ljɛr]	colloquial
populaire [pɔpylɛr]	popular; common
une **expression familière/ populaire**	a popular/colloquial expression
littéraire [literɛr]	literary
utiliser la langue littéraire	use literary language

l'**écriture** f [ekrityr]	(hand)writing
avoir une très belle écriture	have very nice handwriting
écrire [ekrir]	write
Ça s'écrit comment?	How is that spelled?
donner sa réponse **par écrit**	give an answer in writing
prendre des notes [prɑ̃drdenɔt]	take notes

le **cours** [kur]	course
un **cours de géographie**	a geography course

---

cour(s/t,e/se/ses)

Note the difference between:

la cour [kur]	*court (of a prince, of justice), courtyard*
le cours [kur]	*course*
le court (de tennis) [kur]	*(tennis) court*
la course [kurs]	*race, run; course*
les courses [kurs]	*shopping*
court,e [kur, kurt]	*short*

---

copier qc (sur qn) [kɔpje]	copy s.th (from s.o.)
Elle a copié sur sa voisine.	She copied from her neighbor.
recopier [r(ə)kɔpje]	recopy, make a copy of
Je n'ai pas eu le temps de recopier ce qui était écrit au tableau.	I didn't have time to copy what was written on the board.
la **copie** [kɔpi]	exercise, paper, test; copy
Le prof a ramassé les copies.	The teacher collected the tests.

la **lecture** [lɛktyʀ]	reading
Mes enfants n'aiment pas la lecture.	My children do not enjoy reading.
lire [liʀ]	read
un **livre** [livʀ]	book
une **lettre** [lɛtʀ]	letter

expliquer [ɛksplike]	explain
une **explication** [ɛksplikasjɔ̃]	explanation
un **texte** [tɛkst]	text; passage
compréhensible [kɔ̃pʀeɑ̃sibl]	comprehensible
incompréhensible [ɛ̃kɔ̃pʀeɑ̃sibl]	incomprehensible

décrire qc [dekʀiʀ]	describe s.th.
une **description** [dɛskʀipsjɔ̃]	description
faire une **description réaliste** de qc	give a realistic description of s.th.
définir [definiʀ]	define
une **définition** [definisjɔ̃]	definition

résumer [ʀezyme]	sum up, give a summary of
un **résumé** [ʀezyme]	summary; résumé
faire un **bref résumé** de l'action	give a brief summary of the plot
commenter [kɔmɑ̃te]	comment
un **commentaire** [kɔmɑ̃tɛʀ]	commentary

discuter de qc [diskyte]	discuss s.th.
discuter' d'un problème important	discuss an important problem
une **discussion** [diskysjɔ̃]	discussion
engager la discussion	open the discussion
un **débat** [deba]	debate
mener un débat	conduct a debate

une **leçon** [l(ə)sɔ̃]	lesson
réciter [ʀesite]	recite
réciter un poème à son père	recite a poem to one's father
par cœur [paʀkœʀ]	by heart
apprendre une poésie par cœur	learn a poem by heart
retenir qc [ʀ(ə)təniʀ/ʀət(ə)niʀ]	retain s.th.
Il retient tout ce qu'il lit.	He retains everything he reads.
oublier [ublije]	forget

traduire [tʀadɥiʀ]	translate
traduire un texte en français	translate a passage into French
une **traduction** [tʀadyksjɔ̃]	translation

un,e **traducteur, -trice** [tRadyktœR, tRis]	translator
signifier [siɲifje]	mean
Que signifie "the sun" en français ?	What is "the sun" in French?
la **signification** [siɲifikasjɔ̃]	meaning

un **chiffre** [ʃifR]	figure, number
un **nombre** [nɔ̃bR]	number
compter [kɔ̃te]	count
compter jusqu'à 100	count to 100
calculer [kalkyle]	calculate; do arithmetic
calculer mentalement	do arithmetic in one's head

un **problème** [pRɔblɛm]	problem
un **problème de maths**	math problem
une **solution** [sɔlysjɔ̃]	answer, solution
résoudre [RezudR]	solve
Tu sais résoudre ce problème ?	Can you solve this problem?
prouver [pRuve]	prove
une **preuve** [pRœv]	proof
apporter la preuve que la terre tourne autour du soleil	furnish proof that the earth revolves around the sun

une **image** [imaʒ]	image, picture
un **dessin** [desɛ̃]	drawing
dessiner [desine]	draw
dessiner qc **au crayon**	draw s.th. in pencil
les **ciseaux** *m* [sizo]	scissors

For information on *forming the plural of French nouns* of the **ciseaux** type, see p. 38.

le **scotch** [skɔtʃ]	scotch tape

une **bibliothèque** [biblijɔtɛk]	library
un **livre** [livR]	book
emprunter un livre à la bibliothèque municipale	check out a book from the city library
un **bouquin** *fam* [bukɛ̃]	book
un **manuel (scolaire)** [manɥɛlskɔlɛR]	textbook
un **dictionnaire** [diksjɔnɛR]	dictionary
un **dictionnaire unilingue**	monolingual dictionary
un **dictionnaire bilingue**	bilingual dictionary
un **chapitre** [ʃapitR]	chapter
la **table des matières** [tabl(ə)dematjɛR]	table of contents

un **cahier** [kaje]	notebook
une **page** [paʒ]	page
Ouvrez vos manuels à la page 14.	Open your textbooks to page 14.

> For information on the *gender of nouns* ending in **-age**, see p. 70.

un **classeur** [klasœʀ]	file; portfolio
une **feuille** [fœj]	sheet
une **feuille de papier**	a sheet of paper
un **cartable** [kaʀtabl]	school bag
une **serviette** [sɛʀvjɛt]	briefcase

un **stylo** [stilo]	pen
écrire **au stylo**	write with a pen
un **stylo (à) bille**	ballpoint pen
un **stylo (à) plume**	fountain pen
l'**encre** f [ãkʀ]	ink
une **tache d'encre**	ink spot
une **cartouche** [kaʀtuʃ]	cartridge
un **crayon** [kʀɛjɔ̃]	pencil
des **crayons de couleur**	colored pencils
un **taille-crayon** [tajkʀɛjɔ̃]	pencil sharpener
une **gomme** [gɔm]	eraser

un **tableau (noir)** [tablo(nwaʀ)]	blackboard
effacer le tableau	clean the blackboard
la **craie** [kʀɛ]	chalk
une **éponge** [epɔ̃ʒ]	sponge

le **programme** [pʀɔgʀam]	syllabus, curriculum
Cette année, le **programme d'histoire** est très dense.	The history syllabus is very crowded this year.
une **matière** [matjɛʀ]	subject, subject matter
l'**emploi du temps** m [ãplwadytã]	schedule
un emploi du temps chargé	a full schedule
la **récréation**; la **récré** fam [ʀekʀeasjɔ̃, ʀekʀe]	recess, break
la **cour de récré**	playground

les **mathématiques**; les **maths** f fam [matematik, mat]	mathematics, math
l'**algèbre** f [alʒɛbʀ]	algebra
la **géométrie** [ʒeɔmetʀi]	geometry
une **règle** [ʀɛgl]	ruler; rule

tirer un trait **à la règle**	draw a line with the ruler
une **calculette** [kalkylɛt]	pocket calculator
l'**informatique** f [ɛ̃fɔʀmatik]	information technology; computer science
la **physique** [fizik]	physics
la **chimie** [ʃimi]	chemistry
la **biologie** [bjɔlɔʒi]	biology
les **sciences naturelles** f [sjɑ̃snatyʀɛl]	natural sciences
la **philosophie** [filɔzɔfi]	philosophy
une **langue** [lɑ̃g]	language
la **langue maternelle**	native language, mother tongue
une **langue étrangère**	foreign language
le **français** [fʀɑ̃sɛ]	French
l'**anglais** m [ɑ̃glɛ]	English
un dictionnaire français-anglais	a French-English dictionary
l'**allemand** m [almɑ̃]	German
l'**espagnol** m [ɛspaɲɔl]	Spanish
l'**italien** m [italjɛ̃]	Italian
le **latin** m [latɛ̃]	Latin
le **grec** [gʀɛk]	Greek
l'**histoire** f [istwaʀ]	history
l'**Histoire de France**	French history
la **géographie** [ʒeɔgʀafi]	geography
histoire-géo fam [istwaʀʒeo]	history and geography (as a subject)
l'**instruction civique** f [ɛ̃stʀyksjɔ̃sivik]	civics
la **musique** [myzik]	music
l'**éducation musicale** f [edykasjɔ̃myzikal]	music education
l'**éducation artistique** f [edykasjɔ̃aʀtistik]	art education
les **arts plastiques** f [aʀplastik]	visual arts
les **travaux manuels** m [tʀavomanɥɛl]	handicrafts
l'**éducation physique (et sportive), EPS** f [edykasjɔ̃fizik (espɔʀtiv), əpeɛs]	physical education, PE
la **gymnastique**; la **gym** fam [ʒimnastik, ʒim]	gymnastics; gym

le **système éducatif** [sistɛmedykatif]	educational system
le **système scolaire** [sistɛmskɔlɛʀ]	school system
envisager une réforme du système scolaire	consider a reform of the school system
la **scolarité** [skɔlaʀite]	course of study
la **scolarité obligatoire**	compulsory school attendance
une **année scolaire** [aneskɔlɛʀ]	school year
la **rentrée (des classes)** [ʀɑ̃tʀe(deklas)]	beginning of the school year
acheter des **fournitures scolaires** pour la prochaine rentrée	buy school supplies for the new school year
une **école de commerce** [ekɔldəkɔmɛʀs]	trade school
un **établissement d'éducation spécialisée** [etablismɑ̃dedykasjɔ̃spesjalize]	establishment for children with special educational needs
un **centre de formation professionnelle** [sɑ̃tʀdəfɔʀmasjɔ̃pʀɔfɛsjɔ̃nɛl]	vocational training center
un **internat** [ɛ̃tɛʀna]	boarding school
être en pension [ɛtʀɑ̃pɑ̃sjɔ̃]	be in a boarding school
Ses parents l'ont envoyé en pension.	His parents have sent him to a boarding school.
une **matière (principale)** [matjɛʀ(pʀɛ̃sipal)]	(major) subject
une **matière obligatoire**	required subject
une **matière facultative**	elective subject
L'espagnol est ma matière préférée.	Spanish is my favorite subject.
une **option** [ɔpsjɔ̃]	elective; option
choisir une **matière en option**	choose an elective
un **proviseur** [pʀɔvizœʀ]	headmaster, headmistress (of a *lycée*)
un,e **principal,e** [pʀɛ̃sipal]	principal (of a *collège*)
Il a été convoqué au bureau du principal.	He was called to the principal's office.
un,e **surveillant,e**; un,e **pion,ne** *fam* [syʀvɛjɑ̃, jɑ̃t; pjɔ̃, pjɔn]	vice-principal; junior master
surveiller [syʀvɛje]	supervise
aller* en étude/permanence/perm *fam* [aleɑ̃netyd/pɛʀm(anɑ̃s)]	go to work during free periods; do schoolwork under supervision
un,e **analphabète** [analfabɛt]	illiterate

un **cancre** fam [kãkR]
    idler, do-nothing, slacker
tricher [tRiʃe]
    cheat
  Le prof l'a surpris en train de tricher.
    The teacher caught him cheating.
sécher un cours fam [seʃeẽkuR]
    cut a class
  Il fait beau, j'ai bien envie de sécher le cours de physique.
    The weather's nice; I'd really like to cut physics class.
faire l'école buissonnière [fɛRlekɔlbɥisɔnjɛR]
    skip school, play hooky
la **retenue** [Rət(ə)ny/R(ə)təny]
    detention
une **(heure de) colle** fam [(œRdə)kɔl]
    (one hour of) detention
  Le prof m'a donné une heure de colle.
    The teacher gave me an hour of detention.

une **note** [nɔt]
    grade, mark
noter [nɔte]
    (give a) grade, mark
  Ce prof note sévèrement.
    That teacher is a hard marker.
le **bulletin scolaire** [byltẽskɔlɛR]
    school report card
  Son bulletin scolaire n'est pas brillant.
    His report card is not dazzling.
un **résultat** [Rezylta]
    result
le **niveau** [nivo]
    level
  Le niveau de la classe est lamentable.
    The level of the class is pitiful.
la **moyenne** [mwajɛn]
    average
  Il n'aura pas la moyenne en anglais, s'il ne travaille pas mieux.
    He won't have a good average in English if he doesn't do better work.

le **brevet (des collèges)** [bRəvɛ]
    lower secondary school diploma
  Elle a été reçue au brevet.
    She has received her lower secondary school diploma.
le **BEP (brevet d'études profes-sionnelles)** [beəpe]
    general vocational certificate
le **CAP (certificat d'aptitude professionnelle)** [seape]
    occupational certificate (in a specific trade)

un **exposé** [ɛkspoze]
    report
une **dissertation** [disɛRtasjɔ̃]
    essay, composition
  rédiger une dissertation
    write an essay
une **rédaction** [Redaksjɔ̃]
    essay, composition
un **brouillon** [bRujɔ̃]
    rough draft

une **opération** [ɔpeRasjɔ̃]
    operation fundamental
  les quatre **opérations fondamentales**
    the four fundamentals (of arithmetic)

une **addition** [adisjɔ̃]	addition
additionner [adisjɔne]	add
une **soustraction** [sustʀaksjɔ̃]	subtraction
soustraire [sustʀɛʀ]	subtract
une **multiplication** [myltiplikasjɔ̃]	multiplication
la **table de multiplication**	multiplication table
multiplier [myltiplije]	multiply
multiplier **par 3**	multiply by three
une **division** [divizjɔ̃]	division
diviser [divize]	divide
On ne peut pas **diviser par 0**.	You can't divide by 0.

une **équerre** [ekɛʀ]	square (rule)
un **rapporteur** [ʀapɔʀtœʀ]	protractor
un **compas** [kɔ̃pa]	pair of compasses
tracer un cercle au compas	trace a circle with the pair of compasses

8.3 University Study, Science, and Research

l'**université** f [ynivɛʀsite]	university
la **faculté**; la **fac** fam [fakylte, fak]	faculty; university
la **fac(ulté) de lettres**	faculty of arts
la **fac(ulté) des sciences**	faculty of sciences
la **fac(ulté) de droit**	faculty of law
une **grande école** [gʀɑ̃dekɔl]	(elite) university
une **classe préparatoire**; une **prépa** fam [klaspʀepaʀatwaʀ, pʀepa]	preparatory class for an elite university
Il faut deux ans de prépa pour entrer dans cette grande école.	To be admitted to that elite university, you need a two-year preparatory course.

la **science** [sjɑ̃s]	science
les **sciences humaines**	humanities
les **sciences naturelles**	natural sciences
les **sciences économiques**	economics
les **sciences politiques**	political science

(un,e) **scientifique** n; adj [sjɑ̃tifik]	scientist; scientific
le raisonnement scientifique	scientific reasoning
le **progrès** [pʀɔgʀɛ]	progress
le progrès technique	technological progress

la **recherche** [ʀəʃɛʀʃ]	research
faire de la recherche	do research
un **centre de recherche**	research center
un,e **chercheur, -euse** [ʃɛʀʃœʀ, øz]	researcher
un,e **savant,e** [savã, ãt]	scholar; scientist

une **théorie** [teɔʀi]	theory
une **expérience** [ɛkspeʀjãs]	experiment

No experiments!

Expérience has several meanings in English. *Note the difference between:*

une expérience	*1. experiment*
	2. experience
faire/se livrer à des expériences	*make experiments, experiment*
avoir de l'expérience	*have experience*
par expérience	*from experience*
expérimenter	*test, try, experiment with*
expérimenter un nouveau procédé	*test a new procedure*

---

expérimental,e [ɛkspeʀimãtal]	experimental
un **labo(ratoire)** [labo/(ɔʀatwaʀ)]	lab(oratory)
vérifier [veʀifje]	verify, check
démontrer [demɔ̃tʀe]	prove
Je vais **te démontrer par a+b**	I'm going to prove to you in
que j'ai raison.	black and white that I'm right.
une **démonstration** [demɔ̃stʀasjɔ̃]	proof

une **invention** [ɛ̃vãsjɔ̃]	invention
inventer [ɛ̃vãte]	invent
un,e **inventeur, -trice**	inventor
[ɛ̃vãtœʀ, tʀis]	
découvrir [dekuvʀiʀ]	discover
une **découverte** [dekuvɛʀt]	discovery
faire une découverte capitale pour	make a major scientific discovery
la science	

la **médecine** [med(ə)sin]	medicine
la **médecine générale**	general medicine
la **médecine dentaire**	dental medicine, dentistry
la **médecine vétérinaire**	veterinary medicine
la **biologie** [bjɔlɔʒi]	biology
la **psychologie** [psikɔlɔʒi]	psychology

un,e **mathématicien,ne**	mathematician
[matematisjɛ̃, jɛn]	
un,e **physicien,ne** [fizisjɛ̃, jɛn]	physicist

un,e **informaticien,ne** [ɛ̃fɔʀmatisjɛ̃, jɛn]	information technology expert; computer scientist
un,e **chimiste** [ʃimist]	chemist
un,e **biologiste** [bjɔlɔʒist]	biologist

un,e **étudiant,e** [etydjɑ̃, jɑ̃t]	(university) student
un étudiant **en lettres**	student of language and literature
les **études** f [etyd]	studies; education
faire des études de médecine	study medicine
étudier [etydje]	study
étudier le droit	study law

un,e **candidat,e** [kɑ̃dida, at]	candidate
être candidat,e à un examen	examination candidate, examinee
un **examen** [ɛgzamɛ̃]	exam(ination)
passer/réussir un examen	pass an examination
un **concours** [kɔ̃kuʀ]	competitive examination
se préparer à un concours/à un examen	prepare for a competitive examination
être reçu,e à un concours/un examen	pass a competitive examination
Il a échoué au concours d'entrée.	He didn't pass the competitive examination.
une **réussite** [ʀeysit]	success
un **échec** [eʃɛk]	failure
un **certificat** [sɛʀtifika]	certificate; testimonial; diploma
un **diplôme** [diplom]	diploma
Elle a enfin son diplôme d'ingénieur en poche.	She finally has her engineering diploma in her pocket.

s'inscrire [sɛ̃skʀiʀ]	register, matriculate; sign up
Julien s'est inscrit en fac(ulté) de médecine.	Julien has registered in the faculty of medicine.
l'**inscription** f [ɛ̃skʀipsjɔ̃]	registration, matriculation
l'**Ecole des Beaux-Arts** f [ekɔldebozaʀ]	School of Fine Arts
un **IUT (Institut universitaire de Technologie)** [iyte]	Institute of Technology
l'**université populaire** f [univɛʀsitepɔpylɛʀ]	institution offering adult (evening) classes

la **recherche fondamentale** [ʀəʃɛʀʃfɔ̃damɑ̃tal]	basic research

le **CNRS (Centre national de la recherche scientifique)** [seεneʀes]	National Center for Scientific Research
la **biochimie** [bjɔʃimi]	biochemistry
une **réaction chimique** [ʀeaksjɔ̃ʃimik]	chemical reaction
une **réaction en chaîne**	chain reaction
la **classification** [klasifikasjɔ̃]	classification
la classification périodique des éléments	periodic table of elements
la **cellule** [selyl]	cell
cellulaire [selylɛʀ]	cellular
la **biologie cellulaire**	cellular biology
le **gène** [ʒɛn]	gene
la **génétique** [ʒenetik]	genetics
le **génie génétique** [ʒeniʒenetik]	gene technology
la **manipulation** [manipylasjɔ̃]	manipulation
les dangers liés aux **manipulations génétiques**	the dangers involved in manipulation of genes
une **chaire** [ʃɛʀ]	chair, professorship
Il a une **chaire de professeur** à l'université de Paris IV.	He has a professorial chair at the University of Paris IV.
un,e **assistant,e** [asisɑ̃, ɑ̃t]	assistant
un **cours magistral** [kuʀmaʒistʀal]	course (of lectures)
assister à un cours magistral	attend a lecture course
les **travaux pratiques (TP)** [tʀavopʀatik (tepe)]	practical course (with student participation)
les **travaux dirigés (TD)** [tʀavodiʀiʒe (tede)]	directed study; seminar
un **cours par correspondance** [kuʀpaʀkɔʀɛspɔ̃dɑ̃s]	correspondence course
un **cours du soir** [kuʀdyswaʀ]	evening course
suivre un cours du soir	take an evening course
une **UV (unité de valeur)** [yve]	certificate (awarded for the work of a semester or a year)
un **DEUG (diplôme d'études universitaires générales)** [dœg]	DEUG, diploma awarded at the end of the "first cycle" (two years of study)
Il me manque encore trois UV pour avoir le DEUG.	I need three more certificates to get my DEUG.
la **licence** [lisɑ̃s]	diploma awarded after the first year of "second cycle" (one year after DEUG)
faire une **licence d'anglais**	study English, work on a *Licence* in English

la **maîtrise** [mɛtʀiz]	master's degree (about two years after DEUG)
passer sa maîtrise	get one's master's (degree)

une **cité universitaire**; une **cité U** *fam* [siteyniveʀsitɛʀ, sitey]	university housing, residential area for students
J'ai une chambre à la cité universitaire.	I have a room in a student dorm.
le **restaurant universitaire**; le **resto U** *fam* [ʀɛstɔʀɑ̃yniveʀsitɛʀ/ʀɛstoy]	student cafeteria
Quand je peux, j'évite de manger au resto U.	When I can, I avoid eating in the student cafeteria.

French Word	English Equivalent	False Friend	French Equivalent
la démonstration	proof, demonstration	(political) demonstration	la manifestation
un compass	pair of compasses, navigational compass	(pocket) compass	une boussole

9.1 Tools and Skilled Trades

un **outil** [uti]	tool, implement
une **boîte à outils**	toolbox
fixer qc [fikse]	fasten s.th.
accrocher qc [akʀɔʃe]	hang s.th
accrocher un cadre au mur	hang a picture (frame) on the wall
monter qc [mɔ̃te]	put together; assemble, mount s.th.
le **montage** [mɔ̃taʒ]	putting together; assembling, mounting
Le montage de la bibliothèque n'a pas été facile.	Putting up the bookshelves was not easy.
faire marcher qc [fɛʀmaʀʃe]	set s.th. going
Je n'arrive pas à faire marcher le magnétoscope.	I can't get the VCR to start.
réparer [ʀepaʀe]	repair
une **réparation** [ʀepaʀasjɔ̃]	repair

un **marteau** [maʀto]	hammer
se servir de [səsɛʀviʀ]	use
un **clou** [klu]	nail
Sers-toi de ce marteau pour enfoncer le clou.	Use that hammer to drive the nail.
arracher un clou	pull out a nail
une **échelle** [eʃɛl]	ladder
utiliser [ytilize]	use, find use for, utilize
employer [ɑ̃plwaje]	employ, use, make use of
le **mode d'emploi** [mɔddɑ̃plwa]	directions for use
suivre le mode d'emploi	follow the directions for use

une **lampe de poche** [lɑ̃pdəpɔʃ]	flashlight
une **pile** [pil]	battery
Il faut changer les piles de la lampe de poche.	The flashlight batteries have to be replaced.
un **canif** [kanif]	pocketknife
couper [kupe]	cut
Ne joue pas avec le canif, tu vas te couper.	Don't play with the pocketknife; you'll cut yourself.
des **ciseaux** m [sizo]	scissors
découper [dekupe]	cut out; cut up
découper une feuille de papier	cut up a sheet of paper

une **pince** [pɛ̃s]	pliers
une **pince coupante**	wire-cutter pliers
une **pince universelle**	combination pliers
des **tenailles**, une **tenaille** f [t(ə)naj]	pliers, pincers (used for removing nails)

une **vis** [vis]	screw
un **tournevis**	screwdriver
une **clé** [kle]	wrench
une **clé anglaise/à molette**	monkey wrench/adjustable wrench
un **niveau à bulle** [nivoabyl]	spirit level
un **mètre (pliant)** [mɛtrə (plijã)]	(folding) rule
une **hache** ['aʃ]	ax, hatchet
une **scie** [si]	saw
une **scie à métaux**	hacksaw
une **scie circulaire/sauteuse**	circular saw, buzz saw/jigsaw
scier [sje]	saw

l'**outillage** *m* [utijaʒ]	set of tools, gear
une **perceuse (électrique)** [pɛrsøz (elɛktrik)]	(electric) drill
percer [pɛrse]	drill (through)
un **établi** [etabli]	workbench
un **étau** [eto]	vise
une **cheville** [ʃ(ə)vij]	dowel
enfoncer une cheville	put in a dowel pin
un **écrou** [ekru]	nut
un **boulon** [bulɔ̃]	bolt
serrer un boulon	tighten a bolt

un **rabot** [rabo]	plane
raboter [rabɔte]	(smoothe with a) plane
raboter une planche	smoothe a board with a plane
un **burin** [byrɛ̃]	chisel
une **lime** [lim]	file
limer [lime]	file, to
une **truelle** [tryɛl]	trowel

9.2 Office, Office Items

un **bureau** [byro]	office; desk
un **article de bureau**	office item
l'**équipement de bureau**	office equipment
une **salle de réunion** [saldəreynjɔ̃]	conference room

une **table** [tabl]	table
un **tiroir** [tirwar]	drawer
La colle est dans le 1er tiroir du bureau.	The glue is in the first drawer of the desk.

une **chaise** [ʃɛz]	chair, seat
une **étagère** [etaʒɛR]	set of shelves

classer [klase]	sort; file
classer les dossiers **par ordre alphabétique**	file the records in alphabetical order
un **classeur** [klasœR]	file of documents, binder; filing cabinet
une **fiche** [fiʃ]	filing card; slip of paper; memo
un **fichier** [fiʃje]	filing case; card index
remettre un fichier **à jour**	bring a card index up to date

le **papier** [papje]	paper
le **papier à lettres**	writing paper, stationery
l'**en-tête** m [ɑ̃tɛt]	letterhead
le **papier à en-tête**	letterhead paper
une **enveloppe** [ɑ̃v(ə)lɔp]	envelope
un **timbre** [tɛ̃bR]	stamp
un timbre à 30 cents	a 30-cent stamp

un **stylo (à) plume** [stilo(a)plym]	fountain pen
l'**encre** f [ɑ̃kR]	ink
une **cartouche** [kaRtuʃ]	ink cartridge
un **stylo (à) bille** [stilo(a)bij]	ballpoint pen
un **crayon** [kRɛjɔ̃]	pencil
un **taille-crayon**	pencil sharpener
un **marqueur** [maRkœR]	highlighter, marker
souligner un passage important **au marqueur**	underline an important passage with the marker
un **feutre** [føtR]	felt-tipped pen
la **colle** [kɔl]	glue, mucilage, paste
un tube de colle	a tube of glue

un **téléphone** [telefɔn]	telephone
donner/recevoir un coup de téléphone	place/receive a telephone call
téléphoner à qn [telefɔne]	telephone s.o.
J'ai essayé de lui téléphoner, mais c'était occupé.	I tried to phone him, but the line was busy.
appeler qn [ap(ə)le]	call s.o.
rappeler qn [Rap(ə)le]	call s.o. back
Jean a téléphoné; il a demandé que tu le rappelles.	Jean phoned; he asked that you call him back.
un **appel (téléphonique)** [apɛl(telefɔnik)]	(telephone) call
un **répondeur** [Repɔ̃dœR]	answering machine

Il y a trois messages sur le répondeur.	There are three messages on the answering machine.
un **fax** [faks]	fax
envoyer qc par fax	send s.th. by fax
faxer qc à qn [fakse]	fax s.th. to s.o.

photocopier [fɔtɔkɔpje]	(make a) photocopy
une **photocopie** [fɔtɔkɔpi]	photocopy
Cette machine permet de faire des **photocopies couleur.**	That machine lets you make color photocopies.
une **photocopieuse** (un **photocopieur**) [fɔtɔkɔpjøz, fɔtɔkɔpjœʀ]	photocopier
N'oubliez pas votre document dans la photocopieuse.	Don't forget your document in the photocopier.

calculer [kalkyle]	calculate; estimate
des dépenses **calculées au plus juste**	accurately calculated expenditures
une **calculette** [kalkylɛt]	pocket calculator

un **ordinateur** [ɔʀdinatœʀ]	computer
un **micro-ordinateur**	personal computer
une **disquette** [diskɛt]	diskette
une **imprimante** [ɛ̃pʀimɑ̃t]	printer
une **imprimante (à) laser/à jet d'encre**	laser/inkjet printer
un **scanneur/scanner** [skanœʀ/skanɛʀ]	scanner

les **fournitures** f [fuʀnityʀ]	supplies; equipment
les **fournitures de bureau**	office supplies
une **chemise** [ʃ(ə)miz]	folder, cover
un **agenda** [aʒɛ̃da]	appointment book
noter un rendez-vous dans son agenda	enter an appointment in one's appointment book
un **calendrier** [kalɑ̃dʀije]	calendar
un **bloc-notes** [blɔknɔt]	writing pad, notepad

un **trombone** [tʀɔ̃bɔn]	paper clip
une **agrafe** [agʀaf]	staple; fastener, clasp
une **agrafeuse** [agʀaføz]	stapler
une **perforatrice**, une **perforeuse** [pɛʀfɔʀatris, pɛʀfɔʀøz]	hole-punch
le **ruban adhésif** [ʀybɑ̃adezif]	adhesive tape
un **surligneur** [syʀliɲœʀ]	highlighter, underliner
surligner [syʀliɲe]	underline, highlight

un **dictaphone** [diktafɔn]	Dictaphone
dicter [dikte]	dictate
un **télécopieur** [telekɔpjœʀ]	fax machine
une **telélécopie** [telekɔpi]	(tele)fax

9.3 Vocational and Professional Training, Occupations

apprendre qc à qn [apʀɑ̃dʀ]	teach s.th. to s.o.
C'est moi qui lui ai appris le français.	I'm the one who taught him French.
apprendre (à faire) qc [apʀɑ̃dʀ]	learn (to do) s.th.
un,e **apprenti,e** [apʀɑ̃ti]	apprentice
Cette entreprise forme régulière-ment des apprentis.	This firm regularly trains apprentices.
un **apprentissage** [apʀɑ̃tisaʒ]	apprenticeship
faire son apprentissage (chez)	do one's apprenticeship (with, at)
devenir* [dev(ə)niʀ]	become
Il a décidé de devenir pilote.	He has decided to become a pilot.
la **formation professionnelle** [fɔʀmasjɔ̃pʀɔfɛsjɔnɛl]	
un **atelier** [atəlje]	workshop, studio, atelier

étudier [etydje]	study (at a university)
faire des études f [fɛʀdezetyd]	study (at a university)
Ses parents économisent pour lui permettre de faire des études.	His parents are saving so that he can go to college.
une **faculté**; une **fac** fam [fakylte, fak]	faculty
une **université** [univɛʀsite]	university
une **grande école** [gʀɑ̃dekɔl]	elite university
suivre des cours [sɥivʀ(ə)dekuʀ]	take courses
Elle suit des **cours de littérature** à la Sorbonne.	She's taking literature courses at the Sorbonne.

un **examen** [ɛgzamɛ̃]	exam(ination), test
passer un examen	pass an exam
un **concours** [kɔ̃kuʀ]	competitive examination
se présenter à un concours	take part in a competitive examination
un **diplôme** [diplom]	diploma

un **stage** [staʒ]	practical training course; residence
faire un stage en entreprise	do practical training in a company

un,e **stagiaire** [staʒjɛʀ]	trainee, probationer
la **période d'essai** [peʀjɔddesɛ]	probationary period, trial period

l'**industrie** f [ɛ̃dystʀi]	industry
un,e **industriel,le** [ɛ̃dystʀijɛl]	industrialist
un **PDG (président-directeur général)** [pedeʒe]	managing director
un,e **directeur, -trice** [diʀɛktœʀ, tʀis]	manager, director, head
un,e **chef** [ʃɛf]	boss
un **chef d'entreprise**	head of a firm
une **entreprise** [ɑ̃tʀəpʀiz]	concern, business, firm, company; enterprise
Il dirige une **entreprise de travaux publics.**	He manages a construction engineering firm.
un,e **entrepreneur, -euse** [ɑ̃tʀəpʀənœʀ, øz]	entrepreneur; employer; industrialist

un **cadre** [kadʀ]	executive, manager
un **cadre supérieur**	top executive, senior manager
un **cadre moyen**	mid-level executive/manager
un,e **employé,e** [ɑ̃plwaje]	employee
un,e **comptable** [kɔ̃tabl]	bookkeeper, accountant
un,e **secrétaire** [səkʀetɛʀ]	secretary
une **secrétaire de direction**	executive secretary

un,e **ouvrier, -ière** [uvʀije, ijɛʀ]	worker, laborer

Ouvrier

Note the difference between:
un **ouvrier qualifié** — *skilled worker*
un **ouvrier spécialisé (OS)** — *unskilled worker*

un **manœuvre** [manœvʀ]	unskilled laborer
Il **travaille comme manœuvre** sur un chantier.	He's an unskilled laborer at a construction site.
un **contremaître**, une **contremaîtresse** [kɔ̃tʀəmɛtʀ, tʀɛs]	overseer, foreman

l'**administration** f [administʀasjɔ̃]	administration
le **service public** [sɛʀvispyblik]	public service
un,e **fonctionnaire** [fɔ̃ksjɔnɛʀ]	official, civil servant
un,e **facteur, -trice** [faktœʀ, tʀis]	postman, letter carrier
Le facteur fait sa tournée à vélo.	The postman makes his rounds on a bike.
un,e **postier, -ière** [pɔstje, jɛʀ]	postal employee
un **agent (de police)** [aʒɑ̃]	policeman, policewoman

Laissez-moi tranquille ou j'appelle un agent.	Leave me alone, or I'll call a policeman.
un **policier** [pɔlisje]	police officer
un **pompier** [pɔ̃pje]	fireman

l'**enseignement** m [ãsɛɲ(ə)mã]	education, teaching
l'**enseignement public**	public education
l'**enseignement privé/libre**	private education
un,e **enseignant,e** [ãsɛɲã, ãt]	educator, teacher
un,e **instituteur, -trice**; un,e **instit** fam [ɛ̃stitytœʀ, tʀis; instit]	elementary school teacher
un **professeur**; un,e **prof** fam [pʀɔfesœʀ, pʀɔf]	teacher
un **professeur des écoles**	elementary school teacher

Homme ou femme?

For *most nouns designating occupation*, there exist both a *masculine form* and a *feminine form*.

un vendeur	une vendeuse
un acteur	une actrice
un infirmier	une infirmière
un secrétaire	une secrétaire

In addition, for some professions there exists only one (usually masculine) form: **un écrivain, un ingénieur, un maire, un professeur**.

Numerous professions previously open only to men are now practiced by women as well, and over time (and by law) these nouns have acquired a feminine form, which, however, has not become firmly established in all cases. Examples: **une avocate, une juge, une metteuse en scène, une ministre, une députée**.

---

un,e **éducateur, -trice** [edykatœʀ, tʀis]	educator
un,e **travailleur, -euse social,e** [tʀavajœʀ, øz sɔsjal]	social worker

le **commerce** [kɔmɛʀs]	commerce, trade
Le **petit commerce** a du mal à subsister.	It is hard for small shopkeepers to stay in business.
un,e **représentant,e** [ʀəpʀesãtã, ãt]	(sales) representative
un,e **commerçant,e** [kɔmɛʀsã, ãt]	merchant, tradesman, shopkeeper
un,e **marchand,e** [maʀʃã, ãd]	dealer, shopkeeper; merchant
un **marchand de glaces**	ice cream vendor
un,e **vendeur, -euse** [vãdœʀ, øz]	salesman, saleswoman
Elle a trouvé une **place de vendeuse** dans un grand magasin.	She found a job as a saleswoman in a department store.
un,e **boulanger, -ère** [bulãʒe, ɛʀ]	baker

un,e **pâtissier, -ière** [patisje, jɛʀ]	pastry chef
un,e **boucher, ère** [buʃe, ɛʀ]	butcher
un,e **charcutier, -ière** [ʃaʀkytje, jɛʀ]	pork butcher
un,e **bijoutier, -ière** [biʒutje, jɛʀ]	jeweler
un,e **libraire** [libʀɛʀ]	book dealer
un,e **pharmacien,ne** [faʀmasjɛ̃, jɛn]	pharmacist
un,e **opticien,ne** [ɔptisjɛ̃, jɛn]	optician

un,e **cuisinier, -ière** [kɥizinje, jɛʀ]	cook
un,e **serveur, -euse** [sɛʀvœʀ, øz]	server; waiter, waitress
un **garçon** [gaʀsɔ̃]	waiter
Garçon, l'addition, s'il vous plaît!	Waiter, the check, please!

la **médecine** [med(ə)sin]	medicine
la **médecine du travail**	industrial medicine
les **professions médicales** [pʀɔfɛsjɔ̃medikal]	medical professions
un **médecin** [med(ə)sɛ̃]	doctor, physician
Martine est médecin à Paris.	Martine is a doctor in Paris.
un,e **généraliste** [ʒeneʀalist]	general practitioner
un,e **chirurgien,ne** [ʃiʀyʀʒjɛ̃, jɛn]	surgeon
un,e **infirmier, -ière** [ɛ̃fiʀmje, jɛʀ]	hospital attendant, nurse
un,e **dentiste** [dɑ̃tist]	dentist

le **bâtiment** [batimɑ̃]	construction, building (industry)
Le **secteur du bâtiment** est en crise.	The building industry is in crisis.
un,e **architecte** [aʀʃitɛkt]	architect
un **ingénieur** [ɛ̃ʒenjœʀ]	engineer
un,e **artisan,e** [aʀtizɑ̃, an]	artisan, craftsman
un,e **peintre** [pɛ̃tʀ]	painter
un **peintre en bâtiment(s)**	house painter
un,e **électricien, -ienne** [elɛktʀisjɛ̃, jɛn]	electrician

l'**informatique** f [ɛ̃fɔʀmatik]	information technology; computer science
un,e **programmeur, -euse** [pʀɔgʀamœʀ, øz]	programmer
un,e **électronicien,ne** [elɛktʀɔnisjɛ̃, jɛn]	electronics engineer
un,e **technicien,ne** [tɛknisjɛ̃, jɛn]	technician
une **technicienne en électronique**	electronics technician

les **transports en commun** m [trãspɔrãkɔmɛ̃]	public transportation
Il y a une grève des **transports en commun.**	There's a public transit strike.
un **chauffeur** [ʃofœr]	driver, chauffeur
un chauffeur de taxi	taxi driver
un,e **conducteur, -trice** [kɔ̃dyktœr, tris]	driver, conductor
un **conducteur de bus**	bus driver
un,e **pilote** [pilɔt]	pilot
un **pilote de ligne**	airline pilot
une **hôtesse de l'air** [otɛsdəlɛr]	stewardess, flight attendant
un **steward** [stiwart]	steward, flight attendant

l'**agriculture** f [agrikyltyr]	agriculture
un,e **agriculteur, -trice** [agrikyltœr, tris]	farmer, agriculturist
un,e **cultivateur, -trice** [kyltivatœr, tris]	farmer, grower, cultivator
un,e **paysan,ne** [peizã, an]	peasant, farmer
un,e **ouvrier, -ière (agricole)** [uvrije, ijɛr (agrikɔl)]	agricultural worker, farm worker
un,e **jardinier, -ière** [ʒardinje, jɛr]	gardener

les **services** m [sɛrvis]	services
Le prix des services augmente sans arrêt.	The prices of services are increasing constantly.
un,e **garagiste** [garaʒist]	garage owner, auto mechanic
un,e **mécanicien,ne** [mekanisjɛ̃, jɛn]	mechanic
un,e **gardien,ne** [gardjɛ̃, jɛn]	guard
un **gardien de musée**	museum guard
une **femme de ménage** [famdəmenaʒ]	cleaning woman

la **justice** [ʒystis]	justice; courts of justice, law
porter une affaire devant la justice	take a case to court
un,e **juge** [ʒyʒ]	judge
un **juge d'instruction** [ʒyʒdɛ̃stryksjɔ̃]	examining magistrate
un **procureur** [prɔkyrœr]	prosecuting attorney, (public) prosecutor
un,e **avocat,e** [avɔka, at]	attorney, lawyer

les **finances** f [finãs]	finance

le **monde des finances**	financial world
Mes finances sont au plus bas.	My funds are low.
un,e **banquier, -ière** [bãkje, jɛʀ]	banker
un,e **caissier, -ière** [kɛsje, jɛʀ]	cashier, teller

la **politique** [pɔlitik]	politics
Elle s'est lancée dans la politique.	She has tried her luck in politics.
un **homme**/une **femme politique**	politician
[ɔm/fampɔlitik]	
un,e **politicien,ne** *péj* [pɔlitisjɛ̃, jɛn]	politician
un,e **ministre** [ministʀ]	minister
un,e **député,e** [depyte]	deputy (in parliament)
un député socialiste	socialist deputy
un **maire** [mɛʀ]	mayor
passer devant M./Mme le maire	go before the mayor (get married)

l'**armée** *f* [aʀme]	army
s'engager dans l'armée	volunteer for the army
un **militaire** [militɛʀ]	soldier, military man
un,e **soldat,e** [sɔlda, at]	soldier
un **général** [ʒeneʀal]	general

la **marine** [maʀin]	navy
la **marine marchande**	merchant marine
un **marin** [maʀɛ̃]	sailor
un **marin-pêcheur**	professional fisherman
un **capitaine** [kapitɛn]	captain

le **journalisme** [ʒuʀnalism]	journalism
un,e **journaliste** [ʒuʀnalist]	journalist
un **journaliste à la radio/télévision**	radio/TV journalist
un,e **reporter** [ʀ(ə)pɔʀtɛʀ/øʀ]	reporter
un,e **rédacteur, -trice**	editor
[ʀedaktœʀ, tʀis]	
un,e **rédacteur, -trice en chef**	editor-in-chief
un,e **photographe** [fɔtɔgʀaf]	photographer
un **photographe de presse**	press photographer

le **tourisme** [tuʀism]	tourism
Notre région vit du tourisme.	Our region lives off tourism.
un,e **guide** [gid]	travel guide
Suivez le guide.	Follow the guide.
un,e **interprète** [ɛ̃tɛʀpʀɛt]	interpreter

le **spectacle** [spɛktakl] — performance, show, play
  donner un spectacle — put on a play
un,e **acteur, -trice** [aktœʀ, tʀis] — actor, actress
un,e **musicien,ne** [myzisjɛ̃, jɛn] — musician
un,e **artiste** [aʀtist] — artist; performer, player
un **auteur** [otœʀ] — author
  L'auteur de la pièce a été applaudi longuement. — The author of the play was applauded for a long while.
un **écrivain** [ekʀivɛ̃] — writer

---

la **population active** [pɔpylasjɔ̃aktiv] — working population
les **catégories socioprofessionnelles** f [kategɔʀisɔsjopʀɔfesjɔnɛl] — professional categories
la **vie professionnelle** [vipʀɔfesjɔnɛl] — professional life
l'**activité professionnelle** f [aktivitepʀɔfesjɔnɛl] — professional activity
Il est ... de profession. [pʀɔfesjɔ̃] — He's ... by profession.
  Il est danseur de profession. — He's a dancer by profession.

---

le **secteur primaire** [sɛktœʀpʀimɛʀ] — primary sector (agriculture, fishing, mining)
le **secteur secondaire** [sɛktœʀsəgɔ̃dɛʀ] — secondary sector (industry)
le **secteur tertiaire** [sɛktœʀtɛʀsjɛʀ] — tertiary sector (services sector)
(travailler) à son compte [asɔ̃kɔ̃t] — (be) independent
  Il fait des économies pour s'**installer à son compte.** — He's saving so that he can set up on his own.
les **professions libérales** f [pʀɔfesjɔ̃libeʀal] — the independent (or liberal) professions

---

se perfectionner [s(ə)pɛʀfɛksjɔne] — improve oneself
le **perfectionnement** [pɛʀfɛksjɔnmɑ̃] — improvement
  faire un stage de perfectionnement — take a continuing education course
se spécialiser [səspesjalize] — specialize
  Je me suis spécialisé en pédiatrie. — I specialized in pediatrics.
un,e **spécialiste** [spesjalist] — specialist
se qualifier [s(ə)kalifje] — become qualified
qualifié,e [kalifje] — qualified
  On recherche des **employés qualifiés** pour ce travail. — Qualified employees are wanted for this job.
expérimenté,e [ɛkspeʀimɑ̃te] — experienced

On demande un vendeur expérimenté.	An experienced salesman is wanted.
la **qualification** [kalifikasjɔ̃]	qualification
se recycler [sǝR(ǝ)sikle]	undergo retraining, get further training
C'est un métier où on doit se recycler régulièrement.	This is a career in which you have to acquire additional training regularly.
le **recyclage** [R(ǝ)siklaʒ]	retraining, further training

l'**ANPE (Agence nationale pour l'emploi)** f [aɛnpeǝ]	national employment office
être inscrit,e à l'ANPE	be registered with the ANPE
l'**orientation professionnelle** f [ɔRjɑ̃tasjɔ̃pRɔfɛsjɔnɛl]	career counseling
un,e **employeur, -euse** [ɑ̃plwajœR, jøz]	employer
un,e **candidat,e** [kɑ̃dida, at]	applicant, candidate
postuler à/pour [pɔstyle]	apply for
Elle a postulé pour un emploi de puéricultrice.	She's applied for a job as a pediatric nurse.
poser sa candidature [pozesakɑ̃didatyR]	put in one's application
un **curriculum vitae** (un **CV**) [kyRikulɔmvite (seve)]	résumé, curriculum vitae
Prière de joindre à votre candidature un **CV détaillé**.	Please attach a detailed résumé to your application.
les **débouchés** m [debuʃe]	job openings
un secteur où il n'y a pas beaucoup de débouchés	a field in which there are not many openings

occuper un poste/une fonction [ɔkypeɛ̃pɔst/ynfɔ̃ksjɔ̃]	occupy a position
occuper un poste à responsabilité	occupy a responsible position
faire carrière [fɛRkaRjɛR]	make a career
Il a fait carrière dans l'automobile.	He's made a career in the automobile industry.
une **promotion** [pRɔmosjɔ̃]	promotion

un **maçon** [masɔ̃]	mason
un **plombier** [plɔ̃bje]	plumber
un,e **menuisier, -ière** [mǝnɥizje, jɛR]	carpenter
un **couvreur** [kuvRœR]	roofer

l'**hôtellerie** f [ɔ/otɛlRi]	hotel trade

L'hôtellerie profite de l'essor du tourisme.	The hotel trade is profiting from the increase in tourism.
un,e **hôtelier, -ière** [ɔ/otəlje, jɛʀ]	hotel owner, hotelier
la **restauration** [ʀɛstɔʀasjɔ̃]	restaurant trade
La **restauration rapide** est en plein boom.	Fast-food restaurants are booming.
un,e **restaurateur, -trice** [ʀɛstɔʀatœʀ, tʀis]	restaurateur
un,e **gérant,e** [ʒeʀɑ̃, ɑ̃t]	manager

un,e **vétérinaire** [veteʀinɛʀ]	veterinarian
un,e **kinésithérapeute**; un,e **kiné** *fam* [kine(ziteʀapøt)]	physical therapist
un,e **esthéticien, -ne** [ɛstetisjɛ̃, ɛn]	cosmetician

9.4 Work and Working Conditions

travailler [tʀavaje]	work
Il travaille dur pour gagner sa vie.	He works hard to earn his living.
travailler à plein temps/à temps complet	work full-time
travailler à mi-temps	work half-time
travailler à temps partiel	work part-time
travailler à la chaîne	work on an assembly line
travailler à domicile	work at home
le **travail** [tʀavaj]	work
le **travail au noir**	work done on the side
le **temps de travail**	working hours
un **contrat de travail**	employment contract
Chaque année, de nombreux jeunes arrivent sur le **marché du travail**.	Every year many young people enter the job market.
un,e **travailleur, -euse** [tʀavajœʀ, jøz]	worker
un travailleur immigré	foreign worker; migratory worker
le **personnel** [pɛʀsɔnel]	personnel

l'**emploi** *m* [ɑ̃plwa]	employment
être sans emploi	be unemployed
un,e **employé,e** [ɑ̃plwaje]	employee
employer [ɑ̃plwaje]	employ
engager [ɑ̃gaʒe]	hire, engage
Il a été engagé **comme chauffeur**.	He was hired as a driver.

un **poste (de travail)** [pɔst]	position
un **boulot** fam [bulo]	job
vivre de **petits boulots**	make a living doing odd jobs
une **activité** [aktivite]	activity, employment
Il n'a pas d'activité régulière.	He has no regular employment.
actif, -ive [aktif, iv]	employed, engaged in work
un **métier** [metje]	trade; business; calling; craft; profession
Elle exerce le **métier de journaliste**.	She is in the journalistic profession.
un **job** fam [dʒɔb]	job
J'ai trouvé un job pour l'été.	I have found a summer job.

....

gagner [gaɲe]	earn
gagner de l'argent	earn money
gagner sa vie	earn one's living
un **salaire** [salɛR]	salary
demander une **augmentation de salaire**	ask for an increase in salary
un,e **salarié,e** [salaRje]	salaried employee
une **heure supplémentaire**; une **heure sup** fam [œRsyp(lemãtɛR)]	overtime

....

produire [pRɔdɥiR]	produce, make
la **production** [pRɔdyksjɔ̃]	production
un **produit** [pRɔdɥi]	product
importer [ɛ̃pɔRte]	import
l'**importation** f [ɛ̃pɔRtasjɔ̃]	importing, import
exporter [ɛkspɔRte]	export
l'**exportation** f [ɛkspɔRtasjɔ̃]	exporting, export
l'**import-export** m [ɛ̃pɔRɛkspɔR]	import-export
la **vente** [vãt]	sales

....

une **entreprise** [ãtRəpRiz]	enterprise, firm, concern
une **société** [sɔsjete]	company
une **affaire** [afɛR]	business
monter une affaire d'import-export	build up an import-export business
le **siège social** [sjɛʒsɔsjal]	company headquarters

....

un **jour ouvrable** [ʒuRuvRabl]	workday, working day
un **jour férié** [ʒuRfeRje]	holiday
le **congé** [kɔ̃ʒe]	leave; vacation; discharge, dismissal
Je vais prendre 3 jours de congé.	I'm going to take three days off.
donner congé à qn	give s.o. time off; give s.o. notice
les **congés payés**	paid leave

faire le pont [fɛʀl(ə)põ]
On part en Normandie pendant le pont du 1ᵉʳ mai.

take a long weekend
We're going to Normandy during the long weekend of May 1ˢᵗ.

une **offre d'emploi** [ɔfʀdãplwa]
regarder les offres d'emploi dans le journal
une **demande d'emploi** [dəmãddãplwa]
un,e **demandeur, -euse d'emploi** [dəmãdœʀ, øzdãplwa]
Le nombre des demandeurs d'emploi a encore augmenté.
créer (des emplois) [kʀee]
supprimer (des emplois) [sypʀime]
La robotisation supprime des emplois.

vacancy, vacant position
look at the vacancies in the newspaper
job wanted, want ad

job seeker

The number of persons seeking jobs has risen once more.
create (jobs)
eliminate (jobs)

Full automation leads to elimination of jobs.

le **chômage** [ʃomaʒ]
l'**accroissement du taux de chômage**
un,e **chômeur, -euse** [ʃomœʀ, øz]
un **chômeur de longue durée**

un **chômeur en fin de droits**

le **chômage partiel** [ʃomaʒpaʀsjɛl]
l'**allocation (de) chômage** f [alɔkasjõ(d(ə))ʃomaʒ]
toucher une allocation chômage
le **licenciement** [lisãsimã]
licencier [lisãsje]
Il a peur de **se faire licencier**.
renvoyer [ʀãvwaje]

unemployment
increase in the number of unemployed persons
unemployed person
person who is unemployed for a long time

recipient of unemployment benefits
short-time work
unemployment pay

receive unemployment pay
layoff
lay off
He's afraid of being laid off.
dismiss, lay off

l'**économie** f [ekɔnɔmi]
économique [ekɔnɔmik]
la **crise économique**
économiser [ekɔnɔmize]
une **difficulté** [difikylte]
faire face aux difficultés
responsable de [ʀɛspõsabl]
Il est responsable de la production.
une **organisation** [ɔʀganizasjõ]

economy
economic
economic crisis
economize
difficulty
face the difficulties
responsible for
He is responsible for production.
organization

revendiquer [ʀ(ə)vɑ̃dike]
Les ouvriers revendiquent une augmentation de salaire.
lay claim to, demand
The workers are demanding a wage increase.

une **revendication** [ʀ(ə)vɑ̃dikasjɔ̃]
des **revendications salariales**
claim, demand
demands for higher wages, wage claims

une **manifestation**; une **manif** *fam* [manif(ɛstasjɔ̃)]
une **manifestation silencieuse**
demonstration

silent demonstration

une **grève** [gʀɛv]
faire grève
strike
go on strike

un,e **gréviste** [gʀevist]
striker

mener une action [m(ə)neynaksjɔ̃]
take militant action

le **partage du travail** [paʀtaʒdytʀavaj]
job sharing

la **réduction du temps de travail** [ʀedyksjɔ̃dytɑ̃d(ə)tʀavaj]
reduction of working hours

l'**horaire à la carte** *m* [ɔʀɛʀalakaʀt]
flextime

l'**intérim** *m* [ɛ̃teʀim]
une **agence d'intérim**
temporary work
a temp agency

faire les trois huit [fɛʀletʀwa'ɥit]
work three 8-hour shifts (around the clock)

embaucher [ɑ̃boʃe]
Ils embauchent du personnel supplémentaire.
hire
They're hiring additional personnel.

l'**embauche** *f* [ɑ̃boʃ]
hiring, taking on

un **CDD (contrat à durée déterminée)** [sedede]
employment contract with a termination date

un **CDI (contrat à durée indéterminée)** [sedei]
open-ended employment contract

le **traitement** [tʀɛtmɑ̃]
Le traitement des fonctionnaires sera augmenté en janvier.
salary, pay
The salaries of civil servants will be increased in January.

les **revenus** *m* [ʀ(ə)vəny/ʀəv(ə)ny]
income

une **indemnité** [ɛ̃dɛmnite]
toucher une **indemnité de licenciement**
severance pay, severance package
receive severance pay

une **prime** [pʀim]
avoir droit à une **prime de fin d'année**
bonus
have the right to a year-end bonus

les **ressources** *f* [ʀ(ə)suʀs]
(financial) means, resources

le **niveau de vie** [nivod(ə)vi]
standard of living

le **pouvoir d'achat** [puvwaʀdaʃa]
Le pouvoir d'achat des ménages a baissé.
purchasing power
The purchasing power of households has declined.

les **charges annexes (au salaire)** f [ʃaʁʒanɛks] incidental labor costs

les **prestations sociales** f [pʁɛstasjɔ̃sɔsjal] fringe benefits

---

la **main-d'œuvre** [mɛ̃dœvʁ] manpower
  employer de la main-d'œuvre bon marché employ cheap labor
un **travail manuel** [tʁavajmanɥɛl] manual labor
l'**automation**/l'**automatisation** f [ɔtɔmasjɔ̃/ɔtɔmatizasjɔ̃] automation
la **rationalisation** [ʁasjɔnalizasjɔ̃] restructuring, increasing efficiency
rationaliser [ʁasjɔnalize] restructure, make more efficient
  Les entreprises qui ne rationalisent pas leur production sont condamnées à disparaître. The firms that don't streamline their production will inevitably disappear from the market.
la **délocalisation** f [delɔkalizasjɔ̃] relocation (to a foreign country)
délocaliser [delɔkalize] relocate (to a foreign country)
  De nombreuses firmes délocalisent leurs usines. Many firms are moving their plants to a foreign country.
la **mondialisation** [mɔ̃djalizasjɔ̃] globalization

---

une **expansion** [ɛkspɑ̃sjɔ̃] expansion
  l'**expansion économique** economic expansion
la **faillite** [fajit] failure, bankruptcy
  faire faillite go bankrupt, fail
un **dépôt de bilan** [depodbilɑ̃] declaration of bankruptcy
déposer son bilan [depozesɔ̃bilɑ̃] declare bankruptcy

---

les **partenaires sociaux** m [paʁtənɛʁsɔsjo] employers and employees (the two sides of industry)
  Le dialogue a repris entre les partenaires sociaux. The dialogue between management and labor was resumed.
un **conflit social** [kɔ̃flisɔsjal] social conflict
contester [kɔ̃tɛste] protest
une **contestation** [kɔ̃tɛstasjɔ̃] protest
  Ils ont tout accepté sans contestation. They have accepted everything without protest.
lutter [lyte] fight, struggle
  lutter pour l'amélioration des conditions de travail fight for improvement of working conditions
la **lutte** [lyt] fight, struggle
une **consultation de la base** [kɔ̃syltasjɔ̃d(ə)labaz] strike ballot

un **préavis de grève** [pʀeavid(ə)gʀɛv]	announcement of a strike
un **lock-out** [lɔkaut]	lockout
le **SMIC (salaire minimum inter-professionnel de croissance)** [smik]	minimum wage
gagner le SMIC	earn the minimum wage
être payé,e au SMIC	be paid the minimum wage

une **réunion** [ʀeynɔ̃]	meeting, conference, session
se **réunir** [s(ə)ʀeyniʀ]	meet, hold a conference
négocier [negɔsje]	negotiate
Les syndicats ont négocié avec le patronat une augmentation de salaire.	The unions have negotiated a wage increase with the employers.
une **négociation** [negɔsjasjɔ̃]	negotiation
un **syndicat** [sɛ̃dika]	union, association
syndical,e [sɛ̃dikal]	union, union-related
un,e **délégué,e syndical,e**	union representative
un,e **patron,ne** [patʀɔ̃, ɔn]	employer
patronal,e [patʀɔnal]	employer, employer-related
un **accord** [akɔʀ]	agreement
Un accord a été signé entre le patronat et les syndicats.	An agreement between the employers and the unions was signed.
un **accord sur les salaires** [akɔʀsyʀlesalɛʀ]	wage agreement, industrial agreement
un,e **délégué,e du personnel** [delegedypɛʀsɔnɛl]	employees' representative
une **convention collective** [kɔ̃vɑ̃sjɔ̃kɔlɛktiv]	collective wage contract

French Word	English Equivalent	False Friend	French Equivalent
une scie	saw	ski	un ski
scier	saw	ski, go skiing	faire du ski

10.1 Leisure Time, Hobbies, and Games

les **loisirs** *m* [lwaziʀ]
  Comment est-ce que tu **occupes
  tes loisirs** ?
un **hobby** ['ɔbi]
se distraire [s(ə)distʀɛʀ]
une **distraction** [distʀaksjɔ̃]
passer son temps à faire qc
  [pasesɔ̃tɑ̃afɛʀ]
  Il passe son temps à bouquiner.
un **passe-temps** [pastɑ̃]
avoir envie de [avwʀɑ̃vi]
  Tu as envie d'aller au cinéma ?

leisure time, spare time
  What do you do in your spare
  time?
hobby
amuse oneself, relax
amusement, recreation
spend one's time doing s.th.

  He spends his time reading.
pastime
want to
  Do you want to go to the
  movies?

actif, -ive [aktif, iv]
  Mes grands-parents sont encore
  très actifs pour leur âge.
une **activité** [aktivite]
participer à qc [paʀtisipe]
  participer à un stage de judo

active
  My grandparents are still quite
  active for their age.
activity
participate in s.th.
  participate in a judo course

lire [liʀ]
la **lecture** [lɛktyʀ]
  Elle est **plongée** dans sa lecture.
les **mots croisés** *m* [mokʀwaze]
  faire des mots croisés

read
reading
  She's immersed in her reading.
crossword puzzle
  do crossword puzzles

un **jeu** [ʒø]
jouer à (un jeu) [ʒwe]

game
play (a game)

---

i **jouer à/de**

Note the difference between:
jouer à (un jeu)
Ils jouent au foot/aux cartes/aux échecs/
aux Indiens.
jouer de/d' (un instrument)
Elles jouent du piano/de la flûte/de
l'harmonica.

*They play soccer/cards/chess/cowboys
and Indians.*

*They play the piano/the flute/the
harmonica.*

In addition to **jouer de, faire de** can also be used with *instruments.* Examples:
Tu joues de l'accordéon ?
Do you play the accordion?
Il fait du violon ?
Does he play the violin?

– **Non, je fais de la clarinette.**
– No, I play the clarinet.
– **Non, il joue du violoncelle.**
– No, he plays the cello.

les **cartes** f [kaʀt]	cards
les **échecs** m [eʃɛk]	chess
un **jeu de société** [ʒød(ə)sɔsjete]	party game, parlor game
un **puzzle** [pœzl/pœzœl]	puzzle
un puzzle de 5000 pièces	a 5,000-piece puzzle

le **jeu de boules** f [ʒød(ə)bul]	bowls, lawn bowling
la **pétanque** [petãk]	game of pétanque
On fait une partie de pétanque ?	Shall we play a round of pétanque?

bricoler [bʀikɔle]	do crafts, make things with one's hands
le **bricolage** [bʀikɔlaʒ]	fixing things
un **magasin de bricolage**	hardware store; a home improvement center
un,e **bricoleur, -euse** [bʀikɔlœʀ, øz]	craftsperson, hobbyist; home improvement enthusiast
coller [kɔle]	glue
la **colle** [kɔl]	glue, paste, mucilage
la **colle à bois**	wood glue
fabriquer [fabʀike]	make, fabricate
Il a fabriqué ses meubles lui-même.	He made his furniture himself.
la **poterie** [pɔtʀi]	pottery

ℹ️ Making things with one's hands

Engaging in various handicrafts often entails use of the expression **faire de** + *type of activity*.

Nous faisons de la poterie/de la peinture sur soie. *We make pottery/paint on silk.*

Il fait du tricot/crochet. *He knits/crochets.*

---

une **photo** [fɔto]	photo
faire/prendre une photo	take a photo
prendre qn/qc en photo	photograph s.o./s.th.
un **appareil photo** [apaʀɛjfɔto]	camera
une **diapositive**; une **diapo** *fam* [djapo(zitiv)]	slide
projeter des diapos	show slides

une **caméra** [kameʀa]	(TV/video) camera
la **vidéo** [video]	video
une **cassette vidéo**	videocassette
filmer [filme]	film
un **film** [film]	film

la **musique** [myzik]	music

Tu fais de la musique ?	Do you play/make music?
le **rythme** [ʀitm]	rhythm
Elle a le rythme dans le sang.	She's got rhythm in her blood.
jouer de qc [ʒwe]	play s.th.

 For information on the difference between **jouer à** and **jouer de**, see p. 185.

danser [dɑ̃se]	dance
la **danse** [dɑ̃s]	dance
la **peinture** [pɛ̃tyʀ]	painting
faire de la peinture	paint
peindre [pɛ̃dʀ]	paint
un **peintre** [pɛ̃tʀ]	painter
un **peintre du dimanche**	Sunday painter
dessiner [desine]	draw
un **jardin** [ʒaʀdɛ̃]	garden
un **jardin potager**	vegetable garden
jardiner [ʒaʀdine]	do gardening, (work in the) garden
le **jardinage** [ʒaʀdinaʒ]	gardening
une **plante** [plɑ̃t]	plant
planter [plɑ̃te]	plant, to
planter des oignons de tulipes	plant tulip bulbs
cultiver [kyltive]	cultivate, grow
Il cultive des légumes dans son jardin.	He grows vegetables in his garden.
une **fleur** [flœʀ]	flower
l'**herbe** f [ɛʀb]	grass
couper l'herbe sous le pied de qn *loc*	take the wind out of s.o.'s sails
les **mauvaises herbes**	weeds
une **promenade** [pʀɔm(ə)nad]	walk
une **promenade à/en vélo**	bike ride
se promener [s(ə)pʀɔm(ə)ne]	go for a walk
Viens, on va se promener **au grand air.**	Come on, we're going for a walk out in the fresh air.
chasser [ʃase]	hunt
la **chasse** [ʃas]	hunting, hunt
aller* à la chasse	go hunting, hunt
un **fusil de chasse**	hunting rifle
un,e **chasseur, -euse** [ʃasœʀ, øz]	hunter, huntress
pêcher [pɛʃe]	fish
la **pêche (à la ligne)** [pɛʃalaliɲ]	angling, fishing

manger le **produit de sa pêche**	eat the catch
un,e **pêcheur, -euse** [pɛʃœʀ, øz]	fisherman, fisherwoman
un **pêcheur à la ligne**	angler

se détendre [s(ə)detɑ̃dʀ]	relax
Il se détend en écoutant de la musique.	He relaxes by listening to music.
la **détente** [detɑ̃t]	relaxation
se relaxer [səʀ(ə)lakse]	relax
un **divertissement** [divɛʀtismɑ̃]	entertainment, amusement

une **collection** [kɔlɛksjɔ̃]	collection
une **collection de timbres**	stamp collection
collectionner [kɔlɛksjɔne]	collect
un,e **collectionneur, -euse** [kɔlɛksjɔnœʀ, øz]	collector
un **album** [albɔm]	album

une **balade** *fam* [balad]	walk
se balader *fam* [s(ə)balade]	go walking
aller se balader dans la forêt	go walking in the woods
une **randonnée** [ʀɑ̃dɔne]	hike
un,e **randonneur, -euse** [ʀɑ̃dɔnœʀ, øz]	hiker
une **excursion** [ɛkskyʀsjɔ̃]	excursion, outing
le **cyclotourisme** [sikloturism]	bike touring

10.2 Sports

le **sport** [spɔʀ]	sport(s)
faire du sport	engage in sports
(un,e) **sportif, -ive** *n; adj* [spɔʀtif, iv]	sportsman, athlete; sporting, athletic
une **association sportive**	a sports association
une **manifestation sportive**	a sports event
une **rencontre sportive**	a sports competition

s'entraîner [sɑ̃tʀɛne]	train
l'**entraînement** *m* [ɑ̃tʀɛnmɑ̃]	training
un,e **entraîneur, -euse** [ɑ̃tʀɛnœʀ, øz]	trainer
être en forme [ɛtʀɑ̃fɔrm]	be in good shape, be fit
Elle fait du sport pour rester en forme.	He does sports to stay in shape.
(être) fort,e [fɔʀ, fɔʀt]	(be) strong

la **force** [fɔʀs]
  La force de cet athlète est impressionnante.
  transpirer [tʀɑ̃spiʀe]

strength
  That athlete's strength is impressive.
  sweat, perspire

---

un **club** [klœb]
  faire partie d'un **club de foot**
une **équipe** [ekip]
un **match** [matʃ]
  Le match oppose deux équipes de même niveau.
  un **match aller/retour**
un **tournoi** [tuʀnwa]
  disputer un tournoi

club
  belong to a soccer club
team
game, match
  Two equally strong teams are facing each other in the match.
  initial match/return match
tournament
  dispute a tournament

---

un **stade** [stad]
  aller au stade
un **gymnase** [ʒymnaz]
un **terrain de sport** [teʀɛ̃d(ə)spɔʀ]

stadium
  go to the stadium
gymnasium, gym
playing field

---

une **course** [kuʀs]
le **départ** [depaʀ]
  donner le départ d'une course

l'**arrivée** f [aʀive]
  franchir la ligne d'arrivée

race, run
start, starting line
  give/fire the starting shot for a race
goal, finish line
  cross the finish line

---

un **résultat** [ʀezylta]
battre [batʀ]
  Bordeaux a battu Monaco 2 à 1.
gagner (qc/contre qn) [gaɲe]
perdre (qc/contre qn) [pɛʀdʀ]
  J'ai perdu mon dernier match de tennis.
  Strasbourg va certainement perdre contre Lyon.
(un,e) **gagnant,e** n; adj [gaɲɑ̃, ɑ̃t]

  Les deux équipes gagnantes se retrouveront en finale.
(un,e) **perdant,e** n; adj [pɛʀdɑ̃, ɑ̃t]

result, outcome
beat
  Bordeaux beat Monaco 2 to 1.
win (s.th./against s.o.)
lose (s.th./against s.o.)
  I lost my last tennis match.
  Strasbourg will certainly lose against Lyon.
winner, victor; winning, victorious
  The two winning teams will meet each other in the final.
loser; losing

---

un,e **champion,ne** [ʃɑ̃pjɔ̃, jɔn]
un **championnat** [ʃɑ̃pjɔna]

champion
championship

le **championnat du monde** de natation	world championship in swimming
une **compétition** [kɔ̃petisjɔ̃]	competition
une **compétition par équipes**	team competition
une **compétition individuelle**	individual competition
participer à une compétition	participate in a competition
un **exploit** [ɛksplwa]	achievement, feat, exploit
un **record** [ʀ(ə)kɔʀ]	record
détenir un record	hold a record
battre un record	break a record
améliorer un record	improve a record

un,e **amateur, -trice** [amatœʀ, tʀis]	amateur
Ils font du cyclisme, mais **en amateurs**.	They are into biking, but as amateurs.
un,e **professionnel,le**; un,e pro *fam* [pʀɔfɛsjɔnɛl, pʀo]	professional, pro
un,e **joueur, -euse** [ʒwœʀ, øz]	player
un joueur de tennis professionnel	professional tennis player

un **ballon** [balɔ̃]	ball
un **ballon de foot(ball)**	soccer ball
le **foot(ball)** [fut(bol)]	soccer ball
un **but** [by(t)]	goal
le **gardien de but**	goalkeeper
marquer un but	make a goal
le **rugby** [ʀygbi]	rugby
le **volley-ball**; le **volley** *fam* [vɔlɛ(bol)]	volleyball
le **basket-ball**; le **basket** *fam* [baskɛt(bol)]	basketball

une **balle** [bal]	ball
une **balle de tennis**	tennis ball
jouer au tennis [ʒweotenis]	play tennis
une **raquette** [ʀakɛt]	(tennis) racquet
le **ping-pong** [piŋpɔ̃g]	Ping-Pong, table tennis
le **filet** [filɛ]	net
La balle a atterri dans le filet.	The ball landed in the net.
le **golf** [gɔlf]	golf

un **vélo** [velo]	bike
faire du vélo	ride a bike
une **bicyclette** [bisiklɛt]	bicycle
un **VTT (vélo tout terrain)** [vetete]	mountain bike
le **cyclisme** [siklism]	biking, cycling

un,e **cycliste** [siklist]	biker, cyclist
pédaler [pedale]	pedal
un **tour** [tuʀ]	tour, trip

---

le/la tour

Note the difference between:

le tour	*tour, trip; circuit*
le Tour de France	*annual bike race around France*
un tour en voiture	*take a (short) car trip*
faire le tour du monde	*tour the world, take a world tour*
la tour	*tower, tall building*
la Tour Eiffel	*Eiffel Tower*
la tour de contrôle	*control tower*

---

une **étape** [etap]	stage
un **maillot** [majo]	jersey
le maillot jaune	the yellow jersey

les **patins à roulettes** m [patɛ̃aʀulɛt]	roller skates
faire du patin à roulettes	go roller-skating, roller-skate
une **planche à roulettes** [plɑ̃ʃaʀulɛt]	skateboard
un **skateboard** [skɛtbɔʀd]	skateboard

l'**athlétisme** m [atletism]	athletics; track and field events
courir [kuʀiʀ]	run
Il n'a pas couru assez vite.	He didn't run fast enough.
la **course (à pied)** [kuʀs(apje)]	running, run
Elle a abandonné après 15 kilomètres de course.	She gave up after running 15 kilometers.
sauter [sote]	jump
le **saut** [so]	jump
le **saut en longueur**	broad jump, long jump
le **saut en hauteur**	high jump
le **saut à la perche**	pole vault
lancer [lɑ̃se]	throw
lancer une balle	throw a ball

la **gymnastique**; la **gym** fam [ʒim(nastik)]	gymnastics
faire de la gymnastique	do gymnastics
un,e **gymnaste** [ʒimnast]	gymnast

les **sports d'hiver** m [spɔʀdivɛʀ]	winter sports
la **neige** [nɛʒ]	snow

le **ski** [ski]	ski
faire du ski	go skiing
skier [skje]	ski
un,e **skieur, -euse** [skjœʀ, skjøz]	skier
une **piste** [pist]	course
skier **hors-piste**	ski off-course

les **sports nautiques** *m* [spɔʀnotik]	water sports
la **natation** [natasjɔ̃]	swimming
nager [naʒe]	swim
nager **en** piscine/**dans** la mer	swim in a pool/in the ocean
un,e **nageur, -euse** [naʒœʀ, øz]	swimmer

la **voile** [vwal]	sail
faire de la voile	go sailing, sail
un **bateau** [bato]	boat
un **bateau à voiles**	sailboat
la **planche à voile** [plɑ̃ʃavwal]	windsurfing board
le **surf** [sœʀf]	surfing

pratiquer (une discipline sportive) [pʀatike]	practice (a sport)
Simon pratique la natation.	Simon swims/is a swimmer.
un,e **athlète** [atlɛt]	athlete
athlétique [atletik]	athletic
un,e **sportif, -ive de haut niveau** [spɔʀtif/spɔʀtivdəonivo]	high-performance athlete, top competitor

un,e **adversaire** [advɛʀsɛʀ]	opponent
siffler [sifle]	hiss, make catcalls; whistle
un,e **arbitre** [aʀbitʀ]	umpire, referee
la **mi-temps** [mitɑ̃]	halftime
L'arbitre a sifflé la mi-temps.	The umpire blew the whistle for halftime.
une **prolongation** [pʀɔlɔ̃gasjɔ̃]	overtime
une **manche** [mɑ̃ʃ]	set *(tennis)*, run *(skiing)*
Il a remporté la première manche.	He won the first set/run.
un **jeu** [ʒø]	game *(tennis)*
un **supporter** [sypɔʀtɛʀ/œʀ]	supporter, fan

une **victoire** [viktwaʀ]	victory
remporter une victoire	win a victory
victorieux, -euse [viktɔʀjø, jøz]	victorious
vaincre [vɛ̃kʀ]	vanquish

Il a tout essayé pour vaincre son adversaire.	He tried everything possible to defeat his opponent.
un **vainqueur** [vɛ̃kœʀ]	victor, winner
sortir* vainqueur d'une épreuve	emerge as the winner of a contest
(faire) match nul [(fɛʀ)matʃnyl]	(play to a) tie
Les deux équipes ont fait match nul.	The two teams tied.
une **défaite** [defɛt]	defeat
une défaite cuisante	crushing defeat
la **revanche** [ʀ(ə)vɑ̃ʃ]	return match
prendre sa revanche	get even
tirer au sort [tiʀeosɔʀ]	toss a coin, draw lots
le **tirage au sort** [tiʀaʒosɔʀ]	toss, draw

un,e **sauteur, -euse** [sotœʀ, øz]	jumper
un sauteur en longueur/en hauteur	broad/high jumper
un **lanceur, -euse** [lɑ̃sœʀ, øz]	pitcher, thrower
une lanceuse de poids	shot-putter
le **poids** [pwa]	weight
le **disque** [disk]	discus
le **javelot** [ʒavlo]	javelin
le **marteau** [marto]	hammer
le **lancer** [lɑ̃se]	throw, shot
le lancer du poids/du disque	shot put(ting), discus throwing
le **jogging** [dʒɔgiŋ]	jogging
Il fait son jogging tous les matins.	He jogs every morning.
le **footing** [futiŋ]	running, jogging

une **coupe** [kup]	cup
la coupe du Monde	world championship cup
une **médaille** [medaj]	medal
une médaille d'or/d'argent/de bronze	gold/silver/bronze medal
les **Jeux Olympiques** m [ʒøzɔlɛ̃pik]	the Olympics/Olympic Games
un **titre** [titʀ]	title
C'est son deuxième titre olympique.	It's his second Olympic title.
un,e **participant,e** [paʀtisipɑ̃, ɑ̃t]	participant
un,e **favori,te** [favɔʀi, it]	favorite
Comme prévu, la favorite a gagné haut la main.	As predicted, the favorite won easily.
un **défi** [defi]	challenge
lancer un défi à qn	challenge s.o.

le **service** [sɛʀvis]	serve

perdre son service	lose one's serve
la **balle de match** [baldəmatʃ]	match point
mener [m(ə)ne]	lead
mener (par) 4 jeux à 2	lead 4 games to 2
le **jeu décisif** [ʒødesizif]	tiebreak
remporter le jeu décisif	win the tiebreak

le **ski alpin** [skialpɛ̃]	alpine skiing
la **descente** [desɑ̃t]	downhill (race)
un **remonte-pente** [ʀ(ə)mɔ̃tpɑ̃t]	T-bar (lift)
un **téléski** [teleski]	ski lift, T-bar
le **tire-fesses** *fam* [tiʀfɛs]	T-bar
un **télésiège** [telesjɛʒ]	chair lift
le **ski de fond** [skidfɔ̃]	cross-country skiing
le **saut à ski** [soaski]	ski jumping
le **patinage** [patinaʒ]	ice skating
le patinage artistique	figure skating
le patinage de vitesse	speed skating
patiner [patine]	ice-skate
les **patins à glace** *m* [patɛ̃aglas]	ice skates
une **patinoire** [patinwaʀ]	ice-skating rink, ice rink; ice stadium
Le verglas a transformé l'autoroute en patinoire.	The thin coating of ice transformed the highway into an ice rink.
un,e **patineur, -euse** [patinœʀ, øz]	ice skater

grimper [gʀɛ̃pe]	climb
un,e **alpiniste** [alpinist]	mountain climber, mountaineer
faire de l'alpinisme *m* [fɛʀd(ə)lalpinism]	do mountain climbing/mountaineering
escalader [ɛskalade]	climb, scale
escalader la **face nord** du Mont-Blanc	climb the north face of Mont Blanc
une **escalade** [ɛskalad]	scaling, climb(ing)

plonger [plɔ̃ʒe]	dive, take/do a header
Elle a **plongé du tremplin** de 3 mètres.	She took a header from the 3-meter board.
L'eau est si claire, c'est un vrai plaisir d'y plonger.	The water is so clear it's a real pleasure to go diving in it.
un,e **plongeur, -euse** [plɔ̃ʒœʀ, øz]	diver
la **plongée (sous-marine)** [plɔ̃ʒe]	(skin) diving, underwater diving
la **brasse** [bʀas]	breaststroke
nager la brasse	do the breaststroke
le **crawl** [kʀol]	crawl

l'**aviron** *m* [aviʀɔ̃]	rowing; oar

ramer [ʀame]	row
un **canoë** [kanɔe]	canoe
descendre la Dordogne **en** canoë	go down the Dordogne in a canoe
une **régate** [ʀegat]	regatta

les **sports de combat** m [spɔʀdəkɔ̃ba]	martial arts
l'**escrime** f [ɛskʀim]	fencing
la **boxe** [bɔks]	boxing
un **combat de boxe**	boxing match
la **lutte** [lyt]	wrestling
le **judo** [ʒydɔ]	judo
le **culturisme** [kyltyʀism]	bodybuilding
une **salle de culturisme**	bodybuilding studio

l'**équitation** f [ekitasjɔ̃]	riding, horsemanship
faire du cheval [fɛʀdyʃ(ə)val]	ride (a horse)
Je fais du cheval depuis mon enfance.	I've been horseback riding since I was a child.

le **dopage** [dɔpaʒ]	doping (a horse, an athlete)
le **doping** [dɔpiŋ]	doping (a horse, an athlete)
se doper [s(ə)dɔpe]	take drugs
Le contrôle a confirmé que le coureur s'était dopé.	The inspection confirmed that the runner had taken drugs.
la **lutte anti-dopage** [lytɑ̃tidɔpaʒ]	the fight against doping

10.3 Theater, Film, and Television

le **théâtre** [teatʀ]	theater
faire du théâtre	be an actor
une **pièce de théâtre**	play
monter une pièce (de théâtre)	stage a play
une **scène** [sɛn]	stage; scenery; scene
entrer* en scène	appear on stage
mettre en scène	produce, stage; *(film)* direct
la **mise en scène**	production, staging, setting; *(film)* direction
Les spectateurs ont apprécié la mise en scène.	The spectators liked the staging.
un **metteur en scène** [metœʀɑ̃sɛn]	producer; *(film)* director

représenter [ʀ(ə)pʀezɑ̃te]	perform, act (a play)

une **représentation** [ʀ(ə)pʀezɑ̃tasjɔ̃]	presentation, performance
la **première** [pʀəmjɛʀ]	premiere
un **spectacle** [spɛktakl]	show; play; performance
un,e **spectateur, -trice** [spɛktatœʀ, tʀis]	spectator
le **public** [pyblik]	public
Cette pièce a du succès **auprès du grand public**.	This play is successful with the public in general.
un **acte** [akt]	act
une **pièce en trois actes**	a play in three acts
un **entracte** [ɑ̃tʀakt]	intermission, interval (between the acts)
l'**action** f [aksjɔ̃]	action
L'action se déroule à Paris, au 16ᵉ siècle.	The action takes place in Paris, in the sixteenth century.
une **scène** [sɛn]	scene
la 1ᵉʳᵉ scène de l'acte II	the first scene of the second act
une **troupe** [tʀup]	company (of actors), troupe
un,e **comédien, -ienne** [kɔmedjɛ̃, jɛn]	actor, actress; comedian; player
une **vedette** [vədɛt]	star
une **star** [staʀ]	star
un **rôle** [ʀol]	role, part, character
le **rôle principal**	main part
un **rôle secondaire**	secondary part
un **petit rôle**	bit part
un,e **figurant,e** [figyʀɑ̃, ɑ̃t]	super(numerary), walkon, extra
la **distribution** [distʀibysjɔ̃]	casting, cast
Quelle distribution! Rien que des vedettes !	What a cast! Nothing but stars!
un **personnage** [pɛʀsɔnaʒ]	character, part
Quel est le **personnage principal** de la pièce ?	Who is the main character of the play?
jouer [ʒwe]	play
Il joue ce rôle pour la 200ᵉ fois.	He's playing this role for the 200ᵗʰ time.
le **jeu** [ʒø]	playing
interpréter [ɛ̃tɛʀpʀete]	interpret
répéter qc [ʀepete]	rehearse s.th.
une **répétition** [ʀepetisjɔ̃]	rehearsal
la **(répétition) générale**	general rehearsal
Une générale ratée promet une première réussie.	A failed general rehearsal means a successful premiere.
diriger [diʀiʒe]	direct; control
Le metteur en scène dirige sa troupe.	The producer controls his company.

débuter [debyte]	début, make one's début
Elle a débuté au Théâtre de la Ville.	She made her début in the Théâtre de la Ville.
avoir le trac [avwaʀlətʀak]	have stage fright

une **comédie** [kɔmedi]	comedy
une **comédie musicale**	musical (comedy)
comique [kɔmik]	comical, funny
un **drame** [dʀam]	drama, play
dramatique [dʀamatik]	dramatic
une **tragédie** [tʀaʒedi]	tragedy
tragique [tʀaʒik]	tragic

la **caisse** [kɛs]	box office
un **billet** [bijɛ]	ticket
faire la queue [fɛʀlakø]	stand in line
Ils ont fait la queue à la caisse pendant trois heures.	They stood in line at the box office for three hours.
complet, -ète [kɔ̃plɛ, ɛt]	sold out
Ce théâtre **affiche complet** jusqu'à la fin de la saison.	The theater is sold out through the end of the season.
le **vestiaire** [vɛstjɛʀ]	cloakroom
On va laisser les manteaux au vestiaire.	We'll leave the coats in the cloakroom.
le **programme** [pʀɔgʀam]	program
être au programme	be on the program

un **succès** [syksɛ]	success
obtenir un succès fou	have a huge success
applaudir qn/qc [aplodiʀ]	applaud s.o./s.th.
L'actrice principale a été très applaudie.	The leading lady received a lot of applause.
les **applaudissements** m [aplodismɑ̃]	applause
un **échec** m [eʃɛk]	failure, flop
Cette mise en scène a été un **échec total**.	This production was a total flop.
siffler [sifle]	hiss, boo (off the stage)
Il était très mauvais et **il s'est fait siffler**.	He was very bad, and he was booed off the stage

la **salle** [sal]	hall; large room
le **rang** [ʀɑ̃]	row
la **place** [plas]	seat
Il vaut mieux arriver tôt, les places ne sont pas numérotées.	It's better to come early; the seats are not assigned.

un **film** [film]	film
tourner un film	shoot a film
un **film muet/parlant**	a silent/sound film, talking film, talkie
filmer [filme]	film
une **caméra** [kameʀa]	camera
un **studio** [stydjo]	studio
un film tourné entièrement en studio	a film shot entirely in the studio
passer à [pase]	run, be showing
Ce film ne passe plus à Paris depuis longtemps.	This film has not been showing in Paris for a long time.
une **séance** [seɑ̃s]	show
On pourrait aller à la séance de 17 heures.	We could go to the 5 o'clock show.

un,e **acteur, -trice** [aktœʀ, tʀis]	actor, actress
un,e **réalisateur, -trice** [ʀealizatœʀ, tʀis]	(film) director
réaliser [ʀealize]	direct, make (a film)
Ce film a été réalisé avec un petit budget.	This film was made on a small budget.
un,e **cascadeur, -euse** [kaskadœʀ, øz]	stuntman, stuntwoman

regarder la télé(vision) [ʀ(ə)gaʀdelatele(vizjɔ̃)]	watch TV/television
un,e **téléspectateur, -trice** [telespɛktatœʀ, tʀis]	television viewer
le **petit écran** [p(ə)titekʀɑ̃]	TV screen

le **programme** [pʀɔgʀam]	channel; program
une **chaîne** [ʃɛn]	(television) station, channel
une **chaîne publique**	a public television station
une **chaîne privée**	a private (commercial) station
la **première chaîne**	Channel One
une **chaîne payante**	pay TV channel
par câble [paʀkabl]	on cable
En Allemagne, on peut recevoir/capter les chaînes françaises par câble.	In Germany you can get the French TV channels on cable.
par satellite [paʀsatelit]	by satellite
la **télécommande** [telekɔmɑ̃d]	remote (control)
zapper [zape]	zap

une **émission** [emisjɔ̃]	broadcast, program, telecast
une **émission sportive**	sportscast, sports broadcast

un **téléfilm** [telefilm] — made-for-television film
une **série télévisée** [seʀitelevize] — television series
un **jeu télévisé** [ʒøtelevize] — television quiz show, game show
  participer à un jeu télévisé — take part in a game show
un **reportage** [ʀ(ə)pɔʀtaʒ] — report, reporting
  Hier soir, j'ai vu un reportage sur le Maroc à la télé. — Last night I saw a report on Morocco on TV.
un,e **reporter** [ʀ(ə)pɔʀtɛʀ/tœʀ] — reporter

---

assister à [asiste] — attend
  Nous avons assisté à une représentation de *l'Avare*. — We attended a performance of *L'Avare* (comedy by Molière).
l'**auditoire** *m* [oditwaʀ] — audience
  un auditoire attentif — an attentive audience

---

le **décor** [dekɔʀ] — scenery, stage effects
les **costumes** *m* [kɔstym] — costumes
le **rideau** [ʀido] — curtain (theater)
  Le rideau se lève/tombe. — The curtain rises/falls.
les **coulisses** *f* [kulis] — wings (theater)

---

un **triomphe** [tʀiɔ̃f] — triumph, hit
  Sa dernière pièce a été un triomphe absolu. — His last play was an absolute triumph.
triomphal,e [tʀiɔ̃fal] — triumphant
huer ['ɥe] — boo, hoot (off the stage)
un **bide** *fam* [bid] — flop
  Quel bide, toute la troupe s'est fait huer. — What a flop; the whole company was booed off the stage.

---

cinématographique [sinematɔgʀafik] — film, cinema, movie
  l'**industrie cinématographique** — film industry, movie industry
un,e **cinéphile** [sinefil] — movie fan
un **ciné-club** [sineklœb] — film club

---

un **film de science-fiction** [filmdəsjãsfiksjɔ̃] — science-fiction film
le **suspense** [syspɛns] — suspense
un **film policier** [filmpɔlisje] — detective film
un **film d'aventures** [filmdavãtyʀ] — adventure film
un **western** [wɛstɛʀn] — Western
un **documentaire** [dɔkymãtɛʀ] — documentary (film)
un **dessin animé** [desɛ̃anime] — cartoon

un **long-métrage** [lɔ̃metʀaʒ]	full-length feature
un **court-métrage** [kuʀmetʀaʒ]	short film
en noir et blanc [ɑ̃nwaʀeblɑ̃]	in black and white
en couleurs [ɑ̃kulœʀ]	in color
la **télévision en couleurs**	color television

le **scénario** [senaʀjo]	(film) script
un,e **scénariste** [senaʀist]	scriptwriter
la **prise de son** [pʀizdəsɔ̃]	sound recording
le **montage** [mɔ̃taʒ]	editing *(film)*; montage
le **mixage** [miksaʒ]	sound mixing
les **effets spéciaux** *m* [efɛspesjo]	special effects
le **trucage** [tʀykaʒ]	trick shots

un **gros plan** [gʀoplɑ̃]	close-up (shot)
On voit le héros **en gros plan**.	The hero is seen in a close-up.
un **ralenti** [ʀalɑ̃ti]	slow motion
Et maintenant, la même scène **au ralenti**.	And now the same scene in slow motion.
un **retour en arrière**/un **flash-back** [ʀ(ə)tuʀɑ̃naʀjɛʀ, flaʃbak]	flashback
le **générique** [ʒeneʀik]	credits
tenir l'affiche [t(ə)niʀlafiʃ]	be running
Ce film tient l'affiche depuis deux ans.	This film has been running for two years.

une **version** [vɛʀsjɔ̃]	version
en version originale (VO)	in the original version
en version originale sous-titrée	in the original version with subtitles
en version française (VF)	in the French version
doubler [duble]	dub

un **feuilleton** [fœjtɔ̃]	series
un **épisode** [epizɔd]	episode
Le n'y comprends plus rien, j'ai dû manquer un épisode.	I don't understand it anymore; I must have missed an episode.
les **variétés** *f* [vaʀjete]	variety
Elle déteste les émissions de variétés.	She hates variety programs.

10.4 Celebrations

une **fête** [fɛt]	holiday, festival, festivity, party
On a **fait la fête** toute la nuit.	We partied all night long.
la **fête** [fɛt]	name day
Aujourd'hui, c'est la fête de Michel.	Today is Michel's name day.
un **jour de fête**	a holiday, a festive occasion
fêter [fɛte]	celebrate

une **fête de famille** [fɛtdəfamij]	family celebration
un **anniversaire** [anivɛʀsɛʀ]	birthday
Je ne sais pas quoi lui offrir pour son anniversaire.	I don't know what to give him for his birthday.
le **baptême** [batɛm]	baptism
baptiser [batize]	baptize
le **mariage** [maʀjaʒ]	wedding; marriage
les **noces** f [nɔs]	wedding, nuptials
le **voyage de noces**	honeymoon
la **noce** [nɔs]	marriage ceremony, wedding ceremony
la **fête des mères/pères** [fɛtdemɛʀ/pɛʀ]	Mother's/Father's Day

féliciter qn de/pour qc [felisite]	congratulate s.o./on s.th.
On l'a félicité de/pour son succès.	They congratulated him on his success.
les **félicitations** f [felisitasjɔ̃]	congratulations; best wishes
Toutes nos félicitations !	Congratulations!
présenter ses vœux à qn [pʀezɑ̃tesevø]	wish s.o. success/all the best
Je vous présente mes meilleurs vœux.	I wish you all the best.
souhaiter qc à qn [swete]	wish s.o. s.th.
Je te souhaite un joyeux Noël.	I wish you a Merry Christmas.
Bonne année ! [bɔnane]	Happy New Year!
Joyeuses fêtes ! [ʒwajøzfɛt]	Happy holidays!
Bonne fête ! [bɔnfɛt]	Best wishes on your name day!
Bon anniversaire ! [bɔnanivɛʀsɛʀ]	Happy birthday!

inviter qn à [ɛ̃vite]	invite s.o. to
Elle m'a invitée à son anniversaire.	She has invited me to her birthday party.
un,e **invité,e** [ɛ̃vite]	guest
une **invitation** [ɛ̃vitasjɔ̃]	invitation

lancer une invitation à qn — issue an invitation to s.o.
retrouver qn [ʀ(ə)tʀuve] — meet s.o. again
se réunir [s(ə)ʀeyniʀ] — meet, get together
Toute la famille s'est réunie pour fêter les 40 ans de Marcel. — The whole family got together to celebrate Marcel's fortieth birthday.

un **dîner** [dine] — dinner
  faire un bon dîner — eat a good dinner, dine well
un **repas (de fête)** [ʀ(ə)pa] — banquet, (public) dinner
un **festin** [fɛstɛ̃] — banquet, feast, (public) dinner
un **gâteau** [gato] — cake
  souffler les bougies du gâteau d'anniversaire — blow out the candles on the birthday cake
le **champagne** [ʃɑ̃paɲ] — champagne
  sabler le champagne — drink champagne

s'**amuser (à)** [samyze] — have a good time, enjoy oneself (at)
  Vous vous êtes bien amusés à cette fête ? — Did you have a good time at that party?
le **plaisir** [pleziʀ] — pleasure
  Ses yeux brillent de plaisir. — Her eyes are shining with pleasure.

la **joie** [ʒwa] — joy
  sauter de joie — jump for joy
joyeux, -euse [ʒwajø, øz] — joyous, happy
rire [ʀiʀ] — laugh
le **rire** [ʀiʀ] — laugh, laughter
rigoler fam [ʀigɔle] — have fun
l'**ambiance** f [ɑ̃bjɑ̃s] — ambiance, atmosphere
  une ambiance animée — an atmosphere of excitement
l'**émotion** f [emosjɔ̃] — emotion
ému,e [emy] — moved
  être ému,e aux larmes — be moved to tears

un **habit** [abi] — clothes, apparel
  L'habit ne fait pas le moine. prov — It is not the cowl that makes the monk.
s'**habiller** [sabije] — dress
  Habille-toi vite. On est en retard. — Get dressed quickly. We're late.
se faire beau/belle [s(ə)fɛʀbo/bɛl] — dress up

le **réveillon** [ʀevejɔ̃] — midnight repast (on Christmas Eve or New Year's Eve)
le **jour de l'An** [ʒuʀdəlɑ̃] — New Year's Day
(le) **carnaval** [kaʀnaval] — carnival (season)

la **Fête du Travail** [fɛtdytʀavaj]	Labor Day
la **Fête Nationale (14 juillet)**	French national holiday
[fɛtnasjɔnal(katɔʀz(ə)ʒɥijɛ)]	
une **fête foraine** [fɛtfɔʀɛn]	fun fair
un **bal populaire** [balpɔpylɛʀ]	public dance

célébrer [selebʀe]	celebrate
Dimanche, on a célébré le 100ᵉ	On Sunday we celebrated my
anniversaire de mon oncle.	uncle's 100th birthday.
une **cérémonie** [seʀemɔni]	ceremony
une cérémonie officielle	official ceremony
les **noces d'or** f [nɔsdɔʀ]	golden wedding anniversary

un **bal (masqué)** [bal(maske)]	(masquerade) ball
se **déguiser** [s(ə)degize]	disguise oneself
Il's'est déguisé **en pirate**.	He disguised himself as a pirate.
le **déguisement** [degizmã]	disguise

un **banquet** [bãkɛ]	banquet
trinquer à [tʀɛ̃ke]	drink to
Trinquons à la santé des jeunes	Let's drink to the health of the
mariés.	newlyweds.
porter un toast à qn/qc	propose a toast to s.o./s.th.
[pɔʀteɛ̃tost]	

French Word	English Equivalent	False Friend	French Equivalent
une raquette	tennis racquet	rocket	une fusée
la balade	walk, stroll	ballad	la ballade
la voile	sail, canvas	veil	le voile
la boxe	boxing	box	la caisse
le tour	tour, trip	tower	la tour
un habit	clothes, dress	habit	une habitude, une coutume

11.1 Trips and Travel Preparations

les **vacances** f [vakɑ̃s]	vacation
Bonnes vacances !	Have a good vacation!
prendre des vacances	take a vacation
passer ses vacances en Espagne	spend one's vacation in Spain
un,e **vacancier, -ière** [vakɑ̃sje, jɛʀ]	vacationer
le **congé** [kɔ̃ʒe]	leave
prendre un **jour de congé**	take a day off
un,e **touriste** [tuʀist]	tourist
le **tourisme** [tuʀism]	tourism
l'**industrie du tourisme**	tourist industry

un **voyage** [vwajaʒ]	trip, voyage; travel
partir* en voyage	go on a trip, travel
un **voyage organisé**	group trip
voyager [vwajaʒe]	travel
un,e **voyageur, -euse** [vwajaʒœʀ, øz]	traveler
un **tour** [tuʀ]	trip, excursion, tour

> For information on the gender of **tour**, see p. 191.

un **circuit** [siʀkɥi]	circular tour, round-trip
faire un circuit à travers le Massif central	take a round-trip through the Central Massif
un **séjour** [seʒuʀ]	stay, sojourn

une **agence de voyage** [aʒɑ̃sdəvwajaʒ]	travel agency
un **syndicat d'initiative** [sɛ̃dikadinisjativ]	tourist information office
Adressez-vous au syndicat d'initiative.	Go to/Ask the tourist information office.
un **office de/du tourisme** [ɔfisdə/dytuʀism]	tourist information office
un **projet (de voyage)** [pʀɔʒɛ]	travel plan
un **renseignement** [ʀɑ̃sɛɲmɑ̃]	information
se renseigner sur qc [s(ə)ʀɑ̃sɛɲe]	inquire about s.th.
Nous nous sommes renseignés sur les prix des circuits en car.	We've inquired about the prices of bus tours.
une **information** [ɛ̃fɔʀmasjɔ̃]	information
s'informer sur [sɛ̃fɔʀme]	get information on
un **catalogue** [katalɔg]	catalog
un **prospectus** [pʀɔspɛktys]	brochure

recommander qc à qn [r(ə)kɔmɑ̃de]
  Nous vous recommandons l'hôtel Bellevue, il est bien et pas trop cher.
les **documents de voyage** m [dɔkymɑ̃d(ə)vwajaʒ]

recommend s.th. to s.o.
  We recommend the Hotel Bellevue to you; it's good and not too expensive.
travel documents

---

réserver [rezɛrve]
  (faire) réserver une chambre
une **réservation** [rezɛrvasjɔ̃]
  N'oubliez pas de confirmer votre réservation.
annuler [anyle]
  être obligé,e d'annuler son voyage

reserve
  reserve a room
reservation
  Don't forget to confirm your reservation.
cancel
  be forced to cancel one's trip

---

les **bagages à main** m [bagaʒamɛ̃]
une **valise** [valiz]
  (dé)faire sa valise
un **sac** [sak]
  un **sac à dos**
préparer [prepare]
  Je n'ai pas encore eu le temps de préparer mes affaires.
les **préparatifs** m [preparatif]
une **liste** [list]
  On a fait une liste des choses à emporter.

hand luggage
suitcase
  pack/unpack one's suitcase
bag, sack
  backpack
prepare; arrange
  I haven't had time yet to get my affairs in order.
preparations
list
  We made a list of things to take.

---

un **guide** [gid]
une **carte routière** [kartrutjɛr]
un **itinéraire** [itinerɛr]
  Empruntez l'**itinéraire bis** pour éviter les bouchons.

travel guide
road map
itinerary; route, road
  Use the secondary roads to avoid the traffic jams.

---

partir* **(pour)** [partir]
  Elle est partie pour l'Espagne.
  partir seul,e
  partir avec qn
le **départ** [depar]
la **destination** [destinasjɔ̃]
arriver* [arive]
  Nous sommes bien arrivés **à destination**.

travel (to), leave (for)
  She has left for Spain.
  travel alone
  travel with s.o.
departure
destination
arrive
  We arrived safely at our destination.

l'**arrivée** f [aʀive] — arrival

un,e **passager, -ère** [pasaʒe, ɛʀ]	passenger
un,e **contrôleur, -euse** [kɔ̃tʀolœʀ, øz]	inspector, ticket collector
un **contrôle** [kɔ̃tʀol]	inspection, ticket check
un **guichet** [giʃɛ]	(ticket) window
un **billet** [bijɛ]	ticket
un **billet de train/d'avion**	train/plane ticket
composter son billet	cancel/invalidate one's ticket
un **aller simple** [alesɛ̃pl]	one-way ticket
un **aller-retour**/un **aller et retour** [ale(e)ʀ(ə)tuʀ]	round-trip ticket
un **supplément** [syplemɑ̃]	supplement

un **train** [tʀɛ̃]	train
un **train rapide**	fast train, (limited) express
un **train direct**	express train
voyager en train	travel by train
rater *fam*/manquer le train	miss the train
le **TGV (train à grande vitesse)** [teʒeve]	TGV (high-speed train)
prendre le TGV	take the TGV
monter* dans le TGV	get on/board the TGV
descendre* du TGV	get off the TGV
la **correspondance** [kɔʀɛspɔ̃dɑ̃s]	connection; change of trains
attendre la correspondance (pour)	wait for the connection (to)
une **gare** [gaʀ]	train station
la **consigne** [kɔ̃siɲ]	baggage checkroom
la **consigne automatique**	baggage lockers
un **quai** [kɛ]	platform
une **voie** [vwa]	track
Le train pour Bordeaux partira de la voie 12.	The train to Bordeaux leaves from Track 12.
la **classe** [klas]	class
voyager en première (classe)	travel in first class
La seconde (classe) est bondée.	Second class is full to bursting.

l'**horaire** m [ɔʀɛʀ]	schedule
le **retard** [ʀ(ə)taʀ]	delay
On est parti avec **une heure de retard**.	We left an hour late.

une **voiture** [vwatyʀ]	coach, car
un **compartiment** [kɔ̃paʀtimɑ̃]	compartment

un **compartiment non-fumeurs**	a no-smoking compartment
un **wagon-lit** [vagɔli]	sleeping car
une **couchette** [kuʃɛt]	couchette, sleeper
une **voiture-couchettes** [vwatyʀkuʃɛt]	couchette car
un **wagon-restaurant** [vagɔ̃ʀɛstɔʀɑ̃]	dining car

un **avion** m [avjɔ̃]	airplane
prendre l'avion	take the airplane, travel by plane
un **aéroport** m [aeʀɔpɔʀ]	airport
voler [vɔle]	fly
un **vol** [vɔl]	flight

un **bateau** [bato]	ship
un **ferry(-boat)** [feʀi(bot)]	ferry(boat)
un **port** [pɔʀ]	port, harbor
un **port de plaisance**	yacht harbor
à bord [abɔʀ]	on board, aboard
naviguer à bord d'un voilier	sail on board a sailing ship
avoir le mal de mer [avwaʀl(ə)maldəmɛʀ]	be seasick

un **car** [kaʀ]	coach, long-distance bus
prendre le car **pour** Nîmes	take the bus to Nîmes
une **autoroute** [otoʀut]	superhighway
une **autoroute à péage**	tollway, toll road
une **aire** [ɛʀ]	area
une **aire de repos/de pique-nique**	rest/picnic area
une **aire de service**	service and rest area
une **aire de stationnement**	parking area

une **carte d'identité** [kaʀtdidɑ̃tite]	identification card
une **pièce d'identité** [pjɛsdidɑ̃tite]	identification document/paper
présenter une pièce d'identité	present some identification
un **passeport** [paspɔʀ]	passport
se présenter au contrôle des passeports	go to the passport inspection/control point
en règle [ɑ̃ʀɛgl]	in order
Votre passeport n'est pas en règle.	Your passport is not in order.
valable [valabl]	valid
périmé,e [peʀime]	expired
Votre passeport est périmé depuis 6 mois.	Your passport expired six months ago.
un **visa** [viza]	visa

une **frontière** [fʀɔ̃tjɛʀ]	border
la **douane** [dwan]	customs
passer la douane	go through customs
un **douanier** [dwanje]	customs official
déclarer qc [deklaʀe]	declare s.th.
Vous avez quelque chose à déclarer ?	Do you have anything to declare?
fouiller [fuje]	search
Les douaniers nous ont fouillés **des pieds à la tête.**	The customs officials searched us from head to toe.

un **pays** [pei]	country
partir* pour un **pays lointain**	go off to a far-away country
une **région** [ʀeʒjɔ̃]	region, area
une **région touristique**	tourist area
(un,e) **étranger, -ère** *n; adj* [etʀɑ̃ʒe, ɛʀ]	foreigner; foreign
l'**étranger** *m* [etʀɑ̃ʒe]	foreign parts
à l'étranger	abroad
international,e [ɛ̃tɛʀnasjɔnal]	international

visiter qc [vizite]	visit s.th., view s.th.

For information on various ways of expressing the idea of *visiting,* see p. 139.

une **visite** [vizit]	visit
un,e **visiteur, -euse** [vizitœʀ, øz]	visitor
découvrir [dekuvʀiʀ]	discover
une **découverte** [dekuvɛʀt]	discovery
une **aventure** [avɑ̃tyʀ]	adventure
partir à l'aventure	go off on an adventure
un **souvenir** [suv(ə)niʀ]	souvenir, travel memento
un **magasin de souvenirs**	souvenir shop

la **mer** [mɛʀ]	sea, ocean
une maison avec **vue sur la mer**	a house with an ocean view

For information on **mer/mère/maire,** see p. 353.

la **plage** [plaʒ]	beach
le **sable** [sabl]	sand
se baigner [s(ə)beɲe]	swim
Les enfants se sont baignés tous les jours.	The children went swimming every day.
la **baignade** [beɲad]	swimming; swimming area
Baignade interdite.	No swimming.

le **repos** [ʀ(ə)po]	rest, break
prendre un repos bien mérité	enjoy a well-deserved break
se reposer [sǝʀ(ə)poze]	rest

la **campagne** [kɑ̃paɲ]	country, fields
la **montagne** [mɔ̃taɲ]	mountains
la **neige** [nɛʒ]	snow
Il est tombé beaucoup de neige cet hiver.	A lot of snow has fallen this winter.

un **voyage d'études** [vwajaʒdetyd]	educational trip, study trip
un **voyage d'affaires** [vwajaʒdafɛʀ]	business trip
un **voyage d'agrément** [vwajaʒdagʀemɑ̃]	pleasure trip
un **voyage de noces** [vwajaʒdǝnɔs]	honeymoon trip
la **pleine saison** [plɛnsɛzɔ̃]	high season
hors saison [ɔʀsɛzɔ̃]	off season
Si vous le pouvez, allez-y plutôt hors saison.	If you can, go there off season.

un,e **accompagnateur, -trice** [akɔ̃paɲatœʀ, tʀis]	(travel) companion
accompagner qn [akɔ̃paɲe]	accompany s.o.
un **voyagiste**/un **tour opérateur** [vwajaʒist/tuʀɔpeʀatœʀ]	tour operator

un **bac** [bak]	ferry
Les deux rives sont reliées par un bac.	The two banks of the river are linked by a ferry.
une **croisière** [kʀwazjɛʀ]	cruise
s'embarquer [sɑ̃baʀke]	embark, go on board
s'embarquer **pour** la Crète	embark for Crete
débarquer [debaʀke]	disembark, land
faire escale [fɛʀɛskal]	put into a port, call at a port
Ce soir, nous ferons escale à Marseille.	This evening we'll make a port call in Marseille.

le **décollage** [dekɔlaʒ]	takeoff
décoller [dekɔle]	take off, lift off
l'**atterrissage** m [ateʀisaʒ]	landing
atterrir [ateʀiʀ]	land
L'avion a atterri à 8 heures 24.	The plane landed at 8:24.

exotique [εgzɔtik]	exotic
l'**exotisme** *m* [εgzɔtism]	exoticism
le **folklore** [fɔlklɔʀ]	folklore

la **Méditerranée** [mediteʀane]	Mediterranean
l'(**océan**) **Atlantique** *m* [atlɑ̃tik]	Atlantic
la **Manche** [mɑ̃ʃ]	English Channel
la **mer du Nord** [mɛʀdynɔʀ]	North Sea
la **mer Baltique** [mɛʀbaltik]	Baltic Sea

un **parc naturel** [paʀknatyʀεl]	nature park
en plein air [ɑ̃plεnεʀ]	outdoors
un **restaurant en plein air**	an outdoor restaurant
au grand air [ogʀɑ̃tεʀ]	in the fresh/open air
passer ses journées dehors/au grand air	spend one's days out in the open air
se détendre [s(ə)detɑ̃dʀ]	relax
Même en vacances, il n'arrive pas à se détendre.	Even on vacation, he can't manage to relax.
se relaxer [səʀ(ə)lakse]	relax

un **bain de soleil** [bɛ̃dsɔlεj]	sunbath
un **coup de soleil** [kudsɔlεj]	sunburn
en plein soleil [ɑ̃plɛ̃sɔlεj]	in the blazing sun
Il s'est endormi en plein soleil.	He fell asleep in the blazing sun.
les **lunettes de soleil** *f* [lynεtdəsɔlεj]	sunglasses

> For information on *forming the plural of French nouns* of the **lunettes** type, see p. 38.

l'**ambre solaire** *m* [ɑ̃bʀ(ə)sɔlεʀ]	suntan lotion
bronzer [bʀɔ̃ze]	(get a) tan
Je ne bronze jamais, j'attrape seulement des coups de soleil.	I never tan; I just get sunburned.
bronzé,e [bʀɔ̃ze]	tan(ned)
le **bronzage** [bʀɔ̃zaʒ]	tanning

une **excursion** [εkskyʀsjɔ̃]	outing, excursion
faire une **excursion en montagne**	go hiking in the mountains
une **randonnée** [ʀɑ̃dɔne]	hike, outing; long walk
faire une **randonnée à pied**	go on a hike
faire une **randonnée à bicyclette**	go on a bike trip
un **chemin de grande randonnée** (**GR**)	hiking route, trail
un **sentier** [sɑ̃tje]	path

11.2 Accommodations

un **hôtel** [ɔ/otɛl]	hotel
une **pension (de famille)** [pɑ̃sjɔ̃]	private hotel, residential hotel
une **auberge de jeunesse** [obɛʀʒd(ə)ʒœnɛs]	youth hostel
un **club (de vacances)** [klœb]	vacation club
un **village de vacances** [vilaʒdəvakɑ̃s]	vacation village
un **appartement**/une **maison de vacances** [apaʀtəmɑ̃/mɛzɔ̃dvakɑ̃s]	vacation apartment/cottage
libre [libʀ]	free, vacant
complet, -ète [kɔ̃plɛ, ɛt]	full, booked up
L'hôtel affiche complet.	The hotel is full.

une **chambre** [ʃɑ̃bʀ]	room
une **chambre simple**	single room
une **chambre double**	double room
la **clé (clef)** [kle]	key
le **lit** [li]	bed
un **grand lit**	double bed
un lit supplémentaire	extra bed

louer [lwe]	rent
louer un appartement pour 15 jours	rent an apartment for two weeks
une **location** [lɔkasjɔ̃]	(rented) vacation apartment/cottage

la **catégorie** [kategɔʀi]	category, class
le **confort** [kɔ̃fɔʀ]	comfort, convenience
une **chambre tout confort**	a room equipped with all conveniences
confortable [kɔ̃fɔʀtabl]	comfortable
le **luxe** [lyks]	luxury
un **hôtel de luxe**	luxury hotel
une **étoile** [etwal]	star
un **hôtel/restaurant 3 étoiles**	a three-star hotel/restaurant

une **salle de bains** [saldəbɛ̃]	bathroom
une **douche** [duʃ]	shower
Nous avons des chambres avec/ sans douche.	We have rooms with/without a shower.
prendre une douche	take a shower
se doucher [s(ə)duʃe]	shower, take a shower
un **lavabo** [lavabo]	washbasin, sink
les **W.-C.** m [vese]	toilet

une **terrasse** [teʀas]	terrace
un **balcon** [balkɔ̃]	balcony
donner sur [dɔnesyʀ]	overlook, face
Ma chambre donne sur la rue.	My room overlooks/faces the street.
calme [kalm]	quiet
bruyant,e [bʀɥjɑ̃, jɑ̃t]	loud
central,e [sɑ̃tʀal]	central
Nous avons choisi cet hôtel parce qu'il est central.	We chose this hotel because it is centrally located.
une **piscine** [pisin]	swimming pool

la **réception** [ʀesɛpsjɔ̃]	reception (desk)
déposer ses clés à la réception	leave one's keys at the reception desk
le **hall** ['ol]	reception area
l'**ascenseur** m [asɑ̃sœʀ]	elevator

en demi-pension [ɑ̃d(ə)mipɑ̃sjɔ̃]	with breakfast and one main meal
prendre une chambre en demi-pension	take a room with breakfast and one main meal
en pension complète [ɑ̃pɑ̃sjɔ̃kɔ̃plɛt]	with all meals
le **petit déjeuner** [p(ə)tideʒœne]	breakfast
Le petit déjeuner **est compris** dans le prix de la chambre.	Breakfast is included in the price of the room.
le **restaurant** [ʀɛstɔʀɑ̃]	restaurant
le **service** [sɛʀvis]	service
le **personnel** [pɛʀsɔnɛl]	personnel, staff
Le service est lent car ils manquent de personnel.	The service is slow, since they don't have enough personnel.

le **camping** [kɑ̃piŋ]	camping; campground
un **terrain de camping**	campground
faire du camping	go camping, camp (out)
Le **camping sauvage** est interdit ici.	No unauthorized camping is permitted here.
camper [kɑ̃pe]	go camping, camp (out)
une **tente** [tɑ̃t]	tent
monter la tente	put up the tent
une **caravane** [kaʀavan]	camping trailer
un **campingcar** [kɑ̃piŋkaʀ]	camper, camping van

l'**hôtellerie** f [ɔ/otɛlʀi]	hotel trade, hospitality industry
un,e **hôtelier, -ière** [ɔ/otəlje, jɛʀ]	hotel owner, hotelier
le **logement** [lɔʒmɑ̃]	accommodations, lodging
Il faut s'y prendre tôt pour trouver un logement sur la côte.	You have to start looking early to find accommodations on the coast.

une **chambre d'hôte** [ʃãbʀ(ə)dot]	guest room, room with breakfast
un **chalet** [ʃalɛ]	chalet, cottage; country house
un **gîte rural** [ʒitʀyʀal]	vacation quarters in the country

un **prix forfaitaire** [pʀifɔʀfɛtɛʀ]	all-inclusive price
la **nuit(ée)** [nɥi(te)]	night
Combien coûte la nuit(ée), en single/pour une personne ?	How much is it per night for a single room?
la **note** [nɔt]	bill, account
présenter la note	present the bill
La note est salée.	The bill is padded.
hors de prix [ɔʀdəpʀi]	unaffordable
modéré,e [mɔdeʀe]	moderate
un,e **estivant,e** [ɛstivã, ãt]	summer vacationer, summer guest

une **station** [stasjɔ̃]	resort
une **station thermale**	spa resort
une **station balnéaire**	seaside resort
une **station de sports d'hiver**	winter sports resort
une **colonie de vacances**; une **colo** *fam* [kɔlɔnid(ə)vakãs, kolo]	vacation colony/camp
partir en colo(nie de vacances)	go to a vacation colony

11.3 Dining Out

un **restaurant** [ʀɛstɔʀã]	restaurant
aller manger au restaurant	go out to eat in a restaurant
un **hôtel-restaurant** [ɔ/otɛlʀɛstɔʀã]	hotel with its own restaurant
un **bar** [baʀ]	(hotel) bar
un **bistro(t)** [bistʀo]	bistro
un **café** [kafe]	café

un,e **patron,ne** [patʀɔ̃, ɔn]	chef; owner
un,e **chef** [ʃɛf]	chef
un restaurant tenu par un grand chef	a restaurant run by a famous chef
un,e **cuisinier, -ière** [kɥizinje, jɛʀ]	cook
un **garçon** [gaʀsɔ̃]	waiter
Garçon, 2 cafés, s'il vous plaît.	Waiter, two cups of coffee, please.
servir qn/qc [sɛʀviʀ]	serve s.o./s.th.
On vous sert, Madame ?	Have you been served, Madam?
servir qc à qn	serve s.th. to s.o.
un,e **serveur, -euse** [sɛʀvœʀ, øz]	server, waitress

un,e **client,e** [klijɑ̃, ɑ̃t] — customer
la **clientèle** [klijɑ̃tɛl] — clientele, customers
Ce restaurant attire une clientèle internationale. — This restaurant attracts an international clientele.
un,e **consommateur, -trice** [kɔ̃sɔmatœʀ, tʀis] — guest (in a restaurant, etc.)
une **consommation** [kɔ̃sɔmasjɔ̃] — drink, beverage
Ils mettent longtemps à apporter les consommations. — They're taking a long time to bring us the drinks.

la **gastronomie** [gastʀɔnɔmi] — gastronomy, fine dining
gastronomique [gastʀɔnɔmik] — gastronomic
un **menu gastronomique** — (complete) gourmet dinner/meal
une **spécialité** [spesjalite] — specialty
la **spécialité du chef** — specialty of the house
typique de [tipik] — typical of
C'est un plat typique de la région. — This dish is typical of the region.
atypique de [atipik] — not typical of
local,e [lɔkal] — local
une **coutume locale** — local custom
goûter [gute] — try, taste
déguster [degyste] — taste; sip, savor
déguster une douzaine d'huîtres — savor/eat a dozen oysters
une **dégustation** [degystasjɔ̃] — tasting, sampling
une **dégustation de vins** — wine tasting

le **menu** [məny] — menu; complete dinner, set meal
Je prends le menu à 20 euros. — I'll take the complete dinner for 20 euros.
la **carte** [kaʀt] — menu
choisir un plat **à la carte** — order a dish à la carte (from the menu)
la **carte des vins** — wine list
un **plat** [pla] — dish; course
un **plat cuisiné** — ready-cooked dish
le **plat du jour** — special dish of the day
commander [kɔmɑ̃de] — order
une **commande** [kɔmɑ̃d] — order
Pourriez-vous **prendre les commandes**, s'il vous plaît ? — Could you take our orders, please?
proposer [pʀɔpoze] — suggest
Aujourd'hui, nous vous proposons la mousse au chocolat (faite) maison. — Today we suggest that you try the chocolate mousse à la maison.

un **apéritif** [apeʀitif]	aperitif
un **hors-d'œuvre** ['ɔʀdœvʀ]	appetizer, hors d'oeuvre
des hors-d'œuvre variés	assorted appetizers
une **entrée** [ɑ̃tʀe]	first course, starter
le **plat de résistance/principal** [plad(ə)ʀezistɑ̃s/pʀɛ̃sipal]	main course
le **plateau de fromages** [platod(ə)fʀɔmaʒ]	cheese platter
un **dessert** [deseʀ]	dessert
au choix [oʃwa]	alternatively
Vous pouvez prendre au choix du fromage ou un dessert.	You can either have cheese or dessert.
un **digestif** [diʒestif]	digestive, after-dinner drink

la **cave** [kav]	cellar
avoir une cave bien remplie	have a well-stocked cellar
un **vin de pays** [vɛ̃d(ə)pei]	local wine
une **bouteille** [butɛj]	bottle
un **bouchon** [buʃɔ̃]	cork
un **tire-bouchon**	corkscrew
un **verre** [vɛʀ]	glass

What you drink *from what*

Note the difference between:

un verre d'eau	*a glass of water*
un verre à eau	*a water glass*
un verre de vin	*a glass of wine*
un verre à vin	*a wineglass*
une tasse de café	*a cup of coffee*
une tasse à café	*a coffee cup*

---

un **guide (gastronomique)** [gidgastʀɔnɔmik]	(restaurant) guide
le **guide Michelin** [gidmiʃlɛ̃]	Michelin guide
une **étoile** [etwal]	star
Ce restaurant a deux étoiles dans le guide Michelin.	This restaurant has two stars in the Michelin guide.

le **prix** [pʀi]	price
le **tarif** [taʀif]	price
le **tarif des consommations**	beverage prices
l'**addition** f [adisjɔ̃]	bill, check
Apportez-moi un café et l'addition, s'il vous plaît.	Please bring me a cup of coffee and the check, please.

service compris [sɛʀviskɔ̃pʀi]	service included
le **pourboire** [puʀbwaʀ]	tip, gratuity
laisser un pourboire généreux	leave a generous tip
une **réclamation** [ʀeklamasjɔ̃]	complaint
faire une réclamation	complain, make a complaint

un **salon de thé** [salɔ̃d(ə)te]	café, tearoom
un **libre-service** [libʀəsɛʀvis]	self-service restaurant
un **self** *fam* [sɛlf]	self-service restaurant
un **fast-food** [fastfud]	fast-food restaurant
une **brasserie** [bʀasʀi]	(large) pub
un **restauroute/restoroute** [ʀɛstoʀut]	highway restaurant

le **maître d'hôtel** [mɛtʀ(ə)dotɛl]	head waiter
recommandé,e [ʀ(ə)kɔ̃mɑ̃de]	recommended, advisable
Il est recommandé de réserver une table.	It is advisable to reserve a table.
renommé,e [ʀ(ə)nɔme]	renowned, famous
La Bourgogne est renommée pour ses vins.	Burgundy is famous for its wines.
conseiller [kɔ̃seje]	advise, recommend
Quel vin pourriez-vous me conseiller?	Which wine could you recommend to me?
déconseiller [dekɔ̃seje]	advise against

un **grand cru** [gʀɑ̃kʀy]	a great wine
un **pichet** [piʃɛ]	pitcher
une **carafe** [kaʀaf]	carafe
une **carafe d'eau**	a carafe of water
un **seau à glace** [soaglas]	ice bucket
un **glaçon** [glasɔ̃]	ice cube
Tu veux combien de glaçons dans ton whisky?	How many ice cubes do you want in your whisky?

11.4 Sights of Interest

une **visite (guidée)** [vizit(gide)]	guided tour
touristique [tuʀistik]	tourist
Carcassonne est une ville touristique.	Carcassonne is a tourist town.
visiter qc [vizite]	visit, view, see
un,e **visiteur, -euse** [vizitœʀ, øz]	visitor

une **curiosité (touristique)** [kyʀjozite(tuʀistik)]	(tourist) sight, sight of interest
admirer les curiosités de la région	admire the sights of the region

un **monument (historique)** [mɔnymɑ̃ (istɔʀik)]	(historical) monument
un **château** [ʃato]	castle
un **château fort**	medieval citadel
Ce château a été **classé monument historique**.	This castle has been classified as a historical monument.
des **ruines** f [ʀɥin]	ruins
une **église en ruine**	a church in ruins
des **murs** m [myʀ]	walls
un **palais** [palɛ]	palace
un **palais ancien**	an old palace

une **église** [egliz]	church
une **cathédrale** [katedʀal]	cathedral
une **cathédrale romane/gothique**	Romanesque/Gothic cathedral
un **musée** [myze]	museum
le **musée d'art moderne**	museum of modern art

un **quartier** [kaʀtje]	quarter; part of town
une **place** [plas]	square, plaza
un **marché (aux puces)** [maʀʃe(opys)]	(flea) market
une **tour** [tuʀ]	tower
On a une vue splendide du haut de la tour.	You have a fantastic view from the top of the tower.

> For information on the *gender* of **tour**, also see p. 191.

un **pont** [pɔ̃]	bridge

un **plan** [plɑ̃]	(city) map, plan
Il est incapable de lire un plan.	He's incapable of reading a city map.
un **dépliant** [deplijɑ̃]	folding page; leaflet
Tu trouveras tous les détails dans le dépliant.	You'll find all the details in the leaflet.
un **tour (de la ville)** [tuʀ(d(ə)lavil)]	(city) tour
un **circuit touristique** [siʀkɥ ituʀistik]	round-trip tour
l'**entrée** f [ɑ̃tʀe]	entry, entrance
L'entrée au musée est gratuite pour les enfants.	Entrance to the museum is free for children.

un **site** [sit]	site
une **attraction** [atʀaksjɔ̃]	attraction
La Tour Eiffel est une attraction pour les touristes.	The Eiffel Tower is a tourist attraction.
pittoresque [pitɔʀɛsk]	picturesque
La vieille ville est très pittoresque.	The old town is very picturesque.

une **forteresse** [fɔʀtəʀɛs]	fortress
des **remparts** m [ʀɑ̃paʀ]	city ramparts/walls
une **chapelle** [ʃapɛl]	chapel
une **basilique** [bazilik]	basilica
un **arc** [aʀk]	arch
l'**Arc de Triomphe**	the Arch of Triumph
un **parc** [paʀk]	park
une **fontaine** [fɔ̃tɛn]	fountain
un **jet d'eau** [ʒɛdo]	water spray, fountain
une **colonne** [kɔlɔn]	column
un **(spectacle) son et lumière** [(spɛktakl)sɔ̃elymjɛʀ]	sound and light show
assister à un son et lumière	attend a sound and light show
les **heures d'ouverture** f [œʀduvɛʀtyʀ]	opening hours, business hours
la **fermeture hebdomadaire** [fɛʀmətyʀɛbdɔmadɛʀ]	closing day

French Word	English Equivalent	False Friend	French Equivalent
un car	(tour) bus	car	une voiture
valable	valid	valuable	précieux, de grande valeur
la cave	cellar	cave	la caverne

12.1 Visual Arts

l'**art** [aʀ]	art
les **beaux-arts**	fine arts
les **arts plastiques**	visual arts
les **arts graphiques**	graphic arts
une **œuvre d'art**	work of art
un,e **artiste** [aʀtist]	artist
un artiste peintre	painter
artistique adj [aʀtistik]	artistic
un métier artistique	artistic profession

peindre [pɛ̃dʀ]	paint
la **peinture** [pɛ̃tyʀ]	paint; painting
un **peintre** [pɛ̃tʀ]	painter
un **atelier** [atəlje]	atelier, studio
un **modèle** [mɔdɛl]	model
poser [poze]	pose
Dans sa jeunesse, elle a posé pour des peintres célèbres.	In her youth she posed for famous artists.

un **tableau** [tablo]	picture; painting
une **toile** [twal]	canvas; painting
un **cadre** [kadʀ]	frame
un tableau ancien dans un cadre doré	an old picture in a gold frame
encadrer [ãkadʀe]	frame
faire encadrer une toile	have a painting framed
un **portrait** [pɔʀtʀɛ]	portrait
un **autoportrait**	self-portrait
un **paysage** [peizaʒ]	landscape

dessiner [desine]	draw
un **dessin** [desɛ̃]	drawing
un,e **dessinateur, -trice** [desinatœʀ, tʀis]	draftsman; designer
un **crayon** [kʀɛjɔ̃]	pencil
un portrait au crayon	a portrait in pencil

un **original** [ɔʀiʒinal]	original
L'original se trouve au musée du Louvre.	The original is in the Louvre.
une **reproduction** [ʀ(ə)pʀɔdyksjɔ̃]	reproduction

une **copie** [kɔpi]	copy
Ce n'est qu'une copie sans aucune valeur.	It's nothing but a worthless copy.
un **musée** [myze]	museum
exposer [ɛkspoze]	exhibit
une **exposition** [ɛkspozisjɔ̃]	exhibition
une **exposition permanente/temporaire**	a permanent/special exhibition
une **galerie** [galʀi]	(art) gallery
Ses toiles sont exposées dans une galerie.	His paintings are exhibited at a gallery.
visiter qc [vizite]	visit s.th., view s.th.
une **visite** [vizit]	visit
une visite guidée	guided tour
l'**architecture** f [aʀʃitɛktyʀ]	architecture
Notre-Dame de Paris est un exemple célèbre de l'architecture gothique.	Notre-Dame in Paris is a celebrated example of Gothic architecture.
une, e **architecte** [aʀʃitɛkt]	architect
un **projet** [pʀɔʒɛ]	project, plan
un **plan** [plɑ̃]	plan
La Grande Arche a été construite d'après les plans d'Otto von Spreckelsen.	The Grande Arche was built according to the plans of Otto von Spreckelsen.
un **monument** [mɔnymɑ̃]	monument
monumental,e [mɔnymɑ̃tal]	monumental
une œuvre monumentale	a monumental work
créer [kʀee]	create
créer un style nouveau	create a new style
la **créativité** [kʀeativite]	creativity
réaliser [ʀealize]	realize
la **réalisation** [ʀealizasjɔ̃]	realization
La réalisation de ce projet a duré 5 ans.	The realization of this project took five years.
beau, bel; belle [bo, bɛl]	beautiful
la **beauté** [bote]	beauty
laid,e [lɛ, lɛd]	ugly
la **laideur** [lɛdœʀ]	ugliness
célèbre [selɛbʀ]	famous, celebrated
inconnu,e [ɛ̃kɔny]	unknown
anonyme [anɔnim]	anonymous
une œuvre anonyme	an anonymous work

la **peinture à l'huile** [pɛ̃tyʀalɥil]	oil painting
une **aquarelle** [akwaʀɛl]	watercolor
un **nu** [ny]	nude
une **nature morte** [natyʀmɔʀt]	still life

l'**Ecole des Beaux-Arts** (les Beaux-Arts) f [ekɔldebozaʀ]	art academy, school of fine arts
faire ses études aux Beaux Arts	study at the art academy
un **pinceau** [pɛ̃so]	brush
une **palette** [palɛt]	palette
un **pastel** [pastɛl]	pastel
un **fusain** [fyzɛ̃]	charcoal; charcoal drawing
une esquisse au fusain	a charcoal sketch
graver [gʀave]	engrave; imprint, impress
une **gravure** [gʀavyʀ]	engraving, cut, print
un livre illustré par des gravures de Daumier	a book illustrated with engravings by Daumier
un **graveur** [gʀavœʀ]	engraver

l'**impressionnisme** m [ɛ̃pʀesjɔnism]	impressionism
(un,e) **impressionniste** n; adj [ɛ̃pʀesjɔnist]	impressionist; impressionistic
Au musée d'Orsay, il y a une magnifique collection d'œuvres impressionnistes.	In the Musée d'Orsay there is a magnificent collection of impressionist works.
l'**expressionnisme** m [ɛkspʀesjɔnism]	expressionism
(un,e) **expressionniste** n; adj [ɛkspʀesjɔnist]	expressionist; expressionistic
le **cubisme** [kybism]	cubism
le **surréalisme** [syʀealism]	surrealism
l'**art nouveau** m [aʀnuvo]	art nouveau
réaliste [ʀealist]	realistic
figuratif, -ive [figyʀatif, iv]	figurative
abstrait,e [abstʀɛ, ɛt]	abstract
Après une période figurative, il s'est tourné vers l'art abstrait.	After a figurative period, he turned to abstract art.

une **collection** [kɔlɛksjɔ̃]	collection
collectionner [kɔlɛksjɔne]	collect
un,e **collectionneur, -euse** [kɔlɛksjɔnœʀ, øz]	collector

un **faux** [fo]	fake, forgery
Quand on a fait expertiser le tableau, on a découvert que c'était un faux.	When an appraisal of the picture was done, it was found to be a fake.
un,e **faussaire** [fosɛʀ]	forger

sculpter [skylte]	sculpt
la **sculpture** [skyltyʀ]	sculpture
une **statue** [staty]	statue
une **statue de/en bronze**	a bronze statue
Cette statue est une œuvre de Rodin.	That statue is a work by Rodin.
un **buste** [byst]	bust
un buste de Napoléon	a bust of Napoleon
un **bas-relief** [baʀəliɛf]	bas-relief
le **marbre** [maʀbʀ]	marble
une colonne en marbre de Carrare	a column of Carrara marble

modeler [mɔd(ə)le]	model
l'**argile** f [aʀʒil]	clay
un vase en argile	a clay vase
la **poterie** [pɔtʀi]	pottery
faire de la poterie	pot, make pottery
la **céramique** [seʀamik]	ceramics

le **style** [stil]	style
le **style roman**	Romanesque style
le **style gothique**	Gothic style
le **style médiéval**	medieval style
le **style baroque**	Baroque style
le **style classique**	classical style

12.2 Music and Musical Events

la **musique** [myzik]	music
la **musique moderne**	modern music
la **musique folklorique**	folk music
faire de la musique	make music
J'écoute surtout de la musique classique.	I listen primarily to classical music.
une école de musique	school of music
un,e **musicien,ne** [myzisjɛ̃, jɛn]	musician
musical,e [myzikal]	musical

Il a reçu une solide formation musicale.	He has received a solid musical education.
un **son** [sɔ̃]	sound
une **note** [nɔt]	note
savoir lire les notes	know how to read notes
écouter [ekute]	listen to; hear

un **instrument** [ɛ̃stʀymɑ̃]	instrument

> **i** If you want to say what *instrument* you *play*, you must be sure to use the correct *preposition*. See the information on p. 185.

une **flûte** [flyt]	flute
prendre des cours de **flûte à bec**	take recorder lessons
une **guitare** [gitaʀ]	guitar
un **violon** [vjɔlɔ̃]	violin
une **trompette** [tʀɔ̃pɛt]	trumpet
un **clarinette** [klaʀinɛt]	clarinet
un **piano** [pjano]	piano
apprendre le piano	learn to play the piano
un **orgue** (des **orgues** f) [ɔʀg]	organ (church organ)
un **orgue électronique**	electronic organ, keyboard
une **batterie** [batʀi]	percussion instruments

une **mélodie** [melɔdi]	melody
Tout le monde connaît cette mélodie populaire.	Everyone knows this folk melody.
un **air** [ɛʀ]	tune, air
un air gai et entraînant	a gay and lively tune
un **rythme** [ʀitm]	rhythm
un **mouvement** [muvmɑ̃]	movement
le **premier mouvement** de la sonate «Au clair de lune»	the first movement of the Moonlight Sonata.

chanter [ʃɑ̃te]	sing
chanter en direct	sing live
chanter en play-back	sing playback (karaoke)
un,e **chanteur, -euse** [ʃɑ̃tœʀ, øz]	singer
un **chant** [ʃɑ̃]	singing, vocal music
une **chanson** [ʃɑ̃sɔ̃]	song, hit
un **chœur** [kœʀ]	choir; chorus
Chantons tous **en chœur**.	Let's all sing in chorus.
une **chorale** [kɔʀal]	choir
chanter dans une chorale	sing in a choir
un **lied** [lid]	lied, art song
un lied de Schubert	a Schubert lied

un **opéra** [ɔpeʁa]	opera
un **ballet** [balɛ]	ballet
danser [dɑ̃se]	dance
un,e **danseur, -euse** [dɑ̃sœʁ, øz]	dancer
le **jazz** [dʒaz]	jazz
le **rock** [ʁɔk]	rock
un **groupe** [gʁup]	group, band
jouer de la batterie dans un groupe de rock	play the drums in a rock band
la **musique pop** [myzikpɔp]	pop music
le **reggae** [ʁege]	reggae
le **rap** [ʁap]	rap
la **techno** [tɛkno]	techno
un **concert** [kɔ̃sɛʁ]	concert
un **orchestre** [ɔʁkɛstʁ]	orchestra
un **chef d'orchestre**	conductor
diriger [diʁiʒe]	conduct
Le chef d'orchestre a dirigé son ensemble avec une grande précision.	The conductor conducted his ensemble with great precision.
un,e **soliste** [sɔlist]	soloist
un **abonnement** [abɔnmɑ̃]	subscription
prendre un **abonnement pour la saison**	get a season ticket
un,e **abonné,e** [abɔne]	subscriber
s'abonner à qc [sabɔne]	subscribe to s.th.
s'abonner à l'opéra	get an opera subscription
un **billet** [bijɛ]	ticket
une **salle de concert** [saldəkɔ̃sɛʁ]	concert hall
un **music-hall** [myzikol]	music hall
le **parterre** [paʁtɛʁ]	orchestra
J'ai réussi à avoir des places de parterre.	I succeeded in getting orchestra seats.
le **balcon** [balkɔ̃]	balcony
une **loge** [lɔʒ]	box
être aux 1ères loges *loc*	have a front seat
une **représentation** [ʁəpʁezɑ̃tasjɔ̃]	performance, show, presentation
un,e **interprète** [ɛ̃tɛʁpʁɛt]	interpreter
interpréter [ɛ̃tɛʁpʁete]	interpret
Elle interprète Mozart à merveille.	She interprets Mozart wonderfully well.

applaudir [aplodiʀ] — applaud
Le public a applaudi à tout rompre. — The audience applauded thunderously.
les **applaudissements** *m* [aplodismã] — applause
siffler [sifle] — boo, hiss
critiquer [kʀitike] — criticize, critique
un,e **critique** [kʀitik] — critic
Les critiques ont été très sévères. — The critics were very harsh.
la **critique** [kʀitik] — criticism
La critique a été sévère. — The criticism was merciless.

un **micro(phone)** [mikʀo/mikʀɔfɔn] — microphone, mike
un **amplificateur**; un **ampli** *fam* [ãpli(fikatœʀ)] — amplifier
la **sonorisation**; la **sono** *fam* [sɔno/sɔnɔʀizasjɔ̃] — loudspeaker system
La sono est trop forte. — The loudspeaker system is too loud.
un **décibel** [desibɛl] — decibel

enregistrer [ãʀ(ə)ʒistʀe] — record
Ce pianiste a enregistré toutes les sonates de Beethoven. — This pianist has recorded all of Beethoven's sonatas.
un **enregistrement** [ãʀ(ə)ʒistʀəmã] — recording
un **(disque) compact** [kɔ̃pakt] — compact disc
un **CD** [sede] — CD
Son dernier CD est sorti il y a deux semaines. — His/Her last CD came out two weeks ago.

le **conservatoire** [kɔ̃sɛʀvatwaʀ] — conservatory, school of music
Elle a fait ses études au Conservatoire de Paris, où elle a remporté un 1er prix. — She studied at the Paris Conservatory, where she won a first prize.
la **gamme** [gam] — scale
fair ses gammes — play scales, practice
la **gamme majeure** — major scale
la **gamme mineure** — minor scale
l'**harmonie** *f* [aʀmɔni] — harmony
harmonieux, -euse [aʀmɔnjø, jøz] — harmonious
la **mesure** [m(ə)zyʀ] — measure; bar
jouer en mesure — play in time

un **instrument à cordes** [ɛ̃stʀymãakɔʀd] — string instrument

un **instrument à vent** [ɛ̃stʀymãavã]	wind instrument
un **instrument à percussion** [ɛ̃stʀymãapɛʀkysjɔ̃]	percussion instrument

un **alto** *m* [alto]	viola
un **violoncelle** [vjɔlɔ̃sɛl]	cello
une **contrebasse** [kɔ̃tʀəbas]	double bass
une **harpe** ['aʀp]	harp
un **hautbois** ['obwa]	oboe
un **piano à queue** [pjanoakœ]	grand piano

une **symphonie** [sɛ̃fɔni]	symphony
une **sonate** [sɔnat]	sonata
une **sonate pour piano**	piano sonata
un **concerto** [kɔ̃sɛʀto]	concert
un concerto pour violon et orchestre	a concert for violin and orchestra
un **quatuor** [kwatɥɔʀ]	quartet
un **quatuor à cordes**	string quartet
la **musique de chambre** [myzikdəʃɑ̃bʀ]	chamber music
un **morceau** [mɔʀso]	(musical) composition, piece
jouer un **morceau** de musique	play a musical composition

la **musique instrumentale** [myzikɛ̃stʀymãtal]	instrumental music
la **musique orchestrale** [myzikɔʀkɛstʀal]	orchestral music
la **musique vocale** [myzikvɔkal]	vocal music, singing

un **gala** [gala]	gala
un **récital** [ʀesital]	musical recital
donner un **récital** de chant	give a vocal recital
un **festival** [fɛstival]	festival
une **tournée** [tuʀne]	tour
L'orchestre rentre d'une tournée triomphale au Japon.	The orchestra is returning from a successful tour in Japan.

un,e **virtuose** [viʀtɥoz]	virtuoso
Il joue du violon **en virtuose**.	He plays the violin with virtuosity.
le **talent** [talã]	talent
doué,e [due]	gifted
Elle est douée, mais elle ne travaille pas assez.	She is gifted, but she doesn't work enough.
un **enfant prodige** [ãfãpʀɔdiʒ]	child prodigy
une **cantatrice** [kãtatʀis]	cantatrice, (classical) singer

une **diva** [diva]	diva, celebrated singer

12.3 Literature

la **littérature** [liteʀatyʀ]	literature
la **littérature de (quai de) gare**	light fiction, popular literature
la **littérature engagée**	engaged literature
littéraire [liteʀɛʀ]	literary
un **texte littéraire**	literary text
un **texte non-littéraire**	expository text, nonliterary text
le **genre littéraire**	literary genre
un **prix littéraire**	award for literature
les **lettres** f [lɛtʀ]	study of languages and literatures; letters
un **homme**/une **femme de lettres**	writer; man/woman of letters

un **écrivain** [ekʀivɛ̃]	writer
écrire [ekʀiʀ]	write
un **auteur** [otœʀ]	author
Camus est l'auteur de *La peste.*	Camus is the author of *The Plague.*
un,e **romancier, -ière** [ʀɔmɑ̃sje, jɛʀ]	writer (of novels), novelist
un **poète** [pɔɛt]	poet

une **œuvre** [œvʀ]	work
les **œuvres complètes** de Balzac	the complete works of Balzac
un **ouvrage** [uvʀaʒ]	work, piece of work
publier un ouvrage	publish a book/work
un **passage** [pasaʒ]	passage
un **extrait** [ɛkstʀɛ]	excerpt, selection

un **livre** [livʀ]	book
un **bouquin** fam [bukɛ̃]	book
le **titre** [titʀ]	title
une **page** [paʒ]	page

> For information on the *gender of nouns* ending in -age, see p. 70.

un **chapitre** [ʃapitʀ]	chapter
un **volume** [vɔlym]	volume
une encyclopédie en 24 volumes	an encyclopedia in 24 volumes
la **table des matières** [tabl(ə)dematjɛʀ]	table of contents
la **couverture** [kuvɛʀtyʀ]	cover
le **dos du livre** [dodylivʀ]	spine

une **bande dessinée (BD)** [bɑ̃ddesine (bede)]	comic book
un **album** [albɔm]	number, issue
J'ai tous les albums d'Astérix.	I have every issue of Asterix.
un,e **dessinateur, -trice** [desinatœʀ, tʀis]	cartoonist, draftsman
l'**illustration** f [ilystʀasjɔ̃]	illustration
un,e **illustrateur, -trice** [ilystʀatœʀ, tʀis]	illustrator
illustrer qc [ilystʀe]	illustrate s.th.

les **époques littéraires** f [epɔkliteʀeʀ]	the literary epochs
les **courants littéraires** m [kuʀɑ̃liteʀeʀ]	the literary movements/currents
Différents courants littéraires ont marqué le romantisme.	Various literary currents left their mark on romanticism.
le **classicisme** [klasisism]	classicism
le **romantisme** [ʀɔmɑ̃tism]	romanticism
le **réalisme** [ʀealism]	realism
le **naturalisme** [natyʀalism]	naturalism
le **symbolisme** [sɛ̃bɔlism]	symbolism
l'**existentialisme** m [egzistɑ̃sjalism]	existentialism
Sartre est le chef de file de l'existentialisme français.	Sartre is the leading representative of French existentialism.

un **tome** [tɔm]	volume
Cette nouvelle se trouve dans le tome II des œuvres complètes de Maupassant.	This short story is in the second volume of Maupassant's collected works.
les **mémoires** m [memwaʀ]	memoirs
une **anthologie** [ɑ̃tɔlɔʒi]	anthology
une anthologie de la **poésie française**	an anthology of French poetry

une **bulle** [byl]	bubble
Les personnages des BD s'expriment par bulles.	The comic strip characters express themselves in bubbles.
un **scénario** [senaʀjo]	script, story
Goscinny a écrit des scénarios pour Lucky Luke.	Goscinny wrote stories for Lucky Luke.
un,e **scénariste** [senaʀist]	scriptwriter, story writer
l'**humour** m [ymuʀ]	humor

For information on **humour/humeur**, see p. 69.

humoristique [ymɔʀistik]	humorous
un **dessin humoristique**	caricature
une **planche** [plɑ̃ʃ]	page of pictures, illustration

un **éditeur, -trice** [editœʀ, tʀis]	publisher
une **édition** [edisjɔ̃]	edition
acheter un livre dans une **édition** de poche	buy a book in a paperback/ pocketbook edition
une **maison d'édition**	publishing house
(vient de) paraître [vjɛ̃d(ə)paʀɛtʀ]	(just) come out, be published
Son roman vient de paraître dans la collection Folio.	His novel has just been published in the Folio series.

12.4 Prose, Nonfiction

la **prose** [pʀoz]	prose
un **roman** [ʀɔmɑ̃]	novel
un **roman d'aventures**	adventure novel
un **roman policier**/un **polar** *fam*	detective/mystery novel
un **roman de science-fiction**	science-fiction novel
un **roman à l'eau de rose**	trashy novel

une **nouvelle** [nuvɛl]	short story, novella
un **conte** [kɔ̃t]	story, tale; fairy tale
un **conte satirique**	satirical tale
un **conte de fées**	fairy tale
une **biographie** [bjɔgʀafi]	biography
une **autobiographie** [otobjɔtgʀafi]	autobiography
une **légende** [leʒɑ̃d]	legend
un **traité** [tʀɛte]	treatise
un **traité de philosophie**	philosophical treatise
un **essai** [esɛ]	essay
Il a écrit un essai sur la peinture de Renoir.	He wrote an essay on Renoir's painting.
un **discours** [siskuʀ]	speech
faire/prononcer un discours	make/deliver a speech
une **lettre** [lɛtʀ]	letter
Les *lettres persanes* de Montesquieu sont pleines d'ironie.	Montesquieu's *Persian Letters* are full of irony.
un **proverbe** [pʀɔvɛʀb]	proverb

Comme dit le proverbe : *Tout ce qui brille n'est pas or.*	As the proverb says: All that glitters is not gold.

un **article** [aʀtikl]	article
consacrer un long article à un événement	devote a long article to an event
un **document** [dɔkymã]	document
adapter [adapte]	adapt
Il a adapté son roman pour la télévision.	He has adapted his novel for television.
intégral,e [ɛ̃tegʀal]	unabridged, complete
l'**œuvre intégrale** d'un écrivain	the unabridged work of a writer
abrégé,e [abʀeʒe]	abridged
une **version abrégée**	an abridged edition

un **récit** [ʀesi]	account, story; report
une **histoire** [istwaʀ]	story
raconter une histoire drôle	tell a funny story
la **fiction** [fiksjɔ̃]	fiction
C'est de la pure fiction.	That's pure fiction.
fictif, -ive [fiktif, iv]	fictional, made-up, invented
un **portrait** [pɔʀtʀɛ]	portrait
L'écrivain a **dressé un portrait** touchant de son héroïne.	The writer drew a touching portrait of his heroine.

un,e **journaliste** [ʒuʀnalist]	journalist
un **reportage** [ʀ(ə)pɔʀtaʒ]	report
un **compte-rendu** [kɔ̃tʀãdy]	account, report, review
Dans le journal d'hier a/est paru un compte-rendu de sa dernière publication.	In yesterday's paper there was a review of his latest publication.
une **interview** [ɛ̃tɛʀvju]	interview
Le ministre a **accordé une interview** à la télévision.	The minister granted an interview to television.

observer [ɔpsɛʀve]	observe
une **observation** [ɔpsɛʀvasjɔ̃]	observation
faire une observation	make an observation
affirmer [afiʀme]	claim, assert
Il affirme que cette histoire est vraie.	He claims that this story is true.
une **affirmation** [afiʀmasjɔ̃]	claim, assertion
réfléchir à/sur qc [ʀefleʃiʀ]	think about s.th., consider s.th.
J'ai réfléchi à ce problème.	I've thought about this problem.

une **réflexion** [ʀeflɛksjɔ̃]	reflection
s'accorder un **temps de réflexion**	take time for reflection

un **point de vue** [pwɛ̃dvy]	point of view
une **(prise de) position** [(pʀizdə)pozisjɔ̃]	(taking a) position
prendre clairement position sur qc	take a clear position on s.th.
une **opinion** [ɔpiɲɔ̃]	opinion, view
donner son opinion sur qc	give one's opinion on s.th.
un **avis** [avi]	view, opinion
à mon avis	in my opinion
partager l'avis de qn	share s.o.'s view
un **argument** [aʀgymɑ̃]	argument
prouver [pʀuve]	prove
Rien ne prouve que ce soit vrai.	Nothing proves that this is right.
contredire qn [kɔ̃tʀədiʀ]	contradict s.o.

s'engager pour qc [sɑ̃gaʒe]	support s.th., champion s.th.
Ce philosophe s'engage pour la paix dans le monde.	This philosopher supports world peace.
s'adresser à qn [sadʀɛse]	address s.o.
L'auteur s'adresse avant tout à la jeunesse.	The author addresses the youth above all.
une **question** [kɛstjɔ̃]	question
un **problème** [pʀɔblɛm]	problem
Cet essai soulève beaucoup de questions et de problèmes sans les résoudre.	This essay raises many questions and problems without solving them.

une **publication** [pyblikasjɔ̃]	publication
une **anecdote** [anɛkdɔt]	anecdote
Il paraît que cette anecdote est véridique.	It appears that this anecdote is truthful.
un **témoignage** [temwaɲaʒ]	testimony, statement, eyewitness account
un témoignage (im)partial	a biased/an impartial statement
journalistique [ʒuʀnalistik]	journalistic
un **texte journalistique**	newspaper text
captivant,e [kaptivɑ̃, ɑ̃t]	captivating, enthralling
passionnant,e [pasjɔnɑ̃, ɑ̃t]	exciting, thrilling
une description passionnante	an exciting description

un,e **narrateur, -trice** [naʀatœʀ, tʀis]	narrator
un **narrateur omniscient**	an omniscient narrator
narratif, -ive [naʀatif, iv]	narrative

Le poème comporte quelques éléments narratifs.	The poem contains several narrative elements.
la **perspective** [pɛʀspɛktiv]	perspective
Je ne peux pas partager la perspective de l'auteur.	I cannot share the author's perspective.
l'**optique** f [ɔptik]	perspective, standpoint
se placer dans l'**optique du lecteur**	put oneself in the reader's place

une **thèse** [tɛz]	thesis
formuler une thèse	formulate a thesis
une **hypothèse** [ipɔtɛz]	hypothesis
avancer une hypothèse	advance a hypothesis
une **antithèse** [ɑ̃titɛz]	antithesis
une **synthèse** [sɛ̃tɛz]	synthesis
faire la synthèse de qc	sum up/summarize s.th.

mettre en relief [mɛtʀɑ̃ʀəljɛf]	set off, show clearly
mettre en évidence [mɛtʀɑ̃nevidɑ̃s]	make conspicuous, bring to light
souligner [suliɲe]	underline, emphasize
Ce critique met en relief/met en évidence/souligne la gravité du problème.	This critic underlines the seriousness of the problem.
exagérer [ɛgzaʒeʀe]	exaggerate
une **exagération** [ɛgzaʒeʀasjɔ̃]	exaggeration

la **tension** [tɑ̃sjɔ̃]	suspense, tension
Le poète maintient la tension du début à la fin.	The poet maintains the suspense from beginning to end.
le **suspense** [syspɛns]	suspense
le **fil de l'action** [fild(ə)laksjɔ̃]	thread of the plot
interrompre le fil de l'action par un commentaire	interrupt the thread of the plot with a comment
le **fil conducteur** [filkɔ̃dyktœʀ]	main thread (of the plot, etc.)
perdre le fil conducteur du texte	lose the main thread of the text
le **déroulement** [deʀulmɑ̃]	unfolding, development
un **retour en arrière** [ʀ(ə)tuʀɑ̃naʀjɛʀ]	flashback
une **allusion** [a(l)lyzjɔ̃]	allusion
faire allusion à qn/qc	make an allusion to s.o./s.th.
un **lieu commun** [ljøkɔmɛ̃]	s.th. in common

Ce livre accumule les lieux communs.	This book is an accumulation of common things.

une **conviction** [kɔ̃viksjɔ̃]	conviction
ma conviction profonde	my profound conviction
être convaincu,e que [ɛt(ʀə)kɔ̃vɛ̃ky]	be convinced that
Je suis convaincu que cela s'est passé ainsi.	I'm convinced that it happened that way.
une **intention** [ɛ̃tɑ̃sjɔ̃]	intention
avoir l'intention de faire qc	intend to do s.th.
approuver [apʀuve]	approve
lu et approuvé	read and approved

12.5 Poetry

la **poésie** [pɔezi]	poetry
un **poème** [pɔɛm]	poem
un **poète** [pɔɛt]	poet
poétique [pɔetik]	poetic
l'œuvre poétique de Prévert	Prévert's poetic works
lyrique [liʀik]	lyrical
le **lyrisme** [liʀism]	lyricism, lyric poetry

le **sentiment** [sɑ̃timɑ̃]	feeling, sentiment
exprimer ses sentiments dans un poème	express one's feelings in a poem
sentimental,e [sɑ̃timɑ̃tal]	sentimental
l'**humeur** f [ymœʀ]	humor, mood
être d'humeur joyeuse	be in a cheerful mood
l'**état d'âme** m [etadam]	state/frame of mind
l'**atmosphère** f [atmɔsfɛʀ]	atmosphere
Le poète a su créer une atmosphère mélancolique.	The poet knew how to create a melancholy atmosphere.

une **image** [imaʒ]	image
un style **riche en images**	a style rich in images
imagé,e [imaʒe]	ornate, with a wealth of images
une expression imagée	a picturesque expression
une **métaphore** [metafɔʀ]	metaphor
Flaubert apporte un grand soin aux métaphores.	Flaubert takes great pains with metaphors.
un **symbole** [sɛ̃bɔl]	symbol
symbolique [sɛ̃bɔlik]	symbolic

un **recueil** [Rəkœj]	collection, miscellany
un **recueil de poèmes**	collection of poems
un **cycle** [sikl]	cycle
un **sonnet** [sɔnɛ]	sonnet
une **ode** [od]	ode
une **ballade** [balad]	ballad
une **fable** [fabl]	fable
les fables de La Fontaine	the fables of La Fontaine

la **forme** [fɔRm]	form
un **poème à forme fixe**	a poem with a fixed form, fixed rules
une **strophe** [stRɔf]	strophe, stanza
une **strophe de quatre vers**	a four-line stanza
un **refrain** [Rəfrɛ̃]	refrain
un **vers** [vɛR]	verse, line (of poetry)
la **versification** [vɛRsifikasjɔ̃]	art of metrics, versification
un **tercet** [tɛRsɛ]	tercet, triplet
un **quatrain** [katRɛ̃]	quatrain
Le sonnet se compose de deux quatrains et deux tercets.	A sonnet consists of two quatrains and two tercets.

le **rythme** [Ritm]	rhythm
Le rythme saccadé traduit les états d'âme de la protagoniste.	The jerky rhythm reflects the frame of mind of the main character.
un **enjambement** [ɑ̃ʒɑ̃bmɑ̃]	enjambment
une **syllabe** [silab]	syllable
un **octosyllabe** [ɔktɔsilab]	eight-syllable line of poetry
un **alexandrin** (un **dodécasyllabe**) [alɛksɑ̃dRɛ̃ (dodekasilab)]	Alexandrine, twelve-syllable line of poetry
une **allitération** [aliteRasjɔ̃]	alliteration
«Pour qui sont ces serpents qui sifflent sur vos têtes ?» (*Racine*)	"For whom are the snakes intended that hiss above your heads?"
une **césure** [sezyR]	caesura, break

la **rime** [Rim]	rhyme
une **rime pauvre/riche**	a poor/rich rhyme
une **rime plate** (aa bb)	a consecutive (adjacent) rhyme
une **rime croisée** (ab ab)	an alternate rhyme
rimer avec qc [Rime]	rhyme with s.th.
Amour rime avec *toujours*.	*Amour* rhymes with *toujours*.
la **sonorité** [sɔnɔRite]	resonance
sonore [sɔnɔR]	resonant

12.6 Drama

le **théâtre** [teatʀ]	theater
la **tragédie** [tʀaʒedi]	tragedy
une tragédie de Racine	a tragedy by Racine
tragique [tʀaʒik]	tragic
la **comédie** [kɔmedi]	comedy
comique [kɔmik]	comical
le **drame** [dʀam]	drama, play
dramatique [dʀamatik]	dramatic
un auteur dramatique	playwright

une **pièce (de théâtre)** [pjɛs]	play
une **pièce en prose**	play in prose
une **pièce en vers**	play in verse
un **acte** [akt]	act
une pièce en cinq actes	a play in five acts
un **tableau** [tablo]	tableau; scene
un drame en trois tableaux	a drama in three scenes
une **scène** [sɛn]	scene
la scène précédente	preceding scene
la scène suivante	following scene

l'**action** f [aksjɔ̃]	action, plot
L'action se déroule dans l'Antiquité.	The action unfolds in ancient times.
l'**action principale**	main plot
l'**action secondaire**	subplot, secondary plot

un **héros**, une **héroïne** ['eʀo, eʀɔin]	hero, heroine
un,e **protagoniste** [pʀotagɔnist]	protagonist, central figure
Les protagonistes de cette pièce sont dominés par leurs passions.	The main characters of this play are ruled by their passions.
un **dialogue** [djalɔg]	dialogue
un **monologue** [mɔnɔlɔg]	monologue
L'action est interrompue par un long monologue.	The action is interrupted by a long monologue.

une **représentation** [ʀəpʀezɑ̃tasjɔ̃]	performance, production, show
représenter [ʀəpʀezɑ̃te]	perform, depict, portray
la **première** [pʀəmjɛʀ]	premiere
L'auteur a assisté à la **première mondiale** de sa nouvelle comédie.	The author attended the world premiere of his new comedy.
le **metteur en scène** [mɛtœʀɑ̃sɛn]	producer
mettre en scène [mɛtʀɑ̃sɛn]	produce

la **mise en scène** [mizãsɛn]	production
monter une pièce [mõteynpjɛs]	stage a play
la **répétition** [ʀepetisjõ]	rehearsal
la **(répétition) générale**	general rehearsal
le **public** [pyblik]	(theater) public, audience

un **rôle** [ʀol]	role
Il a obtenu un petit rôle dans une pièce de Molière.	He got a small role in a Molière play.
le **premier rôle**	leading role
jouer [ʒwe]	play
Elle joue ce rôle à merveille.	She plays this role admirably.
le **jeu** [ʒœ]	play
un,e **comédien,ne** [kɔmedjɛ̃, jɛn]	comedian; player; actor, actress
un,e **acteur, -trice** [aktœʀ, tʀis]	(*film*) actor, actress
un,e **figurant,e** [figyʀã, ãt]	super(numerary), extra
débuter [debyte]	début, make one's début
avoir le trac [avwaʀl(ə)tʀak]	have stage fright
Avant chaque représentation, il est mort de trac.	Before every show he has terrible stage fright.

le **point de départ** [pwɛ̃d(ə)depaʀ]	starting point
L'action a pour point de départ l'assassinat du roi.	The starting point of the action is the king's murder.
l'**exposition** *f* [ɛkspozisjõ]	introduction, exposition
l'**intrigue** *f* [ɛ̃tʀig]	plot, intrigue
le **mobile** [mɔbil]	motive
Le monologue nous révèle les mobiles du meurtrier.	The monologue reveals to us the murderer's motives.
le **nœud** [nø]	crux, central point
Le nœud du drame se forme à l'acte III, scène 4.	The crux of the drama takes shape in Act III, Scene 4.
le **point culminant** [pwɛ̃kylminã]	climax
le **coup de théâtre** [kudteatʀ]	dramatic surprise
le **malentendu** [malãtãdy]	misunderstanding
Toute l'histoire repose sur un malentendu.	The entire story rests on a misunderstanding.
le **dénouement** [denumã]	dénouement, unraveling
un dénouement heureux	happy ending/outcome
fatal,e [fatal]	fatal, disastrous
une issue fatale	disastrous ending/outcome

le **comique** [kɔmik]	comic art, comedy; comic aspect
le **comique de situation**	comedy of situation

le **comique de caractère**	comedy of character
le **comique de langage**	comedy of language
un **quiproquo** [kipʀɔko]	mistake, mixup

12.7 Working with Texts

un **auteur** [otœʀ]	author
un auteur célèbre	a famous author
un **écrivain** [ekʀivɛ̃]	writer
un écrivain peu connu	a little-known writer
écrire [ekʀiʀ]	write

une **idée** [ide]	idea
exposer ses idées	expound one's ideas
une **pensée** [pɑ̃se]	thought
prendre parti pour/contre [pʀɑ̃dʀpaʀti]	take sides with/against
se révolter (contre) [s(ə)ʀevɔlte]	rebel (against)
critiquer [kʀitike]	criticize
la **critique** [kʀitik]	criticism, critique
s'élever contre [sel(ə)ve]	protest, rise up against
Cet écrivain s'élève contre la violence.	This writer is protesting violence.

distraire [distʀɛʀ]	entertain
Le but de l'auteur est de distraire son public.	The author's goal is to entertain his readers.
amuser [amyze]	entertain

le **genre** [ʒɑ̃ʀ]	genre
le **genre dramatique**	dramatic genre, drama
une **œuvre** [œvʀ]	work
un **chef d'œuvre**	masterpiece
(être) tiré,e de [tiʀe]	(be) drawn from
Ce passage est tiré d'une nouvelle de Le Clézio.	This passage is drawn from a short story by Le Clézio.
le **titre** [titʀ]	title
le **sous-titre**	subtitle

un **sujet** [syʒɛ]	subject, topic
un **sujet d'actualité**	a topical subject
le **thème** [tɛm]	theme, subject
La mort est le thème central de son œuvre.	Death is the central theme of his work.

il s'agit de [ilsaʒidə]
Il s'agit d'un discours sur l'éducation.

it is a matter of, it concerns
It concerns a discourse on education.

il est question de [ilɛkɛstjɔ̃də]
Au premier acte, il est question de la guerre.

it is a question of, it has to do with
In the first act, it is a question of war.

traiter qc/de qc [tʀɛte]
L'auteur traite un sujet délicat.

discuss s.th./deal with s.th.
The author discusses a ticklish subject.

Le texte traite de la religion.

The text deals with religion.

parler de qc [paʀle]

talk about s.th.

---

la **structure** [stʀyktyʀ]

structure

se diviser en [s(ə)divize]
Cet ouvrage se divise en trois récits.

be divided into
This work is divided into three stories.

se composer de [s(ə)kɔ̃poze]

consist of, be composed of

comporter [kɔ̃pɔʀte]
Sa tragédie comporte deux parties principales.

include, comprise
His tragedy includes two main parts.

une **phase** [faz]

phase, stage

un **chapitre** [ʃapitʀ]
chapitre 2, ligne 14

chapter
Chapter 2, line 14

---

une **narration** [naʀasjɔ̃]

narration, narrative

l'**introduction** f [ɛ̃tʀɔdyksjɔ̃]

introduction

le **début** [deby]

beginning, start

le **développement** [dev(ə)lɔpmɑ̃]
Le développement de l'intrigue est interrompu par des retours en arrière.

development
The development of the plot is interrupted by flashbacks.

la **partie principale** [paʀtipʀɛ̃sipal]

main part

le **tournant** [tuʀnɑ̃]
Le tournant de l'action **se situe au** chapitre suivant.

turning point
The turning point of the action is placed in the following chapter.

la **conclusion** [kɔ̃klyzjɔ̃]
un essai dont la conclusion manque de logique

conclusion, end
an essay whose conclusion is devoid of logic

la **fin** [fɛ̃]
à la fin

end
finally, in the end

---

analyser [analize]

analyze

une **analyse (de texte)** [analiz]

(text) analysis

expliquer [ɛksplike]

explain, interpret

une **explication de texte** [ɛksplikasjɔ̃d(ə)tɛkst]

detailed comment on a text

commenter [kɔmãte]	comment
un **commentaire** [kɔmãtɛʀ]	commentary
rédiger un commentaire de texte	write a commentary on the text
peser le pour et le contre	weigh the pros and cons
[pəzel(ə)puʀel(ə)kõtʀ]	
un **avantage** [avãtaʒ]	advantage
un **inconvénient** [ɛ̃kõvenjã]	disadvantage
résumer [ʀezyme]	summarize
un **résumé** [ʀezyme]	summary
faire un bref résumé du passage	make a brief summary of the passage
un **paragraphe** [paʀagʀaf]	paragraph
un **extrait** [ɛkstʀɛ]	excerpt

d'abord [dabɔʀ]	first
Tout d'abord, l'auteur présente ses personnages.	First of all, the author introduces his characters.
pour commencer [puʀkɔmãse]	at the beginning, first
ensuite [ãsɥit]	then
Ensuite, il parle de ses intentions.	Then he speaks about his intentions.
de plus [dəplys]	moreover
en effet [ãnefɛ]	in reality, indeed, in fact
En effet, il explique ses idées d'une manière remarquable.	In fact, he explains his ideas in a remarkable way.
donc [dõk]	then, therefore
enfin [ãfɛ̃]	finally
Enfin, il résume les différents aspects du problème.	Finally, he summarizes the different aspects of the problem.
finalement [finalmã]	finally, at last
pour finir [puʀfiniʀ]	to make a long story short
en conclusion [ãkõklyzjõ]	in conclusion
En conclusion, on peut dire que son argumentation est convaincante.	In conclusion, one can say that his reasoning is convincing.
bref [bʀɛf]	in short
Bref, je trouve que l'auteur a tort.	In short, I think that the author is wrong.
dans l'ensemble [dãlãsãbl]	all in all
Dans l'ensemble, je suis d'accord avec elle.	All in all, I agree with her.
pourtant [puʀtã]	however, nevertheless, yet
Le héros est sincère, et pourtant il n'est pas sympathique.	The hero is sincere, and yet he is not likable.

interpréter [ɛ̃tɛʀpʀete]	interpret

une **interprétation** [ɛ̃tɛʀpʀetasjɔ̃]	interpretation
le **contexte** [kɔ̃tɛkst]	context
replacer un extrait dans son contexte	put an excerpt back in its context
le **plan** [plɑ̃]	plan
un **détail** [detaj]	detail
un **message** [mɛsaʒ]	message
dégager le message d'un texte	extricate the message of a text
la **signification** [siɲifikasjɔ̃]	meaning, significance
un **symbole** [sɛ̃bɔl]	symbol
symboliser [sɛbɔlize]	symbolize

une **méthode** [metɔd]	method
les **moyens (d'expression)** *m* [mwajɛ̃]	means (of expression)
décrire qc [dekʀiʀ]	describe s.th.
une **description** [dɛskʀipsjɔ̃]	description
énumérer [enymeʀe]	enumerate, list
une **énumération** [enymeʀasjɔ̃]	enumeration, list
Ce passage comporte de nombreuses énumérations.	This passage contains numerous enumerations.
une **comparaison** [kɔ̃paʀɛzɔ̃]	comparison
comparer qn/qc à qn/qc [kɔ̃paʀe]	compare s.o./s.th. with s.o./s.th.
une **répétition** [ʀepetisjɔ̃]	repetition

le **déroulement de l'action** [deʀulmɑ̃d(ə)laksjɔ̃]	unfolding of the action
se dérouler [s(ə)deʀule]	unfold; develop, take place
se situer [səsitɥe]	be placed, be incorporated
La scène se situe à la fin de l'acte II.	The scene comes at the end of Act II.
se passer [s(ə)pase]	take place
L'histoire se passe à Marseille.	The story takes place in Marseille.
le **lieu** [ljø]	place
le **temps** [tɑ̃]	time
Molière ne respecte pas toujours les **unités de lieu, de temps** et **d'action**.	Molière does not always respect the unities of place, time, and action.
le **contenu** [kɔ̃t(ə)ny]	content(s)
contenir [kɔ̃t(ə)niʀ]	contain
Cette partie contient beaucoup d'expressions familières.	This part contains many colloquial expressions.
le **fond** [fɔ̃]	subject matter, substance
analyser le fond et la forme	analyze the substance and the form

un **héros**, une **héroïne** ['eʀo; eʀoin]	hero, heroine
le **personnage principal/ central** [pɛʀsɔnaʒpʀɛ̃sipal/sɑ̃tʀal]	principal/main character
un **personnage secondaire** [pɛʀsɔnaʒs(ə)gɔ̃dɛʀ]	secondary character
présenter [pʀezɑ̃te]	introduce, present
Dans le premier chapitre, l'auteur présente les personnages centraux.	In the first chapter the author introduces the main characters.
le **caractère** [kaʀaktɛʀ]	character
Le caractère de chaque protago-niste est décrit avec précision.	The character of each protago-nist is described with precision.
un **type** [tip]	type
C'est le **type même** du héros romantique.	He is the embodiment of the romantic hero.

un **cycle** [sikl]	cycle
Ce poème fait partie d'un cycle.	This poem is part of a cycle.
une **trilogie** [tʀilɔʒi]	trilogy
C'est le **premier volet** d'une trilogie.	This is the first part of a trilogy.
s'intituler [sɛ̃tityle]	be titled
Le roman s'intitule *Germinal*.	The novel is titled *Germinal*.

en premier lieu [ɑ̃pʀəmjeljø]	in the first place
En premier lieu, il faut signaler la clarté de la langue.	In the first place, the clarity of the language must be mentioned.
par conséquent [paʀkɔ̃sekɑ̃]	consequently
pour conclure [puʀkɔ̃klyʀ]	in conclusion, to summarize

le **style** [stil]	style
une poésie écrite dans un **style élaboré**	poetry written in an elaborate style
un **style limpide**	clear style
un **style concis**	concise style
un **style dépouillé**	prosaic, matter-of-fact style
un **style recherché**	refined, elegant style
un **style ampoulé**	high-flown style
un **moyen stylistique** [mwajɛ̃stilistik]	stylistic means
La variété des moyens stylistiques contribue au lyrisme de l'œuvre.	The variety of the stylistic means contributes to the lyricism of the work.
l'**ironie** *f* [iʀɔni]	irony
L'ironie de ce passage est mordante.	The irony of this passage is biting.

une **figure de style** [figyʀdəstil]	stylistic figure
une **métaphore** [metafɔʀ]	metaphor
une **mise en relief** [mizɑ̃ʀəljɛf]	emphasis, accentuation
au sens propre/figuré [osɑ̃spʀɔpʀ/figyʀe]	in the literal/figurative sense
Il utilise cette expression au sens figuré.	He uses this expression in the figurative sense.

French Word	English Equivalent	False Friend	French Equivalent
la gamme	scale	game	le jeu, la partie
une bulle	bubble	bull	un taureau
la fin	end	fin	la nageoire

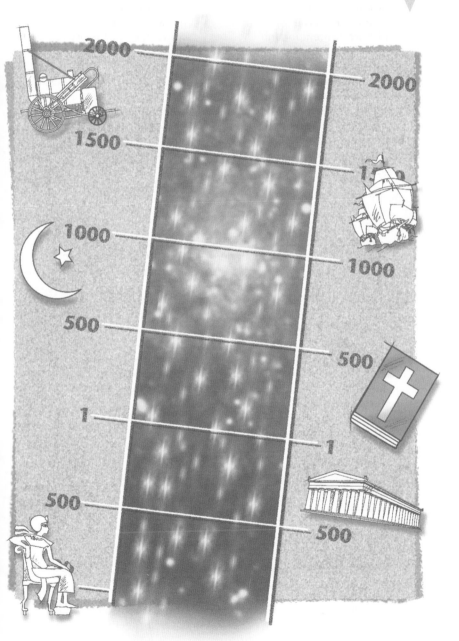

13.1 History

l'**histoire** f [istwaʀ]
history

  l'**histoire ancienne**
  ancient history

  l'**histoire moderne**
  modern history

  l'**histoire contemporaine**
  contemporary history

un,e **historien,ne** [istɔʀjɛ̃, jɛn]
historian

historique [istɔʀik]
historic(al)

  un **événement historique**
  a historic/historical event

avoir lieu [avwaʀljø]
take place

  La guerre de Trente Ans a eu lieu au 17ᵉ siècle.
  The Thirty Years War took place in the seventeenth century.

se passer [s(ə)pase]
happen, take place

  Ce fait historique s'est passé à la fin du 19ᵉ siècle.
  This historical event took place at the end of the nineteenth century.

durer (de ... à) [dyʀe]
last (from . . . until)

  La Première Guerre mondiale a duré de 1914 à 1918.
  World War I lasted from 1914 to 1918.

au début de [odebydə]
at the beginning of

  L'avion a été inventé au début du 20ᵉ siècle.
  The airplane was invented at the beginning of the twentieth century.

à la fin de [alafɛ̃də]
at the end of

  A la fin du règne de Louis XIV, la France était au bord de la ruine.
  At the end of the reign of Louis XIV, France was on the verge of ruin.

remonter à [ʀ(ə)mɔ̃te]
date back to, go back (in time) to

  Cette coopération remonte aux années 80.
  This cooperation dates back to the eighties.

le **siècle** [sjɛkl]
century

av./ap. J.-C. (avant/après Jésus-Christ) [avɑ̃/apʀeʒesykʀi(st)]
B.C./A.D.

  en 1200 ap. J.-C.
  in 1200 A.D.

  au Vᵉ siècle av. J.-C.
  in the fifth century B.C.

---

la **Gaule** [gol]
Gaul

un,e **Gaulois,e** [golwa, waz]
Gaul

un,e **Romain,e** [ʀɔmɛ̃, ɛn]
Roman

romain,e [ʀɔmɛ̃, ɛn]
Roman

gallo-romain,e [galoʀɔmɛ̃, ɛn]
Gallo-Roman

  l'**époque gallo-romaine**
  the Gallo-Roman epoch

---

découvrir [dekuvʀiʀ]
discover

  Christophe Colomb a découvert l'Amérique.
  Christopher Columbus discovered America.

une **découverte** [dekuvɛʀt]	discovery
conquérir [kɔ̃keʀiʀ]	conquer
Les soldats espagnols ont conquis de nouvelles terres pour leur roi.	The Spanish soldiers conquered new lands for their king.
une **conquête** [kɔ̃kɛt]	conquest
fonder [fɔ̃de]	found; establish
une **colonie** [kɔlɔni]	colony
colonial,e [kɔlɔnjal]	colonial
L'Espagne a fondé un grand empire colonial.	Spain founded a large colonial empire.
un,e **esclave** [ɛsklav]	slave

la **monarchie** [mɔnaʀʃi]	monarchy
un **roi** [ʀwa]	king
une **reine** [ʀɛn]	queen
royal,e [ʀwajal]	royal
le **royaume** [ʀwajom]	kingdom
régner [ʀeɲe]	reign, rule
Louis XIV a régné **en souverain absolu**.	Louis XIV reigned as an absolute monarch.
le **règne** [ʀɛɲ]	reign

un **empire** [ãpiʀ]	empire
un **empereur** [ãpʀœʀ]	emperor
Charlemagne a été **sacré empereur** en 800.	Charlemagne was crowned emperor in 800.
une **impératrice** [ɛ̃peʀatʀis]	empress

la **population** [pɔpylasjɔ̃]	population
le **peuple** [pœpl]	people
Le peuple a décidé de prendre le pouvoir.	The people decided to seize power.
une **révolution** [ʀevɔlysjɔ̃]	revolution
la **Révolution** [ʀevɔlysjɔ̃]	French Revolution
la **Marseillaise** [maʀsɛjɛz]	Marseillaise (French national anthem)
Liberté, Egalité, Fraternité [libɛʀte, egalite, fʀatɛʀnite]	Liberty, Equality, Fraternity
"Liberté, Egalité, Fraternité" est la devise de la France.	"Liberté, Egalité, Fraternité" is the motto of France.

la **guerre** [gɛʀ]	war
une **guerre civile**	civil war
déclarer la guerre	declare war
faire la guerre	make war

battre [batʀ]
Napoléon Iᵉʳ a été battu à Waterloo.

beat
Napoleon I was beaten at Waterloo.

occuper [ɔkype]
L'ennemi a occupé presque tout le pays.

occupy
The enemy occupied almost the entire country.

l'**occupation** f [ɔkypasjɔ̃]
sous l'occupation

occupation
under/during the occupation

libérer [libeʀe]
Les troupes alliées ont libéré la France.

liberate, free
The Allied troops liberated France.

la **libération** [libeʀasjɔ̃]

liberation

la **paix** [pɛ]
conclure un traité de paix
vivre en paix
faire la paix

peace
conclude a peace treaty
live in peace
make peace

un **armistice** [aʀmistis]
signer l'armistice

armistice
sign the armistice

la **Première Guerre mondiale** [pʀəmjɛʀgɛʀmɔ̃djal]

World War I

la **Seconde Guerre mondiale** [s(ə)gɔ̃dgɛʀmɔ̃djal]

World War II

la **Collaboration** [kɔ(l)labɔʀasjɔ̃]

the Collaboration (under the Vichy government)

la **Résistance** [ʀezistɑ̃s]

the Resistance (French resistance movement, 1940–44)

Pour libérer son pays, il est entré dans la Résistance.

To liberate his country, he joined the French Resistance.

le **Débarquement** [debaʀkəmɑ̃]

the landing (of Allied forces in Normandy, 1944)

Le Débarquement des Alliés en Normandie a eu lieu le 6 juin 1944.

The landing of the Allies in Normandy took place on June 6, 1944.

une **ère** [ɛʀ]

era

une **époque** [epɔk]
à l'époque des croisades

epoch, age
in the time of the Crusades

la **préhistoire** [pʀeistwaʀ]

prehistory

l'**âge de la pierre/du bronze** [aʒd(ə)lapjɛʀ/dybʀɔ̃z]

Stone/Bronze Age

l'**Antiquité** f [ɑ̃tikite]

antiquity

antique [ɑ̃tik]

antique, ancient

les **Anciens** m [ɑ̃sjɛ̃]

the ancients, the people of antiquity

le **Moyen(-)Age** [mwajɛnaʒ]	Middle Ages
médiéval,e [medjeval]	medieval
Carcassonne est une ville médiévale.	Carcassonne is a medieval town.
les **Croisades** f [kʀwazad]	Crusades
la **Renaissance** [ʀənɛsɑ̃s]	Renaissance
la **Réforme** [ʀefɔʀm]	Reformation
l'**Absolutisme** m [absɔlytism]	absolutism
l'**Ancien Régime** m [ɑ̃sjɛ̃ʀeʒim]	the *Ancien Régime* (period of absolutism in France before 1789)

le **clergé** [klɛʀʒe]	clergy
un **monarque** [mɔnaʀk]	monarch
succéder à [syksede]	succeed, follow
A la mort de Louis XIV, Louis XV lui a succédé.	When Louis XIV died, Louis XV succeeded him.
une **dynastie** [dinasti]	dynasty
la dynastie des Carolingiens	the Carolingian dynasty
la **noblesse** [nɔblɛs]	nobility
Noblesse oblige. *loc*	Rank has its obligations.
(un,e) **noble** n; adj [nɔbl]	noble
un **privilège** [pʀivilɛʒ]	privilege
Les nobles ne voulaient pas renoncer à leurs privilèges.	The nobles did not want to give up their privileges.
la **bourgeoisie** [buʀʒwazi]	bourgeoisie, middle class
(un,e) **bourgeois,e** n; adj [buʀʒwa, waz]	bourgeois; middle-class
le **Tiers-Etat** [tjɛʀzeta]	the Third Estate (the people)
98% de la population appartenaient au Tiers-Etat.	The Third Estate included 98 percent of the population.

les **Etats-Généraux** m [etaʒeneʀo]	the Estates General
la **prise de la Bastille** [pʀizdəlabastij]	the storming of the Bastille
la **guillotine** [gijɔtin]	guillotine
guillotiner [gijɔtine]	guillotine, to
une **exécution** [ɛgzekysjɔ̃]	execution
les **droits de l'homme** m [dʀwad(ə)lɔm]	human rights, rights of man
la **séparation des pouvoirs** [sepaʀasjɔ̃depuvwaʀ]	separation of powers
le **pouvoir législatif**	legislative power
le **pouvoir exécutif**	executive power
le **pouvoir judiciaire**	judicial power

l'**Empire** m [ɑ̃piʀ]	Empire

le Premier Empire (1804-1814)	the First Empire (1804–1814)
le Seconde Empire (1852-1870)	the Second Empire (1852–1870)
la **Guerre franco-allemande** **(1870/71)** [gɛRfRãkoalmãd]	the Franco-German War (1870/71)
la **(Iᵉʳᵉ-Vᵉ) République** [ʀepyblik]	the (First, Fifth) Republic

les **relations franco-allemandes** f [ʀ(ə)lasjɔ̃fʀãkoalmãd]	Franco-German relations
l'**OFAJ (Office franco-allemand pour la jeunesse)** [ɔfaʒ]	the Franco-German Youth Office
la **réunification** [ʀeynifikasjɔ̃]	reunification
la réunification de l'Allemagne	the reunification of Germany
la **CECA (Communauté européenne du charbon et de l'acier)** [seka]	European Coal and Steel Community
le **Marché commun** [maʀʃekɔmɛ̃]	Common Market, European Community
l'**Union européenne** [ynjɔ̃øʀɔpeɛn]	European Union

le **combat** [kɔ̃ba]	combat; fight, battle
combattre [kɔ̃batʀ]	combat; fight
combattre pour la liberté	fight for freedom
la **lutte** [lyt]	fight, battle
lutter [lyte]	fight
une **invasion** [ɛ̃vazjɔ̃]	invasion
envahir (qc) [ãvaiʀ]	invade (s.th.)
Le pays a été envahi par les troupes ennemies.	Enemy troops invaded the country.
un **envahisseur** [ãvaisœʀ]	invader, aggressor
dévaster [devaste]	devastate
La guerre a dévasté les villes et les villages.	The war devastated the towns and villages.
dominer [dɔmine]	dominate
la **torture** [tɔʀtyʀ]	torture
Le prisonnier a été soumis à la torture.	The prisoner was subjected to torture.
torturer [tɔʀtyʀe]	torture

une **victoire** [viktwaʀ]	victory
victorieux, -euse [viktɔʀjø, jøz]	victorious
sortir* victorieux, -euse d'un combat	emerge victorious from a fight
vaincre [vɛ̃kʀ]	vanquish, conquer, defeat
le **vainqueur** [vɛ̃kœʀ]	victor, conqueror
la **gloire** [glwaʀ]	glory

une **défaite** [defɛt]	defeat
une **débâcle** [debakl]	debacle, collapse, disaster
perdre [pɛʀdʀ]	lose
« La France a perdu une bataille! Mais la France n'a pas perdu la guerre! » *(de Gaulle)*	"France has lost a battle! But France has not lost the war!"
le/la **vaincu,e** [vɛ̃ky]	the loser, the conquered
Malheur aux vaincus!	Woe to the vanquished!
les **négociations** f [negɔsjasjɔ̃]	negotiations
les **négociations de paix**	peace negotiations

13.2 Religion

la **religion** [ʀ(ə)liʒjɔ̃]	religion
(un,e) **religieux, -euse** n; adj [ʀ(ə)liʒjø, jøz]	monk, nun; religious person
un religieux de l'ordre des Franciscains	a monk of the Franciscan Order
la **théologie** [teɔlɔʒi]	theology

la **foi** [fwa]	faith, belief
avoir la foi	have faith
croire (à/en) [kʀwaʀ]	believe (in)

---

i | **Whom and in what one believes**

Note the difference between:

croire qn/qc	*believe s.o./s.th.*
Il ne croit même pas ses amis.	*He doesn't even believe his friends.*
Tu crois tout ce qu'on te raconte ?	*Do you believe everything you're told?*
croire à qn/qc	*believe in s.o./s.th.*
Tu crois à l'avenir de l'Europe ?	*Do you believe in the future of Europe?*
croire en Dieu	*believe in God*
Je crois en Dieu, mais pas au diable.	*I believe in God, but not in the Devil.*

(un,e) **croyant,e** n; adj [kʀwajã, jãt]	believer, faithful person
prier [pʀije]	pray
la **prière** [pʀijɛʀ]	prayer
faire ses prières	pray, say one's prayers

(un,e) **chrétien,ne** n; adj [kʀetjɛ̃, jɛn]	Christian
la **foi chrétienne**	the Christian faith

(un,e) **catholique** *n; adj* [katɔlik]	Catholic
un **catholique pratiquant**	a practicing Catholic
le **catholicisme** [katɔlisism]	Catholicism
(un,e) **protestant,e** *n; adj* [pʀɔtɛtɑ̃, ɑ̃t]	Protestant
le **protestantisme** [pʀɔtɛstɑ̃tism]	Protestantism

l'**Eglise** *f* [egliz]	the Church (as an institution)
la séparation de l'Eglise et de l'Etat	the separation of Church and State
une **église** [egliz]	church
une **cathédrale** [katedʀal]	cathedral
le **pape** [pap]	pope
un **prêtre** [pʀɛtʀ]	priest
un **curé** [kyʀe]	a (Catholic) parish priest
M. le **curé**	Father
un **pasteur** [pastœʀ]	a (Protestant) pastor

Dieu [djø]	God
Jésus-Christ [ʒesykʀi(st)]	Jesus Christ
le **ciel** (les **cieux** *poétique, biblique*) [sjɛl, sjø]	heaven
"Notre Père qui es aux cieux."	"Our Father who art in heaven."
un **ange** [ɑ̃ʒ]	angel
le **paradis** [paʀadi]	paradise
le **diable** [djabl]	devil
tirer le diable par la queue *loc*	be hard up
l'**enfer** *m* [ɑ̃fɛʀ]	hell

l'**instruction religieuse** *f* [ɛ̃stʀyksjɔ̃ʀ(ə)liʒjøz]	religious instruction
le **baptême** [batɛm]	baptism
baptiser [batize]	baptize
Ils ont fait baptiser leur fils.	They had their son baptized.
la **(première) communion** [(pʀəmjɛʀ)kɔmynjɔ̃]	(first) communion
la **confirmation** [kɔ̃fiʀmasjɔ̃]	confirmation
le **mariage** [maʀjaʒ]	marriage; wedding
le **mariage civil**	civil wedding
le **mariage religieux**	church wedding

Noël [nɔɛl]	Christmas
Joyeux Noël !	Merry Christmas
le père Noël	Father Christmas
Vendredi Saint [vɑ̃dʀədisɛ̃]	Good Friday
Pâques *f* [pak]	Easter
Joyeuses Pâques !	Happy Easter!

l'**Ascension** f [asɑ̃sjɔ̃]	Ascension Day
la **Pentecôte** [pɑ̃tkot]	Pentecost, Whitsuntide
la **Fête-Dieu** [fɛtdjø]	Corpus Christi Day
l'**Assomption** f [asɔ̃psjɔ̃]	Assumption of the Holy Virgin
la **Toussaint** [tusɛ̃]	All Saints' Day

l'**Islam** m [islam]	Islam
se **convertir** à [s(ə)kɔ̃vɛʀtiʀ]	convert
Il s'est converti à l'Islam.	He converted to Islam.
islamique [islamik]	Islamic, Muslim
(un,e) **musulman,e** n; adj	Muslim
[myzylmɑ̃, an]	
le **ramadan** [ʀamadɑ̃]	Ramadan

le **Judaïsme** [ʒydaism]	Judaism
(un,e) **juif/juive** n; adj [ʒɥif, ʒɥiv]	Jew/Jewess; Jewish
(un,e) **israélite** n; adj [isʀaelit]	Israelite

l'**hindouisme** m [ɛ̃duism]	Hinduism
le **bouddhisme** [budism]	Buddhism
l'**athéisme** m [ateism]	atheism
la **laïcité** [laisite]	nondenominational character (of schools, etc.)
laïque [laik]	nondenominational
aller à l'école laïque	go to a nondenominational school
une **secte** [sɛkt]	sect

la **Bible** [bibl]	Bible
l'**Ancien**/le **Nouveau Testament**	the Old/New Testament
[ɑ̃sjɛ̃/nuvotɛstamɑ̃]	
le **Coran** [kɔʀɑ̃]	Koran, Quran

la **messe** [mɛs]	mass
aller* à la messe	go to mass
dire la messe	say mass
le **péché** [peʃe]	sin
se **confesser** [s(ə)kɔ̃fɛse]	confess
la **confession** [kɔ̃fɛsjɔ̃]	confession
entendre qn en confession	hear s.o.'s confession
être de confession protestante	belong to the Protestant confession
la **liberté du culte** [libɛʀtedykylt]	freedom of worship

un **temple** [tɑ̃pl]	temple; French Protestant church
une **mosquée** [mɔske]	mosque

une **paroisse** [paʀwas]	parish
le curé de notre paroisse	our (Catholic) parish priest
un **prêche** [pʀɛʃ]	sermon
prêcher [pʀɛʃe]	preach
prêcher la tolérance	preach tolerance
bénir [beniʀ]	bless
Le prêtre bénit les fidèles.	The priest blesses the faithful.

le **clergé** [klɛʀʒe]	clergy
un membre du clergé	a member of the clergy
un **évêque** [evɛk]	bishop
un **archevêque** [aʀʃəvɛk]	archbishop
un **moine** [mwan]	monk
Il est gras comme un moine. *loc*	He's as fat as a monk.
une **(bonne) sœur** *fam* [sœʀ]	nun, sister
un **ordre (religieux)** [ɔʀdʀ]	(religious) order
un **couvent** [kuvɑ̃]	convent
entrer au couvent	enter a convent
un **monastère** [mɔnastɛʀ]	monastery

saint,e [sɛ̃, sɛ̃t]	saint
un,e **Saint,e**	a saint
la **Sainte Vierge**	the Holy Virgin
le **Saint Esprit**	the Holy Spirit
sacré,e [sakʀe]	sacred, holy
solennel,le [sɔlanɛl]	solemn
la **communion solennelle**	the solemn first communion
un **miracle** [miʀakl]	miracle
croire aux miracles	believe in miracles
la **résurrection** [ʀezyʀɛksjɔ̃]	resurrection
la **croix** [kʀwa]	cross
faire le signe de croix	make the sign of the cross
pieux, -euse [pjø, pjøz]	pious
un **dogme** [dɔgm]	dogma

13.3 Philosophy

la **philosophie** [filɔzɔfi]	philosophy
un,e **philosophe** [filɔzɔf]	philosopher
philosophique [filɔzɔfik]	philosophical
un conte philosophique	a philosophical tale

penser [pɑ̃se]	think
"Je pense donc je suis."	"I think, therefore I am."
(Descartes)	

la **pensée** [pãse]	thought
un,e **penseur, -euse** [pãsœʀ, øz]	thinker
Descartes était un des grands penseurs de son temps.	Descartes was one of the great thinkers of his time.
une **idée** [ide]	idea
échanger des idées	exchange ideas
une **théorie** [teɔʀi]	theory
émettre une théorie	set forth a theory
théorique [teɔʀik]	theoretical
l'**esprit** *m* [ɛspʀi]	mind, intellect; spirit; wit
spirituel,le [spiʀitɥɛl]	intellectual; spiritual; witty
la **matière** [matjɛʀ]	matter
une **notion** [nosjɔ̃]	notion, concept

les **mœurs** *f* [mœʀ(s)]	morals
le **bien** [bjɛ̃]	the Good
le **mal** [mal]	the Bad, the Evil
moral,e [mɔʀal]	moral
la **morale** [mɔʀal]	morality

---

i **Same sound, different meaning**

The words **moral** and **morale** sound alike, but their meanings are different.
Note the difference between:

le moral	*morale, spirit, mental or moral faculties*
remonter le moral à qn	*cheer s.o. up*
la morale	*morals, morality, ethics*
donner une leçon de morale à qn	*give s.o. a moral lecture*

---

la **raison** [ʀɛzɔ̃]	reason, understanding; sanity
perdre la raison	lose one's mind
raisonner [ʀɛzɔne]	reason; argue
le **raisonnement** [ʀɛzɔnmã]	reasoning; argument
suivre un raisonnement logique	follow a logical reasoning
raisonnable [ʀɛzɔnabl]	reasonable
un **argument** [aʀgymã]	argument
un argument pour/contre	an argument for/against
le **sens** [sãs]	sense; meaning
donner un sens à sa vie	give meaning to one's life
le **symbole** [sɛ̃bɔl]	symbol
le **bon sens** [bɔ̃sãs]	good sense, common sense
agir **en dépit du** bon sens	act against good sense
la **contradiction** [kɔ̃tʀadiksjɔ̃]	contradiction

l'**origine** *f* [ɔʀiʒin]	origin
la **cause** [koz]	cause
causer [koze]	cause, to
un **effet** [efɛ]	effect
A petite cause grands effets. *loc*	Small causes, big effects.
la **volonté** [vɔlɔ̃te]	will

concret, -ète [kɔ̃kʀɛ, ɛt]	concrete
un exemple concret	a concrete example
abstrait,e [abstʀɛ ɛt]	abstract
réel,le [ʀeɛl]	real
Le fait dont je parle est réel.	The event I'm talking about is real.
réaliste [ʀealist]	realistic
la **réalité** [ʀealite]	reality
l'**expérience** *f* [ɛkspeʀjɑ̃s]	experience; experiment
une **expérience vécue**	a personal experience
tenter l'expérience	attempt the experiment

vrai,e [vʀɛ]	true

---

i   For information on *adjectives* whose *meaning changes*, depending on whether they *precede* or *follow* the word modified, see p. 37.

---

la **vérité** [veʀite]	truth
cacher la vérité	hide the truth
véritable [veʀitabl]	true, genuine, real
certain,e [sɛʀtɛ̃, ɛn]	certain
Je suis **sûr et certain**.	I am quite certain.
incertain,e [ɛ̃sɛʀtɛ̃, ɛn]	uncertain
la **certitude** [sɛʀtityd]	certitude, certainty
l'**incertitude** *f* [ɛ̃sɛʀtityd]	incertitude, uncertainty
être dans l'incertitude au sujet de qc	be uncertain about s.th.
l'**erreur** *f* [eʀœʀ]	error
faire erreur	err, make an error
L'erreur est humaine. *loc*	To err is human.
faux, fausse [fo, fos]	false, wrong
faire fausse route	be on the wrong track

une **œuvre** [œvʀ]	work
les œuvres complètes de Voltaire	the complete works of Voltaire
un **ouvrage** [uvʀaʒ]	work, book
un ouvrage philosophique	a philosophical work
une **essai** [esɛ]	essay
un **traité** [tʀɛte]	treatise

la **méthode** [metɔd]	method
la **doctrine** [dɔktʀin]	doctrine
le **modèle** [mɔdɛl]	model
le **principe** [pʀɛ̃sip]	principle
Il est contre **par principe**.	He is opposed out of principle.

l'**individu** m [ɛ̃dividy]	individual
l'**être** m [ɛtʀ]	being
l'**essence** f [esɑ̃s]	essence; main point
l'**existence** f [ɛgzistɑ̃s]	existence, being, life
"L'existence précède l'essence."	"Existence comes before
(Sartre)	essence."
exister [ɛgziste]	exist, live, be in existence
la **mort** [mɔʀ]	death
mourir de sa belle mort	die a natural death
le **néant** [neɑ̃]	nothingness

la **conception** [kɔ̃sɛpsjɔ̃]	thought, notion; conception
concevoir [kɔ̃s(ə)vwaʀ]	conceive; imagine, understand
Il ne peut pas concevoir qu'on	He can't imagine that people
soit d'un autre avis que lui.	have a different opinion from
	his.
le **terme** [tɛʀm]	term, word, expression
un **acte** [akt]	act, deed
juger qn sur ses actes	judge s.o. by his deeds
douter [dute]	doubt, to
douter de l'existence de Dieu	doubt the existence of God
le **doute** [dut]	doubt
mettre qc en doute	place s.th. in doubt
l'**apparence** f [apaʀɑ̃s]	appearance
ne pas se fier aux apparences	not be deceived by appearances
l'**utopie** f [ytɔpi]	utopia
l'**ignorance** f [iɲɔʀɑ̃s]	ignorance
le **hasard** ['azaʀ]	hazard, chance
Nous n'avons rien laissé au	We have left nothing to chance.
hasard.	

élémentaire [elemɑ̃tɛʀ]	elementary, elemental
une question élémentaire	an elementary question
définitif, -ive [definitif, iv]	definitive
empirique [ɑ̃piʀik]	empirical

le **siècle des lumières**	the (Age of) Enlightenment
[sjɛkldelymjɛʀ]	
l'**idéalisme** m [idealism]	idealism

l'**empirisme** m [ãpiʀism]	empiricism
le **matérialisme** [mateʀjalism]	materialism
l'**existentialisme** m [ɛgzistãsjalism]	existentialism
"L'existentialisme est un humanisme." *(Sartre)*	"Existentialism is humanism."

la **métaphysique** [metafizik]	metaphysics
l'**éthique** f [etik]	ethics
l'**esthéthique** f [ɛstetik]	aesthetics
la **logique** [lɔʒik]	logic

French Word	English Equivalent	False Friend	French Equivalent
la misère	misery, want	miser	l'avare
la reine	queen	rein	la rêne

14.1 Constitution, State Institutions

le **pays** [pei]	country, land
les pays de l'Union européenne	the countries of the European Union
l'**Etat** *m* [eta]	state
"L'Etat c'est moi." (*Louis XIV*)	"I am the state."
la **nation** [nasjɔ̃]	nation
la **nationalité** [nasjɔnalite]	nationality, national status
demander la nationalité française	apply for French citizenship
être de nationalité espagnole	be a Spanish national
national,e [nasjɔnal]	national
l'**hymne national**	national anthem
le **drapeau** [dʀapo]	flag
hisser le drapeau tricolore	raise/hoist the Tricolor (French flag)
la **patrie** [patʀi]	fatherland
la **société** [sɔsjete]	society
la **république** [ʀepyblik]	republic
le **président de la République**	the president of the Republic
républicain,e [ʀepyblikɛ̃, ɛn]	republican
la **démocratie** [demɔkʀasi]	democracy
démocratique [demɔkʀatik]	democratic
un **régime démocratique**	a democratic form of government
la **constitution** [kɔ̃stitysjɔ̃]	constitution
constitutionnel,le [kɔ̃stitysjɔnɛl]	constitutional
une **monarchie constitutionnelle**	a constitutional monarchy
un **individu** [ɛ̃dividy]	individual, person
Tous les individus sont égaux devant la loi.	All persons are equal before the law.
individuel,le [ɛ̃dividyɛl]	individual, personal
respecter les libertés individuelles	respect individual freedoms
un,e **citoyen,ne** [sitwajɛ̃, jɛn]	citizen
la **liberté** [libɛʀte]	liberty
l'**égalité** *f* [egalite]	equality
la **fraternité** [fʀatɛnite]	fraternity, brotherhood
un,e **électeur, -trice** [elɛktœʀ, tʀis]	voter
électoral,e [elɛktɔʀal]	electoral, election
se faire inscrire sur une **liste électorale**	register one's name on a list of voters
un,e **candidat,e** [kɑ̃dida, at]	candidate
désigner un candidat	designate a candidate

Elections and voting

une élection	election
l'élection présidentielle	presidential election
être candidat à l'élection présidentielle	be a candidate in the presidential election
les (élections) législatives	legislative elections
se présenter aux élections législatives	be a candidate in the legislative elections
les (élections) régionales	regional elections
les (élections) cantonales	cantonal elections
les (élections) municipales	municipal elections
les (élections) européennes	European elections
les élections anticipées	upcoming elections
envisager des élections anticipées	face upcoming elections
un vote	vote; voting
exercer son droit de vote	exercise one's right to vote
le suffrage	suffrage; vote
le suffrage universel	universal suffrage
le suffrage indirect	indirect suffrage
élire qn au suffrage universel	elect s.o. according to the principle of universal suffrage
le scrutin	ballot, balloting
le scrutin secret	secret ballot
le scrutin/suffrage majoritaire	election by absolute majority
le scrutin/suffrage proportionnel	proportional election
un tour de scrutin	round of voting
au 1er/2e tour	in the first/second round of voting
Il a été élu au deuxième/2e tour.	He was elected in the second round.
dépouiller le scrutin	count the ballots/votes
élire qn	elect s.o.
Les citoyens ont élu un nouveau Président.	The citizens elected a new president.
voter qc	pass s.th.
voter une loi	pass a law
voter pour qn	vote for s.o.

une **loi** [lwa]	law
un **projet de loi**	bill
adopter une loi	adopt/pass a law
approuver une loi	pass a law
promulguer une loi	promulgate a law
rejeter une loi	reject a law
légal,e [legal]	legal
la **voix** [vwa]	voice; vote, suffrage

le/la **Président,e** [pʀezidã, ãt]	president
présidentiel,le [pʀezidãsjɛl]	presidential
les **élections présidentielles**	presidential elections

le **gouvernement** [guvɛʀnəmã]	government
les membres du gouvernement	the members of the government
renverser le gouvernement	overthrow the government
gouvernemental,e [guvɛʀnəmãtal]	governmental
gouverner [guvɛʀne]	govern
un,e **ministre** [ministʀ]	minister
le **ministre de l'Education**	minister of education
le **Premier ministre**	prime minister
le **ministre des Affaires Étrangères**	minister of foreign affairs; secretary of state
le **parlement** [paʀləmã]	parliament
Le Parlement se réunit.	The parliament is meeting/assembling.
(un,e) **parlementaire** n; adj [paʀləmãtɛʀ]	member of parliament; parliamentary
une session parlementaire	session of parliament
une **séance** [seãs]	session
la **liberté de conscience** [libɛʀtedkɔ̃sjãs]	freedom of conscience
la **liberté du culte** [libɛʀtedykylt]	freedom of religion
la **liberté d'opinion** [libɛʀtedɔpinjɔ̃]	freedom of opinion
les **droits fondamentaux** m [dʀwafɔ̃damãto]	fundamental rights
les **droits de l'homme** m [dʀwadlɔm]	rights of man, human rights
la **Déclaration des droits de l'homme**	the Declaration of the Rights of Man
garantir [gaʀãtiʀ]	guarantee
La Constitution garantit le respect des droits fondamentaux.	The Constitution guarantees respect of fundamental rights.
proclamer [pʀɔklame]	proclaim, announce
Les résultats du vote seront proclamés demain.	The results of the vote will be announced tomorrow.
la **proclamation** [pʀɔklamasjɔ̃]	proclamation, announcement
la proclamation de la République	the proclamation of the Republic
l'**autodétermination** f [otodetɛʀminasjɔ̃]	self-determination
se battre pour le **droit à l'auto-détermination**	fight for the right of self-determination
un **référendum** [ʀefeʀɛ̃dɔm/ʀefeʀãdɔm]	referendum
un **plébiscite** [plebisit]	plebiscite
le **fédéralisme** [federalism]	federalism

un **Etat fédéral** [etafederal]	federal state
la **République fédérale d'Allemagne**	Federal Republic of Germany
une **confédération** [kɔ̃federasjɔ̃]	confederation
la **Confédération helvétique**	Swiss Confederation, Helvetic Confederacy
le **Chancelier (allemand)** [ʃɑ̃səlje]	(the German) federal chancellor

la **participation** [paʀtisipasjɔ̃]	participation
La participation au vote a été très faible.	Voter participation was very low.
s'**abstenir** [sapstəniʀ]	abstain (from voting)
Les électeurs ont été **nombreux à s'abstenir.**	Numerous voters abstained from voting.
une **abstention** [apstɑ̃sjɔ̃]	abstention

une **circonscription (électorale)** [siʀkɔ̃skʀipsjɔ̃(elɛktɔʀal)]	constituency, election district
un **bureau de vote** [byʀodvɔt]	election bureau, election offices
une **urne** [yʀn]	ballot box
déposer son bulletin dans l'urne	put one's ballot in the ballot box
un **bulletin (de vote)** [byltɛ̃(dvɔt)]	ballot
un **bulletin blanc**	blank ballot
un **bulletin nul**	invalid ballot

la **majorité** [maʒɔʀite]	majority
obtenir la majorité	obtain a majority
la **majorité absolue**	absolute majority
la **majorité relative**	relative/simple majority
Au 2e tour, la majorité relative suffit.	In the second round of voting, a relative majority is sufficient.
être en ballottage [ɛtʀɑ̃balɔtaʒ]	be in a runoff

un **chef d'Etat** [ʃɛfdeta]	head of government
Les chefs d'Etat de l'UE se sont **réunis à Londres.**	The heads of government of the EU met in London.
le **chef de l'Etat** [ʃɛfdəleta]	head of state
Le chef de l'Etat s'est adressé aux Français dans une allocution télévisée.	The head of state addressed the French people in a televised speech.
le **chef du gouvernement** [ʃɛfdyguvɛʀnəmɔ̃]	head of government
la **cohabitation** [kɔabitasjɔ̃]	cohabitation (cooperation between the president and the government, when it has a different political orientation)
un gouvernement de cohabitation	a cohabitation government

l'**Assemblée nationale** f [asãblenasjɔnal]	French National Assembly
un,e **député,e** [depyte]	deputy
les députés de l'opposition	the opposition deputies
le **Sénat** [sena]	Senate
un,e **sénateur, -trice** [senatœʀ, tʀis]	senator
la **question de confiance** [kɛstjɔ̃dkɔ̃fjɑ̃s]	question of confidence
poser la question de confiance	put the vote of confidence
une **motion de censure** [mosjɔ̃dsɑ̃syʀ]	motion of censure/no-confidence
voter une motion de censure	pass a motion of censure
dissoudre [disudʀ]	dissolve
dissoudre l'Assemblée	dissolve the National Assembly
la **dissolution** [disɔlysjɔ̃]	dissolution
prononcer la dissolution de l'Assemblée	announce the dissolution of the National Assembly
la **législature** [leʒislatyʀ]	legislative period
démissionner avant la fin de la législature	resign before the end of the legislative period
les **indemnités parlementaires** f [ɛ̃dɛmnitepaʀləmɑ̃tɛʀ]	parliamentary pay and allowances

le **Conseil des ministres** [kɔ̃sɛjdeministʀ]	Council of Ministers; cabinet
le/la **ministre des Affaires étrangères**	minister of foreign affairs
le/la **ministre de l'Intérieur**	minister of the interior
le/la **ministre des Finances**	minister of finance
Le chef du gouvernement a renvoyé son ministre des Finances.	The head of the government has dismissed his minister of finance.
le/la **ministre de l'Education nationale**	minister of national education
le/la **garde des Sceaux** [gaʀd(ə)deso]	minister of justice
un,e **secrétaire d'Etat** [s(ə)kʀetɛʀdeta]	secretary of state
la secrétaire d'Etat **à la condition féminine**	secretary of state for women's issues
un **remaniement ministériel** [ʀ(ə)manimɑ̃ministeʀjɛl]	cabinet reshuffle
procéder à un remaniement ministériel	carry out a cabinet reshuffle
démissionner [demisjɔne]	resign
la **démission** [demisjɔ̃]	resignation
donner sa démission	submit one's resignation

succéder à [syksede]
  Jacques Chirac a succédé à François
  Mitterrand comme président de la
  République.
la **succession** [syksesjɔ̃]
  assurer/prendre la succession
  de qn

succeed
  Jacques Chirac succeeded
  François Mitterand as president
  of the Republic.
succession
  succeed s.o., become s.o.'s
  successor

le **pouvoir** [puvwaʀ]
  le **pouvoir législatif**
  le **pouvoir exécutif**
  le **pouvoir judiciaire**
  la **séparation des pouvoirs**
  la **prise du pouvoir**
  être au pouvoir
  François Mitterrand a été au
  pouvoir pendant 14 ans.

power
  legislative power
  executive power
  judicial power
  separation of powers
  seizure of power
  be in power
  François Mitterrand was in power
  for 14 years.

un,e **ressortissant,e** [ʀ(ə)sɔʀtisɑ̃, ɑ̃t]
  les ressortissants français à
  l'étranger
un,e **compatriote** [kɔ̃patʀiɔt]
un,e **patriote** [patʀiɔt]
le **patriotisme** [patʀijɔtism]
le **nationalisme** [nasjɔnalism]
(un,e) **nationaliste** n; adj [nasjɔnalist]
le **chauvinisme** [ʃovinism]
(un,e) **chauvin, -ine** n; adj [ʃovɛ̃, in]
  Il n'est pas nationaliste, il est carré-
  ment chauvin.

national
  the French nationals abroad

compatriot
patriot
patriotism
nationalism
nationalist; nationalistic
chauvinism
chauvinist; chauvinistic
  He's not a nationalist; he's a
  downright chauvinist.

14.2 Public Administration

une **institution** [ɛ̃stitysjɔ̃]
  les institutions de la République
officiel,le [ɔfisjɛl]
  Elle a fait une déclaration
  officielle.
un,e **fonctionnaire** [fɔ̃ksjɔnɛʀ]
une **fonction** [fɔ̃ksjɔ̃]
exercer [ɛgzɛʀse]
  exercer le pouvoir

institution
  the institutions of the Republic
official
  She has made an official
  statement.
official, civil servant
function, duty, office
exercise
  exercise power

occuper [ɔkype]
  occuper un poste important
(être) responsable de [Rɛspɔ̃sabl]
  M. Martin est responsable des
  questions fiscales.

occupy, hold
  hold an important office
(be) responsible for
  Mr. Martin is responsible for tax
  matters.

une **capitale** [kapital]
une **commune** [kɔmyn]
  La France a plus de 36 000
  communes.
communal,e [kɔmynal]
  les bâtiments communaux
un **maire** [mɛR]
  M./Mme le maire
une **mairie** [mɛRi]
l'**hôtel de ville** m [ɔ/otɛldəvil]
un,e **habitant,e** [abitã, ãt]

capital (city)
township
  France has more than 36,000
  townships.
town, municipal
  the municipal buildings
mayor
  Mr./Ms. Mayor
town hall
city hall *(in larger cities)*
inhabitant

une **région** [Reʒjɔ̃]
régional,e [Reʒjɔnal]
  le **Conseil régional**
un **département** [depaRtəmã]

départemental,e [depaRtəmãtal]
  une route départementale
un **arrondissement** [aRɔ̃dismã]

un **canton** [kãtɔ̃]

region, area
regional
  Regional Council
département (French administrative division)
pertaining to a département
  a département highway
arrondissement (subunit of a
  département)
canton (subunit of an
  arrondissement)

les **autorités** f [ɔtɔRite]
  se plaindre **auprès** des autorités
l'**administration** f [administRasjɔ̃]
  travailler dans l'administration
administratif, -ive [administRatif, iv]
  le **service administratif**
la **bureaucratie** [byRokRasi]
bureaucratique [byRokRatik]

the authorities
  complain to the authorities
administration
  work in the administration
administrative
  administrative service
bureaucracy
bureaucratic

la **municipalité** [mynisipalite]
  La fête a été organisée par la
  municipalité.
municipal,e [mynisipal]
  le **Conseil municipal**
un,e **conseiller, -ère** [kɔ̃seje, jɛR]
  une conseillère municipale

municipality
  The festival was organized by
  the municipality.
municipal
  town/city/municipal council
councilman, councilwoman
  town councilwoman

une **demande** [d(ə)mɑ̃d]	request, application, petition
faire une demande **auprès** de qn	present a request/petition to s.o.
un **formulaire** [fɔʀmylɛʀ]	form
remplir un formulaire	fill out a form
un **questionnaire** [kɛstjɔnɛʀ]	questionnaire
un **certificat** [sɛʀtifika]	certificate
faire établir un **certificat de mariage**	have a marriage certificate issued
un **extrait (de naissance)** [ɛkstʀɛ]	(birth) certificate
un **permis** [pɛʀmi]	permit
un **permis de séjour**	residence permit
délivrer un **permis de conduire**	issue a driver's license
prolonger (le passeport/la carte d'identité) [pʀɔlɔ̃ʒe]	renew (the passport/the identification card)

le **fisc** [fisk]	tax authorities, public treasury
fiscal,e [fiskal]	fiscal, tax
la **fraude fiscale**	tax fraud
un,e **percepteur, -trice** [pɛʀsɛptœʀ, tʀis]	tax collector
les **impôts** m [ɛ̃po]	taxes
payer des impôts	pay taxes
les **impôts sur le revenu**	income tax
imposer qn [ɛ̃poze]	tax s.o.
On **impose les contribuables en fonction de** leurs revenus.	The taxpayers are taxed according to their income.
imposable [ɛ̃pozabl]	taxable
Le stagiaire gagne trop peu pour être imposable.	A trainee earns too little to be subject to taxes.
déclarer [deklaʀe]	declare
Il ne déclare pas tout ce qu'il gagne.	He doesn't declare everything he earns.
une **déclaration d'impôts** [deklaʀasjɔ̃dɛ̃po]	tax declaration
remplir une déclaration	fill out a tax declaration
le/la **contribuable** [kɔ̃tʀibyabl]	taxpayer

un **préfet** [pʀefɛ]	prefect (chief administrator of a *département*)
une **préfecture** [pʀefɛktyʀ]	prefecture (headquarters of a *département*)
la **sous-préfecture**	sub-prefecture (headquarters of an *arrondissement*)

la **régionalisation** [ʀeʒjɔnalizasjɔ̃]	regionalization
le **Conseil régional** [kɔ̃sɛjʀeʒjɔnal]	regional council
la **centralisation** [sɑ̃tʀalizasjɔ̃]	centralization
centralisé,e [sɑ̃tʀalize]	centralized
La France est un pays centralisé.	France is a centralized country.
central,e [sɑ̃tʀal]	central
la **décentralisation** [desɑ̃tʀalizasjɔ̃]	decentralization
un partisan de la décentralisation	a supporter of decentralization
décentralisé,e [desɑ̃tʀalize]	decentralized

la **Métropole** [metʀɔpɔl]	mother country
Ils vont quitter la Guadeloupe pour aller en Métropole.	They're going to leave Guadeloupe to move to the mother country.
une **métropole** [metʀɔpɔl]	metropolis
La pollution touche toutes les grandes métropoles.	Pollution affects all the great metropolises.
la **France métropolitaine** [fʀɑ̃smetʀɔpɔlitɛn]	metropolitan France
les **D.O.M.-T.O.M.** *m* [dɔmtɔm]	the overseas *départements* and territories
un **territoire** [teʀitwaʀ]	territory, area of jurisdiction
l'**aménagement du territoire**	area planning

14.3 Parties, Political Systems

(la) **politique** *n; adj* [pɔlitik]	politics; policy; political
faire de la politique	be politically active
un **régime** [ʀeʒim]	regime; form of government
un **régime totalitaire**	totalitarian regime
un **système** [sistɛm]	system, form, regime
instaurer un système démocratique	set up a democratic system

un **homme d'Etat** [ɔmdeta]	statesman
un **homme**/une **femme politique** [ɔm/fampɔlitik]	politician
un,e **politicien,ne** *pej* [pɔlitisjɛ̃, jɛn]	politician
diriger [diʀiʒe]	lead
diriger le pays/la nation	lead the country/the nation
gouverner [guvɛʀne]	govern

le **gouvernement** [guvɛʁnəmã]	government, cabinet
Le Premier ministre forme son gouvernement.	The prime minister forms his cabinet.

un **parti** [paʁti]	party
un **parti conservateur**	conservative party
le **parti gaulliste**	Gaullist party
un **parti libéral**	liberal party
un **parti chrétien-démocrate**	Christian Democratic party
un **parti socialiste**	socialist party
un **parti communiste**	communist party
être majoritaire (au parlement/ gouvernement) [maʒɔʁitɛʁ]	be in the majority (in the parliament/government)
être minoritaire [minɔʁitɛʁ]	be in the minority
indépendant,e [ɛ̃depãdã, ãt]	independent
mener une politique indépendante	conduct an independent policy
l'**opposition** f [ɔpozisjõ]	opposition

la **gauche** [goʃ]	left
l'**extrême gauche**	the far left
la **droite** [dʁwat]	right
l'**extrême droite**	the far right
être de droite/de gauche	be on the right/left (politically)
les **partis de drotie/de gauche**	the parties of the right/left

le **capitalisme** [kapitalism]	capitalism
un,e **capitaliste** [kapitalist]	capitalist
le **socialisme** [sɔsjalism]	socialism
un,e **socialiste** [sɔsjalist]	socialist
le **communisme** [kɔmynism]	communism
un,e **communiste** [kɔmynist]	communist
le **fascisme** [faʃism]	fascism
un,e **fasciste** [faʃist]	fascist
l'**écologie** f [ekɔlɔʒi]	ecology, environmental protection
un,e **écologiste** [ekɔlɔʒist]	ecologist, environmentalist; Green

un **programme** [pʁɔgʁam]	program, (political) platform
Le candidat présente son programme.	The candidate presents his platform.
un **changement** [ʃãʒmã]	change
se prononcer pour le changement	speak out for change
une **initiative** [inisjativ]	initiative
prendre une initiative	take an initiative
une **mesure** [m(ə)zyʁ]	measure
prendre des mesures efficaces contre le chômage	take effective measures to fight unemployment

un,e **dirigeant,e** [diʀiʒã, ãt] | leader (of parties, unions)
avoir confiance en ses dirigeants | have confidence in one's leading politicians

un **leader** [lidœʀ] | leader
le leader de l'opposition | the leader of the opposition
assumer une responsabilité [asymeynʀɛspɔ̃sabilite] | assume responsibility
Elle assume une responsabilité **au sein du gouvernement.** | She assumes responsibility for the government.

adhérer [adeʀe] | belong to
Est-ce que tu adhères à un parti? | Do you belong to a party?
un,e **adhérent,e** [adeʀã, ãt] | member, adherent
un **membre** [mãbʀ] | member
un,e **militant,e** [militã, ãt] | active party member
Nos responsables ne sont pas assez à l'écoute des militants de base. | Our people on top don't listen enough to the party activists down below.
un,e **sympathisant,e** [sɛ̃patizã, ãt] | sympathizer

un **courant politique** [kuʀãpɔlitik] | political current
un courant modéré | a moderate (political) current
une **union** [ynjɔ̃] | union, alliance
l'union de la Gauche | the left-wing alliance
un **groupe parlementaire** [gʀuppaʀləmãtɛʀ] | faction
se rallier à [s(ə)ʀalje] | join
Le député s'est rallié au groupe communiste. | The deputy joined the communist faction.
une **coalition** [kɔalisjɔ̃] | coalition
Les partis de droite ont formé une coalition. | The right-wing parties formed a coalition.
une **alliance** [aljãs] | alliance

le **PS (Parti socialiste)** [peɛs] | socialist party
le **PC (Parti communiste)** [pese] | communist party
les **Verts** [vɛʀ] | the Greens
le **RPR (Rassemblement pour la République)** [ɛʀpeɛʀ] | neo-Gaullists
l'**UDF (Union pour la démocratie française)** f [ydeɛf] | party of the centrist middle classes

le **FN (Front National)** [ɛfɛn]	National Front (right-wing radical party)
un **message** [mesaʒ]	message
Le président de la République a adressé un message clair aux syndicats.	The president of the Republic sent a clear message to the labor unions.
consulter qn [kɔ̃sylte]	consult s.o.
consulter les électeurs (par référendum)	consult the voters (in a referendum)
une **consultation** [kɔ̃syltasjɔ̃]	public opinion poll
un,e **adversaire** [advɛRsɛR]	adversary
une **intrigue** [ɛ̃tRig]	intrigue
être victime d'une intrigue	be the victim of an intrigue
un **scandale** [skɑ̃dal]	scandal
être impliqué dans un scandale politique	be implicated in a political scandal

14.4   Laws, Justice System, Crime

une **loi** [lwa]	law
avoir la loi pour soi	have the law on one's side
respecter une loi	respect/abide by a law
violer une loi	violate/break a law
légal,e [legal]	legal
un procédé parfaitement légal	a perfectly legal procedure
la **légalité** [legalite]	legality
illégal,e [ilegal]	illegal
l'**illégalité** f [ilegalite]	illegality
le **droit** [dRwa]	law
un **étudiant en droit**	law student
le **droit civil**	civil law
la **justice** [ʒystis]	justice
poursuivre qn en justice	prosecute s.o. by law
juste [ʒyst]	just
une **injustice** [ɛ̃ʒystis]	injustice
être victime d'une injustice	be the victim of an injustice
injuste [ɛ̃ʒyst]	unjust
une **affaire** [afɛR]	lawsuit; matter; affair
Il est mêlé à une **affaire de corruption.**	He is mixed up in a bribery affair.

juger qn [ʒyʒe]   try s.o.; pass sentence on s.o.
  être jugé,e pour qc   be tried for s.th.
un **jugement** [ʒyʒmã]   judgment; sentence
  prononcer un jugement   pass sentence
un,e **juge** [ʒyʒ]   judge
  un,e **juge d'instruction**   examining magistrate
un,e **avocat,e (de la défense)**   (defense) lawyer, counsel
[avɔka, at]
  Son avocat a **plaidé non coupable.**   His lawyer entered a plea of not
                                       guilty.

un **jury** [ʒyʀi]   jury
un,e **juré,e** [ʒyʀe]   member of the jury

---

interroger [ɛ̃teʀɔʒe]   interrogate, question; examine
  interroger l'accusé   interrogate the accused
un **interrogatoire** [ɛ̃teʀɔgatwaʀ]   examination
  procéder à un interrogatoire   examine, conduct an examination
une **question** [kɛstjõ]   question
  poser une question   ask a question

---

accuser qn de qc [akyze]   accuse s.o. of s.th.
  Il a été accusé de vol.   He was accused of theft.
une **accusation** [akyzasjõ]   accusation
  porter une accusation grave contre bring a serious accusation
  qn   against s.o.
un,e **accusé,e** [akyze]   defendant, accused (person)
la **vérité** [veʀite]   truth
un **mensonge** [mãsõʒ]   lie
mentir [mãtiʀ]   (tell a) lie
(être) coupable (de qc)   (be) guilty (of s.th.)
[kupabl]
  Il n'était pas coupable du crime.   He was not guilty of the crime.
la **culpabilité** [kylpabilite]   guilt
  avoir **un doute sur la culpabilité**   have a doubt of the defendant's
  de l'accusé   guilt
innocent,e [inɔsã, ãt]   innocent
  être reconnu innocent,e   be declared innocent
l'**innocence** f [inɔsãs]   innocence

---

condamner qn à qc [kõdane]   sentence s.o. to s.th.
  L'accusée a été condamnée à   The defendant was sentenced to
  6 mois de prison.   six months in prison.
la **condamnation** [kõdanasjõ]   sentence, judgment, penalty
  infliger une condamnation à qn   sentence s.o., inflict a penalty on
                                       s.o.

un,e **condamné,e** [kɔ̃dane]	convict; person under sentence
un **condamné à mort**	a person sentenced to death
punir qn de/pour qc [pyniʀ]	punish s.o. for s.th.
une **prison** [pʀizɔ̃]	prison
faire de la prison	do time (in prison)
un,e **prisonnier, -ière**	prisoner
[pʀizɔnje, jɛʀ]	
Un prisonnier s'est évadé.	A prisoner has escaped.
la **liberté** [libɛʀte]	freedom
remettre qn en liberté	set s.o. at liberty
libérer qn [libeʀe]	release s.o., free s.o.
être **libéré pour** bonne conduite	be released for good conduct

les **forces de l'ordre** f [fɔʀsdəlɔʀdʀ]	forces of order
la **police** [pɔlis]	police
un **agent de police**	policeman, policewoman
un **poste (de police)**	police station
un **policier** [pɔlisje]	policeman, policewoman
policier, -ière [pɔlisje, jɛʀ]	police
une **enquête policière**	police investigation
un **gendarme** [ʒɑ̃daʀm]	gendarme, armed police officer
un,e **commissaire** [kɔmisɛʀ]	superintendent, commissioner
un **commissariat** [kɔmisaʀja]	police station
une **enquête** [ɑ̃kɛt]	investigation, inquiry
Le commissaire **mène l'enquête**.	The commissioner is leading the investigation.
enquêter [ɑ̃kɛte]	investigate, inquire
enquêter sur qn/qc	investigate s.th./s.o.
un **flic** fam [flik]	cop

un **crime** [kʀim]	crime
commettre un crime	commit a crime
criminel,le [kʀiminɛl]	criminal
un **acte criminel**	a criminal act
tuer [tye]	kill
blesser [blese]	injure, wound
une **arme** [aʀm]	weapon
une **victime** [viktim]	victim
L'accident a fait de nombreuses victimes.	The accident claimed numerous victims.
arrêter [aʀɛte]	arrest
une **arrestation** [aʀɛstasjɔ̃]	arrest
procéder à une arrestation	conduct an arrest

une **bagarre** [bagaʀ]	scuffle

Une bagarre a opposé deux bandes de jeunes.	Two teen gangs were involved in a scuffle.
la **violence** [vjɔlɑ̃s]	violence; force
céder face à la violence	yield/give way to force
violent,e [vjɔlɑ̃, ɑ̃t]	violent

une **attaque** [atak]	attack
voler [vɔle]	steal, rob
piquer *fam* [pike]	steal, "lift"
un **vol** [vɔl]	theft, robbery
un vol à main armée	armed robbery
un,e **voleur, -euse** [vɔlœʀ, øz]	thief, robber
"**Au voleur !**"	"Stop, thief!"

un **tribunal** [tʀibynal]	court of law; tribunal, bench
passer devant le tribunal	come before the court/judge
une **cour (de justice)** [kuʀ(dəʒystis)]	court (of justice)
le **procès** [pʀɔsɛ]	trial

le **Tribunal correctionnel** [tʀibynalkɔʀɛksjɔnɛl]	criminal court
la **Cour d'assises** [kuʀdasiz]	court of general sessions
en première instance [ɑ̃pʀəmjɛʀɛ̃stɑ̃s]	in the court of first instance
Elle a été condamnée en première instance.	She was convicted in the court of first instance.
faire appel [fɛʀapɛl]	appeal (to a higher court)
L'accusé a l'intention de faire appel.	The defendant intends to appeal.
la **Cour de cassation** [kuʀdəkasasjɔ̃]	court of cassation (highest court of appeals in France)
casser un jugement [kaseɛ̃ʒyʒmɑ̃]	set aside a verdict

le **droit pénal** [dʀwapenal]	penal law
le **droit civil** [dʀwasivil]	civil law
le **code pénal** [kɔdpenal]	penal code
le **code civil** [kɔdsivil]	civil code
un **dossier** [dosje]	case
La justice a décidé de **rouvrir le dossier.**	The court has decided to reopen the case.
un article [aʀtikl]	article; clause

un **cas** [ka]	case
un cas désespéré	hopeless case
prouver [pʀuve]	prove

L'avocat de la défense a prouvé que l'accusé était innocent.	The defense attorney proved that the accused was innocent.
une **preuve** [pʀœv]	proof
apporter la preuve de la culpabilité de qn	furnish proof of s.o.'s guilt
avouer [avwe]	confess
un **aveu** [avœ]	confession, avowal, admission
passer aux aveux	confess, give a confession
nier [nje]	deny
L'accusé nie tout en bloc.	The defendant denies everything.

une **plainte** [plɛ̃t]	complaint
porter plainte	lodge a complaint
déposer une plainte	demand a stated penalty
inculper qn (de qc) [ɛ̃kylpe]	charge s.o. (with s.th.)
Il a été inculpé de meurtre.	He has been indicted for murder.
une **inculpation** [ɛ̃kylpasjɔ̃]	charge, indictment
comparaître (en justice) [kɔ̃paʀɛtʀ]	appear (before the court)
Demain, ils vont **comparaître (en justice) pour** vol à main armée.	Tomorrow they will appear on a charge of armed robbery.
la **détention provisoire** [detɑ̃sjɔ̃pʀɔvizwaʀ]	custody, detention (pending trial)
Elle a fait trois mois de détention provisoire.	She was held in custody for three months.
un,e **délinquant,e** [delɛ̃kɑ̃, ɑ̃t]	delinquent, offender
la **délinquance** [delɛ̃kɑ̃s]	delinquency
La **délinquance juvénile** est en augmentation.	Juvenile delinquency is on the rise.
un,e **prévenu,e** [pʀev(ə)ny]	accused (person), prisoner
un,e **récidiviste** [ʀesidivist]	recidivist
le **non-lieu** [nɔ̃ljø]	dismissal of a charge
obtenir un non-lieu	have the charge dismissed

un **témoin** [temwɛ̃]	witness
appeler un témoin à la barre	call a witness to the witness stand
l'audition des témoins	hearing of witnesses
témoigner pour/en faveur de/ contre qn [temwaɲe]	testify for/in favor of/against s.o.
Ils ont tous témoigné en faveur de l'accusé.	They all testified in favor of the defendant.

déposer en faveur de/contre qn [depoze]	give evidence for/against
une **déposition** [depozisjɔ̃]	deposition; evidence
un **témoignage** [temwaɲaʒ]	testimony
un **faux témoignage**	false testimony
apporter son témoignage sur qc	testify about s.th.
à **charge** [aʃaʀʒ]	for the prosecution
à **décharge** [adeʃaʀʒ]	for the defense
appeler le témoin à charge/à décharge à la barre	call the witnesses for the prosecution/defense to the stand
le **serment** [sɛʀmɑ̃]	oath
prêter serment	take an oath
affirmer qc sous serment	declare s.th. under oath

le **procureur (général)** [pʀɔkyʀœʀ (ʒeneʀal)]	prosecutor (general)
la **défense** [defɑ̃s]	defense
prendre la défense de qn	defend s.o.
plaider [plɛde]	plead
plaider non-coupable	plead not guilty
le **verdict** [vɛʀdikt]	verdict
La cour a prononcé son verdict.	The court has pronounced its verdict.
des **circonstances atténuantes** f [siʀkɔ̃stɑ̃satenyɑ̃t]	mitigating circumstances
accorder des circonstances atténuantes à l'accusé	allow mitigating circumstances in the defendant's case
la **prescription** [pʀɛskʀipsjɔ̃]	statute of limitations
avec préméditation [avɛkpʀemeditasjɔ̃]	with premeditation
un crime commis avec préméditation	a premeditated crime
la **légitime défense** [leʒitimdefɑ̃s]	self-defense
plaider la légitime défense	plead self-defense
se repentir de qc [sǝʀ(ǝ)pɑ̃tiʀ]	repent of s.th.
Il se repent de son crime.	He repents of his crime.

acquitter qn [akite]	acquit s.o.
Le prévenu a été acquitté.	The accused was acquitted.
un **acquittement** [akitmɑ̃]	acquittal
une **amende** [amɑ̃d]	fine, penalty, reparation
L'accusée a été condamnée à une amende sévère.	The accused was sentenced to a hefty fine.
une **sanction** [sɑ̃ksjɔ̃]	sanction, punitive measure
une **peine** [pɛn]	punishment, penalty

En France, **la peine de mort** a été abolie en 1981.	In France, the death penalty was abolished in 1981.
avec sursis [avɛksyʀsi]	suspended
Ils ont été condamnés à 6 mois de prison avec sursis.	They were given a suspended sentence of six months in prison.
la **réclusion à perpétuité** [ʀeklyzjɔ̃apɛʀpetɥite]	imprisonment for life
une **erreur judiciaire** [eʀœʒydisjɛʀ]	miscarriage of justice; mistrial

un,e **contractuel,le** [kɔ̃tʀaktɥɛl]	auxiliary policeman; meter maid
la **police judiciaire (PJ)** *fam* [polisʒydisjɛʀ (peʒi)]	criminal investigation division (CID)
la **Gendarmerie nationale** [ʒɑ̃daʀməʀinasjɔnal]	gendarmerie, rural police
les **CRS (Compagnies républicaines de sécurité)** *f* [seeʀɛs]	security alert police, riot police
rechercher [ʀ(ə)ʃɛʀʃe]	search for, seek
une **piste** [pist]	track, trace, trail, scent
suivre une piste	follow a trail
une **trace** [tʀas]	trace, track; mark, impression
des **empreintes digitales** *f* [ɑ̃pʀɛ̃tdiʒital]	fingerprints
prendre les empreintes digitales de qn	take s.o.'s fingerprints
(un,e) **suspect,e** *n; adj* [syspɛ(kt),ɛkt]	suspect; suspicious
repérer un individu suspect	spot a suspicious person
soupçonner qn [supsɔne]	suspect s.o.
un **soupçon** [supsɔ̃]	suspicion
Les soupçons se portent sur son mari.	The suspicion falls on her husband.
une **rafle** [ʀafl]	raid, police roundup

les **poursuites** *f* [puʀsɥit]	proceedings
abandonner les poursuites contre qn	abandon proceedings against s.o.
un **mandat** [mɑ̃da]	warrant, writ
délivrer un **mandat d'amener**	issue a warrant
un **mandat d'arrêt**	warrant for arrest
mettre qn en examen [mɛtʀɑ̃nɛgzamɛ̃]	institute preliminary proceedings against s.o.
la **garde à vue** [gaʀdavy]	police custody
Il a été mis en garde à vue.	He was placed in police custody.
une **perquisition** [pɛʀkizisjɔ̃]	house search
une **pièce à conviction** *f* [pjɛsakɔ̃viksjɔ̃]	piece of evidence

un **délit** [deli]	misdemeanor, offense
prendre qn en flagrant délit	catch s.o. in the very act
un **meurtre** [mœrtr]	murder
un **assassinat** [asasina]	homicide, assassination
un **assassin** [asasɛ̃]	murderer, assassin
assassiner [asasine]	murder, assassinate
violer [vjɔle]	rape, to
un **viol** [vjɔl]	rape
un **mobile** [mɔbil]	motive
un **alibi** [alibi]	alibi
vérifier un alibi	check an alibi

kidnapper [kidnape]	kidnap
un,e **kidnappeur, -euse**	kidnapper
[kidnapœr, øz]	
enlever qn [ɑ̃l(ə)ve]	kidnap s.o.
un **enlèvement** [ɑ̃lɛvmɑ̃]	kidnapping
une **prise d'otage** [prizdɔtaʒ]	seizure of a hostage
une **rançon** [rɑ̃sɔ̃]	ransom
un **chantage** [ʃɑ̃taʒ]	blackmail
faire chanter qn [fɛrʃɑ̃te]	blackmail s.o.
un **maître-chanteur**	blackmailer
[mɛtr(ə)ʃɑ̃tœr]	

un **malfaiteur** [malfɛtœr]	offender; evil-doer
un **escroc** [ɛskro]	swindler
une **escroquerie** [ɛskrɔkri]	swindling
un **gangster** [gɑ̃gstɛr]	gangster
un,e **cambrioleur, -euse**	burglar
[kɑ̃brijɔlœr, øʒ]	
un **cambriolage** [kɑ̃brijɔlaʒ]	burglary
cambrioler [kɑ̃brijɔle]	burgle
une **bande** [bɑ̃d]	gang, band
un **hold-up** ['ɔldœp]	holdup
un **réseau** [rezo]	ring, network
démanteler un réseau de trafiquants	dismantle a ring of drug dealers
de drogue	
un,e **complice** [kɔ̃plis]	accomplice

14.5 Associations, Unions

une **association** [asɔsjasjɔ̃]	association
un **syndicat** [sɛ̃dika]	union, trade union

syndical,e [sɛ̃dikal]	pertaining to a union
un,e délégué, syndical,e	union delegate
une organisation syndicale	union organization
un,e **syndicaliste** [sɛ̃dikalist]	union member
le **syndicalisme** [sɛ̃dikalism]	union movement

un,e **salarié,e** [salaʀje]	wage earner
un,e **travailleur, -euse**	worker
[tʀavajœʀ, jøz]	
un,e **patron,ne** [patʀɔ̃, ɔn]	employer, boss
le **patronat** [patʀɔna]	management

protester [pʀɔtɛste]	protest, to
une **protestation** [pʀɔtɛstasjɔ̃]	protest
revendiquer [ʀ(ə)vɑ̃dike]	demand
une **revendication** [ʀ(ə)vɑ̃dikasjɔ̃]	demand

une **grève** [gʀɛv]	strike
Une **grève générale** a paralysé le pays.	A general strike has paralyzed the country.
une **grève sauvage**	unauthorized strike
une **grève de solidarité**	solidarity strike
faire (la) grève	go on strike
se mettre en grève	join the strike
être en grève	be on strike
un,e **gréviste** [gʀevist]	striker

une **réunion** [ʀeynjɔ̃]	meeting
se réunir [s(ə)ʀeyniʀ]	meet
une **discussion** [diskysjɔ̃]	discussion
discuter de qc [diskyte]	discuss s.th.
une **solution** [sɔlysjɔ̃]	solution
un **compromis** [kɔ̃pʀɔmi]	compromise
parvenir à un compromis	come to a compromise
un **résultat** [ʀezylta]	result
obtenir un résultat	obtain a result
reprendre le travail	resume work, go back to work
[ʀ(ə)pʀɑ̃dʀlətʀavaj]	

se syndiquer [s(ə)sɛ̃dike]	form a union
adhérer [adeʀe]	belong, be a member
un,e **adhérent,e** [adeʀɑ̃, ɑ̃t]	union member
s'organiser [sɔʀganize]	become organized

les **partenaires sociaux** *m* [paRtənɛRsɔsjo]	employers and employees
un,e **employeur, -euse** [ãplwajœR, øz]	employer
le **comité d'entreprise** [kɔmitedãtRəpRiz]	joint production committee, works council
une **convention collective** [kõvãsjõkɔlɛktiv]	collective wage agreement
un **conflit social** [kõflisɔsjal]	labor dispute(s)
contester [kõtɛste]	protest
une **contestation** [kõtɛstasjõ]	protest (movement)
se rassembler [s(ə)Rasãble]	assemble
un **rassemblement** [Rasãbləmã]	assembly; crowd
lancer un ordre de grève [lãseɛ̃nɔRdR(ə)dəgRɛv]	call (for) a strike
un **débrayage** [debRejaʒ]	walkout, token strike
débrayer [debReje]	walk out
un **piquet de grève** [pikɛdgRɛv]	picket
un,e **briseur, -euse de grève** [bRizœR, øzdəgRɛv]	strikebreaker, scab
un **lock-out** [lɔkaut]	lockout
négocier [negɔsje]	negotiate
une **négociation** [negɔsjasjõ]	negotiation
engager des négociations	engage in negotiations
un,e **négociateur, -trice** [negɔsjatœR, tRis]	negotiator
un **accord** [akɔR]	agreement
un,e **médiateur, -trice** [medjatœR, tRis]	mediator
une **consultation de la base** [kõsyltasjõd(ə)labaz]	strike ballot

14.6 Domestic Politics

l'**identité** *f* [idãtite]	identity
l'identité culturelle	cultural identity
une **minorité** [minɔRite]	minority
être en minorité	be in a minority
Les minorités essaient de préserver leur langue maternelle.	The minorities are trying to preserve their mother tongue.
l'**autonomie** *f* [otonomi]	autonomy

réclamer l'autonomie d'une région	demand the autonomy of a region
autonomiste [otonomist]	pertaining to autonomy
un **mouvement autonomiste**	a movement for autonomy

(un,e) **étranger, -ère** *n; adj* [etʀɑ̃ʒe, ʒɛʀ]	foreigner; foreign
l'**origine** *f* [ɔʀiʒin]	origin
le **pays d'origine**	country of origin
être d'origine espagnole	be of Spanish origin
la **(double) nationalité** [(dublə)nasjɔnalite]	(dual) nationality, (dual) citizenship

l'**immigration** *f* [imigʀasjɔ̃]	immigration
l'**immigration sauvage**	illegal immigration
immigrer [imigʀe]	immigrate
(un,e) **immigré,e** *n; adj* [imigʀe]	immigrant
un **travailleur immigré**	a foreign/migratory worker
une **immigrée clandestine**	an illegal immigrant
l'**émigration** *f* [emigʀasjɔ̃]	emigration
émigrer [emigʀe]	emigrate
un,e **émigré,e** [emigʀe]	emigrant
un,e **réfugié,e** [ʀefyʒje]	refugee
accueillir des réfugiés politiques	accept political refugees
se réfugier [s(ə)ʀefyʒje]	flee
Ills se sont réfugiés à l'étranger.	They fled to another country.

le **racisme** [ʀasism]	racism
On constate une montée inquiétante du racisme.	We note a disturbing increase in racism.
(un,e) **raciste** *n; adj* [ʀasist]	racist
la **discrimination** [diskʀiminasjɔ̃]	discrimination
être victime de la discrimination raciale	be a victim of racial discrimination

la **tolérance** [tɔleʀɑ̃s]	tolerance
l'**intolérance** *f* [ɛ̃tɔleʀɑ̃s]	intolerance
l'**intégration** *f* [ɛ̃tegʀasjɔ̃]	integration
s'intégrer [sɛ̃tegʀe]	become integrated
Pas mal d'immigrés ont des difficultés à s'intégrer.	A good number of immigrants have difficulty becoming integrated.
intégré,e [ɛ̃tegʀe]	integrated
un **permis de séjour** [pɛʀmidseʒuʀ]	residence permit
accorder un permis de séjour à qn	grant s.o. a residence permit

un **permis de travail** [pɛʀmidtʀavaj]	work permit

l'**asile (politique)** m [azil(pɔlitik)]	(political) asylum
un **demandeur d'asile**	asylum seeker
le **droit d'asile**	right of asylum
demander l'asile politique	request political asylum
accorder l'asile politique à qn	grant s.o. political asylum
un pays d'asile	country of asylum
un foyer pour demandeurs d'asile	home for asylum seekers

l'**opposition** f [ɔpozisjɔ̃]	opposition
s'**opposer à** [sɔpoze]	oppose, be opposed to
Les syndicats s'opposent aux propositions du gouvernement.	The unions oppose the government's proposals.

manifester (en faveur de/contre) [manifɛste]	demonstrate (for/against)
une **manifestation**; une **manif** fam [manif(ɛstasjɔ̃)]	demonstration
une manif pacifique/non-violente	a peaceful demonstration
un,e **manifestat,e** [manifɛstã, ãt]	demonstrator
l'**ordre** m [ɔʀdʀ]	order
troubler l'ordre public	disturb the public order
rétablir l'ordre	reestablish order
la **violence** [vjɔlãs]	violence
la **non-violence**	nonviolence

une **révolte** [ʀevɔlt]	revolt, uprising
une révolte armée	an armed uprising
se **révolter contre** [sɔʀevɔlte]	rebel against
une **révolution** [ʀevɔlysjɔ̃]	revolution
(un,e) **révolutionnaire** n; adj [ʀevɔlysjɔnɛʀ]	revolutionary
libérer [libeʀe]	liberate, free, release
Le dictateur a décidé de libérer quelques prisonniers politiques.	The dictator decided to free several political prisoners.
la **libération** [libeʀasjɔ̃]	liberation, freeing

le **terrorisme** [teʀɔʀism]	terrorism
un,e **terroriste** [teʀɔʀist]	terrorist
appartenir à un **réseau terroriste**	belong to a terrorist network
un **attentat** [atãta]	attempt at crime; crime, outrage
commettre un **attentat à la bombe**	attempt a bombing
un **acte de sabotage** [aktdəsabotaʒ]	act of sabotage

les **us et coutumes** m [ysekutym] — ways and customs
Il faut se plier aux us et coutumes du pays où l'on vit. — One has to adapt to the ways and customs of the country where one lives.

les **particularités** f [paʀtikylaʀite] — peculiarities, special features
respecter les particularités d'une culture — respect the special features of a culture
préserver [pʀezɛʀve] — preserve
préserver les traditions de ses ancêtres — preserve the traditions of one's ancestors
un,e **séparatiste** [sepaʀatist] — separatist
le **séparatisme** [sepaʀatism] — separatism

le **Code de la nationalité** [kɔddəlanasjɔnalite] — code of law dealing with citizenship
un,e **Français,e de souche** [fʀɑ̃sɛ/sɛzdəsuʃ] — a Frenchman or woman by origin
(un,e) **clandestin,e** n; adj [klɑ̃dɛstɛ̃, tin] — illegal immigrant; illegal
l'**afflux** m [afly] — influx
L'afflux de clandestins sur le marché du travail pose des problèmes graves. — The influx of illegal immigrants in the labor market poses serious problems.
un,e **Maghrébin,e** [magʀebɛ̃, bin] — person from the Maghreb
un,e **beur**; une **beurette** fam [bœʀ, ʀɛt] — beur (French-born child of immigrants from the Maghreb)

persécuter [pɛʀsekyte] — persecute
Elle a été persécutée **en raison de** ses convictions politiques. — She was persecuted for her political convictions.
la **persécution** [pɛʀsekysjɔ̃] — persecution
l'**exil** m [ɛgzil] — exile
s'**exiler** [sɛgzile] — go into exile
un,e **opposant,e** [ɔpozɑ̃, ɑ̃t] — opponent
Les opposants au régime ont été nombreux à s'exiler. — Numerous opponents of the regime have gone into exile.
s'**expatrier** [sɛkspatʀije] — leave one's country, become an expatriate
Il a préféré s'expatrier pour échapper aux persécutions. — He preferred to leave the country to escape persecution.

la **xénophobie** [gzenɔfɔbi] — xenophobia
xénophobe [gzenɔfɔb] — xenophobe

le **préjugé** [pʀeʒyʒe] — prejudice
Les préjugés ont la vie dure. — Prejudices are long-lived.
le **rejet** [ʀ(ə)ʒɛ] — rejection
rejeter [ʀ(ə)ʒɛte/ʀəj(ə)te] — reject, exclude
La société a tendance à rejeter ceux qui sont différents. — Society tends to cast out those who are different.
la **haine** ['ɛn] — hatred
éprouver de la haine pour qn — feel hatred for s.o.
l'**exclusion** f [ɛksklyzjɔ̃] — exclusion
Il faut donner la priorité à la lutte contre l'exclusion. — One must give priority to the fight against exclusion.
exclure qn (de) [ɛksklyʀ] — exclude s.o. (from)
Les SDF se sentent souvent exclus de la société. — The homeless often feel excluded from society.
l'**expulsion** f [ɛkspylsjɔ̃] — expulsion
expulser qn [ɛkspylse] — expel s.o.
On a expulsé les clandestins du territoire français. — The illegal immigrants were expelled from France.
renvoyer [ʀɑ̃vwaje] — send back
Ils ont été renvoyés dans leur **pays d'origine.** — They were sent back to their countries of origin.

multiculturel,le [myltikyltyʀɛl] — multicultural
se faire naturaliser [səfɛʀnatyʀalize] — become naturalized
la **naturalisation** [natyʀalizasjɔ̃] — naturalization
obtenir [ɔptəniʀ] — obtain
Elle a demandé sa naturalisation, mais elle ne l'a pas obtenue. — She applied for naturalization, but she did not obtain it.
le **droit du sol** [dʀwadysɔl] — jus soli, (citizenship based on the) right of birthplace
La France applique le droit du sol. — France applies the *droit du sol*.
le **droit du sang** [dʀwadysɑ̃] — jus sanguinis, (citizenship based on the) right of blood

la **désobéissance civile** [dezɔbeisɑ̃ssivil] — civil disobedience
appeler à la désobéissance civile — call for civil disobedience
boycotter [bɔjkɔte] — boycott
une **banderole** [bɑ̃dʀɔl] — streamer
Les manifestants ont déployé leurs banderoles. — The demonstrators have unrolled their streamers.
un **tract** [tʀakt] — leaflet
distribuer des tracts — distribute leaflets

militer (en faveur de/contre) [milite]	be active (in favor of/against)
la **lutte** [lyt]	fight
engager la lutte contre	take up the fight against
lutter pour/contre qn/qc [lyte]	fight for/against s.o./s.th.
le **combat** [kɔ̃ba]	combat, battle
Cette association mène un combat acharné contre la discrimination raciale.	This association is waging a fierce battle against racial discrimination.
des **troubles** m [tʀubl]	disturbances, dissensions
des troubles sanglants	bloody disturbances
une **émeute** [emøt]	riot, disturbance
déclencher une émeute	start a riot
se soulever contre [səsul(ə)ve]	rise up against
Le peuple s'est soulevé contre le roi.	The people rose up against the king.
une **insurrection** [ɛ̃syʀɛksjɔ̃]	insurrection
un **coup d'Etat** [kudeta]	coup d'état
prendre le pouvoir à la suite d'un coup d'Etat	seizing power after overthrowing the government

la **répression** [ʀepʀesjɔ̃]	repression, suppression
La réression de la révolte a été sanglante.	The suppression of the revolt was bloody.
la **torture** [tɔʀtyʀ]	torture

14.7 International Relations

l'**étranger** m [etʀɑ̃ʒe]	foreign parts; abroad
Vue de l'étranger, la situation paraît critique.	Seen from abroad, the situation seems critical.
étranger, -ère [etʀɑ̃ze, ʒɛʀ]	foreign
la **politique étrangère**	foreign policy
le **Ministre/Ministère des Affaires étrangères**	minister/ministry of foreign affairs

la **puissance** [pɥisɑ̃s]	power
une **puissance nucléaire**	a nuclear power
une **grande puissance**	a great power
puissant,e [pɥisɑ̃, ɑ̃t]	powerful

la **relation** [ʀ(ə)lasjɔ̃]	relation
les **relations internationales**	international relations

entretenir/rompre des relations diplomatiques	maintain/break off diplomatic relations
la rupture/la reprise des relations diplomatiques	the rupture/resumption of diplomatic relations
les **rapports** *m* [Rapɔʀ]	relations
Les rapports entre les deux pays sont tendus.	Relations between the two countries are tense.
la **tension** [tɑ̃sjɔ̃]	tension
une **crise** [kʀiz]	crisis
faire des propositions pour mettre fin à la crise	make proposals to bring an end to the crisis

une **réunion** [ʀeynjɔ̃]	meeting
un **sommet** [sɔmɛ]	summit
une **réunion au sommet**	summit meeting
une **rencontre** [ʀɑ̃kɔ̃tʀ]	meeting
des **rencontres bilatérales**	bilateral meetings
une **conférence** [kɔ̃feʀɑ̃s]	conference
Une **conférence internationale sur l'environnement** a lieu à Rome.	An international conference on the environment is taking place in Rome.

la **coopération** [kɔɔpeʀasjɔ̃]	cooperation
coopérer [kɔɔpeʀe]	cooperate
coopérer avec d'autres pays dans le domaine économique	cooperate with other countries in the economic sphere
un **échange** [eʃɑ̃ʒ]	exchange
un **échange scolaire**	student exchange
un **jumelage** [ʒymlaʒ]	(sister city) partnership
(être) jumelé,e [ʒymle]	(be) linked in partnership
Strasbourg est jumelé avec Stuttgart.	Strasbourg is linked with Stuttgart as a sister city.

l'**Europe** *f* [øʀɔp]	Europe
européen,ne [øʀɔpeɛ̃, ɛn]	European
l'**Union européenne** *f* (**UE**) [ynjɔ̃øʀɔpeɛn]	the European Union (EU)
le **Marché commun** [maʀʃekɔmɛ̃]	the Common Market
le **Marché intérieur européen** [maʀʃeɛ̃teʀjœʀøʀɔpeɛ̃]	the European domestic market

un **pays en voie de développement** [peiɑ̃vwad(ə)dev(ə)lɔpmɑ̃]	developing country
le **tiers-monde** [tjɛʀmɔ̃d]	the Third World
les **pays du tiers-monde**	the countries of the Third World
la **francophonie** [fʀɑ̃kɔfɔni]	use of the French language

francophone [fʀɑ̃kɔfɔn]	francophone, French-speaking
Le Sénégal est un pays francophone.	Senegal is a French-speaking country.

l'**ONU (Organisation des Nations Unies)** f [ony]	UN (the United Nations)
l'**OTAN (Organisation du traité de l'Atlantique Nord)** f [otɑ̃]	NATO (the North Atlantic Treaty Organization)
la **diplomatie** [diplɔmasi]	diplomacy
un,e **diplomate** [diplɔmat]	diplomat
une **ambassade** [ɑ̃basad]	embassy
un,e **ambassadeur, -drice** [ɑ̃basadœʀ, dʀis]	ambassador, ambassadress
un **consulat** [kɔ̃syla]	consulate
le consulat (général) de France à Francfort	the French Consulate (General) in Frankfurt
un **consul** [kɔ̃syl]	consul
consulaire [kɔ̃sylɛʀ]	consular

l'**hégémonie** f [eʒemɔni]	hegemony
une **rivalité** [ʀivalite]	rivalry
un **désaccord** [dezakɔʀ]	disagreement, discord
être en désaccord avec qn	be at variance with s.o.
la **détérioration** [deteʀjɔʀasjɔ̃]	deterioration
On assiste à une détérioration des relations entre les deux pays.	A deterioration of the relations between the two countries is being seen.
une **querelle** [kəʀɛl]	quarrel
Cette querelle les oppose depuis 20 ans.	That quarrel has put them at odds for 20 years.
un **conflit** [kɔ̃fli]	conflict
un **conflit armé**	armed conflict
la **pression** [pʀesjɔ̃]	pressure
exercer une pression sur qn	exert pressure on s.o.
s'**affronter** [safʀɔ̃te]	confront each other
une **confrontation** [kɔ̃fʀɔ̃tasjɔ̃]	confrontation
La confrontation semble inévitable.	Confrontation seems inevitable.
une **intervention** [ɛ̃tɛʀvɑ̃sjɔ̃]	intervention
une **sanction** [sɑ̃ksjɔ̃]	sanction
décréter des sanctions envers un état	impose sanctions against a state
un **embargo** [ɑ̃baʀgo]	embargo
lever l'embargo contre un pays	lift the embargo against a country

la **neutralité** [nøtralite]	neutrality
une **consultation** [kɔ̃syltasjɔ̃]	consultation
des **consultations bilatérales**	bilateral consultations
la **détente** [detɑ̃t]	détente
poursuivre une **politique de détente**	pursue a policy of détente
une **amélioration** [ameljɔrasjɔ̃]	improvement
un **entretien** [ɑ̃trətjɛ̃]	talk, conversation
un **entretien secret**	a secret talk
un **accord** [akɔr]	accord, agreement
conclure un accord	conclude an agreement
un **pacte** [pakt]	pact
une **entente** [ɑ̃tɑ̃t]	understanding, agreement
un **traité** trete	treaty
signer un traité	sign a treaty
ratifier un traité	ratify a treaty
violer un traité	violate a treaty

un **ennemi héréditaire** [en(ə)mieredit ɛr]	hereditary enemy
un **rapprochement** [raprɔ∫mɑ̃]	rapprochement, reconciliation
Les négociations ont mené à un rapprochement entre les adversaires.	The negotiations led to a rapprochement between the adversaries.
se rapprocher de qn/qc [s(ə)raprɔ∫e]	draw nearer to s.o./s.th.
une **réconciliation** [rekɔ̃siljasjɔ̃]	reconciliation
la **réconciliation franco-allemande**	the Franco-German reconciliation
se réconcilier [s(ə)rekɔ̃silje]	be reconciled
se réconcilier avec son ennemi héréditaire	be reconciled with one's hereditary enemy
un,e **allié,e** [alje]	ally
une **alliance** [aljɑ̃s]	alliance
le **Traité sur la coopération franco-allemande** [tretesyrlakɔɔperasjɔ̃frɑ̃koalmɑ̃d]	the Franco-German Cooperation Treaty

le **Parlement européen** [parləmɑ̃ørɔpeɛ̃]	the European Parliament
siéger [sjeʒe]	be headquartered, have one's seat
Le Parlement européen siège à Strasbourg.	The European Parliament has its seat in Strasbourg.
un **siège** [sjɛʒ]	seat (in Parliament)
le **Conseil de l'Europe** [kɔ̃sɛjdəlørɔp]	Council of Europe

le **Conseil des ministres**   Council of Ministers
[kɔ̃sɛjdəministʀ]
la **Commission européenne**   European Commission
[kɔ̃misjɔ̃øʀɔpeɛn]
la **Banque centrale européenne**   European Central Bank (ECB)
(BCE) [bãksãtʀaløʀɔpeɛn(beseə)]

14.8 Peace, War, Military

la **paix** [pɛ]	peace
faire la paix avec qn	make peace with s.o.
signer un **traité de paix**	sign a peace treaty
la **guerre** [gɛʀ]	war
la **guerre civile**	civil war
une **déclaration de guerre**	declaration of war
faire la guerre à qn/à un pays	make war on s.o./on a country
déclarer la guerre	declare war

un **plan** [plã]	plan
attaquer [atake]	attack, to
une **attaque** [atak]	attack
repousser une attaque	repulse an attack
mener une action [məneynaksjɔ̃]	carry out an operation
une **bataille** [bataj]	battle
la **défense** [defãs]	defense
le **ministre de la Défense**	minister of defense
(l')**ennemi,e** *n; adj* [en(ə)mi]	enemy; hostile
une **nation ennemie**	a hostile nation

(un) **militaire** *n; adj* [militɛʀ]	soldier; military
un **militaire de carrière**	career military man
un,e **soldat,e** [sɔlda, at]	soldier
un **uniforme** [ynifɔ̃ʀm]	uniform
une **caserne** [kazɛʀn]	barracks

une **armée** [aʀme]	army
une **arme** [aʀm]	arm, weapon
une arme conventionnelle	a conventional weapon
une arme chimique	a chemical weapon
une arme nucléaire	a nuclear weapon
L'Inde dispose de l'arme nucléaire.	India has nuclear weapons.
armer qn de qc [aʀme]	arm s.o. with s.th.
un **coup de feu** [kudfø]	shot

Un coup de feu a éclaté au coin de la rue.	A shot rang out at the street corner.
un **fusil** [fyzi]	rifle; gun
une **bombe** [bɔ̃b]	bomb
une **bombe atomique**	atom(ic) bomb
une **mine** [min]	mine
exploser [ɛksploze]	explode
détruire [detʀɥiʀ]	destroy

une **frontière** [fʀɔ̃tjɛʀ]	border, frontier
franchir la frontière franco-allemande	cross the French-German border
un **incident** [ɛ̃sidɑ̃]	incident
Un incident grave s'est produit.	A serious incident has occurred.
l'**occupation** f [ɔkypasjɔ̃]	occupation
occuper [ɔkype]	occupy
L'armée ennemie occupe le pays.	The enemy's army is occupying the country.

un,e **prisonnier, -ière** [pʀizɔnje, jɛʀ]	prisoner
un **prisonnier de guerre**	prisoner of war
un **camp (de prisonniers)** [kɑ̃]	(prisoner of war) camp
un **camp de concentration**	a concentration camp
une **victime** [viktim]	victim
Cette attaque a fait beaucoup de victimes parmi la population civile.	This attack claimed many victims among the civilian population.
(un,e) **blessé,e** n; adj [blese]	wounded, injured
On a évacué les blessés graves en hélicoptère.	The seriously wounded were evacuated by helicopter.
tuer [tɥe]	kill
(un,e) **mort,e** [mɔʀ, mɔʀt]	dead person; dead
La bataille a fait des centaines de morts.	The battle claimed hundreds of dead.

l'**armement** m [aʀməmɑ̃]	armament, arms
la **course aux armements**	arms race
le **contrôle des armements**	arms control
réduire l'armement nucléaire/conventionnel	limit nuclear/conventional arms
le **désarmement** [dezaʀməmɑ̃]	disarmament

hostile [ɔstil]	hostile
les **hostilités** f [ɔstilite]	hostilities
Tout le monde souhaite la fin des hostilités.	Everyone longs for the end of the hostilities.

combattre [kɔ̃batʀ]	combat
un,e **combattant,e** [kɔ̃batɑ̃, ɑ̃t]	combatant, soldier

le **service militaire (obligatoire)** [sɛʀvismilitɛʀ]	(required) military service
le **service civil** [sɛʀvissivil]	civilian service
faire son service militaire/civil	do one's military/civilian service
un **conscrit** [kɔ̃skʀi]	conscript
un **appelé** [ap(ə)le]	soldier called up for service
une **recrue** [ʀəkʀy]	recruit
un,e **volontaire** [vɔlɔ̃tɛʀ]	volunteer
demander des volontaires pour une mission	request volunteers for a mission
s'engager [sɑ̃gaʒe]	enlist, sign up
Il s'est engagé dans la marine pour 5 ans.	He enlisted in the Navy for five years.
un **objecteur de conscience** [ɔbjɛktœʀdəkɔ̃sjɑ̃s]	conscientious objector (CO)
obtenir le **statut d'**objecteur de conscience	obtain conscientious objector status
(un,e) **pacifiste** *n; adj* [pasifist]	pacifist
le **pacifisme** [pasifism]	pacifism
un **déserteur** [dezɛʀtœʀ]	deserter
déserter [dezɛʀte]	desert

une **troupe** [tʀup]	troop
une **division** [divizjɔ̃]	division
un **bataillon** [batajɔ̃]	battalion
un **officier** [ofisje]	officer
un **général** [ʒeneʀal]	general
recevoir un ordre [ʀəsəvwaʀɛ̃nɔʀdʀ]	receive an order
La troupe a reçu l'ordre de se mettre en marche.	The troops have received marching orders.

une **provocation** [pʀɔvɔkasjɔ̃]	provocation
un **avertissement** [avɛʀtismɑ̃]	warning
lancer un dernier avertissement à qn	give s.o. a final warning
un **ultimatum** [yltimatɔm]	ultimatum
L'ultimatum expirera demain à midi.	The ultimatum will expire tomorrow at midday.
un **bombardement** [bɔ̃baʀdəmɑ̃]	bombardment, shelling
bombarder [bɔ̃baʀde]	bombard, bomb
la **dissuasion** [disɥazjɔ̃]	dissuasion
la **force de dissuasion**	force of dissuasion

l'**armée de métier** f [aʀmed(ə)metje]	professional army
l'**armée de terre** f [aʀmedtɛʀ]	ground forces
un **char** [ʃaʀ]	tank
tirer sur [tiʀe]	shoot at
L'armée a tiré sur des civils.	The army shot at civilians.
l'**armée de l'air** f [aʀmedlɛʀ]	air force
un **avion de chasse** [avjɔ̃d(ə)ʃas]	fighter plane
une **fusée** [fyze]	missile
la **marine** [maʀin]	navy
un **sous-marin** [sumaʀɛ̃]	submarine, sub
un **sous-marin nucléaire**	a nuclear submarine
un **porte-avions** [pɔʀtavjɔ̃]	aircraft carrier

les **forces armées** f [fɔʀs(əz)aʀme]	armed forces
la **force de frappe** [fɔʀsdəfʀap]	French nuclear strike force
intervenir* [ɛ̃tɛʀvəniʀ]	intervene
Les forces armées sont intervenues à deux reprises.	The armed forces have intervened twice.
une **intervention** [ɛ̃tɛʀvɑ̃sjɔ̃]	intervention
les **pertes** f [pɛʀt]	losses
On déplore de lourdes pertes.	They complain of heavy losses.

une **agression** [agʀesjɔ̃]	aggression
un **agresseur** [agʀesœʀ]	aggressor
un,e **attaquant,e** [atakɑ̃, ɑ̃t]	attacker
repousser l'attaquant	beat off the attacker
le **couvre-feu** [kuvʀəfø]	curfew
l'**état d'urgence** m [etadyʀʒɑ̃s]	state of emergency
déclarer l'état d'urgence	declare a state of emergency
envahir [ɑ̃vaiʀ]	invade
envahir un pays	invade a country
un **envahisseur** [ɑ̃vaisœʀ]	invader
résister à l'envahisseur	resist the invader
une **invasion** [ɛ̃vazjɔ̃]	invasion
dévaster [devaste]	devastate
un **crime de guerre** [kʀimdəgɛʀ]	war crime
poursuivre qn pour crimes de guerre	prosecute s.o. for war crimes
un,e **criminel,le de guerre** [kʀiminɛldəgɛʀ]	war criminal

résister à [ʀeziste]	resist, offer resistance
la **résistance** [ʀezistɑ̃s]	resistance
un,e **résistant,e** [ʀezistɑ̃, ɑ̃t]	resistance fighter

Les résistants ont saboté la voie ferrée.	The resistance fighters sabotaged the railroad line.
un **traître**, une **traîtresse** [tʀɛtʀ, tʀɛtʀɛs]	traitor
une **trahison** [tʀaizɔ̃]	treason
trahir [tʀaiʀ]	commit treason, betray
Il a trahi sa patrie.	He betrayed his fatherland.
exécuter [ɛgzekyte]	execute
une **exécution** [ɛgzekysjɔ̃]	execution

une **victoire** [viktwaʀ]	victory
remporter la victoire	be victorious, conquer
le **vainqueur** [vɛ̃kœʀ]	victor
sortir* vainqueur de	emerge as victor
vaincre [vɛ̃kʀ]	vanquish, conquer
un,e **vaincu,e** [vɛ̃ky]	conquered person, loser
une **défaite** [defɛt]	defeat
subir une défaite	suffer a defeat
se rendre [s(ə)ʀɑ̃dʀ]	surrender
Les vaincus se sont rendus à l'ennemi.	The losers surrendered to the enemy.

la **fuite** [fɥit]	flight
prendre la fuite	take flight
fuir [fɥiʀ]	flee
La population civile a fui devant l'ennemi.	The civilian population fled from the enemy.
s'enfuir [sɑ̃fɥiʀ]	escape, flee
Ils ont profité de l'obscurité pour s'enfuir.	They took advantage of the darkness to escape.
capituler [kapityle]	capitulate
L'armée a capitulé **sans conditions**.	The army capitulated unconditionally.
la **capitulation** [kapitylasjɔ̃]	capitulation
un **armistice** [aʀmistis]	armistice
violer l'armistice	violate the armistice

French Word	English Equivalent	False Friend	French Equivalent
un parti	(political) party	party (event)	une soirée
le flic	cop, policeman	flick (movie)	le ciné

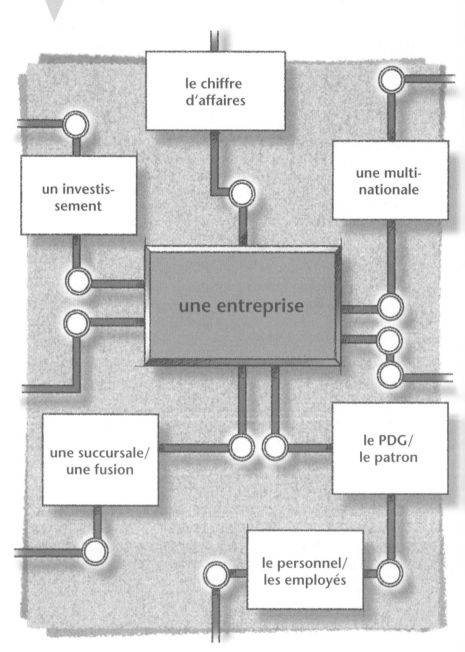

15.1 Agriculture, Fishing, and Mining

l'**agriculture** f [agʀikyltyʀ] — agriculture
agricole [agʀikɔl] — agricultural
  un,e **ouvrier, -ière agricole** — agricultural worker
un,e **agriculteur, -trice** — farmer, agriculturist
[agʀikyltœʀ, tʀis]
un,e **cultivateur, -trice** — farmer, grower, cultivator
[kyltivatœʀ, tʀis]
un,e **paysan,ne** [peizã, an] — peasant, farmer
une **ferme** [fɛʀm] — farm
  passer les vacances à la ferme — spend one's vacation on a farm
un,e **fermier, -ière** — farmer; tenant farmer
[fɛʀmje, jɛʀ]

la **campagne** [kãpaɲ] — country
  Depuis sa retraite, il habite **à la campagne.** — Since his retirement, he has lived in the country.
campagnard,e [kãpaɲaʀ, aʀd] — country, rural, rustic
  La **vie campagnarde** lui plaît beaucoup. — He likes country life very much.

un **champ** [ʃã] — field
  un **champ de blé** — wheat field, grain field
un **pré** [pʀe] — meadow
une **forêt** [fɔʀɛ] — forest

la **culture** [kyltyʀ] — cultivation, growing
  pratiquer la **culture des fruits et légumes** — engage in growing fruits and vegetables
cultiver [kyltive] — cultivate, grow
  la **surface cultivée** — cultivated area/acreage
un **produit** [pʀɔdɥi] — product
  un **produit agricole** — agricultural product
le **rendement** [ʀãdmã] — yield

l'**élevage** m [el(ə)vaʒ] — breeding, raising (of livestock)
élever [el(ə)ve] — breed, raise
  Il élève des chèvres dans le Cantal. — He raises goats in Cantal.
un,e **éleveur, -euse** [el(ə)vœʀ, øz] — breeder, raiser

la **chute des prix** [ʃytdepʀi] — drop in prices
manifester [manifɛste] — demonstrate
  Les éleveurs manifestent contre la concurrence étrangère. — The livestock breeders are demonstrating against foreign competition.

une **manifestation**; une **manif** *fam* [manif(ɛstasjɔ̃)]	demonstration

le **vignoble** [viɲɔbl]	vineyard
Le vignoble français fournit de très grands crus.	The French vineyards produce first-rate wines.
un,e **vigneron,ne** [viɲ(ə)ʀɔ̃, ɔn]	winegrower, vintner
un,e **viticulteur, -trice** [vitikyltœʀ, tʀis]	viticulturist, winegrower
le **vin** [vɛ̃]	wine

la **pêche** [pɛʃ]	fishing
la **pêche au large**	deep-sea fishing
La **pêche à la ligne** est son passe-temps favori.	Fishing with a rod and line is his favorite hobby.
une **canne à pêche**	fishing rod
pêcher [pɛʃe]	fish
un,e **pêcheur, -euse** [pɛʃœʀ, øz]	fisherman, angler
un **marin-pêcheur**	commercial fisherman
un **filet** [filɛ]	net

les **richesses du sous-sol** f [ʀiʃesdysusɔl]	mineral resources
les **matières premières** f [matjɛʀpʀəmjɛʀ]	raw materials
un pays riche/pauvre **en matières premières**	a country rich/poor in raw materials
le **charbon** [ʃaʀbɔ̃]	coal
une **mine** [min]	mine
une **mine à ciel ouvert**	open-pit mine, strip mine
un **mineur** [minœʀ]	miner, mineworker

le **secteur primaire** [sɛktœʀpʀimɛʀ]	primary sector
les **ressources naturelles** f [ʀ(ə)suʀsnatyʀɛl]	natural resources
rural,e [ʀyʀal]	rural
la **population rurale**	rural population
l'**exode rural**	rural exodus
un,e **exploitant,e agricole** [ɛksplwatɑ̃(t)agʀikɔl]	agriculturist, farmer
une **exploitation agricole** [ɛksplwatasjɔ̃agʀikɔl]	farm, agricultural concern
exploiter [ɛksplwate]	work, cultivate
Elle exploite sa ferme avec ses enfants.	She works her farm with her children.
une **coopérative** [k(ɔ)ɔperativ]	coop(erative)

une **coopérative viticole**	winegrowers' cooperative
l'**équipement** m [ekipmɑ̃]	equipment
un **tracteur** [tʀaktœʀ]	tractor

les **primeurs** m [pʀimœʀ]	early vegetables and fruit
la **culture maraîchère** [kyltyʀmaʀeʃɛʀ]	market gardening
un,e **maraîcher, -ère** [maʀeʃe, ɛʀ]	market gardener

l'**engrais** [ɑ̃gʀɛ]	manure, fertilizer
un **pesticide** [pɛstisid]	pesticide
Les arbres fruitiers sont **traités aux pesticides.**	The fruit trees are treated with pesticides.
un **insecticide** [ɛ̃sɛktisid]	insecticide

le **bétail** [betaj]	cattle, livestock
le **pâturage** [patyʀaʒ]	pasture
En automne, le bétail quitte les pâturages et rentre à l'étable.	In fall the cattle leave the pastures and return to the stable.
la **surproduction** [syʀpʀɔdyksjɔ̃]	overproduction
les **quotas** m [kɔta]	quotas
les **quotas laitiers**	milk quotas

viticole [vitikɔl]	winegrowing
une **région viticole**	a winegrowing area
les **vendanges** f [vɑ̃dɑ̃ʒ]	vintage, grape gathering
vendanger [vɑ̃dɑ̃ʒe]	gather/pick the grapes
Cette année ils ont vendangé début septembre.	This year they picked the grapes in early September.

la **pisciculture** [pisikyltyʀ]	fish farming
les **crustacés** m [kʀystase]	crustaceans, shellfish
un restaurant réputé pour ses coquillages et crustacés	a restaurant known for its shellfish

la **houille** ['uj]	bituminous (hard) coal
le **lignite** [liɲit]	lignite, brown coal
une **région minière** [ʀeʒjɔ̃miɲɛʀ]	mining region
une **galerie** [galʀi]	level, drift, heading
un **gisement** [ʒizmɑ̃]	bed, deposit
un **gisement abondant**	a rich deposit
Ce gisement fournit un charbon de haute qualité.	This deposit supplies high-quality coal.
Le gisement est épuisé.	The bed is exhausted.

extraire [εkstRεR]	extract
traiter [tRεte]	process
Traiter les minerais est coûteux.	Processing minerals is costly.

15.2 Industry and Handicrafts

l'**industrie** f [ɛ̃dystRi]	industry
l'**industrie lourde**	heavy industry
l'**industrie automobile**	automobile industry
l'**industrie aéronautique**	aeronautics industry
l'**industrie électronique**	electronics industry
travailler dans l'industrie	work in industry
(un,e) **industriel,le** n; adj	industrialist, manufacturer;
[ɛ̃dystRijɛl]	industrial
une **région industrielle**	industrial region
une **zone industrielle (ZI)**	industrial area
un **secteur industriel**	industrial sector

une **usine** [yzin]	factory
l'**installation** f [ɛ̃stalasjɔ̃]	equipment, plant; installation
La production a augmenté grâce	Production has increased, thanks
à des installations ultra-modernes.	to ultramodern equipment.
s'installer [sɛ̃stale]	establish oneself
De nombreuses entreprises se	Numerous firms have established
sont installées en province.	themselves in the provinces.
une **machine** [maʃin]	machine
un **robot** [Rɔbo]	robot

un,e **travailleur, -euse**	worker
[tRavajœR, øz]	
un,e **ouvrier, -ière** [uvRije, ijɛR]	worker, laborer
un **ouvrier qualifié**	skilled worker
un **ouvrier spécialisé (OS)**	unskilled worker, temporary worker

la **concentration** [kɔ̃sɑ̃tRasjɔ̃]	concentration
se concentrer [s(ə)kɔ̃sɑ̃tRe]	become concentrated
une **crise** [kRiz]	crisis
L'industrie automobile **est en crise.**	The automobile industry is in crisis.
un secteur **touché par la crise**	a sector affected by the crisis

fabriquer [fabRike]	manufacture, make
la **fabrication** [fabRikasjɔ̃]	manufacturing
la **fabrication en (grande) série**	(large) series production

un,e **fabricant,e** [fabʀikã, ãt]	manufacturer, maker
(un,e) **producteur, -trice** *n; adj* [pʀɔdyktœʀ, tʀis]	producer; producing
un **pays producteur de pétrole**	an oil-producing country
produire [pʀɔdɥiʀ]	produce
un **produit** [pʀɔdɥi]	product
Un nouveau produit a été lancé sur le marché.	A new product has been put on the market.
la **production** [pʀɔdyksjɔ̃]	production

un,e **artisan,e** [aʀtizã, an]	artisan, (handi)craftsman
l'**artisanat** *m* [aʀtizana]	(handi)craft, trade
artisanal,e [aʀtizanal]	relating to a craft, artisanal
une **entreprise artisanale**	craftsman's business, workshop
un **atelier** [atəlje]	workshop

s'industrialiser [sɛ̃dystʀijalize]	become industrialized
Cette région s'est fortement industrialisée dans les années 80.	That area became heavily industrialized in the eighties.
l'**industrialisation** *f* [ɛ̃dystʀijalizasjɔ̃]	industrialization
une **industrie(-)clé** [ɛ̃dystʀikle]	key industry
l'**industrie sidérurgique** [ɛ̃dystʀisideʀyʀʒik]	steel industry
l'**industrie métallurgique** [ɛ̃dystʀimetalyʀʒik]	metallurgical industry
l'**industrie textile** [ɛ̃dystʀitekstil]	textile industry
l'**industrie agro-alimentaire** [ɛ̃dystʀiagʀoalimãtɛʀ]	food(-processing) industry
une **industrie de pointe** [ɛ̃dystʀid(ə)pwɛ̃t]	leading industry
l'**industrie chimique et pharmaceutique** [ɛ̃dystʀiʃimikefaʀmasøtik]	chemical and pharmaceutical industry
une **branche** [bʀãʃ]	branch
travailler dans une branche industrielle **en plein essor**	work in a booming branch of industry

la **main-d'œuvre** [mɛ̃dœvʀ]	manpower; labor
avoir besoin de main d'œuvre qualifiée	be in need of qualified manpower
travailler à la chaîne [tʀavajealaʃɛn]	work on an assembly line

l'**implantation** *f* [ɛ̃plãtasjɔ̃]	setting up, establishment
protester contre l'implantation d'une centrale nucléaire	protest the setting up of a nuclear power plant
implanter [ɛ̃plãte]	set up, establish

implanter une usine dans une zone industrielle	set up a factory in an industrial area
l'**essor** m [esɔʀ]	boom
la **récession** [ʀesesjɔ̃]	recession
la **délocalisation** [delɔkalizasjɔ̃]	moving to a foreign country
délocaliser [delɔkalize]	move to a foreign country
Cette firme a délocalisé une partie de sa production.	That firm has moved part of its production to another country.
la **restructuration** [ʀəstʀyktyʀasjɔ̃]	restructuring
restructurer [ʀəstʀyktyʀe]	restructure
la **reconversion** [ʀ(ə)kɔ̃vɛʀsjɔ̃]	changeover, conversion, retooling
se **reconvertir** [səʀ(ə)kɔ̃vɛʀtiʀ]	change over, convert, reshuffle
la **robotisation** [ʀɔbɔtizasjɔ̃]	robotization, full automation
l'**automation**/l'**automatisation** f [ɔtɔmasjɔ̃/ɔtɔmatizasjɔ̃]	automation

les **biens de consommation** m [bjɛ̃d(ə)kɔ̃sɔmasjɔ̃]	consumer goods
les **biens d'équipement** m [bjɛ̃dekipmɑ̃]	capital goods
se lancer dans la production de biens d'équipement	go into production of capital goods
les **produits (semi-)finis** m [pʀɔdɥi(semi)fini]	(semi-)finished products
la **finition** [finisjɔ̃]	finishing

15.3 Company Operations

une **entreprise** [ɑ̃tʀəpʀiz]	enterprise, concern, business
une **entreprise de travaux publics**	civil engineering firm
une **compagnie** (une **Cie**) [kɔ̃paɲi (si)]	company (Co.)
une **firme** [fiʀm]	firm
un **groupe** [gʀup]	group, concern
Cette firme fait partie d'un groupe international.	This firm belongs to an international concern.
le **siège social** [sjɛʒsɔsjal]	company headquarters

un **chef** [ʃɛf]	boss
le **chef d'entreprise**	head of the company
la **direction** [diʀɛksjɔ̃]	management

un,e **directeur, -trice** [diʀɛktœʀ, tʀis]	principal, manager
le **PDG (président-directeur général)** [pedeʒe]	general manager
diriger [diʀiʒe]	direct, head
un,e **patron,ne** [patʀɔ̃, ɔn]	boss

le **personnel** [pɛʀsɔnɛl]	personnel
un **cadre** [kadʀ]	managerial staff member
un **cadre supérieur**	top-level manager
un **cadre moyen**	mid-level manager
un,e **supérieur,e** [sypeʀjœʀ]	superior
un,e **employé,e** [ãplwaje]	employee
un,e **collègue** [kɔlɛg]	colleague
un **poste** [pɔst]	position, post, job
occuper un poste important dans une firme	hold an important position in a firm
une **fonction** [fɔ̃ksjɔ̃]	function
occuper une fonction de cadre supérieur	have a managerial function
responsable de [ʀɛspɔ̃sabl]	responsible for
Il est responsable de l'exportation.	He is in charge of export.

la **concurrence** [kɔ̃kyʀãs]	competition
faire face à la concurrence étrangère	brave the foreign competition
un,e **concurrent,e** [kɔ̃kyʀã, ãt]	competitor
la **perte** [pɛʀt]	loss
produire à perte	produce at a loss

une **maison** [mɛzɔ̃]	business, firm, house
la **maison mère**	head office
une **maison de gros**	wholesale firm
une **multinationale** [myltinasjɔnal]	multinational (company)
une **SA (Société anonyme)** [ɛsa]	private corporation
une **SARL (Société à responsabilité limitée)** [ɛsaɛʀɛl]	limited-liability company
une **PME (Petites et moyennes entreprises)** [peɛmə]	small or medium-sized business
Les PME ont de plus en plus de mal à survivre.	Survival is increasingly hard for small and medium-sized businesses.
une **succursale** [sykyʀsal]	branch (office)
ouvrir une succursale à l'étranger	open a branch in a foreign country

les **effectifs** *m* [efεktif] — effective force, personnel
réduire les effectifs de moitié — reduce personnel by half
un,e **collaborateur, -trice** [kɔ(l)labɔʀatœʀ, tʀis] — coworker
pouvoir compter sur des collaborateurs efficaces — be able to count on effective coworkers
un **manager** [manadʒœʀ/εʀ] — manager
embaucher [ɑ̃boʃe] — hire; employ
L'entreprise embauche des ouvriers qualifiés. — The company is hiring skilled workers.
l'**embauche** *f* [ɑ̃boʃ] — hiring; employment
le **comité directeur** [kɔmitediʀεktœʀ] — board of management
le **conseil de surveillance** [kɔ̃sεjdəsyʀvεjɑ̃s] — supervisory board

les **affaires** *f* [afεʀ] — business
un homme/une femme d'affaires — a businessman/-woman
Il est en Italie **pour affaires**. — He is in Italy on business.
le **chiffre d'affaires** [ʃifʀ(ə)dafεʀ] — turnover
investir dans [ɛ̃vεstiʀ] — invest in
un **investissement** [ɛ̃vεstismɑ̃] — investment
amortir ses investissements — amortize one's investments
une **fusion** [fyzjɔ̃] — merger
fusionner [fyzjɔne] — merge
fusionner pour rester compétitif — merge in order to stay competitive
la **comptabilité** [kɔ̃tabilite] — accounting, bookkeeping
les **frais** *m* [fʀε] — costs
les **charges** *f* [ʃaʀʒ] — secondary costs
le **bénéfice** [benefis] — profit
réinvestir ses bénéfices — reinvest one's profits
un **déficit** [defisit] — loss, deficit
déposer son bilan [depozesɔ̃bilɑ̃] — declare bankruptcy
faire faillite [fεʀfajit] — go bankrupt

15.4 Technology

la **technique** [tεknik] — technology; engineering
la **technique de pointe** — leading technology
technique [tεknik] — technical, technological
le **progrès** [pʀɔgʀε] — progress
un,e **technicien,ne** [tεknisjɛ̃, jεn] — technician; engineer

la **technologie** [tɛknɔlɔʒi]	technology; engineering
les technologies nouvelles	the new technologies
technologique [tɛknɔlɔʒik]	technological
avoir une avance technologique sur qn	have a technological advantage over s.o.

inventer [ɛ̃vɑ̃te]	invent
une **invention** [ɛ̃vɑ̃sjɔ̃]	invention
un,e **inventeur, -trice** [ɛ̃vɑ̃tœʀ, tʀis]	inventor
(un,e) **scientifique** *n; adj* [sjɑ̃tifik]	scientist; scientific
une **méthode** [metɔd]	method
agir avec méthode	proceed in a methodical way

un **moteur** [mɔtœʀ]	motor
automatique [ɔtɔmatik]	automatic
électrique [elɛktʀik]	electric(al)
l'**électricité** *f* [elɛktʀisite]	electricity
une **panne d'électricité**	electrical failure
électronique [elɛktʀɔnik]	electronic
l'**électronique** *f* [elɛktʀɔnik]	electronics
L'électronique fait partie de notre vie quotidienne.	Electronics are part of our daily life.

nucléaire [nykleɛʀ]	nuclear
un **réacteur nucléaire**	nuclear reactor
le **nucléaire** [nykleɛʀ]	nuclear power, nuclear energy
une manifestation contre le nucléaire	a demonstration against nuclear power
une **centrale nucléaire** [sɑ̃tʀalnykleɛʀ]	nuclear power plant
un **incident** [ɛ̃sidɑ̃]	incident
Un incident technique a provoqué l'arrêt de la centrale électrique.	A technical incident led to the shutdown of the electrical plant.

un **équipement** [ekipmɑ̃]	equipment
un **dispositif** [dispozitif]	apparatus, device
le **(service) technico-commercial** [tɛknikokɔmɛʀsjal]	commercial and technical department

le **savoir-faire** [savwaʀfɛʀ]	know-how
L'ingénieur a démontré son savoir-faire.	The engineer demonstrated his know-how.
la **haute technologie** ['ottɛknɔlɔʒi]	high technology

le **transfert de technologie** [trãsfɛrdəteknɔlɔʒi]	technology transfer
le **génie génétique** [ʒeniʒenetik]	genetic engineering
un **parc technologique** [parktɛknɔlɔʒik]	technology park
une **technopole** [tɛknɔpɔl]	technology center
La recherche et l'industrie sont réunies dans les technopoles.	Research and industry are united in technology centers.

spatial,e [spasjal]	(pertaining to) space
un **vaisseau spatial**	spaceship
une **navette/station spatiale**	space shuttle/station
la **navigation spatiale**	space travel
un,e **astronaute** [astrɔnot]	astronaut

une **fusée** [fyze]	rocket
un **satellite** [satelit]	satellite
sur orbite [syrɔrbit]	in orbit
mettre un satellite **sur orbite**	put a satellite in orbit

15.5 Trade and Services

le **commerce** [kɔmɛrs]	trade, commerce
commercial,e [kɔmɛrsjal]	commercial
un **(petit) commerçant** [kɔmɛrsã]	small tradesman, shopkeeper
Les petits commerçants sont contre l'ouverture du centre commercial.	Small shopkeepers are opposed to the opening of the shopping center.

le **marché** [marʃe]	market
aller* faire son marché	go out to do one's shopping
un,e **marchand,e** [marʃã, ãd]	merchant, dealer
une **marchandise** [marʃãdiz]	merchandise
proposer sa marchandise **à bas prix**	offer one's merchandise at low prices
marchander [marʃãde]	deal; haggle
un **magasin** [magazɛ̃]	store, shop

un,e **client,e** [klijã, klijãt]	client, customer
un,e **client,e fidèle**	faithful customer
la **clientèle** [klijãtɛl]	clientele, customers
un,e **consommateur, -trice** [kɔ̃sɔmatœr, tris]	consumer
acheter [aʃ(ə)te]	buy, purchase

un,e **acheteur, -euse** [aʃ(ə)tœʀ, øz]	buyer
un **achat** [aʃa]	purchase
commander [kɔmãde]	order, to
une **commande** [kɔmãd]	order
vendre [vãdʀ]	sell
un,e **vendeur, -euse** [vãdœʀ, øz]	salesperson, salesman/-woman
la **vente** [vãt]	sale(s)
la **vente par correspondance**	mail order sales
la **vente en gros/au détail**	wholesale/retail sales
la **vente aux enchères**	auction sale
les **soldes** m [sɔld]	reductions, clearance sales
un **contrat** [kɔ̃tʀa]	contract
signer un contrat	sign a contract

le **prix** [pʀi]	price
la **facture** [faktyʀ]	invoice, bill
envoyer [ãvwaje]	send
Envoyez-nous votre **bon de commande.**	Send us your order form.
livrer [livʀe]	deliver
la **livraison** [livʀɛzɔ̃]	delivery

un **article** [aʀtikl]	article, item
Cet article est épuisé.	That item is sold out.
la **marque** [maʀk]	brand
une **étiquette** [etikɛt]	price tag
la **garantie** [gaʀãti]	guarantee
un appareil **sous garantie**	an appliance under warranty
faire de la publicité [fɛʀd(ə)lapyblisite]	advertise

l'**offre** f [ɔfʀ]	supply
la **demande** [d(ə)mãd]	demand
Les prix varient **en fonction de** l'offre et de la demande.	The prices vary depending on supply and demand.
importer [ɛ̃pɔʀte]	import, to
l'**importation** f [ɛ̃pɔʀtasjɔ̃]	import
exporter [ɛkspɔʀte]	export, to
l'**exportation** f [ɛkspɔʀtasjɔ̃]	export

le **secteur tertiaire** [sɛktœʀtɛʀsjɛʀ]	services sector
le **commerce intérieur/extérieur** [kɔmɛʀsɛ̃teʀjœʀ/ɛksteʀjœʀ]	domestic/foreign commerce trade
le **commerce de gros/de détail** [kɔmɛʀsdəgʀo/dədetaj]	wholesale/retail trade

la **balance commerciale** [balãskɔmɛʀsjal]	balance of trade
un,e **grossiste** [gʀosist]	wholesaler
un,e **détaillant,e** [detajã, ãt]	retailer
un,e **VRP (Voyageur de commerce, représentant et placier)** [veɛʀpe]	commercial/sales rep(resentative)
une **commission** [kɔmisjɔ̃]	commission
travailler à la commission	work on a commission basis

la **distribution** [distʀibysjɔ̃]	distribution
fournir [fuʀniʀ]	supply
un,e **fournisseur, -euse** [fuʀnisœʀ, øz]	supplier
expédier [ɛkspedje]	ship
expédier qc contre remboursement	ship C.O.D.
un **colis** [kɔli]	package
un **échantillon** [eʃãtijɔ̃]	sample

la **taxe** [taks]	tax
exempt de taxes	tax-free, tax-exempt
le **prix HT (hors taxes)** [pʀiɔʀtaks]	price before taxes
le **prix TTC (toutes taxes comprises)** [pʀitetese]	price after taxes
la **TVA (Taxe à la valeur ajoutée)** [tevea]	value-added tax (VAT)
une **remise** [ʀ(ə)miz]	discount
un **rabais** [ʀabɛ]	reduction in price

un **entrepôt** [ãtʀəpo]	warehouse
le **stock** [stɔk]	stock
être en rupture de stock	be out of stock/undeliverable
écouler le stock	sell the stock

15.6 Money, Banking

l'**argent** *m* [aʀʒã]	money
l'argent de poche	pocket money
avoir de l'argent sur soi	have money on one
compter [kɔ̃te]	count
compter des billets de banque	count banknotes
la **monnaie** [mɔnɛ]	coins, change
avoir de la monnaie	have coins
rendre la monnaie	make change

une **unité monétaire** [ynitemɔnetɛʀ]	monetary unit
un **dollar** [dɔlar]	dollar
un **billet de 100 dollars**	a 100-dollar bill
un **euro** [øʀo]	euro
5 euros **en liquide**	5 euros in cash
plus de 3 euros	more than 3 euros
moins de 3 euros	less than 3 euros
un **cent** [sɛnt]	cent

un **porte-monnaie** [pɔʀt(ə)mɔnɛ]	coin purse
un **portefeuille** [pɔʀt(ə)fœj]	wallet, billfold; portfolio
avoir un portefeuille bien rempli	have a well-filled wallet
gérer son portefeuille	manage one's portfolio

gratuit,e [gʀatɥi, ɥit]	gratis, free
coûter [kute]	cost
Ça coûte trop cher.	That costs too much.
payer [peje]	pay
payer comptant/cash	pay in cash
la **valeur** [valœʀ]	value
dépenser [depɑ̃se]	spend
Il dépense son argent sans compter.	He spends his money without counting it.

économiser [ekɔnɔmize]	economize, save
les **économies** f [ekɔnɔmi]	savings
faire des économies	economize
économe [ekɔnɔm]	economical, thrifty
Il n'est pas avare, il est seulement économe.	He's not a miser; he's just thrifty.
la **fortune** [fɔʀtyn]	fortune
faire fortune	get rich

prêter [pʀete]	lend, loan
Elle lui a prêté 2000 euros.	She loaned him 2000 euros.
un **prêt** [pʀɛ]	loan
accorder un prêt à des conditions intéressantes	grant a loan on favorable conditions
un **crédit** [kʀedi]	credit; trust
faire crédit	give credit
emprunter qc à qn [ɑ̃pʀɛ̃te]	borrow s.th. from s.o.
Je ne sais plus à qui j'ai emprunté ce crayon.	I don't remember who I borrowed this pencil from.
un **emprunt** [ɑ̃pʀɛ̃]	loan; borrowing
rembourser [ʀɑ̃buʀse]	reimburse, pay back

un **remboursement** [ʀɑ̃buʀsəmɑ̃]	repayment, reimbursement
devoir qc à qn [dəvwaʀ]	owe s.th. to s.o.
Vous me devez une grosse somme.	You owe me a large sum.
la **dette** [dɛt]	debt
faire des dettes	run up debts

une **banque** [bɑ̃k]	bank

Don't confuse *banque* and *banc*

*Both the **spelling** and the **pronunciation** differ:*

une banque [bɑ̃k]	*bank*
la BNP (*B*anque *N*ationale de *P*aris)	*BNP (one of the largest French banks)*
un banc [bɑ̃]	*bench*
un banc public	*public bench, park bench*

---

un **banquier** [bɑ̃kje]	banker; bank employee
un **guichet** [giʃɛ]	position, window
la **caisse** [kɛs]	cashier's office, teller's window
passer à la caisse	go to the teller's window
un,e **caissier, -ière** [kɛsje, jɛʀ]	teller, cashier
encaisser [ɑ̃kese]	pay in, bank
changer [ʃɑ̃ʒe]	change
changer de l'argent	change money
changer ses francs en marks	change one's francs to marks
le **change** [ʃɑ̃ʒ]	(money) exchange

un **compte (en banque)** [kɔ̃t(ɑ̃bɑ̃k)]	(bank) account
un **compte courant**	current account
ouvrir un compte	open an account
un numéro de compte	account number
déposer de l'argent sur son compte	deposit money in one's account
retirer de l'argent [ʀ(ə)tiʀed(ə)laʀʒɑ̃]	withdraw money
une **(grosse) somme** [(gʀos)sɔm]	(large) sum
un montant de . . . [mɔ̃tɑ̃də]	an amount of . . .
On a reçu une facture d'un montant de 2500 euros.	We have received an invoice for the amount of 2500 euros.

un **chèque** [ʃɛk]	check
encaisser un chèque	cash a check
un **eurochèque** [øʀoʃɛk]	eurocheque
une **carte bancaire** [kaʀt(ə)bɑ̃kɛʀ]	bank card
une **carte de crédit** [kaʀtdəkʀedi]	credit card
payer par carte (de crédit)	pay by credit card
le **code secret** [kɔdsəkʀɛ]	PIN number

les **sous** *m; fam* [su]	sous; money
ne pas avoir un sou en poche	not have a dime in one's pocket
le **fric** *fam* [fʀik]	"dough"

les **devises** *f* [dəviz]	currency
une **devise forte/faible**	a hard/soft currency
le **taux de change** [todʃɑ̃ʒ]	exchange rate
les **recettes** *f* [ʀ(ə)sɛt]	receipts, returns
la **dévaluation** [devalɥasjɔ̃]	devaluation
dévaluer [devalɥe]	devalue
Le gouvernement a décidé de dévaluer la monnaie.	The government decided to devalue the currency.
l'**inflation** *f* [ɛ̃flasjɔ̃]	inflation

le **coût** [ku]	costs
coûteux, -euse [kutø, øz]	costly, expensive
régler [ʀegle]	pay
régler une facture **en espèces**	pay an invoice in cash
du **liquide** [likid]	cash
payer qc **en liquide**	pay for s.th. in cash

l'**épargne** *f* [epaʀɲ]	saving
épargner [epaʀɲe]	save
un,e **épargnant,e** [epaʀɲɑ̃, ɑ̃t]	saver
un **livret d'épargne** [livʀɛdepaʀɲ]	savings book
la **caisse d'épargne** [kɛsdepaʀɲ]	savings bank
une **tirelire** [tiʀliʀ]	money box

s'endetter [sɑ̃dɛte]	get/run into debt
les **intérêts** *m* [ɛ̃teʀɛ]	interest
le **taux d'intérêt**	interest rate
une **hypothèque** [ipɔtɛk]	mortgage
prendre une hypothèque sur qc	take out a mortgage on s.th.

une **agence** [aʒɑ̃s]	branch office
une **succursale** [sykyʀsal]	branch (office)
un **coffre(-fort)** [kɔfʀə(fɔʀ)]	safe, safety deposit box
louer un coffre à la banque	rent a bank safety deposit box
un **distributeur automatique (de billets)** [distʀibytœʀɔtɔmatik]	ATM, automated teller

un **chéquier** [ʃekje]	checkbook
un **carnet de chèques** [kaʀnɛdʃɛk]	checkbook

faire/rédiger un chèque (á l'ordre de qn) [fɛR/Rediʒeẽ ʃɛk]	make out/issue a check (to the order of s.o.)
la **signature** [siɲatyʀ]	signature
Sur ce chèque, la signature est falsifiée.	The signature on the check is forged.
signer [siɲe]	sign
signer un chèque	sign a check

un **relevé de compte** [ʀəl(ə)ve/ʀ(ə)ləved(ə)kɔ̃t]	bank statement
le **solde** [sɔld]	balance (between balance and credit)
le **découvert** [dekuvɛʀ]	overdraft, uncovered balance
La banque m'a accordé un découvert de 10 000 euros.	The bank has granted me an overdraft of 10,000 euros.
être à découvert	be overdrawn, have a deficit
débiter [debite]	debit
le **débit** [debi]	debit
créditer [kRedite]	credit
Mon compte a été crédité de 1000 euros.	My account was credited with 1000 euros.
virer [viʀe]	transfer, to
un **virement** [viʀmɑ̃]	transfer
un **prélèvement automatique** [pʀelɛvmɑ̃ɔtɔmatik]	automatic deduction; banker's order
verser [vɛʀse]	pay in, deposit
un **versement** [vɛʀsəmɑ̃]	deposit

les **finances** f [finɑ̃s]	finances
un **financier** [finɑ̃sje]	financier
financer [finɑ̃se]	finance
financer l'achat d'une maison	finance the purchase of a house
le **financement** [finɑ̃smɑ̃]	financing

la **Bourse** [buʀs]	Stock Exchange
la **spéculation** [spekylasjɔ̃]	speculation
spéculer [spekyle]	speculate
un,e **spéculateur, -trice** [spekylatœʀ, tʀis]	speculator
une **action** [aksjɔ̃]	stock
la **hausse** ['os]	rise
Mes actions sont **en hausse**.	My stocks are on the rise.
la **baisse** [bɛs]	fall
un **dividende** [dividɑ̃d]	dividend
un **titre** [titʀ]	security, bond, stock
un **placement** [plasmɑ̃]	investment (of money)

placer [plase]	invest (money)
les **fonds d'investissement** *m* [fɔ̃dɛ̃vɛstismɑ̃]	investment funds

15.7 Insurance

une **assurance** [asyʀɑ̃s]	insurance
une **assurance obligatoire**	compulsory insurance
s'**assurer contre qc** [sasyʀe]	insure oneself against s.th.
s'assurer contre les inondations	insure oneself against floods
assurer [asyʀe]	insure
un,e **assuré,e** [asyʀe]	insured (person)

une **compagnie d'assurances** [kɔ̃paɲidasyʀɑ̃s]	insurance company
un **assureur** [asyʀœʀ]	insurer
une **police d'assurance** [pɔlisdasyʀɑ̃s]	insurance policy
un **contrat** [kɔ̃tʀa]	contract

un **accident** [aksidɑ̃]	accident
déclarer un accident	report an accident/damage
une **déclaration** [deklaʀasjɔ̃]	report, notification of loss

une **assurance vie** [asyʀɑ̃svi]	life insurance
une **assurance maladie** [asyʀɑ̃smaladi]	health insurance
une **assurance auto(mobile)** [asyʀɑ̃sɔto/oto(mɔbil)]	auto(mobile) insurance
une **assurance accidents** [asyʀɑ̃saksidɑ̃]	accident insurance
On va **résilier** notre assurance accidents.	We're going to cancel our accident insurance.
une **assurance vieillesse** [asyʀɑ̃svjɛjɛs]	old-age (pension) insurance
J'ai **contracté** une assurance vieillesse, on ne sait jamais.	I've signed up for a pension plan; you never know.
une **assurance dépendance** [asyʀɑ̃sdepɑ̃dɑ̃s]	nursing care insurance
une **assurance responsabilité civile** [asyʀɑ̃sʀɛspɔ̃sabilitesivil]	personal liability insurance
une **assurance tous risques** [asyʀɑ̃stuʀisk]	full comprehensive insurance

cotiser [kɔtize]	pay a contribution
une **cotisation** [kɔtizasjɔ̃]	contribution
les **prestations** f [pʀɛstasjɔ̃]	payments

couvrir qc [kuvʀiʀ]	cover s.th.
Cette assurance couvre à peu près tous les risques.	This insurance covers pretty much all risks.
une **prime** [pʀim]	premium
un **bonus** [bɔnys]	premium rate
Après cet accident, il a perdu son bonus.	After that accident he lost his premium rate.
un **malus** [malys]	extra premium (for covering higher accident rates)

un **constat (à l')amiable** [kɔ̃sta(al)amjabl]	friendly accident report (without police)
un **formulaire** [fɔʀmylɛʀ]	form
Vous pouvez m'aider à remplir ce formulaire?	Can you help me fill out this form?
un **sinistre** [sinistʀ]	disaster, calamity
les **dégâts** m [dega]	damage
s'assurer contre les dégâts des eaux	insure oneself against water damage
les **dommages** m [dɔmaʒ]	damages
les **dommages (et) intérêts** m [dɔmaʒ(e)ɛ̃teʀɛ]	payment of damages, indemnity
dédommager qn [dedɔmaʒe]	compensate s.o.
L'assurance ne m'a toujours pas dédommagé	The insurance company still hasn't compensated me.
indemniser qn de qc/pour qc [ɛ̃dɛmnize]	indemnify s.o. for s.th.
Il a été indemnisé pour ses frais d'hôpital.	He was indemnified for his hospital costs.
une **indemnisation** [ɛ̃dɛmnizasjɔ̃]	indemnification, compensation

la **Sécurité sociale**; la **Sécu** fam [seky(ʀitesɔsjal)]	state social and health insurance
une **caisse d'assurance maladie** [kɛsdasyʀɑ̃smaladi]	health insurance company
une **caisse de retraite** [kɛsdəʀ(ə)tʀɛt]	retirement fund
une **allocation** f [alɔkasjɔ̃]	allocation, allowance
les **allocations familiales**	family/children's allowance
l'**allocation de maternité**	maternity allowance
l'**allocation de chômage**	unemployment benefits
Il n'a pas encore touché son allocation de chômage.	He hasn't gotten his unemployment benefits yet.

les **Assedic (Associations pour l'emploi dans l'industrie et le commerce)** f [asedik]	unemployment insurance
les **charges sociales** f [ʃaʁʒ(ə)sɔsjal]	social contributions
une **mutuelle** [mytɥɛl]	supplementary insurance (company)

French Word	English Equivalent	False Friend	French Equivalent
une manifestation	(political) demonstration	manifestation	une démonstration
la vente	sale(s)	vent	l'issue; le conduit d'air

16.1 Telecommunications

le **téléphone** [telefɔn]
Marc est là? On le demande au
téléphone.
un coup de téléphone
donner un coup de téléphone à qn
répondre au téléphone
téléphoner à qn [telefɔne]
Depuis une heure, il téléphone à
Marie.
un **coup de fil** *fam* [kudfil]
passer un coup de fil à qn
recevoir un coup de fil
le **combiné** [kɔ̃bine]
décrocher/raccrocher (le combiné)
sonner [sɔne]
Le téléphone sonne.

telephone
Is Marc here? He's wanted on
the phone.
telephone call
telephone s.o.
answer the telephone
telephone s.o.
He's been on the phone with
Marie for an hour.
phone call
phone s.o.
receive a call
receiver
pick up/hang up (the receiver)
ring
The phone is ringing.

une **communication (téléphonique)** [kɔmynikasjɔ̃(telefɔnik)]
Je t'entends mal, la communication est très mauvaise.
un **appel** [apɛl]
On a reçu un appel de Marseille.
appeler qn [ap(ə)le]
rappeler qn [ʀap(ə)le]
M. Dubois est en conférence,
veuillez rappeler dans un quart
d'heure.
un,e **correspondant,e**
[kɔʀɛspɔ̃dɑ̃, ɑ̃t]

(telephone) connection, call

I can't hear you well; the connection is very bad.
call
We received a call from Marseille.
call s.o.
call s.o. back
Mr. Dubois is in conference;
please call back in a quarter of
an hour.
correspondant; partner in
conversation

un **numéro** [nymeʀo]
composer/faire un numéro
se tromper de numéro
les **renseignements (téléphoniques)** *m* [ʀɑ̃sɛɲmɑ̃]
le **standard** [stɑ̃daʀ]

number
dial a number
dial the wrong number
(telephone) information

telephone switchboard

la **ligne (téléphonique)**
[liɲ (telefɔnik)]
Les lignes sont encombrées.
La tempête a coupé toutes les
lignes téléphoniques.

(telephone) line

The lines are overloaded.
The storm knocked out all the
phone lines.

être en dérangement [ɛtʀɑ̃deʀɑ̃ʒmɑ̃]	be out of order
La ligne a été en dérangement toute la journée.	The line was out of order all day.
occupé,e [ɔkype]	busy
Impossible de téléphoner à Luc, c'est toujours occupé.	It's impossible to phone Luc; his line is always busy.

un **portable** [pɔʀtabl]	mobile phone; cell phone
une **cabine (téléphonique)** [kabin]	telephone booth
une **télécarte** [telekaʀt]	telephone card
un **téléphone à cartes** [telefɔnakaʀt]	card telephone
un **répondeur (automatique)** [ʀepɔ̃dœʀ]	answering machine
le **bip sonore** [bipsɔnɔʀ]	beeping sound
Vous pouvez laisser votre message après le bip sonore.	You can leave your message after the sound of the beep.

un **fax** [faks]	fax
envoyer un fax	send a fax
faxer qc à qn [fakse]	fax s.th. to s.o.
le **minitel** [minitɛl]	minitel, btx (terminal)

un **annuaire** [anɥɛʀ]	telephone book
les **pages jaunes** f [paʒʒon]	the Yellow Pages
être sur la liste rouge [ɛtʀsyʀlalistəʀuʒ]	have an unlisted number

---

i

Using the phone in France

Allô ! J'écoute.	*Hello! (person receiving call)*
Qui est à l'appareil ?	*Who's calling, please?*
Pouvez-vous me passer ... ?	*May I speak to ...*
Je vous passe ...	*I'll connect you with ...*
Restez en ligne.	*Stay on the line.*
Ne coupez pas.	*Don't hang up.*
Ne quittez pas.	*Please remain on the line.*
Il y a erreur.	*You have the wrong number.*

---

la **télécommunication** [telekɔmynikasjɔ̃]	telecommunications
les **Télécom** [telekɔm]	telecom
le **téléphone de voiture** [telefɔndəvwatyʀ]	car phone
un **publiphone** [pyblifɔn]	public telephone, pay phone
un,e **abonné,e** [abɔne]	telephone customer/subscriber

Il n'y a pas d'abonné au numéro que vous avez demandé.	This is not a working number.
un **numéro vert** [nymerovɛʀ]	toll-free telephone number
l'**indicatif** *m* [ɛ̃dikatif]	prefix
la **tonalité** [tɔnalite]	dial tone

une **télécopie** [telekɔpi]	fax
un **télécopieur** [telekɔpjœʀ]	fax machine

16.2 Postal Service

la **Poste** [pɔst]	Post Office, Postal Service
postal,e [pɔstal]	postal
poster une lettre [pɔsteynlɛtʀ]	mail/post a letter
un **bureau de poste** [byʀodpɔst]	post office
un **guichet** [giʃɛ]	window, (counter) position
Il n'y a qu'un guichet ouvert.	There's only one window open.
une **boîte aux lettres** [bwatolɛtʀ]	mailbox

un,e **facteur, -trice** [faktœʀ, tʀis]	mail carrier
distribuer [distʀibɥe]	deliver
la **distribution** [distʀibysjɔ̃]	delivery
une **tournée** [tuʀne]	round, route
Le facteur commence sa tournée à 8 heures.	The mail carrier starts his route at 8 o'clock.

le **courrier** [kuʀje]	mail
écrire [ekʀiʀ]	write
envoyer [ɑ̃vwaje]	send
recevoir [ʀəs(ə)vwaʀ/ʀ(ə)səvwaʀ]	receive, get
une **lettre** [lɛtʀ]	letter
une **lettre recommandée**	registered letter
en recommandé [ɑ̃ʀ(ə)kɔmɑ̃de]	by registered mail
envoyer qc en recommandé	send s.th. by registered mail
par avion [paʀavjɔ̃]	by airmail
expédier une lettre par avion	send a letter by airmail
une **carte postale** [kaʀt(ə)pɔstal]	postcard
un **imprimé** [ɛ̃pʀime]	printed matter
un **télégramme** [telegʀam]	telegram

une **enveloppe** [ɑ̃v(ə)lɔp]	envelope
une **enveloppe timbrée**	stamped envelope
un **timbre(-poste)** [tɛ̃bʀə(pɔst)]	(postage) stamp

l'**adresse** f [adʀɛs]	address
le **code postal** [kɔdpɔstal]	postal delivery code, ZIP code
le **cachet (de la poste)** [kaʃɛ]	postmark

poste restante [pɔst(ə)ʀɛstãt]	General Delivery
envoyer une lettre poste restante	send a letter General Delivery
la **boîte postale (BP)**	post office box (P.O.)
[bwatpɔstal (bepe)]	
CEDEX (courrier d'entreprise à distribution exceptionnelle) [sedɛks]	(collective post office for specially delivered business and administrative mail)
le **tri** [tʀi]	sorting
un **centre de tri (postal)**	postal sorting center
trier [tʀije]	sort (mail)

un **colis** [kɔli]	package
un **colis contre remboursement**	C.O.D. package
à l'attention de [alatãsjɔ̃də]	attention:
à l'attention de Mme Fournier	Attention: Mrs. Fournier
faire suivre [fɛʀsɥivʀ]	forward
Prière de faire suivre.	Please forward.
par retour du courrier [paʀʀətuʀdykuʀje]	by return mail
répondre à une lettre par retour du courrier	answer a letter by return mail
ci-joint,e [sijwɛ̃, jwɛ̃t]	enclosed
Veuillez trouver ci-joint(s) les documents demandés.	Enclosed please find the documents requested.
l'**expéditeur, -trice** [ɛkspeditœʀ, tʀis]	sender
le/la **destinataire** [dɛstinatɛʀ]	recipient

affranchir [afʀãʃiʀ]	frank (a letter), stamp
affranchir une lettre **au tarif en vigueur**	put sufficient postage on a letter
le **port** [pɔʀ]	postage, postal rate
franco de port	postage-free
les **tarifs postaux** m [taʀifpɔsto]	postage, postal tariffs
la **surtaxe** [syʀtaks]	postage due
le **distributeur (de timbres)** [distʀibytœʀ(dətɛ̃bʀ)]	stamp-vending machine
un **carnet (de timbres)** [kaʀnɛ]	book of stamps

un **mandat** [mãda]	postal money order
un **compte chèque postal (CCP)** [kɔ̃tʃɛkpɔstal (sesepe)]	post office checking account

16.3 Television, Radio

la **télévision**; la **télé** *fam* [tele(vizjɔ̃)]	television, TV
regarder la télé	watch television
un **écran** [ekʀɑ̃]	screen
le **petit écran**	TV screen
une **vedette du petit écran**	TV star

le **programme** [pʀɔgʀam]	television program; channel
Il n'y a rien d'intéressant au programme.	There's nothing interesting on TV.
une **chaîne** [ʃɛn]	TV channel, TV station
une **chaîne publique**	public TV station
une **chaîne privée**	privately operated TV station
sur la première (chaîne)	on Channel One

la **radio** [ʀadjo]	radio
une **station (de radio)**	(radio) station
écouter la radio	listen to the radio

> For information on the difference between **écouter** and **entendre**, see p. 27.

un **poste (de radio)** [pɔst]	radio set
écouter les nouvelles au poste/à la radio	listen to the news on the radio
un **transistor** [tʀɑ̃zistɔʀ]	transistor radio
l'**écoute** *f* [ekut]	listening
Vous êtes **à l'écoute** d'Europe 1.	You are listening to Europe 1.

un **studio** [stydjo]	studio
un **enregistrement** [ɑ̃ʀ(ə)ʒistʀəmɑ̃]	recording
une **émission** [emisjɔ̃]	broadcast
une **émission en direct**	direct broadcast
enregistrer une émission	record a broadcast
un **micro(phone)** [mikʀo(ɔfɔn)]	microphone, mike
le **public** [pyblik]	(radio) public, listeners
un,e **invité,e** [ɛ̃vite]	guest

les **actualités** *f* [aktɥalite]	news
regarder les actualités (télévisées)	watch the (TV) news
informer qn sur qc [ɛ̃fɔʀme]	inform s.o. about s.th.
les **informations**; les **infos** *fam f* [ɛ̃fɔʀmasjɔ̃, ɛ̃fo]	news, information

le **journal (télévisé)** [ʒuʀnal(televize)]	(TV) news journal/program
un **événement/évènement** [evɛnmɑ̃]	event
suivre le cours des événements	follow the course of events
se passer [s(ə)pase]	happen, occur
Pendant 90 minutes il ne s'est rien passé d'intéressant.	For 90 minutes nothing of interest happened.
être au courant (de qc) [ɛtʀokuʀɑ̃]	be informed (about s.th.)
un,e **envoyé,e spécial,e** [ɑ̃vwajespesjal]	special reporter, special correspondent

une **interview** [ɛ̃tɛʀvju]	interview
donner/accorder une interview	give/grant an interview
interviewer [ɛ̃tɛʀvjuve]	interview
un,e **présentateur, -trice** [pʀezɑ̃tatœʀ, tʀis]	presenter; announcer; moderator
un,e **animateur, -trice** [animatœʀ, tʀis]	moderator

la **météo(rologie)** [meteo(ɔʀɔlɔʒi)]	weather report
la **publicité**; la **pub** *fam* [pyb(lisite)]	commercial advertising
Sur les chaînes privées, il y a de plus en plus de pub.	On the privately operated channels, there is more and more advertising.
publicitaire [pyblisitɛʀ]	commercial
un **spot publicitaire**	commercial spot

un **téléviseur** [televizœʀ]	television set
un **poste de télé(vision)** [pɔstdətele]	television set
s'acheter un **poste de télévision portatif**	buy oneself a portable TV set

la **télévision commerciale** [televizjɔ̃kɔmɛʀsjal]	commercial television
un **émetteur** [emɛtœʀ]	station
émettre [emɛtʀ]	broadcast, transmit
émettre 24 heures sur 24	broadcast 24 hours a day
diffuser [difyze]	broadcast, transmit
diffuser de la musique	broadcast music
rediffuser [ʀ(ə)difyze]	broadcast again
Ce débat sera rediffusé demain matin.	This debate will be aired again tomorrow morning.
une **rediffusion** [ʀ(ɛ)difyzjɔ̃]	repeat broadcast, rebroadcast

la **télévision par câble** [televizjɔ̃paʀkabl]	cable television

la **télévision par satellite** [televizjɔ̃paʀsatelit]	satellite television
une **antenne** [ãtɛn]	antenna
une **antenne parabolique**	dish antenna
Je rends l'antenne à nos studios à Paris.	I return you to our Paris studios.
un **décodeur** [dekɔdœʀ]	decoder
une **chaîne codée** [ʃɛnkɔde]	encoded channel
la **réception** [ʀesɛpsjɔ̃]	reception
La réception est très mauvaise.	The reception is very poor.
un **récepteur** [ʀesɛptœʀ]	receiver
capter [kapte]	receive
On n'arrive pas à capter la 5.	We can't get Channel 5.

l'**audimat** m [odimat]	audience
Cette émission fait monter l'audimat.	This broadcast is going to increase the size of the audience.
un,e **auditeur, -trice** [oditœʀ, tʀis]	listener
l'**audience** f [odjãs]	audience, listeners
L'audience des radios locales augmente régulièrement.	The audience of the local stations is growing regularly.
audiovisuel,le [odjovizɥɛl]	audiovisual
radiophonique [ʀadjɔfɔnik]	radio
une **pièce radiophonique**	radio play
la **redevance** [ʀ(ə)dəvãs]	radio/TV tax

les **grandes ondes (GO)** f [gʀãdzɔ̃d (ʒeo)]	long waves
recevoir une émission sur grandes ondes	receive a long-wave broadcast
les **ondes moyennes (OM)**, les **petites ondes** [ɔ̃dmwajɛn, p(ə)titzɔ̃d]	medium waves
les **ondes courtes** f [ɔ̃dkuʀt]	shortwaves
la **modulation de fréquence (FM)** [mɔdylasjɔ̃d(ə)fʀekãs (ɛfɛm)]	FM (frequency modulation)

une **retransmission** [ʀ(ə)tʀãsmisjɔ̃]	transmission, broadcast
retransmettre [ʀ(ə)tʀãsmɛtʀ]	transmit, broadcast
Le concert sera retransmis en modulation de fréquence.	The concert will be broadcast on FM.
en duplex [ãdyplɛks]	on a conference circuit
en différé [ãdifeʀe]	recorded, with time delay
retransmettre un match en différé	broadcast a previously recorded match
un **flash (d'information)** [flaʃ]	news flash, news brief

16.4 Video and Sound Carriers

une **photo** [foto]	photo
prendre une photo	take a photo
prendre qn/qc en photo	take a photo of s.o./s.th.
photographier [fɔtɔgʀafje]	photograph
un **motif** [mɔtif]	subject
un **portrait** [pɔʀtʀɛ]	portrait (photo)
un **appareil photo** [apaʀɛjfoto]	camera
un **polaroïd** [pɔlaʀɔid]	Polaroid
un **flash** [flaʃ]	flash

une **pellicule** [pelikyl]	film
développer un film/une pellicule	develop a film
le **développement** [dev(ə)lɔpmã]	development
un **négatif** [negatif]	negative
le **format** [fɔʀma]	format
une **diapo(sitive)** [djapo(zitiv)]	slide
projeter des diapositives	show slides, project slides
On ne pourra pas regarder de diapos ce soir, le projecteur est en panne.	We can't look at slides this evening; the projector is broken.

un **film** [film]	film
tourner un film	shoot a film
filmer [filme]	film, to
une **caméra** [kameʀa]	camera

le **son** [sɔ̃]	sound, volume
écouter [ekute]	listen to, hear
le **volume** [vɔlym]	volume
Tu ne peux pas **baisser un peu le volume?** On ne s'entend plus!	Can't you turn down the volume a little? We can't hear each other anymore.
enregistrer [ãʀ(ə)ʒistʀe]	record, to
un **enregistrement** [ãʀ(ə)ʒistʀəmã]	recording

un **disque** [disk]	record
un **tourne-disque**	record player
un **CD**, un **compact** [sede, kɔ̃pakt]	CD, compact disc
un **lecteur de compacts/CD**	CD player
une **platine laser** [platinlazɛʀ]	CD player

une **chaîne hi-fi/stéréo** [ʃenifi/steʀeo]	hi-fi/stereo system
une **cassette (K 7)** [kasɛt]	cassette
un **magnétophone** [maɲetɔfɔn]	tape recorder, cassette recorder

un **lecteur de cassettes** [lɛktœʀdəkasɛt]	cassette recorder
une **radiocassette** [ʀadjokasɛt]	radio cassette recorder
un **baladeur**, un **walkman** [baladœʀ, wɔkman]	Walkman
un **lecteur de CD portable**, un **discman** [lɛktœʀdəsedepɔʀtabl, diskman]	portable CD player

(en) couleurs [(ɑ̃)kulœʀ]	(in) color
(en) noir et blanc [(ɑ̃)nwaʀeblɑ̃]	(in) black and white
une photo en couleurs/en noir et blanc	a color/black-and-white photo
net,te [nɛt]	clear
flou,e [flu]	blurred, out of focus
mat,e [mat]	matte
brillant,e [bʀijɑ̃, ɑ̃t]	glossy
une **épreuve** [epʀœv]	print
Vous voulez vos épreuves **en mat** ou **en brillant?**	Do you want your prints matte or glossy?
un **agrandissement** [agʀɑ̃dismɑ̃]	enlargement
agrandir [agʀɑ̃diʀ]	enlarge

un **caméscope** [kameskɔp]	camcorder
un **magnétoscope** [maɲetɔskɔp]	video recorder, VCR
une **vidéocassette** [videokasɛt]	videocassette
un **DVD**, un **lecteur laser vidéo** [devede, lɛktœʀlazɛʀvideo]	DVD player
un **vidéodisque** [videodisk]	video disc, DVD

une **enceinte** [ɑ̃sɛ̃t]	loudspeaker
un **casque** [kask]	headphone

16.5 Newspapers, Magazines, and Books

les **(mass) médias** *m* [(mas)medja]	(mass) media
la **presse** [pʀɛs]	press
un **journal** [ʒuʀnal]	newspaper
un **journal régional/national**	regional/national newspaper
lire [liʀ]	read
la **lecture** [lɛktyʀ]	reading
un,e **lecteur, -trice** [lɛktœʀ, tʀis]	reader
paraître [paʀɛtʀ]	appear, come out
une **revue** [ʀ(ə)vy]	magazine, periodical, journal

une **revue spécialisée**	professional journal
Cette revue paraît le mercredi.	This magazine comes out on Wednesdays.
un **magazine** [magazin]	magazine
un **magazine de mode**	fashion magazine
un **périodique** [peʀjɔdik]	periodical
un **illustré** [ilystʀe]	illustrated magazine

un,e **journaliste** [ʒuʀnalist]	journalist
un,e **reporter** [ʀ(ə)pɔʀtɛʀ/tœʀ]	reporter
un **grand reporter**	special correspondent
un **reportage** [ʀ(ə)pɔʀtaʒ]	reporting, report
un,e **rédacteur, -trice** [ʀedaktœʀ, tʀis]	editor
une **rédactrice en chef**	editor-in-chief
la **rédaction** [ʀedaksjɔ̃]	editing; editorship; editorial offices
rédiger un article [ʀediʒeɛ̃naʀtikl]	write an article
un,e **photographe** [fɔtɔgʀaf]	photographer

la **couverture** [kuvɛʀtyʀ]	cover
le **titre** [titʀ]	title
un **gros titre**	headline; banner
la **une** [layn]	first page, page one
Cette catastrophe a fait la une de tous les journaux.	That catastrophe made page one of all the papers.
la **manchette** [mɑ̃ʃɛt]	headline
le **sommaire** [sɔmɛʀ]	list of contents
une **page** [paʒ]	page

> **i** For information on the *gender of nouns* ending in *-age*, see p. 70.

une **colonne** [kɔlɔn]	column
une **rubrique** [ʀybʀik]	heading, title

un **texte** [tɛkst]	text
un **article** [aʀtikl]	article
Je ne suis pas d'accord avec l'auteur de cet article.	I don't agree with the author of this article.
un **sujet** [syʒɛ]	topic, subject
traiter un sujet sérieux/amusant	deal with a serious/an entertaining subject

l'**information** *f* [ɛ̃fɔʀmasjɔ̃]	information, report, news items
les **informations internationales**	international news
informer [ɛ̃fɔʀme]	inform
une **nouvelle** [nuvɛl]	news

les **nouvelles locales** — local news
Tu as lu les **dernières nouvelles** ? — Have you read the latest news?
de source sûre/de bonne — from a well-informed/reliable
source [dəsuʀsəsyʀ/dəbɔnsuʀs] — source
  Selon une information de source — According to information from a
  sûre, les impôts vont augmenter. — reliable source, taxes are going
  — to rise.

un **détail** [detaj] — detail
  révéler tous les détails du drame — reveal all the details of the drama
un **résumé** [ʀezyme] — summary
  en résumé — in summary
résumer [ʀezyme] — summarize

la **publicité**; la **pub** *fam* [pyb(lisite)] — advertising
une **annonce** [anɔ̃s] — advertisement
  les **petites annonces** — classified ads
  passer une annonce — put in an ad

un **roman feuilleton** [ʀɔmɑ̃fœjtɔ̃] — serial(ized) novel
la **suite** [sɥit] — continuation
à suivre [asɥivʀ] — to be continued

l'**opinion** *f* [ɔpiɲɔ̃] — opinion
la **position** [pozisjɔ̃] — position
  prendre position pour ou contre — take a position for or against
le **point de vue** [pwɛ̃d(ə)vy] — point of view
un **commentaire** [kɔmɑ̃tɛʀ] — commentary
l'**influence** *f* [ɛ̃flyɑ̃s] — influence
influencer [ɛ̃flyɑ̃se] — influence, to
critiquer [kʀitike] — critique; criticize; review
la **critique** [kʀitik] — criticism; critique; review
  Le dernier film de Depardieu a eu — Depardieu's last film received
  de bonnes critiques. — good reviews.
un,e **critique** [kʀitik] — critic, reviewer

un **kiosque** [kjɔsk] — kiosk, newsstand
un **numéro** [numeʀo] — issue
  Le dernier numéro de Paris-Match — The last issue of *Paris-Match* is
  est épuisé. — sold out.
un **abonnement** [abɔnmɑ̃] — subscription
s'abonner à qc [sabɔne] — subscribe to s.th.

un **livre** [livʀ] — book
un **bouquin** *fam* [bukɛ̃] — book

une **librairie** [libʀɛʀi]	bookstore
Mon nouveau livre sort en librairie la semaine prochaine.	My new book will be in the bookstores next week.
un,e **libraire** [libʀɛ̃ʀ]	book dealer
une **bibliothèque** [biblijɔtɛk]	library
un,e **bibliothécaire** [biblijɔtekɛʀ]	librarian

un **chapitre** [ʃapitʀ]	chapter
la **table des matières** [tabl(ə)dematjɛʀ]	table of contents
la **préface**, l'**avant-propos** m [pʀefas, avɑ̃pʀɔpo]	preface, foreword

la **presse du cœur** [pʀɛsdykœʀ]	rainbow press, tabloids
la **presse à sensation/à scandale** [pʀɛsasɑ̃sasjɔ̃/askɑ̃dal]	sensational/yellow/gutter press
un **canard** *fam* [kanaʀ]	(local) rag
J'ai lu ça dans mon canard.	I read it in my local rag.
publier [pyblije]	publish
une **publication** [pyblikasjɔ̃]	publication
imprimer [ɛ̃pʀime]	print
une **imprimerie** [ɛ̃pʀimʀi]	printing shop
la **mise en page** [mizɑ̃paʒ]	layout

un **tirage** [tiʀaʒ]	circulation, print run
à grand tirage	with a high circulation
Cette revue a un tirage de 200 000 exemplaires.	This magazine has a circulation of 200,000 copies.
tirer à [tiʀe]	print; have a print run of ...
Le journal tire à 400 000 exemplaires.	The newspaper has a print run of 400,000 copies.
la **diffusion** [difyzjɔ̃]	distribution
éditer [edite]	publish
une **édition** [edisjɔ̃]	edition
Edition spéciale! Demandez France-Soir !	Special edition! Buy *France-Soir*!
une **édition du soir**	evening edition
une **maison d'édition**	publishing house
un,e **éditeur, -trice** [editœʀ, tʀis]	publisher

un **quotidien** [kɔtidjɛ̃]	daily newspaper
un **hebdo(madaire)** [ɛbdo(ɔmadɛʀ)]	weekly newspaper
un **mensuel** [mɑ̃sɥɛl]	monthly magazine/periodical
un **supplément** [syplemɑ̃]	supplement

un **supplément week-end/du dimanche**	weekend/Sunday supplement

une **agence de presse** [aʒɑ̃sdəpʀɛs]	press agency
un,e **correspondant,e** [kɔʀɛspɔ̃dɑ̃, ɑ̃t]	correspondent
un **éditorial** [editɔʀjal]	editorial
un,e **éditorialiste** [editɔʀjalist]	editorialist, editorial writer

une **enquête** [ɑ̃kɛt]	inquiry, investigation; poll
Nos reporters ont mené l'enquête.	Our reporters conducted the inquiry.
un **sondage** [sɔ̃daʒ]	opinion poll
les **faits divers** *m* [fɛdivɛʀ]	news items, news in brief
un **compte-rendu** [kɔ̃tʀɑ̃dy]	report, account
une **chronique (théâtrale)** [kʀɔnik (teatʀal)]	(theater) column; news summary
un **scoop** [skup]	scoop
Ce n'est pas vraiment un scoop. *loc*	That's not exactly a scoop.
le **courrier des lecteurs** [kuʀjedelɛktœʀ]	letters from readers
le **courrier du cœur** [kuʀjedykœʀ]	advice column

exclusif, -ive [ɛksklyzif, iv]	exclusive
l'**exclusivité** *f* [ɛksklyzivite]	exclusiveness; exclusive rights
Ce reportage **paraît en exclusivité** dans notre magazine.	This reporting appears exclusively in our magazine.
objectif, -ive [ɔbʒɛktif, iv]	objective
l'**objectivité** *f* [ɔbʒɛktivite]	objectivity
subjectif, -ive [sybʒɛktif, iv]	subjective
la **subjectivité** [sybʒɛktivite]	subjectivity
divertissant,e [divɛʀtisɑ̃, ɑ̃t]	entertaining
instructif, -ive [ɛ̃stʀyktif, iv]	informative, instructive

la **tendance (politique)** [tɑ̃dɑ̃s]	(political) tendency
orienté,e [ɔʀjɑ̃te]	oriented, slanted
(être) orienté à droite/à gauche	(be) slanted to the right/left
la **liberté de la presse** [libɛʀted(ə)lapʀɛs]	freedom of the press
la **censure** [sɑ̃syʀ]	censorship
manipuler [manipyle]	manipulate
une **campagne de presse** [kɑ̃paɲdəpʀɛs]	press campaign

un **best-seller** [bɛstsɛlœʀ]	best-seller

un **exemplaire** [εgzãplεʀ]	copy
un **exemplaire broché/relié**	a paper-bound/bound copy
la **reliure** [ʀəljyʀ]	binding
une **brochure** [bʀɔʃyʀ]	stitching; booklet, brochure
les **droits d'auteur** m [dʀwadotœʀ]	copyright

une **collection** [kɔlεksjɔ̃]	(book) series
une **collection de poche**	pocketbook series
une **collection classique**	series of classical authors
Ce roman vient de paraître dans la collection Folio.	This novel has just appeared in the *Folio* series.
les **œuvres complètes (de Molière)** [œvʀεkɔ̃plεt]	the complete works (of Molière)

la **version** [vεʀsjɔ̃]	version
lire un roman **en version originale**	read a novel in the original version
la **version intégrale**	complete (unabridged) version
la **version abrégée et adaptée**	abridged and adapted version
une **faute d'impression** [fotdẽpʀεsjɔ̃]	typo(graphical error)

16.6 Multimedia, Computers

(le) **multimédia** n; adj [myltimedja]	multimedia
l'**informatique** f [ẽfɔʀmatik]	computer science; information technology
le **langage informatique** [lãgaʒẽfɔʀmatik]	programming language
un,e **informaticien, ne** [ẽfɔʀmatisjẽ, jεn]	computer scientist, IT specialist

un **ordinateur** [ɔʀdinatœʀ]	computer
un **PC** [pese]	personal computer, PC
allumer/éteindre son PC	turn on/turn off one's PC
un **portable** [pɔʀtabl]	laptop
un **micro-ordinateur** [mikʀoɔʀdinatœʀ]	microcomputer

le **disque dur** [diskədyʀ]	hard disk
une **disquette** [diskεt]	diskette, floppy
un **lecteur de disquette**	disk drive
introduire la disquette dans le lecteur de disquette	put the diskette in the disk drive
un **cédérom (CD-ROM)** [sedeʀɔm]	CD-ROM
un **lecteur de cédérom**	CD-ROM drive

un **moniteur**, un **écran (couleur)** [mɔnitœʀ, ekʀã(kulœʀ)]	(color) monitor
une **imprimante** [ɛ̃pʀimãt]	printer
une **imprimante (à) laser**	laser printer
une **imprimante à jet d'encre**	inkjet printer
imprimer [ɛ̃pʀime]	print
un **clavier** [klavje]	keyboard
une **touche** [tuʃ]	key
taper [tape]	type
une **souris** [suʀi]	mouse
cliquer [klike]	click (with the mouse)
double-cliquer sur l'icône	double-click on the icon
un **scanneur/scanner** [skanœʀ/skanɛʀ]	scanner
scanner [skane]	scan

un **curseur** [kyʀsœʀ]	cursor
la **flèche** [flɛʃ]	arrow
un **jeu électronique** [ʒøelɛktʀɔnik]	electronic game
un **jeu vidéo** [ʒøvideo]	computer game
une **console de jeux vidéo**	play station
une **manette de jeu** [manɛtdəʒø]	joystick

le **matériel** [mateʀjɛl]	hardware
le **logiciel** [lɔʒisjɛl]	software
le **progiciel** [pʀɔʒisjɛl]	software package
un **programme** [pʀɔgʀam]	program
un **programme anti-virus**	antivirus program
charger/démarrer un programme	load/start a program
programmer [pʀɔgʀame]	program
un,e **programmeur, -euse** [pʀɔgʀamœʀ, øz]	programmer
le **langage de programmation** [lãgaʒdəpʀɔgʀamasjɔ̃]	programming language
installer [ɛ̃stale]	install
Je n'arrive pas à installer ce programme.	I can't manage to install this program.
l'**installation** f [ɛ̃stalasjɔ̃]	installation
le **traitement de texte** [tʀɛtmãd(ə)tɛkst]	word processing (program)
traiter [tʀɛte]	process
traiter des données	process data

un **fichier** [fiʃje]	file
ouvrir/fermer un fichier	open/close a file

Pour revenir au **menu principal**, il faut fermer ce fichier.	To return to the main menu, this file has to be closed.
l'**accès** m [aksɛ]	access
le **mot de passe** [modpas]	password

formater [fɔʀmate]	format
mémoriser [memɔʀize]	store, to
mettre en mémoire [mɛtʀɑ̃memwaʀ]	store, to
sauvegarder [sovgaʀde]	save
Il faut sauvegarder le texte avant de fermer le fichier.	Before the file is closed, the text has to be saved.
mettre à jour [mɛtʀaʒuʀ]	update, bring up to date
Cela fait longtemps que ce fichier n'a pas été mis à jour.	This file hasn't been updated in a long time.
copier [kɔpje]	copy
couper [kupe]	cut
coller [kɔle]	paste
effacer [efase]	delete

Internet, le **Net** m [(ɛ̃tɛʀ)nɛt]	Internet
On a passé 3 heures à surfer/ naviguer sur le Net.	We spent three hours surfing the Net.
le **web/WEB** [wɛb]	the Web
un,e **utilisateur, -trice** [ytilizatœʀ, tʀis]	user
le **modem** [mɔdɛm]	modem
le **service en ligne** [sɛʀvisɑ̃liɲ]	on-line service
l'**autoroute de l'information** f [otoʀutdəlɛ̃fɔʀmasjɔ̃]	information superhighway
télécharger un texte [teleʃaʀʒeɛ̃tɛkst]	download a text
le **courrier électronique** [kuʀjeelɛtʀɔnik]	e-mail
un **mél**, un **e-mail** [mel, imɛl]	an e-mail
une **page d'accueil** [paʒdakœj]	home page

les **données** f [dɔne]	data
un **support de données**	data carrier
une **banque de données**	data bank
le **traitement des données**	data processing
le **transfert des données**	data transfer
entrer des données dans l'ordinateur	enter data in the computer
saisir des données sur ordinateur	call up data on the computer
stocker [stɔke]	store

éditer [edite] — edit
se bloquer [s(ə)blɔke] — crash

---

un **processeur** [prɔsesœr] — processor
un **système d'exploitation** [sistɛmdɛksplwatasjɔ̃] — operating system
une **mémoire** [memwar] — memory
  une **mémoire morte (ROM)** — ROM
  une **mémoire vive (RAM)** — RAM
  la **capacité de mémoire** — memory capacity

---

l'**E.A.O. (enseignement assisté par ordinateur)** [əao] — computer-assisted learning
le **télétravail** [teletravaj] — telecommute
une **image virtuelle** [imaʒvirtɥɛl] — virtual image
un **hypertexte** [ipɛrtɛkst] — hypertext

---

se connecter sur Internet [s(ə)kɔnɛktesyrɛ̃tɛrnɛt] — log on to the Internet
un **fournisseur d'accès** [furnisœrdaksɛ] — provider
un **cybercafé** [sibɛrkafe] — Internet café
l'**explorateur** *m* [ɛksplɔratœr] — browser
un **moteur de recherche** [mɔtœrdər(ə)ʃɛrʃ] — search engine
la **boîte aux lettres (électronique)** [bwatolɛtr(elɛktrɔnik)] — (electronic) mailbox
  relever la boîte aux lettres (électronique) — check the (electronic) mailbox
un **pirate** [pirat] — hacker
pirater un programme [pirateɛ̃prɔgram] — make a pirated copy of a program

French Word	English Equivalent	False Friend	French Equivalent
un magasin	store; warehouse	magazine (periodical)	un magazine
un éditeur	publisher	editor	un rédacteur

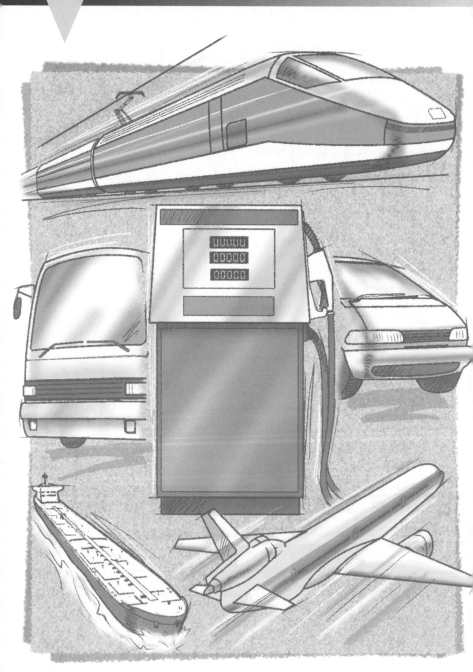

17.1 Individual Transportation

un **moyen de transport** [mwajɛ̃d(ə)tʀãspɔʀ]	means of transportation
une **voiture** [vwatyʀ]	car
aller* quelque part **en voiture**	go somewhere by car
une **voiture de location**	rental car
une **voiture d'occasion**	used car
un **camion** [kamjɔ̃]	truck

une **moto** [moto]	motorcycle
une **mobylette**; une **mob** *fam* [mɔb(ilɛt)]	motor-assisted bicycle
un **scooter** [skutœʀ/skutɛʀ]	motor scooter
un **vélo** [velo]	bike, bicycle
aller* à/en **vélo**	ride a bike

---

i | **Getting around**

En/à + *a noun without an article* generally designates the *way or means of locomotion.*

Nous sommes arrivés en voiture.	*We came by car.*
Elle est partie à/en vélo.	*She left on a bike.*
Ils ont fait une promenade à pied/à cheval.	*They went on a walk/horseback ride.*

Par + *a noun with an article* as a rule designates a *public means of transportation.*

Il est venu par le train/par le car de 8 heures.	*He came on the 8 o'clock train/bus.*

---

faire du vélo	ride a bike
une **bicyclette** [bisiklɛt]	bicycle

un,e **piéton,ne** [pjetɔ̃, ɔn]	pedestrian
un **passage** [pasaʒ]	passage; lane; crossing
un **passage (pour) piétons/clouté**	pedestrian crossing/crosswalk

---

i | For information on the *gender of nouns* ending in -**age**, see p. 70.

---

un **trottoir** [tʀɔtwaʀ]	sidewalk

conduire [kɔ̃dɥiʀ]	drive
Mon père n'aime pas conduire la nuit.	My father doesn't like to drive at night.
la **conduite** [kɔ̃dɥit]	driving; style of driving
Elle a une conduite rapide.	She drives fast.
un,e **conducteur, -trice** [kɔ̃dyktœʀ, tʀis]	driver

circuler [siʀkyle]   drive
On circule mal dans Paris.   Driving in Paris is awful.
la **circulation** [siʀkylasjɔ̃]   traffic
une circulation dense/fluide   heavy/smoothly flowing traffic
le **trafic** [tʀafik]   traffic

démarrer [demaʀe]   start, to
mettre en marche [mɛtʀɑ̃maʀʃ]   start, to
Il n'a pas réussi à mettre (son   He wasn't able to start his
moteur) en marche.   engine.
la **clé (de contact)** [kle(dkɔ̃takt)] (ignition) key
couper le contact   turn off the ignition
arrêter/couper le moteur   stop/turn off the engine
[aʀɛte/kupel(ə)mɔtœʀ]

rouler [ʀule]   drive
rouler à 90 à l'heure   drive 90 km per hour
rouler prudemment   drive with caution
la **vitesse (maximale)**   (maximum) speed
[vitɛs(maksimal)]
à toute vitesse   at maximum speed
La vitesse est limitée à 50 km/h.   The speed is limited to 50 km/h.
avancer [avɑ̃se]   drive on, drive ahead
Avance jusqu'au prochain carrefour. Drive on to the next crossing.
reculer [ʀ(ə)kyle]   drive back
ralentir [ʀalɑ̃tiʀ]   drive more slowly, slow down
Tu devrais ralentir, on roule trop vite. You ought to slow down; we're
                                    going too fast.
s'arrêter [saʀɛte]   stop
Tu aurais dû t'arrêter au feu rouge. You should have stopped at the
                                    red light.
klaxonner [klaksɔne]   sound the horn, honk
Interdiction de klaxonner.   No honking.

le **volant** [vɔlɑ̃]   steering wheel
prendre le volant   take the wheel
être au volant   be behind the wheel, steer
tourner [tuʀne]   turn
un **virage** [viʀaʒ]   curve
Prenez ce virage avec prudence.   Be careful on this curve.
à gauche [agoʃ]   on/to the left
En Grande-Bretagne, on roule à   In Great Britain they drive on
gauche.   the left.
à droite [adʀwat]   on/to the right
tourner à droite   turn to the right

tout droit [tudʀwa]	straight ahead
faire un détour [fɛʀɛ̃detuʀ]	make a detour

passer [pase]	drive through, go through
Tu as le temps de passer.	You have enough time to get through the light.
dépasser [depase]	pass, overtake
Interdiction de dépasser.	No passing.
doubler [duble]	pass, overtake

stationner [stasjɔne]	park, to
stationner en double file	park in a double row
le **stationnement** [stasjɔnmɑ̃]	parking
une zone à **stationnement payant**	a paid-parking zone
Stationnement interdit.	No parking.
se garer [s(ə)gaʀe]	park, to
Il n'y a pas de place pour se garer.	There's no place to park.
un **parking** [paʀkiŋ]	parking lot
un **parking souterrain**	underground parking garage

une **route** [ʀut]	road, way
une **(route) nationale (RN)**	national road, federal highway

> **i** For information on *prepositions* used with **la rue/la route,** see p. 11.

la route de Paris à Versailles	the road from Paris to Versailles
un,e **autoroute (A)** [otoʀut]	superhighway
prendre l'autoroute	take the superhighway
une **entrée** [ɑ̃tʀe]	access (ramp), entrance
une **sortie** [sɔʀti]	exit (ramp)
On quittera l'autoroute à la prochaine sortie.	We'll leave the superhighway at the next exit.
une **rue** [ʀy]	street
un **chemin** [ʃ(ə)mɛ̃]	way
se tromper de chemin	lose one's way
un **carrefour** [kaʀfuʀ]	crossing, crossroads
des **feux de signalisation** *m* [fød(ə)siɲalizasjɔ̃]	traffic lights
un **feu (tricolore)** [fø(tʀikɔlɔʀ)]	(traffic) light
passer au (feu) rouge	go through a red light
griller un feu rouge	run a red light

un **bouchon** [buʃɔ̃]	traffic jam, congestion
Bouchon dans 3 kilomètres !	Slow traffic 3 km ahead!

un **embouteillage** [ãbutɛjaʒ]	traffic jam, bottleneck
Nous partirons tôt pour éviter les embouteillages.	We're leaving early to avoid the traffic jams.
bloquer [blɔke]	block
un accident a bloqué la route.	An accident blocked the road.
une **station-service** [stasjɔ̃sɛrvis]	service station, gas station
l'**essence** f [esãs]	gasoline
faire le plein [fɛrləplɛ̃]	fill it up
le **super sans-plomb** [sypɛrsãplɔ̃]	high-octane lead-free gas
le **gazole**, le **gasoil** [gazɔl, gazwal]	diesel fuel
vérifier [verifje]	check, test
l'**huile** f [ɥil]	oil
Ça fait longtemps que je n'ai pas vérifié le niveau d'huile.	It's been a long time since I checked the oil level.
le **moteur** [mɔtœr]	motor, engine
un **(moteur) diesel** [djezɛl]	diesel (motor)
une **panne** [pan]	breakdown, car trouble, mishap
tomber*/**être en panne**	have a breakdown
On est tombé en panne d'essence.	We've run out of gas.
un **garage** [garaʒ]	repair shop, car garage
emmener la voiture au garage	take the car to the repair shop

For information on the *gender of nouns* ending in **-age**, see p. 70.

---

un,e **garagiste** [garaʒist]	repair shop/garage owner; auto mechanic
réparer [repare]	repair
une **réparation** [reparasjɔ̃]	repair (work)
une **roue** [ru]	wheel
la **roue de secours**	spare wheel
changer une roue	change a wheel
un **pneu** [pnø]	tire
monter les pneus d'hiver	put on the snow tires
la **pression** [presjɔ̃]	pressure
la pression des pneus	tire pressure
gonfler [gɔ̃fle]	pump up, inflate
l'**éclairage** m [eklɛraʒ]	lights
un **phare** [far]	headlight
allumer les phares	turn on the headlights
le **feu arrière** [føarjɛr]	rear light, taillight

le **code de la route** [kɔddəlaʀut] — traffic regulations, road rules
la **priorité** [pʀijɔʀite] — right of way
  Priorité à droite. — Yield to the right.
  respecter la priorité — watch the right of way
  avoir la priorité sur — have the right of way over
un **panneau** [pano] — traffic sign
(un) **sens interdit** [sɑ̃sɛ̃tɛʀdi] — no entry, one-way street
  s'engager dans un sens interdit — enter a one-way street improperly
(un **sens unique** [sɑ̃synik] — one-way street

un **contrôle** [kɔ̃tʀol] — inspection; check
les **papiers** m [papje] — (car) papers/documents
  présenter ses papiers à la police — present one's papers to the police
le **permis (de conduire)** [pɛʀmi] — driver's license
  On lui a retiré le permis de conduire. — His driver's license was taken away.
une **assurance** [asyʀɑ̃s] — insurance
  Il a une **assurance tous risques.** — He has full-coverage insurance.
(être) assuré,e contre qc [asyʀe] — (be) insured against s.th.

un **danger** [dɑ̃ʒe] — danger
  Ce chauffard est un vrai **danger public.** — This bad driver is a real public danger.
dangereux, -euse [dɑ̃ʒʀø, øz] — dangerous
  un virage dangereux — a dangerous curve
un **risque** [ʀisk] — risk
  courir un risque — run a risk
  prendre des risques — take risks
un **accident** [aksidɑ̃] — accident
  L'accident s'est produit à la sortie du village. — The accident occurred at the far edge of the village.

la **police** [pɔlis] — police
un **poste (de police)** [pɔst(dəpɔlis)] — police station, station house
  Il a passé la nuit au poste. — He spent the night in the police station.

un **commissariat** [kɔmisaʀja] — police station, station house
un **agent** [aʒɑ̃] — policeman/-woman
  Pourriez-vous me renseigner, M. l'agent? — Officer, could you give me some information?
un **flic** fam [flik] — cop

un **véhicule** [veikyl] — vehicle
  La police a retrouvé le véhicule utilisé par les voleurs. — The police have found the car used by the thieves.

une **auto(mobile)** [oto/ɔtɔ(mɔbil)]	car, auto(mobile)
un,e **automobiliste** [oto/ɔtɔmɔbilist]	automobile driver
un **motard** [mɔtaʀ]	motorcyclist
un **break** [bʀɛk]	station wagon
une **décapotable** [dekapɔtabl]	convertible
un,e **4x4** (un,e **quatre quatre**) [kat(ʀə)kat(ʀə)]	vehicle with four-wheel drive
une **camionnette** [kamjɔnɛt]	delivery truck
un **vélomoteur** [velomɔtœʀ]	moped
un **deux-roues** [døʀu]	two-wheeler
une **auto-école** [otoekɔl]	driving school
Elle s'est inscrite dans une auto-école.	She signed up at a driving school.

la **boîte de vitesses** [bwatdəvitɛs]	transmission
une boîte de vitesses automatique	an automatic transmission
l'**embrayage** m [ãbʀɛjaʒ]	clutch
embrayer [ãbʀeje]	engage the clutch
débrayer [debʀeje]	disengage the clutch
une **vitesse** [vitɛs]	gear
passer une vitesse	engage a gear
passer en 4ᵉ (vitesse)	shift into fourth (gear)
changer de vitesse	change gear, shift
la **marche avant/arrière** [maʀʃavã/aʀjɛʀ]	forward/reverse gear
passer la marche arrière	engage the reverse gear

accélérer [akseleʀe]	accelerate
l'**accélérateur** m [akseleʀatœʀ]	gas pedal, accelerator
appuyer à fond sur l'accélérateur	step on the gas
une **pédale** [pedal]	pedal
freiner [fʀene]	(apply the) brake
le **frein** [fʀɛ̃]	brake
le **frein à main**	handbrake
donner un coup de frein	tap the brake
ABS (le **système antiblocage**) [abeɛs]	ABS
rouler en pleins phares [ʀuleãplɛ̃faʀ]	drive with the high beams on
rouler en codes (en feux de croisement) [ʀuleãkɔd]	drive with the low beams on

faire demi-tour [fɛʀd(ə)mituʀ]	turn around
une **déviation** [devjasjɔ̃]	detour
A cause des travaux (routiers), il y a des déviations partout.	Because of the roadwork, there are detours everywhere.

tenir sa droite [t(ə)niʀsadʀwat]
Tu es incapable de tenir ta droite.

keep to the right
You're incapable of keeping to
the right.

serrer à droite [seʀeadʀwat]
rater un virage *fam* [ʀateɛ̃viʀaʒ]
zigzaguer [zigzage]
déraper [deʀape]
La voiture a dérapé sur la route
verglacée.
un **chantier** [ʃɑ̃tje]
Chaussée déformée. [ʃosedefɔʀme]
les **gravillons** *m* [gʀavijɔ̃]
Attention, gravillons !

stay to the right
go off the road in a curve
(drive in a) zigzag
skid, go into a skid
The car went into a skid on the
icy road.
roadwork, construction site
Damaged pavement.
fine gravel
Caution, loose gravel!

un **parcmètre** [paʀkmɛtʀ]
un **horodateur** [ɔʀodatœʀ]

parking meter
vending machine for parking
permits

Stationnement interdit !
[stasjɔnmɑ̃ɛ̃tɛʀdi]
Je ne peux pas rester longtemps, je
suis en stationnement interdit.
la **zone bleue** [zonblø]
N'oublie pas ton disque, tu es en
zone bleue.
un,e **contractuel,le** [kɔ̃tʀaktɥɛl]

No parking!

I can't stay long; I'm in a no
parking zone.
blue (short-term) parking zone
Don't forget your parking dial;
you're in a short-term zone.
parking-meter attendant, meter maid

le **réseau routier** [ʀezoʀutje]
une **voie express** [vwaɛkspʀɛs]
emprunter la voie express
une **bretelle** [bʀətɛl]
un **échangeur** [eʃɑ̃ʒœʀ]
le **péage** [peaʒ]
une **autoroute à péage**
un **(boulevard) périphérique**;
le **périph** *fam* [peʀif(eʀik)]
une **rocade** [ʀɔkad]
un **rond-point** [ʀɔ̃pwɛ̃]
s'engager dans un rond-point
un **sens giratoire** [sɑ̃sʒiʀatwaʀ]
une **voie sans issue** [vwasɑ̃zisy]
une **impasse** [ɛ̃pas]
une **piste cyclable** [pist(ə)siklabl]

road network
expressway
take the expressway
access/exit ramp
changeover, exchange
toll
a toll road, a tollway
beltway

bypass
traffic circle
enter a traffic circle
circular traffic
street with no outlet
dead-end street
bike path

un **encombrement** [ɑ̃kɔ̃bʀəmɑ̃]
être coincé dans les encombrements
un **ralentissement** [ʀalɑ̃tismɑ̃]

traffic jam, congestion
be stuck in congested traffic
slow-moving traffic, slowdown

l'**heure d'affluence** f [œʀdaflyãs]	rush hour
les **heures de pointe** f [œʀdəpwɛ̃t]	peak traffic hours
Impossible de circuler **aux heures de pointe.**	During the peak traffic hours, getting anywhere is impossible.
consommer [kɔ̃sɔme]	consume; use
Ma voiture consomme 10 litres au cent.	My car uses 10 liters for every 100 km.
la **consommation** [kɔ̃sɔmasjɔ̃]	consumption, use
un **pot d'échappement** [podeʃapmã]	exhaust pipe
un **pot catalytique** [pokatalitik]	catalytic converter
la **sécurité** [sekyʀite]	safety
une **ceinture de sécurité**	safety belt, seat belt
attacher sa ceinture de sécurité	fasten one's seat belt
un **airbag**, un **coussin gonflable** [ɛʀbag, kusɛ̃gɔ̃flabl]	airbag
crever [kʀəve]	have a flat tire
J'ai crevé.	I've got a flat.
une **crevaison** [kʀəvɛzɔ̃]	puncture
un **cric (d'automobile)** [kʀik]	car jack
le **service de dépannage** [sɛʀvisdədepanaʒ]	towing service
dépanner [depane]	provide road service; tow
une **dépanneuse** [depanøz]	road-service vehicle; tow truck
remorquer [ʀ(ə)mɔʀke]	tow
La dépanneuse nous a remorqués jusqu'au garage le plus proche.	The tow truck towed us to the nearest repair shop.
une **révision** [ʀevizjɔ̃]	inspection
un **centre de contrôle technique** [sãtʀ(ə)dəkɔ̃tʀɔltɛknik]	technical inspection center
un **toit ouvrant** [twauvʀã]	sunroof, sliding roof
la **climatisation**; la **clim** fam [klim(atizasjɔ̃)]	air conditioning, AC
une **bougie** [buʒi]	spark plug
changer les bougies	change the spark plugs
une **vidange** [vidãʒ]	oil change
un **clignotant** [kliɲɔtã]	blinker
mettre le clignotant à gauche	put on the left blinker
un **pare-chocs** [paʀʃɔk]	bumper
un **pare-brise** [paʀbʀiz]	windshield

un **essuie-glace** [esɥiglas]	windshield wiper
un **lave-glace** [lavglas]	windshield washer (unit)

une **infraction** [ɛ̃fʀaksjɔ̃]	infraction
Il a **commis une infraction au** code de la route.	He committed an infraction of the traffic regulations.
une **interdiction (de dépasser)** [ɛ̃tɛʀdiksjɔ̃(d(ə)depase)]	ban (on passing)
respecter une interdiction	comply with a ban
un **excès de vitesse** [ɛksɛdvitɛs]	speeding
une **amende pour** excès de vitesse	a fine for exceeding the speed limit
une **limitation de vitesse** [limitasjɔ̃dvitɛs]	speed limit
(un) **rappel** [ʀapɛl]	reminder of a previous traffic sign

un **chauffard** [ʃofaʀ]	bad driver, reckless driver
un **alcootest** [alkɔtɛst]	alcohol test
Son alcootest a été positif.	His alcohol test was positive.
écraser [ekʀaze]	run over
Elle s'est fait écraser par un chauffard ivre.	She was run over by a drunken driver.
une **collision** [kɔlizjɔ̃]	collision
une **victime** [viktim]	victim
porter secours á qn [pɔʀtes(ə)kuʀ]	lend s.o. aid, help s.o.
les **premiers secours**	first aid
un **témoin** [temwɛ̃]	witness
Selon le témoin de l'accident, elle n'a pas respecté le feu.	According to the witness of the accident, she didn't stop at the red light.

la **carte grise** [kaʀtəgʀiz]	(gray) registration certificate
la **carte verte** [kaʀtəvɛʀt]	(green) proof of insurance
une **vignette** [viɲɛt]	tax sticker

une **contravention** [kɔ̃tʀavɑ̃sjɔ̃]	fixed penalty notice
un **papillon** *fam* [papijɔ̃]	detachable form, slip
Quand elle est revenue, il y avait un papillon sous son essuie-glace.	When she came back, there was a ticket under the windshield wiper.
une **amende** [amɑ̃d]	fine, penalty
un **procès-verbal (PV)** [pʀɔsɛvɛʀbal (peve)]	ticket
La contractuelle lui a mis un PV.	The meter maid gave him a ticket.

17.2 Public Transportation System

le **transport** [tʀãspɔʀ]	transportation, transport
transporter [tʀãspɔʀte]	transport
voyager [vwajaʒe]	travel
voyager en/par le train	travel by train
un **voyage** [vwajaʒ]	trip
Bon voyage !	Have a good trip!
un,e **voyageur, -euse** [vwajaʒœʀ, øz]	traveler

un **(auto)bus** [(oto/ɔtɔ)bys]	bus
un **arrêt de bus/d'autobus**	a bus stop
un **trajet** [tʀaʒɛ]	distance, way
Je fais ce trajet tous les jours.	I travel this way every day.
un **(auto)car** [(oto/ɔtɔ)kaʀ]	coach, long-distance bus
Le car pour Brive partira à 9 heures 15.	The bus to Brive leaves at 9:15.
une **gare routière** [gaʀʀutjɛʀ]	bus station
un **train** [tʀɛ̃]	train
Ce train s'arrête à toutes les gares.	The train stops at all the stations.
un **TGV (train à grande vitesse)** [teʒeve]	TGV (French high-speed train)
le **RER (Réseau express régional)** [ɛʀəɛʀ]	regional suburban/commuter train
un **métro** [metʀo]	metro, subway
une **ligne de métro**	subway line
une **station de métro**	subway station
un **taxi** [taksi]	taxi
appeler un taxi	call a taxi

une **gare** [gaʀ]	railroad station
un **quai** [kɛ]	platform
une **voie** [vwa]	track
Le train pour Brest part de la voie 2.	The train to Brest leaves from Track 2.
les **rails** m [ʀaj]	rails
la **consigne** [kɔ̃siɲ]	baggage checkroom; locker
laisser ses bagages à la consigne (automatique)	leave one's baggage in the checkroom (in the locker)

un **ticket** [tikɛ]	ticket
un **aller simple** [alesɛ̃pl]	one-way ticket
un **aller-retour**, un **aller et retour** [ale(e)ʀ(ə)tuʀ]	round-trip ticket
un aller-retour pour Strasbourg	a round-trip ticket to Strasbourg

valable [valabl]
Votre billet n'est plus valable.
valid
Your ticket is no longer valid.

(en) 1ère classe [(ã)pRǝmjɛRklas]
Elle voyage toujours en 1ère (classe).
(in) first class
She always travels in first class.

(en) 2e class [(ã)dØzjɛmklas]
(in) second class

un **carnet** [kaRnɛ]
Un **carnet de tickets** (de métro), s'il vous plaît.
a book of tickets
A book of (subway) tickets, please.

une **carte orange** [kaRtɔRãʒ]
une carte orange pour trois zones
multi-trip area ticket
a multi-trip pass for three zones

une **réduction** [Redyksjõ]
Il a droit à la **réduction famille nombreuse.**
reduction
He has a right to the large-family reduction.

un **chauffeur** [ʃofœR]
driver

un,e **contrôleur, -euse** [kõRɔlœR, Øz]
montrer son billet au contrôleur
ticket collector
show one's ticket to the ticket collector

un,e **passager, -ère** [pasaʒe, ɛR]
passenger

attendre (le bus ...) [atãdR]
wait for (the bus ...)

une **salle d'attente** [saldatãt]
waiting room

prendre (le métro ...) [pRãdR]
On y va en taxi ou on prend le métro?
take (the metro ...)
Shall we go by taxi or take the subway?

rater (le bus ...) *fam* [Rate]
Si tu ne te dépêches pas, tu vas rater ton bus.
miss (the bus ...)
If you don't hurry, you'll miss your bus.

manquer (le bus ...) [mãke]
miss (the bus ...)

monter* (dans le bus ...) [mõte]
get on/board (the bus ...)

En voiture, s.v.p. ! [ãvwatyRsilvuplɛ]
Les voyageurs pour Lyon en voiture, s'il vous plaît !
All aboard, please!
All those traveling to Lyon, please board!

descendre* (du bus ...) [desãdR]
Elle est tombée en descendant du train.
get off (the bus ...)
She fell while getting off the bus.

changer (de bus ...) [ʃãʒe]
Pour aller à *Odéon*, il faut changer à *Châtelet*.
change (buses ...)
To get to Odéon, you have to change at Châtelet.

la **correspondance** [kɔRespõdãs]
attendre la correspondance
connecting train, connection
wait for the connecting train

les **renseignements** *m* [Rãsɛɲmã]
information

un **horaire** [ɔRɛR]
Renseigne-toi sur les **horaires des trains pour** Nantes.
schedule
Ask for the schedule of trains to Nantes.

le **départ** [depaʀ]	departure
l'**heure de départ**	time of departure
l'**arrivée** f [aʀive]	arrival
l'**heure d'arrivée**	time of arrival
L'arrivée du TGV est prévue pour 18 heures 30.	The TGV is scheduled to arrive at 6:30 P.M.
en avance [ãnavãs]	too early
Nous sommes en avance.	We're too early.
à l'heure [alœʀ]	on time
Le car est parti à l'heure.	The bus left on time.
ponctuel,le [pɔ̃ktɥɛl]	punctual, on schedule
en retard [ãʀ(ə)taʀ]	late, too late
Le train est en retard.	The train is late.
annulé,e [anyle]	canceled
Le vol de 9 heures est **annulé en raison des grèves**.	The 9 A.M. flight was canceled because of the strikes.

une **place** [plas]	seat; place
(faire) réserver une place	reserve a seat
une **place assise/debout**	seat/standing room
une **banquette** [bãkɛt]	bench

la **SNCF (Société nationale des chemins de fer français)** [ɛsɛnseɛf]	French state railway system
un **train de voyageurs** [tʀɛ̃dvwajaʒœʀ]	excursion train
une **locomotive** [lɔkɔmɔtiv]	locomotive
un **wagon** [vagɔ̃]	car
un **wagon-lit**	sleeping car
un **wagon-restaurant**	dining car
un **compartiment** [kɔ̃paʀtimã]	compartment
un **compartiment (non-)fumeurs**	(no-)smoking compartment
une **couchette** [kuʃɛt]	couchette
une **voiture-couchettes**	couchette car

un **avion** [avjɔ̃]	airplane
un **hélicoptère** [elikɔptɛʀ]	helicopter
une **compagnie aérienne** [kɔ̃paɲiaeʀjɛn]	airline company

voler [vɔle]	fly
Au retour, nous volons de nuit.	On the way back we fly at night.
un **vol régulier** [vɔlʀegylje]	regularly scheduled flight
un **(vol) charter** [(vɔl)ʃaʀtɛʀ]	charter flight

une **piste** [pist]	runway

L'avion **se pose sur la piste**.	The airplane is landing on the runway.
un **aéroport** [aeʀɔpɔʀ]	airport
un **aérodrome** [aeʀodʀom]	airfield
une **aérogare** [aeʀogaʀ]	terminal
un **terminal** [tɛʀminal]	terminal
Les vols internationaux partent du terminal B.	The international flights leave from Terminal B.

un **bateau** [bato]	boat, ship
un **ferry(-boat)** [feʀi(bot)]	ferry(boat)
Le ferry transporte des passagers et des voitures.	The ferry transports passengers and cars.
traverser [tʀavɛʀse]	cross
une **traversée** [tʀavɛʀse]	crossing
la traversée de la Manche	the crossing of the English Channel
un **port** [pɔʀ]	port
arriver* à bon port	arrive safely; end happily
un **capitaine** [kapitɛn]	captain
un **marin** [maʀɛ̃]	sailor
à bord [abɔʀ]	on board, aboard
Il était marin à bord du Titanic.	He was a sailor aboard the *Titanic*.
monter* à bord	go on board

les **bagages** m [bagaʒ]	baggage, luggage
les **bagages à main**	hand luggage
un **porteur** [pɔʀtœʀ]	porter
un **chariot** [ʃaʀjo]	baggage cart
mettre ses bagages sur le chariot	put one's baggage on the baggage cart

le **transport** [tʀɑ̃spɔʀ]	transportation, transport
le **transport routier/ ferroviaire/aérien/ maritime/ fluvial**	transportation by road/rail/air/sea/inland shipping
le **réseau (ferroviaire)** [ʀezo(feʀɔvjɛʀ)]	(railroad) network
les **transports en commun** m [tʀɑ̃spɔ̃ɑ̃kɔmɛ̃]	public means of transportation
emprunter les transports en commun	use public transit
un **train de banlieue** [tʀɛ̃d(ə)bɑ̃ljø]	suburban train
faire la navette [feʀlanavɛt]	commute
J'aime mieux faire la navette tous les jours qu'habiter à Paris.	I'd rather commute every day than live in Paris.
desservir [desɛʀviʀ]	stop (at a train station)

Ce train ne dessert pas la gare de Corbeil.	This train doesn't stop at the Corbeil station.
une **rame de métro** [ʀamdəmetʀo]	subway train
La prochaine rame passe dans 3 minutes.	The next subway train will pass through in three minutes.
les **grandes lignes** f [gʀɑ̃dliɲ]	long-distance lines
le **tram(way)** [tʀam(wɛ)]	streetcar

le **terminus** [tɛʀminys]	terminus, final stop
à destination de ... [adɛstinasjɔ̃də]	bound for ...
L'avion à destination de New York est parti à 13 heures 30.	The plane bound for New York took off at 1:30 P.M.
en provenance de ... [ɑ̃pʀɔv(ə)nɑ̃sdə]	coming from ...
Le train en provenance de Lille arrivera en retard.	The train from Lille will arrive late.

composter [kɔ̃pɔste]	date; cancel (after use)
N'oubliez pas de composter votre billet.	Don't forget to cancel your ticket.
un **accès** [aksɛ]	access, entry
Accès interdit !	No access/entry!

l'**enregistrement (des bagages)** m [ɑ̃ʀ(ə)ʒistʀəmɑ̃(debagaʒ)]	check-in (of baggage)
l'**embarquement** m [ɑ̃baʀkəmɑ̃]	boarding
la **carte d'embarquement**	boarding pass
embarquer [ɑ̃baʀke]	board, go on board
un **pilote**, un **commandant de bord** [pilɔt, kɔmɑ̃dɑ̃d(ə)bɔʀ]	pilot, flight captain
un **steward** [stiwaʀt]	steward, flight attendant
une **hôtesse de l'air** [otɛsdəlɛʀ]	stewardess, flight attendant
les **ventes hors-taxes** f [vɑ̃tɔʀtaks]	duty-free shopping
décoller [dekɔle]	take off, lift off
L'avion a décollé de la piste 03.	The plane took off from Runway 03.

le **décollage** [dekɔlaʒ]	takeoff
atterrir [ateʀiʀ]	land
l'**atterrissage** m [ateʀisaʒ]	landing
une **escale** [ɛskal]	intermediate landing, stopover
faire escale	make an intermediate landing/stopover
le **décalage horaire** [dekalaʒɔʀɛʀ]	time difference
Il y a 9 heures de décalage (horaire) entre Paris et San Francisco.	There's a nine-hour time difference between Paris and San Francisco.
un **paquebot** [pak(ə)bo]	passenger ship

French Word	English Equivalent	French	English

un **navire** [naviʀ] (large) ship, vessel
 Le navire **met le cap** sur Tahiti. The ship is heading for Tahiti.
naviguer [navige] sail; navigate
la **navigation** [navigasjɔ̃] sailing; navigation
une **croisière** [kʀwazjɛʀ] cruise
un **équipage** [ekipaʒ] crew
 les **membres d'équipage** crew members
le **mal de mer** [maldəmɛʀ] seasickness

un **semi-remorque** [səmiʀ(ə)mɔʀk] truck/semi-trailer tractor
un **routier** [ʀutje] long-haul truck driver
 Les routiers ont bloqué la route The long-haul truck drivers have
 en signe de protestation. blocked the road as a sign of protest.
un **camionneur** [kamjɔnœʀ] truck driver; mover
la **marchandise** [maʀʃɑ̃diz] merchandise, goods
 un **train de marchandises** freight train
 charger la marchandise sur le camion load the goods on the truck

un **cargo** [kaʀgo] cargo ship, freighter
le **fret** [fʀɛt] freight, cargo
 charger le fret dans la cale stow the freight in the hold
un **pétrolier** [petʀɔlje] tanker
une **péniche** [peniʃ] barge
un **canal** [kanal] canal
 Les péniches naviguent sur les canaux. The barges sail on the canals.
une **écluse** [eklyz] lock (on canals)

French Word	English Equivalent	False Friend	French Equivalent
un car	coach, long-distance bus	car	une voiture

18.1 Universe, Earth

l'**espace** *m* [ɛspas]	(outer) space
lancer une fusée dans l'espace	launch a rocket into outer space
le **ciel** [sjɛl]	sky
le **soleil** [sɔlɛj]	sun
solaire [sɔlɛʀ]	solar
le **système solaire**	solar system
une **étoile** [etwal]	star
une **étoile filante**	falling star
la **lune** [lyn]	moon
être dans la lune *loc*	be absent-minded
la **pleine lune**	full moon
la **lune de miel**	honeymoon
croître [kʀwatʀ]	wax, increase
décroître [dekʀwatʀ]	wane, decrease
lunaire [lynɛʀ]	lunar
la **terre** [tɛʀ]	earth
tourner autour de la terre	revolve around the earth
le **globe (terrestre)** [glɔb(teʀɛstʀ)]	(terrestrial) globe

l'**air** *m* [ɛʀ]	air
être au grand air	be in the fresh air
un **gaz** [gaz]	gas
l'**ozone** *m* [ozon/ɔzɔn]	ozone
l'**oxygène** *m* [ɔksiʒɛn]	oxygen
respirer [ʀɛspiʀe]	breathe
respirer **à pleins poumons**	breathe deeply
la **respiration** [ʀɛspiʀasjɔ̃]	respiration, breathing

l'**univers** *m* [ynivɛʀ]	universe
universel,e [ynivɛʀsɛl]	universal
une **galaxie** [galaksi]	galaxy
la **voie lactée** [vwalakte]	Milky Way
la **constellation** [kɔ̃stelasjɔ̃]	constellation
Cette étoile fait partie de la constellation d'Orion.	That star belongs to the constellation Orion.
une **comète** [kɔmɛt]	comet
tirer des plans sur la comète *loc*	build castles in the air
un **météore** [meteɔʀ]	meteor
un **astre** [astʀ]	star, celestial body
une **année-lumière** [anelymjɛʀ]	light-year
une **éclipse** [eklips]	eclipse
une **éclipse totale/partielle**	total/partial eclipse
une **planète** [planɛt]	planet

un **satellite** [satelit]	satellite
La Lune est un satellite de la Terre.	The moon is a satellite of the earth.
une **orbite** [ɔrbit]	orbit
mettre un satellite **sur orbite**	put a satellite into orbit

le **pôle** [pol]	pole
le pôle Nord/Sud	North/South Pole
le **cercle polaire** [sɛrkl(ə)polɛr]	polar circle
l'**hémisphère** m [emisfɛr]	hemisphere
l'hémisphère nord	the northern hemisphere
la **rotation** [ʀɔtasjɔ̃]	rotation
La rotation de la Terre sur elle-même dure 24 heures.	The rotation of the earth on its axis takes 24 hours.

un **axe** [aks]	axis
l'**équateur** m [ekwatœr]	equator
les **tropiques** m [trɔpik]	tropics
le **tropique du Cancer/du Capricorne**	the Tropic of Cancer/of Capricorn
un **fuseau horaire** [fyzoɔrɛr]	time zone

l'**atmosphère** f [atmɔsfɛr]	atmosphere
graviter [ɡravite]	revolve; gravitate
Le satellite gravite autour de la Terre.	The satellite revolves around the earth.
la **gravitation** [ɡravitasjɔ̃]	gravitation
l'**attraction** f [atraksjɔ̃]	attraction
l'attraction terrestre	earth's gravitational attraction
attirer [atire]	attract
L'aimant attire le fer.	The magnet attracts iron.

l'**astronautique** f [astronotik]	space travel, astronautics
un,e **astronaute** [astronot]	astronaut
un,e **cosmonaute** [kɔsmɔnot]	cosmonaut
une **fusée** [fyze]	rocket
Le lancement de la fusée Ariane s'est bien passé.	The launch of the Ariane rocket was successful.
une **soucoupe volante** [sukupvɔlɑ̃t]	flying saucer
un **OVNI (objet volant non-identifié)** [ɔvni]	UFO (unidentified flying object)
Il croit fermement aux OVNI et aux extraterrestres.	He firmly believes in UFOs and extraterrestrials.

spatial,e [spasjal]	spatial, space
la **recherche spatiale**	space research

un **vaisseau spatial**	spaceship
une **navette/station spatiale**	space shuttle/station
l'**apesanteur** f [apəzãtœʀ]	weightlessness
se trouver **en état d'apesanteur**	be in a state of weightlessness

18.2 Geography

la **géographie** [ʒeɔgʀafi]	geography
une **carte (de géographie)**	a map
géographique [ʒeɔgʀafik]	geographic
le **paysage** [peizaʒ]	landscape
la **nature** [natyʀ]	nature

le **monde** [mɔ̃d]	world
Il a voyagé dans le **monde entier.**	He's traveled all over the world.
la **terre** [tɛʀ]	earth; soil, ground
avoir les pieds sur terre *loc*	have both feet on the ground
un **continent** [kɔ̃tinã]	continent
terrestre [tɛʀɛstʀ]	terrestrial, land
les **animaux terrestres**	land animals
la **surface** [syʀfas]	surface, area
La France a une surface de 550 000 km².	France has an area of 550,000 square km.
un **pays** [pei]	country
une **région** [ʀeʒjɔ̃]	region, area
une **région sauvage**	an untamed area
une **province** [pʀɔvɛ̃s]	province
s'étendre sur [setãdʀ]	extend
Cette forêt s'étend sur 200 hectares.	This forest extends over 200 hectares.
une **frontière** [fʀɔ̃tjɛʀ]	border, frontier, boundary
une **frontière naturelle**	natural boundary

le **relief** [ʀəljɛf]	relief
une **montagne** [mɔ̃taɲ]	mountain(s)
montagneux, -euse [mɔ̃taɲø, øz]	mountainous
une **région montagneuse**	a mountainous region
une **colline** [kɔlin]	hill
un **volcan** [vɔlkã]	volcano
un **volcan en activité**	an active volcano
volcanique [vɔlkanik]	volcanic
une **éruption volcanique**	volcanic eruption

un **sommet** [sɔmɛt]	summit, peak
monter* au sommet	climb to the summit
s'**élever à** [sel(ə)ve]	rise, ascend
Le Mont Blanc s'élève à 4807 m.	Mont Blanc is 4807 meters high.
un **col** [kɔl]	(mountain) pass
une **vallée** [vale]	valley
une **gorge** [gɔRʒ]	gorge
Chaque années, de nombreux touristes visitent les gorges du Verdon.	Every year numerous tourists visit the gorges of Verdon.

la **hauteur** ['otœR]	height
La hauteur de la Tour Montparnasse **est de** 209 m.	The height of the Montparnasse Tower is 209 meters.
haut,e ['o, 'ot]	high
une montagne **haute de** 3000 m	a mountain 3000 meters high
bas,se [ba, bas]	low
L'avion vole très bas.	The plane is flying very low.

les Alpes f [lezalp]	the Alps
les Pyrénées f [lepiRene]	the Pyrenees
le Massif Central [ləmasifsɑ̃tRal]	the Massif Central
les Vosges f [levoʒ]	the Vosges

une **forêt** [fɔRɛ]	forest
la **forêt vierge**	virgin forest
un **bois** [bwa]	wood(s)
se promener **dans les bois**	go for a walk in the woods
la **campagne** [kɑ̃paɲ]	country, fields
un **désert** [dezɛR]	desert
désertique [dezɛRtik]	desertlike, waste, desolate
une région complètement désertique	a completely barren area

l'**eau**, les **eaux** f [o]	water; waters
Les **eaux de pluie** ont grossi la rivière.	The rains caused the stream to swell.
profond,e [pRɔfɔ̃, ɔ̃d]	deep
une eau peu profonde	a shallow body of water
la **profondeur** [pRɔfɔ̃dœR]	depth
La gorge a une profondeur de 250 mètres.	The gorge has a depth of 250 meters.

la **mer** [mɛR]	sea
aller* au bord de la mer	go to the seaside

Watch out for homophones!

In French there are a number of words that are pronounced the same *(homophones)* but are spelled differently and thus have different meanings.
Examples:

la mer [mɛʀ]	*the sea*
la mère [mɛʀ]	*the mother*
le maire [mɛʀ]	*the mayor*

maritime [maʀitim]	maritime
le **climat maritime**	maritime climate
un **océan** [ɔseã]	ocean
les **marées** f [maʀe]	tides
la **marée haute/basse**	high/low tide, flood/ebb tide
à marée haute/basse	at high/low tide, at flood/ebb tide
une **vague** [vag]	wave

un **fleuve** [flœv]	river (flowing into the sea)
La ville est située **au bord d'un fleuve.**	The city is situated on a river.
se jeter dans [səʒ(ə)tedã]	flow into
La Seine se jette dans la Manche.	The Seine flows into the English Channel.
navigable [navigabl]	navigable
une **rivière** [ʀivjɛʀ]	river, stream
couler [kule]	flow
une **source** [suʀs]	source
prendre sa source	have its source
un **lac** [lak]	lake

la Seine [lasɛn]	the Seine
la Loire [lalwaʀ]	the Loire
le Rhône [ləʀon]	the Rhône
la Garonne [lagaʀɔn]	the Garonne
le Rhin [ləʀɛ̃]	the Rhine

une **côte** [kot]	coast
Cet été, nous allons **sur la Côte d'Azur.**	This summer we're going to the Côte d'Azur (Riviera).
une **rive** [ʀiv]	bank
sur la rive droite du fleuve	on the right bank of the river
un **rivage** [ʀivaʒ]	shore; bank, waterside
une **plage** [plaʒ]	beach
le **sable** [sabl]	sand
une plage de sable fin	a beach with fine sand
un **rocher** [ʀɔʃe]	rock
rocheux, -euse [ʀɔʃø, øz]	rocky

La Bretagne a des côtes rocheuses.	Brittany has rocky coasts.
une **île** [il]	island

un **atlas** [atlas]	atlas
un **parallèle** [paʀalɛl]	parallel
à la hauteur du 20ᵉ parallèle	in the latitude of the 20th parallel
un **mèridien** [meʀidjɛ̃]	meridian
être situé,e à [ɛt(ʀə)sitɥe]	be situated/located
... degrés de latitude (nord/sud) [dəgʀed(ə)latityd(nɔʀ/syd)]	... degrees of (northern/southern) latitude
Paris est situé à 48 degrès de latitude nord.	Paris is situated at 48 degrees of northern latitude.
... degrès de longitude (est/ouest) [dəgʀed(ə)lɔ̃ʒityd(ɛst/wɛst)]	... degrees of (eastern/western) longitude
septentrional,e [sɛptɑ̃tʀijɔnal]	northern
méridional,e [meʀidjɔnal]	southern
oriental,e [ɔʀjɑ̃tal]	eastern
occidental,e [ɔksidɑ̃tal]	western

une **chaîne de montagnes** [ʃɛndəmɔ̃taɲ]	mountain chain
l'**altitude** f [altityd]	altitude
Le village est situé à une altitude de 1200 mètres.	The village is situated at an altitude of 1200 meters.
une **pente** [pɑ̃t]	slope, gradient, incline
Le sol descend **en pente douce**.	The ground slopes gently.
un **glacier** [glasje]	glacier
fondre [fɔ̃dʀ]	melt
une **grotte** [gʀɔt]	grotto, cave

le Jura [ləʒyʀa]	the Jura Mountains
les Ardennes [lezaʀdɛn]	the Ardennes
la Forêt-Noire [lafɔʀɛnwaʀ]	the Black Forest

un **plateau** [plato]	plateau
une **plaine** [plɛn]	plain
La Beauce est une plaine fertile.	The Beauce is a fertile plain.
plat,e [pla, plat]	flat, level
en terrain plat	in level terrain
la **superficie** [sypɛʀfisi]	surface
l'**étendue** f [etɑ̃dy]	extent, size
un **bassin** [basɛ̃]	basin
le Bassin parisien	Paris basin

le **sol** [sɔl]	soil, ground

un sol fertile	fertile soil
le **terrain** [teʀɛ̃]	terrain, ground
un terrain aride	arid terrain
boisé,e [bwaze]	wooded
l'**érosion** f [eʀozjɔ̃]	erosion
la **désertification** [dezɛʀtifikasjɔ̃]	degeneration into arid lands, devastation
Le déboisement entraîne un phénomène de désertification.	Deforestation leads to degeneration into arid lands.

l'(océan) **Atlantique** m [latlɑ̃tik]	the Atlantic (Ocean)
la **Méditerranée** [lamediteʀane]	the Mediterranean
la **mer du Nord** [lamɛʀdynɔʀ]	the North Sea
la **mer Baltique** [lamɛʀbaltik]	the Baltic Sea
la **Manche** [lamɑ̃ʃ]	the English Channel
le (océan) **Pacifique** m [ləpasifik]	the Pacific (Ocean)
traverser le Pacifique à la voile	cross the Pacific in a sailboat
l'**océan Indien** m [lɔseɑ̃ɛ̃djɛ̃]	the Indian Ocean

le **lac de Constance** [ləlakdəkɔ̃stɑ̃s]	Lake Constance
le **lac Léman** [ləlaklemɑ̃]	Lake Geneva, Lake Leman
une **mer intérieure** [mɛʀɛ̃teʀjœʀ]	inland sea

un **ruisseau** [ʀɥiso]	brook
un **courant** [kuʀɑ̃]	current
un **torrent** [tɔʀɑ̃]	torrent; mountain stream
L'orage a transformé le ruisseau en torrent rapide.	The storm transformed the brook into a fast-moving torrent.
une **chute d'eau** [ʃytdo]	waterfall
une **cascade** [kaskad]	cascade, small waterfall
en amont [ɑ̃namɔ̃]	upstream
une ville située au bord de la Seine, en amont de Paris	a city situated on the Seine, upstream from Paris
en aval [ɑ̃naval]	downstream
un **affluent** [aflyɑ̃]	tributary
le **confluent** [kɔ̃flyɑ̃]	confluence
Lyon se trouve au confluent du Rhône et de la Saône.	Lyon is located at the confluence of the Rhône and the Saône.
l'**embouchure** f [ɑ̃buʃyʀ]	mouth
Le pont enjambe l'embouchure de la loire.	The bridge spans the mouth of the Loire.
un **étang** [etɑ̃]	pond

la **Marne** [lamaʀn]	the Marne
la **Meuse** [lamøz]	the Meuse
la **Saône** [lason]	the Saône

la **Dordogne** [ladɔʀdɔɲ] — the Dordogne
la **Moselle** [lamɔzɛl] — the Moselle
le **Danube** [lədanyb] — the Danube

une **baie** [bɛ] — bay
un **golfe** [gɔlf] — gulf
une **presqu'île** [pʀɛskil] — peninsula
une **falaise** [falɛz] — cliff
une **dune** [dyn] — dune
le **littoral** [litɔʀal] — seaboard, coastal region
  Les complexes hôteliers défigurent le littoral. — The hotel complexes disfigure the seaboard.

18.3 Climate, Weather

le **climat** [klima] — climate
  le **climat méditerranéen** — Mediterranean climate
  le **climat océanique** — Atlantic climate
  le **climat continental/tropical** — continental/tropical climate
  le **climat polaire** — polar climate
  un **climat rude/(mal)sain** — harsh/(un)healthy climate
une **zone** [zon] — zone
  un pays situé dans la **zone tempérée** — a country situated in the temperate zone
une **saison** [sɛzɔ̃] — season
  la **saison des pluies** — the rainy season

le **temps** [tɑ̃] — weather
la **météo(rologie)** [meteo(ɔʀɔlɔʒi)] — meteorology; weather report
le **bulletin météorologique** [byltɛ̃meteɔʀɔlɔʒik] — weather report
les **prévisions météo(rologiques)** f [pʀevizjɔ̃meteo] — weather prediction, forecast
un **changement** [ʃɑ̃ʒmɑ̃] — change
  A la météo, ils ont annoncé un changement de temps. — In the weather report they announced a change in the weather.
variable [vaʀjabl] — variable
  Le temps sera variable sur la moitié nord du pays. — The weather will be variable in the northern half of the country.

la **pression atomsphérique** [pʀesjɔ̃atmɔsfeʀik] — atmospheric pressure
  La pression **est en hausse/en baisse**. — The pressure is rising/dropping.

les **hautes/basses pressions**	high/low pressure
un **baromètre** [baʀɔmɛtʀ]	barometer
Le baromètre est descendu depuis hier.	The barometer has fallen since yesterday.

la **température** [tɑ̃peʀatyʀ]	temperature
un **degré** [dəgʀe]	degree
(20 degrés) au-dessus/au-dessous de zéro	(20 degrees) above/below zero
plus [plys]	plus
moins [mwɛ̃]	minus
Il fait plus/moins 15.	It's plus/minus 15 degrees.
à **l'ombre** [alɔ̃bʀ]	in the shade
Il fait 35 degrés à l'ombre.	It's 35 degrees in the shade.
un **thermomètre** [tɛʀmɔmɛtʀ]	thermometer
baisser [bese]	drop, fall
La température a **baissé de 15 degrés** depuis hier.	The temperature has dropped 15 degrees since yesterday.
monter* [mɔ̃te]	rise, climb
moyen,ne [mwajɛ̃, ɛn]	average
A Paris, au mois d'août, la température moyenne est de 18,7 degrés.	In Paris the average temperature in August is 18.7 degrees Celsius.
la **moyenne annuelle** [mwajɛnanɥɛl]	the yearly average
Il fait beau. [ilfɛbo]	The weather is fine.
Il fait bon. [ilfɛbɔ̃]	The weather is pleasant.
Il fait chaud. [ilfɛʃo]	It's warm. It's hot.
la **chaleur** [ʃalœʀ]	heat
Quelle chaleur!	What heat! Such heat!
une vague de chaleur	heat wave
(le) **froid** *n; adj* [fʀwa]	cold
Il fait froid.	It's cold.
tiède [tjɛd]	mild
doux, douce [du, dus]	mild
frais, fraîche [fʀɛ, fʀɛʃ]	cool
Les nuits sont fraîches.	The nights are cool.
la **fraîcheur** [fʀɛʃœʀ]	coolness

le **soleil** [sɔlɛj]	sun
Il fait soleil.	It's sunny.
Le soleil brille.	The sun is shining.
Le soleil tape.	The sun is very strong.
Le soleil se lève/se couche.	The sun is rising/is setting.
le **lever/coucher de/du soleil**	sunrise/set
Profitons des rares **rayons de soleil**.	Let's take advantage of the rare rays of the sun.
sec, sèche [sɛk, sɛʃ]	dry

agréable [agʁeabl]	pleasant, agreeable
le **ciel** [sjɛl]	sky

la **pluie** [plɥi]	rain
La pluie tombe sans arrêt depuis 8 jours.	Rain has been falling for a week without a break.
pleuvoir [pløvwaʁ]	rain
Il pleut.	It's raining.
une **goutte** [gut]	drop
un **nuage** [nɥaʒ]	cloud
nuageux, -euse [nɥaʒø, øz]	cloudy, overcast
Le ciel est très nuageux.	The sky is very cloudy.
Il fait mauvais. [ilfɛmovɛ]	The weather is bad.
Il fait lourd. [ilfɛluʁ]	It's humid.
un **orage** [ɔʁaʒ]	thunderstorm
Il y a de l'orage dans l'air.	There's a thunderstorm in the air.
orageux, -euse [ɔʁaʒø, øz]	stormy
un temps orageux	stormy weather
le **tonnerre** [tɔnɛʁ]	thunder
Le tonnerre gronde au loin.	The thunder is rolling in the distance.
un **éclair** [eklɛʁ]	flash of lightning
la **foudre** [fudʁ]	lightning; thunderbolt
La foudre est **tombée sur** sa maison.	Lightning struck his house.
l'**humidité** f [ymidite]	humidity
le **brouillard** [bʁujaʁ]	fog
un **brouillard à couper au couteau** *loc*	a very dense fog

le **vent** [vɑ̃]	wind
un **vent glacial**	an icy wind
Le vent **souffle fort.**	A strong wind is blowing.
Il fait du vent.	It's windy.
La direction du vent a changé.	The wind direction has changed.
une **tempête** [tɑ̃pɛt]	storm
La tempête **s'est calmée** vers le soir.	The storm died down toward evening.

la **neige** [nɛʒ]	snow
un **flocon de neige**	snowflake
La neige tombe **à gros flocons.**	The snow is falling in thick flakes.
neiger [neʒe]	snow
la **glace** [glas]	ice
le **gel** [ʒɛl]	frost
geler [ʒ(ə)le]	freeze
Il gèlera au-dessus de 400 m.	There will be frost above 400 meters.

le **verglas** [vɛʀgla]
La voiture a **dérapé sur une plaque de verglas.**

thin coating of ice
The car skidded on a patch of thin ice.

un **anticyclone** [ãtisiklon]
une **dépression** [depʀɛsjɔ̃]
la **canicule** [kanikyl]
Les personnes âgées supportent mal cette canicule.
une **éclaircie** [eklɛʀsi]
On profite d'une éclaircie pour sortir.
s'**éclaircir** [seklɛʀsiʀ]
Le ciel s'éclaircit.
s'**améliorer** [sameljɔʀe]
une **amélioration** [ameljɔʀasjɔ̃]
Une amélioration arrive par l'ouest.

a high
a low
dog days
Elderly people have a hard time coping with the dog days.
clearing up
We're taking advantage of a break in the weather to go outside.
clear up
The sky is clearing.
improve
improvement
Better weather is approaching from the west.

se couvrir [s(ə)kuvʀiʀ]
Le ciel se couvre rapidement.

become overcast
The sky is quickly becoming overcast.

couvert,e [kuvɛʀ, ɛʀt]
maussade [mosad]
Il fait un temps maussade.
pluvieux, -euse [plyvjø, øz]
un automne pluvieux
(Il fait) un temps de chien. fam
[(ilfɛ)ɛ̃tɑ̃d(ə)ʃjɛ̃]
une **perturbation** [pɛʀtyʀbasjɔ̃]
une **averse** [avɛʀs]
Le soleil **arrive à percer** entre deux averses.
pleuvoir à verse [pløvwaʀavɛʀs]
Ne sors pas sans parapluie, il pleut à verse.
des **précipitations** f [pʀesipitasjɔ̃]
(être) trempé,e [tʀãpe]
Je suis trempé **jusqu'aux os.**
la **brume** [bʀym]
un **arc-en-ciel** [aʀkãsjɛl]

covered, overcast
disagreeable
The weather is disagreeable.
rainy
a rainy autumn
(It's) miserable weather.

disturbance
shower
The sun peeps out between two showers.
pour rain
Don't go out without an umbrella; it's pouring rain.
precipitation
(be) soaked
I'm soaked clear through to the skin.
haze, mist
rainbow

une **brise** [bʀiz]
une brise légère
un **courant d'air** [kuʀãdɛʀ]
Ferme la porte, il y a des courants d'air.

breeze
a light breeze
air current
Close the door, there's a draft.

une **rafale** [ʀafal]	squall; strong gust of wind
une rafale violente	a violent squall

la **gelée** [ʒ(ə)le]	frost
Les **gelées tardives** ont abîmé les fleurs.	Late frosts have ruined the flowers.
un **froid de canard** *fam* [fʀwadkanaʀ]	really cold
le **givre** [ʒivʀ]	frost
la **grêle** [gʀɛl]	hail
le **dégel** [deʒɛl]	thaw

18.4 Substances, Materials

une **matière** [matjɛʀ]	material; matter
un **matériau** [mateʀjo]	(building) material

---

matière – matériau – matériel

Note the difference between:

la matiére	*material; matter*
un pays riche en matières premières	*a land rich in raw materials*
le matériau	*(building) material*
les matériaux de construction	*construction materials*
le matériel	*material, implements*
le matériel de camping	*camping gear*

(un) **solide** *n; adj* [sɔlid]	solid
(un) **liquide** *n; adj* [likid]	liquid
Au-dessous de 0 degré, l'eau passe de l'état liquide à l'état solide.	Below 0 degree Celsius, water passes from the liquid state to the solid state.

un **gaz** [gaz]	gas
des **gaz toxiques**	toxic gases
gazeux, -euse [gazø, øz]	gaseous, gas-containing
de l'**eau gazeuse**	carbonated water, mineral water
se composer de [s(ə)kɔ̃poze]	be composed of
L'air se compose de plusieurs gaz.	Air is made up of several gases.
contenir [kɔ̃t(ə)niʀ]	contain
Ce produit contient du pétrole.	This product contains petroleum.

---

fragile [fʀaʒil]	fragile
fin, fine [fɛ̃, fin]	fine
épais,se [epɛ, epɛs]	thick; bulky

la **pierre** [pjɛʀ]	stone
une maison **en pierre**	a stone house
une pierre précieuse	a precious stone
minéral,e [mineʀal]	mineral
la **chimie minérale**	inorganic chemistry
le **sable** [sabl]	sand
le **ciment** [simɑ̃]	cement
le **béton** [betɔ̃]	concrete
une **construction en béton armé**	a reinforced concrete structure
le **verre** [vɛʀ]	glass
du verre opaque/transparent	opaque/transparent glass

le **métal** [metal]	metal
métallique [metalik]	metallic
le **fer** [fɛʀ]	iron
l'**acier** m [asje]	steel
l'**or** m [ɔʀ]	gold
avoir une **chaîne en or**	have a gold chain
l'**argent** m [aʀʒɑ̃]	silver
un **bijou en argent**	silver jewelry

le **coton** [kɔtɔ̃]	cotton
un t(ee)-shirt **100% coton**	a T-shirt made of 100% cotton
la **soie** [swa]	silk
le **cuir** [kɥiʀ]	leather
la **laine** [lɛn]	wool

le **bois** [bwa]	wood
le **papier** [papje]	paper
le **carton** [kaʀtɔ̃]	cardboard
ranger qc dans une **boîte en carton**	put s.th. into a cardboard box

la **chimie** [ʃimi]	chemistry
chimique [ʃimik]	chemical
un **produit chimique**	chemical, chemical product
le **pétrole** [petʀɔl]	petroleum
un **produit pétrolier**	petroleum product
[pʀɔdɥipetʀɔlje]	
l'**essence** f [esɑ̃s]	gasoline
le **plastique** [plastik]	plastic
Devant le supermarché, il y a un conteneur pour les **bouteilles en plastique.**	In front of the supermarket there's a container for plastic bottles.
la **colle** [kɔl]	glue, paste, mucilage

un **élément** [elemã]	element
un **atome** [atom]	atom
une **molécule** [mɔlekyl]	molecule

une **substance(in)organique** [sypstãs(in)ɔʀganik]	an (in)organic substance
l'**oxygène** m [ɔksiʒɛn]	oxygen
une **bouteille d'oxygène**	a bottle of oxygen
l'**hydrogène** m [idʀɔʒɛn]	hydrogen
le **carbone** [kaʀbɔn]	carbon
l'**azote** m [azɔt]	nitrogen

soluble [sɔlybl]	soluble
Le sel est soluble dans l'eau.	Salt is soluble in water.
inflammable [ɛ̃flamabl]	flammable, inflammable
fondre [fɔ̃dʀ]	melt
La glace fond au-dessus de 0 degré.	Ice melts above 0 degree Celsius.

l'**ardoise** f [aʀdwaz]	slate
un **toit en ardoise**	slate roof
le **grès** [gʀɛ]	sandstone
le **granit** [gʀanit]	granite
la **craie** [kʀɛ]	chalk
le **plâtre** [platʀ]	plaster
l'**argile** f [aʀʒil]	clay
modeler un buste **en argile**	model a bust in clay

la **porcelaine** [pɔʀsəlɛn]	porcelain
un service **en porcelaine** de Sèvres	a Sèvres porcelain service
la **céramique** [seʀamik]	ceramics
le **cristal** [kʀistal]	crystal

un **minerai** [minʀɛ]	mineral, ore
l'exploitation du **minerai de fer**	mining of iron ore
le **cuivre** [kɥivʀ]	copper
l'**étain** m [etɛ̃]	tin; pewter
le **bronze** [bʀɔ̃z]	bronze
le **zinc** [zɛ̃g]	zinc
le **plomb** [plɔ̃]	lead
Tu es lourd comme du plomb.	You're as heavy as lead.
avoir un sommeil de plomb loc	sleep like a brick
le **laiton** [lɛtɔ̃]	brass
un **alliage** [aljaʒ]	alloy
la **tôle** [tol]	sheet iron
la **tôle ondulée**	corrugated iron

souder [sude]	solder, weld, braze

la **fibre** [fibʀ]	fiber
une **fibre naturelle/synthétique**	natural/synthetic fiber
filer [file]	spin
le **lin** [lɛ̃]	linen

le **carburant** [kaʀbyʀɑ̃]	motor fuel
être en panne de carburant	be out of motor fuel
la **pétrochimie** [petʀoʃimi]	petrochemistry
un **pipeline** [piplin/pajplajn]	pipeline
un **oléoduc** [ɔleɔdyk]	oil pipeline
le **mazout** [mazut]	oil fuel (for stoves, etc.)
faire remplir la cuve à mazout	have the heating-oil tank filled
le **goudron** [gudʀɔ̃]	tar
le **polystyrène** [pɔlistiʀɛn]	polystyrene, Styrofoam

18.5 Plants, Gardens, Agriculture

la **végétation** [veʒetasjɔ̃]	vegetation
une **végétation luxuriante**	luxuriant vegetation
végétal,e [veʒetal]	vegetable
une **graisse végétale**	vegetable fat
une **plante** [plɑ̃t]	plant
planter [plɑ̃te]	plant, to
une **plantation** [plɑ̃tasjɔ̃]	planting; plantation
La grêle a détruit les plantations.	The hail destroyed the plantings.
l'**herbe** f [ɛʀb]	grass
pousser [puse]	grow
Ça pousse comme de la mauvaise herbe. *loc*	It grows like a weed.

un **arbre** [aʀbʀ]	tree
un **arbre fruitier**	fruit tree
une **branche** [bʀɑ̃ʃ]	branch, twig
une **feuille** [fœj]	leaf
Le sol est couvert de **feuilles mortes**.	The ground is covered with dead leaves.

un **fruit** [fʀɥi]	fruit
un **fruit mûr/vert**	ripe/unripe, green fruit
les **fruits**	fruit(s)

une **pomme** [pɔm]	apple
une **tarte aux pommes**	apple tart
une **poire** [pwaʀ]	pear
Ce que tu peux **être poire**. *fam*	What a simpleton you can be./You're too good-natured.
une **prune** [pʀyn]	plum
faire qc **pour des prunes** *fam*	do s.th. in vain/for nothing
une **cerise** [s(ə)ʀiz]	cherry
une **pêche** [pɛʃ]	peach
avoir la pêche *fam*	be lucky
un **abricot** [abʀiko]	apricot
la **confiture d'abricots**	apricot jam
une **fraise** [fʀɛz]	strawberry
le **raisin** [ʀɛzɛ̃]	grape
une **grappe de raisins**	bunch of grapes
une **olive** [ɔliv]	olive

une **fleur** [flœʀ]	flower
un **arbre en fleurs**	a flowering tree
offrir un **bouquet de fleurs** à qn	give s.o. a bouquet of flowers
fleurir [flœʀiʀ]	flower, bloom
se fâner [s(ə)fane]	wilt
une **rose** [ʀoz]	rose
Elle est fraîche comme une rose. *loc*	She's as fresh as a daisy.
une **tulipe** [tylip]	tulip
un **jardin** [ʒaʀdɛ̃]	garden
un **(jardin) potager**	vegetable garden
un,e **jardinier, -ière** [ʒaʀdinje, jɛʀ]	gardener
jardiner [zaʀdine]	work in the garden, do gardening
entretenir [ɑ̃tʀət(ə)niʀ]	keep up; maintain
récolter [ʀekɔlte]	reap; gather in
la **récolte** [ʀekɔlt]	harvest
Cette année, la récolte a été bonne/ mauvaise.	This year the harvest was good/poor.

le **légume** [legym]	vegetable
une bonne **soupe de légumes**	a good vegetable soup
la **carotte** [kaʀɔt]	carrot
la **pomme de terre** [pɔmdətɛʀ]	potato
Tu as vu le prix des pommes de terre nouvelles?	Have you seen the price of the new potatoes?
la **patate** *fam* [patat]	potato
le **chou** [ʃu]	cabbage
la **tomate** [tɔmat]	tomato
le **champignon** [ʃɑ̃piɲɔ̃]	mushroom

Je ne suis pas sûr que ce champi-gnon soit comestible. | I'm not sure that this mushroom is edible.

une **racine** [ʀasin]	root
prendre racine	take root, become rooted
une **tige** [tiʒ]	stem
un **tronc** [tʀɔ̃]	trunk
un **bourgeon** [buʀʒɔ̃]	bud
le **feuillage** [fœjaʒ]	leaves, foliage
un **arbre à feuillage persistant**	a tree with evergreen foliage
une **haie** ['ɛ]	hedge
Le jardin est entouré d'une haie.	The garden is surrounded by a hedge.
un **arbuste** [aʀbyst]	bush, shrub

un **chêne** [ʃɛn]	oak
un meuble **en chêne massif**	a piece of solid-oak furniture
un **bouleau** [bulo]	birch
un **hêtre** ['ɛtʀ]	beech
un **orme** [ɔʀm]	elm
un **peuplier** [pøplije]	poplar
un **saule** [sol]	willow
un **pin** [pɛ̃]	pine
une **pomme de pin**	pinecone
un **sapin** [sapɛ̃]	fir
décorer le **sapin de Noël**	decorate the Christmas tree
un **platane** [platan]	elm tree
une allée **bordée de** platanes	an avenue bordered by elm trees
un **tilleul** [tijœl]	linden tree
un **palmier** [palmje]	palm tree

une **vigne** [viɲ]	vine; vineyard
un **pommier** [pɔmje]	apple tree
un **poirier** [pwaʀje]	pear tree
faire le poirier	do a headstand
un **verger** [vɛʀʒe]	orchard
un **noisetier** [nwaz(ə)tje]	hazelnut tree or bush
un **noyer** [nwaje]	walnut tree
un **pêcher** [pɛʃe]	peach tree
un **cerisier** [s(ə)ʀizje]	cherry tree
un **prunier** [pʀynje]	plum tree
secouer qn comme un prunier *loc, fam*	shake s.o. hard
un **olivier** [ɔlivje]	olive tree

un **cassis** [kasis]	black currant bush

la **liqueur**/la **crème de cassis**	liqueur made from black currants
une **groseille** [gʀɔzɛj]	red currant
la **gelée de groseilles**	red currant jelly
une **mûre** [myʀ]	blackberry
une **ronce** [ʀɔ̃s]	blackberry bush

une **pâquerette** [pakʀɛt]	daisy
une **jonquille** [ʒɔ̃kij]	daffodil
une **violette** [vjɔlɛt]	violet
le **lilas** [lila]	lilac
le **muguet** [mugɛ]	lily of the valley
le **coquelicot** [kɔkliko]	poppy
une **marguerite** [maʀgəʀit]	daisy
effeuiller la marguerite	pluck the daisy (she loves me, she loves me not ...)
un **tournesol** [tuʀnəsɔl]	sunflower
une **salade à l'huile de tournesol**	a salad dressed with sunflower oil
la **bruyère** [bʀyjɛʀ]	heather
le **genêt** [ʒənɛ]	broom
un **œillet** [œjɛ]	carnation
le **glaïeul** [glajœl]	gladiolus
un **lys** [lis]	lily
un **bouton** [butɔ̃]	bud
un **bouton de rose**	rosebud

une **courgette** [kuʀʒɛt]	zucchini
une **aubergine** [obɛʀʒin]	eggplant
un **artichaut** [aʀtiʃo]	artichoke
un **poivron** [pwavʀɔ̃]	(green) pepper
un **concombre** [kɔ̃kɔ̃bʀ]	cucumber
une **salade** [salad]	lettuce; salad greens
des **épinards** m [epinaʀ]	spinach
mettre du beurre dans les épinards fam	make life more comfortable

moissonner [mwasɔne]	reap, gather in, mow (grain)
la **moisson** [mwasɔ̃]	(grain) harvest
les **céréales** f [seʀeal]	grains
le **blé** [ble]	wheat
un **champ de blé**	wheat field, grain field
le **maïs** [mais]	corn
du **maïs transgénique**	genetically modified corn
le **froment** [fʀɔmɑ̃]	wheat
la **farine de froment**	wheat flour
l'**orge** f [ɔʀʒ]	barley

le **seigle** [sɛgl]	rye
du **pain de seigle**	rye bread
l'**avoine** f [avwan]	oats
le **colza** [kɔlza]	rape, rapeseed
la **betterave** [bɛtʀav]	beet
la **betterave à sucre**	sugar beet

semer [səme]	sew
une **graine** [gʀɛn]	grain, seed
labourer [labuʀe]	plow, till
une **charrue** [ʃaʀy]	plow
l'**engrais** m [ãgʀɛ]	fertilizer; manure
Les engrais sont indispensables à l'agriculture intensive.	Fertilizers are indispensable for intensive farming.
irriguer [iʀige]	irrigate
l'**irrigation** f [iʀigasjɔ̃]	irrigation
l'**arrosage** m [aʀozaʒ]	watering
L'arrosage des jardins est interdit en période de grande sécheresse.	Watering gardens is prohibited during periods of great drought.
un **arrosoir** [aʀozwaʀ]	watering can
les **vendanges** f [vãdãʒ]	vintage, grape gathering
Dans trois jours, nous commencerons à faire les vendanges.	In three days we'll start to pick the grapes.
vendanger [vãdãʒe]	gather grapes

18.6 Animals, Keeping an Animal

la **faune** [fon]	fauna, animal kingdom
la **faune et la flore** des régions tropicales	the fauna and flora of the tropical regions
un **animal** [animal]	animal
un **animal domestique**	domestic animal
utile [ytil]	useful
nuisible [nɥisibl]	harmful
Les rats sont des animaux nuisibles.	Rats are pests.
une **bête** [bɛt]	animal
une **bête sauvage**	a wild animal
une **race** [ʀas]	breed
un **chien de race**	pedigreed dog

un **cheval**, des **chevaux** [ʃ(ə)val, o]	horse
un **taureau** [tɔʀo]	bull
une **vache** [vaʃ]	cow
la **maladie de la vache folle (ESB)**	mad cow disease (BSE)

un **bœuf**, des **bœufs** [bœf, bø]	ox
Qui vole un œuf vole un bœuf. *prov*	It starts with little things and ends with big ones.
un **veau** [vo]	calf
un **mouton** [mutɔ̃]	sheep
une **chèvre** [ʃɛvʀ]	goat
ménager la chèvre et le chou *loc*	run with the hare and hunt with the hounds
un **cochon** [kɔʃɔ̃]	pig

---

i **Not for vegetarians!**

Note the difference between:

un cochon	*pig*
C'est donner de la confiture aux cochons. *loc*	*That's casting pearls before swine.*
le porc	*pork*
une côtelette de porc	*pork chop*
Les musulmans ne mangent pas de porc.	*Muslims do not eat pork.*

---

une **étable** [etabl]	stall
rentrer les vaches à l'étable	bring the cows into the stall

la **volaille** [vɔlaj]	poultry, fowl
un **coq** [kɔk]	rooster
Le coq chante *cocorico*.	The rooster says *cock-a-doodle-doo*.
une **poule** [pul]	hen, fowl
avoir la chair de poule	have goose bumps
un **poussin** [pusɛ̃]	chick, newly hatched chicken
un **canard** [kanaʀ]	duck

un,e **chien,ne** [ʃjɛ̃, ʃjɛn]	dog, bitch
Attention, **chien méchant**.	Beware of the dog!
un temps à ne pas mettre un chien dehors *loc*	weather you wouldn't put a dog out in
aboyer [abwaje]	bark
mordre [mɔʀdʀ]	bite
une **niche** [niʃ]	doghouse
un,e **chat,te** [ʃa, ʃat]	cat
avoir un chat dans la gorge *loc*	have a frog in one's throat

une **souris** [suʀi]	mouse
Quand le chat n'est pas là, les souris dansent. *prov*	When the cat's away, the mice will play.
un **rat** [ʀa]	rat
un **hamster** ['amstɛʀ]	hamster
un **cochon d'Inde** [kɔʃɔ̃dɛ̃d]	guinea pig
un **lapin** [lapɛ̃]	rabbit, bunny

un **oiseau** [wazo]	bird
un **drôle d'oiseau** *fam*	an odd bird, a funny fellow
l'**aile** *f* [ɛl]	wing
le **bec** [bɛk]	beak
un **nid** [ni]	nest
faire son nid	make a nest
un **œuf**, des **œufs** [ɛ̃nœf, dezø]	egg, eggs
pondre un œuf	lay an egg
une **cage** [kaʒ]	cage

For information, on the *gender of nouns* ending in -age, see p. 70.

un **perroquet** [peʀɔkɛ]	parrot
un **pigeon** [piʒɔ̃]	dove, pigeon

un **poisson** [pwasɔ̃]	fish
un **poisson de mer**	sea fish
un **poisson d'eau douce**	freshwater fish
un **poisson rouge**	goldfish
un **aquarium** [akwaʀjɔm]	aquarium
une **truite** [tʀɥit]	trout
un **hareng** ['aʀɑ̃]	herring

un **serpent** [sɛʀpɑ̃]	snake, serpent
un **serpent venimeux**	poisonous snake
un **crocodile** [kʀɔkɔdil]	crocodile
des **larmes de crocodile**	crocodile tears

un,e **lion,ne** [ljɔ̃, ljɔn]	lion, lioness
la **part du lion**	lion's share
un,e **tigre, -esse** [tigʀ, tigʀɛs]	tiger, tigress
un **loup**, une **louve** [lu, luv]	wolf, she-wolf
avoir une faim de loup *loc*	be as hungry as a wolf
un **singe** [sɛ̃ʒ]	monkey
être malin comme un singe *loc*	be as sly as a fox

(le) **mâle** *n; adj* [mal]	male
une **girafe mâle**	a male giraffe
(la) **femelle** *n; adj* [fəmɛl]	female
La jument est la femelle du cheval.	The mare is a female horse.
un **mammifère** [mamifɛʀ]	mammal
un **carnivore** [kaʀnivɔʀ]	carnivore
un **herbivore** [ɛʀbivɔʀ]	herbivore
une **espèce** [ɛspɛs]	species
une **espèce protégée**	a protected species

une espèce **en voie de disparition**	a species threatened by extinction

un **étalon** [etalɔ̃]	stallion
une **jument** [ʒymɑ̃]	mare
un **poney** [pɔnɛ]	pony
un **âne**, une **ânesse** [an, anɛs]	ass, donkey; she-ass
une **écurie** [ekyʀi]	stable, mews

apprivoiser [apʀivwaze]	tame
dresser [dʀɛse]	train
dompter [dɔ̃(p)te]	break in, tame

la **queue** [kø]	tail
Le chien remue la queue.	The dog wags its tail.
la **gueule** [gœl]	mouth (of an animal)
se jeter dans la gueule du loup *loc*	venture into the lion's den
une **patte** [pat]	paw; foot; leg (of animal)

---

jambe – patte

Note the difference between:

la **jambe**	*(human) leg*
la **patte**	*(animal's) leg, paw, foot*
L'homme a deux jambes et le chien a quatre pattes.	*Man has two legs, and a dog has four.*

---

un **prédateur** [pʀedatœʀ]	predator
une **proie** [pʀwa]	prey
Le faucon s'est jeté sur sa proie.	The falcon pounced on its prey.
le **gibier** [ʒibje]	game
une **trace** [tʀas]	spoor, trail; track, footprint
la **chasse** [ʃas]	hunt, hunting
aller* à la **chasse au gros gibier**	go big game hunting
chasser [ʃase]	hunt

un **troupeau** [tʀupo]	herd
Le chien de berger rassemble le troupeau de moutons.	The sheepdog gathers the herd of sheep.
une **brebis** [bʀəbi]	ewe
un **agneau** [aɲo]	lamb
innocent, e comme l'agneau qui vient de naître *loc*	innocent as a newborn lamb

la **basse-cour** [baskuʀ]	poultry yard
une **oie** [wa]	goose

une **dinde** [dɛ̃d]	turkey
un **cygne** [siɲ]	swan

une **cigogne** [sigɔɲ]	stork
La cigogne est un **oiseau migrateur**.	The stork is a migratory bird.
un **aigle** [ɛgl]	eagle
un **moineau** [mwano]	sparrow
une **mésange** [mezɑ̃ʒ]	titmouse
un **merle** [mɛʀl]	blackbird
une **hirondelle** [iʀɔ̃dɛl]	swallow
Une hirondelle ne fait pas le printemps. *prov*	One swallow doesn't make a spring.
une **alouette** [alwɛt]	lark
un **rossignol** [ʀɔsiɲɔl]	nightingale

un **insecte** [ɛ̃sɛkt]	insect
une **larve** [laʀv]	larva
une **mouche** [muʃ]	fly
Quelle mouche t'a piqué ? *fam*	What's gotten into you?
une **guêpe** [gɛp]	wasp
avoir une **taille de guêpe**	have a wasplike waist
un **moustique** [mustik]	mosquito
un **papillon** [papijɔ̃]	butterfly
une **coccinelle** [kɔksinɛl]	ladybug
une **fourmi** [fuʀmi]	ant
avoir des fourmis dans les jambes *loc*	have pins and needles in one's legs

une **abeille** [abɛj]	bee
l'**apiculture** f [apikyltyʀ]	apiculture, beekeeping
un,e **apiculteur, -trice** [apikyltœʀ, tʀis]	apiculturist, beekeeper

un **requin** [ʀəkɛ̃]	shark
une **baleine** [balɛn]	whale
un **dauphin** [dofɛ̃]	dolphin

un **reptile** [ʀɛptil]	reptile
ramper [ʀɑ̃pe]	crawl, creep
un **lézard** [lezaʀ]	lizard
une **vipère** [vipɛʀ]	viper, poisonous snake
une **tortue** [tɔʀty]	tortoise
une **grenouille** [gʀənuj]	frog

un **fauve** [fov]	wild animal
un **ours**, des **ours** [uʀs]	bear

| un **renard** [ʀ(ə)naʀ] | fox |
| rusé comme un renard *loc* | as crafty as a fox |

18.7 Ecology, Environmental Protection, and Catastrophes

l'**écologie** *f* [ekɔlɔʒi]	ecology; environmental protection
un, e **écologiste** [ekɔlɔʒist]	ecologist; environmentalist; Green
écologique [ekɔlɔʒik]	ecological
biologique [bjɔlɔʒik]	biological
l'**agriculture bio(logique)**	organic farming
s'**engager** [sɑ̃gaʒe]	become involved/active in
s'engager dans le mouvement écologiste	get involved in the environmental movement
l'**engagement** *m* [ɛ̃gaʒmɑ̃]	involvement
agir [aʒiʀ]	act
Ils agissent **avec conviction**.	They act out of conviction.
une **action** [aksjɔ̃]	action
Les écologistes mènent des actions contre les industries polluantes.	The environmentalists lead a campaign against industries that pollute the environment.
la **nature** [natyʀ]	nature
l'équilibre entre l'homme et la nature	the balance between man and nature
l'**environnement** *m* [ɑ̃viʀɔnmɑ̃]	environment
la **protection de l'environnement**	protection of the environment
protéger l'environnement	protect the environment

l'**air** *m* [ɛʀ]	air
l'**air pur/pollué**	clean/polluted air
l'**eau** *f* [o]	water
l'**eau potable**	drinking water
Eau non potable !	Not drinking water!
propre [pʀɔpʀ]	clean

 For information on *adjectives* that *change their meaning* depending on whether they *precede* or *follow* the word modified, see p. 8

polluer [pɔlɥe]	pollute
Les produits chimiques polluent les rivières.	Chemicals pollute the rivers.
polluant,e [pɔlɥɑ̃, ɑ̃t]	polluting, environmentally harmful
non-polluant,e [nɔ̃pɔlɥɑ̃, ɑ̃t]	nonpolluting, pollutant-free

dégager un gaz polluant/non-polluant	emit an environmentally harmful/a nonpolluting gas
la **pollution** [pɔlysjɔ̃]	pollution
un,e **pollueur, -euse** [pɔlyœʀ, øz]	polluter

détruire [detʀɥiʀ]	destroy
la **destruction** [destʀyksjɔ̃]	destruction
l'**écosystème** m [ekosistɛm]	ecosystem
la **disparition** [dispaʀisjɔ̃]	disappearance; extinction
contaminé,e [kɔ̃tamine]	contaminated
la **contamination** [kɔ̃taminasjɔ̃]	contamination

les **gaz d'échappement** m [gazdeʃapmɑ̃]	exhaust gases
le **smog** [smɔg]	smog
les **pluies acides** f [plɥiasid]	acid rain
la **mort des forêts** [mɔʀdefɔʀɛ]	death of forest trees due to exhaust gases

un **CFC (chlorofluorocarbone)** [seɛfse]	chlorofluorocarbon
une **bombe aérosol** [bɔ̃baeʀɔsɔl]	aerosol spray (can)
la **couche d'ozone** [kuʃdozon/dɔzɔn]	ozone layer
Le **trou dans la couche d'ozone** est inquiétant.	The hole in the ozone layer is disturbing.
l'**effet de serre** m [efɛd(ə)sɛʀ]	greenhouse effect
le **réchauffement de l'atmos-phère** [ʀeʃofmɑ̃d(ə)latmɔsfɛʀ]	global warming, warming of the atmosphere

un **danger** [dɑ̃ʒe]	danger
Attention, **danger de mort.**	Caution, danger!
dangereux, -euse [dɑ̃ʒʀø, øz]	dangerous
une **menace** [mənas]	threat, menace
La pollution des eaux représente une menace sérieuse.	Water pollution is a serious threat.
menacer [mənase]	threaten, menace

le **bruit** [bʀɥi]	noise
bruyant,e [bʀyjɑ̃, ɑ̃t]	loud
Le moteur de la moto est trop bruyant.	The motorcycle engine is too loud.
calme [kalm]	calm, quiet, tranquil
le **silence** [silɑ̃s]	silence
silencieux, -euse [silɑ̃sjø, øz]	silent
une forêt calme et silencieuse	a calm and silent forest

les **ordures** f [ɔʀdyʀ]	refuse, garbage, trash
les ordures ménagères	household garbage
le **tri des ordures**	separation of garbage
la **poubelle** [pubɛl]	garbage can
le **ramassage** [ʀamasaʒ]	collection; removal
effectuer le ramassage des **vieux papiers**	pick up old paper
la **décharge** [deʃaʀʒ]	garbage dump
porter ses ordures à la décharge publique/municipale	bring one's garbage to the public/municipal dump
une **déchetterie** [deʃɛtʀi]	garbage collecting point, garbage treatment facility

une **bouteille (non) consignée** [butɛj(nɔ̃)kɔ̃siɲe]	(non-)returnable bottle
une **bouteille en (matière) plastique** [butɛjɑ̃(matjɛʀ)plastik]	plastic bottle
le **verre usagé** [vɛʀyzaʒe]	old glass
biodégradable [bjodegʀadabl]	biodegradable
un produit biodégradable	a biodegradable product
recyclable [ʀ(ə)siklabl]	recyclable
un emballage recyclable	recyclable packaging
le **recyclage** [ʀ(ə)siklaʒ]	recycling
recycler [ʀ(ə)sikle]	recycle
du **papier recyclé**	recycled paper

une **centrale nucléaire** [sɑ̃tʀalnykleɛʀ]	nuclear power plant
un **réacteur** [ʀeaktœʀ]	(nuclear) reactor
radioactif, -ive [ʀadjoaktif, iv]	radioactive
un nuage radioactif	a radioactive cloud
la **radioactivité** [ʀadjoaktivite]	radioactivity
mesurer la radioactivité	measure the radioactivity

un **accident** [aksidɑ̃]	accident
un accident tragique	a tragic accident
un horrible accident	a horrible accident
une **catastrophe**, une **cata** fam [kata(stʀɔf)]	catastrophe
une **catastrophe naturelle**	natural catastrophe
catastrophique [katastʀɔfik]	catastrophic
un **incendie** [ɛ̃sɑ̃di]	conflagration, fire
un **incendie de forêt**	forest fire
le **feu** [fø]	fire
prendre feu	catch fire

brûler [bʀyle]	burn
la **fumée** [fyme]	smoke
Il n'y a pas de fumée sans feu. *prov*	Where there's smoke there's fire.
une **explosion** [ɛksplozjɔ̃]	explosion
exploser [ɛksploze]	explode
une **inondation** [inɔ̃dasjɔ̃]	flood, inundation
inonder [inɔ̃de]	flood, inundate
Le fleuve est sorti de son lit et a inondé la plaine.	The river left its banks and flooded the plain.

l'**énergie** f [enɛʀʒi]	energy
une **source d'éergie**	source of energy
l'**énergie nucléaire**	nuclear energy, atomic energy
l'**énergie solaire/éolienne**	solar/wind energy
l'**énergie géothermique**	geothermal energy
les **énergies douces/renouvelables**	alternative/renewable energy sources
La recherche se penche sur les énergies renouvelables.	Research focuses on renewable energy sources.
électrique [elɛktʀik]	electric(al)
le **courant électrique**	electrical current
l'**électricité** f [elɛktʀisite]	electricity
le **charbon** [ʃaʀbɔ̃]	coal
le **gaz** [gaz]	gas
le **gaz naturel**	natural gas
le **pétrole** [petʀɔl]	petroleum

un **site** [sit]	site, location
préserver [pʀezɛʀve]	preserve, protect
préserver les sites naturels	preserve natural monuments/wonders
sauvage [sovaʒ]	wild
désert,e [dezɛʀ,t]	deserted, unpopulated

les **déchets** m [deʃɛ]	waste, refuse
éliminer les déchets	remove refuse
une **usine de traitement des déchets**	refuse treatment plant
la **collecte sélective (des déchets)** [kɔlɛktselɛktiv]	separate collection (of refuse)
un **conteneur à verre/papier (usagé)** [kɔ̃tənœʀavɛʀ/papje]	container for glass/paper
la **récupération** [ʀekypeʀasjɔ̃]	recovery, recycling
le **compostage** [kɔ̃pɔstaʒ]	composting
l'**élimination** f [eliminasjɔ̃]	removal
l'**incinération** f [ɛ̃sineʀasjɔ̃]	incineration
une **usine d'incinération des déchets**	refuse incineration plant

les **ressources naturelles** *f* [ʀ(ə)suʀsnatyʀɛl]	natural resources
gaspiller [gaspije]	waste
Fais attention à ne pas gaspiller l'eau.	Be careful not to waste water.
le **gaspillage** [gaspijaʒ]	waste, squandering
l'**écotaxe** *f* [ekotaks]	environmental tax, ecotax
un **capteur solaire** [kaptœʀsɔlɛʀ]	solar collector
une **éolienne** [eɔljɛn]	windwheel
la **bioénergie** [bjoenɛʀʒi]	bioenergy

l'**émission** *f* [emisjɔ̃]	emission
l'émission d'oxyde/de dioxyde de soufre/de gaz carbonique	emission of sulfur oxide/sulfur dioxide/carbon dioxide
émettre [emɛtʀ]	emit
un **produit toxique** [pʀɔdɥitɔksik]	a toxic substance
la **nuisance** [nɥizɑ̃s]	(environmental) harm
nocif,-ive [nɔsif, iv]	harmful
se dégrader [s(ə)degʀade]	become degraded
Pendant des années, la qualité de l'eau s'est dangereusement dégradée.	Over the years the water quality has become dangerously degraded.
la **dégradation** [degʀadasjɔ̃]	degradation, destruction
la **dégradation de l'environnement**	the destruction of the environment
la **détérioration** [deteʀjɔʀasjɔ̃]	deterioration
se détériorer [s(ə)deteʀjɔʀe]	deteriorate
les **dégâts** *m* [dega]	damage
causer des dégâts importants	cause major damage
la **marée noire** [maʀɛnwaʀ]	oil pollution
la **biosphère** [bjɔsfɛʀ]	biosphere

les **métaux lourds** *m* [metoluʀ]	heavy metals
un sol contaminé par des métaux lourds	soil contaminated with heavy metals
un **détergent** *m* [detɛʀʒɑ̃]	detergent
l'**engrais** *m* [ɑ̃gʀɛ]	fertilizer
un **insecticide** [ɛ̃sɛktisid]	insecticide
un **pesticide** [pɛstisid]	pesticide
les **nitrates** *m* [nitʀat]	nitrates

la **nappe phréatique** [napfʀeatik]	groundwater
une **station d'épuration** [stasjɔ̃depyʀasjɔ̃]	purification plant
les **égoûts** *m* [egu]	sewers, sewer system
les **eaux usées** *f* [oyze]	wastewater, sewage

l'**uranium** *m* [yʀanjɔm]   uranium
la **radiation** [ʀadjasjɔ̃]   radiation
  être exposé à des radiations   be exposed to radiation
l'**irradiation** *f* [iʀadjasjɔ̃]   irradiation
le **stockage** [stɔkaʒ]   storage
le **retraitement** [ʀ(ə)tʀɛtmɑ̃]   reconversion
  une **usine de retraitement**   reconversion plant
retraiter [ʀ(ə)tʀete]   reconvert
  Cette usine retraite des déchets   This plant reconverts radioactive
  radioactifs.   waste.

un **désastre** [dezastʀ]   disaster
désastreux, -euse [dezastʀø, øz]   disastrous
imprévu,e [ɛ̃pʀevy]   unforeseen, unexpected
imprévisible [ɛ̃pʀevizibl]   unforeseeable
  avoir des répercussions imprévisi-   have unforeseeable repercussions
  bles sur la santé   on health
prévisible [pʀevizibl]   foreseeable

le **déboisement** [debwazmɑ̃]   deforestation
déboiser [debwaze]   deforest, clear (of trees)
aménager [amenaʒe]   manage, regulate the felling of trees
l'**aménagement** *m* [amenaʒmɑ̃]   management (of a forest)
  l'**aménagement du territoire**   area planning
l'**assainissement** *m* [asenismɑ̃]   redevelopment; drainage
  le **reboisement** [ʀ(ə)bwazmɑ̃]   reforestation
reboiser [ʀ(ə)bwaze]   reforest, plant (trees)
renaturer [ʀ(ə)natyʀe]   return to nature

une **tornade** [tɔʀnad]   tornado
un **ouragan** [uʀagɑ̃]   hurricane
une **avalanche** [avalɑ̃ʃ]   avalanche
  Risque d'avalanches !   Danger of avalanches!
un **tremblement de terre**   earthquake
[tʀɑ̃bləmɑ̃d(ə)teʀ]
un **cataclysme** [kataklism]   cataclysm, natural catastrophe
un **glissement de terrain**   landslide, landslip
[glismɑ̃d(ə)teʀɛ̃]
une **éruption (volcanique)**   (volcanic) eruption
[eʀypsjɔ̃(vɔlkanik)]
  Le volcan est **entré en éruption.**   The volcano has started to erupt.
une **coulée de lave** [kuled(ə)lav]   stream of lava
la **sécheresse** [seʃ(ə)ʀɛs]   drought
  une région **touchée par la**   an area affected by drought
  sécheresse

un **sinistre** [sinistʀ]	calamity; disaster; grim event
sinistré,e [sinistʀe]	affected by a disaster
déclarer une région zone sinistrée	declare a region a disaster area

18.8 Town, Country, Buildings, and Infrastructure

une **ville** [vil]	town, city
la **ville** de Toulouse	the town of Toulouse
une **ville** de province	provincial town
la **vieille ville**	old town
une **ville satellite**	satellite town
une **ville nouvelle**	new town, newly created town
habiter [abite]	live in, inhabit
habiter (dans) une ville	live in a town
Ses parents **habitent (à) Lille.**	His parents live in Lille.
un,e **habitant,e** [abitã, ãt]	inhabitant
une **capitale** [kapital]	capital (city)
un,e **citadin,e** [sitadɛ̃, in]	townsman, town citizen
Ils ne connaissent pas la campagne, ce sont des citadins.	They don't know the rural areas; they're town dwellers.
un **village** [vilaʒ]	village
un,e **villageois,e** [vilaʒwa, az]	villager
la **campagne** [kɑ̃paɲ]	country
aller* s'installer à la campagne	move to the country
un,e **campagnard,e** [kɑ̃paɲaʀ, aʀd]	countryman/-woman, rustic
le **centre** [sɑ̃tʀ]	center
le **centre-ville**	center of town, city center
central,e [sɑ̃tʀal]	central
habiter un quartier central	live in a centrally located part of town
les **environs** m [ɑ̃viʀõ]	environs, vicinity, surroundings
la **banlieue** [bɑ̃ljø]	suburbs
dans la **proche banlieue** d'une ville	in the nearby suburbs of a city
un **quartier** [kaʀtje]	quarter, part of town, neighborhood
un **quartier chic/populaire**	an elegant/modest neighborhood
un **quartier ouvrier/industriel**	a working-class/industrial neighborhood
l'**espace** m [ɛspas]	space, area
un **terrain** [teʀɛ̃]	lot, plot (of ground)
un **terrain à bâtir**	building site
s'étendre sur [setɑ̃dʀ]	extend over, cover

La zone industrielle s'étend sur 3 kilomètres.	The industrial area extends over three km.

un **projet** [pRɔʒɛ]
  un projet de modernisation
transformer [tRɑ̃sfɔrme]
  transformer le quartier de la gare
une **transformation** [tRɑ̃sfɔrmasjɔ̃]

project
  modernization project
transform
  transform the railroad station area
transformation, rebuilding

démolir [demɔliR]
  Les vieux immeubles ont été démolis.
construire [kɔ̃stRɥiR]
  faire construire une maison
une **construction** [kɔ̃stRyksjɔ̃]
reconstruire [R(ə)kɔ̃stRɥiR]

demolish, tear down
  The old buildings were demolished.
construct, build
  have a house built
construction, building (structure)
reconstruct, rebuild

un **bâtiment** [batimɑ̃]
  un bâtiment ancien
une **maison** [mɛzɔ̃]
  une maison neuve
une **villa** [vila]
un **pavillon** [pavijɔ̃]
un **immeuble** [imœbl]
une **tour** [tuR]

building
  an old building
house
  a new house
villa
small house
real estate, real property
tower

For information on the *gender* of **tour**, see p. 191.

---

un,e **HLM** (une **habitation à loyer modéré**) [aʃɛlɛm]

rent-controlled housing

une **rue** [Ry]
  jouer dans la rue
  une **rue commerçante**
  une rue animée
un **chemin** [ʃ(ə)mɛ̃]
une **voie** [vwa]
une **avenue** [av(ə)ny]
un **boulevard** [bulvaR]
une **chaussée** [ʃose]
  Attention, chaussée déformée !
un **trottoir** [tRɔtwaR]
un **carrefour** [kaRfuR]
un **parking** [paRkiŋ]
  un **parking souterrain**

street
  play in the street
  shopping street
  a busy street
way
way, street
avenue
boulevard
pavement
  Caution, bumpy pavement!
sidewalk
crossing, crossroads
parking lot
  underground parking garage

une **place** [plas]	square, plaza
une **cour** [kuʀ]	courtyard
Mon appartement **donne sur** la cour de l'immeuble.	My apartment faces the courtyard of the building.
un **pont** [pɔ̃]	bridge
un **pont suspendu**	suspension bridge

une **route** [ʀut]	road, way, route
sur la route de Dijon	on the road to Dijon
Route barrée.	Road closed.
une **(route) nationale (RN)**	national road, federal highway
un,e **autoroute (A)** [ɔtɔ/otoʀut]	superhighway
un **garage** [gaʀaʒ]	car repair shop, automotive garage

> For information on the *gender of nouns* ending in **-age**, see p. 70.

une **station-service** [stasjɔ̃sɛʀvis]	service station, gas station

un **magasin** [magazɛ̃]	store, shop
un **grand-magasin**	department store
un **supermarché** [sypɛʀmaʀʃe]	supermarket
un **hypermarché** [ipɛʀmaʀʃe]	large supermarket, warehouse store
une **grande surface** [gʀɑ̃dsyʀfas]	supermarket, consumer warehouse
un **centre commercial** [sɑ̃tʀ(ə)kɔmɛʀsjal]	shopping center
une **galerie marchande** [galʀimaʀʃɑ̃d]	shopping passage
un **marché** [maʀʃe]	market
un **marché couvert**	covered market
les **halles** f ['al]	covered market halls

un **hôpital** [ɔpital]	hospital
un **hôpital universitaire**	university hospital
un **CHU (centre hospitalier universitaire)** [seaʃy]	university hospital center
une **clinique** [klinik]	clinic; nursing home
une **clinique privée**	private clinic
une **maison de retraite** [mɛzɔ̃dʀətʀɛt]	retirement home
un **cimetière** [simtjɛʀ]	cemetery

une **mairie** [mɛʀi]	town hall
un **hôtel de ville** [otɛldəvil]	city hall (in a larger city)
la **poste** [pɔst]	post office

une **gare** [gaʀ]	railroad station
une **gare routière**	bus station
un **musée** [myze]	museum
visiter un musée	visit a museum
un **théâtre** [teatʀ]	theater
un **centre culturel** [sɑ̃tʀ(ə)kyltyʀɛl]	cultural center
une **prison** [pʀizɔ̃]	prison
être aimable comme une porte de prison *loc*	be cranky, be snappish

un **terrain de sport** [teʀɛ̃d(ə)spɔʀ]	playing field, sports field
un **stade** [stad]	stadium
une **piscine** [pisin]	swimming pool
une **piscine couverte**	indoor swimming pool
un **gymnase** [ʒimnaz]	gym(nasium)
une **salle de sport** [sald(ə)spɔʀ]	gym(nasium)

une **crèche** [kʀɛʃ]	nursery
laisser son enfant à la crèche	leave one's child at the nursery
un **jardin d'enfants** [ʒaʀdɛ̃dɑ̃fɑ̃]	kindergarten
une **école** [ekɔl]	school
une **(école) maternelle** [matɛʀnɛl]	kindergarten (for children three to six years old)
une **école primaire** [ekɔlpʀimɛʀ]	primary school
un **collège** [kɔlɛʒ]	junior high school
un **lycée** [lise]	high school
une **université** [ynivɛʀsite]	university

un **monument historique** [mɔnymɑ̃istɔʀik]	a historic monument
un **château** [ʃato]	castle, chateau
des **ruines** *f* [ʀɥin]	ruins
un château **en ruines**	a castle in ruins
une **église** [egliz]	church
une **cathédrale** [katedʀal]	cathedral

urbain,e [yʀbɛ̃, ɛn]	urban
les **transports urbains**	urban transit
l'**urbanisation** *f* [yʀbanizasjɔ̃]	urbanization
l'**urbanisme** *m* [yʀbanism]	city planning
s'**urbaniser** [syʀbanize]	become urbanized
Cette région s'est urbanisée rapidement.	This region became urbanized rapidly.
se **dépeupler** [s(ə)depœple]	become depopulated
La campagne se dépeuple au profit de la ville.	The countryside is losing its population to the towns.

l'**exode rural/urbain** m [εgzɔdʀyʀal/yʀbε̄]	rural/urban exodus
les **ruraux** m, pl [ʀyʀo]	rural inhabitants

une **métropole** [metʀɔpɔl]	metropolis
une **agglomération** [aglɔmeʀasjɔ̄]	extended area
L'agglomération lyonnaise comprend Lyon et sa banlieue.	The extended Lyon area includes the town of Lyon and its suburbs.
une **cité** [site]	city, town
une **cité-dortoir**	bedroom town
un **hameau** ['amo]	hamlet, small village

la **périphérie** [peʀifeʀi]	periphery, edge of town
un **quartier résidentiel** [kaʀtjeʀezidɑ̄sjεl]	(upscale) residential area
un **faubourg** [fobuʀ]	outskirts, suburb

un **promoteur immobilier** [pʀɔmɔtœʀimɔbilje]	builder, building firm
un **chantier** [ʃɑ̄tje]	construction site
Tout le quartier **est en chantier**.	The whole neighborhood is one big construction site.
restaurer [ʀεstɔʀe]	restore
la **restauration** [ʀεstɔʀasjɔ̄]	restoration
rénover [ʀenɔve]	renovate
rénover un bâtiment vétuste	renovate a dilapidated building
la **rénovation** [ʀenɔvasjɔ̄]	renovation
s'améliorer [sameljɔʀe]	improve
une **amélioration** f [ameljɔʀasjɔ̄]	improvement
se dégrader [s(ə)degʀade]	become dilapidated
la **dégradation** [degʀadasjɔ̄]	dilapidation

un **édifice** [edifis]	building, edifice
une **résidence secondaire** [ʀezidɑ̄ss(ə)gɔ̄dεʀ]	second residence; vacation home
une **maison de campagne** [mεzɔ̄dkɑ̄paɲ]	country house
un **pâté de maisons** [patedmεzɔ̄]	block (of houses)
faire le tour du pâté de maisons	go around the block
un **grand ensemble** [gʀɑ̄tɑ̄sɑ̄bl]	large housing development
un **taudis** [todi]	slum, hovel, hole
délabré,e [delabʀe]	ramshackle, tumbledown
habiter une maison complètement délabrée	live in a totally ramshackle house

une **piste cyclable** [pist(ə)siklabl]	bicycle path
une **voie sans issue** [vwasɑ̃zisy]	no-outlet street, dead-end street
une **voie piétonne** [vwapjetɔn]	pedestrian path
une **zone piétonne** [zɔnpjetɔn]	pedestrian zone
une **zone industrielle (ZI)** [zɔnɛ̃dystʀiɛl]	industrial area

un **parc** [paʀk]	park
le parc du château de Chantilly	the park of the chateau of Chantilly
un **jardin public** [ʒaʀdɛ̃pyblik]	public park
un **square** [skwaʀ]	square, small park in a town

un **échangeur** [eʃɑ̃ʒœʀ]	superhighway changeover/exchange
un **(boulevard) périphérique**; le **périph** *fam* [peʀif(eʀik)]	beltway
emprunter le boulevard périphérique	use the outer beltway
une **rocade** [ʀɔkad]	bypass road
desservir [desɛʀviʀ]	lead into; serve
La rocade dessert la zone industrielle.	The bypass leads into the industrial area.

un **port** [pɔʀ]	port
un **port maritime/fluvial**	maritime/inland port
un **port de plaisance**	yacht basin
un **quai** [kɛ]	wharf, pier, quay

French Word	English Equivalent	False Friend	French Equivalent
un axe	axis	ax	une hache
le golfe	gulf	golf	le golf
la burme	haze, mist	broom	le balai

19.1 Days of the Week and Dates

une **semaine** [s(ə)mɛn]	week
hebdomadaire [ɛbdɔmadɛʀ]	weekly
le **week-end** [wikɛnd]	weekend
quinze jours [kɛ̃zʒuʀ]	two weeks
une **quinzaine (de jours)**	about two weeks
[kɛ̃zɛn (d(ə)ʒuʀ)]	

The preposition *in* in statements of time

If *in* designates a *period of time within which* an event occurs, then use **en** + *noun group*.
However, if *in* refers to a *future point in time*, then use **dans** + *noun group*.
Examples:

Elle a écrit ce livre en quinze jours.	*She wrote that book in two weeks.*
Dans quinze jours, on sera en vacances.	*In two weeks, we'll be on vacation.*
Valérie viendra dans un mois.	*Valérie will come in a month.*

---

les **jours de la semain** *m*	weekdays
[ʒuʀd(ə)las(ə)mɛn]	
lundi [lɛ̃di]	Monday
mardi [maʀdi]	Tuesday
mercredi [mɛʀkʀədi]	Wednesday
jeudi [ʒødi]	Thursday
vendredi [vɑ̃dʀədi]	Friday
samedi [samdi]	Saturday
dimanche [dimɑ̃ʃ]	Sunday

(le) dimanche

Note:
Days of the week unaccompanied by an article designate a day of the *current, past,* or *coming* week:

dimanche prochain	*next Sunday*
dimanche dernier	*last Sunday*
Luc vient/viendra dimanche.	*Luc is coming on Sunday.*

Days of the weeks are *accompanied by the definite article* if something occurs on a regular basis.

Le dimanche, je fais la grasse matinée.	*On Sundays I sleep really late.*

---

le **jour** [ʒuʀ]	day
couler des jours heureux *loc*	spend happy days
Le jour se lève.	Day is breaking.

> **ℹ️ How to talk about days of the week and dates**
>
> | | |
> |---|---|
> | Quel jour sommes-nous aujourd'hui ? | *What day of the week is it today?* |
> | C'est quel jour aujourd'hui ? | *What day of the week is it today?* |
> | (Aujourd'hui,) Nous sommes vendredi. | *Today is Friday.* |
> | On est mercredi. | *It's Wednesday.* |
> | C'est jeudi. | *It's Thursday.* |
> | Nous sommes le combien ? | *What is the date?* |
> | On est le combien aujourd'hui ? | *What is today's date?* |
> | Nous sommes le 1er avril/le 13 mai. | *It's April 1st/May 13th.* |
> | On est le 6 (mai). | *It's the 6th (of May).* |
> | Aujourd'hui, c'est le 13 (juin). | *Today is the 13th (of June).* |

---

la **journée** [ʒuʀne]
  On n'a rien fait **de toute la journée**.

day (time)
  We did nothing all day.

quotidien,ne [kɔtidjɛ̃, jɛn]
  Donne-nous aujourd'hui notre pain quotidien. *(extrait du Notre Père)*

daily
  Give us this day our daily bread (from the Lord's Prayer)

la **date** [dat]
  un **ami de longue date**

date
  a friend of long standing

---

aujourd'hui [oʒuʀdɥi]

today

demain [d(ə)mɛ̃]
  après-demain
  A partir de demain, je me mets au régime.

tomorrow
  day after tomorrow
  Starting tomorrow I'm going on a diet.

hier [jɛʀ]
  avant-hier
  Je m'en souviens **comme si c'était hier**.

yesterday
  day before yesterday
  I remember it as if it were yesterday.

---

le **lendemain** [lɑ̃dmɛ̃]
  le **surlendemain**
  Il est reparti le lendemain de son arrivée.

(on) the following day
  the day after next
  He left again on the day following his arrival.

la **veille** [vɛj]
  la **veille au soir**
  l'**avant-veille**

(on) the eve, (on) the day before
  (on) the previous evening
  two days before

en huit [ɑ̃ɥit]
  Je serai de retour **lundi en huit**.

in a week
  I'll be back a week from Monday.

d'ici le/la ... [disilə/la]
  Nous ne la verrons pas **d'ici la semaine prochaine**.

in ... , ... from today, until ...
  We won't see them until next week.

19.2 Time and Time of Day

le **temps** [tã]	time
Le temps passe vite.	Time passes quickly.
l'**heure** *f* [œʀ]	time (of day); hour
demander l'heure à qn	ask s.o. the time of day
un **quart** d'heure	a quarter of a hour
une **demi-/demie** heure	half an hour
la **minute** [minyt]	minute
J'en ai pour une minute.	I only need a minute.
la **seconde** [s(ə)gɔ̃d]	second

Asking and giving the time of day

Quelle heure est-il ?/Il est quelle heure ?	*What time is it? It is what time?*
Vous avez l'heure ?	*Do you have the exact time?*
A quelle heure ... ?	*What time ... ?*
A quelle heure y a-t-il un train pour Bordeaux ?	*What time is there a train to Bordeaux?*
Il est ...	*It is ...*
... 9 heures (du matin/du soir).	*... 9 o'clock (in the morning/evening)*
... 9 h 05 (neuf heures cinq).	*... five after nine.*
... 9 h 15 (neuf heures et quart).	*... a quarter after nine.*
... 9 h 30 (neuf heures et demie).	*... half past nine.*
... 9 h 45 (dix heures moins le quart).	*... a quarter to ten.*
... 9 h 55 (dix heures moins cinq).	*... five to ten.*

pile [pil]	... on the dot, on the stroke of ...
précis,e [pʀesi]	exactly
Le cours commence **à 8 heures pile/précises**.	Class begins at 8 o'clock on the dot.
vers [vɛʀ]	toward, about
Nous arriverons **vers 6 heures du soir**.	We'll arrive about 6 in the evening.
presque [pʀɛsk]	almost

le **matin** [matɛ̃]	morning
de bon matin	in the early morning

le matin, ce matin, le lendemain

Note the difference between:

ce matin/**ce** soir, etc.	*this morning/this evening*
le matin/**le** soir, etc.	*in the morning/in the evening*
demain matin/soir	*tomorrow morning/evening (viewed from the present time)*
le lendemain matin/soir	*on the following morning/evening (viewed from a different time)*

de bonne heure [d(ə)bɔnœʀ] — early
Mon grand-père se couche toujours de bonne heure. — My grandfather always goes to bed early.

la **matinée** [matine] — morning, forenoon
dans la matinée — during the morning
faire la grasse matinée *loc* — sleep late in the morning

(le) **midi** [midi] — noon, midday
Elle déjeune ici tous les midis. — She eats here every day at noon.

l'**après-midi** *m/f* [apʀɛmidi] — (in the) afternoon
en fin d'après-midi — in the late afternoon

le **soir** [swaʀ] — (in the) evening

la **soirée** [swaʀe] — evening

la **nuit** [nɥi] — night
La nuit tombe tôt en cette saison. — Night falls early at this time of year.

minuit [minɥi] — midnight
Nous sommes rentrés **à minuit et demi**. — We came home at 12:30 A.M.

---

une **montre** [mɔ̃tʀ] — (wrist)watch
regarder l'heure à sa montre — look at one's watch
avancer sa montre d'une heure — set one's watch ahead an hour
Ma montre **avance de** cinq minutes. — My watch is five minutes fast.

en avance [ɑ̃navɑ̃s] — (too) early
Nous avons tout notre temps, nous sommes en avance. — We have plenty of time; we're too early.

retarder [ʀ(ə)taʀde] — be slow; put/set back

en retard [ɑ̃ʀ(ə)taʀd] — (too) late
Tu vas encore **arriver en retard**, si tu ne te dépêches pas. — You're going to arrive late again if you don't hurry.

à l'heure [alœʀ] — on time, punctual
Le train est toujours à l'heure. — The train is always on time.

ponctuel,le [pɔ̃ktɥɛl] — punctual

Il fait jour. [ilfɛʒuʀ] — It's light./It's day.
Il fait nuit. [ilfɛnɥi] — It's night./It's dark.
Il fait noir. [ilfɛnwaʀ] — It's dark.
Il fait noir comme dans un four. *loc* — It's pitch dark.

---

l'**heure d'été** *f* [œʀdete] — summertime, daylight saving time
mettre sa montre à l'heure d'été — put one's watch on daylight saving time

l'**heure d'hiver** *f* [œʀdivɛʀ] — wintertime
Demain on passe à l'heure d'hiver, il faut retarder le réveil d'une heure. — Tomorrow we change to winter time; we have to put the alarm back an hour.

pendant des heures [pɑ̃dɑ̃dezœʀ] — for hours

de jour [dəʒuR]	during the day, in the daytime
de nuit [dənɥi]	at night
Ils voyagent toujours de nuit.	They always travel at night.

l'**aube** f [ob]	dawn, daybreak
se lever avant l'aube	get up before dawn
le **crépuscule** [kRepyskyl]	dusk, twilight
le **lever de/du soleil**	sunrise
[ləved(ə)/dysɔlɛj]	
Les oiseaux chantent dès de lever du soleil.	The birds start singing at sunrise.
le **coucher de/du soleil**	sunset
[kuʃed(ə)/dysɔlɛj]	

un **réveil** [Revɛj]	alarm clock
une **pendule** [pãdyl]	clock, timepiece
remettre les pendules à l'heure loc	clarify, make clear
une **horloge** [ɔRlɔʒ]	clock
régler [Regle]	set
régler sa montre **sur la pendule de la cuisine**	set one's watch by the kitchen clock

19.3 Months and Seasons

le **mois** [mwa]	month
Le mois de mai a 31 jours.	The month of May has 31 days.
trois fois par mois	three times a month
mensuel,le [mãsɥɛl]	monthly
une **revue mensuelle**	monthly periodical

janvier [ʒãvje]	January
février [fevRije]	February
mars [maRs]	March
avril [avRil]	April
mai [mɛ]	May
juin [ʒɥɛ̃]	June
juillet [ʒɥijɛ]	July
Nous partons en vacances **au mois de/en juillet**.	We go on vacation in July.
août [u(t)]	August
septembre [sɛptãbR]	September
octobre [ɔktɔbR]	October
novembre [nɔvãbR]	November
décembre [desãbR]	December

début ... [deby]	(at the) beginning of ...
Début janvier, je vais aller à Paris.	At the beginning of January, I'm going to go to Paris.
au début du mois de ...	at the beginning of the month of ...
fin ... [fɛ̃]	(at the) end of ...
Il viendra **fin janvier**.	He will come at the end of January.
à la fin du mois de ...	at the end of the month of ...
un **an** [ɑ̃]	year
par an	per year, annually
une **année** [ane]	year
Bonne année !	Happy New Year!
l'**année scolaire**	school year
annuel,le [anɥɛl]	annual, yearly
faire son **rapport annuel** sur qc	make's one's annual report on s.th.
une **saison** [sɛzɔ̃]	season
Il fait beau pour la saison.	It's nice weather for this time of year.
le **printemps** [pʁɛ̃tɑ̃]	spring
au printemps	in spring
l'**été** m [ete]	summer
en été	in summer
l'**automne** m [otɔn/ɔtɔn]	autumn, fall
en automne	in autumn
l'**hiver** m [ivɛʁ]	winter
en hiver	in winter
pendant tout l'hiver	all winter long
le **calendrier** [kalɑ̃dʁije]	calendar
un **trimestre** [tʁimɛstʁ]	trimester
L'année scolaire française est divisée en trimestres.	The French school year is divided into trimesters.
un **semestre** [semɛstʁ]	semester
bimensuel,le [bimɑ̃sɥɛl]	twice a month, bimonthly
un **magazine bimensuel**	a bimonthly magazine
une **année bissextile** f [anebisɛkstil]	leap year
printanier, -ière [pʁɛ̃tanje, jɛʁ]	springlike
une journée printanière	a springlike day
estivale,e [ɛstival]	summery, pertaining to summer
le Festival estival de Paris	the Paris Summer Festival
automnal,e [otɔnal/ɔtɔnal]	autumnal, fall-like
hivernal,e [ivɛʁnal]	wintry
saisonnier, -ière [sɛzɔnje, ɛʁ]	seasonal

19.4 Other Time Concepts

le **temps** [tã]	time
avoir le temps de faire qc	have time to do s.th.
passer du/son temps à faire qc	spend one's time doing s.th.
gagner du temps	gain time
perdre son temps à faire qc	waste one's time doing s.th.
Il est temps de faire qc.	It's time to do something.
Je trouve le temps long.	I'm bored.
court,e [kuʀ, kuʀt]	short
Le temps m'a paru court.	The time seemed short to me.

la **durée** [dyʀe]	duration
durer [dyʀe]	last; take (time)
un **moment** [mɔmã]	moment
attendre le bon moment	wait for the right moment
Ce n'est pas le moment.	This isn't the right moment.
longtemps [lɔ̃tã]	long, a long while
Je n'en ai pas pour longtemps.	I don't need long.
un **siècle** [sjɛkl]	century

le **passé** [pase]	past
passé,e [pase]	past
se souvenir du temps passé	remember bygone days
autrefois [otʀəfwa]	formerly, in former times
ancien,ne [ãsjɛ̃, jɛn]	ancient, old; bygone, former

For information on *adjectives* with *different meanings* depending on whether they *precede* or *follow* the word modified, see p. 37.

---

récent,e [ʀesã, ãt]	recent
récemment	recently

le **présent** [pʀezã]	present
présent,e [pʀezã, ãt]	present
maintenant [mɛ̃t(ə)nã]	now
en ce moment [ãs(ə)mɔmã]	at this time

l'**avenir** *m* [av(ə)niʀ]	future
faire des **projets d'avenir**	make plans for the future
le **futur** [fytyʀ]	future
futur,e [fytyʀ]	future
Je vous présente mon future mari.	I present my future husband to you.

prochain,e [pʁɔʃɛ̃, ɛn] — next

bientôt [bjɛ̃to] — soon

Les enfants vont bientôt rentrer de l'école. — The children are going to return from school soon.

ensuite [ãsɥit] — after, afterwards, then

---

l'**origine** *f* [ɔʁiʒin] — origin

le **commencement** [kɔmãsmã] — beginning

commencer [kɔmãse] — begin, start

J'ai **commencé à** apprendre l'espagnol. — I've begun learning Spanish.

Il a **commencé par** crier, puis il s'est calmé. — First he shouted, then he calmed down.

recommencer [ʁ(ə)kɔmãse] — begin again

aller faire qc [alefeʁ] — be going to do s.th.

Je vais passer tout à l'heure. — I'm going to come by right now.

se mettre à faire qc [s(ə)mɛtʁafeʁ] — start to do s.th.

Il faut que je me mette à préparer les affaires. — I have to start putting things in order.

venir de faire qc [v(ə)niʁd(ə)feʁ] — have just done s.th.

Il y a longtemps que tu es là ? – Non, je viens d'arriver. — Have you been here long? No, I've just arrived.

être en train de faire qc [ɛtʁãtʁɛ̃d(ə)feʁ] — be (in the act of) doing something

Ne me dérange pas, je suis en train de lire. — Don't bother me; I'm busy reading.

au milieu de [omiljødə] — in the middle of

Elle s'est réveillée au milieu de la nuit. — She woke up in the middle of the night.

au bout de [obudə] — after

Au bout d'un quart d'heure, j'en ai eu assez. — After a quarter of a hour, I had enough.

finir [finiʁ] — finish, end

Elle a **fini de** manger. — She's finished eating.

Ils ont **fini par** nous donner raison. — They ended by admitting we were right.

la **fin** [fɛ̃] — end

terminer [tɛʁmine] — finish, complete

Il ne termine jamais ce qu'il a commencé. — He never completes what he's started.

---

avant (de) [avã] — before

Passe me voir avant 6 heures. — Come see me before 6 o'clock.

Réfléchis **avant de** parler. — Think before you speak.

il y a [ilja] — ago

On a déménagé il y a 5 ans. — We moved five years ago.

d'abord [dabɔʀ]
at first, at first sight
depuis [depɥi]
since
Je ne l'ai pas vu depuis son retour.
I haven't seen him since his return.
à partir de [apaʀtiʀdə]
starting from
pendant [pãdã]
during
Ne me dérange pas pendant ma sieste.
Don't disturb me during my afternoon nap.
entre [ãtʀ]
between
Je prends mes vacances entre le 25 juin et le 10 juillet.
I'm taking my vacation between June 25th and July 10th.
jusqu'à [ʒyska]
until
Je serai à la maison jusqu'à 8 heures.
I'll be at home until 8 o'clock.
après [apʀɛ]
after, afterward
Tu peux m'appeler après 9 heures.
You can call me after 9 o'clock.
Et qu'est-ce que tu feras après ?
And what will you do afterward?

quand? [kã]
when?
tout de suite [tutsɥit]
at once, right away, immediately
Je l'ai reconnu tout de suite.
I recognized him right away.
tout à l'heure [tutalœʀ]
just
par la suite [paʀlasɥit]
later on, subsequently, afterward
Au début, je le trouvais sympa, mais par la suite, je n'ai eu que des problèmes avec lui.
At first I found him likable, but later on I had nothing but problems with him.

ne ... jamais [nəʒamɛ]
never
Je n'ai jamais dit ça.
I never said that.
Jamais le jardin n'a été aussi beau.
The garden has never been so beautiful.

rarement [ʀaʀmã]
rarely
de temps en temps [d(ə)tãzãtã]
from time to time, now and then
la fois [fwa]
time (occasion)
C'est la deuxième fois que ma voiture tombe en panne.
It's the second time my car has had a breakdown.
quelquefois [kɛlkəfwa]
sometimes
Je les rencontre quelquefois au cinéma.
I sometimes meet her at the movies.
parfois [paʀfwa]
sometimes
régulièrement [ʀegyljɛʀmã]
regularly
Ils rendent régulièrement visite à leur tante.
They visit their aunt regularly.
souvent [suvã]
often
toujours [tuʒuʀ]
always
tout le temps [tul(ə)tã]
all the time, always
Il est tout le temps dans la lune. *loc*
His thoughts are always elsewhere.

en même temps [ãmɛmtã]	at the same time
Ils sont partis en même temps que moi.	They left at the same time as I.
à la fois [alafwa]	at one time, simultaneously
Tu ne peux pas faire deux choses à la fois.	You can't do two things at one time.
tout à coup [tutaku]	suddenly
Tout à coup, elle s'est mise à pleurer.	Suddenly she started to cry.
peu à peu [pøapø]	bit by bit, little by little
Sa santé s'améliore peu à peu.	His health is improving bit by bit.
soudain [sudɛ̃]	suddenly
J'étais en train de dormir quand, soudain, j'ai entendu un cri.	I was sleeping when, suddenly, I heard a shout.

tôt [to]	soon, quickly
déjà [deʒa]	already
Quoi ? Il est déjà minuit ?	What? It's already midnight?
tard [taʀ]	late
Tôt ou tard, tu admettras que j'ai raison.	Sooner or later you'll admit that I'm right.

avant que + *subj* [avãkə]	before
On va rentrer avant qu'il pleuve.	We're going home before it rains.
depuis que [dəpɥikə]	since
Je ne l'ai pas vu depuis qu'il est revenu.	I haven't seen him since he came back.
pendant que [pãdãkə]	while
Ma mère garde mon bébé pendant que je travaille.	My mother watches my baby while I work.
après que [apʀɛkə]	after
Il a fait la vaisselle après que les invités étaient partis.	He did the dishes after the guests had left.

un **instant** [ɛ̃stã]	instant
Il est arrivé **à l'instant où** j'allais partir.	He arrived the instant I was leaving.
une **époque** [epɔk]	epoch, time
à l'époque	at that time, at the time
une **période** [peʀjɔd]	period, time

l'autre jour [lot(ʀə)ʒuʀ]	recently, the other day
L'autre jour, j'ai rencontré Michel.	I ran into Michel the other day.
de mon temps [d(ə)mõtã]	in my day

De mon temps, il n'y avait pas de cartes de crédit.
In my day there were no credit cards.

jadis [ʒadis]
formerly, once upon a time
Jadis, on s'éclairait à la bougie.
Formerly we used candles for lighting.

auparavant [opaʀavã]
before, previously
Il est allé chez elle, mais auparavant, il lui a téléphoné.
He went to her house, but he telephoned her beforehand.

pour le moment [puʀl(ə)mɔmã]
for the moment, at this time
Je suis sans emploi, pour le moment.
I'm unemployed at the moment.

à présent [apʀezã]
at present, now

actuellement [aktyɛlmã]
now, currently
Actuellement, les fraises sont très bon marché.
Currently, strawberries are quite cheap.

contemporain,e [kɔ̃tãpɔʀɛ̃, ɛn]
contemporary
la musique contemporaine
contemporary music

à l'avenir [alav(ə)niʀ]
in (the) future
A l'avenir, il écoutera les conseils de ses amis.
In the future he will listen to his friends' advice.

éternel,le [etɛʀnɛl]
eternal
croire à la **vie éternelle**
believe in eternal life

l'éternité f [etɛʀnite]
eternity
Ça a duré une éternité.
That took an eternity.

cesser (de faire) qc [sese]
stop (doing) s.th.
Il a cessé de pleuvoir.
It has stopped raining.

aboutir à [abutiʀ]
result in, lead to
S'il continue comme ça, il n'aboutira à rien.
If he keeps on like that, he won't amount to anything.

dès [dɛ]
from, since, as early as
dès l'aube
since daybreak

dès que [dɛkə]
as soon as
Je t'aiderai dès que j'aurai fini mon travail.
I'll help you as soon as I've finished my work.

au cours de [okuʀdə]
in the course of
On se verra au cours du mois de septembre.
We'll see each other in the course of the month of September.

entre-temps [ãtʀətã]
in the meantime, meanwhile
J'arrive dans 5 minutes. Entre-temps, sers-toi quelque chose à boire.
I'll be there in five minutes. In the meantime, pour yourself something to drink.

tant que [tãkə]
as long as

Tant qu'il sera là, elle n'aura pas la paix.	As long as he's there, she'll have no peace.
en l'espace de [ɑ̃lɛspasdə]	within, in the space of
En l'espace de 20 minutes, la tempête a tout détruit.	Within 20 minutes, the storm destroyed everything.

à ce moment-là [as(ə)mɔmɑ̃la]	at that moment
C'est à ce moment-là que je l'ai vu.	Just at that moment, I saw him.
sur le coup [syʀl(ə)ku]	right away; at the first moment
Sur le coup, je n'ai pas compris ce qui se passait.	I didn't understand right away what was going on.
Il a été tué **sur le coup.**	He was killed on the spot.
immédiat,e [imedja, jat]	immediate
une réaction immédiate	an immediate reaction
immédiatement	immediately

simultané,e [simyltane]	simultaneous
deux actions simultanées	two simultaneous actions
simultanément	simultaneously
de suite [d(ə)sɥit]	one after another, consecutively
Elle a eu deux accidents de suite.	She had two accidents one after another.

au plus tôt [oplyto]	at the earliest
au plus tard [oplytaʀ]	at the latest
Je serai là, au plus tard à 4 heures.	I'll be there at 4 o'clock at the latest.
d'avance [davɑ̃s]	in advance, ahead of time
Je peux te dire d'avance que ça ne marchera pas.	I can tell you ahead of time that that won't work.
un **délai** [delɛ]	delay; time extension, reprieve
Je demande un **délai de réflexion.**	I request time for reflection.
prolonger [pʀɔlɔ̃ʒe]	prolong, extend
Il voudraient prolonger leur séjour d'une semaine.	They would like to extend their stay by a week.

19.5 Spatial Relationships

l'**espace** m [ɛspas]	space
le temps et l'espace	time and space
dans [dɑ̃]	in

Je n'ai plus rien dans mon porte-monnaie.

I have nothing more in my wallet.

dedans [d(ə)dã]
Ce sac est lourd; qu'est-ce qu'il y a dedans ?

in it
This bag is heavy; what's in it?

à l'intérieur (de) [alɛ̃teʀjœʀ]
Il est à l'intérieur de la maison.

inside
He is inside the house.

dehors [dəɔʀ]
Allez jouer dehors.

outdoors
Go play outdoors.

à l'extérieur (de) [alɛksteʀjœʀ]

outside (of)

---

avant [avã]
Il faut tourner à gauche avant la mairie.

in front of, before
You have to turn left in front of the town hall.

après [apʀɛ]
L'accident s'est produit 5 kilomètres après Tours.

after, behind
The accident occurred five km beyond Tours.

devant [d(ə)vã]
Devant la maison, il y a deux grands arbres.

before, in front of
In front of the house there are two large trees.

derrière [dɛʀjɛʀ]
Il se cache derrière le mur.

behind
He's hiding behind the wall.

---

sur [syʀ]
Le livre est posé sur la table.

on
The book is lying on the table.

sous [su]
Le crayon est tombé sous le bureau.

under, beneath
The pencil fell under the desk.

dessus [d(ə)sy]
un gâteau avec des cerises dessus
au-dessus de
L'avion vole au-dessus des nuages.

on, upon, above
a cake with cherries on it
on top of, above
The plane flies above the clouds.

dessous [dəsu]
au-dessous de

underneath
under, underneath, below

---

le **bas** [ba]
dans le **tiroir du bas**
le **haut** ['o]
sur l'**étagère du haut**
l'**arrière** m [aʀjɛʀ]
à l'arrière de
Je n'aime pas être assis à l'arrière du bus.
l'**avant** m [avã]
à l'avant de
le **fond** [fɔ̃]

the lower part, the bottom
in the bottom drawer
the upper part, the top
on the top shelf
the rear part, the back
in the back of
I don't like sitting in the back of the bus.
the front part, the front
in the front of
bottom, lowest part

le **coin** [kwɛ̃]	corner
au coin de la rue	on the street corner
le **côté** [kote]	side
Le carré a 4 côtés égaux.	A square has four sides of equal length.
le **bout** [bu]	end
au bout de	at the end of
Elle nous attend au bout du quai.	She's waiting at the end of the platform.
le **bord** [bɔR]	edge
supérieur,e [sypeRjœR]	upper
le bord supérieur de la page	the upper edge of the page
inférieur,e [ɛ̃feRjœR]	lower

---

de côté [d(ə)kote]	sideways, to one side
faire un **pas de côté**	step to the side
à côté (de) [akote]	by, near, next to
Assieds-toi **à côté de moi**.	Sit down near me.
de face [dəfas]	in front, abreast of
la **droite** [dRwat]	the right (side)
tenir sa droite	keep to the right
la **gauche** [goʃ]	the left (side)
Sur votre gauche, vous pouvez voir la tour Eiffel.	On your left you can see the Eiffel Tower.
de près [d(ə)pRɛ]	close, from close up
de loin [d(ə)lwɛ̃]	far, from afar
Je l'ai reconnue de loin.	I recognized her from afar.

à l'extrémité de [alɛkstRemitedə]	at the far end of
Un drapeau flotte à l'extrémité du mât.	A flag flutters at the very end of the pole.
côte à côte [kotakot]	side by side
Ils sont assis côte à côte.	They are sitting side by side.
en bas (de) [ɑ̃ba]	below, at the bottom (of)
en haut (de) [ɑ̃'o]	above, on top (of)
en haut d'une côte	on top of a hill
en avant (de) [ɑ̃navɑ̃]	to the front, at the front (of)
Il marche en avant du groupe.	He is marching in front of the group.
en arrière (de) [ɑ̃naRjɛR]	to the back, in back (of)
au premier plan [opRəmjeplɑ̃]	in the foreground
Au premier plan du tableau, on voit un cheval.	In the foreground of the picture one sees a horse.
au second plan [os(ə)gɔ̃plɑ̃]	in the background

à la hauteur de [alaˈotœʀdə]	at a height of
le long de [ləlɔ̃də]	along
Des roses poussent le long du mur.	Roses grow along the wall.
vis-à-vis (de) [vizavi]	across (from), opposite
Sa chambre est vis-à-vis de la mienne.	Her room is across from mine.
le **milieu** [miljø]	middle
au milieu de	in the middle of
Il y a un arbre au milieu du jardin.	There is a tree in the middle of the garden.

hors de qc [ɔʀdə]	out of, outside of
Il a couru hors de la pièce.	He ran out of the room.
en dehors (de) [ãdəɔʀ]	outside (of)
La maison est en dehors du village.	The house is outside of the village.

19.6 Length, Circumference, Distance

la **dimension** [dimãsjɔ̃]	dimension
prendre les dimensions de qc	take the dimensions of s.th.
la **longueur** [lɔ̃gœʀ]	length
long, longue [lɔ̃, lɔ̃g]	long
La table est **longue de** 2 mètres.	The table is 2 meters long.
avoir 10 mètres **de long**	be 10 meters long
court,e [kuʀ, kuʀt]	short
Elle a **les cheveux courts.**	She has short hair.
large [laʀʒ]	wide
Un terrain de **100 mètres de long sur 30 (mètres) de large.**	A lot 100 meters long by 30 meters wide.
la **largeur** [laʀʒœʀ]	width
étroit,e [etʀwa, wat]	narrow
un chemin étroit	a narrow path
haut,e [ˈo, ˈot]	high, tall
La maison est **haute de** 13 mètres.	The house is 13 meters high.
La tour a 50 mètres **de haut.**	The tower is 50 meters high.
la **hauteur** [ˈotœʀ]	height
dans le sens de la largeur/hauteur	in terms of width/height
bas,se [ba, bas]	low
un plafond bas	a low ceiling
profond,e [pʀɔfɔ̃, ɔ̃d]	deep
la **profondeur** [pʀɔfɔ̃dœʀ]	depth

le **tour** [tuʀ] — circumference
autour de [otuʀdə] — around
entouré,e de [ãtuʀedə] — surrounded by
  un jardin entouré d'une clôture — a garden surrounded by a fence

près (de) [pʀɛ] — near
  Il y a un arrêt de bus près de l'école. — There is a bus stop near the school.
proche (de) [pʀɔʃ] — close (to)
  C'est la station de métro **la plus proche**. — It is the closest subway station.
les **environs** m [ãviʀɔ̄] — surroundings, vicinity
  Ils habitent **dans les environs de** Mulhouse. — They live in the vicinity of Mulhouse.

loin (de) [lwɛ̄] — far (from)
  Nous habitons en banlieue, pas loin de Marseille. — We live in a suburb, not far from Marseille.
  On voit les bateaux passer **au loin**. — One sees the ships passing in the distance.

éloigné,e [elwaɲe] — distant, removed
lointain,e [lwɛ̄tɛ̄, ɛn] — distant, faraway
  Je rêve souvent de pays lointains. — I often dream of faraway lands.
à ... m/km d'ici [amɛtʀ/kilɔmɛtʀdisi] — ... m/km from here
  La prochaine station-service est à 400 m d'ici. — The next gas station is 400 meters from here.

jusqu'à [ʒyska] — as far as; up to; down to
  aller à pied jusqu'à la poste — go on foot as far as the post office
entre [ãtʀ] — between
  Il y a 1000 km entre Dunkerque et Nice. — Dunkirk and Nice are 1000 km apart.

le **périmètre** [peʀimɛtʀ] — perimeter
la **circonférence** [siʀkɔ̄feʀãs] — circumference
la **limite** [limit] — limit
limité,e [limite] — limited
délimité,e [delimite] — bounded
  une propriété délimitée par un mur — a property bounded by a wall

la **distance** [distans] — distance
  Le feu rouge se trouve à une distance de 150 mètres. — The red light is located at a distance of 150 meters.
distant,e de [distã, ãtdə] — apart

Les deux villes sont distantes de 5 km.	The two towns are five km apart.
d'ici à ... [disia]	from here to ...
Il y a 3 km d'ici à la maison la plus proche.	It's three km from here to the next house.

19.7 Place and Direction

l'**endroit** m [ɑ̃dʀwa]	place, spot
par endroits	in places
le **lieu** [ljø]	place
le **lieu de naissance**	place of birth
un **lieu public**	a public place
le **point** [pwɛ̃]	point
le **point de départ**	point of departure
local,e [lɔkal]	local
les traditions locales	the local traditions

la **place** [plas]	place
ranger quelque chose à sa place	put something in its place
la **situation** [sitɥasjɔ̃]	situation; site; position
la situation géographique	the geographical position
situé,e [sitɥe]	situated
Cette maison est située en plein centre.	This house is situated right in the center.
la **position** [pozisjɔ̃]	position, situation

où [u]	where
Où est mon sac?	Where is my bag?
ici [isi]	here
là [la]	there
là-bas [laba]	there, over there
Tu vois ce château là-bas?	Do you see that castle over there?
là-haut [la'o]	up there
là-dessus [lad(ə)sy]	on that
Monte là-dessus, tu verras mieux.	Climb on top of that; you'll see better.
là-dedans [lad(ə)dɑ̃]	in there
Allume la lumière, il fait noir là-dedans.	Turn on the light; it's dark in there.
là-dessous [lad(ə)su]	under there
par terre [paʀtɛʀ]	on the floor, on the ground
Ramasse ces papiers qui traînent par terre.	Pick up those papers that are lying around on the floor.

à [a]	in
à Montpellier/au Portugal	in Montpellier/in Portugal
en [ɑ̃]	in
en Angleterre	in England
chez [ʃe]	at, to, in (the house of, etc.)
Je l'ai invité chez moi.	I invited him to my house.

---

partout [paʀtu]	everywhere
nulle part [nylpaʀ]	nowhere, not ... anywhere
Je l'ai cherché partout, mais je ne l'ai vu nulle part.	I looked for him everywhere, but I didn't see him anywhere.
quelque part [kɛlk(ə)paʀ]	somewhere
Je ne sais pas qui c'est, mais je l'ai déjà vu quelque part.	I don't know who that is, but I've seen him somewhere before.
autre part [ot(ʀə)paʀ]	elsewhere, somewhere else
ailleurs [ajœʀ]	elsewhere, somewhere else
Si tu ne te plais pas ici, va ailleurs.	If you don't like it here, go somewhere else.

---

la **direction** [diʀɛksjɔ̃]	direction
la **bonne/mauvaise direction**	the right/wrong direction
en direction de	in the direction of
se diriger vers [s(ə)diʀiʒe]	steer toward
Le bateau se dirige vers le port.	The ship is steering toward the port.
le **sens** [sɑ̃s]	direction
dans le **sens des aiguilles d'une montre**	(in a) clockwise (direction)
l'**orientation** f [ɔʀjɑ̃tasjɔ̃]	orientation
avoir le sens de l'orientation	have a good sense of orientation
s'orienter vers qc [sɔʀjɑ̃te]	get one's bearings regarding s.th.

---

tout droit [tudʀwa]	straight ahead
Continue tout droit jusqu'à la gare.	Keep on straight ahead as far as the railroad station.
droit,e [dʀwa, at]	straight
une avenue toute droite	an avenue as straight as an arrow
horizontal,e [ɔʀizɔ̃tal]	horizontal
vertical,e [vɛʀtikal]	vertical
à droite de [adʀwatdə]	to the right of
à gauche de [agoʃdə]	to the left of
On met le couteau à droite de l'assiette et la fourchette à gauche.	You put the knife to the right of the plate and the fork to the left.

en avant [ãnavã]	forward, ahead
En avant, marche!	Forward, march!
en arrière [ãnaʀjɛʀ]	backwards
faire un pas en arrière	take a step backwards
vers [vɛʀ]	toward

le **nord (N)** [nɔʀ]	north
Lille est situé **dans le Nord** de la France.	Lille is in northern France.
au nord (de)	north (of)
au nord de la Loire	north of the Loire
le **sud (S)** [syd]	south
au sud (de)	south (of)
l'**est (E)** *m* [ɛst]	east
à l'est (de)	east (of)
l'**ouest (O)** *m* [wɛst]	west
à l'ouest (de)	west (of)

opposé,e [ɔpoze]	opposite, opposing
repartir* dans la direction opposée	set out again in the opposite direction
en sens inverse [ãsãsẽvɛʀs]	in the opposite direction
Elle est partie en sens inverse.	She went off in the opposite direction.
parallèle à [paʀalɛl]	parallel to
La rue de la Gare est parallèle à la rue Balzac.	The rue de la Gare runs parallel to the rue Balzac.
perpendiculaire à [pɛʀpãdikylɛʀ]	perpendicular to
de haut en bas [də'o(t)ãba]	from top to bottom
de long en large [dəlõãlaʀʒ]	up and down; to and fro
marcher de long en large	walk up and down
à travers [atʀavɛʀ]	across
voyager à travers la France	travel across France

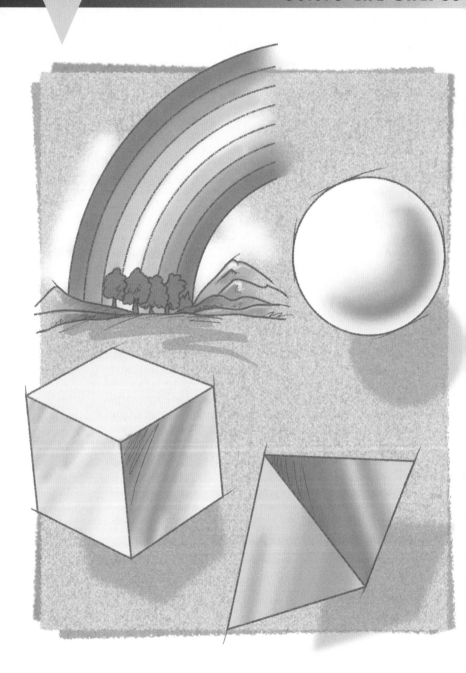

20.1 Colors

une **couleur** [kulœʀ]	color
riche en couleurs	colorful, many-colored

Showing your colors

Note the difference between:

la couleur	*color*
la télé(vision) en couleurs	*color television*
un homme/une femme de couleur	*man/woman of color*
la peinture	*color, paint; painting; picture*
un pot de peinture	*pot of paint*
Il fait de la peinture.	*He paints.*
Je ne peux pas le voir en peinture. *fam*	*I can't stand him.*

---

coloré,e [kɔlɔʀe]	colored
du **verre coloré**	colored glass
incolore [ɛ̃kɔlɔʀ]	colorless
un liquide incolore	a colorless liquid
colorier [kɔlɔʀje]	color, stain
un **album à colorier**	coloring book
un **ton** [tɔ̃]	tone
une **nuance** [nɥɑ̃s]	shade, hue
uni,e [yni]	plain and unpatterned
un tissu uni	plain, unpatterned material
multicolore [myltikɔlɔʀ]	multicolored
un papillon multicolore	a multicolored butterfly

blanc, blanche [blɑ̃, blɑ̃ʃ]	white
Tu commences à avoir des **cheveux blancs.**	You're starting to get white hairs.
noir,e [nwaʀ]	black
gris,e [gʀi, gʀiz]	gray

bleu,e [blø]	blue
jaune [ʒon]	yellow
rouge [ʀuʒ]	red
vert,e [vɛʀ, vɛʀt]	green
violet,te [vjɔlɛ, ɛt]	violet
Il porte une cravate violette.	He's wearing a violet tie.
rose [ʀoz]	pink, rose(-colored)

orange [ɔʀɑ̃ʒ]	orange
des chaussettes orange	orange socks
marron [maʀɔ̃]	brown
azur [azyʀ]	azure, blue

Colors

Adjectives denoting color are normally *variable in form*:

Elle a acheté deux **jupes** vert**es**.   *She bought two green skirts.*

However, they are *invariable* if they are *nouns used as adjectives* or if they are *compound adjectives*:

Elle a les **yeux marron**.   *She has brown eyes.*

Elle m'a offert trois **chemises bleu clair**.   *She gave me three light blue shirts.*

---

blond,e [blɔ̃, blɔ̃d]	blond
brun,e [bʀɛ̃, bʀyn]	brown, dark
une **bière blonde/brune**	a light/dark beer
roux, rousse [ʀu, ʀus]	red-haired, sandy
Elle a **les cheveux roux**.	She has red hair.

---

teindre [tɛ̃dʀ]	dye, color
Elle s'est fait teindre **en roux**.	She had her hair dyed red.
la **teinte** [tɛ̃t]	tint, color, shade
déteindre [detɛ̃dʀ]	fade, lose color
Sa chemise a déteint au lavage.	His shirt faded in the wash.

---

criard,e [kʀijaʀ, jaʀd]	loud, shrill
une nappe **aux couleurs criardes**	a tablecloth in loud colors
mauve [mov]	mauve
beige [bɛʒ]	beige
ocre [ɔkʀ]	ocher
châtain [ʃatɛ̃]	chestnut, auburn
Elle est châtain.	She has auburn hair.
Elle a les cheveux **châtain foncé**.	She has deep chestnut-colored hair.
lilas [lila]	lilac

---

bleu marine [blømaʀin]	dark blue, navy blue
Elle est belle, ta chemise bleu marine.	Your navy blue shirt is really pretty.
bleu ciel [bløsjɛl]	sky blue
bleu turquoise [bløtyʀkwaz]	turquoise blue
La mer est bleu turquoise.	The sea is turquoise blue.
rouge sang [ʀuʒsɑ̃]	blood red
vert foncé [vɛʀfɔ̃se]	dark green
une jupe vert foncé	a dark green skirt
vert pomme [vɛʀpɔm]	apple green
gris clair [gʀiklɛʀ]	light gray

une cravate gris clair	a light gray tie
doré,e [dɔʀe]	golden, gold-colored
argenté,e [aʀʒɑ̃te]	silvery, silver-colored
clair,e [klɛʀ]	light
Il a **les yeux clairs.**	He has light eyes.
foncé,e [fɔ̃se]	dark
pâle [pal]	pale
Elle a **le teint pâle.**	She has a pale complexion.
vif, vive [vif, viv]	strong, bright
une robe **rouge vif**	a bright red dress
sombre [sɔ̃bʀ]	dark
brillant,e [bʀijɑ̃, ɑ̃t]	shiny
mat,e [mat]	matte

20.2 Shapes

la **forme** [fɔʀm]	shape, form
une boîte **en forme de** cœur	a heart-shaped box
former [fɔʀme]	shape, form
Les enfants forment un cercle	The children form a circle
autour du sapin.	around the fir tree.
(se) déformer [(sə)defɔʀme]	distort (become distorted)
La chaleur déforme le plastique.	Heat distorts plastic.
Le plastique se déforme sous	Plastic loses its shape under the
l'effet de la chaleur.	influence of heat.
uniforme [ynifɔʀm]	uniform
une **figure** [figyʀ]	figure
une figure géométrique	a geometric figure
une **silhouette** [silwɛt]	silhouette, shape, outline
le **point** [pwɛ̃]	dot
un **trait** [tʀɛ]	straight line; stroke
tirer un trait **à la règle**	draw a straight line with the ruler
une **ligne** [liɲ]	line
une **(ligne) droite**	straight line
rond,e [ʀɔ̃, ʀɔ̃d]	round
La terre est ronde.	The earth is round.
un **cercle** [sɛʀkl]	circle
un **demi-cercle**	semicircle, half-circle
le **bord** [bɔʀ]	edge
le bord de la table	edge of the table

un **coin** [kwɛ̃]	corner
une **pointe** [pwɛ̃t]	point
pointu,e [pwɛ̃ty]	pointed, sharp
Attention, le couteau est pointu.	Be careful; the knife is sharp.
régulier, -ière [ʀegylje, jɛʀ]	regular
irrégulier, -ière [iʀegylje, jɛʀ]	irregular, uneven
une surface irrégulière	an uneven surface

un **angle** [ãgl]	angle
un **angle droit**	right angle
un **angle aigu/obtus**	acute/obtuse angle
un **triangle** [tʀijãgl]	triangle
triangulaire [tʀijãgylɛʀ]	triangular
un **rectangle** [ʀɛktãgl]	rectangle
rectangulaire [ʀɛktãgylɛʀ]	rectangular
un **carré** [kaʀe]	square
carré,e [kaʀe]	square
une **croix** [kʀwa]	cross
marquer qc d'une croix	mark s.th. with a cross
une **courbe** [kuʀb]	curve
un **arc** [aʀk]	arc
tracer un arc de cercle	describe an arc
ovale [ɔval]	oval

une **sphère** [sfɛʀ]	sphere
sphérique [sfeʀik]	spherical
un **hémisphère** [emisfɛʀ]	hemisphere
Nous vivons dans l'**hémisphère Nord**.	We live in the northern hemisphere.
un **cube** [kyb]	cube
cubique [kybik]	cubical
la **racine cubique** d'un nombre	the cube root of a number
une **pyramide** [piʀamid]	pyramid
un **cylindre** [silɛ̃dʀ]	cylinder
cylindrique [silɛ̃dʀik]	cylindrical

21.1 Designations of Quantity

combien ? [kɔ̃bjɛ̃] how much?
Combien coûte ce parfum ? How much does this perfume cost?
la **quantité** [kɑ̃tite] quantity
le **nombre** [nɔ̃bʀ] number
nombreux, -euse [nɔ̃bʀø, øz] numerous
L'accident a fait de nombreuses The accident claimed numerous
victimes. victims.
plusieurs [plyzjœʀ] several
Il y a plusieurs mois que je ne l'ai I haven't seen him for several
pas vu. months.
quelques [kɛlkə] a few; some, any
On en reparlera dans quelques We'll talk about it again in a few
années. years.
quelques-uns/quelques-unes some
[kɛlkəzɛ̃, zyn]
Je ne les connais pas tous, mais j'en I don't know all of them, but
ai déjà rencontré quelques-uns. I've already met some of them.

compter [kɔ̃te] count
compter sur ses doigts count on one's fingers
comparer qn/qc à qn/qc compare s.o./s.th. with s.o./s.th.
[kɔ̃paʀe]
contenir [kɔ̃t(ə)niʀ] contain, hold
Cette bouteille contient un litre. That bottle contains one liter.

ne ... rien [nəʀjɛ̃] nothing, not ... anything
Je n'**en** sais rien. I don't know anything about it.
Rien ne va plus. Nothing works anymore.
ne ... rien du tout [nəʀjɛ̃dytu] nothing at all, not ... anything at
  all
Je n'**y** comprends rien du tout. I understand nothing at all
  about it.
ne ... pas (de) [nəpa] no, not, not any
Je ne vois pas de solution. I see no solution.
ne ... pas du tout [nəpadytu] no, not, not any at all
Elle n'a pas d'argent du tout. She has no money at all.
ne ... pas un,e seul,e not a single
[nəpa(z)ɛ̃/ynsœl]
Ils ne parlent pas un seul mot They don't speak a single word
d'allemand. of German.
ne ... aucun,e [nəokɛ̃/kyn] none; not any
Tu n'as aucune raison de te mettre You don't have any reason to get
en colère. angry.
aucun,e (de) ... ne [okɛ̃/ynnə] no one; not any

Aucun de ces deux tableaux ne me plaît.

Neither one of those two pictures pleases me.

ne ... plus (de) [nəply]
Je n'ai plus de monnaie.

no more, not any more
I don't have any more change.

ne ... plus du tout [nəplydytu]
Il faut passer à la boulangerie, on n'a plus du tout de pain.

no more, not any more at all
We have to go to the bakery; we don't have any more bread at all.

---

peu (de) [pø]
Il a peu de chances de réussir.
Tu peux me prêter un peu d'argent ?

little
He has little chance of succeeding.
Can you loan me a little money?

un (tout) petit peu (de)
très peu (de)

a (very) little
very little

ne ... pas grand-chose
[nəpagʀɑ̃ʃoz]
Je n'**y** connais pas grand-chose.

not much

I don't understand much of it.

presque pas (de) [pʀɛskəpas]
Cette année il n'y a presque pas eu de neige.

almost no, almost none
This year there was almost no snow.

---

beaucoup (de) [boku]
pas mal (de) *fam* [pamal]
Il y avait pas mal de gens à la manifestation.

much
quite a few
There were quite a few people at the demonstration.

bien du/de la/de l'/des [bjɛ̃]
Je vous souhaite bien du plaisir.

plenty of, many of
Have lots of fun.

plein (de) *fam* [plɛ̃]
un **tas (de)** *fam* [ɛ̃ta]
J'ai un tas de problèmes en ce moment.

full (of)
a lot (of)
I have a lot of problems at the moment.

énormément (de) [enɔʀmemɑ̃]
Cette femme a énormément de courage.

a great deal (of)
This woman has a great deal of courage.

tant (de) [tɑ̃]
Ne bois pas tant (d'alcool).

so much (of)
Don't drink so much (alcohol).

trop (de) [tʀo]

too much (of)

---

un **verre (de)** [ɛ̃vɛʀ]
se servir un verre de jus d'orange

a glass (of)
pour oneself a glass of orange juice

une **bouteille (de)** [ynbutɛj]
une **boîte (de)** [ynbwat]
un **paquet (de)** [ɛ̃pakɛ]
un paquet de biscuits

a bottle (of)
a box, a can (of)
a package (of)
a package of cookies

une **part** [ynpaʀ]	a part, a share
Ne t'inquiète pas, tu auras ta part du gâteau.	Don't worry; you'll get your share of the cake.
une **partie** [ynpaʀti]	a part, a portion
Une partie du public a sifflé la pièce.	Part of the audience booed the play.
la **plupart du/de la/des** [laplypaʀ]	most of the
La plupart du temps, il travaille.	Most of the time he works.
La plupart des spectateurs sont partis avant la fin du film.	Most of the spectators left before the end of the film.
la **moitié** [lamwatje]	half
le **reste** [ləʀɛst]	the rest, the remainder
le **double** [lədubl]	twofold, twice as much
doubler [duble]	double
En trois ans, il a doublé sa fortune.	In three years he doubled his fortune.
la **majorité** [lamaʒɔʀite]	the majority
La grande majorité des élèves trouve les vacances trop courtes.	The great majority of the pupils think the vacations are too short.

plus (de/que) [ply]	more (than)
autant (de/que) [otɑ̃]	as much (as)
moins (de/que) [mwɛ̃]	less (than)

---

i **More or less**

After **plus/moins** use **que** if a *comparison* is being made; use **de** if a *statement of quantity* is being made. Examples:

Tu gagnes **plus** d'argent **que** moi.	*You earn more money than I.*
Il gagne **plus de** 10 000 francs.	*He earns more than 10,000 francs.*
Elle mange **moins que** moi.	*She eats less than I.*
Ça vaut **moins de** 100 francs.	*That's worth less than 100 francs.*

---

tout, toute, tous, toutes [tu, tut, tus, tut]	all, every, each
C'est un événement dont **tout le monde** parle.	It's an event that everyone is talking about.
Tous leurs enfants vivent à l'étranger.	All of her children live abroad.
Toutes mes filles sont mariées.	All of my daughters are married.
le **tout** [lətu]	the whole (thing)
l'**ensemble** *m* [lɑ̃sɑ̃bl]	the whole, the general effect
chaque [ʃak]	each, every
Chaque jour, il quitte la maison à 7 heures.	Every day he leaves the house at 7 o'clock.

chacun,e [ʃakɛ̃, yn]
Il y en a assez pour chacun.

each, every one; everyone
There is enough for everyone.

le **maximum** [ləmaksimɔm]
Je peux dépenser 200 euros **au maximum.**

the maximum, the most
I can spend 200 euros at most.

le **minimum** [ləminimɔm]
Il fait vraiment le minimum d'efforts.
au minimum

the minimum, the least
He really makes the minimum of effort.
at least

un **groupe** [ɛ̃grup]
un petit groupe de curieux
une **foule** [ynful]
Il y avait une foule immense devant le stade.

a group
a small group of curious people
a crowd (of people)
There was a huge crowd in front of the stadium.

une **masse (de)** [ynmas]
en masse
davantage [davɑ̃taʒ]
Veux-tu davantage de dessert?
en trop [ɑ̃trɔ]
On lui a rendu ce qu'il avait payé en trop.
la **majeure partie** [lamaʒœrparti]
tout au plus [tutoplys]
Nous resterons là-bas 8 jours tout au plus.

a mass, a large number
en masse, in a body
more
Do you want more dessert?
too much
They returned to him what he had paid in excess.
the greatest part
at most
We'll stay there a week at most.

considérable [kɔ̃sideRabl]
élevé,e [el(ə)ve]
Le prix de cette voiture est très élevé.
limité,e [limite]
Je ne dispose que d'une somme limitée.
restreint,e [Restrɛ̃, ɛ̃t]
Ses moyens sont restreints.

considerable
high, steep
The price of that car is quite high.
limited
I have only a limited sum at my disposal.
limited, restricted
His means are limited.

21.2 Numbers and Counting Words

Cardinal Numbers

0	zéro	[zeʀo]	40	quarante	[kaʀãt]
1	un,e	[ɛ̃/yn]	41	quarante et un/une	[kaʀãteɛ̃/yn]
2	deux	[dø]	50	cinquante	[sɛ̃kãt]
3	trois	[tʀwa]	60	soixante	[swasãt]
4	quatre	[katʀ]	61	soixante et un/une	
5	cinq	[sɛ̃k]	62	soixante-deux	
6	six	[sis]	69	soixante-neuf	
7	sept	[set]	70	soixante-dix	
8	huit	['ɥit]	71	soixante et onze	
9	neuf	[nœf]	72	soixante-douze	
10	dix	[dis]	79	soixante-dix-neuf	
11	onze	['ɔ̃z]	80	quatre-vingts	[katʀəvɛ̃]
12	douze	[duz]	81	quatre-vingt-un/une	[katʀəvɛ̃ɛ̃/yn]
13	treize	[tʀɛz]	82	quatre-vingt-deux	[katʀəvɛ̃dø]
14	quatorze	[katɔʀz]	89	quatre-vingt-neuf	
15	quinze	[kɛ̃z]	90	quatre-vingt-dix	
16	seize	[sez]	91	quatre-vingt-onze	
17	dix-sept	[disset]	92	quatre-vingt-douze	
18	dix-huit	[dizɥit]	99	quatre-vingt-dix-neuf	
19	dix-neuf	[diznœf]	100	cent	[sã]
20	vingt	[vɛ̃]	101	cent un/une	[sãɛ̃/yn]
21	vingt et un/une	[vɛ̃teɛ̃/yn]	110	cent dix	
22	vingt-deux	[vɛ̃tdø]	200	deux cents	
30	trente	[tʀãt]	1 000	mille	[mil]
31	trente et un/une	[tʀãteɛ̃/yn]	1 001	mille un/une	
32	trente-deux	[tʀãtdø]	2 000	deux mille	

1 000 000	**un million**	[ɛ̃miljɔ̃]	1 000 000 000	**un milliard**	[ɛ̃miljar]

With *dates* and *names of rulers*, the *cardinal number* (except in the case of the number 1) is used:
le deux/trois mai (le 2-5-2000 or le 2/5/2000);
Napoléon III (trois), Louis XIV (quatorze);
but: le 1er (premier) avril; Napoléon 1er (premier).
In accordance with the spelling reforms of 1990, the *individual elements of compound numbers* may also be linked with hyphens:
1284 = mille-deux-cent-quatre-vingt-quatre.

Ordinal Numbers

1er	le premier	[pʀəmje, jɛʀ]
1re	la première	[pʀəm jɛʀ]
2^e	le/la deuxième	[døzjɛm]
2^e	le/la second,e	[s(ə)gɔ̃, ɔ̃d]
20^e	le/la vingtième	[vɛ̃tjɛm]
21^e	le/la vingt et unième	[vɛ̃teynjɛm]
22^e	le/la vingt-deuxième	[vɛ̃tdøzjɛm]
71^e	le/la soixante et onzième	[swasɑ̃teɔ̃zjɛm]
100^e	le/la centième	[sɑ̃tjɛm]
1000^e	le/la millième	[miljɛm]

une **dizaine (de)** [yndizɛn]	ten; about ten
une **douzaine (de)** [ynduzɛn]	a dozen; about twelve
une douzaine d'œufs	a dozen eggs
une **quinzaine (de)** [ynkɛ̃zɛn]	about fifteen
une quinzaine de jours	about two weeks
une **vingtaine (de)** [ynvɛ̃tɛn]	about twenty
une **centaine (de)** [ynsɑ̃tɛn]	about one hundred
il y a une centaine d'années	about a hundred years ago
un **millier (de)** [ɛ̃milje]	about one thousand

un **demi** [ɛ̃d(ə)mi]	half
une demi-/demie heure	half an hour
une heure et demie	an hour and a half
un **tiers** [ɛ̃tjɛʀ]	third (part), one-third
un **quart** [ɛ̃kaʀ]	quarter, fourth (part), one-fourth
un quart d'heure	a quarter of an hour
un **cinquième** [ɛ̃sɛ̃kjɛm]	fifth (part), one-fifth
un **centième** [ɛ̃sɑ̃tjɛm]	hundredth (part)
deux cinquièmes [døsɛ̃kjɛm]	two-fifths
un **pour cent** [ɛ̃puʀsɑ̃]	one percent
Plus de 10% des Français aimeraient que leur fille épouse un Allemand.	More than 10 percent of the French would like their daughter to marry a German.

le **double** [lədubl]	twice as much; double
Ça coûte le double de ce que je voulais dépenser.	That costs twice as much as I wanted to spend.
le **triple** [lətʀipl]	three times as much; triple
... fois [fwa]	... times
Ça coûte trois fois rien. *loc*	That costs next to nothing.

un **chiffre** [ʃifʀ]	figure, number

un **nombre** [nɔ̃bʀ]	number
un **nombre entier**	a whole number
un **nombre premier**	a prime number
un **nombre (im)pair**	an (un)even number
un **nombre cardinal**	cardinal number
un **nombre ordinal**	ordinal number
un **numéro** [nymeʀo]	number
l'**ordre** *m* [ɔʀdʀ]	order
par ordre croissant/décroissant	in increasing/decreasing order
une **unité** [ynite]	unit

compter [kɔ̃te]	count
calculer [kalkyle]	do arithmetic; calculate, compute
le **calcul** [kalkyl]	arithmetic; calculation, computation
le **calcul mental**	mental arithmetic
une **erreur de calcul**	error in arithmetic
se tromper dans ses calculs	make a mistake in one's calculations
la **somme** [sɔm]	sum
la **différence** [difeʀɑ̃s]	difference
plus [plys]	plus
moins [mwɛ̃]	minus

le **total** [tɔtal]	total
Au total, ça fait 75 euros.	That makes a total of 75 euros.
le **résultat** [ʀezylta]	result

égal,e [egal]	equal
deux quantités égales	two equal quantities
l'**égalité** *f* [egalite]	equality
supérieur,e [supeʀjœʀ]	higher, greater, above
La température est **supérieure à la normale**.	The temperature is higher than normal.
inférieur,e [ɛ̃feʀjœʀ]	lower, less, below

exact,e [ɛgza(kt), ɛgzakt]	exact
Avez-vous l'heure exacte?	Do you have the exact time?
précis,e [pʀesi, iz]	precise
Je serai là à 15 heures précises.	I'll be there precisely at 3 P.M.
environ [ɑ̃viʀɔ̃]	about, around
Il a environ 35 ans.	He's about 35 years old.
à peu près [apøpʀɛ]	pretty near, nearly
correspondre à qc [kɔʀɛspɔ̃dʀə]	correspond to s.th.
Ça correspond à peu près à mes calculs.	That roughly corresponds to my calculations.
(c'est) juste [ʒyst]	(that is) correct/right

(c'est) faux [fo] Le résultat est juste/faux.	(that is) incorrect/wrong The result is correct/incorrect.

une **opération** [ɔpeʀasjɔ̃]	operation
une **addition** [adisjɔ]	addition
additionner [adisjɔne]	add
une **soustraction** [sustʀaksjɔ̃]	subtraction
soustraire [sustʀɛʀ]	subtract
une **multiplication** [myltiplikasjɔ̃]	multiplication
multiplier [myltiplije] multiplier **par** trois	multiply multiply by three
une **division** [divizjɔ̃]	division
diviser [divize] diviser **par** deux	divide divide by two

la **virgule** [viʀgyl] deux virgule cinq	comma two comma five (2,5 = 2.5)
recompter [ʀ(ə)kɔ̃te] J'ai recompté trois fois pour être sûr.	count again, recount I've recounted it three times, just to be sure.

21.3 Measures and Weights

la **mesure** [m(ə)zyʀ]	measure
une **unité de mesure**	a unit of measure
mesurer [məzyʀe] mesurer une pièce	measure measure a room
la **taille** [taj]	height, size
petit,e [p(ə)ti, it]	small
minuscule [minyskyl]	tiny, minuscule
grand,e [gʀɑ̃, gʀɑ̃d]	large
immense [imɑ̃s]	immense, huge
gros,se [gʀo, gʀos]	fat
énorme [enɔʀm] Elle a fait une énorme bêtise.	enormous, gigantic She did something enormously stupid.

la **dimension** [dimɑ̃sjɔ̃] Vous connaissez les dimensions de votre bureau?	dimension, size Do you know the dimensions of your office?
la **longueur** [lɔ̃gœʀ]	length
long, longue [lɔ̃, lɔ̃g]	long
court,e [kuʀ, kuʀt]	short

la **largeur** [laʀʒœʀ]	width
dans le sens de la largeur	in terms of width
large [laʀʒ]	wide
la **hauteur** ['otœʀ]	height
haut,e ['o, 'ot]	high, tall
La Tour Eiffel est **haute de** 320 mètres.	The Eiffel Tower is 320 meters high.
bas,se [ba, bas]	low
la **profondeur** [pʀɔfɔ̃dœʀ]	depth
profond,e [pʀɔfɔ̃, ɔ̃d]	deep
un lac profond	a deep lake
un **millimètre** [milimɛtʀ]	millimeter
un **centimètre** [sɑ̃timɛtʀ]	centimeter
un **mètre** [mɛtʀ]	meter
un **kilomètre** [kilɔmɛtʀ]	kilometer
un kilomètre **de long**	one kilometer long
un kilomètre **à l'heure (km/h)**	one kilometer per hour (km/h)

le **poids** [pwa]	weight
peser [pəze]	weigh
Pierre pèse 70 kilos.	Pierre weighs 70 kilos.
la **balance** [balɑ̃s]	scales, balance
La balance indique 80 kilos.	The scales show 80 kilos.
la **masse** [mas]	mass
lourd,e [luʀ, luʀd]	heavy
léger, -ère [leʒe, leʒɛʀ]	light

Light and easy

Note these common phrases:

léger, -ère	*light (in weight; **opposite: lourd,e**); trifling (**opposite: grave**)*
des bagages légers/lourds	*light/heavy baggage*
une blessure légère/grave	*a slight/serious injury*
facile	*easy (to do; **opposite: difficile**)*
un devoir facile/difficile	*an easy/difficult task*
C'est facile/difficile à dire.	*That's easy/hard to say.*

---

net,te [nɛt]	net
le **poids net**	net weight
brut,e [bʀyt]	gross
le **bénéfice brut**	gross profit
un **gramme (de)** [gʀam]	gram
un **kilo(gramme) (de)** [kilo, kilɔgʀam]	kilo(gram)
un kilo de pommes de terre	a kilo of potatoes

une livre (de) [livʀ]	pound (454 grams)

la **surface** [syʀfas]	surface
carré,e [kaʀe]	square
une pièce de 15 mètres carrés (m²)	a room 15 meters square (m²)

le **volume** [vɔlym]	volume
le **contenu** [kɔ̃t(ə)ny]	content(s)
un **litre** [litʀ]	liter
un litre de lait	a liter of milk
cube [kyb]	cubic
un **mètre cube** (m³)	cubic meter (m³)

l'**échelle** *f* [eʃɛl]	scale
à l'**échelle (de)** 1/100 000ᵉ	on the scale of 1 : 100,000
la **graduation** [gʀadɥasjɔ̃]	scale; division into degrees; graduation

une **tonne** [tɔn]	ton
Elle/Il en fait des tonnes. *loc, fam*	She/He is laying it on thick.
un **quintal** [kɛ̃tal]	hundredweight, 100 kilograms

la **superficie** [sypɛʀfisi]	surface
un **are** [aʀ]	area (land measurement equaling 119.6 square yards)
un **hectare** [ɛktaʀ]	hectare
un terrain de 3 hectares	a three-hectare lot

le contexte

une catégorie

faire partie de

comparer

un point commun

22.1 Classification

classer [klase]
Tu devrais classer les photos dans un album.
le **classement** [klasmã]
une **catégorie** [kategɔʀi]
un **ordre** [ɔʀdʀ]
classer des objets **par ordre de taille**
ordonner [ɔʀdɔne]
une **suite (de)** [sɥit]
une **série (de)** [seʀi]
Cette **série de timbres** n'est pas complète.

sort, class, classify; file
You should arrange the photos in an album.
classing, classification; filing
category, class
order
classify objects by size

arrange, put in order
series, succession, set
series
This stamp series is not complete.

une **sorte (de)** [sɔʀt]
une **espèce (de)** [ɛspɛs]
Nous habitons une espèce de château.
correspondre à qc [kɔʀɛspɔ̃dʀ]

sort, kind
species, kind
We live in a kind of castle.

correspond to s.th.

un **signe** [siɲ]
un **signe particulier**
spécial,e [spesjal]
général,e [ʒeneʀal]
Elle manque de **culture générale**.
principal,e [pʀɛ̃sipal]
la **rue principale**
un **détail** [detaj]
constituer [kɔ̃stitɥe]
former [fɔʀme]
Les différents éléments constituent/ forment un ensemble.

sign
a special sign
special
general
She lacks a good general education.
main, principal
main street
detail
constitute
form
The different elements constitute/form a whole.

une **qualité** [kalite]
Je préfère la qualité à la quantité.
préféré,e [pʀefeʀe]
St-Exupéry est mon auteur préféré.
important,e [ɛ̃pɔʀtã, ãt]
l'**importance** f [ɛ̃pɔʀtãs]
une affaire de **la plus haute importance**
négligeable [negliʒabl]
C'est un détail négligeable.

quality
I'll take quality over quantity.
favorite, preferred
St-Exupéry is my favorite author.
important
importance
a matter of the greatest importance
negligible, unimportant
It's an unimportant detail.

premièrement [pRəmjɛRmã] (in the) first (place), firstly
deuxièmement [døzjɛmmã] (in the) second (place), secondly
Premièrement, je n'ai pas envie First, I don't want to go there,
d'y aller, et deuxièmement, je n'ai and second, I don't have time.
pas le temps.
d'abord [dabɔR] at first
ensuite [ãsɥit] then, afterward
puis [pɥi] then
Ils ont d'abord eu une fille, puis First they had a girl, then two
deux garçons. boys.
finalement [finalmã] finally
enfin [ãfɛ̃] at last, finally
Il a enfin trouvé un logement. Finally he found a place to live.

la **classification** [klasifikasjɔ̃] classification
procéder à la classification de qc set about classifying s.th.
la **disposition** [dispozisjɔ̃] disposition, arrangement

en premier lieu [ãpRəmjeljø] in the first place
En premier lieu, je tiens à First of all, I want to thank Mr.
remercier M. Bernard pour son Bernard for his efficient help.
aide efficace.
occuper la première place occupy first place
[ɔkypelapRəmjɛRplas]
être en tête de [ɛtRãtɛt] be at the top of
Il est en tête du Top 50. He's at the top of the hit charts.
passer* au second plan fade into the background
[paseos(ə)gɔ̃plã]
en dernier lieu [ãdɛRnjeljø] last of all, lastly

22.2 Degree, Comparison, Contexts

fort,e [fɔR, fɔRt] strong, great
une forte majorité a strong majority
faible [fɛbl] weak; slight
un faible pourcentage a small percentage
à peu près [apøpRɛ] pretty near, nearly so
moyen,ne [mwajɛ̃, jɛn] average
Vichy est une ville moyenne. Vichy is an average-sized town.
en moyenne on the average
largement [laRʒəmã] largely, fully, plentifully

énorme [enɔʀm]	enormous, huge
Il a gagné une somme énorme au loto.	He won an enormous amount in the lottery.
Il a gagné **énormément** d'argent.	He earned/won a huge sum of money.
fantastique [fãtastik]	fantastic
génial *fam* [ʒenjal]	inspired; great, super
hyper/méga/giga *fam* [ipɛʀ/mega/ʒiga]	total(ly), awesome(ly)
J'ai trouvé ce film hyper nul.	I thought the film was totally awesome.
C'était une soirée méga cool.	It was a totally cool evening.
terrible [tɛʀibl]	terrible
J'ai été témoin d'un terrible accident.	I was witness to a terrible accident.
extrême [ɛkstʀɛm]	extreme(ly)
Ils vivent dans une extrême pauvreté.	They live in extreme poverty.
Il fait **extrêmement** froid.	It is extremely cold.

comparer qn/qc à qn/qc [kɔ̃paʀe]	compare s.o./s.th. to/with s.o./s.th.
On le compare souvent à son père.	He is often compared with his father.
la **comparaison** [kɔ̃paʀɛzɔ̃]	comparison
le **rapport** [ʀapɔʀ]	relation; harmony; connection
établir des rapports avec qn	establish relations with s.o.
Le succès du chanteur est **sans rapport avec** son talent.	The singer's success has no relation to his talent.
Le prix de ce vêtement n'est pas **en rapport avec** sa qualité.	The price of this article of clothing is not in keeping with its quality.
par rapport à	in comparison to
le **point commun** [pwɛ̃kɔmɛ̃]	common thing, common point

la **relation** [ʀ(ə)lasjɔ̃]	relation, relationship
une **relation de cause à effet**	a causal relationship
égal,e [egal]	equal
diviser qc en deux parts égales	divide s.th. into two equal parts
pareil,le [paʀɛj]	like, equal, similar
Je n'ai jamais dit une **chose pareille**.	I never said anything like that.
samblable [sãblabl]	similar
ressembler à [ʀ(ə)sãble]	resemble
ressemblant,e [ʀ(ə)sãblã, ãt]	like, similar
la **ressemblance** [ʀ(ə)sãblãs]	similarity, resemblance

comme [kɔm]	like, as
Il est bête comme ses pieds. *loc, fam*	He's a real blockhead.
aussi ... que [osikə]	as ... as
Je cours aussi vite que toi.	I run just as fast as you.
autant/tant ... que [otãkə]	as much as
Il n'est pas aussi (si) gros que Daniel, parce qu'il ne mange pas autant (tant) que lui.	He's not as fat as Daniel, because he doesn't eat as much as he.
plus ... que [plykə]	more ... than
Elle est plus grande que son frère.	She is bigger than her brother.
moins ... que [mwɛ̃kə]	less ... than

le **contraire** [kɔ̃tʀɛʀ]	contrary
au contraire de	in contrast to
contrairement à [kɔ̃tʀɛʀmã]	in opposition to
Contrairement à ce qu'ils ont annoncé à la météo, il fait beau.	Despite the weather report, the weather is good.
la **différence** [difeʀãs]	difference
à la différence de	contrary to
différent,e de [difeʀã, ãt]	different
Ses idées sont différentes des miennes.	His ideas are different from mine.
l'**opposition** *f* [ɔpozisjɔ̃]	opposition; contrast
s'opposer à [sɔpoze]	oppose, be opposed to
(être) opposé,e à qc [ɔpoze]	(be) opposed to s.th.
Ils sont opposés à cette décision.	They are opposed to this decision.
à l'opposé de [alɔpoze]	contrary to
A l'opposé de mon père, ma mère aime bien ma nouvelle coiffure.	Contrary to my father, my mother likes my new hairdo.

le **contexte** [kɔ̃tɛkst]	context
sortir qc de son contexte	take s.th. out of its context
le **lien** [ljɛ̃]	bond, tie, link
être lié,e à/avec [ɛt(ʀə)lje]	be linked/friendly with
Sa façon de voir les choses est liée à son enfance malheureuse.	His way of seeing things is linked with his unhappy childhood.
Nous sommes très liés avec les Dupont.	We are close friends of the Duponts.
faire partie de [fɛʀpaʀti]	belong to
Elle fait partie des artistes les plus doués de sa génération.	She is one of the most gifted artists of her generation.
dépendre de [depãdʀ]	depend on

Tout dépend de sa décision.

la **dépendance** [depɑ̃dɑ̃s]

Everything depends on his/her decision.

dependence

---

comparé,e à [kɔ̃paʀe]
comparable à [kɔ̃paʀabl]
similaire [similɛʀ]
Ils ont fait des expériences similaires.

compared/in comparison with/to
comparable with/to
similar
They have had similar experiences.

---

de plus en plus [d(ə)plyzɑ̃ply]
Elle est de plus en plus gentille.
de moins en moins
[d(ə)mwɛ̃zɑ̃mwɛ̃]
Nous nous voyons de moins en moins.
de mieux en mieux
[d(ə)mjøzɑ̃mjø]
de pire en pire [d(ə)piʀɑ̃piʀ]

more and more, increasingly
She is increasingly nice.
less and less

We see each other less and less.

better and better

worse and worse

---

la **parenté** [paʀɑ̃te]
l'**analogie** f [analɔʒi]
procéder **par analogie**

relationship, kinship
analogy
proceed in an analogous way

---

la **distinction** [distɛ̃ksjɔ̃]
se distinguer de [s(ə)distɛ̃ge]
Il se distingue de ses frères par sa taille.
le **contraste** [kɔ̃tʀast]
contraster avec [kɔ̃tʀaste]
Sa voix douce contraste avec son physique de brute.
différer de [difeʀe]
être en contradiction avec
[ɛtʀɑ̃kɔ̃tʀadiksjɔ̃]

distinction
differ from
He differs from his brothers by his size.
contrast
contrast with
His soft voice contrasts with his rough exterior.
differ from
be in opposition to, contradict

à l'inverse de [alɛ̃vɛʀs]
inversement [ɛ̃vɛʀsəmɑ̃]
et vice versa [evisvɛʀsa]
Elle aime son mari et vice versa.

in contrast to
inversely
and vice versa
She loves her husband and vice versa.

en revanche [ɑ̃ʀ(ə)vɑ̃ʃ]
Je n'aime pas Lyon, en revanche Marseille me plaît beaucoup.

on the other hand
I don't like Lyon, but on the other hand, I like Marseille a lot.

22.3 Properties

léger, -ère [leʒe, ɛʀ]	light
avoir **le sommeil léger**	sleep lightly
lourd,e [luʀ, luʀd]	heavy
Cette valise est trop lourde.	This suitcase is too heavy.

> For information on **léger/lourd,** see p. 418.

plein,e [plɛ̃, ɛn]	full
Le verre est **à moitié plein.**	The glass is half full.
complet, -ète [kɔ̃plɛ, ɛt]	complete
vide [vid]	empty
dur,e [dyʀ]	hard
mou, molle [mu, mɔl]	soft
épais,se [epɛ, ɛs]	thick, dense
un brouillard épais	a dense fog
mince [mɛ̃s]	slender, thin
étroit,e [etʀwa, wat]	narrow
une rue étroite	a narrow street

froid,e [fʀwa, fʀwad]	cold
Bois ton thé avant qu'il (ne) soit trop froid.	Drink your tea before it gets too cold.
tiède [tjɛd]	luke(warm), tepid
Il n'a pas inventé l'eau tiède. *loc*	He won't set the world on fire.
chaud,e [ʃo, ʃod]	warm; hot

visible [vizibl]	visible
invisible [ɛ̃vizibl]	invisible
"L'essentiel est invisible pour les yeux." (*St-Exupéry*).	"What is essential is invisible to the eye."
lisible [lizibl]	legible
illisible [ilizibl]	illegible

vieux, vieil, vieille [vjø, vjɛj]	old
un vieux pull; un vieil anorak; une vieille chemise	an old sweater; an old parka; an old shirt
ancien,ne [ɑ̃sjɛ̃, jɛn]	old, ancient; former
un monument ancien	an old building

> For information on *adjectives* that *change their meaning* depending on whether they *precede* or *follow* the word modified, see p. 37.

neuf, neuve [nœf, nœv]	new

nouveau, nouvel; nouvelle [nuvo, nuvɛɛl]	new; other
un nouveau film; un nouvel opéra; une nouvelle pièce	a new film; a new opera; a new play

> For information on the difference between **nouveau** and **neuf**, see p. 100.

actuel,le [aktɥɛl]	present, of the present time
moderne [mɔdɛʀn]	modern

bon,ne [bɔ̃, bɔn]	good
meilleur,e [mɛjœʀ]	better
excellent,e [ɛkselɑ̃, ɑ̃t]	excellent
médiocre [medjɔkʀ]	mediocre
mauvais,e [movɛ, ɛz]	bad
être de mauvaise humeur	be in a bad mood
normal,e [nɔʀmal]	normal
anormal,e [anɔʀmal]	abnormal
ordinaire [ɔʀdinɛʀ]	ordinary, common, usual, everyday
du **vin ordinaire**	simple table wine
rare [ʀaʀ]	rare
étrange [etʀɑ̃ʒ]	strange, funny
bizarre [bizaʀ]	bizarre, funny
Elle m'a regardé **d'un air bizarre.**	She looked at me in a funny way.
ridicule [ʀidikyl]	ridiculous
se rendre ridicule	make oneself ridiculous

facile [fasil]	easy
C'est plus facile à dire qu'à faire.	It's easier said than done.
difficile [difisil]	difficult
une langue difficile à apprendre	a difficult language to learn

> For information on the usage of *light/easy* and *heavy/difficult*, see p. 418.

nécessaire [neseseʀ]	necessary
utile [ytil]	useful
inutile [inytil]	useless
essentiel,le [esɑ̃sjɛl]	essential
aller* droit à l'essentiel	go straight to the essence of the matter

exact,e [egza(kt), egzakt]	exact, correct
Ma montre **indique l'heure exacte.**	My watch shows the correct time.
inexact,e [inegza(kt), inegzakt]	inexact, incorrect
précis,e [pʀesi, iz]	precise
imprécis,e [ɛ̃pʀesi, iz]	imprecise

vrai,e [vʀɛ]   true
  Ce n'est pas vrai.   That's not true.

> For information on *adjectives* that *change their meaning* depending on whether
> they *precede* or *follow* the word modified, see p. 38.

faux, fausse [fo, fos]   false, wrong
  L'adresse qu'on m'a donnée est   The address I was given is
  fausse.   wrong.
vague [vag]   unclear, vague
  Je n'ai qu'une vague idée sur la   I have only a vague idea of the
  question.   problem.
direct,e [diʀɛkt]   direct
indirect,e [ɛ̃diʀɛkt]   indirect

rapide [ʀapid]   rapid, fast

> **fast**
>
> *Note:*
> **vite** *(fast)* is an *adverb;* in *adjectival use,* employ the word **rapide**.
> Elle court **vite**/rapidement.   *She runs fast.*
> *But:* Ils sont **rapides**.   *They are fast.*

vif, vive [vif, viv]   lively
  avoir une intelligence vive   have a lively intelligence
lent,e [lɑ̃, lɑ̃t]   slow
  Roulez lentement !   Drive slow!

cher, chère [ʃɛʀ]   expensive, dear
bon marché [bɔ̃maʀʃe]   cheap, inexpensive
  En ce moment, les fraises sont   At the moment, strawberries are
  bon marché.   inexpensive.
  Les pommes de terre sont   Potatoes are cheaper than
  meilleur marché que les asperges.   asparagus.

> **Good, better, best**
>
> Note the irregular comparative forms of the following adjectives and adverbs:
>
> | | | |
> |---|---|---|
> | **bon,ne** *(good)* | **meilleur,e** | **le/la meilleur,e** |
> | **mauvais,e** *(bad)* | **pire** | **le/la pire** |
> | **bien** *(well)* | **mieux** | **le mieux** |
> | **peu** *(little)* | **moins** | **le moins** |
> | **beaucoup** *(much)* | **plus** | **le plus** |

clair,e [klɛʀ]   clear
  tirer au clair   clarify

obscur,e [ɔpskyʀ]	dark
une nuit obscure	a dark night
coloré,e [kɔlɔʀe]	colored
incolore [ɛ̃kɔlɔʀ]	colorless
transparent,e [tʀɑ̃spaʀɑ̃, ɑ̃t]	transparent
opaque [ɔpak]	opaque

efficace [efikas]	effective, efficacious
un remède efficace contre le mal de tête	an effective headache remedy
inefficace [inefikas]	ineffective
indispensable [ɛ̃dispɑ̃sabl]	indispensable
Ta présence est **indispensable à** mon bonheur.	Your presence is indispensable to my happiness.

22.4 Way and Manner

la **manière (de)** [manjɛʀ]	manner, way
de manière que/à	so that
De quelle manière ?	In what way?
la **façon (de)** [fasɔ̃]	way, manner, style, mode
de façon que/à	so that
De quelle façon ?	In what way?
de toute façon	at any rate

---

de manière que, etc.

After the conjunctions **de façon que, de manière que, de sorte que,** the *indicative* is used in the subordinate clause if it is a question of an *actual consequence.* If an *intention* is being expressed, the *subjunctive* is required.
Examples:

Il pleut de façon/manière/sorte qu'on ne **peut** pas sortir.	*It's raining so heavily that one can't go out.*
Exprime-toi de façon/manière/sorte qu'on te **comprenne.**	*Express yourself so that you can be understood.*
Viens de bonne heure de sorte qu'on **puisse** regarder le match à la télé.	*Come early, so that we can watch the match on TV.*
Il est venu de bonne heure de sorte qu'on **a pu** regarder le match à la télé.	*He came early so that we could watch the match on TV.*

If the *subject is the same* in the main clause and the subordinate clause, an *infinitive construction* is preferable:

Il parle lentement, **de manière à être compris.**	*He speaks slowly so that he can be understood.*
Crie fort, **de façon à être entendu/de façon qu'on t'entende.**	*Scream loudly so that you can be heard.*

une **sorte (de)** [sɔʀt]	manner, way
de **sorte que**	so that
le **mode** [mɔd]	mode, way, manner
le **mode d'emploi**	directions for use

le **moyen** [mwajɛ̃]	means, way
trouver le moyen de faire qc	find a way to do s.th.
Comment ? [kɔmɑ̃]	How?
Comment ça va ?	How are you?
ainsi [ɛ̃si]	thus, so, in this manner
Si tu t'y prends ainsi, tu n'y arriveras jamais.	If you go about it in that way, you'll never succeed.
aussi [osi]	also, too
même [mɛm]	even
J'ai même eu le temps de laver la voiture.	I even had time to wash the car.
très [tʀɛ]	very, quite
Elle est très adroite.	She's very skillful.

bien *adv* [bjɛ̃]	well
Les plantes poussent bien avec cette pluie.	Plants grow well in this rain.
vraiment [vʀɛmɑ̃]	really
Est-ce que tu as vraiment dit ça ?	Did you really say that?
seulement [sœlmɑ̃]	only
autrement [otʀəmɑ̃]	otherwise, differently
Je ne pouvais pas faire autrement.	I couldn't act any other way.

en général [ɑ̃ʒeneʀal]	in general
En général, nous prenons nos vacances en été.	In general we take our vacation in summer.
généralement [ʒeneʀalmɑ̃]	generally, usually
d'habitude [dabityd]	customarily, usually
Comme d'habitude.	As usual.
normalement [nɔʀmalmɑ̃]	normally
surtout [syʀtu]	above all, chiefly
Surtout, ne faites pas ça !	Just don't do it!

devoir [dəvwaʀ]	have to, must, be obliged to
Il doit avoir environ 40 ans.	He must be about 40.
il faut que + *subj* [ilfokə]	it is necessary that
Il faut que tu ailles voir ce film.	You absolutely have to see that film.
vouloir [vulwaʀ]	wish, want, need
pouvoir [puvwaʀ]	be able (can)

---

pouvoir/savoir

Note the difference between:

pouvoir	*be able, can (under certain circumstances)*
Vous faites trop de bruit, je ne peux pas dormir.	*You're making too much noise; I can't sleep.*
savoir	*know how to, can (through study)*
Il ne sait ni lire ni écrire.	*He can neither read nor write.*

---

vraisemblablement [vʀɛsãblabləmã]
  Nous serons vraisemblablement absents jusqu'au 15.

probably
  We'll probably be away until the 15th.

au fond [ofɔ̃]
  Au fond, elle n'est pas si méchante.

at bottom
  At bottom, she's not so mean.

en principe [ãpʀɛ̃sip]
en particulier [ãpaʀtikylje]
particulièrement [paʀtikyljɛʀmã]
exclusivement [ɛksklyzivmã]
  Elle se nourrit exclusivement de produits bio.

in principle
in particular
particularly
exclusively
  She eats exclusively organic foods.

22.5 Cause, Effect, Goal, Purpose

la **cause** [koz]
  à cause de
  C'est à cause de toi qu'on a raté le train.

cause
  because of
  It's because of you that we missed the train.

causer [koze]
  Sa santé nous cause des soucis.

cause
  His state of health causes us anxiety.

grâce à [gʀasa]
  C'est grâce à vous que j'ai eu cet emploi.

thanks to, owing to
  It's thanks to you that I got this job.

la **raison (pour laquelle)** [ʀɛzɔ̃]
  Je ne connais pas la raison pour laquelle elle n'est pas venue.
  Pour quelle raison?

the reason (why/for)
  I don't know why she didn't come.
  Why? For what reason?

le **motif** [mɔtif]
Pourquoi ? [puʀkwa]

motive, motivation
Why?

parce que [paʀs(ə)kə]

because

puisque [pɥiskə]
  On est parti sans elle puisqu'elle
  n'arrivait pas.
since, as, seeing that
  Since she didn't come, we left
  without her.

comme [kɔm]
  Comme il était déjà tard, il est
  allé se coucher.
as, since, because
  As it was already late, he went to
  bed.

car [kaʀ]
for, because

c'est pour cela/ça que
[sɛpuʀs(ə)la/sakə]
therefore, that's why

c'est pourquoi [sɛpuʀkwa]
  Elle travaille beaucoup, c'est pour
  cela qu'/ça qu'/c'est pourquoi elle
  est fatiguée.
therefore, that's why
  She works a lot; that's why she is
  tired.

alors [alɔʀ]
then

donc [dɔ̃k]
  J'avais raté le train, je ne pouvais
  donc plus arriver à l'heure.
then, therefore; consequently
  I missed the train; consequently
  I couldn't arrive on time.

pour [puʀ]
  Elle travaille dur pour nourrir sa
  famille.
in order to
  She works in order to feed her
  family.

pour que + *subj* [puʀkə]
  Je fais tout pour qu'il soit content.
so that
  I do everything to satisfy him.

---

le **but** [byt]
  poursuivre un but
  avoir pour but
  dans le but de
goal, end, aim
  pursue a goal
  have as an aim
  with the object of

atteindre [atɛ̃dʀ]
  Il a atteint tous les buts qu'il
  s'était fixés.
attain, achieve
  He has attained all the goals he
  had set for himself.

l'**objectif** *m* [ɔbʒɛktif]
  se fixer un objectif
objective, purpose, goal
  establish a goal for oneself

---

l'**effect** *m* [efɛ]
  Ce médicament ne produit aucun
  effet sur lui.
effect
  This medication has no effect on
  him.

  en effet
  in reality, in fact, indeed

le **résultat** [ʀezylta]
result

entraîner [ɑ̃tʀɛne]
entail, involve

---

le **mobile** [mɔbil]
  On ne connaît toujours pas le
  mobile du crime.
motive
  We still don't know the motive
  for the crime.

le **hasard** ['azaʀ]
  par hasard
chance
  by chance

la **fin** [fɛ̃]	end, purpose
La fin justifie les moyens. *loc*	The end justifies the means.
afin que + *subj* [afɛ̃kə]	so that
Il a parlé lentement afin que nous comprenions tout.	He spoke slowly, so that we would understand everything.
afin de + *inf* [afɛ̃də]	in order to
Prenez un taxi afin d'arriver à l'heure.	Take a taxi in order to arrive on time.
aboutir à [abutiʀ]	lead to
Les négociations ont abouti à un résultat satisfaisant.	The negotiations led to a satisfactory result.
l'**intention** *f* [ɛ̃tɑ̃sjɔ̃]	intention
avoir l'intention de faire qc	intend to do s.th.

la **conséquence** [kɔ̃sekɑ̃s]	consequence
avoir pour conséquence	result in s.th.
tirer les conséquences	draw the consequences
par conséquent [paʀkɔ̃sekɑ̃]	as a consequence
Tu as désobéi, par conséquent tu seras puni.	You disobeyed; as a consequence, you will be punished.
résulter de [ʀezylte]	result, follow from
Il ne peut rien résulter de bon de cette dispute.	Nothing good can result from this argument.
il en résulte que	the result is that

22.6 State, Motion, and Change

être [ɛtʀ]	be
l'**état** *m* [eta]	state
Quand nous avons acheté la maison, elle était en mauvais état.	When we bought the house, it was in a bad state.
une **situation** [sitɥasjɔ̃]	situation
être situé,e [ɛt(ʀə)sitɥe]	be situated
La maison est située près de la rivière.	The house is situated close to the river.
se trouver [s(ə)tʀuve]	be located
L'hôtel se trouve à 200 mètres de la gare.	The hotel is 200 meters from the railroad station.
exister [ɛgziste]	exist
Est-ce que le Père Noël existe vraiment, papa?	Does Santa Claus really exist, Papa?
l'**existence** *f* [ɛgzistɑ̃s]	existence

mettre [mɛtʀ]	put, place
Elle met des fleurs dans un vase.	She is putting flowers in a vase.
poser [poze]	lay, place
poser les assiettes sur la table	lay the plates on the table
enlever [ãl(ə)ve]	take away, remove
placer [plase]	place, put
placer un bon mot dans la conversation	insert a witty remark into the conservation
déplacer [deplase]	put in a different place
remplacer [ʀãplase]	replace
Elle a remplacé son tourne-disque par un lecteur de CD.	She has replaced her record player with a CD player.
installer [ẽstale]	install, set up
Elle installe son fauteuil face à la télé.	She is putting her armchair in front of the TV.

porter [poʀte]	carry
une valise **lourde à porter**	a suitcase that is heavy to carry
apporter [apoʀte]	bring
Apporte-moi une bière, s'il te plaît.	Bring me a beer, please.
emporter qc [ãpoʀte]	take s.th. with/along
Si tu vas en Norvège, n'oublie pas d'emporter des vêtements chauds.	If you're going to Norway, don't forget to take along warm clothes.
remporter qc [ʀãpoʀte]	take s.th. along again

> For information on **porter/mener** and their compounds, see p. 140.

conduire qn à [kɔ̃dɥiʀ]	take s.o. to; drive s.o. to
Tu pourrais me conduire à la gare?	Could you take me to the train station?
mener qn à [m(ə)ne]	accompany s.o. to
mener un enfant à l'école	take a child to school
amener qn [am(ə)ne]	bring s.o. along
J'ai amené mon bébé, j'espère que ça ne vous dérange pas.	I've brought my baby along; I hope that won't bother you.
emmener qn [ãm(ə)ne]	take s.o. along
Je suis en voiture. Veux-tu que je t'emmène ?	I've got the car. Shall I take you with me?

lever [l(ə)ve]	lift, raise
lever le doigt	lift a finger
soulever [sul(ə)ve]	lift, raise up

Je ne peux pas soulever ce sac, il est trop lourd.	I can't lift this bag; it's too heavy.
appuyer sur qc [apɥije]	press (on) s.th.
Pour mettre la machine en marche, appuie sur ce bouton.	To start the machine, press this button.

enfermer [ãfɛʀme]	lock in
cacher [kaʃe]	hide
ranger [ʀɑ̃ʒe]	straighten up; arrange
déranger [deʀɑ̃ʒe]	disarrange; put in disarray

tirer [tiʀe]	pull
Arrête de **tirer les cheveux à** ta petite sœur.	Stop pulling your little sister's hair.
pousser [puse]	push
repousser [ʀ(ə)puse]	push away; spurn
Elle n'a pas d'amis, tout le monde la repousse.	She has no friends; everyone spurns her.
tourner [tuʀne]	turn
(se) retourner [ʀ(ə)tuʀne]	turn (oneself) around
J'ai passé la nuit à **me retourner dans mon lit**.	I spent the night turning and tossing in my bed.

lancer [lɑ̃se]	throw
A toi de **lancer les dés**.	It's your turn to throw the dice.
jeter [ʒ(ə)te]	throw (away)
jeter qc à la poubelle	throw s.th. in the trashcan
lâcher [laʃe]	loosen, let go
ramasser [ʀamase]	gather; collect; pick up
Ramasse ce papier, s'il te plaît.	Pick up the paper, please.

commencer qc [kɔmɑ̃se]	start s.th.
finir qc [finiʀ]	finish s.th.

---

commencer – finir

Note the difference between:

commencer à/de fair qc	*start to do s.th.*
Qui commence à lire ?	*Who'll start to read?/Who'll read first?*
commencer par faire qc	*do s.th. first*
Elle a commencé par préparer la salade.	*She started by making the salad.*
finir de faire qc	*finish doing s.th.*
Il n'a pas encore fini de manger.	*He hasn't finished eating.*
finir par faire qc	*finish by doing s.th.*
Elle a fini par s'endormir.	*She ended up going to sleep.*

continuer à/de [kɔ̃tinye]
Nous continuons à/de travailler.
abandonner [abɑ̃dɔne]
Il a abandonné ses études.
terminer [tɛrmine]
Termine tes carottes, si tu veux
du dessert.

continue (to)
We're continuing to work.
give up
He dropped out of college.
finish
Finish your carrots if you want
some dessert.

la **position** [pozisjɔ̃]
rester [rɛste]
immobile [im(m)ɔbil]
l'**immobilité** f [imɔbilite]

position
stay, remain
immobile, motionless
immobility

changer [ʃɑ̃ʒe]
Il a beaucoup changé depuis
l'année dernière.
Elle a **changé de** coiffure.
un **changement** [ʃɑ̃ʒmɑ̃]
inchangé,e [ɛ̃ʃɑ̃ʒe]
Je l'ai trouvée inchangée, toujours
aussi jeune.
une **évolution** [evɔlysjɔ̃]
évoluer [evɔlɥe]
Les relations parents-enfants ont
beaucoup évolué.
se développer [(s(ə)dev(ə)lɔpe]
un **développement** [dev(ə)lɔpmɑ̃]
un **progrès** [prɔgrɛ]

change
He's changed a lot since last
year.
She has changed her hairdo.
change
unchanged
I found her unchanged, still just
as young.
evolution
evolve, change
Relations between parents and
children have changed greatly.
develop
development
progress

ajouter (qc à qc) [aʒute]
supprimer [syprime]
Si tu veux maigrir, il faut supprimer le chocolat.
remplir [rɑ̃plir]
remplir un formulaire
vider [vide]
Il a vidé son verre **d'un trait**.

add (s.th. to s.th.)
omit, cut out
If you want to lose weight, you
have to cut out chocolate.
fill out
fill out a form
empty
He emptied his glass in one
gulp.

boucher [buʃe]
boucher un trou
déboucher [debuʃe]
déboucher une bouteille
couvrir [kuvrir]
recouvrir [r(ə)kuvrir]
envelopper [ɑ̃v(ə)lɔpe]

stop (up), obstruct
stop a gap
open; uncork
uncork a bottle
cover
cover again; cover up
wrap up

plier [plije]	fold

casser [kase]	break, ruin
arracher [aʀaʃe]	pull out
abîmer [abime]	damage

devenir* [dəv(ə)niʀ/d(ə)vənir]	become
Elle veut devenir architecte plus tard.	She wants to become an architect later.
transformer [tʀɑ̃sfɔʀme]	change, transform
une **transformation** [tʀɑ̃sfɔʀmasjɔ̃]	change, transformation
augmenter [ɔgmɑ̃te]	increase, rise
Le prix de l'essence a encore augmenté.	The price of gasoline has risen again.
une **augmentation** [ɔgmɑ̃tasjɔ̃]	increase
diminuer [diminɥe]	decrease, drop
Le bruit diminue d'intensité.	The noise is decreasing.
une **diminution** [diminysjɔ̃]	decrease
monter* [mɔ̃te]	rise
baisser [bese]	fall
Sa vue a beaucoup baissé.	His vision has decreased greatly.

traverser [tʀavɛʀse]	cross, traverse
parcourir [paʀkuʀiʀ]	travel through
Il a parcouru toute l'Afrique.	He has traveled all over Africa.

les **circonstances** f [siʀkɔ̃stɑ̃s]	circumstances
modifier [mɔdifje]	modify, alter, change
modifier une loi	change a law
une **modification** [mɔdifikasjɔ̃]	modification, change
une **alternative** [altɛʀnativ]	alternative
varier [vaʀje]	vary
Le docteur m'a conseillé de varier mon alimentation.	The doctor advised me to vary my diet.
la **variation** [vaʀjasjɔ̃]	variation

effectuer [efɛktɥe]	effect, accomplish, carry out
effectuer un achat	effect a purchase
achever [aʃ(ə)ve]	finish, complete; achieve
Nous avons enfin achevé de payer la maison.	We have finished paying for the house at last.
s'améliorer [sameljɔʀe]	improve
faciliter [fasilite]	facilitate, make easy

Son équipement ultra-moderne lui facilite le travail.	His ultramodern equipment makes work easy for him.
s'aggraver [sagʀave]	worsen
Son état de santé s'est encore aggravé.	His state of health has worsened again.

briser [bʀize]	break
Le verre s'est brisé en tombant par terre.	The glass broke when it fell on the floor.
déchirer [deʃiʀe]	tear up
rompre [ʀɔ̃pʀ]	break; break up
Elle a rompu avec Jean.	She has broken up with Jean.
interrompre [ɛ̃teʀɔ̃pʀ]	interrupt
Ne m'interromps pas quand je parle.	Don't interrupt me when I'm talking.
une **interruption** [ɛ̃teʀypsjɔ̃]	interruption

éloigner qc de [elwaɲe]	put s.th. far or farther away from
approcher qc de [apʀɔʃe]	put s.th. closer to
Approche la chaise de la table.	Put the chair closer to the table.
rapprocher qc de [ʀapʀɔʃe]	put s.th. closer to

renverser [ʀɑ̃vɛʀse]	overturn, spill
Elle a renversé un verre de vin sur le tapis.	She spilled a glass of wine on the carpet.
secouer [s(ə)kwe]	shake
secouer la nappe	shake out the tablecloth

23.1 Speaking, Informing, Asking, Answering

parler [paʀle]
Il parle avec l'accent de Toulouse.

Je lui parlerai de tes problèmes.

la **parole** [paʀɔl]
  adresser la parole à qn
  prendre la parole

speak, talk
  He speaks with a Toulouse
  accent.
  I'll talk to him/her about your
  problems.
word
  address s.o.
  take the floor

---

s'exprimer [sɛkspʀime]
une **expression** [ɛkspʀesjɔ̃]
  une **expression familière**
une **conversation** [kɔ̃vɛʀsasjɔ̃]
  détourner la conversation
discuter de qc [diskyte]
  Je ne peux discuter de rien avec
  mes parents.
une **discussion** [diskysjɔ̃]
bavarder [bavaʀde]
bavard,e [bavaʀ, aʀd]

express oneself
expression
  a colloquial expression
conversation
  get off the subject
discuss s.th.
  I can't discuss anything with my
  parents.
discussion
talk, chat
talkative, chatty

---

dire qc à qn [diʀ]
raconter qc à qn [ʀakɔ̃te]
un **mot** [mo]
une **phrase** [fʀaz]
un **discours** [diskuʀ]
un **dialogue** [djalɔg]
prononcer [pʀɔnɔ̃se]
  On ne prononce pas le *t* à la fin
  de *mot*.
  Au début de la réception, il a
  prononcé un discours.

say s.th. to s.o.
tell s.th. to s.o.
word
sentence, phrase
talk, speech
dialogue
pronounce
  The *t* at the end of *mot* is not
  pronounced.
  At the beginning of the reception, he gave a speech.

---

appeler [ap(ə)le]
un **appel** [apɛl]
  Le Président a lancé un appel à la
  population.
la **voix** [vwa]
  à haute voix/à voix haute
  à voix basse
  Parle à voix basse, le bébé dort.

call
call, appeal
  The President issued an appeal
  to the population.
voice
  loudly and clearly
  in a low voice
  Speak in a low voice; the baby is
  sleeping.

se taire [s(ə)tɛʀ]
  Tais-toi, je voudrais écouter les
  informations.

be quiet
  Be quiet; I want to hear the
  news.

une **remarque** [ʀ(ə)maʀk]	remark
faire une remarque	make a remark
remarquer [ʀ(ə)maʀke]	remark upon; notice; observe
faire remarquer qc à qn	call s.o.'s attention to s.th.
Je te fais remarquer que tu t'es	I call your attention to the fact
encore trompé.	that you were mistaken again.
à propos de [apʀɔpodə]	with respect to, in connection with

répéter [ʀepete]	repeat
redire [ʀ(ə)diʀ]	repeat, say again
Je le lui ai dit et redit, mais il ne	I've told it to him again and again,
me croit toujours pas.	but he still doesn't believe me.
insister sur qc [ɛ̃siste]	insist on s.th.
rappeler qc à qn [ʀap(ə)le]	remind s.o. of s.th.
rappeler à qn de faire qc	remind s.o. to do s.th.
[ʀap(ə)le]	

> For information on **rappeler** and the various words used with it, see p. 64.

ajouter [aʒute]	add
Je dois ajouter que j'ai toujours été	I must add that I was always
content de son travail.	satisfied with his work.

déclarer [deklaʀe]	declare
déclarer qc sur l'honneur	declare s.th. on one's word of honor
une **déclaration** [deklaʀasjɔ̃]	declaration, statement
affirmer [afiʀme]	affirm, assert, declare, claim
J'affirme que je n'ai jamais vu cet	I maintain that I have never
homme.	seen that man.
Il affirme avoir tout payé.	He claims to have paid for everything.
une **affirmation** [afiʀmasjɔ̃]	affirmation, claim
nier [nje]	deny
Elle nie m'avoir vu.	She denies having seen me.

présenter (ses idées) [pʀezɑ̃te]	present (one's ideas)
défendre (ses opinions) [defɑ̃dʀ]	defend (one's opinions)
influencer [ɛ̃flyɑ̃se]	influence
L'avocat cherche à influencer le jury.	The lawyer is trying to influence the jury.
persuader [pɛʀsɥade]	persuade
Tu n'as pas réussi à nous persuader	You haven't succeeded in persuad-
de tes bonnes intentions.	ing us of your good intentions.
assurer [asyʀe]	assure

Je vous assure que je n'y suis pour rien.

I assure you that I can't help it.

démontrer [demɔ̃tʀe]
Je peux vous démontrer que j'ai raison.
une **démonstration** [demɔ̃stʀasjɔ̃]
L'avocat de la défense a **fait la démonstration de** l'innocence de l'accusé.
prétendre [pʀetɑ̃dʀ]
Il prétend que sa famille est très riche.
Elle prétend bien connaître le Président de la République.

demonstrate, prove
I can prove to you that I'm right.
demonstration, proof
The defense attorney has proved the innocence of the accused.

claim, pretend; intend; maintain
He claims that his family is very rich.
She pretends to know the President of the Republic well.

promettre [pʀɔmɛtʀ]
Il m'a promis monts et merveilles.
loc
Je lui ai promis de revenir l'année prochaine.
une **promesse** [pʀɔmɛs]
tenir ses promesses

promise
He promised me the earth.

I've promised her to come back next year.
promise
keep one's promises

informer qn de qc [ɛ̃fɔʀme]
Je vous informerai de ma décision, **le moment venu.**
une **information** [ɛ̃fɔʀmasjɔ̃]
renseigner qn (sur qc) [ʀɑ̃seɲe]
Il nous a renseignés sur les horaires des trains.
se renseigner (sur)
un **renseignement** [ʀɑ̃seɲmɑ̃]
donner des renseignements à qn
expliquer [ɛksplike]
une **explication** [ɛksplikasjɔ̃]

inform s.o. of s.th.
I will inform you of my decision when the time comes.
information
give s.o. information (about s.th.)
He gave us information about the train schedule.
inform oneself (about)
information
give information to s.o.
explain
explanation

préciser [pʀesize]
décrire [dekʀiʀ]
Je lui ai décrit le chemin avec précision, il ne peut pas se perdre.
une **description** [dɛskʀipsjɔ̃]

state precisely, specify
describe
I described the way to him precisely; he can't get lost.
description

demander qc à qn [d(ə)mãde]   ask s.o. s.th.; ask s.o. for s.th.

 For information on **demander** and the words used with it, see p. 66.

une **question** [kɛstjɔ̃]	question
poser une question	ask a question

répondre à [Repɔ̃dR]   answer
Il m'a répondu sèchement.   He answered me gruffly.
Elle n'a pas répondu à ma   She hasn't answered my
question.   question.
une **réponse** [Repɔ̃s]   answer, response
donner une réponse à qn   give a response to s.o.

un **entretien** [ãtRətjɛ̃]   conversation
avoir un entretien avec qn **au sujet**   have a conversation with s.o. on
de qc   the subject of s.th.
s'entretenir avec [sãtRət(ə)niR]   converse with
un,e **interlocuteur, -trice**   interlocutor, partner in
[ɛ̃tɛRlɔkytœR, tRis]   conversation
un **échange de vues** [eʃãʒdəvy]   exchange of views

convaincre [kɔ̃vɛ̃kR]   convince
une **conviction** [kɔ̃viksjɔ̃]   conviction
Il a parlé avec conviction.   He spoke with conviction.
convaincant,e [kɔ̃vɛ̃kã, ãt]   convincing

exagérer [ɛgzaʒeRe]   exaggerate
une **exagération** [ɛgzaʒeRasjɔ̃]   exaggeration
se vanter de qc [s(ə)vãte]   boast of s.th.
Il se vante de pouvoir soulever   He boasts that he can lift 100
100 kilos.   kilos.
(un,e) **vantard,e** n; adj [vãtaR, aRd]   boaster; boastful
un **prétexte** [pRetɛkst]   pretext
sous prétexte de   under the pretext of

proclamer [pRɔklame]   proclaim
C'est un scandale, je le proclame   It's a scandal; I tell you that loud
haut et fort.   and clear.
chuchoter [ʃyʃɔte]   whisper
Elle lui a chuchoté quelque chose à   She whispered something in his
l'oreille.   ear.

avertir [avɛʀtiʀ]	inform; warn
Je l'ai averti qu'il allait avoir des ennuis.	I warned him that he would have a hard time of it.
un **avertissement** [avɛʀtismã]	warning
donner un avertissement à qn	give a warning to s.o.

signaler qc à qn [siɲale]	point out s.th. to s.o.
Je te signale que tu as pris la mauvaise route.	I'm pointing out to you that you've taken the wrong road.
indiquer [ɛ̃dike]	indicate, show
Pourriez-vous m'indiquer le chemin de la poste ?	Could you show me the way to the post office?
évoquer [evɔke]	mention
Il n'évoque jamais les années qu'il a passées à l'étranger.	He never mentions the years he spent abroad.
interroger [ɛ̃teʀɔʒe]	interrogate, question
La police l'a interrogé pendant trois heures.	The police interrogated him for three hours.
une **interrogation** [ɛ̃teʀɔgasjɔ̃]	question
un **interrogatoire** [ɛ̃teʀɔgatwaʀ]	interrogation
subir un interrogatoire	be interrogated
soumettre qn à un interrogatoire	interrogate s.o.

23.2 Excusing, Regretting, Consoling

demander pardon à qn [d(ə)mãdepaʀdɔ̃]	beg s.o.'s pardon
Pardon ! [paʀdɔ̃]	Pardon me! Sorry!
pardonner qc à qn/à qn d'avoir fait qc [paʀdɔne]	pardon s.o. for s.th./for having done s.th.
Elle ne lui a jamais pardonné de l'avoir quittée.	She has never forgiven him for having left her.
s'excuser [sɛkskyze]	excuse oneself, apologize
Je me suis excusé auprès d'elle.	I apologized to her.
Excuse(z)-moi !	Excuse me!
Tu m'en veux ? [tymãvø]	Are you mad at me?
C'est (de) ma faute. [sɛ(d(ə))mafot]	It's my fault.

regretter [ʀ(ə)gʀete]	regret

Je regrette d'avoir été méchant avec toi.	I regret having been mean to you.
Tous mes regrets. [tumeʀ(ə)gʀɛ]	I'm very sorry.
(Je suis) Désolé, e ! [dezɔle]	(I'm) Sorry!

(C'est) Dommage ! [dɔmaʒ]	(That's a) Pity! (That's) Too bad!
Tu ne peux pas venir samedi ?	Can't you come on Saturday?
Dommage !	That's too bad!
Tant pis ! [tãpi]	So much the worse! Never mind!
Je regrette, il ne reste plus de gâteau pour toi. – Tant pis.	I'm sorry, there's no cake left for you. Never mind.
Tant pis pour lui, il n'avait qu'à faire attention !	So much the worse for him; he should have paid attention.
Tant mieux ! [tãmjø]	So much the better!
malheureusement [maløʀøzmã]	unfortunately
Hélas ! [elas]	Alas!
Nous espérions qu'il guérirait, mais hélas, il est mort.	We hoped he would recover, but alas, he died.

Ne t'en fais pas. [n(ə)tãfɛpa]	Don't worry about it.
Ne t'en fais pas pour moi, ça ira très bien.	Don't worry about me; it will go just fine.
Il n'y a pas de mal. [ilnjapadmal]	There's no harm in it./It doesn't matter.

consoler qn [kɔ̃sɔle]	console s.o.
Mon/Ma pauvre. [mɔ̃/mapovʀ]	You poor thing.
Tu es resté à l'hôpital tout l'été ? Mon pauvre.	You spent all summer in the hospital? Poor thing.
rassurer qn [ʀasyʀe]	reassure s.o.
Tes parents sont inquiets ? Téléphone-leur pour les rassurer.	Your parents are worried? Call them to reassure them.
Ça ne fait rien. [san(ə)fɛʀjẽ]	That doesn't matter.
Ce n'est pas grave. [s(ə)nɛpagʀav]	It's not serious.
Ce n'est rien. [s(ə)nɛʀjẽ]	It's nothing.
Ça va passer. [savapase]	That will pass.
Ça peut arriver à tout le monde. [sapøaʀiveatulmɔ̃d]	That can happen to anybody.

avoir honte [avwaʀˈɔ̃t]	be ashamed
J'ai honte de m'être comporté si bêtement.	I'm ashamed of having acted so stupidly.
être gêné,e [ɛt(ʀə)ʒɛne]	be embarrassed
Il est tellement grossier que **j'en suis gêné pour lui.**	He is so boorish that I'm really embarrassed for him.

23.3 Allowing, Forbidding, Suggesting, Advising

permettre qc à qn/à qn de faire qc [pɛʀmɛtʀ]
permit/allow s.o. s.th./s.o. to do s.th.

Je lui ai permis d'aller au cinéma.
I allowed him to go to the movies.

la **permission** [pɛʀmisjɔ̃]
permission

demander la permission de faire qc
ask permission to do s.th.

donner à qn la permission de faire qc
give s.o. permission to do s.th.

autoriser qc/qn à faire qc [ɔtɔʀize]
authorize s.th./s.o. to do s.th.

l'**autorisation** f [ɔtɔʀizasjɔ̃]
authorization

accorder à qn l'autorisation de faire qc
grant s.o. authorization to do s.th.

s'il te/vous plaît [siltə/vuplɛ]
please

---

empêcher qn de faire qc [ãpɛʃe]
prevent s.o. from doing s.th.

interdire qc à qn/à qn de faire qc [ɛ̃tɛʀdiʀ]
forbid s.o. s.th./s.o. to do s.th.

Elle a interdit à ses enfants de regarder des films d'horreur.
She has forbidden her children to watch horror films.

une **interdiction** [ɛ̃tɛʀdiksjɔ̃]
prohibition, ban

Interdiction de fumer.
No smoking.

défendre qc à qn/à qn de faire qc [defãdʀ]
forbid s.o. s.th./s.o. to do s.th.

Je te défends de me parler sur ce ton.
I forbid you to speak to me in that tone.

défense de ... [defãs]
... prohibited

Défense d'entrer.
No entry.

---

proposer (à qn) de faire qc [pʀɔpoze]
propose/suggest (to s.o.) doing s.th.

Je lui ai proposé d'aller au théâtre.
I suggested to him/her that we go to the movies.

une **proposition** [pʀɔpozisjɔ̃]
proposal, proposition, suggestion

rejeter une proposition
reject a proposal

conseiller qc à qn/à qn de faire qc [kɔ̃seje]
recommend s.th. to s.o./advise s.o. to do s.th.

Le docteur m'a conseillé un séjour à la montagne.
The doctor recommended a stay in the mountains to me.

Je vous conseille de passer par Nancy.
I advise you to drive through Nancy.

un **conseil** [kɔ̃sɛj]
advice

il n'y a qu'à faire qc fam [ilnijaka]
all you need to do is ...

il suffit de faire qc [ilsyfi]
J'attends votre réponse, il suffit de me passer un coup de fil.

it suffices to do s.th.
I am waiting for your reply; calling me on the phone is sufficient.

il faut/faudrait que + *subj* [ilfo/fodʀɛkə]
Il faudrait que vous vous reposiez.

one must/ought to/should

You ought to rest.

il vaut/vaudrait mieux que + *subj* [ilvo/vodʀɛmjøkə]
Il vaut mieux que nous partions tout de suite.

it is/would be better if/that

It's better that we leave right away.

prier qn de faire qc [pʀije]
Je vous prie de vous taire et de m'écouter.

ask s.o. to do s.th.
Please be quiet and listen to me.

obliger qn à faire qc [ɔbliʒe]
forcer qn à faire qc [fɔʀse]
Tu ne peux pas la forcer à aimer Frédéric.

oblige s.o. to do s.th.
force s.o. to do s.th.
You can't force her to love Frédéric.

recommander qc à qn/à qn de faire qc [ʀ(ə)kɔmɑ̃de]
Je lui ai recommandé de réserver une chambre d'hôtel.
une **recommandation** [ʀ(ə)kɔmɑ̃dasjɔ̃]

recommend s.th. to s.o./that s.o. do s.th.
I recommended that he reserve a hotel room.
recommendation

donner un ordre [dɔneɛ̃nɔʀdʀ]
donner à qn l'ordre de faire qc
ordonner à qn de faire qc [ɔʀdɔne]
déconseiller à qn de faire qc [dekɔ̃sɛje]
Je te déconseille de prendre la route le 1ᵉʳ août.

give an order
give s.o. an order to do s.th.
order s.o. to do s.th.
advise s.o. against doing/not to do s.th.
I advise you not to leave town on August 1ˢᵗ.

23.4 Pain, Anger, Aggression

avoir mal (à) [avwaʀmal]
J'ai mal à la tête.
Ça fait mal.
Je me suis fait mal.
Aïe ! [aj]

have pain (in)
I have a headache.
That hurts.
I've hurt myself.
Ow! Ouch!

en avoir assez [ɑ̃navwaʀase]
J'en ai assez de l'attendre.

have enough of s.th.
I'm tired of waiting for him/her.

Ça suffit ! [sasyfi]	That's enough!
Arrête ! [aʀɛt]	Stop!

Zut ! *fam* [zyt]	Darn! Heck!
Zut, alors ! Je ne trouve plus mon portefeuille.	Well; darn it! I can't find my wallet.
Mince ! *fam* [mɛ̃s]	Golly! Gosh!
Mince, alors !	Well, gosh darn it all!
Merde ! *pop* [mɛʀd]	Damn it! Shit!
Quel,le ... ! [kɛl]	What a(n) ... !
Quel idiot, celui-là !	What an idiot that guy is!

énerver qn [enɛʀve]	get on s.o.'s nerves
Arrête de chanter cette chanson stupide, tu m'énerves.	Stop singing that stupid song; you're getting on my nerves.
embêter qn [ãbɛte]	bore s.o., annoy s.o.

se disputer [s(ə)dispyte]	argue, quarrel
Mes enfants n'arrêtent pas de se disputer.	My children never stop quarreling.
une **dispute** [dispyt]	argument, quarrel
crier [kʀije]	shout, yell
crier après qn	shout at s.o.
un **cri** [kʀi]	shout, yell
pousser un cri de douleur	emit a cry of pain

menacer [mənase]	threaten
une **menace** [mənas]	threat
mettre ses menaces à exécution	carry out one's threats
agressif, -ive [agʀesif, iv]	aggressive
l'**agressivité** *f* [agʀesivite]	aggressiveness
attaquer [atake]	attack, to
une **attaque** [atak]	attack
une **attaque verbale**	verbal attack

uen **plainte** [plɛ̃t]	complaint
se plaindre de qn/qc [s(ə)plɛ̃dʀ]	complain about/of s.o./s.th.
Ma fille se plaint de maux de ventre.	My daughter complains of a stomachache.
Ça brûle. [sabʀyl]	It burns.
Ça pique. [sapik]	It burns/scratches/stings.

gronder [gʀɔ̃de]	scold, reprimand
Il a peur de se faire gronder par ses parents.	He's afraid of being scolded by his parents.

gueuler *fam* [gœle] — bawl (insults)
engueuler qn *fam* [ãgœele] — swear at s.o.
  Pierre et Juliette ont passéé la soirée à s'engueuler. — Pierre and Juliette spent the evening swearing at each other.
une **engueulade** *fam* [ãgœelad] — bawling out, giving hell

contredire qn [kɔ̃tRədiR] — contradict s.o.
  Chaque fois qu'il ouvre la bouche, vous le contredisez. — Every time he opens his mouth, you contradict him.
une **contradiction** [kɔ̃tRadiksjɔ̃] — contradiction
avoir l'esprit de contradiction — like to contradict
un **malentendu** [malãtãdy] — misunderstanding
provoquer [pRɔvoke] — provoke
  Tu dis ça pour me provoquer, ou quoi ? — Are you saying that to provoke me?
une **provocation** [pRɔvokasjɔ̃] — provocation
interrompre [ɛ̃teRɔ̃pR] — interrupt
  Il m'a interrompu au beau milieu de ma phrase. — He interrupted me right in the middle of my sentence.
couper la parole à qn [kupelapaRɔl] — interrupt s.o., cut s.o. off
  Je voudrais vous expliquer mon point de vue sans que vous me coupiez la parole. — I'd like to explain my point of view to you without you interrupting me.

C'est un scandale ! [sɛ(t)ɛ̃skãdal] — It's a scandal!
C'est scandaleux ! [sɛskãdalø] — It's scandalous!
C'est inadmissible ! [sɛ(t)inadmisibl] — It's unacceptable!
en avoir marre *fam* [ãnavwaRmaR] — have enough of it
  J'en ai marre. — I've had enough of it.
en avoir ras le bol *fam* [ãnavwaRRalbɔl] — be fed up with it, be sick of it
Tu me casses les pieds. *fam* [tym(ə)kaslepje] — You're driving me up the wall.
Tu es vache. *fam* [tyɛvaʃ] — You're mean.
  Tu es vache avec lui, quand-même. — You're really mean to him.

jurer [ʒyRe] — curse, to
un **juron** [ʒyRɔ̃] — curse
une **injure** [ɛ̃ʒyR] — insult
injurier [ɛ̃ʒyRje] — insult, call names
  Il l'a injuriée devant tout le monde. — He called her names in front of everyone.

grossier, -ière [gRosje, jɛR] — crude, rude, unmannerly
  C'est un gamin grossier et mal élevé. — He's a rude and ill-bred boy.

un **gros mot** [gromo] — curse word, swear word
Je me demande où mon fils a appris tous ces gros mots. — I ask myself where my son learned all these curse words.
une **insulte** [ɛ̃sylt] — insult
insulter [ɛ̃sylte] — insult, to
Tu ne vas pas te laisser insulter par ce sale type, non ? — You're not going to let that awful creep insult you, are you?
Menteur ! Menteuse ! [mɑ̃tœr, øz] — Liar!
Espèce de ... ! [ɛspɛsdə] — What a(n) ... !
Espèce d'idiot ! — What an idiot!
(un,e) **imbécile** n; adj [ɛ̃besil] — imbecile; imbecilic
(un,e) **con,ne** n; adj, pop [kɔ̃, kɔn] — fool, idiot; foolish, idiotic
une **connerie** pop [kɔnri] — nonsense, garbage
Arrête de dire des conneries. — Stop dishing out such garbage.
un,e **abruti,e** fam [abryti] — stupid person, dummy
Regarde cet abruti qui double dans le virage. — Look at that dummy who's passing in the curve.
(un,e) **débile** n; adj, fam [debil] — feeble-minded (person)
Tu es débile, ou quoi ? — Are you feeble-minded, or what?
Salaud ! Salope ! fam [salo, salɔp] — Scoundrel! Louse!
Salopard ! fam [salɔpar] — Swine!

C'est ridicule. [sɛridikyl] — That's ridiculous.
C'est du vol ! [sɛdyvɔl] — That's highway robbery!
C'est une honte ! [sɛ(t)ynə'ɔ̃t] — That's a disgrace!
C'est insupportable. [sɛ(t)ɛ̃sypɔrtabl] — That's intolerable.
C'est dégoûtant ! [sɛdegutɑ̃] — That's disgusting!
C'est dégueulasse ! pop [sɛdegœlas] — That's horrible/nasty/disgusting!
Arrête de roter, c'est dégueulasse ! — Stop belching; it's disgusting!
C'est le comble ! [sɛl(ə)kɔ̃bl] — That's the limit!
Quelle horreur ! [kɛlɔrœr] — How horrible!

La ferme ! fam [lafɛrm] — Shut up!
La ferme ! Tu as assez dit de bêtises comme ça. — Shut up! You've already said enough stupid things.
Ta gueule ! fam [tagœl] — Shut your trap!
Toi, ta gueule ! On (ne) t'a rien demandé. — You, shut your trap! Nobody asked your opinion.
Fiche le camp !/Fous le camp ! fam [fiʃləkɑ̃/ful(ə)kɑ̃] — Get lost!/Get out of here!
Dégage ! fam [degaʒ] — Get lost!

Fiche-moi/Fous-moi la paix !   Leave me alone!
fam [fiʃmwa/fumwalapɛ]

23.5 Agreeing, Confirming, Qualifying, Refusing

donner son accord [dɔnesɔ̃nakɔʀ]	give one's agreement
accepter [aksɛpte]	accept
J'accepte tes excuses.	I accept your apology.
Il a accepté de m'aider.	He agreed to help me.
Oui. ['wi]	Yes.
Bien sûr ! [bjɛ̃syʀ]	Of course!
Entendu. [ɑ̃tɑ̃dy]	All right. Of course.
Entendu, je passerai te chercher à 8 heures.	All right, I'll come by for you at 8 o'clock.
Bien entendu.	Of course./Naturally.
D'accord. [dakɔʀ]	Agreed.

Naturellement. [natyʀɛlmɑ̃]	Naturally.
Absolument. [absɔlymɑ̃]	Absolutely.
Vous êtes d'accord avec elle ? – Absolument.	Do you agree with her? Absolutely.
Parfaitement. [paʀfɛtmɑ̃]	Exactly./Just so./Decidedly.
Exactement. [ɛgzaktəmɑ̃]	Exactly.

Volontiers. [vɔlɔ̃tje]	Gladly./With pleasure.
Vous buvez quelque chose ? – Volontiers, j'ai très soif.	Will you have something to drink? With pleasure; I'm very thirsty.
Pourquoi pas ? [puʀkwapa]	Why not?
Si tu veux. [sityvø]	If you wish.

Bof ! [bɔf]	Well!
Il était comment, ce film ? – Bof ! Pas très bon, je suis déçu.	How was that film? Well, not very good. I'm disappointed.
Peut-être. [pøtɛtʀ]	Perhaps.
On verra. [ɔ̃vɛʀa]	We'll see.

être contre [ɛt(ʀə)kɔ̃tʀ]	be against
Cette idée est mauvaise. Je suis absolument contre.	That idea is bad. I'm absolutely against it.
s'opposer à qc [sɔpoze]	be opposed to s.th.
Il s'est opposé à ma candidature.	He opposed my candidacy.

Non. [nɔ̃] No.
Pas du tout. [padytu] Not at all.
Pas question. [pakɛstjɔ̃] Out of the question.
  Pas question que je te prête ma Lending you my car is out of the
  voiture. question.
Rien à faire. [ʀjɛ̃nafɛʀ] It's no use.
Jamais de la vie. [ʒamɛdlavi] Never in this world.
Ça (ne) va pas, non ? *fam* Are you in your right mind?
[sa(n)vapanɔ̃]
  Mais qu'est-ce que vous faites What are you doing in my
  dans mon jardin ? Ça (ne) va pas, garden? Are you in your right
  non ? mind?
Et puis quoi, encore ? Anything else?/Is that all?
[epɥikwaɑ̃kɔʀ]
  Tu voudrais que nous te donnions You want us to give you 1000
  1000 euros. Et puis quoi, encore ? euros. Is that all?

---

bien *adv* [bjɛ̃] fine
  Bien, pusique c'est comme ça, je Fine; if that's how it is, I'm
  m'en vais. leaving.
sûrement [syʀmɑ̃] surely
certainement [sɛʀtɛnmɑ̃] certainly
évidemment [evidamɑ̃] evidently, obviously; of course
  J'ai attendu, mais évidemment, il I waited, but he didn't come, of
  n'est pas venu. course.
sans doute [sɑ̃dut] doubtless, no doubt

> ### ℹ Beyond all doubt?
>
> *Note the difference between:*
> sans doute *doubtless, no doubt*
> Elle a sans doute raison. *Doubtless she's right.*
> Elle prendra sans doute le train de *No doubt she'll take the 3 P.M. train.*
> 15 heures.
> sans aucun doute *without any doubt, quite definitely*
> Tu es sûr que c'était Jean ? – Sans *Are you sure it was Jean? Without any*
> aucun doute. *doubt.*

---

tout à fait [tutafɛ] quite, entirely
complètement [kɔ̃plɛtmɑ̃] completely
  Il a complètement raté son examen. He completely failed his exam.
en tout cas [ɑ̃tuka] in any case

---

par exemple (p. ex.) [paʀɛgzɑ̃pl] for example (e.g.)
en effet [ɑ̃nefɛ] in reality; indeed; in fact
  Il ne pourra pas venir dimanche. En He can't come on Sunday; in
  effet, il est gravement malade. fact, he's seriously ill.

Vous avez vu ce match ? – Je l'ai vu, en effet.

Did you see that match? I saw it indeed.

vraiment [vʀɛmã]
really

en fait [ãfɛt]
in fact, actually

En fait, c'est tout simple, une fois qu'on a compris.

Actually it's quite easy, once you've understood it.

C'est un fait que ... [sɛ(t)ɛ̃fɛkə]
It is a fact that ...

---

ainsi [ɛ̃si]
so, thus, in this way

Venez tôt, ainsi vous pourrez déjeuner avec nous.

Come early; that way you can have lunch with us.

de toute manière [dətutmanjɛʀ]
either way

De toute manière, quoique tu fasses, elle sera vexée.

Either way, whatever you do, she'll be cross.

de toute façon [dətutfasɔ̃]
at any rate, anyway

---

d'ailleurs [dajœʀ]
besides, moreover

Tu n'as qu'à le lui demander toi-même; d'ailleurs il sera là demain.

You can ask him yourself; besides, he'll be there tomorrow.

après tout [apʀɛtu]
after all

Tu pourrais lui écrire; après tout, c'est ta mère.

You could write to her; after all, she's your mother.

finalement [finalmã]
finally, in the end

enfin [ãfɛ̃]
at last, after all

Ce n'est pas très agréable, mais, enfin, on s'y habitue.

It's not very pleasant, but you finally get used to it.

en réalité [ãʀealite]
in reality

autrement dit [otʀəmãdi]
in other words

Elle ne me regarde plus, elle me parle à peine ... autrement dit, elle ne m'aime plus.

She doesn't look at me anymore; she barely talks to me ... in other words, she no longer loves me.

bref [bʀɛf]
in short, in brief

Et après tous ces ennuis, on nous a aussi volé notre voiture. Bref, des vacances affreuses.

And after all that unpleasant-ness, our car was stolen too. In short, a horrible vacation.

---

seulement [sœlmã]
only

uniquement [ynikmã]
solely

Elle est venue de Londres unique-ment pour te voir.

She came from London solely to see you.

simplement [sɛ̃pləmã]
simply

Je voudrais simplement dire que je ne suis pas d'accord.

I'd simply like to say that I don't agree.

au moins [omwɛ̃]	at least
du moins [dymwɛ̃]	at least
Du moins, c'est mon avis.	At least, that's my opinion.
plus ou moins [plyzumwɛ̃]	more or less

tout de même [tudmɛm]	all the same
Tu aurais tout de même pu te raser.	You could have shaved all the same.
quand même [kɑ̃mɛm]	nevertheless, all the same
plutôt [plyto]	rather, sooner, instead
Cette jupe ne te va pas, prends plutôt l'autre.	That skirt doesn't suit you; take the other one instead.

approuver [apʀuve]	approve (of)
J'approuve entièrement la décision de Claire.	I entirely approve of Claire's decision.
une **approbation** [apʀɔbasjɔ̃]	approval
effectivement [efɛktivmɑ̃]	actually
D'accord, nous partirons ce soir. C'est effectivement la meilleure solution.	All right, we'll leave this evening. That's actually the best solution.
éventuellement [evɑ̃tɥɛlmɑ̃]	possibly; on occasion
le cas échéant [ləkazeʃeɑ̃]	in that case, if necessary
Le cas échéant, on pourrait s'arrêter à Orléans pour dîner.	In that case we could stop in Orléans for dinner.

refuser qc à qn/de faire qc [ʀ(ə)fyze]	refuse s.o. s.th./to do s.th.
Je refuse d'écouter ces bêtises.	I refuse to listen to this nonsense.
un **refus** [ʀ(ə)fy]	refusal
à aucun prix [aokœ̃pʀi]	under no circumstances
Je ne lui en parlerai à aucun prix.	Under no circumstances will I tell him about it.
à tout prix [atupʀi]	at all costs
Viens vite, il faut que je te parle à tout prix.	Come quickly; I have to speak to you at all costs.

à coup sûr [akusyʀ]	most definitely
Si on va à cette fête, on va s'ennuyer à coup sûr.	If we go to that party, we'll most definitely be bored.
précisément [pʀesizemɑ̃]	precisely, exactly

Mais c'est précisément ce que j'essaie de dire depuis une heure.	But that's precisely what I've been trying to tell you for an hour.
sans faute [sɑ̃fot]	without fail
Alors, à jeudi, sans faute !	Well, until Thursday, without fail!

totalement [tɔtalmɑ̃]	totally
décidément [desidemɑ̃]	definitely, positively
Toi, décidément, on ne te changera jamais !	Definitely, nobody will ever change you!
en somme [ɑ̃sɔm]	in short; on the whole
pur et simple [pyʀesɛ̃pl]	pure and simple, clearly
C'est une escroquerie pure et simple.	That's crooked behavior, pure and simple.
nettement [nɛtmɑ̃]	clearly
Elle est nettement plus âgée que lui.	She's clearly older than he.

également [egalmɑ̃]	equally; also, too
J'aime la musique classique, mais également le reggae.	I like classical music, but I like reggae too.
habituellement [abitɥɛlmɑ̃]	habitually, as a rule
Habituellement, nous faisons une promenade après le déjeuner.	As a rule we take a walk after lunch.
d'ordinaire [dɔʀdinɛʀ]	ordinarily, usually
obligatoirement [ɔbligatwaʀmɑ̃]	compulsorily
forcément [fɔʀsemɑ̃]	necessarily, inevitably; well, of course
Tu connais Paul ? – Forcément, c'est mon oncle.	Do you know Paul? Well, of course; he's my uncle.

à la rigueur [alaʀigœʀ]	if absolutely necessary
Ce n'est pas idéal, mais ça peut aller à la rigueur.	It's not ideal, but it can work if absolutely necessary.
sous (toute) réserve [su(tut)ʀezɛʀv]	with reservation
faute de mieux [fotdəmjø]	for want of something better
Faute de mieux, allons au musée, ça nous fera passer le temps.	For want of something better, let's go to the museum; that will help us pass the time.
sans plus [sɑ̃plys]	nothing more, but that's all
Ils ont été polis, sans plus.	They were polite, nothing more.

au fond [ofɔ̃]	at bottom, in the main
Au fond, cette idée n'est pas si bête.	At bottom, this idea is not so bad.
tout compte fait [tukɔ̃tfɛ]	all in all
en fin de compte [ɑ̃fɛ̃dkɔ̃t]	to sum up, finally

pour ainsi dire [puRɛ̃sidiR]
Il n'a pour ainsi dire rien mangé.

étant donné que [etɑ̃dɔnekə]
Etant donné qu'ils ne s'entendaient plus, il valait mieux qu'ils se séparent.

so to speak, as it were
He ate nothing, so to speak.
in view of the fact that
In view of the fact that they weren't getting along anymore, it was better that they separate.

---

malgré tout [malgRetu]
Nous nous voyons rarement, mais nous sommes malgré tout restés bons amis.

d'autant plus que ...
[dotɑ̃ply(s)kə]
Il lui faudrait un appartement plus grand, d'autant plus qu'elle attend un bébé.

d'un côté ... de l'autre
[dɛ̃kotedəlotR]
D'un côté ça m'embête de passer Noël chez ma belle-mère, mais de l'autre, ça lui fera tellement plaisir.

d'une part ... d'autre part
[dynpaRdotRəpaR]

in spite of everything
We see each other rarely, but in spite of everything we've stayed good friends.
all the more as ...

She ought to have a bigger apartment, all the more as she's expecting a baby.
on the one hand ... on the other hand
On the one hand it bores me to spend Christmas at my mother-in-law's, but on the other it will really make her happy.
on the one hand ... on the other hand

23.6 Praising and Thanking, Criticizing

féliciter qn de/pour qc [felisite]
Je vous félicite de votre courage.

Félicitations ! [felisitasjɔ̃]
un **compliment** [kɔ̃plimɑ̃]
Tout le monde lui fait **des compliments sur** sa nouvelle coiffure.

congratulate s.o. on s.th.
I congratulate you on your courage.
Congratulations!
compliment
Everyone compliments her on her new hairdo.

---

remercier qn de qc [R(ə)mɛRsje]
Je vous remercie de m'avoir aidé.

Merci. [mɛRsi]
le **remerciement** [R(ə)mɛRsimɑ̃]

thank s.o. for s.th.
I thank you for having helped me.
Thanks.
thanks

Bravo ! [bʀavo] — Bravo!
Bien ! [bjɛ̃] — Good!
Super ! [sypɛʀ] — Super!
Génial ! [ʒenjal] — Brilliant!
Ça y est ! [sajɛ] — That's it!/Way to go!
Voilà ! [vwala] — There!/There you have it!
  Voilà ! Tu as presque fini. — There! You're almost done.
Pas mal. [pamal] — Not bad.
Pas terrible. [patɛʀibl] — Not so terrific.
Nul./Nulle. [nyl] — Miserable./Wretched.
  Ne lis pas ce livre, il est absolument nul. — Don't read that book; it's absolutely wretched.

critiquer [kʀitike] — criticize
dire du bien/du mal de qn/qc [diʀdybjɛ̃/dymal] — say good/bad things about s.o./s.th.
  On m'a dit beaucoup de bien de ce restaurant. — I've heard a lot of good things about this restaurant.
conner raison/tort à qn [dɔneʀɛzɔ̃/tɔʀ] — side with/against s.o.

reprocher qc à qn/à qn d'avoir fait qc [ʀ(ə)pʀɔʃe] — reproach s.o. for s.th./s.o. for having done s.th.
  Je lui reproche de ne pas m'avoir dit la vérité. — I reproach him for never having told me the truth.
un **reproche** [ʀ(ə)pʀɔʃ] — reproach
  faire des reproches à qn **sur qc** — reproach s.o. because of s.th.
condamner [kɔ̃dane] — condemn

louer qn pour qc [lwe] — praise s.o. for s.th.
une **louange** [lwɑ̃ʒ] — eulogy, commendation, praise
  chanter les louanges de qn/qc — sing s.o.'s/s.th.'s praises
la **reconnaissance** [ʀ(ə)kɔnɛsɑ̃s] — gratitude, thankfulness
  manifester sa reconnaissance envers qn — show one's gratitude toward s.o.
(être) reconnaissant,e (à qn de qc) [ʀ(ə)kɔnɛsɑ̃, ɑ̃t] — (be) grateful (to s.o. for s.th.)
  Elle n'a rien dit, et je lui en suis très reconnaissant. — She said nothing, and I'm very grateful to her for that.

blâmer qn de/pour qc [blame] — blame/criticize s.o. for s.th.
un **blâme** [blam] — blame, reproach, reprimand

23.7 Taking a Position and Evaluating

une **opinion** [ɔpinjɔ̃]
opinion
   partager l'opinion de qn (sur qc)
   share s.o.'s opinion (on s.th.)
un **avis** [avi]
opinion, way of thinking, judgment

   donner son avis
   give one's opinion
   être du même avis que
   be of the same opinion as
   être d'(un) avis contraire/opposé
   be of the opposite opinion
   A mon avis, tu n'aurais pas dû lui dire ça.
   In my opinion, you shouldn't have said that to him.
être en accord avec qn [ɛtRɑ̃nakɔR]
be in agreement with s.o.

être en désaccord avec qn [ɛtRɑ̃dezakɔR]
be in disagreement with s.o.

(être) favorable à [favɔRabl]
(be) favorable to, about
   Le directeur a été favorable à mon projet.
   The director was favorable about my project.

protester contre qc [pRɔtɛste]
protest against s.th.
contester qc [kɔ̃tɛste]
dispute/challenge/contest s.th.
   Le joueur a contesté la décision de l'arbitre.
   The player contested the referee's decision.
s'élever contre qc [sel(ə)ve]
rise up against s.th.

Ça m'est égal. [samɛ(t)egal]
It's all the same to me.
Et après ? [eapRɛ]
Well? What of it?
   Et après ? Qu'est-ce que ça peut te faire ?
   What of it? What business is it of yours?
Et alors ? [ealɔR]
Well? So what?

considérer que [kɔ̃sideRe]
consider/think that
   Je considère que c'est stupide.
   I think that it's stupid.
   Je **le considère comme** un jeune homme plein de talent.
   I consider him a very talented young man.
juger que [ʒyʒe]
consider/think/believe that
   Fais-le, si tu juges que c'est nécessaire.
   Do it, if you believe that it's necessary.
être sûr,e (de qc/que) [ɛt(Rə)syR]
be sure (of s.th./that)

   Je suis sûr de le connaître.
   I'm sure that I know him.
   J'étais pourtant sûr que tu le connaissais.
   Still, I was sure that you knew him.
être certain,e (de qc/que) [ɛt(Rə)sɛRtɛ̃, ɛn]
be certain (of s.th/that)

Je suis **sûre et certaine** de l'avoir vu dimanche.	I'm quite certain that I saw him on Sunday.

une **conclusion** [kɔ̃klyzjɔ̃]
  Le tribunal est arrivé à la conclusion que l'accusé est coupable.
positif, -ive [pozitif, iv]
négatif, -ive [negatif, iv]

conclusion
  The court came to the conclusion that the accused was guilty.
positive
negative

relatif, -ive [ʀ(ə)latif, iv]
dépendre de [depɑ̃dʀ]
  Je ne peux rien te promettre, ça dépendra du temps qu'il fera.
évident,e [evidɑ̃, ɑ̃t]
  Il est évident que j'ai raison.
clair,e [klɛʀ]
confus,e [fɔ̃fy, yz]

relative
depend on
  I can't promise you anything; it depends on the weather.
evident, clear
  It's clear that I'm right.
clear
confused

il est courant que + *subj* [ilɛkuʀɑ̃]
  Il est courant qu'il fasse mauvais en cette saison.
il est (im)possible que + *subj* [ilɛ(ɛ̃)pɔsibl]
  Il est possible qu'il pleuve demain.

it is usual that
  It's usual that the weather is bad this time of year.
it is (im)possible that
  It's possible that it will rain tomorrow.

il est probable que [ilɛpʀɔbabl]
  Il est probable qu'il viendra.
il est improbable que + *subj* [ilɛ(t) ɛ̃pʀɔbabl]

it is probable that
  It's probable that he will come.
it is improbable that

juste [ʒyst]
faux, fausse [fo, fos]
correct,e [kɔʀɛkt]
exact,e [egza(kt), egzakt]
  Il est exact que nous nous connaissons depuis longtemps.

right
wrong
correct
correct, exact
  It's true that we've known each other for a long time.

important,e [ɛ̃pɔʀtɑ̃, ɑ̃t]
l'**importance** *f* [ɛ̃pɔʀtɑ̃s]
  de toute première importance
principal,e [pʀɛ̃sipal]
  Tu n'es pas blessé, c'est le principal.
secondaire [s(ə)gɔ̃dɛʀ]

important
importance
  of the utmost importance
principal, main, chief
  You're not injured; that's the main thing.
secondary

C'est une question tout à fait secondaire.	It's a completely secondary issue.

bien adv [bjɛ̃] — well
Qu'est-ce que tu chantes bien ! — How well you sing!
mieux [mjø] — better
Tu aurais pu mieux faire. — You could have done better.
bon,ne [bɔ̃, bɔn] — good
meilleur,e [mɛjœʀ] — better; best
C'est le meilleur pianiste que je connaisse. — He's the best pianist I know.
parfait,e [paʀfɛ, ɛt] — perfect
Comme ça, c'est parfait. — It's perfect like that.
préférable [pʀefeʀabl] — better, preferable
Il aurait été préférable que tu te taises. — It would have been better for you to be quiet.
préférer [pʀefʀe] — prefer
mal [mal] — poorly, badly
Tu ne trouves pas qu'ils ont mal joué ? — Don't you think they played badly?
mauvais,e [mo/ɔvɛ, ɛz] — bad
pire [piʀ] — worse
de pire en pire — worse and worse

un **avantage** [avɑ̃taʒ] — advantage
un avantage inestimable — an inestimable advantage
agréable [agʀeabl] — agreeable, pleasant
pratique [pʀatik] — practical
Pour aller au bureau, je prends le bus, c'est plus pratique. — To get to the office, I take the bus; it's more practical.

il semble que [ilsɑ̃bl] — it seems that
Il semble que le temps devient/devienne meilleur. — It seems that the weather is improving.
il me semble que [i(l)m(ə)sɑ̃bl] — it seems to me that
Il me semble que Lucas a encore grossi. — It seems to me that Lucas has gained weight again.
avoir l'impression f **que** [avwaʀlɛ̃pʀesjɔ̃] — have the impression that
avoir le sentiment que [avwaʀl(ə)sɑ̃timɑ̃] — have the feeling that
trouver que [tʀuve] — think that
Tu ne trouves pas que Pascal **a mauvaise mine** ? — Don't you think Pascal looks bad?
trouver qn/qc + adj [tʀuve] — think/find s.o./s.th.

Je trouve les nouveaux voisins très gentils.

I think the new neighbors are quite nice.

personnellement [pɛʀsɔnɛlmɑ̃]
Moi, personnellement, je lui aurais dit ce que j'en pense.
personally
Personally, I would have told him what I think of it.

de mon côté [d(ə)mɔ̃kote]
De mon côté, je pense que Valérie a pris la bonne décision.
for my own part
For my own part, I think that Valérie made the right decision.

pour ma part [puʀmapaʀ]
Moi, pour ma part, je préfère la mer à la montagne.
for my part, as for me
As for me, I prefer the sea to the mountains.

franchement [fʀɑ̃ʃmɑ̃]
Là, franchement, tu exagères !
frankly
Frankly, there you're exaggerating!

heureusement (que) [øʀøzmɑ̃]
Heureusement qu'on a retrouvé les clés.
luckily, fortunately
Luckily we found the keys again.

malheureusement [maløʀøzmɑ̃]
Malheureusement, il n'est jamais là quand on a besoin de lui.
unluckily, unfortunately
Unfortunately, he's never there when you need him.

le **goût** [gu]
avoir bon/mauvais goût
J'ai trouvé sa réflexion **de très mauvais goût.**
taste
have good/bad taste
I thought his remark was in very bad taste.

beau, bel; belle [bo, bɛl]
Qu'il est beau, ce bijou !
pretty
What a pretty piece of jewelry!

magnifique [maɲifik]
magnificent, wonderful

splendide [splɑ̃did]
Tu as vu ce but ? Splendide !
splendid
Did you see that goal? Fantastic!

laid,e [lɛ, lɛd]
ugly

charmant,e [ʃaʀmɑ̃, ɑ̃t]
charming

le **charme** [ʃaʀm]
Elle n'est pas belle, mais elle a du charme.
charm
She's not pretty, but she is charming.

mignon,ne [miɲɔ̃, ɔn]
sweet, cute

aimable [ɛmabl]
Merci beaucoup, vous êtes trop aimable.
friendly, kind
Thank you, you're too kind.

adorable [adɔʀabl]
adorable, charming, delightful

Tu ferais ça pour moi ? Tu es vraiment adorable.	You would do that for me? You're really sweet.

idéal,e [ideal]
  Il fait un temps idéal pour un piquenique.

ideal
  It's ideal weather for a picnic.

formidable [fɔʀmidabl] — fantastic

grave [gʀav] — serious, bad
  Hervé est malade ? **Rien de grave,** j'espère.
  Hervé is ill? Nothing serious, I hope.

terrible [teʀibl] — terrible

---

impressionnant,e [ɛ̃pʀesjɔnã, ãt] — impressive
intéressant,e [ɛ̃teʀɛsã, ãt] — interesting
amusant,e [amyzã, ãt] — entertaining, amusing
original,e [ɔʀiʒinal] — original; unusual
  avoir des idées originales — have original ideas

---

banal,e [banal] — banal; trivial, petty, commonplace
  Ce n'est pas banal, ce qui t'est arrivé.
  What happened to you is not a trivial matter.

médiocre [medjɔkʀ] — mediocre
fatigant,e [fatigã, ãt] — tiring, fatiguing
ennuyeux, -euse [ãnɥijø, jøz] — boring
bête [bɛt] — dumb
  Ce n'est pas bête, ce que tu dis.
  What you're saying is not dumb.

désagréable [dezagʀeabl] — disagreeable
pénible [penibl] — troublesome
  Ce que tu peux être pénible, par moments !
  You can really be troublesome at times!

détestable [detɛstabl] — detestable

---

simple [sɛ̃pl] — simple
élémentaire [elemãtɛʀ] — elementary
facile [fasil] — easy
difficile [difisil] — difficult, hard
dur,e [dyʀ] — difficult, hard
  Tu n'y arriveras pas, c'est trop dur.
  You won't get it done; it's too hard.

étonner qn [etɔne] — astonish s.o.
  Ça m'etonnerait qu'il soit à l'heure.
  It would astonish me if he were on time.

s'étonner [setɔne] — be astonished, wonder
  Je m'étonne toujours de l'intelligence de mon chien.
  I'm always astonished by the intelligence of my dog.

étonnant,e [etɔnã, ãt]
astonishing, amazing

l'étonnement *m* [etɔnmã]
astonishment, amazement

(être) surpris,e [syʀpʀi, iz]
(be) surprised

Nous sommes surpris que tu n'aies pas encore compris.
We're surprised that you haven't understood yet.

la **surprise** [syʀpʀiz]
surprise

Elle n'a pas pu cacher sa surprise quand elle l'a vu.
She couldn't hide her surprise when she saw him.

surprenant,e [syʀpʀənã, ãt]
surprising

---

bizarre [bizaʀ]
bizarre, strange

Je **trouve bizarre** qu'elle n'ait pas téléphoné.
I find it strange that she hasn't phoned.

étrange [etʀãʒ]
strange

incroyable [ɛ̃kʀwajabl]
unbelievable, incredible

Incroyable, mais vrai, Véronique s'est mariée !
Incredible, but true: Véronique has gotten married!

un,e **drôle de ...** [dʀol]
a funny, strange, curious ...

Ça, c'est drôle.
That's funny.

Hein ? [ˈɛ̃]
What?/ Huh?

Quoi ? [kwa]
What?

Quoi ? C'est ta sœur ? Mais vous ne vous ressemblez pas !
What? That's your sister? But you don't look at all alike.

Comment ? [kɔmã]
(I beg your) Pardon?

Ah, bon ? [abɔ̃]
Oh yes? Oh, (is that) so?

Ah, bon, c'était pour rire ? Tu m'as fait peur.
Oh, so that was just a joke? You really scared me.

Tiens, tiens ! [tjɛ̃tjɛ̃]
Really! You don't say so!

Tiens, tiens ! C'est à cette heure-ci qu'on rentre ?
Really! You're coming home at this time?

Eh bien ! [ˈe/ˈɛbjɛ̃]
Well, well!

Dis/Dites donc ! [di/ditdɔ̃k]
You don't say! I declare!

Dis-donc ! Qu'est-ce que tu as grandi !
I declare! You've gotten so tall!

Oh, là là ! [olala]
Dear me! Good grief!

Oh, là là ! Quand ma mère va voir ça, elle va être en colère.
Good grief! When my mother sees that, she'll be furious.

Sans blague ! [sãblag]
You don't say! No kidding!

Elle a eu des jumeaux ? Sans blague !
She gave birth to twins? No kidding?

Voyons ! [vwajɔ̃]
Now then! Come, come! Let's see!

Pas possible ! [papɔsibl]
Not possible!

Ça alors ! [saalɔʀ]
Well, I never! I say!

Ça ne vaut rien. [san(ə)voʀjɛ̃]   That's worthless.
Je m'en moque/fiche *fam/*   I don't care.
fous *fam.* [j(ə)mɑ̃mɔk/fiʃ/fu]
   Elle peut penser ce qu'elle veut, je   She can think whatever she
   m'en fiche.   wants; I don't care.
Ça ne me (te, le ...) regarde pas.   That doesn't concern me (you,
[san(ə)mər(ə)gaʀdpa]   him ...).
   Je peux sortir avec qui je veux, ça   I can go out with whomever I
   ne vous regarde pas.   want; that doesn't concern you.
selon [s(ə)lɔ̃]   according to
   Selon moi, cette théorie est   In my opinion, this theory is
   absurde.   absurd.
d'après [dapʀɛ]   according to
   D'après mes parents, je devrais   According to my parents, I
   travailler plus.   should work more.

---

apprécier [apʀesje]   estimate, value, judge; appreciate
une **appréciation** [apʀesjasjɔ̃]   estimation, appreciation
   porter une appréciation sur   give an estimate of
un **jugement** [ʒyʒmɑ̃]   judgment
un **préjugé** [pʀeʒyʒe]   prejudice
   lutter contre **les préjugés racistes**   fight against racist prejudices

---

capital,e [kapital]   important; main; chief
   un événement capital   an important event
primordial,e [pʀimɔʀdjal]   essential, decisive
   jouer un rôle primordial   play an essential role
la **perfection** [pɛʀfɛksjɔ̃]   perfection
   Yann joue du violon **à la**   Yann plays the violin to
   perfection.   perfection.
l'**imperfection** *f* [ɛ̃pɛʀfɛksjɔ̃]   imperfection
exceptionnel,le [ɛksɛpsjɔnɛl]   exceptional
   Elle est d'une adresse   She has exceptional skill.
   exceptionnelle.
remarquable [ʀ(ə)maʀkabl]   remarkable
unique [ynik]   unique
   Nous avons assisté à un spectacle   We went to an absolutely unique
   absolument unique.   play.
convenable [kɔ̃vnabl]   suitable, proper; convenient

(in)suffisant,e [(ɛ̃)syfizɑ̃, ɑ̃t]   (un)satisfactory
catastrophique [katastʀɔfik]   catastrophic
la **catastrophe**; la **cata** *fam*   catastrophe
[kata(stʀɔf)]

En ce moment, au bureau, c'est la cata(strophe); presque tout le monde est malade.	At the moment there's a catastrophe in the office; almost everybody is ill.

ressentir qc comme ... [ʀ(ə)sãtiʀ]
Je ressens sa réflexion comme un affront.

feel s.th. to be ...
I feel his remark to be an insult.

mystérieux, -euse [misteʀjø, jøz] — mysterious
moche *fam* [mɔʃ] — ugly, dowdy
hideux, -euse ['idø, øz] — hideous
affreux, -euse [afʀø, øz] — awful, frightful
horrible [ɔʀibl] — horrible
épouvantable [epuvãtabl] — appalling, dreadful, shocking
Les acteurs étaient bons, mais j'ai trouvé la mise en scène épouvantable.
The actors were good, but I thought the staging was dreadful.

curieux, -euse [kyʀjø, jøz] — curious, strange
frappant,e [fʀapã, ãt] — striking
Qu'est-ce que tu ressembles à ton frère, c'est frappant.
It's striking how much you resemble your brother.
inexplicable [inɛksplikabl] — inexplicable
invraisemblable [ɛ̃vʀɛsãblabl] — improbable
inouï,e [inwi] — unheard of, unprecedented
Mais c'est inouï, ce que tu dis là.
But what you're saying is unheard of.

(être) émerveillé,e [emɛʀveje] — (be) astonished
l'**émerveillement** *m* [emɛʀvejmã] — astonishment
Le spectacle a **plongé** les spectateurs **dans l'émerveillement**.
The play sent the audience into raptures.
stupéfait,e [stypefɛ, ɛt] — stupefied, dumbfounded, thunderstruck

Je suis stupéfait de voir comme ta fille a grandi.
I'm dumbfounded to see how much your daughter has grown.
la **stupéfaction** [stypefaksjõ] — stupefaction
Je n'en crois pas mes yeux/mes oreilles.
I don't believe my eyes/ears.
[ʒ(ə)nãkʀwapamezjø/mezɔʀɛj]

23.8 Exhorting and Wishing

encourager qn à faire qc
[ãkuʀaʒe]
Nous l'avons encouragé à continuer.

encourage s.o. to do s.th.

We encouraged him to keep on.

un **encouragement** [ãkuʀaʒmã]	encouragement

Attention ! [atãsjõ]	Watch out! Caution!
Allez, allez ! [aleale]	Come on, come on! Let's go!
Allez, allez ! Dépêchez-vous un peu.	Come on, come on! Hurry up a little.
Vas-y ! [vazi]	Get going! Get a move on!
Vas-y, saute, ce n'est pas haut !	Get going! Jump, it's not high!
Halte ! ['alt]	Stop!
Stop ! [stɔp]	Stop!

Tais-toi ! [tɛtwa]	Be quiet!
Silence ! [silãs]	Quiet!
Chut ! [ʃyt]	Shhhh!

Va-t'en ! [vatã]	Get lost!/Get away from here!
Laisse-moi tranquille ! [lɛsmwatʀãkil]	Leave me alone!

Au secoure ! [os(ə)kuʀ]	Help!
A l'aide ! [alɛd]	Help!
Au voleur ! [ovɔlœʀ]	Stop, thief!

souhaiter qc à qn [swɛte]	wish s.o. s.th.
Je vous souhaite une bonne nuit.	I wish you a good night.
un **souhait** [swɛ]	wish
un **vœu** [vø]	wish
Je vous adresse tous mes vœux de bonheur.	I wish you every happiness.
Mes meilleurs vœux (pour la nouvelle année).	Best wishes (for the new year).
A tes/vos souhaits ! [ate/voswɛ]	To your health! God bless you!
Atchoum ! – A tes souhaits !	Achoo! God bless you!

Félicitations ! [felisitasjõ]	Congratulations!
Toutes nos félicitations aux jeunes mariés !	Our congratulations to the young couple!
Bonne fête ! [bɔnfɛt]	Happy name day!
Bon anniversaire ! [bɔnaniveʀsɛʀ]	Happy birthday!
Bonne année ! [bɔnane]	Happy New Year!
Bonne année, bonne santé !	Good health and happiness in the new year!
Joyeux Noël ! [ʒwajønɔɛl]	Merry Christmas!
Joyeuses Pâques ! [ʒwajøzpak]	Happy Easter!
Bonne chance ! [bɔnʃãs]	Good luck!

Bon appétit. [bɔnapeti]   Bon appétit. Enjoy your meal.
Bonne journée. [bɔnʒuʀne]   Have a nice day.
Bonne nuit. [bɔnnɥi]   Good night.

Bonnes vacances. [bɔnvakɑ̃s]   Enjoy your vacation.
Bon voyage. [bɔ̃vwajaʒ]   Bon voyage. Have a pleasant
                                     journey.
Bonne route. [bɔnʀut]   Have a good trip.

23.9 Phrases Used in Letters

Letters keep friendship alive

Le destinataire :	**Monsieur (M.), Madame (Mme), Mademoiselle (Melle)** + *nom*	*Recipient*
Le lieu et la date :	**Toulouse, le 1ᵉʳ avril 2000; Lyon, le 2 avril 2000**	*Place and date*
Le début dans une letter officielle :	**Madame, Monsieur // Mesdames, Messieurs // Monsieur/Messieurs // Madame/Mesdames // Mademoiselle/ Mesdemoiselles // Monsieur le Directeur/Madame la Directrice**	*Opening of a formal letter*
Le début dans une lettre à des personnes qu'on connaît (un peu) :	*voir plus haut ou:* **Chère Madame, Cher Monsieur, ...** *(on écrit rarement le nom de famille);* **Cher Philippe; Chère Florence ... Bien chers tous**	*Opening of a letter to acquaintances*
On met une virgule après l'appel :	**Monsieur,**	*The opening is followed by a comma.*
Le premier mot de la lettre prend une majuscule.	**Chère Florence,** **C̲'est avec beaucoup de ...**	*The first word of the letter is capitalized.*
Formules de fin dans une lettre officielle :	**Je vous prie de croire, Monsieur/ Madame ..., à l'expression de mes sentiments/salutations distingué(e)s. Je vous prie d'agréer/de recevoir, Messieurs/Mesdames, l'expression de mes ...**	*Closing of a formal letter: Sincerely yours/Yours truly*
	Dans l'attente de votre réponse, je vous prie de croire, Mademoiselle ..., à l'expression de mes salutations les meilleures.	*In anticipation of your reply*
Formules de fin dans une lettre à des amis :	**Amitiés // (Bien) Amicalement // Meilleures salutations // Bien à toi/vous**	*Phrases used at the end of a letter to friends: Yours/Best regards/Cordially*
Formules de fin dans une lettre à de très bons amis :	**Salut // Affectueusement // Grosses bises**	*Phrases used at the end of a letter to very good friends*

La signature se trouve à droite, en bas.		The signature is found at the bottom, on the right.
Dans des lettres commerciales, on intercale :		In business correspondence, one inserts:
	N/réf. : ... (Notre référence) V/réf. : ... (Votre référence) Objet :	Our reference ... Your reference ... re:
Quelques formules utiles :		Some useful phrases:
	J'ai bien reçu votre lettre du + date	I have received your letter of (date)
	Je vous remercie de ...	Thank you for ...
	En réponse à votre lettre ...	In response to your letter ...
	Je voudrais savoir si ...	I would like to know whether ...
	En référence à votre/ma lettre ...	In reference to your/ my letter ...
	Je vous prie de bien vouloir ...	I request that you ...
	Nous vous serions reconnaissants de ...	We would be grateful to you for ...
	A la suite de votre courier du + date	In reply to your letter of (date)
	Je vous adresse ci-joint ...	Enclosed ...
	Je suis heureux d'apprendre ...	I am happy to learn ...
	Veuillez répondre par retour du courrier.	Please reply by return mail.
	... aussitôt que possible	... as soon as possible
	Transmettez mes amitiés à ...	Please give my regards to ...

French Word	English Equivalent	False Friend	French Equivalent
le gout	taste	gout	la goutte

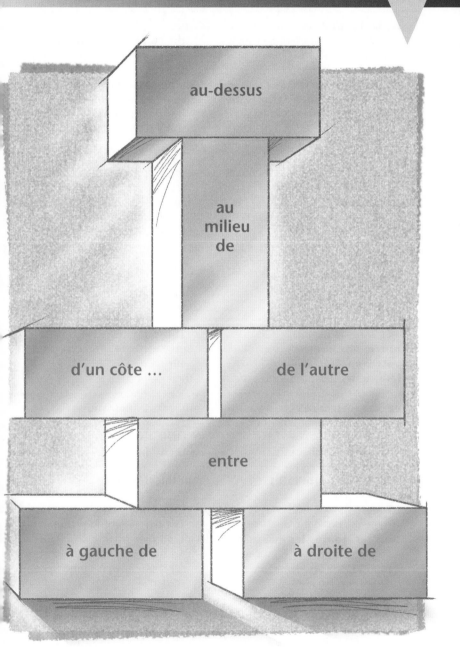

au-dessus

au milieu de

d'un côte ...   de l'autre

entre

à gauche de   à droite de

24.1 Adjuncts and Pronouns

le, la, l'; les [lə, la, le]
le client, l'air; la cliente, l'eau; les clients, les clientes

the
the customer, the air; the customer, the water; the customers, the customers

du, de la, de l'; des [dy, d(ə)la, de]
du pain, de l'air; de la farine, de l'eau; des bonbons, des fraises

of the, from the, by the; some, any
some bread, some air; some flour, some water; some candies, some strawberries

au, à la, à l'; aux [o, ala, o]
je vais au marché, ... à l'arrêt de bus; ... à la banque, ... à l'école; ... aux Etats-Unis

to the
I'm going to the market, ... to the bus stop; ... to the bank, ... to school; ... to the United States

un, une; des [ɛ̃, yn, de]
un client, une cliente; des clients, des clientes

a, an
a customer, a customer; customers, customers

mon, ma; mes [mɔ̃, ma, me]
ton, ta; tes [tɔ̃, ta, te]
son, sa; ses [sɔ̃, sa, se]
C'est son porte-monnaie.
C'est sa montre.
Ce sont ses parents.

my
your
his, her, its
That's his/her wallet.
That's his/her watch.
Those are his/her parents.

notre; nos [nɔtʀ, no]
votre; vos [vɔtʀ, vo]
leur; leurs [lœʀ]

our
your
their

ce, cet, cette; ces [sə, sɛt; se]
ce livre, cet appartement *m*; cette chaise, cette orange
ces livres; ces chaises

this, that; these, those
this book, this apartment; this chair, this orange; these books, these chairs

tout le(l'), toute la(l')
[tul(ə), tutla]
Tout le monde est venu.
Toute la famille est là.

all the, the whole

Everybody came.
The whole family is there.

tous les, toutes les [tule, tutle]
Tous mes amis sont en vacances.
Toutes ces fleurs viennent de mon jardin.

all, all the
All my friends are on vacation.
All these flowers come from my garden.

tout, tous, toutes [tu, tus, tut]
Tout s'est bien passé.
Ils sont tous partis.
Les photos? Il nous les a toutes montrées.

all; every, each
Everything went well.
They have all left.
The photos? He showed them all to us.

chaque [ʃak]
Chaque invité a eu un petit cadeau.
chacun,e [ʃakɛ̃, yn]
Chacun a pu donner son avis.
ne ... aucun,e/aucun,e ... ne
[okɛ̃, okyn]
Il n'a eu aucune réaction.
Aucune (carte postale) ne m'a
plu.
certains, certaines [sɛʀtɛ̃, ɛn]
Certaines personnes ne sont
jamais contentes.
différents, différentes
[difeʀɑ̃, ɑ̃t]
Nous avons goûté des fromages
de différentes régions de France.
divers,es [divɛʀ, ɛʀs]
On en a parlé à diverses
personnes.
plusieurs [plyzjœʀ]
On a arrêté plusieurs suspects.
quelques [kɛlkə]
quelqu'un [kɛlkɛ̃]

Quelqu'un a téléphoné ?
quelques-uns/quelques-unes
[kɛlkəzɛ̃, kɛlkəzyn]
Tu as lu tous les livres de Jules
Verne ? – Non, seulement
quelques-uns.
ne ... personne/personne ... ne
[pɛʀsɔn]
On n'a rencontré personne.
Personne n'a appelé.
pas un,e seul,e [pa(z)ɛ̃/ynsœl]
Pas un (seul) magasin n'était
ouvert.
quelque chose [kɛlkəʃoz]
ne ... rien/rien ... ne [ʀjɛ̃]
Je n'ai rien vu.
Rien ne va plus.
un,e **autre; d'autres** [otʀ]
Montrez-moi un autre/d'autres
modèle(s).
le/la même; les mêmes [mɛm]

each, every
Each guest got a little gift.
each, each one, every one, everyone
Everyone could give his opinion.
none, no one, not one; not any;
anyone, any
He showed no reaction.
I didn't like any (postcard).

certain
Certain people are never
satisfied.
different; various, several

We tasted cheeses from different
regions of France.
diverse, various
We spoke with various people
about it.
several, some
Several suspects were arrested.
some, any; a few
someone, somebody; anyone,
anybody
Did anyone phone?
some, any; a few

Have you read all of Jules
Verne's books? No, only a few.
no one, nobody; not anyone, not
anybody
We didn't meet anybody.
No one phoned.
not a single, not one
Not a single shop had opened.

something
nothing, not anything
I didn't see anything.
Nothing is possible anymore.
other; another, different
Show me another model.

the same

Nous sommes du même avis.	We are of the same opinion.
un,e tel,le; de tels, telles [tɛl]	such a(n)
Il ne faut pas rater une telle occasion.	One should not miss such an occasion.

je (j') [ʒə]	I
me (m') [mə]	me; to me
Il m'a regardé.	He looked at me.
Il m'a donné un conseil.	He gave me a piece of advice.
moi [mwa]	I; me; myself
Sans moi.	Count me out.

tu [ty]	you
te (t') [tə]	you; to you
Tu t'appelles comment ?	What is your name?
Je te dois encore 20 euros.	I still owe you 20 euros.
toi [twa]	you; yourself
C'est pour toi.	That's for you.

il [il]	he; it
le (l') [lə]	him; it
Je le vois souvent.	I see him often.
elle [ɛl]	she; it
Elle est très sympathique.	She is very likeable.
C'est Monique qui vient d'arriver ?	Is it Monique who just arrived?
– Oui, c'est elle.	Yes, it's she.
la (l') [la]	her; it
Si tu la vois, dis-lui de m'appeler.	If you see her, tell her to call me.
lui [lɥi]	him, to him; her, to her
Je lui ai dit de venir.	I told him/her to come.
se (s') [sə]	oneself, himself, herself, itself
Elle s'est regardée dans la glace.	She looked at herself in the mirror.
soi [swa]	oneself, himself, herself, itself
Chacun pour soi et Dieu pour tous. *loc*	Everyone for himself and God for all.
on [ɔ̃]	one, they, we, I, you, people, somebody
On s'est bien amusé(s).	We had a good time.
Ici, on parle espagnol.	Spanish is spoken here.

nous [nu]	we, us, to us; ourselves
Nous avons faim.	We are hungry.
Ecris-nous de temps en temps.	Write us now and then.

vous [vu]	you, to you; yourself
Elle vous a reconnus ?	Did she recognize you?

Servez-vous une bière. | Pour yourself a beer.

ils *m*, **elles** *f* [il, ɛl] — they
les [le] — them
Je les ai invité(e)s. | I invited them.
leur [lœR] — them, to them
Je leur ai apporté des fleurs. | I brought them some flowers.
eux *m*, **elles** *f* [ø, ɛl] — them
Nous pensons souvent à eux/elles. | We often think of them.
se (s') [sə] — themselves, to themselves; each other
Ils se voient souvent. | They see each other often.
Elles aiment se promener seules. | They like going for a walk alone.

en [ã] — of him/her/it, of them/their; from/by/about him, etc.
Il en a parlé. | He talked about it.
Il y a assez de pommes ? – Oui, nous en avons pris trois kilos. | Are there enough apples? Yes, we bought three kilos of them.
y [i] — by/for/in/at/to him/her/it/them
Je m'y intéresse beaucoup. | I'm very interested in it.

ceci [səsi] — this, this thing
cela, ça [s(ə)la, sa] — that, that thing
Donne-moi cela/ça. | Give me that.

qui [ki] — who, that, which, what
C'est une femme qui sait ce qu'elle veut. | That's a woman who knows what she wants.
que (qu') [kə] — whom, that, which, what
C'est une vedette que j'admire. | She's a star whom I admire.
quoi [kwa] — what
Il ne savait plus quoi dire. | He no longer knew what to say.
Par quoi est-ce qu'on commence ? | With what shall we begin?
ce qui [s(ə)ki] — what (that which)
Je ne sais pas ce qui est arrivé. | I don't know what happened.
ce que (ce qu') [s(ə)kə] — what (that which)
Dis-moi ce que tu en penses. | Tell me what you think of it.

dont [dõ] — whose, of which, of whom, from whom, etc.
un film dont on parle beaucoup | a film about which much is being said
où [u] — where; in which
une région où j'ai passé trois ans | a region in which I spent three years

lequel (duquel, auquel) [ləkɛl] — who, whom, that, which

un événement auquel nous pensons tous	an event about which we all think
laquelle (de laquelle, à laquelle) [lakɛl]	who, whom, that, which
C'est une situation dans laquelle je ne voudrais pas être.	It's a situation in which I would not want to be.
lesquels (desquels, auxquels) [lekɛl]	who, whom, that, which
lesquelles (desquelles, auxquelles) [lekɛl]	who, whom, that, which

celui(-ci/-là), celle(-ci/-là) [səlɥi(si/la), sɛl(si/la)]	the one, that; this one/that one
Si tu n'as pas d'anorak, mets celui de Julien.	If you don't have a parka, take Julien's.
ceux(-ci/-là), celles(-ci/-là) [sø(si/la), sɛl(si/la)]	the ones; these/those
Ceux-ci sont trop petits, prends celui-là.	These are too small; take those.

le mien, la mienne; les miens, les miennes [mjɛ̃, mjɛn]	mine, my own
le tien, la tienne; les tiens, les tiennes [tjɛ̃, tjɛn]	yours, your own
Ce pull-là, c'est le mien ou le tien ?	That sweater is mine or yours?
le sien, la sienne; les siens, les siennes [sjɛ̃, sjɛn]	his, his own; hers, her own; its, its own
le, la nôtre; les nôtres [notʀ]	ours, our own
le, la vôtre; les vôtres [votʀ]	yours, your own
le, la leur; les leurs [lœʀ]	theirs, their own

24.2 Interrogatives

est-ce que [ɛskə]	*Formula used to introduce a question*
Qui? [ki]	Who?
Qui est là ?	Who is there?
De qui est ce tableau ?	By whom is that picture?
A qui est cette clé ?	To whom does this key belong?
Que? [kə]	What?
Que veux-tu ?	What do you want?
Quoi? [kwa]	What?
De quoi parlez-vous ?	What are you talking about?
A quoi pensez-vous ?	What are you thinking about?

Qui est-ce qui ? [kiɛski]
  Qui est-ce qui vient avec moi ?
Qui est-ce que ? [kiɛskə]
  Qui est-ce qu'elle a appelé ?
Qu'est-ce qui ? [kɛski]
  Qu'est-ce qui est arrivé ?
Qu'est-ce que ? [kɛskə]
  Qu'est-ce que c'est ?

Who?
  Who is coming with me?
Whom?
  Whom did she call?
What?
  What has happened?
What?
  What is it?

Lequel ? (Duquel ? Auquel ?)
[ləkɛl]
  J'adore cet acteur. – Lequel ?
**Laquelle ? (De laquelle ? A
laquelle ?)** [lakɛl]
  Nous pensons toujours à cette
  chanson. – A laquelle ?
**Lesquels ? (Desquels ?
Auxquels ?)** [lekɛl]
  J'ai reçu une lettre de mes amis. –
  Desquels ?
**Lesquelles ? (Desquelles ?
Auxquelles ?)** [lekɛl]
  Vous avez vu ces belles voitures ?
  – Lesquelles ?

Which (one)?

  I adore that actor. Which one?
Which one?

  We still think about that song.
  About which one?
Which ones?

  I've received a letter from my
  friends. From which ones?
Which ones?

  Did you see those beautiful cars?
  Which ones?

Quel ? Quelle ? [kɛl]
  Quel âge avez-vous ?/Vous avez
  quel âge ?
Quels? Quelles ? Quel(le)s ? [kɛl]
  Par quelles villes êtes-vous passés ?

What? Which? What sort of?
  How old are you?

What? Which? What sort of?
  Through which towns did you
  pass?

Où ? [u]
  Où habitez-vous ?/Vous habitez
  où ?
D'où ? [du]
  D'où vient ce bruit ?

Where?
  Where do you live?

Where (from)?
  Where is that noise coming
  from?

Quand ? [kɑ̃]
  Quand est-ce qu'on mange ?
Comment ? [kɔmɑ̃]
  Comment vas-tu ?
Combien ? [kɔ̃bjɛ̃]
  Combien ça coûte ?/Ça coûte
  combien ?
Pourquoi ? [puʀkwa]

When?
  When do we eat?
How?
  How are you?
How much?
  How much does that cost?

Why?

Pourquoi est-ce que tu ne m'aimes plus ?

Why don't you love me anymore?

24.3 Conjunctions

et [e]
and

ou [u]
or

Voulez-vous du thé ou du café ?
Would you like tea or coffee?

ou bien [ubjɛ̃]
or (else)

Dépêche-toi, ou bien je pars sans toi.
Hurry, or I'll go without you.

mais [mɛ]
but

par contre [paʀkɔ̃tʀ]
by contrast, on the other hand

Il est complètement idiot. Sa sœur, par contre, est très intelligente.
He's a complete idiot. His sister, on the other hand, is very intelligent.

pourtant [puʀtã]
however, yet, still, nevertheless

Il ne me croit pas, je dis pourtant la vérité.
He doesn't believe me, yet I'm telling the truth.

quand même [kãmɛm]
even though, all the same, nevertheless

Elle est malade mais elle ira quand même à cette réunion.
She is ill, but she's going to this meeting all the same.

d'abord [dabɔʀ]
at first, at first sight

puis [pɥi]
then, after that

ensuite [ãsɥit]
after, afterward, then

enfin [ãfɛ̃]
at last, finally, at length

J'ai enfin trouvé du travail.
I've found work at last.

car [kaʀ]
for, because

c'est pourquoi [sɛpuʀkwa]
that's why, therefore

donc [dɔ̃k]
then, therefore, accordingly

Entrez donc.
Do come in.

Je n'ai pas vu ce film; je ne peux donc pas en parler.
I didn't see that film; therefore I can't talk about it.

ainsi [ɛ̃si]
thus, so, in this/that way

Passe par la rue Voltaire, ainsi tu arriveras plus vite.
Take rue Voltaire; you'll get there faster that way.

quand [kã]
when

Quand il était petit, il voulait devenir pompier.
When he was little, he wanted to be a fireman.

Je ne sais pas quand il viendra.
I don't know when he'll come.

Quand tu le verras, dis-lui bonjour de ma part.	When you see him, give him my regards.
pendant que [pãdãkə]	while
Pendant qu'il dort, il ne fait pas de bêtises.	While he's asleep, he doesn't play any pranks.
depuis que [dəpɥikə]	since
Depuis qu'il a déménagé, il n'a pas donné de ses nouvelles.	Since he moved, we haven't heard from him.
avant que + *subj* [avãkə]	before
Tu devrais téléphoner avant qu'il (ne) soit trop tard.	You ought to call before it's too late.
après que [apʀɛkə]	after
jusqu'à ce que + *subj* [ʒyskas(ə)kə]	until
Reste ici jusqu'à ce que je revienne.	Stay here until I return.

⋯⋯⋯⋯⋯⋯⋯⋯⋯⋯⋯⋯⋯⋯⋯⋯⋯⋯⋯⋯⋯⋯⋯⋯⋯⋯⋯⋯⋯

comme [kɔm]	as, since, because
Comme je n'avais pas de farine, je n'ai pas pu faire de tarte.	Since I had no flour, I couldn't bake a cake.
parce que [paʀs(ə)kə]	because
puisque [pɥiskə]	since, as, seeing that
Ce n'est pas la peine de l'inviter puisqu'elle ne viendra pas.	You don't even need to invite her, since she won't come.

⋯⋯⋯⋯⋯⋯⋯⋯⋯⋯⋯⋯⋯⋯⋯⋯⋯⋯⋯⋯⋯⋯⋯⋯⋯⋯⋯⋯⋯

que [kə]	that; as
J'espère que tu vas bien.	I hope that you're well.
Il a le même âge que moi.	He is the same age as I.
pour que + *subj* [puʀkə]	so that
Je le lui ai bien expliqué pour qu'il comprenne.	I explained it well to him, so that he would understand it.
de sorte que [dəsɔʀt(ə)kə]	so that

> For information on the mood (subjunctive/indicative) used following **de sorte que, de façon que, de manière que**, see p. 429.

⋯⋯⋯⋯⋯⋯⋯⋯⋯⋯⋯⋯⋯⋯⋯⋯⋯⋯⋯⋯⋯⋯⋯⋯⋯⋯⋯⋯⋯

tandis que [tãdikə]	while, whereas
J'aime bien voyager tandis que ma femme préfère rester à la maison.	I like to travel, while my wife prefers to stay at home.
alors que [alɔʀkə]	while, whereas; even though
Il n'est pas venu alors qu'il l'avait promis.	He didn't come, even though he had promised to do so.
quoique + *subj* [kwakə]	although, though
bien que + *subj* [bjɛ̃kə]	although, though
Quoiqu'/Bien qu'il fasse froid, il se promène en t-shirt/tee-shirt.	Although it is cold, he's running around in a T-shirt.

sans que + *subj* [sãkə]
Ils sont partis sans que je l'aie remarqué.

without, unless
They left without my noticing it.

---

si [si]
même si [mɛmsi]
Même si (l')on me proposait beaucoup d'argent, je ne sauterais pas en parachute.
à condition que + *subj* [akɔ̃disjɔ̃kə]
Nous pouvons vous accompagner, à condition qu'on y aille tout de suite.

if
even if
Even if someone offered me a lot of money, I wouldn't make a parachute jump.
on condition, provided that
We can go with you, provided that we leave right now.

---

d'un côté ... de l'autre [dɛ̃koted(ə)lotʀ]
D'un côté, je l'aime bien, de l'autre, elle m'énerve.

on the one hand ... on the other hand
On the one hand, I like her a lot; on the other, she gets on my nerves.

d'une part ... d'autre part [dynpaʀdotʀ(ə)paʀ]
sinon [sinɔ̃]
Va au lit maintenant, sinon tu n'arriveras pas à te lever demain.

on the one hand ... on the other hand
otherwise
Go to bed now; otherwise you won't be able to get up in the morning.

autrement [otʀəmã]
en revanche [ãʀ(ə)vãʃ]
Il est insupportable, sa femme, en revanche, est charmante.
cependant [s(ə)pãdã]
ou ... ou [uu]
Ou tu te décides enfin ou on part sans toi.
or [ɔʀ]
Il rêvait d'une belle voiture; or il était pauvre.
par conséquent [paʀkɔ̃sekã]
Il a raté son train, c'est pourquoi/par conséquent il a dû prendre un taxi.
voilà pourquoi [vwalapuʀkwa]

otherwise
however; in return
He is unbearable; his wife, however, is charming.
yet, still, however, nevertheless
either ... or
Either you make up your mind at last, or we'll go without you.
but; now; well
He dreamed of a beautiful car, but he was poor.
consequently
He missed his train; consequently he had to take a taxi.
that's why

---

au moment où [omɔmãu]
dès que [dɛkə]
Je t'aiderai dès que j'aurai fini mon travail.
tant que [tãkə]

the instant that, just as
as soon as
I'll help you as soon as I've finished my work.
as long as

Tant que tu resteras avec moi, je serai heureux.	As long as you stay with me, I'll be happy.

d'autant plus que [dotãply(s)kə] — (so much) the more; since, seeing that
Je voudrais déménager, d'autant plus que je travaille loin d'ici. — I'd like to move, seeing that I work far away from here.
afin que + *subj* [afɛ̃kə] — so that
On lui a prêté de l'argent afin qu'elle puisse payer son loyer. — We loaned her money so that she can pay her rent.
malgré que + *subj* [malgrekə] — although
Il a une belle situation malgré qu'il ait quitté l'école à 16 ans. — He has a good job, although he left school at 16.
pourvu que + *subj* [purvykə] — provided (that)
Il viendra demain, pourvu que cela vous convienne. — He'll come tomorrow, provided that it suits you.
de manière que [d(ə)manjɛrkə] — so that
de façon que [d(ə)fasɔ̃kə] — so that

24.4 Auxiliary Verbs

avoir [avwar] — have
être [ɛtr] — be
aller faire qc [ale] — be going to do s.th.
Tu vas écrire à Paul ? — Are you going to write to Paul?
venir de faire qc [v(ə)nir] — have (only) just done s.th.
On vient de faire des courses. — We have just done the shopping.
être en train de faire qc [ɛtrãtrɛ̃] — be about to do s.th.

devoir faire qc [devwar] — have to do s.th.
vouloir faire qc [vulwar] — want to do s.th.
pouvoir faire qc [puvwar] — be able to do s.th.
Peux-tu traduire ce texte ? – Non, je n'ai pas envie. — Can you translate this passage? No, I don't want to.
savoir faire qc [savwar] — know how to do s.th.
Sais-tu traduire ce texte ? – Non, je ne comprends pas le russe. — Can you translate this passage? No, I don't understand Russian.

faire faire qc [fɛr] — have s.th. done
Il a fait réparer sa voiture. — He had his car repaired.
laisser faire qc [lese] — allow s.th. to be done
Il laisse son fils conduire sa voiture. — He lets his son drive his car.

sembler faire qc [sãble]   seem to do s.th.
  Tu sembles avoir des problèmes.   You seem to have problems.
paraître faire qc [parɛtr]   seem to do s.th.
  Elle paraît être d'accord.   She seems to be in agreement.
avoir qc à faire [avwar]   have s.th. to do
  Laisse-moi tranquille, j'ai un   Leave me alone; I have work to
  travail à finir.   finish.
passer pour [pasepur]   be considered (to be)
  Il passe pour un bon cuisinier.   He is considered (to be) a good
                                             cook.

24.5 Negations

ne ... pas (du tout) [nəpa(dytu)]   not (at all)
ne ... pas encore [nəpa(z)ãkɔr]   not yet
  On n'a pas encore dîné.   We haven't eaten dinner yet.
ne ... pas un,e seul,e   not a single
[nəpa(z)ɛ̃/ynsœl]
  Il n'a pas bu une seule goutte   He didn't drink a single drop of
  d'alcool.   alcohol.
ne ... plus (du tout)   not anymore (at all)
[nəply(dytu)]
ne ... jamais [nəʒamɛ]   never
  Nous ne sommes jamais allés en   We have never been to Belgium.
  Belgique.
ne ... personne/personne ... ne   no one, nobody, not anyone
[nəpɛrsɔn]
  Ils ne connaissent personne, ici.   They don't know anyone here.
  Personne ne me comprend.   Nobody understands me.
ne ... rien/rien ... ne [nərjɛ̃]   nothing, not anything
  On n'a rien vu.   We didn't see anything.
  Rien n'est plus beau que les   Nothing is nicer than vacation.
  vacances.
ne ... rien du tout [nərjɛ̃dytu]   nothing at all, not anything at all
  Je n'y comprends rien du tout.   I don't understand anything at
                                             all about it.
ne ... aucun,e/aucun,e ... ne   none, not one, not any; any(one)
[nəokɛ̃/okyn]
  Tu n'as aucune raison d'être   You have no reason to be
  fâché.   offended.
  Aucun de ces films ne m'a plu.   I didn't like any of those films.
ne ... ni ... ni [nənini]   neither ... nor
  Elle n'aime ni la bière ni le vin.   She likes neither beer nor wine.
ne ... que [nəkə]   only
  Il n'y a que deux solutions.   There are only two solutions.

ne ... guère *litt* [nəgɛʀ]   hardly, scarcely, barely
ne ... nulle part [nənylpaʀ]   nowhere, not anywhere
  Tu n'iras nulle part sans mon   Without my permission, you're
  autorisation.   not going anywhere.

24.6 Adverbs and Adverbial Expressions

bien [bjɛ̃]   well; very
  Tu vas bien ?   Are you well?
mieux [mjø]   better
  Il joue très bien du piano, mais   He plays the piano well, but the
  encore mieux du violon.   violin even better.
  Elle joue **de mieux en mieux**.   She plays better and better.
  Tu n'en veux pas ? **Tant mieux**, il   You don't want any of it? So
  y en aura plus pour nous.   much the better; there'll be
        more for us.

mal [mal]   poorly, badly
Tant pis ! [tɑ̃pi]   Too bad! Never mind!
  Il ne vient pas ? Tant pis !   He isn't coming? Never mind!
  Tant pis pour toi !   That serves you right!

ici [isi]   here
  Vous êtes d'ici ?   Are you from here?
là [la]   there
là-bas [laba]   (over) there
  Qui est cet homme là-bas ?   Who is that man over there?
partout [paʀtu]   everywhere
  Nous avons voyagé un peu   We've traveled pretty much
  partout dans le monde.   everywhere in the world.
ailleurs [ajœʀ]   somewhere else, elsewhere
  Si tu n'es pas bien ici, tu n'as   If you don't like it here, you can
  qu'à aller ailleurs.   go somewhere else.

hier [jɛʀ]   yesterday
aujourd'hui [ojuʀdɥi]   today
demain [d(ə)mɛ̃]   tomorrow

déjà [deʒa]   already
  Il est déjà trois heures.   It is already 3 o'clock.
bientôt [bjɛ̃to]   soon
  A bientôt.   See you soon.
parfois [paʀfwa]   sometimes
souvent [suvɑ̃]   often, frequently

Je lis parfois un livre, mais **le plus souvent** je regarde la télévision.

Sometimes I read a book, but most often I watch TV.

toujours [tuʒuʀ]
always; still

encore [ɑ̃kɔʀ]
still

Ils sont encore là ?
Are they still there?

tôt [to]
early

tard [taʀ]
late

Tôt ou tard, tu t'apercevras que nous avons raison.
Sooner or later, you'll see that we're right.

avant [avɑ̃]
previously, before

Avant, j'allais souvent au cinéma.
Previously, I often went to the movies.

maintenant [mɛ̃t(ə)nɑ̃]
now

après [apʀɛ]
afterward, later

soudain [sudɛ̃]
suddenly

longtemps [lɔ̃tɑ̃]
long, a long while

Je n'en ai pas pour longtemps.
I don't need long.

vite [vit]
quickly, fast

Viens vite !
Come quickly!

très [tʀɛ]
very

Cet enfant est très poli.
This child is very polite.

assez (de) [ase]
enough

J'ai assez mangé.
I've had enough to eat.

Tu as dit assez de bêtises pour aujourd'hui.
You've talked enough nonsense for today.

beaucoup (de) [boku]
many, much, a great deal

Merci beaucoup.
Thank you very much.

tant (de) [tɑ̃]
so much, so greatly

Je n'ai jamais vu tant d'argent à la fois.
I've never seen so much money at one time.

Ils se sont tant aimés.
They loved each other so much.

tellement (de) [tɛlmɑ̃]
so, so much, so far

Il a tellement changé que je ne l'ai pas reconnu.
He has changed so much that I didn't recognize him.

plus (de) [ply]
more

trop (de) [tʀo]
too (much)

Il est malade, il a mangé trop de chocolat.
He is sick; he ate too much chocolate.

C'est vraiment trop bête.
It's really too stupid.

peu (de) [pø]
little; few

Le soir, on mange très peu.
In the evening we eat very little.

moins (de) [mwɛ̃]
less

C'est moins loin qu'on (ne) pensait.
It's less far than we thought.

aussi [osi]
also, too; as; so

Je ne savais pas que tu étais aussi bête.	I didn't know that you were so silly.
plutôt [plyto]	rather; sooner
Dans l'ensemble, ils sont plutôt sympathiques.	On the whole, they're rather likeable.
presque [pʀɛsk]	almost
surtout [syʀtu]	above all, chiefly
peut-être [pøtɛtʀ]	perhaps, maybe
Il est peut-être fatigué, mais il est surtout paresseux.	Maybe he is tired, but above all he's lazy.
sans doute [sãdut]	doubtless, no doubt
Vous avez sans doute raison.	No doubt you're right.
même [mɛm]	even
Bien sûr qu'elle est venue, elle est même arrivée en avance.	Of course she came; she even arrived early.
c'est-à-dire [sɛtadiʀ]	that is (to say)
par exemple (p. ex.) [paʀɛgzãpl]	for example (e.g.)

volontiers [vɔlɔ̃tje]	gladly, willingly, with pleasure
Vous en voulez encore ? – Volontiers.	Would you like some more? With pleasure.
exprès [ɛkspʀɛ]	expressly, purposely, on purpose
Excusez-moi, je ne l'ai pas fait exprès.	Excuse me; I didn't do it on purpose.
à peine [apɛn]	hardly
Elle est à peine plus grande que toi.	She is hardly bigger than you.
en vain [ãvɛ̃]	in vain
On a essayé en vain de le joindre au téléphone.	We tried in vain to reach him by phone.

24.7 Prepositions

à [a]	to, at, in, into, on, by, for, from, *etc.*
Il est parti à 6 heures.	He left at 6 o'clock.
Il va à Toulouse.	He's going to Toulouse.
Elle est repartie à pied.	She continued on foot.
de [də]	of; out of, from; by; with; between; *etc.*
Nous serons absents de lundi à jeudi.	We will be away from Monday to Thursday.
Il vient de Quimper.	He comes from Quimper.
Je meurs de faim.	I'm dying of hunger.
en [ã]	in; to; within; at; by; through; *etc.*
On a fait la route en 4 heures.	We made the trip in four hours.
Nous habitons en Bretagne.	We live in Brittany.

dans [dã]
Il fait froid dans cette maison.
On va venir dans 2 heures.

in, within; into; through
It's cold in this house.
We're going to come in two hours.

---

depuis [dəpɥi]
Il pleut depuis deux semaines.
il y a [ilija]
Il y a un quart d'heure qu'elle est partie.
pendant [pãdã]
Le magasin est fermé pendant tout le mois d'août.
jusque [ʒysk(ə)]
Je vous ai attendus jusqu'à 6 heures.
Il est allé jusqu'en Inde.
vers [vɛʀ]
On arrivera vers midi.
Toutes ces voitures se dirigent vers Reims.
au bout de [obudə]
Au bout de 2 heures, on était tous fatigués.
Au bout de 20 kilomètres, il a abandonné.

since, for
It's been raining for two weeks.
ago
She left a quarter of a hour ago.

during
The store is closed during the entire month of August.
as far as; up to; until
I waited for you until 6 o'clock.

He has traveled as far as India.
toward, to; about
We will arrive about noon.
All these cars are driving toward Reims.
after, at the end of
After two hours we all were tired.
He gave up after 20 kilometers.

---

avant [avã]
Ils sont arrivés avant nous.
On s'est arrêté un peu avant Nancy.
après [apʀɛ]
Après 20 heures, tous les magasins sont fermés.
Tournez à gauche après l'hôpital.
devant [d(ə)vã]
Je vous attends devant le cinéma.

before
They arrived before us.
We stopped a little before Nancy.
after
After 8 P.M. all the stores are closed.
Turn left after the hospital.
in front of
I'll wait for you in front of the movie theater.

derrière [dɛʀjɛʀ]
C'est la maison derrière l'église.
par [paʀ]
Ils sont passés par Poitiers.

behind
It's the house behind the church.
through, by
They went through Poitiers.

---

sur [syʀ]
sous [su]
au-dessus (de) [od(ə)sy]
Nous habitons au-dessus des Martin.

on
under
on top of, above
We live above the Martins.

au-dessous (de) [od(ə)su]
En Bretagne, la température descend rarement au-dessous de zéro.

below
In Brittany the temperature rarely drops below zero.

à côté de [akotedə]
à droite de [adʀwatdə]
à gauche de [agoʃdə]
Asseyez-vous à droite/à gauche du président.

be, near
to the right of
to the left of
Sit to the right/to the left of the president.

au milieu de [omiljødə]

in the midst of

entre [ɑ̃tʀ]
Sur cette photo, je suis entre Julie et Pierre.

between
In this photo, I'm between Julie and Pierre.

parmi [paʀmi]
On a trouvé cette lettre parmi de(s) vieux papiers.

among
This letter was found among some old papers.

chez [ʃe]
Il habite toujours chez ses parents.

at the house, office, etc. of
He still lives with his parents.

près de [pʀɛdə]
un village près de Montpellier

near, close to
a village near Montpellier

loin de [lwɛ̃də]
Ce n'est pas loin de la mer.

far from
It's not far from the ocean.

avec [avɛk]
sans [sɑ̃]
Je prends mon café avec du lait mais sans sucre.

with
without
I take my coffee with milk, but without sugar.

pour [puʀ]
contre [kɔ̃tʀ]
la **lutte contre la drogue**

for
against
the fight against drugs

envers [ɑ̃vɛʀ]
J'ai été injuste envers vous.

toward
I was unjust toward you.

malgré [malgʀe]
Malgré la chaleur, il va faire du jogging.

despite
Despite the heat, he is going jogging.

sauf [sof]
Tout le monde était d'accord sauf Jacques.

except
Everyone except Jacques was in agreement.

à cause de [akozdə]
On ne voit rien à cause du brouillard.

because of
One sees nothing because of the fog.

grâce à [gʀasa]
Le film est très réussi grâce aux excellents acteurs.

thanks to
The film is very successful, thanks to the excellent actors.

au cours de [okuʀdə]
Au cours des dernières années, le chômage a augmenté.

in the course of
In the course of the last few years, unemployment has increased.

dès [dɛ]
Nous nous sommes levés dès l'aube.

from, since, as early as
We've been up since dawn.

autour de [otuʀdə]
Il y a un jardin tout autour de la maison.

around, surrounding
There's a garden all around the house.

à travers [atʀavɛʀ]
La route passe à travers la forêt.

through
The road runs through the forest.

au lieu de [oljødə]
Viens m'aider au lieu de me critiquer.

instead of
Come help me instead of criticizing me.

au sujet de [osyʒɛdə]
On ne sait rien de précis au sujet de cet accident.

on the subject of, about
Nothing definite is known about this accident.

à l'aide de [alɛddə]
Il est monté sur le toit à l'aide d'une échelle.

with the help of
He climbed onto the roof with the help of a ladder.

d'après [dapʀɛ]
D'après la radio, les ouvriers **sont** toujours **en grève**.

according to
According to the radio, the workers are still on strike.

selon [s(ə)lɔ̃]
Selon la météo, il fera beau demain.

according to
According to the weather report, the weather will be good tomorrow.

quant à [kãta]
Quant à Dominique, il n'a toujours rien compris.

as for, with regard to
As for Dominique, he still hasn't understood anything.

excepté [ɛksɛpte]
Tout le monde est venu excepté Luc.

except
Everyone came except Luc.

24.8 Linguistic Terminology

> **Levels of Language and Style**
>
> | | |
> |---|---|
> | la langue | *language* |
> | la langue parlée | *the spoken language* |
> | la langue écrite | *the written language* |
> | la langue courante | *the everyday language* |
> | Exemple: Quand il a bu, il raconte n'importe quoi. | *Example: When he's been drinking, he talks pure nonsense.* |
> | la langue familière *(fam)* | *casual, colloquial language* |
> | la langue populaire *(pop)* | *highly colloquial language, slang* |
> | Exemple: Quand il est rond, il déconne à plein tube. | *Example: When he's loaded, he talks a lot of nonsense.* |
> | la langue littéraire/soutenue *(litt)* | *literary/elevated language* |
> | Exemple: L'excès de boisson rend ses propos confus. | *Example: Excess consumption of alcohol causes his speech to be confused.* |
> | la langue des jeunes | *language of young people, youth slang* |
> | La langue des jeunes contient beaucoup d'expressions familières. | *The language of young people contains many colloquial expressions.* |

la **lettre** [lɛtʀ]	letter
A est la première lettre de l'alphabet.	A is the first letter of the alphabet.
le **son** [sɔ̃]	sound
la **voyelle** [vwajɛl]	vowel
une **voyelle nasale**	a nasal vowel
la **consonne** [kɔ̃sɔn]	consonant
une **consonne sonore**	a voiced consonant
la **liaison** [ljɛzɔ̃]	liaison, speech-sound redistribution
Faites la liaison entre ces deux mots.	Run these two words together.
la **syllabe** [silab]	syllable

le **point** [pwɛ̃]	period
les **deux points**	colon
le **point d'exclamation**	exclamation point
le **point d'interrogation**	question mark
la **virgule** [viʀgyl]	comma
le **point-virgule**	semicolon
l'**accent** *m* [aksɑ̃]	accent
l'accent aigu *(é)*	acute accent
l'accent grave *(è)*	grave accent
l'accent circonflexe *(ê)*	circumflex accent
la **cédille** *(ç)* [sedij]	cedilla
le **tiret** [tiʀɛ]	dash
le **trait d'union** [tʀɛdynjɔ̃]	hyphen

la **parenthèse** [paʀɑ̃tɛz]	parenthesis
ouvrir/fermer une parenthèse	open/close a parenthesis
les **guillemets** *m* [gijmɛ]	quotation marks
entre guillemets	in quotation marks

le **mot** [mo]	word
le **nom** [nɔ̃]	noun
le **substantif** [sypstɑ̃tif]	substantive
le **genre** [ʒɑ̃ʀ]	gender
masculin,e [maskylɛ̃, in]	masculine
féminin,e [feminɛ̃, in]	feminine
le **nombre** [nɔ̃bʀ]	number
s'**accorder en genre et en nombre**	agree in gender and in number
le **singulier** [sɛ̃gylje]	singular
le **pluriel** [plyʀjɛl]	plural

le **sujet** [syʒɛ]	subject
le **complément** [kɔ̃plemɑ̃]	object; complement
le **complément d'objet** (l'objet)	object
le **complément d'objet direct**	direct object
le **complément d'objet indirect**	indirect object

l'**article** *m* [aʀtikl]	article
l'**article défini**	the definite article
l'**article indéfini**	the indefinite article
l'**article partitif** (le **partitif**)	the partitive article

le **déterminant** [detɛʀminɑ̃]	determinative word, adjunct
le **déterminant démonstratif**	the demonstrative adjunct
le **déterminant possessif**	the possessive adjunct
le **déterminant interrogatif**	the interrogative adjunct
le **déterminant indéfini**	the indefinite adjunct

l'**adjectif** *m* [adʒɛktif]	adjective
l'**accord** *m* [akɔʀ]	agreement
Faites l'accord de l'adjectif avec le nom.	Make the adjective agree with the noun.
accorder qc avec qc [akɔʀde]	put s.th. in agreement with s.th.
Accordez le verbe avec le sujet.	Put the verb in agreement with the subject.
l'**adverbe** *m* [advɛʀb]	adverb
les **adverbes de lieu/temps**	adverbs of place/time
les **adverbes de manière**	adverbs of manner
la **place** [plas]	position, place
Le sens d'un adjectif peut changer selon la place qu'il occupe.	The meaning of an adjective can change in accordance with the place it occupies.

les **degrés (de signification)** *m* [dəgre]	degrees of comparison
le **positif** [pozitif]	positive
le **comparatif** [kɔ̃paratif]	comparative
le **superlatif** [sypɛrlatif]	superlative

le **numéral** [nymeral]	numeral
le **nombre** [nɔ̃br]	number
un **nombre pair/impair**	an even/uneven number
un **nombre/numéral cardinal**	cardinal number
un **nombre/numéral ordinal**	ordinal number
la **fraction** [fraksjɔ̃]	fraction

le **pronom** [prɔnɔ̃]	pronoun
le **pronom personnel**	personal pronoun
le **pronom personnel conjoint/ disjoint**	conjunctive/disjunctive personal pronoun
le **pronom adverbial**	adverbial pronoun
le **pronom réfléchi**	reflexive pronoun
le **pronom relatif**	relative pronoun
le **pronom sujet/objet**	pronoun subject/object
le **pronom démonstratif**	demonstrative pronoun
le **pronom possessif**	possessive pronoun
le **pronom indéfini**	indefinite pronoun
le **pronom interrogatif**	interrogative pronoun

le **verbe** [vɛrb]	verb
un **verbe (in)transitif**	a transitive/an intransitive verb
un **verbe pronominal**	a reflexive verb
la **forme** [fɔrm]	form
la **forme simple/composée**	the simple/compound form
la **conjugaison** [kɔ̃ʒygɛzɔ̃]	conjugation
la **conjugaison (ir)régulière**	the (ir)regular conjugation
conjuguer [kɔ̃ʒyge]	conjugate
Conjuguez le verbe *aller* au futur simple.	Conjugate the verb *aller* in the future.
le **radical** [radikal]	root
la **terminaison** [tɛrminɛzɔ̃]	ending
la **négation** [negasjɔ̃]	negation

le **mode** [mɔd]	mood
l'**infinitif** *m* [ɛ̃finitif]	infinitive
l'**indicatif** *m* [ɛ̃dikatif]	indicative
le **subjonctif** [sybʒɔ̃ktif]	subjunctive
l'**impératif** *m* [ɛ̃peratif]	imperative

le **temps** [tã]	tense
le **présent** [pʀezã]	present
Mettez le verbe au présent.	Put the verb in the present.
le **passé** [pase]	past
l'**imparfait** m [ɛ̃paʀfɛ]	imperfect
le **passé simple** [pasekɛ̃pl]	past historic, past definite
le **passé composé** [pasekɔ̃poze]	perfect, past indefinite
le **plus-que-parfait** [plyskəpaʀfɛ]	pluperfect
le **passé autérieur** [paseãteʀjœʀ]	past anterior
le **futur simple** [fytyʀsɛ̃pl]	simple future
le **futur composé** [fytyʀkɔ̃poze]	compound future
le **futur antérieur** [fytyʀãteʀjœʀ]	future anterior
le **conditionnel présent** [kɔ̃disjɔnɛlpʀezã]	present conditional
le **conditionnel passé** [kɔ̃disjɔnɛlpase]	past conditional
le **participe présent** [paʀtisippʀezã]	present participle
le **participe passé** [paʀtisippase]	past participle
la **voix active**, l'**actif** m [vwaaktiv/aktif]	active voice
la **voix passive**, le **passif** [vwapasiv/pasif]	passive voice

la **phrase** [fʀaz]	sentence
la **phrase/proposition déclarative**	declarative sentence/clause
la **phrase/propos. interrogative**	interrogative sentence/clause
la **phrase/propos. exclamative**	exclamatory sentence/clause
la **phrase/propos. impérative**	imperative sentence/clause
la **phrase/propos. principale**	principal clause, independent clause
la **phrase/propos. subordonnée**	subordinate clause, dependent clause
le **style** (le **discours**) **(in)direct** [stil (diskuʀ)(ɛ̃)diʀɛkt]	(in)direct discourse
la **concordance des temps** [kɔ̃kɔʀdãsdetã]	sequence of tenses
respecter la concordance des temps	abide by the sequence of tenses
la **mise en relief** [mizãʀəljɛf]	emphasis

l'**interrogation** f [ɛ̃teʀɔgasjɔ̃]	question, interrogative construction
l'**interrogation par intonation**	question using intonation
l'**interrogation par inversion**	question using inversion
le **mot interrogatif** [moɛ̃teʀɔgatif]	interrogative word

la **préposition** [pʀepozisjɔ̃]	preposition
la **conjonction** [kɔ̃ʒɔ̃ksjɔ̃]	conjunction

Index of All French Entries

The index contains all the main entries found in the basic and advanced vocabulary sections. All the words of the basic vocabulary appear in **boldface**, while the advanced vocabulary entries are in normal roman type.

à 402, 483
à ... m/km d'ici 400
à aucun prix 454
A bientôt. 128
à bord 208, 345
à carreaux 104
à cause de 485
à ce moment-là 396
A ce soir. 128
à charge 276
à condition que 478
à côté (de) 398, 485
à coup sûr 454
à décharge 276
A demain. 128
à destination de ... 346
à droite (de) 334, 402, 485
à feu doux 96
à gauche (de) 334, 402, 485
à genoux 34
à jeun 91
à l' 470
à la 470
à la fin de 246
à la fois 394
à la hauteur de 399
à la rigueur 455
à l'aide de 486
A l'aide ! 466
à laquelle 474, 475
à l'attention de 318
à l'avenir 395
à l'endroit 97
à l'envers 97
à l'étroit 115
à l'extérieur 397
à l'extrémité de 398
à l'heure 344, 388
à l'intérieur 397

à l'inverse de 425
à l'ombre 357
à l'opposé de 424
à partir de 393
à peine 483
à peu près 416, 422
A plus tard. 128
à point 92
à pois 104
à présent 395
à propos de 441
A qui est ... ? 145
à rayures 104
à son compte 176
à suivre 325
à talons aiguilles/hauts/ plats 101
A tes/vos souhaits ! 466
A tout à l'heure. 128
à tout prix 454
à travers 403, 486
à volonté 68
A votre santé ! 91
abandonner 436
abcès 46
abeille 371
abîmer 437
abonné,e 226
abonné,e 316
abonnement 226, 325
s'abonner 226, 325
aboutir 395, 433
aboyer 368
abrégé,e 232
abricot 364
abruti,e 450
ABS 338
absence 149
absent,e 149
Absolument. 451
absolutisme 249
s'abstenir 263
abstention 263

abstrait,e 256
abstrait,e 223
abus 54
accélérateur 338
accélérer 338
accent 487
accepter 67, 134, 451
accès 330
accès 346
accessoire 105
accident 44, 311, 337, 374
accompagnateur, -trice 210
accompagner 140
accompagner 210
accomplir 81
accord 488
accord 183, 280, 288
accord sur les salaires 183
accorder 488
accorder 82
accouchement 21
accoucher 21
accourir 33
accro 53
accrocher 166
s'accroître 136
accueil 144
accueillir 144
accusation 272
accusé,e 272
accuser 272
achat 107, 305
acheter 107, 304
acheteur, -euse 305
achever 438
acide 86
acier 361
acquérir 82, 146
acquisition 82, 146
acquittement 276
acquitter 276

acte 196, 237
acte 33, 257
acte de sabotage 282
acteur, -trice 176, 198, 238
actif 490
actif, -ive 30, 76, 179, 185
action 30, 76, 196, 237, 372
action 146, 310
activité 30, 76, 179, 185
activité professionnelle 176
actualités 319
actuel,le 427
actuellement 395
acupuncture 52
adaptation 134
adapter 232
s'adapter 134
addition 216
addition 160, 417
additionner 160, 417
adhérent,e 270, 279
adhérer 270, 279
adjectif 488
administratif, -ive 266
administration 171
administration 266
admirateur, -trice 58
admiration 58
admirer 58
ado(lescent,e) 11, 24, 129
adolescence 24
adopter 144
adoptif, -ive 127
adorable 58, 461
adorer 58
adresse 10, 77, 318
s'adresser 233
adroit,e 77
adulte 11, 24
adverbe 488
adversaire 192, 271
aérer 121
aérodrome 345
aérogare 345

aéroport 208, 345
affaire 179, 271
affaires 302
affamé,e 91
affection 21
affection 142
affectueux, -euse 142
affirmation 232, 441
affirmer 232, 441
affluent 355
afflux 283
affranchir 318
affreux, -euse 36, 465
s'affronter 287
afin de 433
afin que 433, 479
afrique 14
âge 11, 25
âge de la pierre/du bronze 248
âge ingrat 131
âgé,e 11, 25
agence 309
agence de presse 327
agence de voyage 205
agenda 169
agent 337, 171
agglomération 382
aggravation 45
s'aggraver 45, 438
agir 30, 77, 372
agité,e 73
agneau 88
agneau 370
agrafe 169
agrafeuse 169
agrandir 323
agrandissement 323
agréable 69, 138, 358, 460
agresseur 292
agressif, -ive 448
agression 131
agression 292
agressivité 448
agricole 295
agriculteur, -trice 174, 295

agriculture 174, 295
Ah, bon ? 463
aide 50
aide sociale 134
aider 135
Aïe ! 447
aigle 371
aiguille 103
ail 92
aile 369
ailleurs 402, 481
aimable 69, 137, 461
aimer 20, 58
aîné,e 13, 127
ainsi 430, 453, 476
air 225, 349, 372
airbag 340
aire 208
aisé,e 133
ajouter 94, 436, 441
Albanie 16
album 230
album 188
alcool 54, 91
alcoolique 54
alcoolisme 54
alcootest 56, 341
alexandrin 236
algèbre 156
algérie 16
algérien,ne 16
alibi 278
aliment 85
alimentation 85
allégé,e 87
Allemagne 14
allemand 157
allemand,e 14
aller 104
aller 30
aller bien/mal 42
aller chercher 139
aller en boîte 130
aller en étude/permanence/perm 158
aller faire 392, 479
aller simple 207, 342
aller voir 139

allergie 44
allergique 44
aller-retour, aller et retour 207, 342
Allez, allez ! 466
alliage 362
alliance 105, 270, 288
allié,e 288
allitération 236
Allô ! 128
allocation 312
allocation (de) chômage 180
s'allonger 34
allumer 120
allumette 54
allusion 234
alors 432
alors que 477
alouette 371
Alpes 352
alpiniste 194
alternative 437
altitude 354
alto 228
amabilité 69, 137
amant 21
amateur, -trice 190
ambassade 287
ambassadeur, -drice 287
ambiance 138, 202
ambitieux, -euse 75
ambition 75
ambre solaire 211
ambulance 51
amélioration 48, 288, 359, 382
s'améliorer 48, 359, 382, 437
aménagement 377
aménager 377
amende 276, 341
amener 140, 434
amer, -ère 86
américain,e 15
Amérique 14
ameublement 119
ami,e 21, 129, 137

amical,e 137
amitié 137
amour 20
amoureux, -euse 21, 58
ampli(ficateur) 227
ampoule 47
amusant,e 71, 462
amuser 239
s'amuser 58, 202
an 11, 390
analogie 425
analphabète 158
analyse (de texte) 240
analyser 65, 240
ananas 90
ancêtre 127
ancien Régime 249
Ancien Testament 253
ancien,ne 391, 426
anciens 248
âne, ânesse 370
anecdote 233
anesthésie 52
ange 252
angine 46
anglais 157
anglais,e 14
angle 408
Angleterre 14
angoisse 62
animal 367
animateur, -trice 320
année 390
année bissextile 390
année scolaire 158
année-lumière 349
anniversaire 23, 201
annonce 325
annuaire 316
annuel,le 390
annulé,e 344
annuler 206
anonyme 222
anorak 98
anormal,e 427
ANPE 177
antenne 321
anthologie 230

antibiotique 52
anticyclone 359
antipathie 138
antipathique 138
antique 248
antiquité 248
antithèse 234
anxieux, -euse 62
août 389
apercevoir 29, 82
s'apercevoir 29, 82
apéritif 216
apesanteur 351
apiculteur, -trice 371
apiculture 371
appareil 120
appareil dentaire 53
appareil photo 186, 322
apparence 35, 257
appartement 112
appartement de vacances 212
appartement en copropriété 115
appartenance à une religion 13
appartenir 145
appauvri,e 136
appel 168, 315, 440
appelé 291
appeler 168, 315, 440
appendicite 46
appétissant,e 93
appétit 85
applaudir 197, 227
applaudissements 197, 227
apporter 434
appréciation 464
apprécier 142, 464
apprendre 149, 170
apprenti,e 170
apprentissage 170
apprivoiser 370
approbation 454
approcher 438
s'approcher 33
approuver 235, 454

appuyer 435
s'appuyer 34
après 393, 397, 482, 484
après que 394, 477
après tout 453
après-midi 388
après-rasage 39
aquarelle 223
aquarium 369
arbitraire 68
arbitre 192
arbre 363
arbuste 365
arc 219, 408
arc-en-ciel 359
archevêque 254
architecte 112, 173, 222
architecture 112, 222
Ardennes 354
ardoise 362
are 419
argent 108, 306, 361
argenté,e 105
argenté,e 407
argile 224, 362
argument 233, 255
arme 273, 289
armée 175, 289
armée de l'air 292
armée de métier 292
armée de terre 292
armement 290
armer 289
armistice 248
armistice 293
armoire 117
arracher 437
arracher 53
s'arranger 144
arrestation 273
Arrête ! 448
arrêter 273
s'arrêter 30, 334
arreter le moteur 334
arrière 397
arrière-grand-mère 127
arrière-grand-père 127

arrière-grands-parents 127
arrière-petite-fille 126
arrière-petit-fils 126
arrière-petits-enfants 126
arrivée 31, 189, 207, 344
arriver 31, 78, 128, 206
arrogant,e 74
arrondissement 266
arrosage 367
arrosoir 367
art 221
art nouveau 223
artère 19
artichaut 92, 366
article 107, 232, 305, 324, 488
article 274
artisan,e 173, 299
artisanal,e 299
artisanat 299
artiste 176, 221
artistique 221
arts plastiques 157
ascenseur 114, 213
ascension 253
asie 14
asile 282
aspect physique 35
asperges 89
s'asphyxier 47
aspirateur 121
assainissement 377
assaisonner 92
assassin 278
assassinat 278
assassiner 278
Assedic 313
Assemblée nationale 264
s'asseoir 33
assez 482
assiette 95
assis,e 33
assistant,e 163
assister 199
association 130, 278
Assomption 253
assorti,e 104

assumer une responsabilité 270
assurance 311, 337
assurance accidents 311
assurance auto(mobile) 311
assurance dépendance 311
assurance maladie 311
assurance responsabilité civile 311
assurance tous risques 311
assurance vie 311
assurance vieillesse 311
assuré,e 337, 311
assurer 311, 441
s'assurer 311
assureur 311
astre 349
astronaute 304, 350
astronautique 350
atelier 170, 221, 299
athée 13
athéisme 253
athlète 192
athlétique 192
athlétisme 191
Atlantique 211, 355
atlas 354
atmosphère 235
atmosphère 350
atome 362
attaquant,e 292
attaque 44, 274, 289, 448
attaquer 289, 448
atteindre 432
attendre 139, 343
attendre un enfant 21
attentat 282
attentif, -ive 149
attentif, -ive 76
Attention ! 466
atterrir 210, 346
atterrissage 210, 346
attirer 350
attraction 219, 350

attraper 33
attribuer 82
atypique 215
au 470
au bout de 392, 484
au choix 88, 216
au cours de 395, 486
au début de 246
au fond 431, 455
au grand air 211
au lieu de 486
au milieu de 392, 485
au moins 454
au moment où 478
au plus tard 396
au plus tôt 396
au premier plan 398
Au revoir. 128
au second plan 398
Au secours ! 466
au sens propre/figuré 244
au sujet de 486
Au voleur ! 466
aube 389
auberge de jeunesse 212
aubergine 92, 366
aucun,e ... ne 410, 471, 480
au-dessous 485
au-dessus 484
audience 321
audimat 321
audiovisuel,le 321
auditeur, -trice 321
auditif, -ive 29
auditoire 199
augmentation 437
augmentation 136
augmenter 108, 437
aujourd'hui 386, 481
auparavant 395
auquel 473, 475
ausculter 51
aussi 430, 482
aussi ... que 424
Australie 14
autant 412
autant ... que 424

auteur 176, 229, 239
auto(mobile) 338
autobiographie 231
autobus 342
autocar 342
autodétermination 262
auto-école 338
automation/automatisa-
  tion 182, 300
automatique 303
automnal,e 390
automne 390
automobiliste 338
autonomie 280
autonomiste 281
autorisation 446
autoriser 446
autoritaire 72, 149
autorité 130, 149
autorités 266
autoroute 208
autoroute (A) 335, 380
autoroute de l'informa-
  tion 330
autour de 400
autour de 486
autre(s) 471
l'autre jour 394
autre part 402
autrefois 391
autrement 430
autrement 478
autrement dit 453
Autriche 15
autrichien,ne 15
aux 470
auxquelles 474, 475
av./ap. J.-C. 246
avalanche 377
avaler 85
avancer 30, 334
avant 392, 397, 482, 484
avant que 394, 477
avantage 241, 460
avant propos 326
avare 70
avec 485
avec préméditation 276

avec sursis 277
avenir 391
aventure 209
avenue 11, 379
averse 359
avertir 444
avertissement 291, 444
aveu 275
aveugle 27
avion 208, 344
avion de chasse 292
aviron 194
avis 65, 233, 458
avocat,e 174, 272
avoine 367
avoir 145, 479
avoir à faire 480
avoir besoin 108
avoir bonne/mauvaise
  mine 42
avoir chaud/froid 43
avoir de la classe 76
avoir de la famille 125
avoir de la peine 78
avoir de la volonté 72
avoir des boutons 36
avoir des problèmes 135
avoir des vertiges 46
avoir du goût 104
avoir du mal 78
avoir du succès 142
avoir envie 66, 85, 108,
  185
avoir honte 445
avoir la gueule de bois 56
avoir la trouille 76
avoir l'air 35
avoir le cœur sur la main
  73
avoir le mal de mer 208
avoir le sentiment que
  460
avoir le trac 197, 238
avoir les jambes molles 46
avoir lieu 246
avoir l'impression que
  460
avoir mal 43, 447

avoir mal à la gorge 43
avoir pitié 135
avoir sommeil 42
avoir un faible pour 73
avortement 23
avorter 23
avouer 275
avril 389
axe 350
azote 362
azur 405

B

bac(calauréat) 152
bac 210
bagages 345
bagages à main 206
bagarre 131, 273
bague 105
baguette 87
baie 356
baignade 209
se baigner 209
baignoire 116
bain 36
bain de soleil 211
baiser 21
baisse 310
baisser 108, 357, 437
se baisser 33
baisser les yeux 29
bal 203
bal populaire 203
balade 188
se balader 188
baladeur 323
balai 119
balance 418
balance commerciale 306
balayer 120
balcon 115, 213, 226
baleine 371
ballade 236
balle 190
balle de match 194
ballet 226
ballon 190

banal,e 462
banane 90
bande 129
bande 278
bande dessinée (BD) 230
banderole 284
banlieue 378
banque 308
Banque centrale européenne (BCE) 289
banquet 203
banquette 344
banquier 308
banquier, -ière 175
baptême 201, 252
baptiser 201, 252
bar 214
baraqué,e 35
barbe 38
baromètre 357
bas 98, 397
bas,se 352, 399, 418
basilique 219
basket(-ball) 190
baskets 99
bas-relief 224
basse-cour 370
bassin 354
bataille 289
bataillon 291
bateau 192, 208, 345
bâtiment 112, 173, 379
bâtir 112
batterie 225
batteur 121
battre 142, 189, 248
battre 96
bavard,e 73, 440
bavarder 440
beau, bel, belle 34, 222, 461
beaucoup 411, 482
beau-père 127
beauté 34, 222
beaux-parents 127
bébé 24, 124
bec 369

beige 406
belge 15
Belgique 15
belle-fille 127
belle-mère 127
bénéfice 302
bénin, bénigne 45
bénir 254
BEP 159
béret (basque) 98
best-seller 327
bétail 297
bête 72, 367, 462
bêtise 72
béton 112, 361
betterave 367
beur; beurette 283
beurre 87
beurré,e 55
bible 253
bibliothécaire 326
bibliothèque 155, 326
bicyclette 190, 333
bide 199
Biélorussie 16
bien 255, 430, 452, 460, 481
bien cuit,e 92
bien du/de la/de l'/des 411
bien que 477
Bien sûr ! 451
Bien ! 457
bien(s) 146
bien-être 145
biens de consommation 300
biens d'équipement 300
bientôt 392, 481
bière 91
bifteck 88
bijou, bijoux 104
bijou-fantaisie 105
bijoutier, -ière 173
bikini 98
bilingue 14
billet 197, 207, 226
billet (de banque) 109

bimensuel,le 390
biochimie 163
biodégradable 374
bioénergie 376
biographie 231
biologie 157, 161
biologique 372
biologiste 162
biosphère 376
bip sonore 316
biscotte 87
bistro(t) 214
bizarre 71, 427, 463
blâme 457
blâmer 457
blanc, blanche 405
blé 366
blessé,e 44, 290
blesser 273
blesser (se) 44
blessure 44
bleu 47
bleu ciel 406
bleu marine 406
bleu turquoise 406
bleu,e 405
bloc-notes 169
blond,e 35, 406
bloquer 336
se bloquer 331
blouse 101
blouson 98
body 101
bœuf 88, 368
Bof ! 451
boire 54, 85
bois 352, 361
boisé,e 355
boisson 85
boîte 94, 411
boîte aux lettres 317
boîte aux lettres (électronique) 331
boîte d'allumettes 55
boîte de vitesses 338
boîte postale (BP) 318
bol 95
bombardement 291

bombarder 291
bombe 290
bombe aérosol 373
Bon anniversaire ! 201, 466
Bon appétit. 467
bon marché 108, 428
bon sens 255
Bon voyage. 467
bon,ne 70, 86, 427, 460
bonbon 90
bonheur 58
Bonjour ! 128
Bonne année ! 201, 466
Bonne chance ! 466
Bonne fête ! 201, 466
Bonne journée. 467
Bonne nuit ! 128, 467
Bonne route. 467
Bonnes vacances. 467
bonnet 98
Bonsoir ! 128
bonté 70
bonus 312
bord 398, 407
borné,e 75
Bosnie-Herzégovine 16
bosse 47
bottes 99
bouche 18
boucher 436
boucher, -ère 106
boucher, ère 173
boucherie 106
bouchon 216, 335
boucle d'oreille 105
bouddhisme 253
bouger 30
bougie 340
boulanger, -ère 106, 172
boulangerie 106
bouleau 365
boulevard 11, 379
boulon 167
boulot 12, 179
bouquin 155, 229, 325
bourgeois,e 133
bourgeois,e 249

bourgeoisie 133
bourgeoisie 249
bourgeon 365
bourse 310
bousculer 137
bout 398
bouteille 216, 411
bouteille (non) consignée 374
bouteille en (matière) plastique 374
boutique 106
bouton 103, 118, 366
boxe 195
boycotter 284
bracelet 105
branche 363
branche 299
bras 19
brasse 194
brasserie 217
brave 76
Bravo ! 457
break 338
brebis 370
bref 241, 453
Brésil 15
brésilien,ne 15
bretelle 339
brevet 159
bricolage 186
bricoler 186
bricoleur, -euse 186
brillant,e 323, 407
brioche 87
brique 112
briquet 54
brise 359
briser 438
briseur, -euse de grève 280
britannique 14
broche 105
brochure 328
broder 103
broderie 103
bronchite 46
bronzage 211

bronze 362
bronzé,e 36, 211
bronzer 211
brosse 119
brosse (à cheveux) 37
brosse (à dents) 37
se brosser les dents 37
brouillard 358
se brouiller 131
brouillon 159
bruit 27, 373
brûlant,e 43, 86
brûler 375
se brûler 44
brûlure 44
brume 359
brun,e 35, 406
brushing 38
brut,e 418
brutal,e 74
brutalité 74
brute 74
bruyant,e 213, 373
bruyère 366
building 115
Bulgarie 16
bulle 230
bulletin (de vote) 263
bulletin météorologique 356
bulletin scolaire 159
bureau 117, 167
bureau de poste 317
bureau de tabac 106
bureau de vote 263
bureaucratie 266
bureaucratique 266
burin 167
bus 342
buste 224
but 66, 148, 190, 432
buveur, -euse 54

ça 473
Ça (ne) va pas, non ? 452

Ça alors ! 463
Ça brûle. 448
Ça m'est égal. 458
Ça ne fait rien. 445
Ça ne me (te, le ...) regarde pas. 464
Ça ne vaut rien. 464
Ça peut arriver à tout le monde. 445
Ça pique. 448
Ça suffit ! 448
Ça va passer. 445
Ça y est ! 457
cabine 316
cabinet dentaire 50
cabinet médical 49
cabinet(s) 114
cacher 435
cachet 52
cachet (de la poste) 318
cadet,te 13, 127
cadre 117, 171, 221, 301
café 87, 214
cafetière 97, 121
cage 369
cahier 156
caisse 108, 197, 308
caisse d'assurance maladie 312
caisse de retraite 312
caisse d'épargne 309
caissier, -ière 108, 175, 308
calcul 416
calculer 155, 169, 416
calculette 157, 169
caleçon 101
calendrier 169, 390
calmant 52
calme 71, 213, 373
calmer 141
camarade 137
cambriolage 278
cambrioler 278
cambrioleur, -euse 278
came 54
camembert 89
se camer 54

caméra 186, 198, 322
caméscope 323
camion 333
camionnette 338
camionneur 347
camp (de prisonniers) 290
campagnard,e 295, 378
campagne 210, 295, 352, 378
campagne de presse 327
camper 213
camping 213
campingcar 213
Canada 15
canadien,ne 15
canal 347
canapé 119
canard 88, 368
canard 326
cancer 47
cancre 159
candidat,e 162, 260
candidat,e 177
canicule 359
canif 166
cannelle 92
canoë 195
cantatrice 228
canton 266
CAP 159
capable 77
capacité 80
capitaine 175, 345
capital 145
capital,e 464
capitale 266, 378
capitalisme 269
capitaliste 269
capitulation 293
capituler 293
capter 321
capteur solaire 376
captivant,e 233
car 208, 342, 432, 476
caractère 68, 243
caractériser 69
caractéristique 69

carafe 97, 217
caravane 213
carbone 362
carburant 363
caresser 21, 138
cargo 347
carie 53
carnaval 202
carnet 343
carnet (de timbres) 318
carnet de chèques 309
carnivore 369
carotte 89, 364
carré 408
carré,e 419
carré,e 408
carrefour 335, 379
carrelage 118
cartable 156
carte 215
carte bancaire 308
carte de crédit 308
carte d'identité 13, 208
carte grise 341
carte orange 343
carte postale 317
carte routière 206
carte verte 341
cartes 186
carton 361
cartouche 156, 168
cartouche de cigarettes 55
cas 274
cascade 355
cascadeur, -euse 198
caserne 289
casque 323
casquette 98
casse-croûte 92
casser 437
se casser le bras 48
casser un jugement 274
casserole 96
cassette 322
casseur, -euse 132
cassis 365
cata(strophe) 374

cata(strophe) 464
cataclysme 377
catalogue 205
catalogue 109
catastrophique 374
catastrophique 464
catégorie 212, 421
catégories socioprofes-sionnelles 176
cathédrale 218, 252, 381
catholicisme 252
catholique 12, 252
cause 256, 431
causer 256, 431
cave 114, 216
CD 227, 322
CDD 181
CDI 181
CD-ROM 328
ce 470
Ce n'est pas grave. 445
Ce n'est rien. 445
ce que (ce qu') 473
ce qui 473
CECA 250
ceci 473
cécité 29
céder 81
cédérom 328
CEDEX 318
cédille 487
ceinture 103
cela 473
célèbre 222
célébrer 203
célibataire 12, 125
celle (-ci/-la) 474
celles (-ci/-la) 474
cellulaire 163
cellule 163
celui (-ci/-la) 474
cendre 55
cendrier 55
censure 327
cent 307
centaine 415
centenaire 25
centième 415

centime 307
centimètre 418
central,e 213, 378
central,e 268
centrale nucléaire 303, 374
centralisation 268
centralisé,e 268
centre 378
centre commercial 106, 380
centre culturel 381
centre de contrôle tech-nique 340
centre de formation pro-fessionnelle 158
cependant 478
céramique 224, 362
cercle 407
cercle polaire 350
cercueil 26
céréales 366
cérémonie 203
cerise 90, 364
cerisier 365
certain(e)s 471
certain,e 256, 458
certainement 452
certificat 162
certificat 267
certificat (médical) 51
certitude 256
cerveau 19
ces 470
cesser 395
C'est (de) ma faute. 444
C'est dégoûtant ! 450
C'est dégueulasse ! 450
C'est du vol ! 450
C'est inadmissible ! 449
C'est insupportable. 450
C'est le comble ! 450
c'est pour cela/ça que 432
c'est pourquoi 432, 476
C'est ridicule. 450
C'est scandaleux ! 449
C'est un fait que ... 453

499

C'est un scandale ! 449
C'est une honte ! 450
c'est-à-dire 483
césure 236
cet 470
cette 470
ceux (-ci/-la) 474
CFC 373
chacun,e 413, 471
chagrin 61
chaîne 104, 198, 319
chaîne codée 321
chaîne de montagnes 354
chaine hi-fi 322
chaire 163
chaise 117, 168
chalet 214
chaleur 357
chaleureux, -euse 142
chambre 114, 212
chambre d'hôte 214
champ 295
champagne 91, 202
champignon 89, 364
champion,ne 189
championnat 189
chance 141
chancelier (allemand) 263
change 308
changement 269, 356, 436
changer 97, 308, 343, 436
se changer 97
chanson 225
chant 225
chantage 278
chanter 79, 225
chanteur, -euse 225
chantier 339, 382
chapeau 98
chapelle 219
chapitre 155, 229, 240, 326
chaque 412, 471
char 292
charbon 296, 375

charcuterie 106
charcutier, -ière 106, 173
se charger 81
charges 116, 302
charges annexes 182
charges sociales 313
chariot 108, 345
charmant,e 69, 461
charme 69, 461
charmer 142
charrue 367
charter 344
chasse 187
chasse 370
chasser 187
chasser 370
chasseur, -euse 187
chat,te 368
châtain 36, 406
château 218, 381
chaud,e 28, 36, 86, 100, 426
chauffage 116
chauffard 341
chauffe-eau 121
chauffer 120
chauffeur 174, 343
chaussée 379
Chaussée déformée. 339
chausser 102
chaussettes 98
chaussons 101
chaussures 99
chauve 36
chauvin, -ine 265
chauvinisme 265
chef 171, 214, 300
chef de l'Etat 263
chef d'Etat 263
chef du gouvernement 263
chemin 335, 379
cheminée 114
chemise 98
chemise 169
chemise de nuit 99
chemisier 98
chêne 365

chèque 308
chéquier 309
cher, chère 108, 428
chercher 79
chercheur, -euse 161
chéri,e 129
cheval, chevaux 367
cheveux 18, 35
cheville 20, 167
chèvre 368
chez 402, 485
chic 99
chien,ne 368
chiffon 119
chiffre 155, 415
chiffre d'affaires 302
chimie 157, 361
chimique 361
chimiste 162
Chine 16
chinois,e 16
chirurgien,ne 49, 173
choc 44
chocolat 87
chœur 225
choisir 79, 108
choix 79
cholestérol 46
chômage 134, 180
chômage partiel 180
chômeur, -euse 134, 180
chorale 225
chou 364
chou-fleur 92
chrétien,ne 12, 251
chronique (théâtrale) 327
CHU 380
chuchoter 443
Chut ! 466
chute 31, 44
chute d'eau 355
chute des prix 295
ciboulette 92
cidre 91
ciel 252, 349, 358
cigare 54
cigarette 54
cigogne 371

ci-joint,e 318
cil 20
ciment 361
cimetière 380
cimetière 26
ciné-club 199
cinématographique 199
cinéphile 199
cinquième 415
circonférence 400
circonscription 263
circonstances 437
circonstances atténuantes 276
circuit 205
circuit touristique 218
circulation 334
circuler 334
ciseaux 38, 155, 166
ciseaux 103
citadin,e 378
cité 382
cité u(niversitaire) 164
citoyen,ne 260
clair,e 459
clair,e 36, 407, 428
clandestin,e 283
claquage 48
clarinette 225
classe 133, 151, 207
classe préparatoire 160
classement 421
classer 168, 421
classeur 156, 168
classicisme 230
classification 163, 422
clavier 329
clé 167
clé (clef) 114, 212
clé (de contact) 334
clean 53
clergé 249, 254
client,e 107, 215, 304
clientèle 107, 215, 304
cligner (des yeux) 29
clignotant 340
clim(atisation) 340
climat 356

clinique 49, 380
cliquer 329
clochard,e 134
clope 55
clou 166
club 189
club (de vacances) 212
CNRS 163
coalition 270
cocaïne 54
coccinelle 371
cochon 368
cochon d'Inde 368
cocotte-minute 96
code civil 274
code de la nationalité 283
code de la route 337
code pénal 274
code postal 11, 318
code secret 308
cœur 19
coffre 309
cohabitation 263
se coiffer 37
coiffeur, -euse 37
coiffure 37
coin 116, 398, 408
coke 54
col 352
col 102
colère 70
colis 306, 318
collaborateur, -trice 302
collaboration 248
collant 98
colle 168, 186, 361
colle 159
collecte sélective (des déchets) 375
collection 188, 223, 328
collectionner 188, 223
collectionneur, -euse 188, 223
collège 151, 381
collègue 137, 301
coller 186, 330
collier 105

colline 351
collision 341
colo(nie) de vacances 214
colonial,e 247
colonie 247
colonne 324
colonne 219
colonne vertébrale 20
coloré,e 405
coloré,e 429
colorier 405
colza 367
combat 250, 285
combattant,e 291
combattre 250, 291
combien ? 108, 410, 475
combiné 315
comédie 197, 237
comédien,ne 196, 238
comète 349
comique 71, 197, 237
comique 238
comité d'entreprise 280
comité directeur 302
commandant de bord 346
commande 215, 305
commander 215, 305
commander 109
comme 424, 432, 477
commencement 392
commencer 392, 435
Comment ? 430, 463, 475
commentaire 154, 241, 325
commenter 154, 241
commerçant,e 172, 304
commerce 172, 304
commerce de gros/détail 305
commerce intérieur/extérieur 305
commercial,e 304
commissaire 273
commissariat 273, 337
commission 306

commission européenne 289
commode 117
commotion cérébrale 47
communal,e 266
communauté 133
commune 266
communication (télé-phonique) 315
communion 252
communisme 269
communiste 269
compact 227, 322
compagne 21
compagnie 144
compagnie (Cie) 300
compagnie aérienne 344
compagnie d'assurances 311
compagnon 21
comparable 425
comparaison 242, 423
comparaître 275
comparatif 489
comparé,e 425
comparer 65, 242, 410, 423
compartiment 207, 344
compas 160
compatriote 265
compétence 80
compétent,e 80
compétition 190
complément 488
complet, -ète 197, 212, 426
complètement 452
complexé,e 75
complice 278
compliment 139, 456
compliqué,e 71
comportement 73
comportement sexuel 22
comporter 240
se comporter 73
se composer 240, 360
composition 152

compostage 375
composter 346
compréhensible 154
compréhensif, -ive 75, 131
compréhension 64, 149
compréhension 131
comprendre 63, 149
comprimé 50
compromis 279
comptabilité 302
comptable 171
compte (en banque) 308
compte chèque postal (CCP) 318
compter 155, 306, 410, 416
compte-rendu 232
compte-rendu 327
con,ne 450
concentration 149, 298
se concentrer 149, 298
conception 22, 257
concerné,e 140
concert 130, 226
concerto 228
concevoir 82, 257
concierge 113
conciliant,e 76
conclure 67
conclusion 240, 459
concombre 92, 366
concordance des temps 490
concours 162, 170
concret, -ète 256
concubinage 127
concurrence 301
concurrent,e 301
condamnation 272
condamné,e 273
condamner 272, 457
conditionnel passé 490
conditionnel présent 490
conditions de vie 136
condoléances 26

conducteur, -trice 174, 333
conduire 333, 434
conduite 333
confédération 263
conférence 286
se confesser 253
confession 253
confiance 61, 131
se confier 131
confirmation 252
confiture 87
conflit 130
conflit 287
conflit social 182, 280
confluent 355
confondre 67
confort 117, 212
confortable 100, 117, 212
confrontation 287
confus,e 459
confus,e 67
confusion 67
congé 179, 205
congélateur 94
congeler 94
conjonction 490
conjugaison 489
conjugal,e 26
conjuguer 489
connaissance 64
connaissances 148
connaître 64, 137, 148
se connecter 331
connerie 450
conquérir 247
conquête 247
consciencieux, -euse 75
conscrit 291
conseil 446
Conseil de l'Europe 288
conseil de surveillance 302
Conseil des ministres 264, 289
conseil régional 268
conseiller 446

conseiller 217
conseiller, -ère 266
conséquence 433
conservatoire 227
conserve 94
considérable 413
considérer 458
consigne 207, 342
consolation 141
consoler 141, 445
consommateur, -trice 215, 304
consommation 215
consommation 340
consommer 340
consonne 487
constat (à l')amiable 312
constatation 68
constater 68
constellation 349
constituer 421
constitution 260
constitution 35
constitutionnel,le 260
construction 112, 379
construire 112, 379
consul 287
consulaire 287
consulat 287
consultation 49
consultation 271, 288
consultation de la base 182, 280
consulter 49
consulter 271
contagieux, -euse 45
contamination 373
contaminé,e 373
contaminer 45
conte 231
contemporain,e 395
conteneur à verre/papier (usagé) 375
contenir 242, 360, 410
content,e 59
contenu 242, 419
contestation 182, 280
contester 458

contester 182, 280
contexte 242, 424
continent 13, 351
continuer 436
contractuel,le 277, 339
contradiction 255
contradiction 449
contraindre 144
contrainte 144
contraire 424
contrairement 424
contraste 425
contraster 425
contrat 305, 311
contravention 341
contre 485
contrebasse 228
contredire 131, 233
contredire 449
contremaître, contremaîtresse 171
contribuable 267
contrôle 152, 207, 337
contrôle des naissances 23
contrôleur, -euse 207, 343
convaincant,e 443
convaincre 443
convalescence 48
convenable 464
convention collective 183, 280
conversation 440
se convertir 253
conviction 235, 443
coopération 286
coopérative 296
coopérer 286
coordonnées 10
copain, copine 21, 129, 137
copie 153, 222
copier 153, 330
coq 368
coquelicot 366
coran 253
corbeille à pain 95

corde (à linge) 102
cordial,e 142
cornichon 92
corps 18
corpulence 35
corpulent,e 35
correct,e 152, 459
correspondance 207, 343
correspondant,e 151, 315
correspondant,e 327
correspondre 416, 421
corrigé 152
cosmonaute 350
costume 98
costumes 199
côte 353
côte à côte 398
côté 398
côtelette 89
cotisation 312
cotiser 312
coton 361
coton 39, 51, 102
cou 19
couche d'ozone 373
couché,e 33
coucher 21
se coucher 33
coucher de/du soleil 389
couchette 208, 344
coude 19
coudre 103
couette 119
coulée de lave 377
couler 353
couleur 405
couleurs 323
coulisses 199
couloir 114
coup 142
coup de feu 289
coup de fil 315
coup de soleil 211
coup de théâtre 238
coup d'Etat 285
coup d'œil 29

coupable 272
coupe 92, 193
coupe de cheveux 37
couper 94, 166, 330
couper (se) 44
couper la parole 449
couper le moteur 334
couple 24, 124
coupure 44
cour 380
cour (de justice) 274
cour d'assises 274
cour de cassation 274
courage 72
courageux, -euse 72
courant 355
courant (électrique) 118
courant d'air 359
courant politique 270
courants littéraires 230
courbatures 46
courbe 408
courgette 366
courir 31, 191, 138
couronne 53
courrier 317
courrier des lecteurs 327
courrier du cœur 327
courrier électronique
330
cours 153
cours du soir 163
cours élémentaire (CE)
150
cours magistral 163
cours moyen (CM) 151
cours par correspondance
163
cours préparatoire (CP)
150
course 31, 189, 191
court,e 35, 100, 391,
399, 417
court-circuit 121
court-métrage 200
cousin,e 125
coussin 117
coussin gonflable 340

coût 309
couteau 95
coûter 108, 307
coûteux, -euse 109, 309
coûts 109
couvent 254
couvert 95
couvert,e 359
couverture 229, 324
couvre-feu 292
couvreur 177
couvrir 436
couvrir 312
se couvrir 97
se couvrir 359
crack 55
craie 156
craie 362
craindre 60
crainte 60
craintif, -ive 76
crâne 19
cravate 105
crawl 194
crayon 156, 168, 221
création 78
créativité 222
crèche 381
crédit 307
créditer 310
créer 78, 180, 222
crème 38, 90
crème Chantilly 93
crème fraîche 89
crêpe 93
crépuscule 389
crevaison 340
crever 340
cri 448
criard,e 406
cric 340
crier 448
crime 273
crime de guerre 292
criminel,le 273
criminel,le de guerre 292
crise 44, 286, 298
cristal 362

critique 130, 227, 239,
325
critiquer 227, 239, 325,
457
Croatie 16
crochet 103
crocodile 369
croire 65, 251
croisades 249
croisière 210, 347
croissant 87
croître 349
croix 254, 408
Croix-Rouge 51
croyant,e 251
CRS (Compagnies républi-
caines de sécurité) 277
cru,e 86
crudités 88
crustacés 297
cube 419
cube 408
cubique 408
cubisme 223
cuillère (cuiller) 95
cuillerée 95
cuir 361
cuir 102
cuisine 93, 114
cuisiner 93
cuisinier, -ière 93, 173,
214
cuisinière 121
cuisse 20
cuit,e 86
cuivre 362
culotte 101
culpabilité 272
cultivateur, -trice 174,
295
cultivé,e 148
cultiver 187, 295
culture 148, 295
culture maraîchère 297
culturisme 195
curé 252
curieux, -euse 73
curieux, -euse 465

curiosité 73, 218
curriculum vitae (CV) 177
curseur 329
cybercafé 331
cycle 236, 243
cyclisme 190
cycliste 191
cyclotourisme 188
cygne 371
cylindre 408
cylindrique 408

D

d'abord 241, 393, 422, 476
D'accord. 451
d'ailleurs 453
Danemark 15
danger 337, 373
dangereux, -euse 337, 373
danois,e 15
dans 396, 484
dans l'ensemble 241
danse 32, 187
danser 32, 130, 187, 226
danseur, -euse 226
Danube 356
d'après 464, 486
date 386
date de naissance 12
dauphin 371
d'autant plus que 456, 479
d'avance 396
davantage 413
de 483
de bonne heure 388
de bonne source 325
de côté 398
de face 398
de façon que 479
de grand standing 116
de haut en bas 403
de jour 389
de l' 470
de la 470

de laquelle 474, 475
de loin 398
de long en large 403
de manière que 479
de mieux en mieux 425
de moins en moins 425
de mon côté 461
de mon temps 394
de nuit 389
de pire en pire 425
de plus 241
de plus en plus 425
de près 398
de profession 176
de sorte que 477
de source sûre 325
de suite 396
de temps en temps 393
de toute façon 453
de toute manière 453
dealer/dealeur 55
débâcle 251
déballer 110
débarquement 248
débarquer 210
débarrasser 120
débat 154
débile 450
débit 310
débiter 310
déboisement 377
déboiser 377
déboucher 436
débouchés 177
debout 32
débrayage 280
débrayer 280, 338
se débrouiller 78
début 240, 390
débuter 197, 238
décalage horaire 346
décapotable 338
décéder 26
décembre 389
décentralisation 268
décentralisé,e 268
déception 62, 143
décès 26

décevoir 142
décharge 374
déchets 121, 375
déchetterie 374
déchirer 103, 438
déchirure 48
décibel 227
décidément 455
décider 77
se décider 77
décision 77
déclaration 311, 441
déclaration d'impôts 267
déclarer 209, 441
déclarer 267
se déclarer 45
décodeur 321
décollage 210, 346
décoller 210, 346
déconseiller 217, 447
décontracté,e 71
décor 199
découper 94, 166
décourager 135
découvert 310
découverte 161, 209, 247
découvrir 161, 209, 246
décrire 154, 242, 442
décroître 349
déçu,e 62
dedans 397
dédommager qn 312
défaite 193, 251, 293
défaut 69
défendre 441, 446
défense 289
défense 276
défense de ... 446
défi 193
déficit 302
définir 154
définitif, -ive 257
définition 154
(se) déformer 407
défunt,e 26
Dégage ! 450
dégâts 312, 376

dégel 360
dégoût 60
dégoûté,e 60
dégradation 376, 382
se dégrader 376, 382
degré 357
degrés 489
degrés de latitude 354
degrés de longitude 354
déguisement 203
se déguiser 203
dégustation 215
déguster 215
dehors 397
déjà 394, 481
déjeuner 85
délabré,e 382
délai 396
délégué,e du personnel 183
délimité,e 400
délinquance 275
délinquance juvénile 132
délinquant,e 275
délit 278
délivrer 135
délocalisation 182, 300
délocaliser 182, 300
demain 386, 481
demande 305
demande 267
demande d'emploi 180
demander 66, 443, 444
demandeur, -euse d'emploi 180
démangeaison 46
se démaquiller 39
démarrer 334
déménagement 113
déménager 113
se démettre 48
demi 415
démission 264
démissionner 264
démocratie 260
démocratique 260
démodé,e 103
démolir 379

démonstration 161, 442
démontrer 161, 442
démuni,e 134
dénouement 238
dent 19, 50
dentelle 103
dentier 53
dentifrice 37
dentiste 50, 173
déodorant 39
dépanner 340
dépanneuse 340
départ 31, 189, 206, 344
département 266
départemental,e 266
dépasser 335
se dépêcher 31
dépendance 425
dépendant,e 53, 135
dépendre 135, 424, 459
dépenser 108, 307
se dépeupler 381
déplacer 434
se déplacer 33
dépliant 218
déposer 276
déposer son bilan 182, 302
déposition 276
dépôt de bilan 182
dépressif, -ive 47
dépression 61, 359
dépression nerveuse 47
déprimé,e 61
depuis 393, 484
depuis que 394, 477
député,e 175
député,e 264
déranger 435
déraper 339
dermato(logue) 51
déroulement 234
déroulement de l'action 242
se dérouler 242
derrière 397, 484
derrière 20
des 470

dès 395, 486
dès que 395, 478
désaccord 287
désagréable 69, 462
désarmement 290
désastre 377
désastreux, -euse 377
descendance 127
descendants 127
descendre 32, 343
descendre 127
descente 32
descente 194
description 154, 242, 442
déséquilibré,e 75
désert 352
désert,e 375
déserter 291
déserteur 291
désertification 355
désertique 352
désespéré,e 59
désespérer 59
désespoir 59
se déshabiller 97
déshérités 136
se désintéresser 83
désintérêt 83
désintoxication 53
se désintoxiquer 53
désir 66
désirer 21, 66, 107
désobéissance civile 284
Désolé,e ! 445
désordonné,e 75
désordre 119
desquelles 474, 475
dessert 90, 216
desservir 345, 383
dessin 155, 221
dessin animé 199
dessinateur, -trice 221, 230
dessiner 155, 187, 221
dessous 397
dessus 397
destinataire 318

destination 206
destiner 83
destruction 373
détail 242, 325, 421
détaillant,e 306
déteindre 406
se détendre 34, 188, 211
détendu,e 138
détenir 146
détente 34, 188, 288
détention provisoire 275
détergent 376
détérioration 287, 376
se détériorer 376
déterminant 488
déterminé,e 75
détestable 462
détester 58
détourner le regard 29
détruire 131, 290, 373
dette 308
DEUG 163
deuil 26, 61
deux cinquièmes 415
deuxièmement 422
deux-pièces 115
deux-roues 338
dévaluation 309
dévaluer 309
devant 397, 484
dévaster 250, 292
développement 240,
    322, 436
se développer 436
devenir 170, 437
déviation 338
deviner 67
devinette 67
devises 309
devoir 308, 430, 479
devoirs 152
dévorer 91
d'habitude 430
diabète 46
diable 252
diagnostic 51
dialogue 130, 237, 440
diamant 105

diapo(sitive) 186, 322
diarrhée 46
d'ici à ... 401
d'ici le/la ... 386
dictaphone 170
dictée 152
dicter 170
dictionnaire 155
diesel 336
Dieu 252
différence 416, 424
différent(e)s 471
différent,e 424
différer 425
difficile 71, 427, 462
difficulté 135, 152, 180
diffuser 320
diffusion 326
digérer 91
digestif 216
digicode 115
digne de foi 74
dimanche 385
dimension 399, 417
diminuer 437
diminution 437
dinde 88
dinde 371
dîner 86, 202
diplomate 72
diplomate 287
diplomatie 287
diplôme 162, 170
dire 440
dire du bien/du mal 457
direct,e 428
directeur, -trice 171, 301
direction 300, 402
dirigeant,e 270
diriger 79, 196, 226,
    268, 301
se diriger 30, 402
Dis/Dites donc ! 463
discipline 149
discman 323
discothèque 130
discours 231, 440
discret, -ète 73

discrétion 73
discrimination 281
discussion 154, 279, 440
discuter 154, 279, 440
disparition 373
disposer 146
dispositif 303
disposition 422
dispute 141, 448
se disputer 448, 141
disque 322
disque 193
disque dur 328
disquette 169, 328
dissertation 159
dissolution 264
dissolvant 39
dissoudre 264
dissuasion 291
distance 400
distant,e 400
distinction 425
distingué,e 76
distinguer 65
se distinguer 425
distraction 185
distraire 239
se distraire 185
distribuer 33, 317
distributeur (de timbres)
    318
distributeur automatique
    109, 309
distribution 196, 317
distribution 306
diva 229
divers,es 471
divertissant,e 327
divertissement 188
dividende 310
diviser 160, 417
se diviser 240
division 160, 291, 417
divorce 12, 26, 125
divorcé,e 12, 125
divorcer 26, 125
dizaine 415
docteur 49

doctrine 257
document 232
documentaire 199
documents de voyage 206
dodécasyllabe 236
dogme 254
doigt 19
doigt de pied 20
domicile 10
domination 144
dominer 144, 250
Dommage ! 445
dommages 312
dommages (et) intérêts 312
dompter 370
D.O.M.-T.O.M. 268
don 150
donc 241, 432, 476
données 330
donner 33
se donner la peine 81
donner raison/tort à 457
donner son accord 451
donner sur 213
donner un coup de main à 121
donner un ordre 447
dont 473
dopage 195
se doper 195
doping 195
d'ordinaire 455
Dordogne 356
doré,e 105
doré,e 407
d'origine 12
dormir 28
dos 19
dos du livre 229
dose 55
dossier 274
D'où ? 475
douane 209
douanier 209
double 412, 415

doublé,e 104
doubler 335, 412
doubler 200
doublure 104
douche 36, 116, 212
se doucher 212
doué,e 150, 228
douleur 43
doute 67, 257
douter 67, 257
doux, douce 28, 357
douzaine 415
draguer 21, 138
dramatique 197, 237
drame 197, 237
drap 120
drapeau 260
dresser 370
drogue 53
drogué,e 53
se droguer 53
droit 271
droit civil 274
droit de garde 126
droit du sang 284
droit du sol 284
droit pénal 274
droit,e 402
droite 269, 398
droits d'auteur 328
droits de l'homme 249, 262
droits fondamentaux 262
drôle 71, 463
du 470
du moins 454
du toc 105
d'un côté ... de l'autre 456, 478
dune 356
d'une part ... d'autre part 456, 478
duplex 115
duquel 473, 475
dur,e 28, 86, 426, 462
durée 391
durer 246, 391
DVD 323

dynamique 72
dynastie 249

E

E.A.O. 331
eau 352, 372
eau (minérale) 90
eau de toilette 39
eaux usées 376
échange 151, 286
échange de vues 443
échangeur 339, 383
échantillon 306
s'échapper 34
écharpe 105
échec 78, 151, 162, 197
échecs 186
échelle 166
échelle 419
échographie 52
échouer 78, 151
éclair 358
éclairage 336
éclairage 118
éclaircie 359
s'éclaircir 359
éclairer 118
éclipse 349
écluse 347
école 150, 381
école de commerce 158
Ecole des Beaux-Arts 162, 223
ecole maternelle 150
école primaire 381
écologie 269, 372
écologique 372
écologiste 269, 372
économe 307
économie 180
économies 307
économique 180
économiquement faible 136
économiser 180, 307
écosystème 373
écotaxe 376

écoute 319
écouter 27, 79, 225, 322
écran 319, 329
écraser 341
écrire 80, 153, 229, 239, 317
écriture 153
écrivain 176, 229, 239
écrou 167
ecstasy 53
écurie 370
édifice 115, 382
éditer 326, 331
éditeur, -trice 231, 326
édition 231, 326
éditorial 327
éditorialiste 327
édredon 119
éducateur, -trice 148, 172
éducation 24, 148
éducation artistique 157
éducation musicale 157
éducation physique 157
éduquer 24, 148
effacer 330
effectifs 302
effectivement 454
effectuer 437
effet 256, 432
effet de serre 373
effets spéciaux 200
efficace 75, 429
s'effondrer 63
s'efforcer 81
effort 78
égal,e 416, 423
également 455
egalité 247, 260, 416
église 218, 252, 381
égoïsme 70
égoïste 70
égoûts 376
Egypte 16
Eh bien ! 463
élaborer 81
élancé,e 35
s'élancer 33

électeur, -trice 260
électoral,e 260
électricien, -ienne 173
électricité 117, 303, 375
électrique 120, 303, 375
électrocardiogramme (ECG) 52
électronicien,ne 173
électronique 303
élégant,e 99
élément 362
élémentaire 462
élémentaire 257
élevage 295
élève 151
élevé,e 413
élever 24, 148, 295
s'élever 239, 352, 458
éleveur, -euse 295
élimination 375
elle 472
elles 473
éloigné,e 400
éloigner 438
s'éloigner 33
e-mail 330
emballage 110
emballer 110
embarrassé,e 62
embargo 287
embarquement 346
embarquer 346
s'embarquer 210
embarras 62
embauche 181, 302
embaucher 181, 302
embêter 448
embouchure 355
embouteillage 336
embrasser 21, 138
embrayage 338
embrayer 338
émerveillé,e 465
émerveillement 465
émetteur 320
émettre 320, 376
émeute 285
émigration 281

émigré,e 281
émigrer 13, 281
émission 198, 319
émission 376
emménager 113
emmener 140, 434
émotion 58, 202
empêcher 67, 446
empereur 247
empire 247
Empire 249
empirique 257
empirisme 258
emploi 178
emploi du temps 156
employé,e 171, 178, 301
employer 166, 178
employeur, -euse 177, 280
s'empoisonner 46
emporter 434
empreintes digitales 277
emprunt 307
emprunter 307
ému,e 58, 202
en 402, 473, 483
en amont 355
en argent 105
en arrière 403
en arrière 398
en aval 355
en avance 344, 388
en avant 403
en avant 398
en avoir assez 447
en avoir marre 449
en avoir ras le bol 449
en bas 398
en ce moment 391
en conclusion 241
en couleurs 200
en dehors 399
en demi-pension 213
en dernier lieu 422
en différé 321
en duplex 321
en effet 241, 452
s'en faire 63

en fait 453
en fin de compte 455
en général 430
en haut 398
en huit 386
en l'espace de 396
en même temps 394
en noir et blanc 200
en or 105
en particulier 431
en pension complète 213
en plein air 211
en plein soleil 211
en premier lieu 243, 422
en première instance 274
en principe 431
en promotion 109
en provenance de ... 346
en réalité 453
en recommandé 317
en règle 208
en retard 344, 388
en revanche 425, 478
en sens inverse 403
en somme 455
s'en sortir 132
en tout cas 452
en trop 413
en vain 483
En voiture, s.v.p. ! 343
en vouloir à 62, 132
encadrer 221
encaisser 308
enceinte 21
enceinte 323
Enchanté,e. 129
encombrement 339
encore 482
encouragement 466
encourager 135, 465
encre 156, 168
s'endetter 309
endive 92
s'endormir 28
endroit 401
énergie 72, 375
énergique 72

énervant,e 71
énerver 448
s'énerver 141
enfance 24
enfant 11, 24, 124
enfant prodige 228
enfer 252
enfermer 435
enfin 241, 422, 453, 476
enflé,e 47
s'enfuir 34, 293
engagement 372
engager 178
s'engager 233, 372
s'engager 81, 291
engrais 297, 367, 376
engueulade 449
engueuler 449
enjambement 236
enlèvement 278
enlever 97, 120, 278, 434
ennemi héréditaire 288
ennemi,e 289
ennui 63
s'ennuyer 140
s'ennuyer 63
ennuyeux, -euse 462
énorme 417, 423
énormément 411
enquête 273
enquête 327
enquêter 273
enregistrement 227, 319, 322
enregistrement (des bagages) 346
enregistrer 227, 322
enseignant,e 148, 172
enseignement 148, 172
enseigner 148
ensemble 412
ensemble 101
ensuite 241, 392, 422, 476
entendre 27, 79
s'entendre bien/mal 131
Entendu. 451

entente 288
enterrement 26
enterrer 26
en-tête 168
enthousiasme 61
entorse 48
entouré,e 400
entracte 196
entraînement 188
entraîner 432
s'entraîner 188
entraîneur, -euse 188
entre 393, 400, 485
entrecôte 89
entrée 31, 87, 114, 216, 218, 335
entrepôt 306
entrepreneur, -euse 171
entreprise 171, 179, 300
entrer 31
entre-temps 395
entretenir 364
s'entretenir 443
entretien 288, 443
énumération 242
énumérer 242
envahir 250, 292
envahisseur 250, 292
enveloppe 168, 317
envelopper 436
envers 485
envie 62
envieux, -euse 62
environ 416
environnement 372
environs 378, 400
envisager 68
envoyé,e spécial,e 320
envoyer 305, 317
éolienne 376
épais,se 86, 100, 360, 426
s'épanouir 145
épargnant,e 309
épargne 309
épargner 309
épaule 19
épicé,e 92

épicer 92
épicerie 106
épices 92
épicier, -ière 106
s'épiler 39
épinards 366
épingle 103
épisode 200
éplucher 94
épluchures 121
éponge 156
éponge 38
époque 248, 394
époques littéraires 230
épouse 12, 126
épouser 26
épousseter 121
épouvantable 465
époux 12, 126
épreuve 135
épreuve 323
EPS 157
épuisé,e 45
équateur 350
équerre 160
équilibré,e 74
équipage 347
équipe 189
équipement 121, 297, 303
équiper 116
équitation 195
ère 248
érosion 355
érotique 22
érotisme 22
erreur 64, 256
erreur judiciaire 277
éruption (volcanique) 377
escalade 194
escalader 194
escale 346
escalier 114
escalope 89
escarpins 101
esclave 247
escrime 195
escroc 278

escroquerie 278
espace 112, 349, 378, 396
Espagne 15
espagnol 157
espagnol,e 15
espéce 421
espéce 369
Espcé de ... ! 450
espérance 59
espérance de vie 25
espérer 59
espoir 59
esprit 255
essai 77, 231, 256
essayer 77
essayer 104
essence 336, 361
essence 257
essentiel,le 427
essor 300
essorer le linge 102
essuie-glace 340
essuyer 119
s'essuyer 37
est (E) 403
est-ce que 474
esthéthique 258
esthéticien, -ne 178
estival,e 390
estivant,e 214
estomac 19
Estonie 16
et 476
Et alors ? 458
Et après ? 458
Et puis quoi, encore ? 452
et vice versa 425
étable 368
établi 167
établissement d'éducation spécialisée 158
étage 114
étagère 117, 168
étain 362
étalage 109
étalon 370

étang 355
étant donné que 456
étape 191
Etat 260
état 433
état (de santé) 42
état civil 12
état d'âme 235
état d'esprit 69
état d'urgence 292
Etat fédéral 263
Etats-Généraux 249
Etats-Unis 15
étau 167
été 390
éteindre 120
s'étendre 351, 378
étendre le linge 102
étendue 354
éternel,le 395
éternité 395
éternuer 43
éthique 258
étiquette 305
étoffe 102
étoile 212, 216, 349
étonnant,e 463
étonnement 463
étonner 462
s'étonner 462
étouffer 47
étrange 427, 463
étranger 209, 285
étranger, -ère 13, 209, 281, 285
être 145, 433, 479
être 257
être à l'aise 145
être attiré,e 142
être au courant 320
être bien/mal avec 142
être bien/mal portant,e 45
être contre 451
être convaincu,e 235
être décidé,e à 77
être en accord 458
être en ballottage 263

être en conflit 135
être en contact 138
être en contradiction 425
être en dérangement 316
être en désaccord 458
être en forme 42, 188
être en pension 158
être en tête de 422
être en train de faire 392, 479
être gêné,e 445
être hostile 143
être le/la/les ... 145
être lié,e 424
être majoritaire 269
être bien/mal en point 45
être minoritaire 269
être situé,e 354
être situé,e 433
étroit,e 100, 399, 426
études 162
étudiant,e 162
étudier 162, 170
euro 109, 307
eurochèque 308
Europe 14, 286
européen,ne 286
eux 473
s'évanouir 47
événement 320
éventuellement 454
évêque 254
évidemment 452
évident,e 459
évier 118
éviter 67
évoluer 436
évolution 436
évoquer 444
exact,e 416, 427, 459
Exactement. 451
exagération 234, 443
exagérer 234, 443
examen 49, 162, 170
examiner 49
excellent,e 427
excepté 486

exceptionnel,le 464
excès de vitesse 341
excitation 61
exciter 22
exclu,e 137
exclure 284
exclusif, -ive 327
exclusion 137, 284
exclusivement 431
exclusivité 327
excursion 188, 211
s'excuser 444
exécuter 293
exécution 249, 293
exemplaire 328
exercer 265
s'exercer 32
exercice 32, 45, 152
exigeant,e 68, 150
exigence 68
exiger 68, 150
exil 283
s'exiler 283
existence 23, 433
existence 257
existentialisme 230, 258
exister 23, 433
exister 257
exode rural/urbain 382
exotique 211
exotisme 211
expansion 182
s'expatrier 283
expédier 306
expéditeur, -trice 318
expérience 161, 256
expérimental,e 161
expérimenté,e 176
explication 154, 442
explication de texte 240
expliquer 154, 240, 442
exploit 190
exploitant,e agricole 296
exploitation agricole 296
exploiter 296
explorateur 331
exploser 290, 375
explosion 375

exportation 179, 305
exporter 179, 305
exposé 159
exposer 222
exposition 222
exposition 238
exprès 483
expression 153, 440
expressionnisme 223
expressionniste 223
s'exprimer 440
expulser 284
expulsion 284
extérieur 115
extraire 298
extrait 229, 241
extrait (de naissance) 267
extrême 423

F3 115
fable 236
fabricant,e 299
fabrication 298
fabriquer 186, 298
fac(ulté) 160, 170
façade 115
se fâcher 141
facile 427, 462
faciliter 437
façon 429
façon de voir les choses 69
facteur, -trice 171, 317
facture 305
faculté 80
faible 42, 72, 141, 422
faiblesse 42, 141
faillite 182
faim 85
faire appel 274
faire attention 79, 149
se faire beau/belle 202
faire carrière 177
faire chanter 278
faire chauffer 94
faire de la peine 143

faire de la publicité 305
faire de l'alpinisme 194
faire de son mieux 81
faire demi-tour 338
faire des études 170
faire des progrès 149
faire du cheval 195
faire du feu 120
se faire du souci 62
faire du sport 130
faire du tort 74
faire escale 210
faire exprès de faire 79
faire faillite 302
faire faire 479
faire la bise 138
faire la connaissance 138
faire la cour 21
faire la cuisine 120
faire la navette 345
faire la queue 108, 197
faire l'amour 21
faire le lit 120
faire le plein 336
faire le pont 180
faire l'école buissonnière 159
faire les courses 107
faire les trois huit 181
(se) faire mal 43
faire marcher 139, 166
se faire naturaliser 284
faire partie 424
faire pitié 135
faire qc avec/sans peine 82
faire qc avec/sans succès 82
faire qc en cachette 82
faire qc en personne 82
faire qc en vain 81
faire qc volontiers 82
faire semblant 79
faire ses adieux 144
faire suivre 318
faire un détour 335
faire un prix 109

faire une gaffe 143
se faire une idée 82
faire une scène 144
faire/rédiger un chèque 310
faits divers 327
falaise 356
familier, -ière 153
famille 124
fan 130
se fâner 364
fantastique 423
farine 95
fascisme 269
fasciste 269
fast-food 217
fatal,e 238
fatigant,e 71, 462
fatigue 28, 42
fatigué,e 28, 42
fatiguer 42
faubourg 382
faune 367
faussaire 224
fausse-couche 22
faute 152
faute de mieux 455
faute d'impression 328
fauteuil 117
fauve 371
faux 417
faux 224
faux, fausse 256, 428, 459
favorable 458
favori,te 193
fax 169, 316
faxer 169, 316
fécond,e 23
fécondation 23
féconder 23
fécondité 23
fédéralisme 262
félicitations 201, 456, 466
féliciter 139, 201, 456
femelle 369
féminin,e 11, 488

femme 11, 124
femme de ménage 174
femme politique 175, 268
fenêtre 116
fer 361
ferme 295
fermeture éclair 103
fermeture hebdomadaire 219
fermeture velcro 103
fermier, -ière 295
ferry(-boat) 208, 345
fesses 20
festin 202
festival 228
fête 201
fête de famille 201
fête des mères/pères 201
Fête du Travail 203
fête foraine 203
Fête Nationale 203
Fête-Dieu 253
fêter 201
feu 374
feu (tricolore) 335
feu arrière 336
feuillage 365
feuille 156, 363
feuille de maladie/de soins 51
feuilleton 200
feutre 168
feux de signalisation 335
février 389
fiancé,e 12, 125
se fiancer 26
fibre 363
fibres synthétiques 102
fiche 168
Fiche le camp ! 450
Fiche-moi/Fous-moi la paix ! 451
fichier 168, 329
fictif, -ive 232
fiction 232

fidèle 22, 142
fidélité 142
fier, fière 72
fierté 72
fièvre 43
figurant,e 196, 238
figuratif, -ive 223
figure 18, 407
figure de style 244
fil 103
fil conducteur 234
fil de l'action 234
filer 363
filet 89, 190, 296
fille 24, 124, 129
film 186, 198, 322
film d'aventures 199
film de science-fiction 199
film policier 199
filmer 186, 198, 322
fils 24, 124
fin 240, 390, 392
fin 433
fin, fine 100, 360
finalement 241, 422, 453
financement 310
financer 310
finances 174
finances 310
financier 310
fines herbes 92
finir 392, 435
finition 300
finlandais,e 15
Finlande 15
firme 300
fisc 267
fiscal,e 267
fixer 166
flan 93
flash 322
flash (d'information) 321
flash-back 200
flèche 329
flemmard,e 75
fleur 187, 364

fleurir 364
fleuve 353
flic 273, 337
flipper 55
flirter 21
flou,e 323
flûte 225
FN 271
foi 251
foie 88
foie 20
fois 393, 415
folklore 211
foncé,e 36, 407
fonction 265, 301
fonctionnaire 171, 265
fonctionner 120
fond 242, 397
fonder 247
fonder une famille 125
fondre 354, 362
fonds d'investissement 311
fontaine 219
foot(ball) 190
footing 193
force 141, 189
force de frappe 292
forcément 455
forcer 447
se forcer 81
forces armées 292
forces de l'ordre 273
forêt 295, 352
Forêt-Noire 354
format 322
formater 330
formation 148
formation professionnelle 170
forme 407, 489
forme 236
former 148, 407, 421
formidable 462
formulaire 267, 312
fort,e 35, 141, 188, 422
fort,e/faible en 150
forteresse 219

fortune 133, 307
fortuné,e 136
foudre 358
fouetter 96
fouiller 209
foulard 105
foule 413
se fouler 48
foulure 48
four 94, 116
fourchette 95
fourmi 371
fournir 306
fournisseur d'accès 331
fournisseur, -euse 306
fournitures 169
fourrure 103
Fous le camp ! 450
fraction 489
fracture 48
fracture sociale 137
se fracturer 48
fragile 42, 360
fragile 35
fraîcheur 357
frais 302
frais, fraîche 87, 357
fraise 90, 364
framboise 90
franc 109, 307
franc, franche 74
français 157
Français,e de souche 283
français,e 14
France 14
France métropolitaine 268
franchement 461
francophone 287
francophonie 286
frappant,e 465
frapper 142
fraternel,le 126
fraternité 247, 260
frein 338
freiner 338
fréquenter 142
frère 125

fret 347
fric 309
frigidaire 94
frigide 22
frigo 94, 116
fringues 97
frisée 92
frites 89
friteuse 96
froid 357
froid de canard 360
froid,e 28, 36, 86, 138, 426
froissé,e 99
fromage 89
froment 366
front 18
frontière 13, 209, 290, 351
frotter 119
frotter 38
fruit 363
fruits 90
fruits de mer 88
fugue 132
fuguer 132
fuir 293
fuite 34, 293
fumée 54, 375
fumer 53
fumeur, -euse 54
furieux, -euse 141
fusain 223
fuseau horaire 350
fusée 292, 304, 350
fusil 290
fusion 302
fusionner 302
futur 391
futur antérieur 490
futur composé 490
futur simple 490
futur,e 391

.... **G** ....

gaffer 143
gagnant,e 189

gagner 179, 189
gai,e 71
gaieté (gaîté) 71
gala 228
galaxie 349
galerie 222
galerie 297
galerie marchande 380
gallo-romain,e 246
gamin,e 25
gamme 227
gangster 278
gant 105
garage 115, 336, 380
garagiste 174, 336
garantie 120, 305
garantir 262
garçon 124, 129, 173, 214
garde à vue 277
garde des Sceaux 264
se garder 81
garder le lit 43
gardien,ne 113, 174
gare 207, 342, 381
gare routière 342
se garer 335
Garonne 353
gasoil 336
gaspillage 376
gaspiller 376
gastronomie 215
gastronomique 215
gâté,e 76
gâteau 90, 202
gâteau sec 93
gauche 269, 398
gaufre 93
Gaule 246
Gaulois,e 246
gaz 117, 349, 360, 375
gaz d'échappement 373
gazeux, -euse 360
gazole 336
gel 358
gelée 360
geler 358
gendarme 273

Gendarmerie nationale 277
gendre 127
gène 163
gêner 143
général 175
général 291
général,e 421
généralement 430
généraliste 49, 173
génération 136
généreux, -euse 70
générique 200
générosité 70
genêt 366
génétique 45, 163
génial 423, 457
génie génétique 163, 304
genou 19
genre 239, 488
gens 132
gentil,le 69, 138
gentillesse 69
géographie 157, 351
géographique 351
géométrie 156
gérant,e 178
geste 28
gibier 88
gibier 370
gifle 143
gifler 143
giga 423
gisement 297
gîte rural 214
givre 360
glace 90, 118, 358
glacier 354
glaçon 217
glaïeul 366
glissement de terrain 377
glisser 34
globe 349
gloire 250
golf 190
golfe 356
gomme 156
gonfler 336

gorge 19, 352
gosse 25
goudron 55, 363
gourmand,e 91
gourmandise 91
gourmet 91
goût 28, 86, 461
goûter 28, 85, 215
goutte 358
gouttes 52
gouvernement 262, 269
gouvernemental,e 262
gouverner 262, 268
grâce à 431, 485
graduation 419
graffiti 132
graine 367
graisse 96
grammaire 152
gramme 418
grand cru 217
grand ensemble 382
grand,e 34, 417
grande école 160, 170
grande surface 106, 380
Grande-Bretagne 14
grandes lignes 346
grandes ondes (GO) 321
grandir 24, 28
grand-mère 125
grand-père 125
grands-parents 125
granit 362
gras,se 35, 86
gratuit,e 108, 307
grave 462
graver 223
graveur 223
gravillons 339
gravitation 350
graviter 350
gravure 223
grec 157
grec, grecque 15
Grèce 15
greffe 53

grêle 360
grenier 115
grenouille 371
grès 362
grève 181, 279
gréviste 181, 279
grignoter 91
griller 94
grimper 194
grippe 43
gris clair 406
gris,e 405
gronder 448
gros mot 450
gros plan 200
gros,se 34, 45, 417
groseille 366
grossesse 22
grossier, -ière 74, 449
grossir 29, 45
grossiste 306
grotte 354
groupe 129, 133, 226, 300, 413
groupe parlementaire 270
gruyère 89
guêpe 371
guéri,e 48
guérir 48
guérison 48
guerre 247, 289
Guerre franco-allemande 250
gueule 370
gueuler 449
guichet 207, 308, 317
guide 175, 206, 216
guide Michelin 216
guillemets 488
guillotine 249
guillotiner 249
guitare 225
gym(nastique) 157, 191
gymnase 189, 381
gymnaste 191
gynéco(logue) 50

H

habile 80
habileté 80
s'habiller 97, 202
habit 202
habitant,e 113, 266, 378
habiter 10, 113, 378
habits 97
habituellement 455
hache 167
haie 365
haine 60, 284
haïr 60
hall 213
hall d'entrée 115
halles 380
Halte ! 466
hameau 382
hamster 368
hanche 20
handicap 48
handicapé,e 48
hareng 88, 369
haricots verts 89
harmonie 227
harmonieux, -euse 227
harpe 228
hasard 257, 432
hasch(isch) 53
hausse 310
haut 397
haut,e 352, 399, 418
hautbois 228
haute technologie 303
hauteur 352, 399, 418
hebdo(madaire) 326
hebdomadaire 385
hectare 419
hégémonie 287
Hein ? 463
Hélas ! 445
hélicoptère 344
hématome 47
hémisphère 350, 408
herbe 187, 363
herbes de Provence 92
herbivore 369

héréditaire 45
héritage 146
hériter 146
héritier, -ière 146
héroïne 54
héros, héroïne 237, 243
hésitant,e 76
hésitation 77
hésiter 77
hétéro(sexuel,le) 22
hêtre 365
heure 387
heure d'affluence 340
heure d'été 388
heure d'hiver 388
heure sup(plémentaire) 179
heures de pointe 340
heures d'ouverture 219
heureusement 461
heureux, -euse 58
hideux, -euse 465
hier 386, 481
hindouisme 253
hirondelle 371
histoire 157, 232, 246
histoire-géo 157
historien,ne 246
historique 246
hiver 390
hivernal,e 390
HLM 112, 379
hobby 185
hold-up 278
hollandais,e 15
Hollande 15
homéopathie 52
homme 124
homme d'Etat 268
homme politique 175, 268
homo(sexuel,le) 22
Hongrie 16
honnête 71
honnêteté 71
honoraires 51
honte 60
hôpital 49, 380

horaire 207, 343
horaire à la carte 181
horizontal,e 402
horloge 389
horodateur 339
horrible 62, 465
hors de 399
hors de prix 214
hors saison 210
hors-d'œuvre 87, 216
hospitalier, -ière 49
hostile 290
hostilité 143
hostilités 290
hôtel 212
hôtel de ville 266, 380
hôtelier, -ière 178, 213
hôtellerie 177, 213
hôtel-restaurant 214
hôtesse de l'air 174
hôtesse de l'air 346
houille 297
huer 199
huile 95, 336
humeur 69, 235
humide 99
humidité 358
humiliation 143
humilier 143
humoristique 231
humour 74, 230
hydrogène 362
hygiène 38
hyper 423
hypermarché 106, 380
hypertexte 331
hypocrisie 74
hypocrite 74
hypothèque 309
hypothèse 234

.... **I** ....

ici 401, 481
idéal,e 462
idéalisme 257
idéaliste 73
idée 63, 239, 255

identité 280
idiot,e 72
ignorance 257
ignorer 148
il 472
il est (im)possible que 459
il est courant que 459
il est (im)probable que 459
il est question de 240
Il fait beau. 357
Il fait bon. 357
Il fait chaud. 357
Il fait jour. 388
Il fait lourd. 358
Il fait mauvais. 358
Il fait noir. 388
Il fait nuit. 388
il faut/faudrait que 430, 447
il me semble que 460
Il n'y a pas de mal. 445
il n'y a qu'à 446
il s'agit de 240
il semble que 460
il suffit de 447
il vaut/vaudrait mieux 66, 447
il y a 392, 484
île 354
illégal,e 271
illégalité 271
illisible 426
illustrateur, -trice 230
illustration 230
illustré 324
illustrer 230
ils 473
image 155, 235
image virtuelle 331
imagé,e 235
imagination 65
s'imaginer 65
imbécile 450
imitation 79, 139
imiter 78, 139
immédiat,e 396

517

immense 417
immeuble 112, 379
immigration 13, 134, 281
immigré,e 13, 134, 281
immigrer 13, 134, 281
immobile 436
immobilité 436
imparfait 490
impasse 339
impatience 141
impatient,e 141
impératif 489
impératrice 247
imperfection 464
imper(meable) 98
implantation 299
implanter 299
impoli,e 73
importance 421, 459
important,e 421, 459
importation 179, 305
importer 179, 305
import-export 179
imposable 267
imposer 68, 267
impôts 267
imprécis,e 427
impression 65
impressionnant,e 462
impressionnisme 223
impressionniste 223
imprévisible 377
imprévu,e 377
imprimante 169, 329
imprimé 317
imprimé,e 104
imprimer 329
imprimer 326
imprimerie 326
imprudence 73
imprudent,e 73
impuissance 22
impuissant,e 22
inactif, -ive 76
incapable 77
incapacité 80
incendie 374

incertain,e 256
incertitude 256
inchangé,e 436
incident 290, 303
incinération 375
incolore 405
incolore 429
incompétence 80
incompétent,e 80
incompréhensible 154
incompréhension 131
inconfortable 117
inconnu,e 222
inconvénient 241
incroyable 463
inculpation 275
inculper 275
Inde 16
indemnisation 312
indemniser 312
indemnité 181
indemnités parlemen-
   taires 264
indépendant,e 135, 269
indicatif 489
indicatif 317
indien,ne 16
indifférence 75
indifférent,e 75
indigeste 93
indigestion 46
indiquer 444
indirect,e 428
indiscret, -ète 73
indiscrétion 73
indispensable 429
individu 260
individu 257
individuel,le 260
indulgence 149
indulgent,e 149
industrialisation 299
s'industrialiser 299
industrie 171, 298
industrie agro-alimentaire
   299
industrie chimique et
   pharmaceutique 299

industrie de pointe 299
industrie métallurgique
   299
industrie sidérurgique
   299
industrie textile 299
industrie(-)clé 299
industriel,le 171, 298
inefficace 429
inexact,e 427
inexplicable 465
infarctus 44
infection 46
inférieur,e 398, 416
infidèle 22
infidélité 142
infinitif 489
infirme 48
infirmier, -ière 49, 173
inflammable 362
inflammation 46
inflation 309
influence 325
influencer 325, 441
informaticien,ne 162, 328
information 205, 324, 442
informations 319
informatique 157, 173, 328
informer 319, 324, 442
s'informer 205
infos 319
infraction 341
ingénieur 173
inhumain,e 70
initiative 269
injure 449
injurier 449
injuste 71, 271
injustice 71, 271
innocence 272
innocent,e 272
inondation 375
inonder 375
inouï,e 465
inquiet, -ète 62

inquiéter 137
s'inquiéter 61
inquiétude 61, 137
inscription 162
s'inscrire 162
insecte 371
insecticide 297, 376
insensible 70
insister 441
insolent,e 73
installation 298, 329
installer 116, 329, 434
s'installer 113, 298
instant 394
instit(uteur, -trice) 151, 172
institut de beauté 39
institution 265
instructif, -ive 327
instruction 150
instruction civique 157
instruction religieuse 252
instruit,e 150
instrument 225
instrument à cordes 227
instrument à percussion 228
instrument à vent 228
insuffisant,e 464
insulte 450
insulter 450
insurrection 285
intégral,e 232
intégration 134, 281
intégré,e 281
s'intégrer 134, 281
intellectuel,le 63
intelligence 63
intelligent,e 63
intention 68, 235, 433
interdiction 446
interdiction (de dépasser) 341
interdire 446
intéressant,e 462
s'intéresser 80, 140
intérêt 80

intérêts 309
intérieur 115
intérim 181
interlocuteur, -trice 443
internat 158
international,e 209
internet 330
interphone 115
interprétation 242
interprète 175, 226
interpréter 196, 226, 241
interro(gation) 152, 490
interrogation 444
interrogatoire 272
interrogatoire 444
interroger 152, 272
interroger 444
interrompre 438, 449
interrupteur 118
interruption 438
intervenir 292
intervention 287, 292
interview 232, 320
interviewer 320
intestin 20
s'intituler 243
intolérance 135, 281
intolérant,e 75
intoxication 46
intrigue 238, 271
introduction 240
inutile 427
invalide 48
invasion 250, 292
inventer 78, 161, 303
inventeur, -trice 161, 303
invention 78, 161, 303
inversement 425
investir 302
investissement 302
invisible 426
invitation 139, 201
invité,e 201, 319
inviter 139, 201
involontaire 68
invraisemblable 465

irlandais,e 15
Irlande 15
ironie 243
irradiation 377
irrégulier, -ière 408
irrigation 367
irriguer 367
Islam 253
islamique 253
israélite 253
Italie 15
italien 157
italien,ne 15
itinéraire 206
IUT 162
I.V.G. 23
ivre 55, 92
ivresse 55
ivrogne 55

J

jadis 395
jalousie 62, 143
jaloux, -ouse 62, 143
Jamais de la vie. 452
jambe 19
jambon 87
janvier 389
Japon 16
japonais,e 16
jardin 115, 187, 364
jardin d'enfants 150, 381
jardin public 383
jardinage 187
jardiner 187, 364
jardinier, -ière 174, 364
jaune 405
javelot 193
jazz 226
je (j') 472
Je m'en moque/fiche/fous 464
Je n'en crois pas à mes yeux/mes oreilles 465
jean 97
Jésus-Christ 252

jet d'eau 219
jeter 435
se jeter 353
jeu 185, 196, 238
jeu 192
jeu de boules 186
jeu de société 186
jeu décisif 194
jeu électronique 329
jeu télévisé 199
jeu vidéo 329
jeudi 385
jeune 11, 24, 129
jeune fille 129
jeune homme 129
jeunes 132
jeunes gens 129
jeunesse 24, 129, 132
Jeux Olympiques 193
job 179
jogging 101, 193
joie 58, 202
joint 53
joli,e 34
jonquille 366
joue 18
jouer 185, 187, 196, 238
jouer au tennis 190
joueur, -euse 190
jouir 22
jour 385
jour de l'An 202
jour férié 179
jour ouvrable 179
journal 323
journal (télévisé) 320
journalisme 175
journaliste 175, 232, 324
journalistique 233
journée 386
jours de la semaine 385
joyau 105
Joyeuses fêtes ! 201
Joyeuses Pâques ! 466
Joyeux Noël ! 466
joyeux, -euse 202
joyeux, -euse 61
Judaïsme 253

judo 195
juge 174, 272
juge d'instruction 174
jugement 272
jugement 67, 464
juger 272, 458
juger 67
juif/juive 13, 253
juillet 389
juin 389
jumeau, jumelle 126
jumelage 286
jumelé,e 286
jument 370
jupe 97
Jura 354
juré,e 272
jurer 449
juron 449
jury 272
jus (de fruits) 90
jusqu'à 393, 400
jusqu'à ce que 477
jusque 484
juste 70, 271, 416, 459
justice 71, 174, 271

.... K ....

K 7 322
kidnapper 278
kidnappeur, -euse 278
kilo(gramme) 107, 418
kilomètre 418
kiné(sithérapeute) 178
kiosque 325
kitchenette 114
klaxonner 334

.... L ....

là 401, 481
la (l') 470, 472
La ferme! 450
la plupart du/de la/des
    412
la une 324
là-bas 401, 481

labo(ratoire) 161
labourer 367
lac 353
lac de Constance 355
lac Léman 355
lâche 76
lâcher 435
là-dedans 401
là-dessous 401
là-dessus 401
là-haut 401
laïcité 253
laid,e 34, 222, 461
laideur 34, 222
laine 361
laine 102
laïque 253
Laisse-moi tranquille !
    466
laisser faire 479
lait 87
laiton 362
laitue 92
lampadaire 118
lampe 118
lampe de poche 166
lancer 191, 435
lancer 193
lancer un ordre de grève
    280
lanceur, -euse 193
langage 153
langage de programma-
    tion 329
langage informatique
    328
langue 14, 19, 153, 157
lapin 88, 368
laque 38
laquelle 474, 475
large 100, 399, 418
largement 422
largeur 399, 418
larve 371
latin 157
laurier 92
lavabo 116, 212
lavage 119

lave-glace 341
laver 99, 119
se laver 36
laverie (automatique) 102
lave-vaisselle 121
layette 101
le (l') 470, 472
le cas échéant 454
le long de 399
le/la leur 474
le/la mien,ne 474
le/la nôtre 474
le/la sien,ne 474
le/la tien,ne 474
le/la vôtre 474
leader 270
leçon 154
lecteur de cassettes 323
lecteur de CD portable 323
lecteur laser video 323
lecteur, -trice 323
lecture 80, 154, 185, 323
légal,e 261, 271
légalité 271
légende 231
léger, -ère 87, 100, 418, 426
législature 264
légitime défense 276
légume 89, 364
lendemain 386
lent,e 31, 72, 428
lequel 473, 475
les 470, 473
les leurs 474
les mien(ne)s 474
les nôtres 474
les sien(ne)s 474
les tien(ne)s 474
les vôtres 474
lesbienne 22
lesquelles 474, 475
lesquels 474, 475
lessive 99, 120
Lettonie 16
lettre 154, 231, 317, 487
lettres 229

leur 470, 473
leurs 470
lever 434
se lever 32
lever de/du soleil 389
lèvre 18
levure 95
lézard 371
liaison 487
liaison 22, 142
libération 248, 282
libérer 248, 282, 273
se libérer 135
liberté 247, 260, 273
liberté de la presse 327
liberté de conscience 262
liberté d'opinion 262
liberté du culte 253, 262
libraire 106, 173, 326
librairie 106, 326
libre 135, 212
libre-service 217
licence 163
licenciement 180
licencier 180
lied 225
lien 424
lien 126
lieu 242, 401
lieu de naissance 12
lieu commun 234
ligne 407
ligne 39
ligne (téléphonique) 315
lignite 297
lilas 366, 406
lime 167
limer 167
limitation de vitesse 341
limite 400
limité,e 400, 413
limonade 91
lin 363
linge 99, 120
lingerie 101
lion,ne 369
liquide 360

du liquide 309
lire 80, 154, 185, 323
lisible 426
liste 206
liste rouge 316
lit 117, 212
litre 107, 419
littéraire 153, 229
littérature 229
littoral 356
Lituanie 16
livraison 305
livre 107, 154, 155, 229, 325, 419
livrer 305
livret d'épargne 309
local,e 215, 401
locataire 113
location 113, 212
lock-out 183, 280
locomotive 344
loge 226
logement 113
logement 213
loger 113
logiciel 329
logique 64
logique 258
loi 261, 271
loin (de) 400, 485
lointain,e 400
Loire 353
loisirs 185
long, longue 100, 399, 417
long,ue 35
long-métrage 200
longtemps 391, 482
longueur 399, 417
look 131
lotion 39
louange 457
loubard,e 132
loucher 29
louer 113, 212
louer 457
loup, louve 369
lourd,e 86, 418, 426

loyer 113
LSD 55
lui 472
lumbago 48
lumière 117
lunaire 349
lundi 385
lune 349
lunettes de soleil 211
lutte 182, 195, 250, 285
lutte anti-dopage 195
lutter 182, 250, 285
luxe 212
Luxembourg 15
luxembourgeois,e 15
luxueux, -euse 115
lycée 151, 381
lycéen,ne 151
lyrique 235
lyrisme 235
lys 366

.... **M** ....

ma 470
mâcher 91
machine 120, 298
machine à laver 121
maçon 177
Madame/Mesdames 128
madame, mesdames 10
mademoiselle, mesde-moiselles 10
Mademoiselle/Mesde-moiselles 128
magasin 106, 304, 380
magazine 324
maghreb 16
maghrébin,e 16, 283
magnétophone 322
magnétoscope 323
magnifique 461
mai 389
maigre 35, 45, 86
maigrir 29, 45
maillot 191
maillot de bain 98

maillot de corps 101
main 19
main-d'œuvre 182, 299
maintenant 391, 482
maire 175, 266
mairie 266, 380
mais 476
maïs 366
maison 112, 379
maison 301
maison de campagne 382
maison de retraite 380
maison de vacances 212
maître, maîtresse de maison 121
maître d'hôtel 217
maître-chanteur 278
maîtresse 21
maîtrise 164
majeur,e 12, 126
majeure partie 413
majorité 412
majorité 13, 127, 263
mal 255, 460, 481
mal de gorge 43
mal de mer 347
mal tourner 132
mal, maux 43
malade 43, 49
maladie 43
maladie mentale 47
maladresse 77
maladroit,e 77
malchance 142
mâle 369
malentendant,e 29
malentendu 238, 449
malfaiteur 278
malgré 485
malgré que 479
malgré tout 456
malhabile 80
malheur 59
malheureusement 445, 461
malheureux, -euse 59
malhonnête 71
malhonnêteté 71

malin, maligne 45, 76
maltraiter 137
malus 312
maman 124
mamie 125
mammifère 369
manager 302
manche 102, 192, 211
Manche 355
manchette 324
mandat 277, 318
manette de jeu 329
manger 85
manière 429
manif(estation) 181, 282, 296
manifestant,e 282
manifester 282, 295
manifester 60
manipulation 163
manipuler 327
manœuvre 171
manque 55
manquer 343
manteau 98
manucure 39
manuel 155
maquillage 39
maraîcher, -ère 297
marbre 224
marchand,e 107, 172, 304
marchander 107, 304
marchandise 107, 304
marchandise 347
marche 30, 116
marché 106, 218, 304, 380
marche avant/arrière 338
Marché commun 286
Marché commun 250
Marché intérieur européen 286
marcher 30
mardi 385
marée noire 376
marées 353
marginal,e 137

marguerite 366
mari 11, 124
mariage 24, 201, 252
marié,e 11, 124
se marier 24
marijuana 53
marin 175, 345
marine 175
marine 292
maritime 353
mark 307
marmite 96
Marne 355
maroc 16
marocain,e 16
marque 305
marqueur 168
marraine 127
marron 405
mars 389
marseillaise 247
marteau 166
marteau 193
mascara 39
masculin,e 11, 488
masse 418
masse 413
Massif Central 352
mat,e 323, 407
match 189
match nul 193
matérialisme 258
matériau 112, 360
matériel 329
maternel,le 126
maternelle 150, 381
mathématicien,ne 161
mathématiques 156
maths 156
matière 156, 255, 360
matière 158
matières premières 296
matin 387
matinée 388
maussade 359
mauvais,e 427, 460
mauve 406
maximum 413

mayonnaise 89
mazout 363
me (m') 472
mec 131
mécanicien,ne 174
méchanceté 70
méchant,e 70
mécontent,e 71
médaille 193
médecin 49, 173
médecine 49, 161, 173
médecines douces 52
médias 323
médiateur, -trice 280
médical,e 49
médicament 50
médiéval,e 249
médiocre 427, 462
Méditerranée 211, 355
méfiance 61
se méfier 61
mega 423
mégot 55
meilleur,e 427, 460
mel 330
mélancolie 61
mélancolique 61
mélanger 94
mélodie 225
melon 90
membre 270
membre de la famille 125
même 430, 483
même si 478
même(s) 471
mémé 125
mémoire 67, 150, 331
mémoires 230
mémoriser 330
menace 373, 448
menacer 373, 448
ménage 119
ménage 26
ménagère 121
mendiant,e 134
mendier 134
mener 434
mener 194

mener une action 181, 289
mensonge 272
mensuel 326
mensuel,le 389
mentalité 73
menteur, -euse 74, 450
mentir 272
menton 19
menu 215
menuisier, -ière 177
mépris 62, 143
mépriser 62, 143
mer 209, 352
mer Baltique 211, 355
mer du Nord 211, 355
mer intérieure 355
Merci. 456
mercredi 385
mercurochrome 51
Merde ! 448
mère 24, 124
mère de famille 12
méridien 354
méridional,e 354
merle 371
mes 470
mésange 371
message 242
message 271
messe 253
mesure 269, 417
mesure 227
mesurer 417
métal 361
métallique 361
métaphore 235
métaphore 244
métaphysique 258
métaux lourds 376
météo(rologie) 320, 356
météore 349
méthadone 55
méthode 242, 303
méthode 257
métier 12, 179
mètre 418
mètre (pliant) 167

Index

métro 342
métropole 268, 382
metteur en scène 195, 237
mettre 97, 434
se mettre à 392
se mettre à table 85
mettre à jour 330
mettre au monde 22
mettre en évidence 234
mettre en examen 277
mettre en marche 334
mettre en mémoire 330
mettre en relief 234
mettre en scène 237
mettre la table 120
meuble 117
meublé,e 115
meurtre 278
Meuse 355
mexicain,e 15
Mexique 15
micro(phone) 227, 319
microbe 46
microfibres 102
micro-ordinateur 328
midi 388
miel 87
mieux 460, 481
mignon,ne 36
mignon,ne 461
milieu 133
milieu 399
militaire 175, 289
militant,e 270
militer 285
millier 415
millimètre 418
mince 35, 426
Mince ! 448
mine 290, 296
minerai 362
minéral,e 361
mineur 296
mineur,e 13, 127
minimum 413
ministre 175, 262
minitel 316

minorité 280
minuit 388
minuscule 417
minute 387
miracle 254
miroir 118
mise en page 326
mise en relief 490
mise en relief 244
mise en scène 238
misère 134
mi-temps 192
mixage 200
MJC 130
mob(ylette) 333
mobile 238, 278, 432
moche 36, 465
mode 99, 430, 489
mode d'emploi 166
modèle 221
modèle 104, 257
modeler 224
modem 330
modéré,e 214
moderne 99, 427
modeste 74
modestie 74
modification 437
modifier 437
modulation de fréquence (FM) 321
mœurs 255
moi 472
moine 254
moineau 371
moins 357, 412, 416, 482
moins ... que 424
mois 389
moisson 366
moissonner 366
moitié 412
molécule 362
moment 391
mon 470
mon amour 129
mon cher, ma chère 129
mon chou 129

mon lapin 129
Mon/Ma pauvre. 445
mon/ma petit(e) 129
mon trésor 129
mon vieux, ma vieille 129
monarchie 247
monarque 249
monastère 254
mondialisation 182
monde 351
moniteur 329
moniteur, trice 150
monnaie 109, 306
monologue 237
monoparental,e 127
monsieur, messieurs 10
Monsieur/Messieurs 128
montage 166
montage 200
montagne 210, 351
montagneux, -euse 351
montant 308
montée 32
monter 32, 166, 343, 357, 437
monter une pièce 238
montre 104, 388
montrer 33
monument (historique) 218, 222, 381
monumental,e 222
se moquer 60, 139
moquette 118
moral,e 255
morale 255
morceau 107
morceau 228
mordre 368
mort 25
mort 257
mort des forêts 373
mort,e 25, 290
mortel,le 25
Moselle 356
mosquée 253
mot 152, 440, 488
mot de passe 330
mot interrogatif 490

motard 338
moteur 303, 336
moteur de recherche 331
motif 322, 431
motion de censure 264
motivation 148
motiver 149
moto 333
mots croisés 185
mou, molle 28, 72, 86, 426
mouche 371
mouchoir 105
mouillé,e 99
moule 96
moules 88
mourir 25
mousse au chocolat 90
mousseux 91
moustache 39
moustique 371
moutarde 95
mouton 88, 368
mouvement 30, 225
moyen 430
moyen de contraception 23
moyen de transport 333
moyen stylistique 243
Moyen(-)Age 249
moyen,ne 133, 357, 422
moyenne 159
moyenne annuelle 357
moyens (d'expression) 242
muguet 366
multicolore 405
multiculturel,le 284
multimédia 328
multinationale 301
multiplication 160, 417
multiplier 160, 417
municipal,e 266
municipalité 266
mur 116
mûre 366
murs 218
muscle 19

musclé,e 35
musée 218, 222, 381
musical,e 224
music-hall 226
musicien,ne 176, 224
musique 157, 186, 224
musique de chambre 228
musique instrumentale 228
musique orchestrale 228
musique pop 226
musique vocale 228
musulman,e 13, 253
mutuelle 313
myope 29
mystérieux, -euse 465

N

nager 32, 192
nageur, -euse 192
naissance 23
naître 23
nana 131
nappe 95
nappe phréatique 376
narrateur, -trice 233
narratif, -ive 233
narration 240
natation 32, 192
nation 13, 260
national,e 260
nationalisme 265
nationaliste 265
nationalité 13, 260, 281
naturalisation 284
naturalisme 230
nature 351, 372
nature morte 223
naturel,le 71
Naturellement. 451
navigable 353
navigation 347
naviguer 347
navire 347
ne ... aucun,e 410, 471, 480
ne ... guère 481

ne ... jamais 393, 480
ne ... ni ... ni 480
ne ... nulle part 481
ne ... pas 410
ne ... pas (du tout) 410, 480
ne ... pas encore 480
ne ... pas grand-chose 411
ne ... pas un,e seul,e 410, 480
ne ... personne 471, 480
ne ... plus 411
ne ... plus (du tout) 411, 480
ne ... que 480
ne ... rien 410, 471, 480
ne ... rien du tout 410, 480
Ne t'en fais pas. 445
néant 257
nécessaire 427
néerlandais,e 15
négatif 322
négatif, -ive 459
négation 489
négligeable 421
négligence 83
négliger 83
négociateur, -trice 280
négociation 183, 251, 280
négocier 183, 280
neige 191, 210, 358
neige 54
neiger 358
nerf 19
nerveux, -euse 71
net 330
net,te 418
net,te 323
nettement 455
nettoyage 119
nettoyer 99, 119
se nettoyer 37
neuf, neuve 100, 426
neutralité 288
neveu 125

névrosé,e 47
nez 18
niche 368
nicotine 55
nid 369
nièce 125
nier 441
nier 275
nitrates 376
niveau 159
niveau à bulle 167
niveau de vie 136, 181
noble 249
noblesse 249
noce 201
noces 201
noces d'or 203
nocif, -ive 376
Noël 252
nœud 105
nœud 238
noir et blanc 323
noir,e 405
noir,e 55
noisetier 365
nom 488
nombre 155, 410, 416, 488, 489
nombreux, -euse 410
Non. 452
non-lieu 275
non-polluant,e 372
nord (N) 403
normal,e 427
normalement 430
Norvège 15
norvégien,ne 15
nos 470
nostalgie 61
nostalgique 61
note 225
note 159, 214
noter 159
notion 255
notre 470
nouilles 89
se nourrir 85
nourrisson 25

nourriture 85
nous 472
Nouveau Testament 253
nouveau, nouvel, nouvelle 100, 427
nouvelle 231, 324
novembre 389
noyer 365
nu 223
nuage 358
nuageux, -euse 358
nuance 405
nucléaire 303
nuisance 376
nuisible 367
nuit 388
nuit(ée) 214
Nul./Nulle. 457
nulle part 402
numéral 489
numéro 11, 315, 325, 416
numéro de téléphone 11
numéro vert 317
nuque 20

O

obéir 150
objecteur de conscience 291
objectif 66, 432
objectif, -ive 327
objectivité 327
obligatoirement 455
obliger 447
obscur,e 429
obsèques 26
observation 27, 80, 232
observer 27, 80, 232
obtenir 284
occidental,e 354
occupation 248, 290
occupé,e 316
occuper 248, 266, 290
occuper la première place 422

occuper un poste/une fonction 177
océan 353
océan Indien 355
ocre 406
octobre 389
octosyllabe 236
ode 236
odeur 27
œil, yeux 18
œillet 366
œuf,œufs 87, 369
œuvre 229, 239, 256
œuvres complètes 328
OFAJ 250
office de/du tourisme 205
officiel,le 265
officier 291
offre 305
offre d'emploi 180
offre spéciale 109
Oh, là là ! 463
oie 370
oignon 89
oiseau 369
oléoduc 363
olive 364
olivier 365
omelette 88
on 472
On verra. 451
oncle 125
ondes courtes 321
ondes moyennes (OM) 321
ongle 39
ONU (Organisation des Nations Unies) 287
opaque 429
opéra 226
opération 50
opération 159, 417
opérer 50
ophtalmo(logue) 50
opinion 64, 233, 325, 458
opposant 283
opposé,e 424

opposé, e 403
s'opposer 67, 282, 424, 451
opposition 269, 282, 424
opticien,ne 173
optimisme 75
optimiste 75
option 158
optique 234
or 361
or 478
orage 358
orageux, -euse 358
orange 90, 405
orbite 350
orchestre 226
ordinaire 427
ordinateur 169, 328
ordonnance 51
ordonner 421
ordonner 447
ordre 282, 416, 421
ordre (religieux) 254
ordures 374
oreille 18
oreiller 120
oreillons 46
organe 19
organisation 79, 180
organiser 79
s'organiser 279
orge 366
orgue 225
orgueil 74
orgueilleux, -euse 74
oriental,e 354
orientation 402
orientation profession-nelle 177
orienté,e 327
s'orienter 402
original 221
original,e 71, 462
origine 256, 281, 392
ORL 50
orme 365
orphelin,e 12

orteil 20
orthographe 152
orthopédiste 51
os 18
oser 78
OTAN (Organisation du traité de l'Atlantique Nord) 287
otite 46
oto-rhino(laryngologiste) 50
ou 476
ou ... ou 478
ou bien 476
où 401, 473, 475
oubli 83
oublier 65, 154
oublier 83
ouest (O) 403
Oui. 451
ouïe 29
ouragan 377
ours 371
outil 166
outillage 167
ouvert,e 74
ouvrage 229, 256
ouvre-bouteille 91
ouvrier, -ière 133, 171, 174, 298
ovale 408
OVNI 350
oxygène 349
oxygène 362
ozone 349

.... P ....

pacemaker 52
Pacifique 355
pacifisme 291
pacifiste 291
pacte 288
page 156, 229, 324
page d'accueil 330
pages jaunes 316
pain 87
paix 248, 289

palais 218
pâle 36, 46, 407
palette 223
palier 115
pâlir 29
palmier 365
panne 336
panneau 337
pansement 51
pantalon 97
pantoufles 101
papa 124
pape 252
papeterie 106
papier 168, 361
papier peint 118
papiers 337
papiers d'identité 13
papillon 341, 371
papy/papi 125
paquebot 347
pâquerette 366
Pâques 252
paquet 411
paquet-cadeau 110
par 484
par alliance 126
par avion 317
par câble 198
par cœur 154
par conséquent 243, 433, 478
par contre 476
par exemple (p. ex.) 452, 483
par la suite 393
par retour du courrier 318
par satellite 198
par terre 401
paradis 252
paragraphe 241
paraître 323
paraître 231
paraître faire 480
parallèle 354, 403
parapluie 105
parc 219, 383
parc naturel 211

parc technologique 304
parce que 431, 477
parcmètre 339
parcourir 31, 437
Pardon ! 444
pardonner 444
pare-brise 340
pare-chocs 340
pareil,le 423
parent,e 126
parenté 126, 425
parenthèse 488
parents 24, 124
paresse 72, 149
paresseux, -euse 72, 149
parfait,e 460
Parfaitement. 451
parfois 393, 481
parfum 90
parfum 39
se parfumer 39
parfumerie 107
parking 335, 379
parlement 262
Parlement européen 288
parlementaire 262
parler 79, 152, 240, 440
parmi 485
paroisse 254
parole 440
parquet 118
parrain 127
part 412
partage du travail 181
partager 79
partenaires sociaux 182,
    280
parterre 226
parti 269
participant,e 193
participation 263
participe passé 490
participe présent 490
participer 185
particularités 283
particulièrement 431
partie 412
partie principale 240

partir 31, 128, 206
partout 402, 481
pas 30
Pas du tout. 452
pas mal 411
Pas mal. 457
Pas possible ! 463
Pas question. 452
Pas terrible. 457
pas un,e seul,e 471
passage 229, 333
passager, -ère 207, 343
passé 391, 490
passé antérieur 490
passé composé 490
passé simple 490
passé,e 391
passeport 13, 208
passer 335
passer à 198
se passer 242, 246, 320
passer au second plan
    422
passer pour 480
passer son temps 185
passe-temps 185
passif 490
passion 60
passionnant,e 233
pastel 223
pasteur 252
patate 364
pâte 95
pâte brisée 96
pâte feuilletée 96
pâte levée 96
pâté 87
pâté de maisons 382
paternel,le 126
pâtes 89
patience 141
patient,e 49, 141
patinage 194
patiner 194
patineur, -euse 194
patinoire 194
patins à glace 194
patins à roulettes 191

pâtisserie 106
pâtisseries 90
pâtissier, -ière 106, 173
patrie 260
patrimoine 146
patriote 265
patriotisme 265
patron,ne 214, 279, 301
patron,ne 183
patronal,e 183
patronat 279
patte 370
pâturage 297
paupière 20
pauvre 134
pauvreté 134, 145
pavillon 112, 379
payer 109, 307
payer cash 109
payer comptant 109
pays 13, 209, 260, 351
pays en voie de
    développement 286
paysage 221, 351
paysan,ne 174, 295
pays-Bas 15
PC 328
PC 270
PDG 171, 301
péage 339
peau 18
pêche 90, 187, 296, 364
péché 253
pêcher 187, 296
pêcher 365
pêcheur, -euse 188, 296
pédale 338
pédaler 191
pédé 22
pédiatre 51
pédicure 39
peigne 37
se peigner 37
peignoir 101
peindre 187, 221
peine 276
peintre 173, 187, 221
peinture 187, 221

peinture à l'huile 223
pellicule 322
pendant 393, 484
pendant des heures 388
pendant que 394, 477
pendule 389
pénible 462
péniche 347
pensée 63, 239, 255
penser 63, 254
penseur, -euse 255
pension (de famille) 212
pension alimentaire 126
pente 354
Pentecôte 253
pépé 125
percepteur, -trice 267
perceptible 29
percer 167
perceuse 167
perdant,e 189
perdre 79, 189
perdre 251
perdre connaissance 47
perdre de vue 140
père 24, 124
père de famille 12
perfection 464
perfectionnement 176
(se) perfectionner 81, 176
perforatrice, perforeuse 169
perfusion 52
périmé,e 13, 208
périmètre 400
période 394
période d'essai 171
périodique 324
périph(érique) 339, 383
périphérie 382
perle 105
permettre 446
permis 267
permis (de conduire) 337
permis de séjour 281
permis de travail 282
permission 446

perpendiculaire 403
perquisition 277
perroquet 369
persécuter 283
persécution 283
persil 92
personnage 196
personnage principal/central 243
personnage secondaire 243
personnalité 73
personne ... ne 471, 480
personnel 178, 213, 301
personnellement 461
personnes âgées 136
perspective 234
persuader 441
perte 79, 301
pertes 292
perturbation 359
peser 418
se peser 39
peser le pour et le contre 241
pessimisme 75
pessimiste 75
pesticide 297, 376
pétanque 186
pétard 53
petit commerce 106
petit déjeuner 85, 213
petit écran 198
petit,e 34, 417
petite-fille 125
petites ondes 321
petit-fils 125
petits-enfants 125
petits pois 89
pétrochimie 363
pétrole 361, 375
pétrolier 347
peu 411, 482
peu à peu 394
peuple 247
peuplier 365
peur 59
peureux, -euse 75

peut-être 451, 483
phare 336
pharmacie 49
pharmacien,ne 49, 173
phase 240
philosophe 254
philosophie 157, 254
philosophique 254
photo 186, 322
photocopie 169
photocopier 169
photocopieuse (photocopieur) 169
photographe 175, 324
photographier 322
phrase 440, 490
physicien,ne 161
physique 157
physique 35
piano 225
piano à queue 228
pichet 217
pièce 114, 237
pièce à conviction 277
pièce d'identité 208
pied 19
pierre 112, 361
pierre précieuse 105
piéton,ne 333
pieux, -euse 254
pigeon 369
pile 120, 166, 387
pilote 174
pilote 346
pilule 23, 52
pin 365
pince 166
pince (à linge) 102
pinceau 223
ping-pong 190
pion,ne 158
pipe 54
pipeline 363
piquer 274
(se) piquer 54
piquet de grève 280
piqûre 50
pirate 331

pirater un programme 331
pire 460
pisciculture 297
piscine 213, 381
piste 192, 344
piste 277
piste cyclable 339, 383
pitié 60
pittoresque 219
placard 117
place 11, 197, 218, 344, 380, 401, 488
placement 146, 310
placer 434
placer 311
plafond 116
plage 209, 353
plaider 276
plaie 47
se plaindre 448
plaine 354
plainte 275, 448
plaire 60
plaisir 60, 202
plaisir 22
plan 66, 112, 218, 222, 242, 289
planche 231
planche à roulettes 191
planche à voile 192
plancher 116
planète 349
planning familial 126
plantation 363
plante 187, 363
planter 187, 363
plaque de cuisson 121
plastique 361
plat 93, 215
plat de résistance/ principal 216
plat,e 354
platane 365
plateau 97, 354
plateau de fromages 216
platine laser 322

plâtre 48, 362
plébiscite 262
plein 411
plein,e 426
pleine saison 210
pleurer 59
pleurnicher 61
pleuvoir 358
pleuvoir à verse 359
plier 437
plomb 362
plombage 53
plomber une dent 53
plombier 177
plombs 121
polonais,e 16
plongée 194
plonger 194
plongeur, -euse 194
pluie 358
pluies acides 373
pluriel 488
plus 357, 412, 416, 482
plus ... que 424
plus ou moins 454
plusieurs 410, 471
plus-que-parfait 490
plutôt 454, 483
pluvieux, -euse 359
PME 301
pneu 336
pneumonie 46
poche 102
poêle 116
poêle 96
poème 235
poésie 235
poète 229, 235
poétique 235
poids 34, 418
poids 193
poignet 20
poil 20
poing 20
point 401, 407, 487
point commun 423
point culminant 238
point de départ 238

point de vue 65, 233, 325
pointe 408
pointu,e 408
pointure 101
poire 90, 364
poirier 365
poison 46
poisson 88, 369
poitrine 19
poivre 95
poivré,e 86
poivrer 95
poivron 92, 366
polaroïd 322
pôle 350
poli,e 73, 138
police 273, 337
police d'assurance 311
police judiciaire (PJ) 277
policier 172, 273
policier, -ière 273
politesse 73
politicien,ne 175, 268
politique 175, 268
polluant,e 372
polluer 372
pollueur, -euse 373
pollution 373
Pologne 16
polystyrène 363
pommade 51
pomme 90, 364
pomme de terre 89, 364
pommier 365
pompier 172
ponctuel,le 344, 388
poney 370
pont 218, 380
populaire 133, 153
population 132, 247
population active 176
porc 88
porcelaine 362
port 208, 345
port 318, 383
portable 316, 328
porte 113, 116

porte-avions 292
portefeuille 109, 307
porte-monnaie 307
porter 97, 434
se porter bien/mal 45
porter secours 137, 341
porter un toast 203
porteur 345
portrait 221, 232, 322
portugais,e 15
Portugal 15
poser 221, 434
poser sa candidature 177
positif 489
positif, -ive 459
position 233, 325, 401, 436
posséder 113, 145
possession 145
postal,e 317
poste 301, 317, 380
poste (de police) 337
poste (de radio) 319
poste (de travail) 179
poste de télé(vision) 320
poste restante 318
poster une lettre 317
postier, -ière 171
postuler 177
pot catalytique 340
pot de crème 39
pot d'échappement 340
potage 92
pote 131
poterie 186
poterie 224
poubelle 120, 374
pouce 20
poudre 39
poule 368
poulet 88
poumon 20
pour 432, 485
pour ainsi dire 456
pour cent 415
pour commencer 241
pour conclure 243
pour finir 241

pour le moment 395
pour ma part 461
pour que 432, 477
pourboire 217
Pourquoi pas ? 451
Pourquoi ? 431, 475
poursuites 277
poursuivre 144
pourtant 241, 476
pourvu que 479
pousser 363, 435
poussière 120
poussin 368
pouvoir 430, 479
pouvoir 265
pouvoir d'achat 181
pratique 460
pratiquer 192
pré 295
préavis de grève 183
précaire 136
précaution 48
prêche 254
prêcher 254
précieux, -euse 105
précipitations 359
se précipiter 33
précis,e 387, 416, 427
précisément 454
préciser 442
prédateur 370
préface 326
préfecture 267
préférable 460
préféré,e 421
préférer 66, 460
préfet 267
préhistoire 248
préjugé 67, 284, 464
prélèvement automatique 310
première 196, 237
première classe 343
Première Guerre mondiale 248
premièrement 422
prendre 33, 343
s'en prendre 62

prendre des notes 153
prendre froid 43
prendre le pouls 51
prendre parti 239
prendre sa température 44
prendre un verre 54
prendre une cuite 55
prépa 160
préparatifs 206
préparation 77
préparer 77, 94, 206
préposition 490
prés 400
prés de 485
presbyte 29
prescription 276
prescrire 50
présence 149
présent 391, 490
présent,e 149, 391
présentateur, -trice 320
présenter 33, 128, 243, 441
présenter ses vœux 201
préservatif 23
préserver 283, 375
Président,e 261
présidentiel,le 261
presque 387, 483
presque pas (de) 411
presqu' île 356
presse 323
presse à sensation/à scandale 326
presse du cœur 326
pressing 102
pression 336
pression 287
pression atmosphérique 356
prestations 312
prestations sociales 182
prestige 145
prêt 307
prétendre 442
prêter 307
prétexte 443

prêtre 252
preuve 155
preuve 275
prévenu,e 275
prévisible 377
prévision 68
**prévisions météo(rolo-
giques)** 356
prévoir 67
prier 251
prier 447
prière 251
prime 181, 312
primeurs 297
primordial,e 464
principal,e 421, 459
principal,e 158
principe 257
printanier, -ière 390
printemps 390
priorité 337
prise de la Bastille 249
prise de sang 52
prise de son 200
prise d'otage 278
prison 273, 381
prisonnier, -ière 273,
290
priver 144
privilège 136, 249
privilégié,e 136
prix 109, 216, 305
prix forfaitaire 214
prix HT 306
prix TTC 306
pro(fessionnel,le) 190
problème 130, 155, 233
procès 274
processeur 331
procès-verbal (PV) 341
prochain,e 392
proche 400
proclamation 262
proclamer 262, 443
procureur 174
procureur 276
producteur, -trice 299
production 179, 299

produire 179, 299
produit 179, 295, 299
produit de beauté 39
produit d'entretien 121
produit pétrolier 361
produit toxique 376
produits finis 300
produits laitiers 89
prof(esseur) 151, 172
profession 12
professions libérales 176
professions médicales
173
profond,e 352, 399, 418
profondeur 352, 399,
418
progiciel 329
programme 156, 197,
198, 269, 319, 329
programmer 329
programmeur, -euse
173, 329
progrès 160, 302, 436
proie 370
projet 66, 205, 222, 379
projeter 81
prolétariat 137
prolongation 192
prolonger 267, 396
promenade 187
se promener 187
promesse 442
promettre 442
promoteur immobilier
382
promotion 177
pronom 489
prononcer 440
proposer 65, 215, 446
proposition 65, 446
propre 36, 100, 119,
145, 372
propreté 36, 119
propriétaire 113, 134,
145
propriété 113, 134
prose 231
prospectus 205

prospère 146
prospérité 136, 146
protagoniste 237
protection 136
protéger 136
protestant,e 12, 252
protestantisme 252
protestation 279
protester 279, 458
prouver 155, 233
prouver 274
proverbe 231
province 351
proviseur 158
provocation 143, 291,
449
provoquer 143, 449
prudence 72
prudent,e 72
prune 90, 364
prunier 365
PS 270
psy(chiatre) 51
psychologie 161
pub(licité) 320
pubertaire 131
puberté 22, 131
public 196, 238, 319
publication 233, 326
publicitaire 320
publicité 325
publier 326
publiphone 316
puis 422, 476
puisque 432, 477
puissance 285
puissant,e 285
pull 98
punir 273
punir 144, 150
punition 144, 150
pur et simple 455
pur,e 87
purée 89
puzzle 186
pyjama 99
pyramide 408
Pyrénées 352

Q

quai 207, 342
quai 383
qualification 177
qualifié,e 176
se qualifier 176
qualité 69, 100, 421
quand 476
quand ? 393, 475
quand même 454, 476
quant à 486
quantité 410
quart 415
quartier 218, 378
quartier résidentiel 382
quart-monde 137
quatrain 236
quatre quatre (4×4) 338
quatuor 228
que (qu') 473, 477
Que ? 474
Quel(le) ? 475
Quels ? Quelles ? 475
Quel,le ... ! 448
Quelle horreur ! 450
quelque chose 471
quelque part 402
quelquefois 393
quelques 410, 471
quelques-un(e)s 410, 471
quelqu'un 471
querelle 287
Qu'est-ce que ? 475
Qu'est-ce qui ? 475
question 152, 233, 272, 443
question de confiance 264
questionnaire 267
queue 370
qui 473
Qui ? 474
Qui est-ce que ? 475
Qui est-ce qui ? 475
quintal 419
quinzaine 385, 415

quinze jours 385
quiproquo 239
quitter 140
quoi 473
Quoi ? 463, 474
quoique 477
quotas 297
quotidien 326
quotidien,ne 386

R

rabais 306
rabot 167
raboter 167
raccourcir 102
race 367
racine 365
racisme 281
raciste 281
raconter 440
radiateur 116
radiation 377
radical 489
radio 319
radio(graphie) 52
radioactif, -ive 374
radioactivité 374
radiocassette 323
radiographier 52
radiophonique 321
rafale 360
rafle 277
rafraîchissant,e 93
rage 70
rails 342
raisin 90, 364
raison 63, 255, 431
raisonnable 73, 255
raisonnement 255
raisonner 255
ralenti 200
ralentir 334
ralentissement 339
râleur, -euse 74
se rallier 270
rallonger 102
ramadan 253

ramassage 374
ramasser 435
rame de métro 346
ramener 140
ramer 195
ramper 371
rançon 278
rancunier, -ière 74
randonnée 188, 211
randonneur, -euse 188
rang 197
ranger 119, 435
rap 130, 226
rapide 31, 72, 428
rappel 341
rappeler 168, 315, 441
se rappeler 64
rappeur, -euse 130
rapport 423
rapporteur 160
rapports 138, 286
rapports sexuels 22
rapprochement 288
rapprocher 438
se rapprocher 33, 288
raquette 190
rare 427
rarement 393
se raser 39
rasoir 39
rassemblement 280
se rassembler 280
rassurer 445
rat 368
rater 152, 343
rater un virage 339
rationalisation 182
rationaliser 182
rayé,e 104
rayon 109
rayons 52
réacteur 374
réaction 28, 77
réaction chimique 163
réagir 28, 77
réalisateur, -trice 198
réalisation 78, 222
réaliser 78, 198, 222

réalisme 230
réaliste 256
réaliste 73, 223
réalité 256
reboisement 377
reboiser 377
récent,e 391
récepteur 321
réception 213
réception 321
récession 300
recette 94
recettes 309
recevoir 139, 317
recevoir un ordre 291
réchauffement de
  l'atmosphère 373
réchauffer 94
recherche 161
recherche fondamentale
  162
rechercher 277
rechute 45
récidiviste 275
récit 232
récital 228
réciter 154
réclamation 217
réclamer 82
réclusion à perpétuité 277
récolte 364
récolter 364
recommandation 447
recommandé,e 217
recommander 206
recommander 447
recommencer 392
récompense 143, 149
récompenser 143, 149
recompter 417
réconciliation 144, 288
se réconcilier 144, 288
reconnaissance 457
reconnaissant,e 457
reconnaître 65
reconnaître 29
reconstruire 379
reconversion 300

se reconvertir 300
recopier 153
record 190
recoudre 103
recouvrir 436
récré(ation) 156
recrue 291
rectangle 408
rectangulaire 408
recueil 236
reculer 31, 334
récupération 375
récupérer 48
recyclable 374
recyclage 374
recyclage 177
recycler 374
se recycler 177
rédacteur, -trice 175,
  324
rédaction 324
rédaction 159
redevance 321
rediffuser 320
rediffusion 320
rédiger un article 324
redire 441
se redresser 34
réduction 108, 343
réduction 136
réduction du temps de
  travail 181
réel,le 256
référendum 262
réfléchi,e 76
réfléchir 63, 232
réflexe 28
réflexion 63, 233
réforme 249
refouler 60
refrain 236
réfrigérateur 94, 116
refroidir 94
refroidissement 46
réfugié,e 281
se réfugier 281
refus 454
refuser 67

refuser 454
regard 27, 80
regarder 27, 80
regarder la télé(vision)
  198
régate 195
reggae 226
régime 44, 86, 268
région 209, 266, 351
région minière 297
régional,e 266
régionalisation 268
règle 156
régler 309, 389
règles 22
règne 247
régner 247
regret 141
regretter 141, 444
régulier, -ière 408
régulièrement 393
rein 20
reine 247
rejet 284
rejeter 134
rejeter 284
se réjouir 61
relatif, -ive 459
relation 138, 285, 423
relations franco-
  allemandes 250
se relaxer 188, 211
relevé de compte 310
relief 351
religieux, -euse 251
religion 11, 251
reliure 328
remaniement ministériel
  264
remarquable 464
remarque 80, 441
remarquer 27, 80, 441
remboursement 308
rembourser 307
rembourser 51
remède 52
remerciement 456
remercier 456

se remettre 49
remettre en question 131
remise 306
remonte-pente 194
remonter 246
remorquer 340
remparts 219
remplacer 434
remplir 436
remporter 434
remuer 33, 96
renaissance 249
renard 372
renaturer 377
rencontre 286
rencontrer 128
se rencontrer 129
rendement 295
rendez-vous 49
rendre 33
se rendre 33, 293
se rendre compte 65
renfermé,e 75
renommé,e 217
renoncer 67
rénovation 382
rénover 382
renseignement 205, 442
renseignements 315, 343
(se) renseigner 205, 442
rentrée 158
rentrer 31
renverser 438
renvoyer 180
renvoyer 284
réparation 166, 336
réparer 166, 336
repartir 31
(se) répartir 82
répartition 82
repas 85
repas (de fête) 202
repassage 99
repasser 99, 120
se repentir 276
répéter 196, 441
répétition 196, 238, 242

répondeur 168, 316
répondre 443
réponse 443
reportage 199, 232, 324
reporter 175, 199, 324
repos 42, 210
se reposer 33, 42, 210
repousser 139, 435
reprendre des forces 49
reprendre le travail 279
représentant,e 172
représentation 196, 226, 237
représenter 195, 237
répression 285
repriser 103
reproche 141, 457
reprocher 141, 457
reproduction 221
reproduction 22
reptile 371
républicain,e 260
république 260
République (Ière-Ve) 250
République tchèque 16
requin 371
RER 342
réseau 278
réseau (ferroviaire) 345
réseau routier 339
réservation 206
réserver 206
résidence 113
résidence secondaire 382
résignation 62
se résigner 62
Résistance 248
résistance 292
résistant,e 292
résister 292
résolu,e 68
résolution 68
résoudre 78, 155
respecter 135
respiration 349
respirer 349
responsabilité 135

responsable 135, 180, 266, 301
ressemblance 423
ressemblant,e 423
ressembler 423
ressentir 60, 465
ressortissant,e 265
ressources 136, 181
ressources naturelles 296, 376
restaurant 213, 214
restaurant universitaire 164
restaurateur, -trice 178
restauration 178, 382
restaurer 382
restauroute/restoroute 217
reste 412
rester 30, 435
resto U 164
restreint,e 413
restructuration 300
restructurer 300
résultat 189, 279, 416, 432
résultat 159
résulter 433
résumé 154, 241, 325
résumer 154, 241, 325
résurrection 254
retard 207
retarder 388
retenir 64, 154
retenue 159
retirer de l'argent 308
retouche 102
retoucher 102
retour 31
retour en arrière 200, 234
(se) retourner 31, 435
retraite 25
retraité,e 25
retraitement 377
retraiter 377
retransmettre 321
retransmission 321
rétrécir 102

retrouvailles 145
retrouver 79, 140, 202
réunification 250
réunion 279, 286
réunion 183
se réunir 202, 279
se réunir 183
réussir 78, 151
réussite 78, 151, 162
revanche 193
rêve 65
réveil 28
réveil 389
se réveiller 28
réveillon 202
revendication 181, 279
revendiquer 181, 279
revenir 30
revenus 136, 181
rêver 65
révision 340
revoir 140
révolte 130, 282
se révolter 239, 282
révolution 247, 282
révolutionnaire 282
revue 323
rez-de-chaussée 114
Rhin 353
Rhône 353
rhumatismes 47
rhume 43
riche 133
richesse 133, 145
richesses du sous-sol 296
ridé,e 36
rideau 118, 199
ridicule 427
rien ... ne 471, 480
Rien à faire. 452
rigoler 58, 202
rime 236
rimer 236
rincer 38
rire 58, 202
risque 337
risquer 77
risque-tout 75

rivage 353
rivalité 287
rive 353
rivière 353
riz 89
RMIste 134
robe 97
robe de chambre 99
robinet 118
robot 298
robotisation 300
rocade 339, 383
rocher 353
rocheux, -euse 353
rock 226
roi 247
rôle 196, 238
romain,e 246
Romain,e 246
roman 231
roman feuilleton 325
romancier, -ière 229
romantisme 230
rompre 144, 438
ronce 366
rond,e 407
rond-point 339
rose 364, 405
rossignol 371
rotation 350
rôti 88
rôtir 94
roue 336
rouge 405
rouge à lèvres 39
rouge sang 406
rougeole 46
rougir 29
rouler 334
rouler en codes (en feux
   de croisement) 338
rouler en pleins phares
   338
roumanie 16
route 10, 335, 380
routier 347
roux, rousse 35, 406
royal,e 247

royaume 247
RPR 270
ruban adhésif 169
rubéole 46
rubrique 324
rue 10, 335, 379
rugby 190
ruines 218, 381
ruisseau 355
rupture 144
rural,e 296
ruraux 382
ruse 76
rusé,e 76
russe 15
Russie 15
rythme 187, 225
rythme 236

S

sa 470
SA 301
sable 209, 353, 361
sac 105, 206
sacré,e 254
sage 72
saignant,e 92
saigner 44
sain,e 42
saint,e 254
saison 356, 390
saisonnier, -ière 390
salade 89
salade 366
saladier 97
salaire 179
salarié,e 179, 279
Salaud ! 450
sale 37, 100, 119
salé,e 86
saler 95
saleté 37, 119
salir 119
salle 197
salle à manger 114
salle d'attente 49, 343
salle de bains 114, 212

salle de concert 226
salle de réunion 167
salle de séjour 114
salle de sport 381
salon 114
salon de thé 217
Salopard ! 450
Salope ! 450
salopette 101
saluer 128
Salut ! 128
samedi 385
SAMU (Service d'aide médicale d'urgence) 51
sanction 276, 287
sandales 99
sang 18, 44
sangloter 61
sans 485
Sans blague ! 463
sans doute 452, 483
sans faute 455
sans plus 455
sans que 478
sans-abri 134
sans-papiers 136
santé 42
Saône 355
sapin 365
sardine 88
SARL 301
satellite 304, 350
satisfaction 75
satisfait,e 75
sauce 88
saucisson 87
sauf 485
saule 365
saumon 88
saut 31, 191
saut à ski 194
sauter 31, 191
sauteur, -euse 193
sauvage 375
sauvegarder 330
sauver 50, 136
se sauver 34
savant,e 161

saveur 91
savoir 64, 148
savoir faire 479
savoir-faire 80, 303
savon 36
scandale 271
scandinave 15
scanner 329
scanneur/scanner 169, 329
scanneur/scanner 52
scénario 200, 230
scénariste 200, 230
scène 195, 196, 237
scie 167
science 160
sciences naturelles 157
scientifique 160, 303
scier 167
scolarité 158
scoop 327
scooter 333
scotch 155
sculpter 224
sculpture 224
SDF 134
se (s') 472, 473
séance 198, 262
seau à glace 217
sec, sèche 37, 87, 99, 357
sèche-cheveu(x) 38
sèche-linge 102, 121
sécher 37, 99
sécher un cours 159
sécheresse 377
secondaire 459
seconde 387
seconde classe 343
Seconde Guerre mondiale 248
secouer 438
secrétaire 171
secrétaire d'Etat 264
secte 253
secteur primaire 176, 296
secteur secondaire 176
secteur tertiaire 176, 305

Sécu(rité sociale) 51, 312
sécurité 340
seigle 367
sein 20
Seine 353
séjour 205
sel 95
self 217
selon 464, 486
semaine 385
semblable 423
sembler faire 480
semer 367
semestre 390
semi-remorque 347
sénat 264
sénateur, -trice 264
sénile 25
sens 64, 255, 402
sens giratoire 339
sens interdit 337
sens unique 337
sensibilité 70
sensible 70
sentier 211
sentiment 20, 58, 235
sentimental,e 235
sentir 27
se sentir 58
se sentir bien/mal 42
séparation 12, 26, 125
séparation des pouvoirs 249
séparatisme 283
séparatiste 283
séparé,e 12, 125
se séparer 128
se séparer 26
septembre 389
septentrional,e 354
Serbie 16
série 421
série télévisée 199
sérieux, -euse 73
serment 276
séropositif, -ive 47
serpent 369
serré,e 100

serrer à droite 339
serrer la main 138
serrure 114
serveur, -euse 173, 214
serviable 74
service 213
service 193
service civil 291
service compris 217
service de dépannage 340
service en ligne 330
service militaire 291
service public 171
services 174
serviette 37, 95, 156
servir 85, 214
se servir 85, 166
servir de modèle 149
ses 470
seul,e 140
seulement 430, 453
sévère 70, 149
sévérité 70
sexe 11, 21
sexuel,le 21
sexy 21
shamp(o)oing 38
(se) shooter 54
short 97
si 478
Si tu veux. 451
SIDA 47
siècle 246, 391
siècle des lumières 257
siège 288
siège social 179, 300
siéger 288
siffler 197, 227
siffler 192
signaler 444
signature 310
signe 421
signe particulier 13
signer 310
signification 155, 242
signifier 155
s'il te/vous plaît 446

silence 27, 373
Silence ! 466
silencieux, -euse 27, 373
silhouette 407
similaire 425
simple 462
simplement 453
simultané,e 396
sincère 74
sincérité 74
singe 369
singulier 488
sinistre 312, 378
sinistré,e 378
sinon 478
sirop 91
site 219, 375
situation 401, 433
situation de famille 11
situé,e 401
se situer 242
skateboard 191
ski 192
ski alpin 194
ski de fond 194
skier 192
skieur, -euse 192
slip 98
slip de bain 98
slovaque 16
Slovaquie 16
Slovénie 16
SMIC 183
smog 373
SNCF 344
snob 76
social,e 133
socialisme 269
socialiste 269
société 133, 179, 260
sœur 125
sœur 254
sofa 119
soi 472
soie 361
soie 102
soif 85
soigné,e 39

soigner 50
soin 50
soins dentaires 50
soir 388
soirée 388
sol 114
sol 354
solaire 349
soldat,e 175, 289
solde 310
soldes 108, 305
sole 88
soleil 349, 357
solennel,le 254
solidaire 137
solidarité 137
solide 360
soliste 226
solitude 140
soluble 362
solution 155, 279
sombre 407
sommaire 324
somme 308, 416
sommeil 28
sommet 286, 352
son 27, 225, 322, 470, 487
son et lumière 219
sonate 228
sondage 327
songer 68
sonner 113, 315
sonnet 236
sonnette 113
sono(risation) 227
sonore 236
sonorité 236
sorte 421, 430
sortie 31, 335
sortir 31, 129
sortir en boîte 130
souci 135
soucoupe 95
soucoupe volante 350
soudain 394, 482
souder 363
souffrance 61

souffrir 45, 61
souhait 466
souhaiter 66, 201, 466
soûl,e 55, 92
soulever 434
se soulever 285
souligner 234
soupçon 143, 277
soupçonner 143, 277
soupe 87
soupe à l'oignon 92
souper 91
soupière 97
souple 35, 104
souplesse 35
source 353
sourcil 20
sourd,e 29
sourire 58
souris 329, 368
sous 397, 484
sous 309
sous (toute) réserve 455
sous-marin 292
soustraction 160, 417
soustraire 160, 417
sous-vêtements 98
soutenir 135
soutien-gorge 98
souvenir 209
se souvenir 64
souvent 393, 481
spacieux, -euse 115
sparadrap 51
spatial,e 304, 350
spécial,e 421
se spécialiser 176
spécialiste 49
spécialiste 176
spécialité 215
spectacle 176, 196
spectateur, -trice 196
spéculateur, -trice 310
spéculation 310
spéculer 310
sperme 22
sphère 408
sphérique 408

spirituel,le 255
splendide 461
sport 188
sportif, -ive 188
sportif, -ive de haut
    niveau 192
sports de combat 195
sports d'hiver 191
sports nautiques 192
square 383
stade 189, 381
stage 170
stagiaire 171
standard 315
star 196
station 214
station d'épuration 376
stationnement 335
Stationnement interdit !
    339
stationner 335
station-service 336, 380
statue 224
steak 88
stereo 322
stérile 23
stérilité 23
steward 174
steward 346
stimulateur cardiaque 52
stock 306
stockage 377
stocker 330
Stop ! 466
store 118
strophe 236
structure 240
studio 198, 319
studio 115
stupéfaction 465
stupéfait,e 465
stupéfiant 54
stupide 72
stupidité 72
style 224, 243
style (discours)
    (in)direct 490
stylo 156

stylo (à) bille 168
stylo (à) plume 168
subir 63
subjectif, -ive 327
subjectivité 327
subjonctif 489
substance (in)organique
    362
substantif 488
succéder 249, 265
succès 197
succession 265
succursale 301, 309
sucre 87
sucré,e 86
sucrette 87
sud (S) 403
Suède 15
suédois,e 15
suffisant,e 464
suicide 25
se suicider 25
Suisse 15
suisse, Suisse, Suissesse
    15
suite 325, 421
suivre 30
suivre des cours 170
sujet 239, 324, 488
super sans-plomb 336
Super ! 457
superficie 354, 419
supérieur,e 301, 398,
    416
superlatif 489
supermarché 106, 380
supplément 207
supplément 326
supporter 63, 192
supposer 65
supprimer 180, 436
sur 397, 484
sur le coup 396
sur orbite 304
sûr,e 458
surdité 29
sûrement 452
surf 192

surface 351, 419
surligner 169
surligneur 169
surmonter 60
surprenant,e 463
surpris,e 463
surprise 463
surproduction 297
surréalisme 223
surtaxe 318
surtout 430, 483
surveillant,e 158
surveiller 158
survêtement 101
survie 23
survivre 23
suspect,e 277
suspense 199, 234
svelte 35
sweat 98
syllabe 487
syllabe 236
symbole 235, 242, 255
symbolique 235
symboliser 242
symbolisme 230
sympa(thique) 69, 138
sympathie 69, 138
sympathisant,e 270
symphonie 228
symptômes 45
syndical,e 279
syndical,e 183
syndicalisme 279
syndicaliste 279
syndicat 278
syndicat 183
syndicat d'initiative 205
se syndiquer 279
synthèse 234
système 268
système d'exploitation 331
système éducatif 158
système nerveux 19
système scolaire 158

T

ta 470
Ta gueule ! 450
tabac 54
tabagisme 55
table 95, 117, 167
table de nuit/de chevet 117
table des matières 155, 229, 326
tableau 117, 156, 221, 237
tablier 101
tache 99
tâche 80
tag 132
tagueur, -euse 132
taille 19, 34, 100, 417
taille-crayon 156
tailleur 101
se taire 440
Tais-toi ! 466
talent 150, 228
talon 20
tandis que 477
tant 411, 482
tant ... que 424
Tant mieux ! 445
Tant pis ! 445, 481
tant que 395, 478
tante 125
taper 329
tapis 118
tard 394, 482
tarif 216
tarifs postaux 318
tarte 90
tartine 87
tas 411
tasse 95
taudis 382
taureau 367
taux d'alcoolémie 56
taux de change 309
taxe 306
taxi 342

tchèque 16
te (t') 472
technicien,ne 173, 302
technico-commercial 303
technique 302
techno 226
technologie 303
technologique 303
technopole 304
tee-shirt 98
teindre 406
teint 36
teinte 406
teinturerie 102
tel(le)s 472
tel,le 472
télé(vision) 319
télécarte 316
télécharger un texte 330
télécommande 198
télécommunication 316
Télécoms 316
télécopie 170, 317
télécopieur 170, 317
téléfilm 199
télégramme 317
téléphone 168, 315
téléphone à cartes 316
téléphone de voiture 316
téléphoner 168, 315
télésiège 194
téléski 194
téléspectateur, -trice 198
télétravail 331
téléviseur 320
télévision commerciale 320
télévision par câble 320
télévision par satellite 321
tellement (de) 482
témoignage 233, 276
témoigner 275
témoin 275, 341
tempérament 69
température 357
tempête 358
temple 253

temps 242, 356, 387, 391, 490
temps de chien 359
tenaille(s) 166
tendance 327
tendon 19
tendre 21, 33, 70, 86
tendresse 21, 70
tenir 33
tenir à ce que 68
tenir compte 82
tenir l'affiche 200
tenir sa droite 339
tennis 99
tension 286
tension 45, 234
tente 213
tercet 236
terme 257
terminaison 489
terminal 345
terminer 392, 436
terminus 346
terrain 378
terrain 355
terrain de sport 189, 381
terrasse 115, 213
terre 349, 351
terrestre 351
terreur 62
terrible 423, 462
terrifier 62
territoire 268
terrorisme 282
terroriste 282
tes 470
testament 146
tête 18
têtu,e 75
texte 154, 324
TGV 207, 342
thé 87
théâtre 195, 237, 381
théière 97
thème 239
théologie 251
théorie 64, 161, 255

théorique 64, 255
thérapie 53
thermomètre 43, 357
thèse 234
thon 88
thym 92
ticket 342
tiéde 28, 36, 86, 357, 426
Tiens, tiens ! 463
tiers 415
Tiers-Etat 249
tiers-monde 286
tige 365
tigre, -esse 369
tilleul 365
timbre(-poste) 168, 317
timide 75
timidité 75
tirage 326
tirage au sort 193
tiré,e 239
tire-bouchon 91
tire-fesses 194
tirelire 309
tirer 435
tirer 326
se tirer d'affaire 81
tirer au sort 193
tirer sur 292
tirer une conclusion 67
tiret 487
tiroir 117, 167
tissu 102
titre 229, 239, 324
titre 193, 310
toi 472
toile 221
toilette 36
toilettes 114
toit 114
toit ouvrant 340
tôle 362
tolérance 135, 281
tolérant,e 75
tolérer 135
tomate 89, 364
tombe 26
tomber 31

tomber dans les pommes 47
tome 230
ton 405, 470
tonalité 317
tonne 419
tonnerre 358
top 50 130
se tordre 48
tornade 377
torrent 355
tortue 371
torture 250, 285
torturer 250
tôt 394, 482
total 416
totalement 455
toubib 50
touche 329
toucher 28
toucher 60
toujours 393, 482
tour 112, 191, 205, 218, 379, 400
tourisme 175, 205
touriste 205
touristique 217
tournant 240
tournée 317
tournée 228
tourner 334, 435
tournesol 366
tournoi 189
tour-opérateur 210
tous 470
Tous mes regrets. 445
Toussaint 253
tousser 43
tout(e) 412, 470
tout à coup 394
tout à fait 452
tout à l'heure 393
tout au plus 413
tout compte fait 455
tout de même 454
tout de suite 393
tout droit 335, 402
tout le temps 393

tout(e), tous, toutes 412
toutes 470
toux 43
toxico(mane) 55
toxicomanie 55
trace 277, 370
tract 284
tracteur 297
traducteur, -trice 155
traduction 154
traduire 154
trafic 334
trafic de drogue 55
trafiquant,e 55
tragédie 197, 237
tragique 197, 237
trahir 293
trahison 293
train 207, 342
train de banlieue 345
train de voyageurs 344
traîner 34
trait 407
trait d'union 487
traité 231, 256
traité 288
Traité sur la coopération
   franco-allemande 288
traitement 50
traitement 181
traitement de texte 329
traiter 50, 240, 329
traiter 144, 298
traiteur 109
traître, traîtresse 293
trajet 342
tram(way) 346
tranche 107
tranquille 71
transfert de technologie
   304
transformation 379, 437
transformer 112, 379,
   437
transfusion sanguine 52
transistor 319
transparent,e 429
transpirer 43, 189

transport 342
transport 345
transporter 342
transports en commun
   345
transports en commun
   174
trapu,e 35
travail 178
travail manuel 182
travailler 178
travailler à la chaîne 299
travailleur, -euse 149,
   178, 279, 298
travailleur, -euse social,e
   172
travaux dirigés (TD) 163
travaux manuels 157
travaux ménagers 121
travaux pratiques (TP)
   163
traversée 345
traverser 345, 437
traversin 119
tremblement de terre 377
trembler 43
trempé,e 46, 359
très 430, 482
tri 318
triangle 408
triangulaire 408
tribunal 274
tribunal correctionnel 274
tricher 159
tricot 103
tricot de corps 101
tricoter 103
trier 318
trilogie 243
trimestre 390
trinquer 92, 203
triomphal,e 199
triomphe 199
triple 415
triste 71
tristesse 71
troisième âge 25, 133
trombone 169

tromper 22, 142
se tromper 64
trompette 225
tronc 365
trop 411, 482
tropiques 350
trottoir 333, 379
trou 103
troubler 63
troubles 45, 285
trouillard,e 76
troupe 196
troupe 291
troupeau 370
trousse de toilette 39
trouver 79, 460
se trouver 30, 433
trucage 200
truelle 167
truite 88, 369
t-shirt 98
tu 472
Tu es vache. 449
Tu me casses les pieds.
   449
Tu m'en veux ? 444
tube 130
tuer 142, 273, 290
tuile 112
tulipe 364
Tunisie 16
tunisien,ne 16
turc, turque 16
Turquie 16
tutoyer 138
TVA 306
type 243
typique 215

 U

UDF 270
Ukraine 16
ultimatum 291
un(e) 470
uni,e 405
uni,e 26, 104
uniforme 289, 407

union 270
Union européenne 250, 286
union libre 127
unique 464
uniquement 453
unité 416
unité monétaire 307
univers 349
universel,e 349
université 160, 170, 381
université populaire 162
uranium 377
urbain,e 381
urbanisation 381
s'urbaniser 381
urbanisme 381
urgent,e 44
urne 263
us et coutumes 283
USA 15
usage 152
usé,e 100
usine 298
utile 367, 427
utilisateur, -trice 330
utiliser 166
utopie 257
UV 163

V

vacances 205
vacancier, -ière 205
vaccin 52
vacciner 52
vache 367
vague 353, 428
vaincre 192, 250, 293
vaincu,e 251, 293
vainqueur 193, 250, 293
vaisselle 95, 120
valable 13, 208, 343
valeur 307
valise 206
vallée 352
vanille 92
vanité 74

vaniteux, -euse 74
vantard,e 443
se vanter 443
variable 356
variation 437
varicelle 46
varié,e 93
varier 437
variétés 200
vase 118
Vas-y ! 466
Va-t'en ! 466
veau 88, 368
vedette 196
végétal,e 363
végétation 363
véhicule 337
veille 386
veine 19
velcro 103
vélo 190, 333
vélomoteur 338
velours 103
vendanger 297, 367
vendanges 297, 367
vendeur, -euse 107, 172, 305
vendre 107, 305
vendredi 385
Vendredi Saint 252
se venger 74
venir 30
venir de faire 392, 479
vent 358
vente 179, 305
vente par correspondance 109
ventes hors-taxes 346
ventre 19
verbe 489
verdict 276
verger 365
verglas 359
vérifier 161, 336
véritable 256
vérité 64, 256, 272
verlan 132
verre 95, 216, 361, 411

verre usagé 374
vers 387, 403, 484
vers 236
versement 310
verser 90
verser 310
versification 236
version 200, 328
vert foncé 406
vert pomme 406
vert,e 405
vertical,e 402
verts 270
vertu 73
vestiaire 197
vêtement 97
vétérinaire 178
veuf, veuve 12, 125
vexé,e 63
vexer 143
viande 88
vice 73
victime 273, 290
victime 341
victoire 192, 250, 293
victorieux, -euse 192, 250
vidange 340
vide 426
vidéo 186
vidéocassette 323
vidéodisque 323
vide-ordures 121
vider 91, 436
vie 23, 42
vie de famille 125
vie professionnelle 176
vieillard 25
vieillesse 133
vieillesse 25
vieillir 25
vierge 22
vieux 136
vieux, vieil, vieille 25, 426
vif, vive 428
vif, vive 407
vigne 365
vigneron,ne 296

vignette 341
vignoble 296
villa 112, 379
village 378
village de vacances 212
villageois,e 378
ville 378
vin 91, 296
vin de pays 216
vinaigre 95
vinaigrette 89
vingtaine 415
viol 278
violence 131, 274, 282
violent,e 131, 274
violer 278
violet,te 405
violette 366
violon 225
violoncelle 228
vipère 371
virage 334
virement 310
virer 310
virginité 22
virgule 487
virgule 417
virtuose 228
virus 46
vis 167
visa 208
visage 18
vis-à-vis 399
visible 27, 426
visite 139, 209, 217, 222
visite à domicile 49
visiter 209, 217, 222
visiteur, -euse 209, 217
visuel,le 27
vite 31, 482
vitesse 338
vitesse (maximale) 334
viticole 297
viticulteur, -trice 296
vitre 116
vitrine 107
vivant,e 23, 42

vivre 23, 42
vocabulaire 152
vœu 466
voie 207, 342, 379
voie express 339
voie lactée 349
voie piétonne 383
voie sans issue 339, 383
voilà pourquoi 478
Voilà ! 457
voile 192
voir 26
voisin,e 113, 137
voiture 207, 333
voiture couchette 208
voix 261, 440
voix active 490
voix passive 490
vol 32, 208, 274
vol régulier 344
volaille 368
volant 334
volcan 351
volcanique 351
voler 32, 33, 208, 274, 344
volet 118
voleur, -euse 274
volley(-ball) 190
volontaire 68, 291
volonté 66, 256
volontiers 483
Volontiers. 451
volume 229, 322, 419
vomir 46
vos 470
Vosges 352
votre 470
vouloir 66, 430, 479
vous 472
voûté,e 36
vouvoyer 138
voyage 205, 342
voyage d'affaires 210
voyage d'agrément 210
voyage de noces 210
voyage d'études 210
voyager 205, 342

voyageur, -euse 205, 342
voyagiste 210
voyelle 487
Voyons ! 463
vrai,e 64, 256, 428
vraiment 430, 453
vraisemblablement 431
VRP 306
VTT (vélo tout terrain) 190
vue 27
vulgaire 76

W

wagon 344
wagon-lit 208
wagon-restaurant 208
walkman 323
W.-C. 114, 212
web/WEB 330
week-end 385
western 199

X

xénophobe 283
xénophobie 283

Y

y 473
yaourt 89
yog(h)ourt 89
Yougoslavie 16

Z

zapper 198
zigzaguer 339
zinc 362
zonard,e 132
zone 356
zone bleue 339
zone industrielle (ZI) 383
zone piétonne 383
Zut ! 448